PROGRAMMING MICROSOFT® VISUAL INTERDEV™ 6.0

*Nicholas D. Evans, Ken Miller,
and Ken Spencer*

Microsoft Press

PUBLISHED BY
Microsoft Press
A Division of Microsoft Corporation
One Microsoft Way
Redmond, Washington 98052-6399

Library of Congress Cataloging-in-Publication Data
  Evans, Nicholas D.
      Programming Microsoft Visual InterDev 6.0 / Nicholas D. Evans, Ken
  Miller, Ken Spencer.
          p.   cm.
      Includes index.
      ISBN 1-57231-814-7
        1. Microsoft Visual InterDev.   2. Web sites--Design.   I. Miller,
   Ken, 1959– . II. Spencer, Ken, 1951– . III. Title.
   TK5105.8885.M55E93   1999
   005.2'76--dc21   98-31911
                                                            CIP

Printed and bound in the United States of America.

1 2 3 4 5 6 7 8 9   QMQM   4 3 2 1 0 9

Distributed in Canada by ITP Nelson, a division of Thomson Canada Limited.

A CIP catalogue record for this book is available from the British Library.

Microsoft Press books are available through booksellers and distributors worldwide. For further information about international editions, contact your local Microsoft Corporation office or contact Microsoft Press International directly at fax (425) 936-7329. Visit our Web site at mspress.microsoft.com.

Acquisitions Editor: Eric Stroo
Project Editor: Devon Musgrave
Technical Editor: Marc Young

Contents

Contents

Part III Scripting the Scripting Object Model

Contents

Part V Developing n-Tier Applications

Contents

Part VI   Security

Acknowledgments

We'd like to thank all the staff at Microsoft Press and the Microsoft Visual InterDev Product group for all their excellent support and encouragement throughout this project. We would particularly like to extend our sincere thanks to Eric Stroo, Devon Musgrave, David Clark, Anne Hamilton, David Lazar, and Greg Leake. Without your patience and cooperation, this book would not have been possible.

Nick Evans, Ken Spencer, and Ken Miller

My sincere thanks and appreciation go to my wife, Michele, and my sons, Andrew and David, for allowing me to spend time on this project and for supporting me every step of the way.

Nick Evans

I would like to extend many thanks to my wife, Trisha, and my two sons, Jeffrey and Kenny. They have continued to support me over the years in my writing efforts and without their encouragement, projects like this would not have been possible.

To Ken Miller, who has been my business partner in one way or another for many years: thanks for your support and help. You've always been there to help with whatever task needs to be done, and I really appreciate it.

Ken Spencer

To every conference attendee who's asked a question and every reader who's written, e-mailed, phoned, or faxed: thank you for reminding me that no matter how good the tool or how well it is understood, real-world practitioners routinely encounter worthwhile problems for which the answer is not obvious. Trying to solve these problems keeps me entertained and employed!

To my son Jeffrey, in whose eyes I see that wonderment at technology that first got me interested in computers: thanks for reminding me how much fun exploring the unknown can be.

Ken Miller

Introduction

"Once every five years or so, a software development tool comes along that completely revolutionizes the way software applications are constructed. Some recent examples include Lotus Notes for groupware and PowerBuilder and Visual Basic for client-server applications. These products offer unique features that allow developers to create complex applications quickly and easily using an Integrated Development Environment—they are the tools that spring to mind when you think of groupware or client-server software.

"This type of application has been sorely needed in the Web development arena. For the past several years, Web developers have had to work with a variety of elementary tools in order to construct Web applications. Connecting databases to these Web applications has been even harder because of the nature of HTML and the HTTP protocol.

"Microsoft Visual InterDev is the new Web application development tool that was introduced along with the Visual Studio 97 suite of tools in early 1997. It is Microsoft's component integration tool for assembling components created using products such as Visual Basic, Visual C++, and Visual J++.

"Visual InterDev promises to become the de facto standard for constructing dynamic, data-driven Web applications for the entire software industry. In fact, many Web sites and applications have already been created using Visual InterDev, and you can expect to see many more as time goes by."

This was the prediction I made in the introduction to *Inside Microsoft Visual InterDev* (Microsoft Press, 1997), and today, a year later, those words still stand. In fact, according to independent statistics, Visual InterDev has indeed become the de facto standard for development of dynamic, data-driven Web applications. The list of Internet, intranet, and extranet sites using this technology reads like a who's who of the major corporations throughout the world, including Compaq, Dell, Hallmark, Barnes and Noble, CNNSI, Marriott, CompUSA, and many others.

In this book, we'll look under the hood of Visual InterDev 6.0 and explore the unique features that make it such an exciting new product. The book is divided into six parts, which cover everything from getting started to more complex topics such as advanced database topics, three-tier architectures (incorporating Microsoft Visual Basic 6.0 components and Microsoft Transaction Server 2.0), and the incorporation of digital certificates (using Microsoft Certificate Server).

Part I, *Getting Started with Visual InterDev*, introduces you to the product and covers product installation; the integrated development environment; and how to create, maintain, and debug your applications

Part II, *Creating Applications*, introduces you to the new Scripting Object Model, the Data Environment, design-time controls, and using Dynamic HTML features. These are all exciting new features in Visual InterDev 6.0 that increase developer productivity and enhance the end-user experience when running Visual InterDev–created applications.

Part III, *Scripting the Scripting Object Model*, covers scripting design-time controls, using forms (including the new Form Manager), using Active Server Pages (ASP), and integrating client-side Microsoft ActiveX controls and Java applets.

Part IV, *Advanced Database Development*, goes into detail about using the Visual Database Tools (including Data View, Database Designer, Query Designer, and the source code editor), scripting the Data Environment, working with *Recordset* objects, employing stored procedures, and using client database features. These rich database tools make it easy to create powerful Web applications without having to leave the Visual InterDev development environment.

Part V, *Developing n-Tier Applications*, discusses how to build n-tier applications using Visual InterDev 6.0, Visual Basic 6.0, and Microsoft Transaction Server. Both transactional applications as they relate to COM components and transactional ASP pages are discussed. There is also a comprehensive chapter on how to use the built-in server-side components available from the Visual InterDev Toolbox and a chapter on Microsoft Message Queue Server.

Finally, Part VI, *Security*, looks at adding security with chapters on standard security and the incorporation of client-side digital certificates for more advanced user authentication using Microsoft Certificate Server.

The CD-ROM contains a wealth of software that illustrates the techniques outlined in the book. It also includes sample applications that illustrate how to wire together complete, transactional, three-tier applications using Visual InterDev 6.0, Visual Basic 6.0, Microsoft Internet Information Server 4.0, Microsoft Transaction Server 2.0, Microsoft Certificate Server, and Microsoft SQL Server. A key sample application that is referred to throughout the book is a sample Internet banking application named VI-Bank.

This book is essential reading for anyone interested in the next generation of Web application development. Whether your background is in client/server development or Web application development, knowledge of Visual InterDev will enable you to rapidly construct the Internet, intranet, and extranet Web applications of today and tomorrow.

Nick Evans

Part I

Getting Started with Visual InterDev

Chapter 1

Introducing Microsoft Visual InterDev 6.0

The World Wide Web began its life as a platform for sharing documents over the Internet, but now it is used for much more than simple document publishing. In fact, most commercial and corporate Internet sites can be more accurately described as *Web applications* because they require complex programming logic and a myriad of automated, back-end processes to create a compelling, informative experience for their target users. Web technology is also experiencing widespread growth as an effective platform for deploying internal, corporate *intranet* applications and external, business-to-business *extranet* applications.

Dynamic Web applications must be able to coordinate a variety of components and processing that are necessary to provide user interactivity and up-to-date information (for example, real-time data and access to dynamic information stored in databases). These Web applications have server-side processing, commonly accomplished with the use of ASP (Active Server Pages) or CGI (common gateway interface) applications, to process forms, respond to user input, and format database information into HTML (hypertext markup language) pages constructed on the fly. Often the applications must integrate with existing systems within an organization, such as product and customer databases, as well as order processing systems and various other transaction-oriented systems. On the client, the Web pages themselves increasingly contain programming logic such as Microsoft JScript or Microsoft VBScript (Visual Basic, Scripting Edition), as well as embedded software components such as Java applets and ActiveX controls that can provide advanced functionality to users.

Microsoft Visual InterDev 1 was one of the first integrated, visual tools for building dynamic Web applications, and it provided developers the ability to quickly build powerful ASP applications using design-time controls, ActiveX components, and other technologies. As powerful as Visual InterDev 1 was, however, it did not provide a graphical development environment, an object-based development paradigm, or a complete object model for development and thus did not satisfy the needs of many developers.

VISUAL INTERDEV 6.0

Visual InterDev 6 adds to the strengths of Visual InterDev 1 by providing a graphical editor, powerful new development tools, new object-based language extensions complete with events, and much more. Visual InterDev 6 brings the development methodology available with Microsoft Visual Basic to the Web development process. You can glimpse the power of the Visual InterDev 6 integrated development environment (IDE) in Figure 1-1.

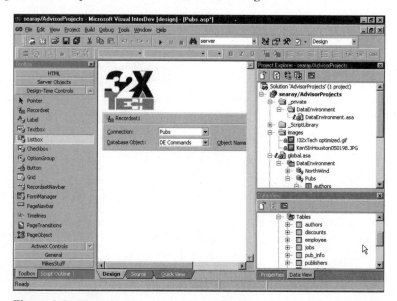

Figure 1-1. *The Visual InterDev 6 IDE provides many new features that let you be more productive when developing applications.*

As a member of the Microsoft visual tools family, Visual InterDev 6 was designed from the ground up for developing, deploying, and managing Web applications; for authoring and debugging ASP Web pages and HTML pages; for building VBScript and JScript applications; for achieving and maintaining database integration with Web applications; and as a connection point for Web authors to Microsoft Visual Studio.

Visual InterDev now includes the following core features:

- **Site Designer**   To quickly prototype Web sites, use the graphical Site Designer. In the Site Designer, you can create pages, links, navigation features, hierarchichal structures, and more—all with an easy-to-use drag-and-drop interface.

- **Cascading style sheets (CSS)**   You can edit style sheets easily in the CSS editor. You can create or modify style sheets for a set of Web pages. You can even preview any page to see how it would look if a style sheet were applied.

- **WYSIWYG page editor**   This new editor includes Design view, which lets you edit and create content in a WYSIWYG workspace. In addition to Design view, other views such as Script and Preview make writing, viewing, and debugging easier.

- **Statement completion**   Statement completion helps you create error-free script statements by presenting you with the names of all available methods and properties when you type in an object name.

- **Data environment**   You can now create and modify data-related objects in a single location—the graphical data environment. In the data environment, you can also drag and drop objects onto ASP Web pages to automatically create data-bound controls at design time. Oracle users will be pleased to hear that the data environment provides the same advanced support for Oracle as it does for Microsoft SQL Server.

- **Data-bound design-time controls**   Design-time controls offer you a richer, more functional, and aesthetically pleasing interface for creating data-enriched pages. Data-bound controls make it simple to incorporate data into your ASP or HTML pages that can "talk" to a database. The controls included with this version of Visual InterDev allow you to target a wide range of browsers or to narrow your focus to take advantage of the unique features of Microsoft Internet Explorer 4.

- **Dynamic HTML** Visual InterDev 6 supports Dynamic HTML (DHTML) in Internet Explorer 4 and other DHTML-capable browsers. The Visual InterDev 6 editor helps you create script for DHTML objects and events by presenting statement completion options for the object model and by displaying the object model hierarchy in the Navigation pane in Script view. As well as scripting directly to the Internet Explorer 4 object model, you can choose to have your design-time controls create client-side data-binding script.

- **Developer isolation** You can work on local versions of project files, which gives you the ability to test and debug your files before updating the master server. You can also work in master mode, in which files are saved both locally and to the master server.

- **Debugging tools** Visual InterDev 6 comes with a debugger that helps you test and debug script and Java components. You can use the debugger with VBScript and JScript, as well as with applications written in Sun Microsystems' Java and run using the Microsoft Java Virtual Machine.

- **Deployment** The ability to build and distribute components and packages from your production server is another important feature of Visual InterDev 6.

VISUAL INTERDEV'S ROLE IN VISUAL STUDIO

Visual InterDev 6 is available both as a stand-alone product and as part of Visual Studio 6. Visual InterDev 6 fully interoperates with the other tools in Visual Studio, including Microsoft FrontPage, Visual Basic, Microsoft Visual J++, Microsoft Visual C++, and other Microsoft technologies. As a key component of Visual Studio, Visual InterDev 6 is used to integrate components and applications created with other Visual Studio tools into seamless Web applications.

Visual Studio provides the "shell," or framework, that hosts Visual InterDev 6. Aspects of the Visual InterDev interface, such as the Project Explorer and Toolbox, are actually part of Visual Studio and are shared by several Visual Studio applications as well as by Visual InterDev. For example, Visual J++ also uses the Project Explorer and Toolbox features of the interface.

Microsoft Visual Studio is a complete development tools suite that provides a network programmer with easy-to-use tools for building solutions. Visual Studio is available in two editions: Professional Edition, which includes the core development tools that noncorporate developers are likely to use, and Enterprise Edition, which includes all the features of Professional Edition plus other tools and technologies that are needed in enterprise development. The following extensive list includes all of the Enterprise Edition's components:

- Visual Basic 6, Enterprise Edition

- Visual C++ 6, Enterprise Edition

- Visual InterDev 6, Enterprise Edition

- Visual J++ 6, Enterprise Edition

- Microsoft Visual FoxPro 6, Enterprise Edition

- Microsoft Visual Modeler 2

- Microsoft Repository 2

- Visual Studio Analyzer

- Visual Component Manager

- Microsoft Visual SourceSafe 6

- Enterprise Visual Database tools:

  - New schema design tools, including support for Oracle 7.*x* and later and SQL Server 6.5 and later

  - Stored Procedure and function editor for Microsoft SQL Server and Oracle

  - Stored Procedure debugging for SQL Server 6.5 and later

  - ODBC and OLE DB drivers for SQL Server, Oracle, SNA VSAM (Virtual Storage Access Method), and DB/2 databases (AS400 and mainframe)

- SQL Server 6.5, Developer Edition

- SNA Server 4, Developer Edition

- Microsoft Windows NT 4 Option Pack (Internet Information Server 4, Microsoft Transaction Server 2, Message Queue Server 1)

- Microsoft BackOffice Server 4.5, Developer Edition (SQL Server, Exchange Server, Systems Management Server, SNA Server, Windows NT Server, Windows NT Option Pack, Proxy Server, Site Server, and the BackOffice Server Service Packs)

- Visual Studio 6 Service Packs—via fulfillment

- MSDN Library

Visual Studio 6 is a powerful collection of development tools to allow you to build almost any type of application. The inclusion of the BackOffice development tools adds the ability to build enterprise applications and to test them in a workstation environment. Then you can deploy the applications in a full production environment.

VISUAL INTERDEV AND WINDOWS DNA

Visual InterDev 6 is part of Microsoft's Windows DNA (Distributed interNet Applications architecture). Windows DNA includes all the tools, servers, middleware, and database support required for building high-powered, integrated applications. Windows DNA is designed to address the various aspects of a distributed system such as a client/server or Web solution.

Visual InterDev is based on Microsoft's powerful Web application development framework, the Active Server framework, which enables Active Server scripting. Active Server scripting is script logic that is embedded in Web pages but that executes on the Web server instead of in the browser. Active Server scripting can be used to create Web applications with advanced server-side processing, including multitier Web applications that can use components developed in languages such as Visual Basic, Visual C++, and Visual J++. The use of server-side components also makes it easier to integrate internal legacy systems within an Internet or intranet solution while preserving all the benefits of Web technology—open standards, cost-effective deployment, cross-platform browsing, and low-bandwidth access. Finally, Visual InterDev includes integrated client-side scripting tools, and it is extensible by third-party components such as Java applets and ActiveX controls that can be added to Web pages and integrated using the Visual InterDev scripting tools.

Even though writing Active Server scripts with Visual InterDev is relatively easy, the scripts provide a powerful environment for Internet and intranet applications. For example, you can incorporate sophisticated functionality through Active Server components.

Active Server components provide the ability to process data and generate useful information, which extends the capabilities of the Web site. For example, using Visual InterDev, you can easily integrate server-side components written in Java, Visual Basic (4 or later), C, C++, or other languages that can create Component Object Model (COM) components. The Active Server framework allows these components to be tightly integrated into the Web application as either out-of-process components (EXEs), in-process components (DLLs), or remote components that leverage Distributed COM (DCOM) for multitier applications (remote EXEs). Server-side components can be limited to a page or globally accessible throughout an application so that a single instance can be shared by all users. Server-side components can also provide an effective way to integrate legacy systems directly into a Web application.

Active Server Pages

An ASP file consists of straight ASCII text in one or more of three forms: text, HTML, or script. An ASP Web page is an HTML page that contains server-side scripting. Server-side scripts are designated with an opening (<%) tag and a closing (%>) tag and are processed before the page is sent to the browser. The following code demonstrates a simple ASP Web page that contains server-side scripting and HTML.

```
<HTML>
<p>
<%FOR  i=3 TO 7%>
<FONT SIZE=<%=i%>>
Hello World!<BR>
</FONT>
<% Next %>
</HTML>
```

In this example, a simple loop is performed to display *Hello World!* in an increasing font size within an HTML page.

When a user requests a URL with an ASP filename extension, the Active Server engine reads through the file from top to bottom, executing any commands and then sending pure HTML back to the user's browser.

Active Server scripting is completely integrated with HTML pages. To enable the Active Server engine to read a file, all you have to do is give the file an .asp file extension. Thus, you can change the extension of an existing HTML file from .htm to .asp to easily make it an ASP Web page. You can then make the HTML dynamic by adding Active Server script to the ASP pages. The host language of Active Server scripting is VBScript. However, you can use the <SCRIPT> tags to include scripts from other scripting languages, such as Perl and JScript.

Visual InterDev 6 enhances ASP by adding a server-side run-time library. This run-time library is implemented in JScript in the initial release of Visual InterDev 6. It is scheduled to move to a series of COM components in a future update to Visual InterDev.

The run-time library provides an object-based language interface. Design-time controls, which we'll discuss in the next section, are implemented by the run-time library and can be addressed as objects. The run-time library also makes it easy to do remote scripting from a browser to the server. This lets script in the browser call script functions on the server, which can improve the performance of your application.

DESIGN-TIME CONTROLS

Design-time controls are an important feature of Visual InterDev. They provide all the benefits of component software as provided by standard ActiveX controls, such as plug-and-play functionality and visual editing at design time. However, design-time controls generate HTML-based content, which is viewable on any platform and any browser. Design-time controls can also generate the server-side or client-side scripting required to accomplish simple or complex tasks within a Web site. In essence, they are visual helper components that help you construct dynamic Web applications based on HTML, client script, and server script.

It is hard to overstate the importance of design-time controls for Visual InterDev. This product derives maximum extensibility using design-time controls, given that third-party software vendors and corporations can seamlessly extend the tool with custom design-time controls to add specialized functionality. Design-time controls can be developed in any language that supports COM, such as C, C++, Java, and Visual Basic. Visual InterDev 6 can also host Java applet design-time controls.

Visual InterDev 6 builds on Microsoft's ActiveX Data Objects (ADO) foundation by providing special design-time controls that generate much of the server-side scripting, including the ADO calls necessary to establish database connections within a Web site, perform queries, and display results. In many cases, you can use the design-time controls to create data-driven Web sites with little additional programming required. Visual InterDev 6 enables you to view and develop directly in Active Server scripting using the ADO component for maximum flexibility.

The new design-time controls included in Visual InterDev 6 are designed to reduce the time it takes you to build applications. The new controls are more granular than those included in Visual InterDev 1. For instance, now you have not only data controls like the new Recordset control, but also Button, Textbox, Listbox, and other controls that let you pull them together like components in a Visual Basic application.

Microsoft supplies a growing set of design-time controls on its Visual InterDev Web site (at *http://msdn.microsoft.com/vinterdev/*), in effect allowing the live upgrading of the tool with new functionality. And over time independent software vendors (ISVs) will also provide hundreds of design-time controls compatible with Visual InterDev, just as hundreds of ActiveX controls (OCXs) are now available for use with Visual Basic. Visual InterDev also supports standard ActiveX controls as a way to extend Web pages with client-side software components that execute within the browser.

DATABASE CONNECTIVITY

Powerful database connectivity options and visual database tools are integral to Visual InterDev. Its database connectivity features are based on the industry database access standard ODBC, and its visual tools work with any database supporting ODBC, including Oracle, SQL Server, Microsoft Access, Visual FoxPro, Borland dBASE, Borland Paradox, Informix, Sybase, IBM DB/2, and many others. In addition, Visual InterDev lets you create highly scalable database solutions, even for Internet applications with thousands of concurrent users, because it leverages the Active Server framework. The core database components of Visual InterDev include:

- Data Environment
- Data View
- Visual database tools (including the Query Designer and the Database Designer)
- Database design-time controls

The integrated database access tools are also based on ADO, which provides scalable, object-oriented database connectivity to any ODBC data source. In addition, Visual InterDev can be used with alternate data access components developed by third parties.

The Data Environment

Visual InterDev 6 changes the way we work with databases and attach them to Web pages. Just as Visual InterDev 1 took a significant step in changing how developers approach this issue, Visual InterDev 6 makes an even more drastic step by adding the Data Environment as well as many other database automation features. The Data Environment collects your data connection and data manipulation code in one place. It provides a standard interface for creating data-related objects and for placing them on Web pages. And it also provides a layer of abstraction, allowing you to create and modify objects that represent your data independently of the database.

The Data Environment is an object layer around ADO. ADO is still used to access the back-end database, and you can script either ADO or Data Environment commands. ADO is used to provide world-class database connectivity within Visual InterDev applications. Specifically designed for Web-based data access, ADO provides an object-based approach to data access over the Web. Via ActiveX scripting, connections to databases can be easily established to any

ODBC data source, and a variety of methods within the component provide you with a powerful set of database commands for manipulating data and creating data-driven Web pages.

ADO lets you manipulate database-defined data types, including binary large objects (BLOBs), such as GIF and JPG images, that are retrieved from databases and dynamically written into Web pages. In addition, ADO provides a rich set of properties for setting locking levels, cursor options, query and login time-outs, transaction support, result set scrolling, error handling, and more. ADO provides an easy-to-use, object-based approach to database programming. Using VBScript or JScript, ADO gives you maximum flexibility to develop powerful database functionality within your Web applications.

Data View

Visual InterDev gives you an integrated view into any ODBC data source being used within a Web site. Data View provides a visual interface to all the databases being used. Figure 1-2 shows the browsing of a database within a Web site directly in Visual InterDev.

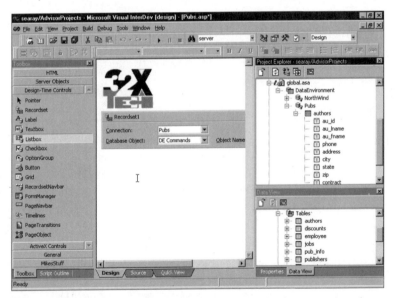

Figure 1-2. *The Data View pane at the bottom right shows an open data source to a SQL Server database, including its tables. (You can also see the Recordset1 design-time control near the center of the editor page.)*

Besides depicting each database connection being used in the site, Data View provides a live connection to each database, letting you work directly with each database within the IDE during Web site development. For example, you can open any database to view tables, defined views, and stored procedures.

Data View can provide detailed information about objects and properties within each database, including table definitions and field types, key structures, and stored procedures. Data View works in conjunction with the Query Designer and Database Designer features; it provides a sophisticated database development, administration, and maintenance system that is tightly integrated with the Visual InterDev IDE. Data View works against any OLE DB or ODBC-compliant data source and can show multiple connections against heterogeneous databases.

Query Designer

Visual InterDev provides a sophisticated SQL Query Designer that works against any ODBC data source. The integrated Query Designer provides an extremely easy-to-use interface for visually constructing even the most complex SQL statements. You can open live views of data sources, and you can drag tables directly into a design pane of the Query Designer window to build their queries. As the user selects fields from tables, the SQL pane shows the dynamically constructed SQL statement. You can directly modify the SQL statement, and the changes are reflected in the design pane. In addition, the query builder lets you execute any SQL statement to test it, displaying the results in a results pane. The Query Designer also lets you easily create complex queries across multiple tables and databases by automatically creating SQL joins and visually depicting these relationships in the design pane. Figure 1-3 on the following page shows a view of the Query Designer.

The SQL pane is a live pane and can be used to create stored procedures, execute arbitrary data definition language (DDL) commands directly against any ODBC data source, or perform ad hoc SQL queries. Visual InterDev thus provides a complete, tightly integrated database development and administration tool for Web developers. The Query Designer works in conjunction with the Query control (a design-time control) so that once developed and tested in the Query Designer, the HTML and server scripting necessary to execute the query is generated and embedded in the appropriate ASP Web page.

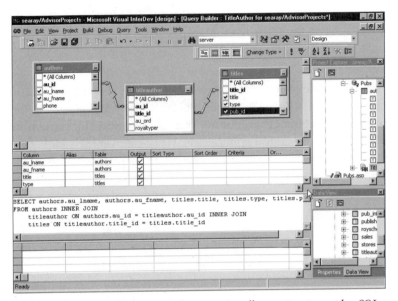

Figure 1-3. *The Query Designer lets you visually construct complex SQL queries against any ODBC data source.*

The Database Designer

In addition to providing the visual Query Designer, which works against any ODBC-compliant database, Visual InterDev also provides a complete Database Designer for users of SQL Server, Microsoft Access, and Oracle databases. The Database Designer is based on an extensible architecture, so support for other database systems can later be added. Using the Database Designer, you can modify the structure and properties of existing databases. Plus, database administration operations that used to take hours can now be done with a couple of mouse clicks.

For example, you can use the Database Designer to change the data type on a field (for instance, from a type CHAR to a type INT) with a simple drop-down selection. Visual InterDev then simply changes the field type, which ordinarily requires manual DDL operations to export the entire table, drop the table, create a new table with the new data type, and import the data into the new table. The Database Designer can generate DDL scripts that can be reviewed and submitted to database administrators for review and execution in controlled database environments.

The Database Designer can also be used to set up database designs (such as key structures and properties) and logical relationships between tables (such as foreign key relationships with automatic triggers and cascading updates, inserts, and deletes). This tool provides a powerful and flexible database environment that simplifies the most complex SQL Server administration tasks.

Scalability

Some database tools for Web applications offer visual aids to ease the development of data-driven Web sites, but often they do not provide the scalability required for commercial Internet sites or large-scale production intranet sites that host mission-critical applications. Visual InterDev provides both ease of use with extensive visual tools and the scalability required for large-scale, data-driven Web sites. For example, global database connections can be established for an entire site, and the Active Server framework pools these database connections across users. Pooling, connection caching, and time-out values are all established automatically based on default properties, but you can easily customize them within Visual InterDev.

Visual InterDev also makes it easy to connect to multiple heterogeneous databases within a Web site, returning or updating data that has been visually integrated within a single HTML page for the user. For example, Visual InterDev can be used to return data from an Oracle database running on a UNIX server, as well as data from a DB/2 database running on an IBM mainframe, all integrated within a single HTML page for the user.

DEVELOPING MULTITIER APPLICATIONS WITH ACTIVEX SERVER COMPONENTS

The Active Server framework allows Web applications to extend server-side functionality with custom or third-party components called ActiveX server components. ActiveX server components are OLE Automation Servers that support COM. Visual InterDev and ActiveX server components enable you to easily create multitier Web applications that include components that encapsulate specific processing logic. For example, a component that provides financial modeling and analysis functions can be used to build portions of a financial services Web application.

Using Visual InterDev, you can create ASP Web pages that execute the ActiveX component on the Web server and use its functions to return financial modeling information to users in dynamically constructed HTML pages. Because the component executes on the server, the content can be viewed on any platform by any browser. ActiveX server components can be integrated into Web applications using either server-side VBScript or server-side JScript. ActiveX server components can be created in any programming language that supports COM, such as C, C++, COBOL, Pascal (Delphi), Java, and Visual Basic.

Extending Visual InterDev Applications

ActiveX server components are an extremely important feature of Visual Inter-Dev. ActiveX server components need not be constrained by the safety restrictions imposed by VBScript and JScript because they execute on a controlled server as opposed to on users' desktops. They can thus be used to extend Active Server scripting with capabilities such as direct access to the file system and access to machine and network resources. As COM components, they can be driven by VBScript and JScript and they can execute as either in-process dynamic-link libraries (DLLs) or out-of-process executables.

For lightweight components designed as in-process DLLs, performance can be dramatically improved over CGI solutions. This is because no context switching between processes is incurred as Web users browse pages that use the component. In addition, ActiveX server components can be instantiated once and shared between all users connected to the Web site for more efficient use of server resources.

Integrating Legacy Systems into Web Applications

ActiveX server components provide a convenient and effective way to tightly integrate a Web application with internal and legacy systems. Components can be used to wrap existing business functionality created in Visual Basic, C, C++, COBOL, Java, or other tools, exposing that functionality via COM. For example, a client-server insurance processing application written in Visual Basic can be exposed as a set of ActiveX components that can be called directly from Web pages via Active Server scripting. In this fashion, Visual InterDev and the Active Server framework help protect and extend an organization's investment in existing tools and systems, ranging from mainframe applications to more recently deployed client-server applications. Visual InterDev can be used to effectively integrate the functionality of these systems directly into the Web site via ActiveX server components.

Distributing ActiveX Server Components Using DCOM

Because ActiveX Server Components are COM objects, out-of-process server components can be seamlessly distributed over a server network using DCOM. This means that components requiring a lot of processing can be distributed to application servers that work with the Web server to efficiently process requests from users browsing the site. For example, a price look-up component that performs complex pricing calculations can be built as an ActiveX Server Component and distributed via DCOM to execute on a specialized application server.

Figure 1-4 demonstrates how DCOM can be used in large installations to add flexibility and power to your Web site.

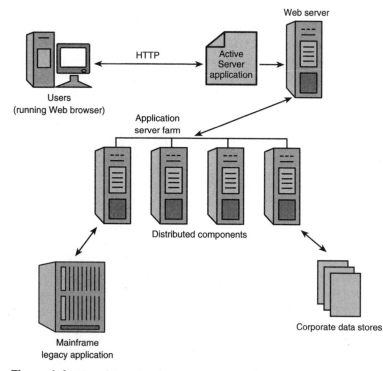

Figure 1-4. *Visual InterDev lets corporations take advantage of distributed ActiveX components via DCOM.*

The advantage of DCOM is that distributed computing is achieved with transparency. Because DCOM provides complete network transparency, you can program DCOM components using the same scripting logic as if the components were running locally on the Web server. Thus, DCOM components can provide greater scalability and fault tolerance for mission-critical Web applications. Also, distributed solutions built with DCOM components and Visual Inter-Dev offer more effective load balancing and the ability to create higher-performance applications for enterprise-class Web applications. You can also use Microsoft Transaction Server technology to provide online transaction processing (OLTP) and monitoring capabilities to Web applications built using distributed DCOM components.

You can also use Microsoft Message Queue Server (MSMQ) to build powerful features into your Web applications. MSMQ is a middleware application that provides asynchronous messaging services between application components.

DEVELOPING WEB PAGES

Besides offering an integrated, visual environment for developing the next generation of server-based Web applications and data-driven Web sites, Visual InterDev 6 provides integrated tools for developing Web pages, including those with client-side scripting, ActiveX controls, and Java applets.

ActiveX Controls and Java Applets

Visual InterDev includes integrated support for adding ActiveX controls, Java applets, and Netscape plug-ins to Web pages. When working with ActiveX controls, you are presented with a visual representation of the control that lets you visually modify the component to fit your needs. A visual property table, similar to the Visual Basic property table, lets you easily modify a component's properties without ever needing to see or work with source code.

The resulting property pages automatically generate all the HTML syntax (based on the World Wide Web Consortium's, or W3C's, industry standard <OBJECT> tag) to bring the component into the Web page and execute it. Perhaps most important, the ActiveX controls are displayed in true WYSIWYG fashion directly in the editor, and they can even be dragged, dropped, and sized directly within the page. With over 1000 ActiveX controls currently available and providing a wide range of functionality ranging from multimedia to multipoint conferencing to real-time data feeds, Visual InterDev 6 offers true extensibility.

Visual InterDev's integrated editors also provide support for easily inserting Java applets and Netscape plug-ins into a Web page. You can visually set characteristics such as size and position, and the editor displays the frame for the Java applet or Netscape plug-in within the document.

Client-Side Scripting in HTML Pages

Visual InterDev 6 also includes Script Outline, which provides access to the methods, properties, and events of the objects on the page. Script Outline makes it easy to add interactivity to Web pages, based on actions and events associated with ActiveX controls and the Visual InterDev 6 object model.

WYSIWYG Editor

Visual InterDev 6 includes a WYSIWYG editor. The Design View visual editor (shown as the Design tab in Visual InterDev) is a true WYSIWYG editor, supporting drag-and-drop editing, toolbar and menu functions, in-place editing, and more. Design View is similar to a Visual Basic form, and it allows you to precisely place multiple ActiveX controls by giving you exact control over *x*, *y* coordinates and *z*-ordering (layering) of controls.

The new Design View editor allows you to work with pages in standard HTML or DHTML. You simply flip the switch on an object, and then you can use the DHTML positioning features to locate the object any place on a page. You can also type directly on a page and within controls and tables, and work directly with images. Figure 1-2, already shown on page 12, shows an ASP Web page in Design View.

The Visual InterDev 6 IDE offers the following editing features:

- **Toolbox control customization**   You can right-click the Toolbox to add and delete individual controls from third-party vendors.

- **Toolbox custom tabs**   You can add new Toolbox tabs by using the Toolbox popup menu.

- **Toolbox object templates**   You can drag objects from the form back to the Toolbox, creating an object template. This template captures all the properties that you set, and it can be used to easily incorporate objects with custom properties into new pages. Groups of controls can also be used as object templates in this manner.

- **Multiple level undo/redo**   You can easily undo most edit operations.

- **Control alignment/spacing/sizing**   You can automatically align, size, and space controls for easier layout.

- **Control drag-and-drop**   You can position controls exactly with drag-and-drop editing. Also, you can drag controls from one page to another.

- **Control layering (*z*-ordering)**   You can set object layering by right-clicking any control.

- **HTML Outline**   The HTML Outline displays the HTML on a page and allows you to navigate to any point in the editor.

MANAGING WEB SITES

Managing the typical Web site has turned out to be complicated for most organizations. Problems range from organizing the various files on the site to repairing page links when they break. Visual InterDev includes extensive site management features to help alleviate these problems.

Site Management Features in the Project System

The Visual InterDev site management features begin with the integrated project system that presents a live view of the site as it exists on the Web server. The project system lets you create new Web sites; view content on an existing site; and create, add, and modify folders and files within a site. Specific site management features within the project system include:

- **Creation of new Web sites with Web site wizards**   The wizards step you through the process of creating a new site on the chosen Web server.

- **Direct file manipulation of any item in a Web site**   You can copy, delete, add, rename, and edit any file in the site from within the IDE by using the File View feature.

- **Ability to import content files and directory trees into a Web site**   You can use the Import File and Import Folder commands to import existing content from any local or network resource into a site.

- **Copy Web command**   You can move an entire site from one server to another by using the Copy Web command. This is useful, for example, for moving a site from a staging server to a production server.

- **Object properties**   You can right-click any object in a site, and Visual InterDev will present a property page that contains useful information related to that object, such as file size, modification date, and all incoming and outgoing links to the file.

Automatic Link Repair

The Visual InterDev project system can track links within a Web site and ensure that they are valid. For example, if you rename a file, the system detects all the pages throughout the site that reference that name as part of a URL reference (hyperlink), and it edits these references to prevent broken links. In addition, if a file is moved or if a site is physically restructured through your use of Visual InterDev, the system automatically repairs links in this manner. Finally, if a page or a file is deleted, Visual InterDev notifies you of all the references to that file within the site.

Link View

Besides providing you with automatic link repair and site management capabilities through File View, Visual InterDev also has a unique Web visualization tool called Link View. Link View presents a graphical view of the Web site, visually showing the logical relationship of pages within the site. For example, you can use Link View to visually depict the links from a particular HTML page to other pages both inside and outside the site. You can expand or collapse the view to any level you want, showing as many pages or sections of the site as you want. Link View depicts all broken links in red.

Besides diagramming links, Link View also depicts specific information about each file, using visual icons to depict its file type, such as HTML pages, Active Server Pages, GIF/JPG images, ActiveX controls, and Java applets. You can launch an editor on any file by simply double-clicking the file name.

You can also filter the view Link View gives you so that only specific information is depicted. For example, you can filter the view to show (in any combination):

- HTML pages
- Multimedia files
- Executables
- Documents
- External files
- Primary links
- Secondary links

Multiuser Development and Integration with Visual SourceSafe

Visual InterDev provides integrated source management for users of Microsoft Visual SourceSafe. Organizations using Visual SourceSafe can place a Web project under source control. Source management is especially helpful when teams of people work on the same Web site, since it provides explicit check-in and check-out capabilities for all files in the site. In addition, the Visual Source-Safe revision tracking and merging features help you protect your work—for example, these features let you roll back to an earlier version of a file or compare two versions of the same file.

Visual InterDev integrates with Visual SourceSafe so that you can put any project under source control without having to install Visual SourceSafe itself on your workstation. All Visual SourceSafe features execute on the server. For Visual InterDev projects under source control, the Visual SourceSafe integration features include the following:

- **Automatic creation of Visual SourceSafe projects**   The New Web Wizards ask you if you want to put a new Web project under source control, and then they let you specify an existing or new Visual SourceSafe project. If you specify a new project, Visual Inter-Dev creates the Visual SourceSafe project on the appropriate network drive.

- **Check-in/check-out files**   When you request to edit a file in the Web site, Visual InterDev explicitly checks the file out of the Visual SourceSafe project before opening the file. If another user has already checked it out (for instance, when another Visual InterDev user or FrontPage user is working on the same project), you are notified and permitted to see only a read-only copy.

- **Visual depiction of file locking status**   Within the project system, icons depict files that a user has checked out as well as read-only files checked out by other users working on the Web site.

- **Automatic addition of elements to a Visual SourceSafe project**   As you create new files for a Web site, Visual InterDev puts these elements under source control, using the Visual SourceSafe project set up for the site. For example, if you import a folder that contains 10 files and 2 subfolders, Visual InterDev adds these elements to the Visual SourceSafe project. If you create a new file, such as a new HTML page, Visual InterDev creates the new entry in the Visual SourceSafe project and checks the element out to you for editing.

EDITING CONTENT

Visual InterDev also includes Microsoft FrontPage 98 to enable you to use FrontPage and the multimedia content-editing tool Microsoft Image Composer, which lets you easily develop images for use in a Web application.

Microsoft Image Composer

The Image Composer is especially useful for developers who need to modify or create images to fit a Web site, and it is designed for developers who are not graphics professionals. It recognizes most popular image formats, including Adobe Photoshop files, and makes it easy to save images into .gif or .jpg formats for use on the Web. You can arrange, customize, and create images in the Image Composer for use on Web sites developed and maintained in Visual InterDev. You can launch the Image Composer from Visual InterDev by clicking a toolbar icon or directly on images from within the IDE. The Image Composer has a command that saves images to the Visual InterDev project. For more detailed information on this tool, see the Microsoft Image Composer online documentation.

AN OPEN AND EXTENSIBLE ARCHITECTURE

The open and extensible architecture of Visual InterDev is a critical aspect of the tool since it provides a high degree of flexibility. Visual InterDev delivers on the promise of openness by:

- Supporting the HTML/HTTP Internet standards

- Supporting ODBC for connectivity to all popular database systems

- Delivering "thin-client" cross-browser and cross-platform Web applications

- Providing full client-side and server-side extensibility via ActiveX controls and Java applets

- Supporting VBScript and JScript client-side and server-side scripting, as well as other scripting languages through third-party scripting engines

Chapter 2

Using the Integrated Development Environment

THE VISUAL INTERDEV IDE AND PROJECT SYSTEM

The Microsoft Visual InterDev 6 integrated development environment (IDE) is much like the one provided by Microsoft Visual Basic. The interface provides a drag-and-drop environment, a Toolbox, a Task List, and a built-in WYSIWYG editor. The menus and toolbars have changed from those in Visual InterDev 1, along with almost every other part of the working environment.

Users of Microsoft development tools will be immediately familiar with the new IDE, and new users should find it intuitive and easy to use. The IDE provides an integrated, global work area for Visual InterDev Web projects. You can open multiple projects simultaneously within the work area. For example, you might want to create a Visual InterDev Web page for use in one project and then open another project and reuse the same page. Opening both projects in the IDE allows you to simultaneously test and modify those projects.

Views and Windows

Visual InterDev 6 includes several views in its main window for working with HTML and Active Server Pages (ASP) Web pages:

- **Design view**   Displays the page in WYSIWYG view, almost as you would see it in a browser. You can create and modify pages in this view.

- **Quick view**   Displays pages as they appear in Internet Explorer 4. However, server script does not execute and data-bound controls (DTCs) do not display data.

- **Source view**   Displays the source code for pages. Objects such as DTCs and HTML intrinsic controls are shown as they appear in a rendered Web page. Pages can be created and modified in this view.

In the Design and Source views, the HTML Outline window, which you can access in the bottom left corner of the IDE, shows the HTML tags for the particular Web page you are viewing. You can create and modify pages by using this window.

In Source view only, the Script Outline window shows the properties, events, and methods for the objects on the viewed Web page.

Figure 2-1 shows the IDE in Source view displaying the script for a page. You change the view in the IDE by clicking a different tab at the bottom of the current view.

The Project Explorer window

The Visual InterDev 6 IDE includes a main Project Explorer window that lets you view and navigate a Web site using the Windows Explorer–based metaphor. The Project Explorer presents the entire site, including the site's content (such as HTML pages, GIF and JPG images, controls and applets, Active Server script files, and other files) and its complete subdirectory structure. Displaying a hierarchical list of the items in a Visual InterDev project or solution (which we'll discuss soon), the Project Explorer provides you with a window into your project and serves as your central point for working with file and data type objects. Take another look at Figure 2-1 to see an example of the Project Explorer displaying a project's structure.

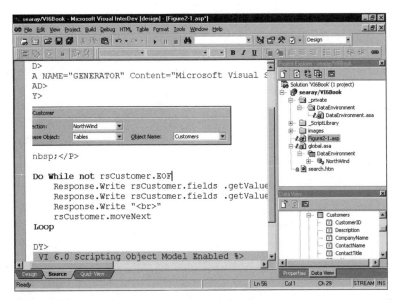

Figure 2-1. *Visual InterDev's integrated development environment provides multiple ways into your project, including three main views and various windows depicting information and enabling you to modify the project.*

The Project Explorer interface is quite intuitive. You can drag items from Project Explorer and drop them into the editor and you can drag items from Windows Explorer and drop them in Project Explorer. Project Explorer also features a context menu that you can access by right-clicking any item in the window.

To make items in Project Explorer active, select the item with the mouse or move the cursor. Once an item is active, you can rename it, display its properties, and take other actions. Note also that Project Explorer is automatically updated every time you change a setting, insert or change a file, or perform any action with Developer Studio. Project Explorer actions work just like those in Windows Explorer. For instance, to copy a file, you must hold down the Control key when you drag and drop the file. If you do not hold down the Control key, the file will be moved instead of copied. You can rename a file by clicking on the file and pressing F2 or by right-clicking the file and selecting Rename. You can also rename a file by clicking it once, waiting a second, and then clicking it again.

You can also select multiple items in the window by using the same techniques used in Windows Explorer. To select multiple contiguous items, click the first item and then, while holding down the Shift key, click the last item of the group you want to select. You can also use either the up or down arrow key with the Shift key to select contiguous items. Select multiple noncontiguous items by clicking the first item and then, while holding down the Ctrl key, clicking any additional items you want in the selection. You can expand and collapse the project lists and folders in the project by clicking the + or − icon to the left of the project name or item. If you want to edit or examine a particular element of the site, double-click the file. Visual InterDev will display the Open File dialog box, asking you if you want to retrieve a working copy or open the file in read-only mode. You can also check the Use As Default Response check box to make your answer the default for future files. If you select Get Working Copy, the file is retrieved from the site, copied to your workstation, and opened in the appropriate editor for that file type. Once you make the desired changes, you can save the changes locally or save the file on the Web server.

You can reset your default answer by using Tools | Options and displaying the Projects | Web Projects properties. The options under When Opening A File control what happens when you double-click a file in Project Explorer.

Finally, you can also preview a page in a browser by right-clicking the page in Project Explorer and selecting View In Browser or Browse With.

The Properties window

The Properties window lists the design-time properties for selected objects and their current settings. As you work with objects, the Properties window will be updated continually to display the current properties for the current object. As you change properties, the changes are applied immediately.

Figure 2-2 shows the Properties window, containing the properties for the Textbox design-time control.

You can display the properties in a category format by clicking the Categorized button on the Properties window toolbar.

The first property shown in the Properties window in Figure 2-2 is Custom. You can click the ellipsis to the right of Custom, or click the Property Pages button (that is, the third button) on the Properties window toolbar, to make Visual InterDev 6 display the Properties page for the object. Figure 2-3 shows the Custom property pages for the Textbox object shown in Figure 2-2.

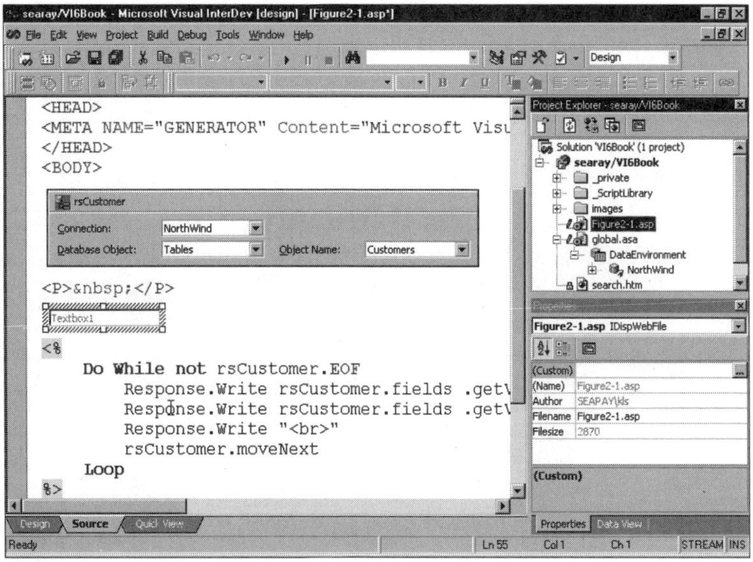

Figure 2-2. *The Properties window displays the properties for an object and allows you to change them at design time.*

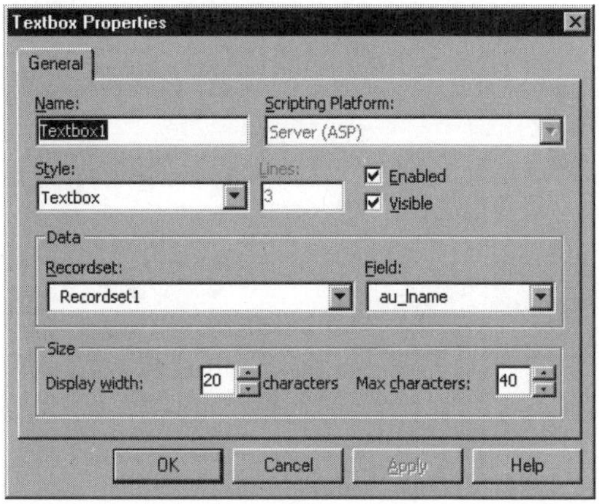

Figure 2-3. *The Properties page for an object organizes the properties and can provide additional features beyond those in the Properties window.*

The Properties window and the Properties page will display properties for the currently selected item. In the design window, just click on the item, and the property display will update. You can also use the drop-down list at the top of the Properties window to display the properties for another item.

The Data View window

Visual InterDev 6 has a new Data View window display, as shown in Figure 2-4.

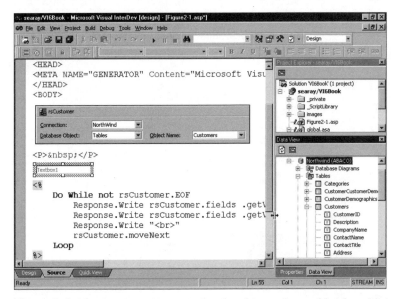

Figure 2-4. *The new Data View window has been enhanced by the addition of its own toolbar and the enrichment of its context menu.*

Data View is available at any time in a project's Data Environment. (See Chapter 12 for more information about the Data Environment.) You can use Data View for many different tasks, including:

- Providing a view into a database that your project has a connection to

- Supplying tables to drop into Query Designer

- Providing access to the Stored Procedure and Trigger editors

- Copying SQL Script to the clipboard

- Displaying the properties for a table or a column

- Providing access to database diagrams and table design features

The Toolbox

The Toolbox displays design-time controls, ActiveX controls, Java applets, Java Beans, HTML intrinsic controls, and HTML and code scraps. The elements displayed in the Toolbox are based on the editor you are using and are enabled only when the associated editor is active.

While each Visual Studio application has its own default set of Toolbox items, the Toolbox always contains the pointer tool. The pointer is used to resize or move a control that has been drawn on a form.

You can work in the following ways with the Toolbox:

- Drag Toolbox items and controls from the Toolbox and drop them onto pages in one of the editors.

- Double-click a Toolbox item to insert it at the current cursor position in the page currently open in an editor.

- Place new items in the Toolbox by dropping them onto the Toolbox. For example, you can drag an item, such as an ActiveX control, from the Windows Explorer and drop it onto the Toolbox. You can also drag text from the editor to the Toolbox, thereby creating a named code fragment that you can reuse. And you can paste items from the clipboard onto the Toolbox by right-clicking the Toolbox and selecting Paste.

- Rearrange items on a Toolbox tab by dragging them to a new location.

- Delete an item from the Toolbox.

- View Toolbox items in a list view format by selecting List View (which is the default setting) from the context menu when you right-click the Toolbox window.

- Customize the Toolbox by creating tabs for custom groups that contain Toolbox items.

Note that items that you add to the Toolbox and changes that you make there appear only on the machine on which they were added or created.

You can add your own tabs to the Toolbox by following these steps:

1. Right-click the Toolbox.

2. Select Add Tab from the context menu.

3. Type the name for the new tab.

As mentioned, the Toolbox can be extended by adding other controls or text. You can add items to the Toolbox by dragging them and dropping them onto the Toolbox. You generally add ActiveX controls to the Toolbox by using the Customize interface:

1.   Right-click the Toolbox.

2.   Select Customize Toolbox from the context menu.

3.   Click the check box beside the component you want to add. You can also click the Browse button to look for the component's executable file.

Projects and Solutions

Your work with Visual InterDev 6 will be based upon *projects* and *solutions*. There are two kinds of projects you can create with Visual InterDev—Web projects and database projects, both of which we'll discuss in this book. A project is a collection of all the files in a project, the settings for that project when it was last saved, and the configuration of Developer Studio when the project was last saved.

A Visual InterDev 6 Web project consists of, simply put, a Web site. Unlike with traditional client-server tools, when you open a Web project with Visual InterDev, you are actually opening a live view of a site as it exists on the Web server. The server can be a personal development server running on your workstation, but more typically it is a staging or production Web server running on a network. The IDE is thus a complete Web site management tool that lets you easily modify the structure of a site (for example, by adding a subdirectory) and edit, add, move, rename, and delete files and folders on the site.

A solution is a container for projects. A solution might contain only one project, or it might contain multiple projects. The information for a solution is stored in an .sln file named for the solution. For instance, a solution named 32XStuff has a solution file named 32Xstuff.sln. This file is stored in the parent directory of the first project in the solution. The "File Types" section at the end of this chapter contains more information on project-related and solution-related file types.

Multiple projects can be opened simultaneously in a solution. Solutions in Visual InterDev 6 provide the same context as that provided by the Workspace in Visual InterDev 1. If there's only one project in a directory and the solution file has the same name, when you open a project file (*.v?p) the solution file is automatically opened. This enables to you to have a project participate in multiple solutions.

The project model is multiuser, allowing multiple developers to work on the same site simultaneously. Check-in and check-out capabilities are provided via integration with the Microsoft Visual SourceSafe version control system. The project system uses the Microsoft FrontPage server-side extensions, which are available for all major Web servers in both the Microsoft Windows NT and UNIX environments. Visual InterDev users and FrontPage users can also work together, simultaneously, on the same sites.

The IDE makes it easy for you to create new sites via wizard technology and to import content, including entire directory trees, into existing sites. You can also browse pages in the project directly from the IDE. This is an important productivity feature because you do not have to pull up a separate Web browser window to view a site under construction. The View in Browser option uses the default browser on your system. When you use this feature, the page you are viewing actually runs in the browser, including all Java applets, ActiveX controls, ActiveX documents, scripting, style sheets, and HTML/DHTML features such as tables and frames.

The IDE also provides a Browse With feature so that you can set up another browser (for example, Netscape Navigator) and with three mouse clicks preview any page of a project in a separate window running that browser.

And you can use the IDE's text editor or HTML editor to edit files in your projects. By default, the IDE associates itself with many file extensions in Windows, including:

- ***.txt**   Text files
- ***.asp**   Active Server Pages files
- ***.html**   HTML files
- ***.htm**   HTML files
- ***.java**   Java application source files
- ***.bat**   DOS batch files
- ***.cmd**   OS/2 and NT command files

To use the IDE's editors to open one of these files, right-click on the file from within Windows Explorer and choose Edit With Visual Studio. If you are using Visual InterDev and you have a file in your project that has an extension that the IDE does not recognize, select the file in Project Explorer, right-click it, and then choose the Open With... command. The Open With... dialog box will display all of the IDE's internal editors so that you can choose one and make it the default editor for that file type.

If you want to open a project's file without loading the whole project, choose the File|Open File command.

The IDE can also open Word files, Excel files, or any file type that can be hosted as an active document. Use the File|Open File command to open these files. The IDE will transform to host Word, but you'll still have all your docking windows available. This is useful when using Word to document specifications or schedules in a project, and you can read or update them without leaving the IDE.

Using Menus and the Keyboard

There are often several ways to accomplish a given task within Developer Studio. Standard Windows-based elements such as toolbars, menus, context menus, and drag-and-drop operations are available for different tasks and sometimes for the same task. The Developer Studio menus contain many options for Visual InterDev projects. You can use the menus to open a Web site or a file, insert a data source into a project, or rearrange the windows displayed within Developer Studio. Be aware that Developer Studio menus can change, depending on the other applications you have installed on your system. For example, if you have Microsoft Visual J++ installed, you will see Build, Debug, and other options that are specific to Visual J++.

The material in this chapter, unless otherwise stated, assumes a default installation of Visual InterDev with no additional Developer Studio–hosted products installed.

As you move around within Developer Studio, notice also that the IDE's menus change in response to your actions. For instance, when you place the cursor in a file, several new options appear on the Edit menu. Other menu options are also added and removed as the context of the current environment changes.

The next few paragraphs describe the various menus.

The File menu is the far-left menu and is used for most file-related tasks, such as creating new files, projects, and solutions; opening existing files, projects, and solutions; and, of course, saving files, projects, and solutions. The File menu also contains other utility commands for file-related tasks.

The Edit menu contains commands related to manipulating text and other attributes within an Edit window. For instance, the standard Cut, Copy, Paste, and Undo commands are located here. The commands on the Edit menu can change, depending on where the cursor is when the Edit menu is selected. For instance, the bottom part of the menu will show the Advanced and Insert File As Text commands when the cursor is located in an HTML page, but you won't see those entries when you are editing a text file.

The View menu contains commands that change Visual InterDev's display characteristics. These include the Refresh command for updating the display and the View Links command, which displays the Link View for the current page and the Broken Links report for troubleshooting links in a site. The View menu also includes the View In Browser and Browse With commands for previewing Web pages.

The Project menu contains commands for inserting new items into the current solution and performing general project-level actions. A command can be as simple as one that inserts a new file into the current project or can be more complex, such as one that inserts an entire project into the current solution. The Project menu also contains commands that work on either an entire project or an entire Web site, such as the Deploy Solution command.

The Tools menu provides direct access to setting Visual InterDev options and customizing the Toolbox. You will also find the View Links On WWW command on the Tools menu.

The Window menu contains items familiar to anyone who has used a multiple-document interface (MDI) application such as Microsoft Word or Microsoft Excel.

Although context-sensitive help is available on a seemingly endless array of subjects throughout Visual InterDev simply by pressing the F1 key, the Help menu also provides access to this information.

You can customize Visual InterDev menus with these steps:

1. Right-click a menu, and select Customize from the context menu.

2. Click the Commands tab to display the Customize dialog box.

3. Select the Command Category that contains the command you need.

4. Select the command you need from the Commands list.

5. Drag the command, and drop it where you want it to appear on the menu.

6. Close the Customize dialog box.

Regarding the keyboard, several keystrokes are especially useful in Visual InterDev. The Esc key will take you from any tool window back to the current document window. Pressing Shift-Esc will close any tool window.

Drag-and-drop actions and popup menus

Developer Studio makes the most of point-and-click technology. The easiest way to do almost anything is to either drag-and-drop an element or right-click the mouse to display a popup menu. Once you get acquainted with the IDE, your productivity will take another big jump over what you can accomplish in other environments. Until you become more familiar with Developer Studio, experiment with dragging and dropping elements and right-clicking the mouse instead of looking through every menu and toolbar. We have documented a lot in this book, but we've also left a few pleasant surprises for you to discover.

You can click the right mouse button at any time to display a context-sensitive (popup) menu of frequently used commands relating to the area in which you click the mouse. This method works throughout Developer Studio in views, Project Explorer, and other areas. For instance, if you right-click over an HTML page, the menu shown in Figure 2-5 appears.

Figure 2-5. *These menu commands work within an HTML page.*

Any item on the menu that is not relevant to the current cursor position is grayed out, indicating that the item is unavailable. The available items on a menu change as you move the cursor. Even within a given window—say, an HTML file—the popup menu can change. For instance, if you right-click a design-time control, the Show Run-Time Text command is available. If you right-click anywhere else, the Show Run-Time Text command is not on the menu and thus is not available.

If you right-click over a filename in Project Explorer, the menu shown in Figure 2-6 appears.

We recommend that you spend some time right-clicking around in the IDE in different places to familiarize yourself with the available options. Each IDE area has a different set of options that are designed to work with the particular item you click on. For instance, you can customize a toolbar by right-clicking it.

Drag-and-drop options also work in many places. You can drop the URL for a file into an HTML page by simply grabbing the filename in the File View of the Project pane and dropping it into a page in the Edit window. To insert a Data Command, just grab the command in Project Explorer and drop it into an ASP Web page. It doesn't get any easier than this!

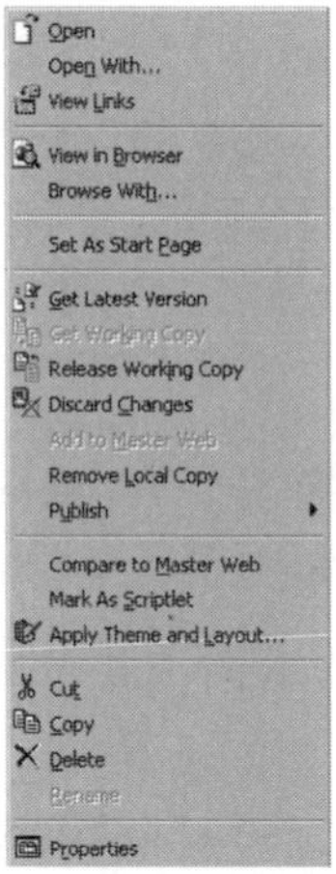

Figure 2-6. *These menu commands are available for files in Project Explorer.*

Table 2-1 illustrates some of the elements that you can drag-and-drop into a page that is open in Design or Source view. Remember, not all drag-and-drop elements are included in this table.

Drag-and-Drop Element	Source View	Description
Data Command	Project Explorer	Inserts a Recordset design-time control
Data Command Fields	Project Explorer	Inserts a design-time control for each field and links it to the Recordset
File	Project Explorer	Inserts the URL for a file into the file open in the editor, complete with an anchor tag
Graphic File	Project Explorer	Inserts an IMG tag
View	Data View	Inserts the SQL for the view
Stored Procedure	Data View	Inserts the SQL for the stored procedure
Toolbox item	Toolbox	Inserts the text or object
Text or object	Source or Design View Editors	Drag text or an object and drop it onto another location on a page
Text	Source View Editor	Insert text from a file into the Toolbox

Table 2-1. *Drag-and-drop elements in the editors.*

Using the Find Command

The Find dialog box lets you do different types of searches from one window. You can use the Find command to search within any of the following:

- The current document (the default)
- All open documents
- The current selection
- The current project folder
- Any number of folders that you choose

You can activate Find by pressing Ctrl-F or through Edit | Find and Replace.

If you want to search in multiple folders, type the paths separated by commas in the Look In: combo box. To refresh the results list when you are doing a multifile search, click the Find button. To step among the results in the results list, press F3. In addition to finding text, you can do automatic search-and-replace operations with Find. You can also dock the Find window by dragging its title bar to the Project Explorer or another window. Doing this can be helpful when you are stepping through large numbers of hits in the results list. If you want to hide a column in the results list of the Find window, simply drag the divider to the right of the column's heading to size the column down to zero.

Toolbars

Visual InterDev 6 provides numerous toolbars that are used to accomplish different tasks. These toolbars, like the IDE's menus, operate from a standard set of commands that are provided by Visual InterDev and Visual Studio. The toolbars contain buttons that are shortcuts to some commonly used menu items. You only need to click a toolbar button once to activate a task.

You can customize toolbars by changing their location, adding commands, removing commands, resizing them, and more. This allows you to customize the interface that Visual InterDev provides.

You can add commands to toolbars following steps similar to those for adding a command to a menu:

1. Right-click a blank spot on a toolbar, and select Customize from the context menu.

2. Click the Commands tab.

3. Select the Command Category that contains the command you need.

4. Select the command you need from the Commands list.

5. Drag the command, and drop it where you want it to appear on the toolbar.

6. Close the Customize dialog box.

To remove commands from a toolbar:

1. Point the mouse at the item you wish to remove from a toolbar.

2. Press and hold down the Alt key.

3. Drag the button from the toolbar into an open area and release it.

To move a toolbar, drag the toolbar to another location. You can also dock the toolbars to one side of the IDE or to a window. To resize a toolbar, grab the corner of a toolbar and drag it to its new size. You can resize any toolbar that is not docked. Docked toolbars do not display a title. If you make a toolbar shorter, the buttons will wrap and the toolbar will change its aspect ratio to accommodate the buttons.

Configuring the Interface

Developer Studio toolbars and windows are free-floating and dockable. A dockable object can be free-floating within the Developer Studio interface or docked to one of the borders. For instance, the toolbars that appear at the top of Developer Studio are merely docked there. You can click on the double bars of a docked toolbar and drag the toolbar, thereby undocking it, as shown with the Query toolbar in Figure 2-7 on the following page. You can even drag it to the bottom of the window and release it, docking it to the bottom of the window frame. Likewise, the Project Explorer window that displays your Web site and its files is merely docked. You can drag it from the border or even maximize it to fill the entire Developer Studio parent window.

When you enable a toolbar, by default it floats freely in Developer Studio. You can grab a toolbar with the mouse and drag it to any location. When you drag a toolbar or a window to a docking location (such as the top of the Developer Studio environment), it changes shape to fit that location and the title bar for the toolbar disappears. Drag the toolbar into place and drop it to complete the docking operation. To make a toolbar free-floating again, simply grab it with the mouse and drag it out of a docking location.

To drag a toolbar that is not docked, place the mouse over the toolbar's title bar and then click the left mouse button and drag. To drag a toolbar that is docked, place the mouse over the toolbar but outside of any toolbar button, and then click the left mouse button and drag. (If you have trouble finding a point outside of all toolbar buttons, click the double bars.) If you double-click a docked toolbar, it moves to its previous floating position.

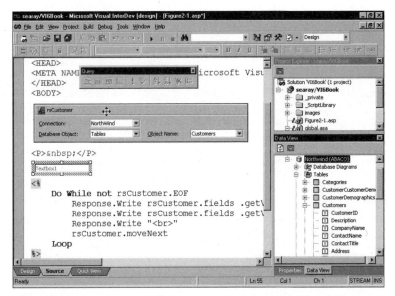

Figure 2-7. *The Query toolbar has been undocked and left free-floating.*

You can hide a toolbar you don't need by right-clicking a blank spot on the toolbars and clicking the toolbar's name on the popup list to deselect the toolbar you wish to hide. You can reenable that toolbar by using this same method and then selecting the name of the desired toolbar.

You can dock windows in the IDE on top of each other by dragging the title bar of one docking window to another. To switch among the windows, use the tabs that appear at the bottom of the docked set. If you want to separate the windows, drag one of the tabs to another location outside the current window.

Visual InterDev 6 uses named window layouts for configuration information. You can see this in Figure 2-7. Notice the list box just above the right end of the Query toolbar? This is the window layout name that we are currently using. You can change window layouts by selecting one from the list.

Visual InterDev 6 has several standard window layouts:

- **Debug**   Used when Visual InterDev switches to debug mode

- **Design**   Used in design mode, displays Project Explorer, Data View, and the Toolbox

- **DevStudio**   The normal Developer Studio mode; changes the interface to a Visual InterDev 1 look

- **Edit HTML**   Used when editing HTML; displays Project Explorer, HTML outline, and the Properties window

■ **Full Screen** Hides all windows and displays the edit window full screen

■ **Visual Basic** Changes the interface to a Visual Basic look and feel

The window layouts are nice because you can reconfigure the interface with the click of a mouse. When you wish to flip back to another window layout, click again and it's right back. And not only can you quickly change the interface, you can create your own named window layouts:

1. Change the configuration.

2. Select Define Window Layout from the View menu.

3. Enter the name for your view.

4. Click Add.

The IDE now supports multiple monitors. Using Windows 98 or Windows NT 5, you can place the IDE or its docking windows on a secondary monitor. This is especially helpful for debugging because you can have your running application on one monitor and your code on the other.

The IDE supports different keyboard schemes. By default, Visual Studio ships with Visual Basic, Developer Studio, and Visual C++ 2 keyboard bindings. You can also create your own keyboard scheme by using Tools|Options and selecting the Environment/Keyboard node in the tree.

Task List

The Task List is new for Visual Studio 6. The Task List helps you customize, categorize, and manage work associated with your project. The Task List does this by displaying your tasks, specially marked comments, named shortcuts, warnings, and detected errors. Some errors, such as SmartEditor and comment errors, are generated as you type in the Editor window. You can also add named shortcuts and other items within the Task List itself at any time.

You can display the Task List by pressing Ctrl-Alt-K or by choosing Task List from the Other Windows command on the View menu.

You can add a task to the Task List by taking these steps:

1. Click the first line in the Description column where it says "Click here to add a new task."

2. Enter the task description.

3. Click the leftmost column to change the task's priority.

You can sort tasks with these steps:

1. Right-click anywhere in the Task window.

2. Choose Sort By from the context menu.

3. Choose the type of sort from the context menu.

You can also add shortcuts to a comment in your code and later jump to the comment's location in the editor. Figure 2-8 shows the Task List with two comments that have shortcuts. You can see the second comment just past the Loop command.

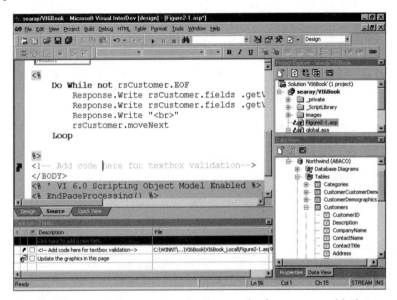

Figure 2-8. *The Task List can track all types of information and link it to specific locations in files.*

You can insert shortcuts to comments using these steps:

1. Insert a valid comment in the code window.

2. Right-click the comment, and choose Add Shortcut from the context menu.

Now you can jump to the location of the comment at any time by double-clicking the shortcut icon in the Task List line containing the comment.

The text editor automatically looks for code comments with tags like "TODO" or "HACK" and puts those lines of code on the Task List. To add your own comment tags that the editor will scan for, use Tools|Options and choose the Environment/Task List node.

The Task List lets you type in your own tasks and associate them with the current solution. When you open that solution in the future, the tasks that you entered will be shown. If someone else uses the same solution file, your tasks are not shared—they are saved on your machine only.

You can also tie any line of code to a task in the Task List. To tie a line of code to a task:

1. Open the file in the text editor.

2. Place the cursor on the line you want to tie to a task.

3. Press Ctrl-K and then Ctrl-H.

When the shortcut appears on the task list, click in the description field and give it an appropriate name. This is also helpful for marking where you were last working in a file or for describing a problem you were trying to solve and the next steps to take.

You can check off a completed task by clicking the complete box just to the left of the task's description.

You can also filter the tasks that are displayed in the Task List:

1. Right-click anywhere in the Task window.

2. Choose Show Tasks from the context menu.

3. Select the tasks that you want to display.

To delete tasks from the Task List:

1. Right-click the task you want to delete.

2. Choose Delete Task from the context menu.

3. Confirm the deletion by answering Yes.

CREATING A WEB PROJECT

Visual InterDev Web projects are considered applications because they consist of various components, such as pages that can update a database, pages that pull information from a database, multimedia pages, and ActiveX components. As you can see, Visual InterDev applications can be complex. They can also include links to pages across the Internet.

Oftentimes you must manage both the creation of a Web site and its long-term maintenance. Using a source code management system makes it easier to create and maintain a Web site, and it improves the development process. It both reduces the number of interaction problems when developers write over other developers' pages and facilitates the reuse of various project elements.

The first step in creating a Web project is to start Visual InterDev. Then take the following steps:

1. Choose New Project from the File menu, or click the New Project icon on the toolbar. The New Project dialog box appears, as shown in Figure 2-9.

2. Double-click the New Web Project icon.

3. Enter the name for your new site in the Name text box.

4. Click either Close Current Solution to start a new solution or Add To Current Solution to add this new project to the current solution.

5. Enter the name of the server that will host the site.

6. Select either Master or Local mode.

7. Click Next.

8. If you want to create a new Web site with the same name as your project, click Next or Finish. Clicking Finish will bypass the final dialogs and create the site. If you want to change the site's name, do so before clicking Next or Finish.

If you clicked Next in step 8, you will be presented with two more wizard steps. These final two steps allow you to supply a *layout* or *theme* to the project. Layouts and themes supply the look for an application. If you choose them at this step, Visual InterDev will copy the appropriate files into your application but will not assign the layouts or themes to files—you must do that later.

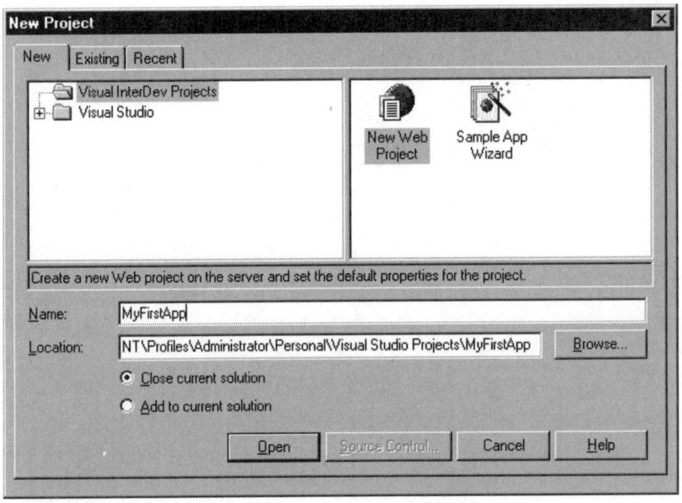

Figure 2-9. *The New Project dialog box provides a list of icons and wizards you can use to create a new project.*

Each option in the New Project dialog box creates a different type of project and takes you step by step through the project creation process. You can quickly create a site and then begin adding content, such as Web pages or database connections or a combination of these and other items. The content is what matters most, and Visual InterDev is designed to let you spend most of your time on that.

When prompted, you must supply the name of the server that will host the site. After you step through the wizard, Visual InterDev communicates with the Web server and creates the new site on the server under the Web server's root directory. It creates a directory with the name you specify for the site and creates an Images directory under it. A new virtual root with the same name, which points to the new Web directory, is also created on the server. If you want to change the name of the site's parent directory, make your changes and then click Next or Finish. Visual InterDev also sets the permissions on the site so that pages can be read and scripts can be executed.

The New Project Wizard automatically creates a file named global.asa, which is the site's default startup file. If you want users to be able to search your site, select the Enable Full Text Searching For Pages In This Web check box. When this option is selected, the wizard creates a file named search.htm, which provides a full-text search page for your site. The New Project Wizard will also copy the scripting library into the _ScriptLibrary directory.

You can also connect your project to an existing site by selecting the Connect To An Existing Web Application On *Name* option button during the creation process instead of selecting Create A New Web. This will connect your project to the existing site and build a mirror of the site's structure in your local working directory.

Creating a new Web project can take a lot of time when either the server that is hosting the site or the network connection between the site running Visual InterDev and the server is busy. Visual InterDev will keep you updated. The information appears in the status line at the bottom of the Developer Studio interface and in several informational messages displayed as small forms.

WEB PROJECT TYPES

The New Project dialog box also provides several options for creating projects. Each project type generates a project or site with certain characteristics. If you have installed Microsoft Visual J++, other options will appear. Table 2-2 on the following page shows several useful project types for use with Visual InterDev. The project type is prefixed with the folder containing it.

Folder/Project Type	Description
Database Projects/ Database Project	Adds a database project. Database projects are useful for managing databases and working with the database structure without tying it to a Web project.
Distribution Units/ Cabinet	Creates a distribution project. You can use this wizard to create a new project that you can use to store items to go into the cab file. From the project, you can also build the cab file.
Distribution Units/Zip	Creates a new zip file project. You can use this wizard to create a new project that you can use to store items to go into the zip file. From the project, you can also build the zip file.
Distribution Units/ Self Extracting Setup	Creates a new self-extracting setup file project. You can use this wizard to create a new project that you can use to store items to go into the self-extracting setup file. From the project, you can also build the setup file.
Visual InterDev Projects/New Web Project	Creates a new Web application. This is the option you will use most to create new Web applications.
Visual InterDev Projects/Sample App Wizard	Installs sample applications.

Table 2-2. *Selected Visual Studio project types.*

Using these project types can save you a lot of time. For instance, if you use the New Web Project option, you can select from different background theme options; Visual InterDev then links the appropriate theme to your site. This saves you time and reduces your testing and debugging cycle. Figure 2-10 shows Project Explorer with the theme files this wizard typically generates. The wizard also loads stylesheets for the site into the _Themes directory. You can modify these stylesheets to provide global formatting for your site and then use them to create other stylesheets by copying one to a new name.

As Microsoft and other companies generate new wizards, you can expect to see additional options for new types of projects. Developer Studio and Visual InterDev are extensible and provide a framework for additional features such as new wizards.

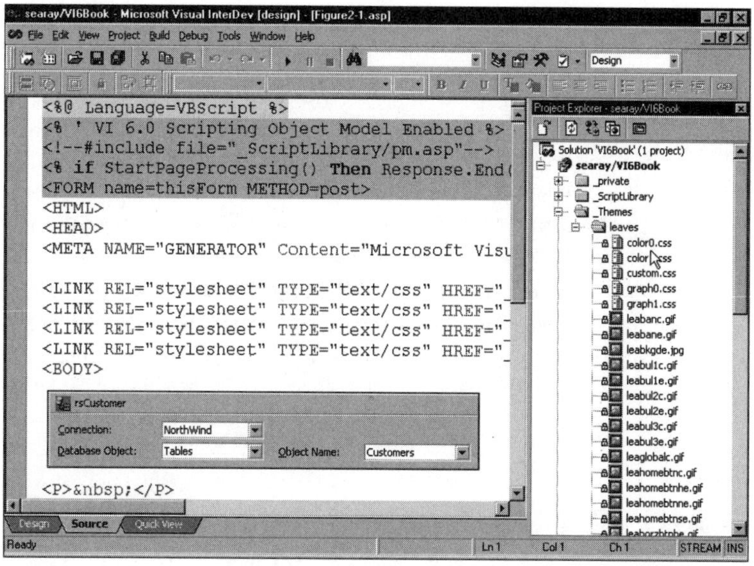

Figure 2-10. *A typical directory structure for a simple Web site.*

OPENING EXISTING SITES

Users who work on a site with Visual InterDev should define their own projects; that is, they should not share projects in a single directory on a server. When the working files are shared on a server, all users should have their own working directories. Below is a sample directory structure for a server:

```
\Users
    \KenSpencer
        \Projects
            \WebABC
            \WebXYZ
            \WebNew
    \KenMiller
        \Projects
            \WebABC
            \WebXYZ
            \WebNew
    \NickEvans
        \Projects
            \WebABC
            \WebXYZ
            \WebOld
```

This sample structure supports Ken Spencer, Ken Miller, and Nick Evans; each person has his own working files for each Web project he is working on. Each person is working on WebABC and WebXYZ as well as other Web projects.

If a user is also working on Visual C++ or Visual J++ projects, each application can follow the same directory structure. Visual Studio remembers your working directory each time you save a workspace or a project. Simply save a workspace to a new directory, and the next time you save it, the workspace will default to that directory structure.

Working on an existing site is the same as creating a new project and then connecting to an existing site. The site is loaded into your project, which you can then work on. Create a new project using the New Web Project Wizard, and connect to an existing Web site. You now have a distributed project workspace on your computer pointing to the same site.

Managing Files and Folders Within a Project

Visual InterDev lets you manage a site's various files and folders. You can create new files and folders, copy files and folders, delete files and folders, and so forth.

Figure 2-8, shown on page 42, shows the Project Explorer for a typical Web site. This is a simple site with a few folders and several files. It was created with the New Web Project Wizard.

You should carefully plan the directory structure of your site. The Visual InterDev tools help you manage the site, but you must take the time to create the proper structure to hold the various files for the site. For instance, the site wizards automatically create the Images folder for a site. If you select a color theme in a wizard or after you have created a project, Visual InterDev creates the appropriate folders to hold those components and copies the files into the new folders. In a typical department, you might have subdepartments that report to the parent department. If so, create appropriate folders for each.

Adding New Items

You can add items such as folders, files, graphics, and other items to a site by using the IDE. To add a new folder:

1. Right-click the site name or parent folder.

2. Select New Folder.

3. In the New Folder dialog box, enter the new folder's name.

If you right-click any folder in the site, the New Folder command appears on the popup menu. If you choose the New Folder command for a subfolder, the new folder is created under the selected folder.

The Add Item command on the Project menu (and on the toolbar and Project Explorer popup menu) provides tools that let you add many other items to a project. Figure 2-11 shows the Add Item properties with the New tab selected. The New tab contains several options for new files.

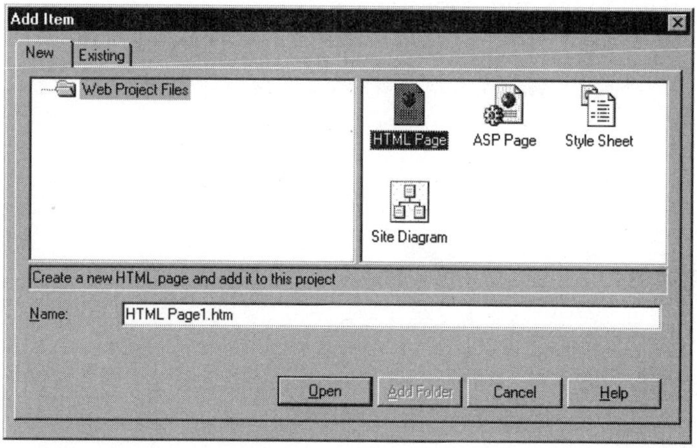

Figure 2-11. *The Add Item dialog box with the New tab selected.*

Table 2-3 describes the standard options for new files. Select the appropriate file type when creating a new file. Selecting the HTML Page option, for instance, creates a new HTML document complete with the appropriate tags at the beginning and end of the file.

Option	*File Type*
Active Server Page	(.asp) ASP file that contains server scripting
HTML Page	(.htm) HTML file
Style Sheet	(.css) cascading style sheet
Site Diagram	(.wdm) site diagram for building and managing Web pages

Table 2-3. *Options on the New tab.*

To add a new file to a project, take the following steps:

1. Right-click the site name in Project Explorer.

2. Choose Add from the popup menu.

3. Select the file type to add.

4. Enter the file's name.

5. Click Open. The new file is created.

The new file is automatically created in the site on the server, and it shows up in Project Explorer page. A copy of the file is placed in the Visual InterDev working directory.

Adding an Existing File or Folder

You can also add existing files and folders to your site in one of several ways. The following sets of step-by-step instructions demonstrate the flexibility you have in managing files.

To add an existing file to a site, take these steps:

1. Right-click the project name or the folder to which you want to add the files in Project Explorer.

2. Choose the Add command from the popup menu.

3. Select Add Item from the submenu.

4. Click the Existing tab.

5. Select the file or files to add.

6. Click Open.

Each file you selected is added to the project.

To add the contents of an existing folder to your project:

1. In Windows Explorer, select the folder to be added.

2. Drag the folder and drop it onto its new location in Project Explorer.

The folder's contents are added to the current project.

You can also add an existing file to your site using drag-and-drop by dragging a file or folder from Windows Explorer and dropping it on the File View page of the Project Workspace. The file is copied to the Web site, and a local working copy is downloaded to your system. You simply need to add the links in your project to the files.

Deleting a File or a Folder

Deleting a file or a folder is as simple as deleting a file in Windows Explorer. Take the following steps:

1. In Project Explorer, select the file or folder to delete.

2. Press the Delete key, or right-click the file or folder and choose the Delete command.

3. Click Yes when you're asked whether you want to delete the file or folder.

The file or folder is deleted from both your local working copy and the Web site.

Renaming a File or a Folder

Renaming a file or a folder is similar to deleting a file. Just take the following steps:

1. Select the file or folder you want to rename.

2. Right-click the file or folder, and select Release Working Copy.

3. Right-click the file or folder, and choose the Rename command. (Or press F2. Or click the file or folder twice—slowly.)

4. Enter the new name for the file or folder.

5. Press the Enter key.

The file or folder is renamed on both your local working copy and the Web site. Any links within your project to the file or the folder are updated automatically.

Working with Sites

A Visual InterDev Web project contains all the files associated with your Web pages as well as a set of project definition files that Visual InterDev uses to maintain and manage the project itself. A Web project is only a reference to a collection of Web files on the Web server; it is not the Web application itself. The application's master files are contained on the Web server hosting the application. You can have a Web application without a project, but not a Web project without a Web application.

In a multideveloper environment, each developer creates a Web project that references the same Web application residing on the Web server. You should refresh or synchronize your local working copy of a site occasionally during the day to make sure it is synchronized with the Web site master copy. If other people are working on the same site, your local copy can get out of sync with the master copy. In fact, everyone's local copy can get out of sync when multiple people make changes. This can cause problems such as broken links and loss of source documents as one copy overwrites another.

To refresh your local working copy, select the Project you wish to refresh in Project Explorer and then choose Refresh from the View menu. Refreshing your local working copy picks up any changes to files or folders and any new files that have been added. Files or folders deleted on the Web site are not deleted on your local working copy. This can cause your local working copy to include files that the Web site does not. It also lets you place the files back on the server if you think they have been deleted erroneously.

Refreshing a project does not replace any local write-enabled copy of your files with files from the server. If the master files have changed, your local copies will remain the same.

You can also synchronize a project or files with the master site. Synchronizing a site does not retrieve a list of new files from the server, but it does synchronize all changes to files. To synchronize a project or multiple files, select the Project or files you want to synchronize in Project Explorer and then select Synchronize from the Project | Web Project menu.

Visual InterDev 6 contains a feature that allows you to isolate your development site from the master site. The files for the Web application reside in two places: the project directory of the developer workstation and the virtual directory on the master Web server. When you are working in a project, you are working on the local files. How changes you save are made to the version on the master Web server depends on the mode the project is in: local or master.

In local mode, changes made to the files are not immediately saved to the master Web server. The new versions are sent to the master Web server only when you explicitly request that the master Web server be updated. If you used the New Project Wizard to create your project and you have a Web server on your workstation, the project is set in local mode by default. In master mode, changes are saved to the local version and the master version at the same time, each time you save a file.

If you are working online, when you save files they will be saved on your local system. They may also update the master Web project depending upon the mode the project is in, as shown in Table 2-4.

Mode	*Action*
Local	The page is saved locally.
Master	The page is saved locally and updated on the master Web server.

Table 2-4. *Local and master modes.*

Moving a File or a Folder

Visual InterDev automates many aspects of site creation and management. Moving files and folders is a good example. If you need to move a file or a folder, open Project Explorer, drag the file or folder to its new location, and drop it in. When you drop the file or folder in its new location, Visual InterDev automatically fixes all the links to the files that were moved.

When you move files and folders, the site is automatically updated. The changes are also reflected in your local working copy of the site, but not to other users who have the site open. They must refresh their local working copy to see the changes.

If you receive a message that your working files are out of sync, you must manually resolve the issue with the file(s) shown. For example, suppose you move a file called feedback.htm to the Images directory on another system and then choose the Refresh command from the View menu. Visual InterDev discovers the discrepancy between the local files and those on the Web server and tries to resolve it. When it cannot guarantee that it has resolved the links, a dialog box appears to tell you that your working files are out of sync. If you look at your working directory in Windows Explorer, you can see that the file is still there. (See Figure 2-12.)

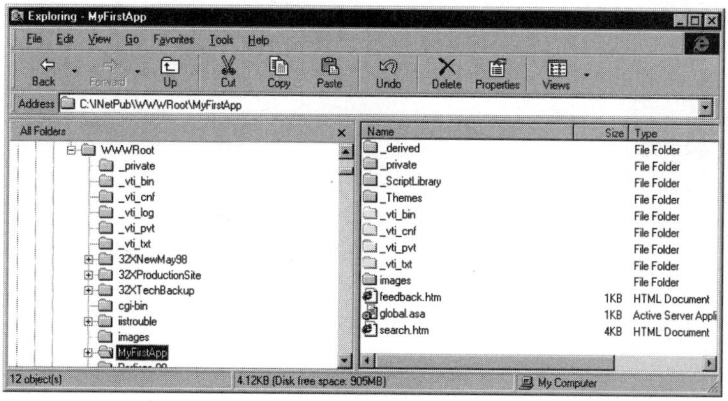

Figure 2-12. *The feedback.htm file appears in Windows Explorer.*

While Figure 2-12 shows that feedback.htm is still in the root directory for the Web site, the File View page of the Project Workspace in Figure 2-13 on the following page shows that the file has been moved within the Web site.

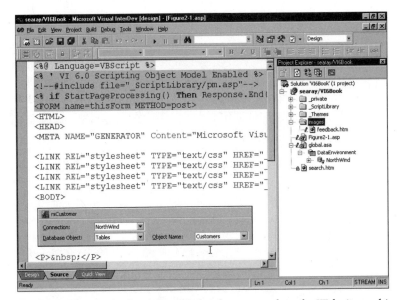

Figure 2-13. *The feedback.htm file has been moved on the Web site and in Project Explorer.*

Figures 2-12 and 2-13 demonstrate how a workspace can get out of sync with a Web site. You can either delete feedback.htm from the working copy or use it to manually update the server. For instance, you can move feedback.htm to the Images directory and replace the existing feedback.htm file that was retrieved from the site. Or you can simply delete feedback.htm from the working copy's root directory and use the new copy retrieved from the server.

Visual InterDev might also inform you that a file you are trying to open has a newer version on the Web server. If this occurs, you can select the new file from the dialog box, and your working copy will be updated automatically. The automatic update does not update pages with links to the moved files if the pages are not in your project. Visual InterDev has no way of knowing about those links.

These scenarios all suggest why it is a good idea to use a tool such as Microsoft Visual SourceSafe to manage your Web applications. This is the only way you can assure that your Web pages and associated files are in sync and are protected.

Copying a Web Site

Visual InterDev lets you copy a Web site to another site. You can copy a site to either another server or another site on the same server using the same steps:

1. In Project Explorer, select the project name or a component of the project to copy.

2. Choose the Copy Web Application command from the Project | Web Project menu, or click the Copy Web Application button on the Project Explorer toolbar. The Copy Project dialog box appears.

3. Enter the destination server name, or use the default name to copy the site on the same server.

4. Enter the name of the site for the destination server.

5. If you are copying the project to a new Web, uncheck the Add To Existing Web Project check box.

6. Click OK.

Figure 2-14 shows the Copy Project dialog box with the current server as the default destination server.

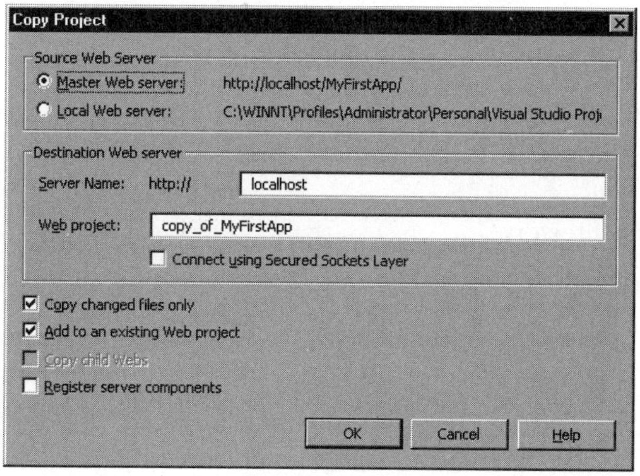

Figure 2-14. *The Copy Project dialog box.*

If the server requires you to connect using Secure Sockets Layer (SSL), you must select the Connect Using Secured Sockets Layer check box.

File Status

Visual InterDev tracks the status of each file in your project. A file that is a working copy is considered updatable and is shown with a pencil icon in Project Explorer. Any changes you make to a working copy of a file are updated to the Web site whenever you save the file. The changes are also saved locally in the working directory.

A lock icon to the left of the file indicates a released file, which is not updatable. You can release a working copy of a file when you no longer need to update it. Releasing the file will delete the file from the working directory. The next time you try to edit the file, Visual InterDev can automatically retrieve a new copy from the site (that is, a copy of the server version of the file is downloaded to your working directory). If you try to open a file and do not have a working copy of that file, Visual InterDev will prompt you with the dialog box shown in Figure 2-15.

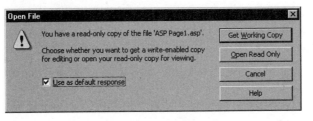

Figure 2-15. *The Open File dialog box allows you to determine what action to take regarding working copies of files.*

When the Open File dialog box is displayed, you can click Get Working Copy and Visual InterDev will retrieve a working copy of the file from the server and open it. If you want only to read the file, click Open Read Only. You can also check the Use As Default Response check box and Visual InterDev will use this answer in the future rather than displaying this dialog box to prompt you.

If you wish to reset your response to the Open File question, you can do this with Tools | Options. Figure 2-16 shows Tools | Options with the Web Projects settings displayed. The settings in the When Opening A File area control what Visual InterDev does when you open a file and do not have a working copy. If you set the default answer and wish to change it, you must change it here.

The Open File settings help ensure that you always work with the most current copy of a file. Releasing a file does not keep you from updating the file further; it simply marks the file as released from the working directory by displaying the gray icon on the FileView page.

To release a working copy of a file, right-click the filename and choose the Release Working Copy command. When you double-click a released file to open it for editing, Visual InterDev contacts the server and retrieves a new copy of the file.

To retrieve a working copy of both the released and current files, right-click the file you want to retrieve and choose the Get Working Copy command.

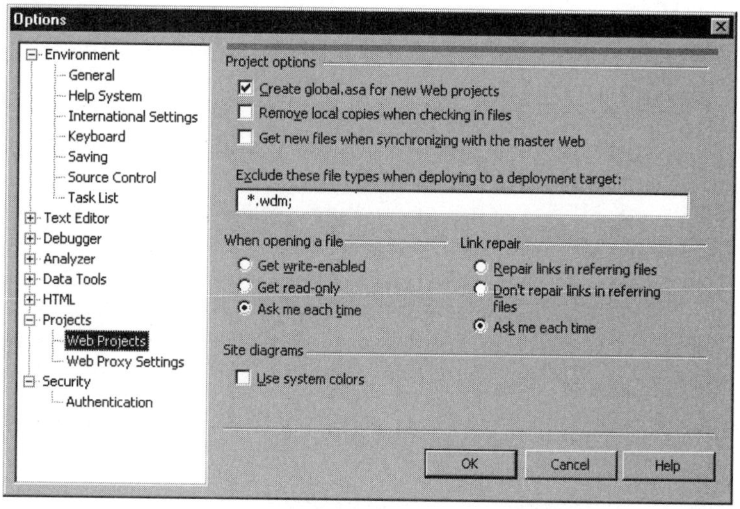

Figure 2-16. *The Tools | Options page allows you to change system options such as the default answer to the Open File dialog box.*

If you try to save a file and do not have a working copy, the Save Of Read-Only File dialog box shown in Figure 2-17 appears. This dialog box lets you determine how Visual InterDev should update the file.

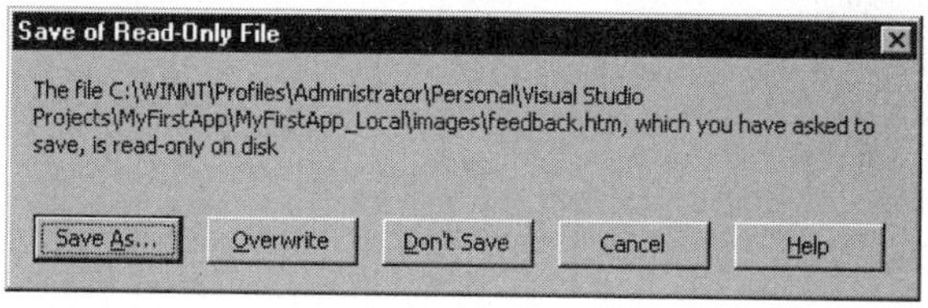

Figure 2-17. *The Save Of Read-Only File dialog box.*

The Save Of Read-Only File dialog box lets you specify whether to keep the existing file (Save As) or update the read-only file (Overwrite). Before clicking one of the buttons, make sure you pick the right file.

If you try to open a project and your file copy is either newer or older than the same file on the server, the Confirm Update dialog box might appear. You can then accept the suggested update with one mouse click. Be sure to carefully resolve issues with file versions; you can easily have a file that is older or newer than the server version and incorrectly overwrite one or the other.

You can select multiple files and use both the Release and Get options on all selected files simultaneously. This lets you treat files as a group and perform the tasks faster. Use Ctrl-Click or Shift-Click to select the files. Do not hold down the mouse button and drag to select files because Developer Studio treats this as a drag operation. After you select the files, right-click a selected file and then choose Get Working Copy or Release Working Copy from the popup menu.

Using Visual InterDev with an Existing Web Site

You can use Visual InterDev with any existing Web site. You first need to create a new workspace that incorporates the site you want to work with. You can then use that workspace just as if you had created a new site from scratch.

The options for creating the new workspace and incorporating it into the existing site depend on whether the site was created with a server that had the Microsoft FrontPage Server Extensions installed. The FrontPage Server Extensions provide the interface between the Web server and Visual InterDev. You can automatically load sites created on servers running the FrontPage Server Extensions into a Visual InterDev project.

For sites without the FrontPage Server Extensions, the process is slightly more complex. The steps for both options are shown below.

To load a site on a server that has the FrontPage Server Extensions installed, use the same New project steps we covered earlier in this chapter, except connect the new project to an existing site. Your new project will contain the existing site, which you can use just like any other that you create with Visual InterDev.

To load a site that was not created on a FrontPage Server Extensions–enabled server, perform the steps below. The files that you wish to load must exist on a file share that is accessible with Windows Explorer. Make sure you complete each step, or you will have extra files on your server.

1. Create a new site on the target server.

2. Find the parent folder for the Web site with Windows Explorer.

3. Select all the files and folders in the folder that contains the site you want to add, and drop them on the project in Project Explorer. This will add the entire contents of files and folders to the parent folder for the new Web site.

4. Test the new site to verify that it contains the correct files and works the way you want it to.

The contents of the existing site's folders are added to the current project. The new site contains all the files that were added from the original site plus any new ones that the Web Project Wizard created, such as global.asa, search.htm, and the Images folder.

MANAGING A SITE USING LINK VIEW

The Link View feature provides a graphical representation of the structure of a Web site. The graphical display shows the pages in the site and the links between them. Link View can depict a wide variety of objects in a site with various graphical icons. These objects include standard HTML pages, ASP Web pages, images, audio and video files, executables, and protocols such as Mail To, as well as data connections, data commands, data range headers, and generic designer controls. Link View is an extremely powerful tool for troubleshooting large sites with complex functionality. You can even chase links from one page to another and quickly determine when links are missing or corrupt.

To open a Link View window:

1. Choose View Links On WWW from the Tools menu.

2. Enter the URL of the site you want to view. This can be any site to which you have a valid connection, including sites located on the Internet if you have an open connection.

3. Click OK.

The Link View window opens, with the site you selected shown in the middle. If you are connecting to a large site, you might want to pause the verification of each page when Link View first appears. To pause the verification step, choose Pause Verification from the Tools menu. To resume verification, choose the Resume Verification command.

The Link View toolbar also appears if it was not visible before. It has a number of commands that let you adjust the filtering of the objects shown in the Link View. Table 2-5 on the following page shows its commands.

Most toolbar commands work on the currently selected object. You can also work with multiple objects.

You can also open a Link View window on a current object in your project. An object's popup menu should include a View Links command whenever applicable.

To open Link View on an object in the current project, take the following steps:

1. Select the object(s) in Project Explorer on which to open Link View.

2. Right-click the selection.

3. Choose View Links from the popup menu.

Command	Description
Expand Links	Expands the links from the current page
Verify Links	Verifies links
Change Diagram Layout	Changes between the two layout views
Show In Links	Shows the links from other pages to the currently selected page or file
Show Out Links	Shows the links from the currently selected page to other pages or files
Show In and Out Links	Shows the links from the currently selected page to other pages or files and from other pages to the currently selected page or file
Show Repeated Links	Show links that are repeated in a page
Show Links Inside Pages	Show internal links
Show All Objects	Shows all objects in the site
Show HTML Pages	Shows only HTML pages (Active Layouts, Active Server Pages, global Active Server Page, Style Sheets) in the site
Show Multimedia Files	Shows only multimedia files (audio, images, image maps, video, and virtual reality) in the site
Show Documents	Shows only documents (Word, text, Excel, and so forth) in the site
Show Executable Files	Shows only executable files in the site
Show Other Protocols	Shows all protocols (Mail To, News, Telnet, and Unknown) used by the site
Show External Files	Shows all external files that are referenced by pages and files in the site
Zoom Link View	Controls the percentage the Link View window is scaled

Table 2-5. *Link View toolbar commands.*

You must expand an object to display its links. Figure 2-18 shows a sample object expanded by selecting default.asp (from the AdventureWorks sample application) and then selecting the toolbar's Expand Links option.

The arrows between the objects in a site are color-coded to indicate the link's status. You can see the broken link to 32x3dshaded.jpg in Figure 2-18. If a broken link exists, Link View provides a graphical clue that the link is broken. Table 2-6 describes the link colors.

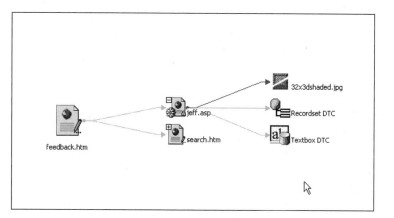

Figure 2-18. *The links between a selected page and other pages and files.*

Color	Meaning
Gray (default)	Links to and from unselected objects.
Red	Broken links that cannot be resolved. The links might not actually be broken; they might simply be unreachable at the moment. (For example, they might be Internet pages to which you do not currently have a connection.)

Table 2-6. *Link colors in Link View.*

The icons representing the various objects in Link View provide a graphical indicator of the object's type and its status. The Visual InterDev Help file shows the icons for each type of object. To access Help for that view, press F1 while Link View is displayed.

You can also open a new Link View on an object currently displayed in Link View by taking the following steps:

1. In the Link View window, select the object(s) on which to open Link View.

2. Right-click the selection, and choose the View Links command from the popup menu.

3. A new Link View window opens with the new display. To alternate between the current view and the previous view, you can use the Next and Previous commands on the Window menu.

The display within Link View changes as you move from object to object. When you select an object, all of the links to that object turn blue. The object also changes color to indicate that it is selected.

You can view the links to and from an object by clicking on it. Visual InterDev also shows all the connections to and from that page. To view an object's full URL, place the cursor over the object for a second or so. The tooltip for an object changes if the link is broken.

The link status tooltips and URL tooltips that Link View displays are useful for tracking problems in a site. If only one link has a problem, it is most likely related to some type of access to that object. If a lot of links to the same server are down, there might be a problem with that server.

Link View normally shows an error code when it displays the broken link tooltip. The error number is displayed from winInet.dll. This .dll file is the same one that Internet Explorer uses for its Internet connection. Appendix B lists all the winInet.dll error messages.

You can zoom the Link View in and out using the Zoom Link View list box on the Link View toolbar.

The popup menu for link objects also provides options that work with multiple pages. If you right-click an object or a group of selected objects, you can choose Expand Links to display the links for all pages. The Preview In Browser command opens the object in the default browser. The Open command opens the object in Edit mode.

To send mail to the address specified by the Mail To command, right-click the Mail To icon and then choose Preview In Browser. To open a file for editing, double-click an object in a Link View for your project. This provides quick access to files within a complex project. The Open command also performs this task. You can also right-click an image and choose Preview In Browser to display it. To save the page in your project, choose Save As from the File menu.

You can drag icons for an object from Link View into Internet Explorer, Word, Exchange Mail, or other applications that support drag-and-drop.

You might occasionally need to refresh Link View, particularly when others are working on a site while you have the Link View window open. The Refresh command on the View menu updates the Link View display and performs a new verification on all objects in the site.

Directory Structure

Visual InterDev 6 uses several directories you should be aware of. You should be aware of the directories and what Visual InterDev 6 stores there, and you should understand what you can move and what you should not move.

The Visual InterDev program is stored, by default, in this structure:

```
C:\Program Files
    Microsoft Visual Studio
        VIntDev98
            bin
            Layouts
            Samples
            Script Library
            Templates
            Themes
```

If you have installed the Server Tools, you will also see the SrvSetup folder. Normally, you should leave the program files in their default locations. You may want to change the directories that store your Layouts and Templates.

In addition to these directories, you will find some files that are used by Visual Studio and Visual InterDev 6 in the Common Files directory.

```
C:\Program Files
    Common Files
        Designer
        Microsoft Shared
        Services
```

In the VIntDev98 directory structure, you might want to consider moving the Themes directory to a network share, if you have lots of users who use themes and work on a network.

Your project files are stored, by default, in your profile area:

```
C:\Winnt\Profiles\user
    \Personal\Visual Studio Projects
        \projectname
```

Projectname will be the name of your project.

Microsoft Internet Information Server (IIS) also uses a directory structure as a container for Web site and application files. The default IIS Web directory tree is illustrated at the top of the following page.

In this example tree, WWWroot contains one Web application, *projectname*. The directories starting with an underscore (_) are system directories that contain files used by IIS, FrontPage Server Extensions, or Visual InterDev 6. For instance, in this tree you can see the DataEnvironent directory under the _private directory. The DataEnvironent directory contains files used by the DE run-time engine.

```
C:\InetPub
   WWWroot
      projectname
         _derived
         Layouts
         _private
               DataEnvironment
               ProgrammingModel
         _ScriptLibrary
         _Themes
         _vti_bin
         _vti_cnf
         _vti_pvt
         _vti_txt
         images
```

File Types

Visual InterDev creates several files when you either start a new Web site or add to a site. Some of the files are standard files such as HTML or text files, while others are specific to Visual InterDev. Other files that you will use frequently with a Web site project include ActiveX servers, ActiveX components, and source files for ASP Web pages. New file types are also added as new types of pages or applications are created. You can also create your own file types for Web sites.

Visual InterDev Web sites and workspaces use the following file types most often:

- .sln files (Visual Studio Solution files) that store information about the current solution

- .vip files (Visual InterDev Project) that store information about Visual InterDev projects

- .opt files (Workspace options files) that store workspace settings

- .htm files that are standard HTML files

- .asp files that contain ActiveX server script and HTML code

- .asa files that are global ASP files for an entire site

- .ocx files that are ActiveX controls

- .alx files (ActiveX Layout files)

- .exe files that are standard executable files

- Other executable files that are often shared between applications

- .dll (dynamic-link libraries) files that are ActiveX server-side components

- .reg files used to register ActiveX components

- .cab files that are setup files containing one or more compressed files

- .stm files that contain HTML and VBScript and are used as include files for ASP Web pages

- .inc files that contain HTML and VBScript and are used as include files for ASP Web pages

This list does not include all the standard file types used in a Web site that represent different application needs, such as GIF, JPG, and WAV.

Chapter 3

Debugging Applications

OVERVIEW

Microsoft Visual Studio 6 includes a built-in debugger with its own complete set of windows and its own toolbar. The debugger allows you to debug both Microsoft Visual InterDev and Visual J++ applications and components. You can also use the debugger to step into the code of components used in Visual InterDev applications written in Microsoft Visual Basic and Visual C++, as long as you have the source code for the application or component.

This chapter will demonstrate how to use the debugger to debug Active Server Pages (ASP) script, client-side script, and Visual Basic components. You'll see how you can use this tool both locally on a system and against an application running remotely on a server. Figure 3-1 on the following page shows the debugger interface.

The Visual InterDev debugging process is similar to debugging a Visual Basic application. You can:

■ Set breakpoints in your application

■ Step into the application code

■ Display the contents of variables

■ Change the values of variables

■ Execute commands in the Immediate window

■ Make corrections to the code

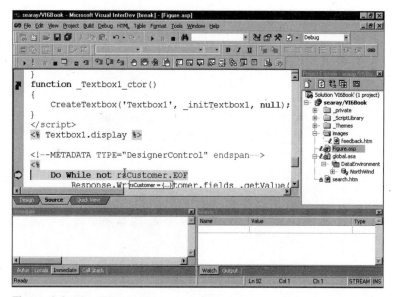

Figure 3-1. *The debugger in Source view.*

Table 3-1 describes some of the windows that are available for use in the debugger for Visual InterDev applications. The control sequence to activate the window is shown in parentheses after the window's name.

> **NOTE** To debug client-side script in Microsoft Internet Explorer, you must be using Internet Explorer 4 and you must have enabled the Visual Inter-Dev debugger.

Window Name	*Description*
Immediate (Ctrl+Alt+I)	Used to display information about the application's state and to interact with the application by executing commands and setting variables.
Watch (Ctrl+Alt+W)	Used to display watch expressions, which generally show the value of variables in the application, to change the values of variables, and to display the contents of object properties.
Locals (Ctrl+Alt+L)	Used to display the value of variables that are within the scope of the current procedure. Variables are displayed as long as they have a value. You can use the Locals window to determine when a variable is initialized and when it is destroyed.

Table 3-1. *Useful Visual InterDev Windows for debugging.*

You can debug server script in any of these ways:

- Run a page containing the script to debug from within a Visual InterDev solution.

- Attach the Visual InterDev debugger to a process (page) already running in Internet Explorer.

- Respond to a syntax or run-time error in a script; this is called *just-in-time* debugging.

- Include a statement in script that starts the debugger.

Some of these methods will be discussed later in this chapter. There is also more information on debugging in the Visual InterDev documentation and on the Microsoft Visual Studio Web site (*http://msdn.microsoft.com/vstudio*).

DEBUGGING STRATEGIES

Debugging Visual InterDev applications is a difficult task for a system to handle. When an ASP application is set for debugging, Internet Information Server (IIS) makes the application an out-of-process application, which means that the application runs in a separate memory space. This results in the application running much slower than when the application runs in the IIS process. For this reason, you do not want to turn on debugging for a production application, at least not for long.

Each breakpoint in a page stops and starts the Web server. This also impacts the performance of all other applications running on the site and their state management. Turning on buffering in IIS 4 for applications that are being debugged will speed up those applications.

To properly debug an application, you should have a local Web server on the system on which you are running Visual InterDev or you should use a dedicated development server. You can remotely debug an application, but only one developer can be remotely debugging an application on an IIS system at a time. This means that your development team can actively have only one debug session per development server.

Using a local Web server for debugging alleviates this problem. In that case, you can develop, test, debug, and then deploy the application to the development server when you are ready. This will make the process much easier to manage and much more productive.

> **NOTE** Microsoft highly recommends that you do not use the Active Desktop mode of Internet Explorer 4 when you are debugging.

Setting up an Application for Debugging

You must perform several steps before beginning to debug an application. First set the start page for the application. In Project Explorer, right-click the page you want to start with, and then select Set As Start Page from the context menu.

Before you can debug an application, you must also enable debugging for the application. You can change this setting in Visual InterDev 6 or in IIS 4. To change the Visual InterDev debug settings for a Web project, use the project's Properties dialog box, as shown in Figure 3-2.

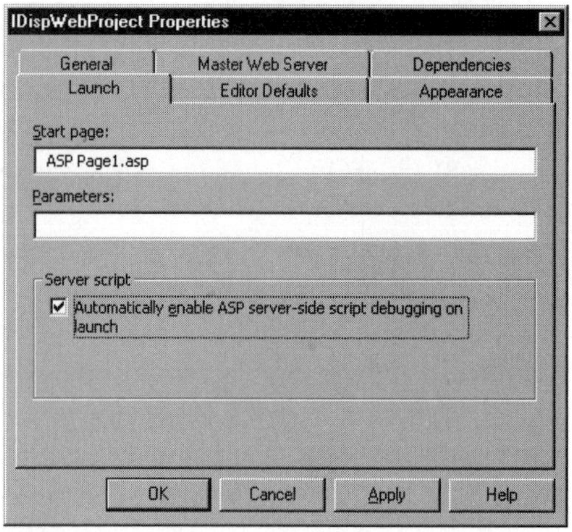

Figure 3-2. *A project's Properties dialog box, showing the debugging option.*

First display the project's Properties dialog box by right-clicking the project in Project Explorer and then selecting Properties from the context menu. On the Launch tab, check the option Automatically Enable ASP Server-side Script Debugging On Launch box under Server Script to enable debugging.

When you enable debugging in Visual InterDev, Visual InterDev lets you debug each time you launch a page within the particular project. This does not affect other applications or other developers. Each time you start the application in debug mode, Visual InterDev will perform the following tasks:

- Set the IIS application to run in its own memory space (that is, out of process).

- Enable the IIS application's debugging options.

- Set up a Microsoft Transaction Server (MTS) package to allow you to attach the debugger to the Web application. The package's identification is set when you first start the debugging session by asking you to provide your name and password.

You can also enable debugging by using the Internet Server Manager subcomponent of IIS. Figure 3-3 shows these debug settings.

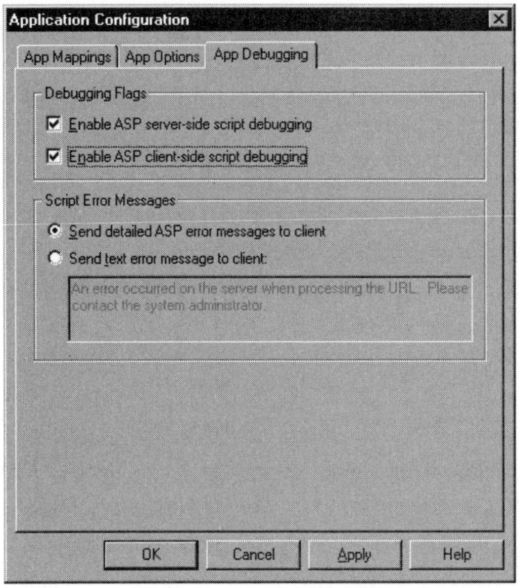

Figure 3-3. *You can also use the IIS Internet Service Manager to enable debugging.*

To display the debug options, select the site in the Internet Service Manager and display its properties. Click the Configuration button, and then click the App Debugging tab. Next check either the Enable ASP Server-side Script Debugging option or the Enable ASP Client-side Script Debugging option. Click OK or Apply to update the settings.

Setting the debug properties with the Internet Service Manager enables this setting for all users of this application. Also, keep in mind that the application will run much slower with these settings turned on.

If you enabled the debug options with Visual InterDev, the first time you launch the application in the debugger after having changed the debugging properties, you might be prompted for a Microsoft Windows NT account and password that has authority to enable debugging on the server.

Debugging ASP Script

Visual InterDev provides tools you can use to debug either client or server code, but each requires a slightly different approach. Let's take a look at debugging server code.

To debug server script from within a Visual InterDev solution:

1. Open the project containing the server script you want to debug.

2. Set the startup page for the application by right-clicking the page you want to run first and choosing Set As Start Page from the context menu.

3. Set a breakpoint in the server script you want to debug.

4. Choose Start on the Debug menu to launch the project.

Visual InterDev now attaches the debugger to the document running on the server. In Internet Explorer, navigate to the .asp file that contains the script you want to debug. When server script execution reaches the line with the breakpoint, the debugger will display the page in the Visual InterDev editor. The current line will be highlighted when the application stops in the editor.

If the .asp file you are debugging is part of your project and you have a working copy, you can fix any errors, save the file, and then click Restart on the Debug menu to restart the debug process.

If debugging is enabled for an application and the server encounters a syntax error or a run-time error in server script, it displays an error message in the requesting browser. Responding Yes to this message will start the debug process. Visual InterDev is launched, and the debugger attaches itself to the script with the error and displays the page in the editor. If the page is part of a project in Visual InterDev, open the project and the page, fix any errors, save the file, and then deploy it to the server. Then refresh the page in Internet Explorer.

If server debugging is not enabled for the application, errors are displayed in the browser as text in the page and you must manually start the debug process in Visual InterDev.

Debugging Global.asa

Debugging Global.asa is a bit more problematic than debugging an ASP Web page. Global.asa is event-based and cannot be started directly (unlike an ASP Web page). The trick is to force a breakpoint in Global.asa's code and start another page that will cause the events in Global.asa to fire.

You can set a breakpoint in Global.asa just as you can in other pages. You can also insert statements in your code that will stop the script language. Either of the statements in Table 3-2 will stop execution and explicitly start the debugger.

Script Language	*Stop and Debug Statement*
VBScript	Stop
JScript	Debugger

Table 3-2. *Debug statements for script languages.*

Stepping Through an Application

The Visual InterDev debugger lets you step through the code in your application line by line, checking variables and testing values as you go. This is the process we have used for years in Visual Basic to quickly test applications and get them into production.

The Debug toolbar's Step buttons or the shortcut keys are the easiest way to walk through the code when the debugger stops at a breakpoint or when you start the application. The commands you use to step through your code are described in Table 3-3.

Debug Menu Command	Button	Action
Step Into (F11)		Moves you to the next script line. If the script calls another procedure, Step Into allows you to step through the lines of the called procedure as well.
Step Over (F10)		Moves you to the next script line. If the script calls another procedure, the procedure is executed but the debugger does not step through the called procedure's individual lines.
Step Out (Shift+F11)		Lets you stop stepping through lines of a procedure before reaching its end.

Table 3-3. *The debugging step commands.*

The Run To Cursor command (Ctrl+F10) or its toolbar button is also useful. When you place the cursor in a page and click Run To Cursor, Visual InterDev will execute the code up to that line. Then you can step through it.

Using Breakpoints

Developers use breakpoints to stop execution of code at a particular point. For instance, if you wish to test a certain line of code, you place a breakpoint on that line. Then, when you run the code in the debugger, the application stops on the line containing the breakpoint and the debugger goes into "break" mode. When the debugger is in break mode, you can inspect variables, execute commands, change the next line to execute, and so forth. Most of your debugging activities will be done in break mode.

You can use a breakpoint (or a statement that will stop execution) to specify a place in a script at which you want to stop and examine the state of a process. You can then step into or step over lines of script individually to find errors. Breakpoints show up as red octagons to the left of a line of script, as shown in Figure 3-4.

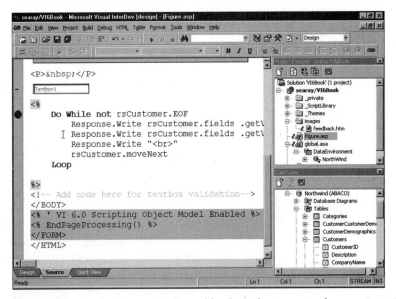

Figure 3-4. *Breakpoints are indicated by the red octagon in the margin to the left of a line.*

It's easy to set a breakpoint:

1. Open the file you're debugging.

2. Place the cursor in the line of script in which you want to set a breakpoint.

3. From the Debug menu, choose Insert Breakpoint.

You can also set a breakpoint by placing the cursor in a line of script and pressing F9 or by clicking in the margin left of the line.

The Breakpoints window displays a list of the breakpoints in your solution, as shown in Figure 3-5. (To open the Breakpoints window, select Breakpoints from the Debug menu or press Ctrl+B.) You can use this window to review the list of breakpoints, clear all the breakpoints in the solution, disable and enable breakpoints, and more.

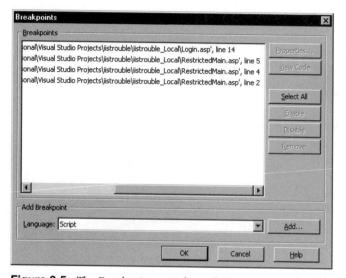

Figure 3-5. *The Breakpoints window allows you to configure each breakpoint in a solution and to review all the breakpoints for that solution.*

One of the nice features of the debugger is the ability to set parameters on a breakpoint. One of the parameters you can set is a condition that must be met for that breakpoint to stop the execution of the code. Figure 3-6 on the following page shows the properties of a breakpoint with a condition set.

To set a breakpoint's properties, display the Breakpoints window, select the desired breakpoint, and then click Properties. If you are setting a condition, you can set it to break when the condition is true by changing the radio button to the right of the condition.

Breakpoint conditions are extremely useful when you are debugging an application that can have a wide range of values and you only need to test certain values. For instance, you might have a loop in your application that iterates 1000 times. Instead of stepping through each of those iterations, you can use a condition to trigger the breakpoint to stop on the particular iteration you are looking for. You can also use conditions in this manner when you are returning large amounts of data from a database and want to check only certain conditions.

The Breakpoints window is also useful for removing breakpoints. When you have finished debugging your application and are ready to deploy it, you can bring up the Breakpoints window and delete either all or some of the breakpoints.

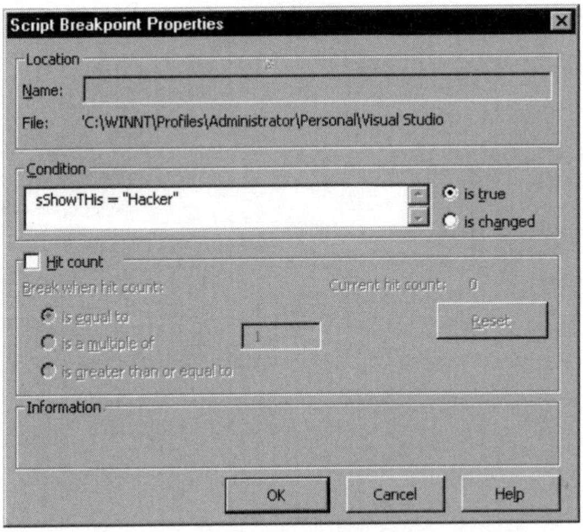

Figure 3-6. *Breakpoint properties allow you to control how the breakpoint is triggered.*

Using the Debug Windows

The Immediate window is one of the most used debug windows. It is used to interact with your running Web application. You can enter commands and execute them, display the values of variables, execute functions, and much more. The Immediate window is your central point of contact with the application.

Figure 3-7 shows a simple page that is in break mode. In the example shown, the application has a *Select Case* statement based upon the *sShowThis* variable. One of the tricks to testing a *Select Case* statement is to test it with all of its possible values. This process is usually time-consuming as you run the application several times and try to force the variables through each value change. You might choose to test a *Select Case* statement by programmatically changing the variable, but doing so still takes time.

The debugger allows us to debug these types of statements dynamically. For instance, let's debug our *Select Case* statement in Figure 3-7 by changing all of its options. You can see that *sShowThis* currently has a value of 999 and that the cursor is stopped on the *Stop* statement, thus putting the application in break mode. (You can tell which line is the current line because the line will be yellow-highlighted and will have a small arrow in the left margin pointing at it.)

To continue debugging this page, press F11 to step to the next line. We will continue stepping through the page by pressing F11 until the cursor reaches the *End Select* statement. At this point, we will have tested the *Select Case* statement for the 999 condition. We still need to test for a value of 1020 and any values other than 1020 and 999, such as "". To test these other conditions,

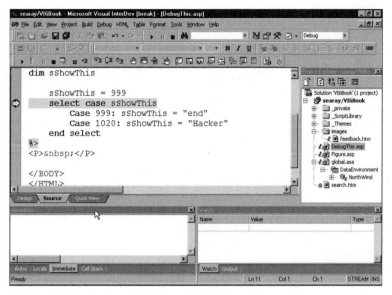

Figure 3-7. *Once the application is in break mode, you can interact with it line by line.*

we need to restart the *Select Case* statement. To do this, move the cursor to the *Select Case* line and select Set Next Statement from the Debug menu (Ctrl+Shift+F10). This will move the pointer to that line, and the line will now execute when you press F11 again. So, how do we reset the variable for the new condition? Simply enter a variable definition command into the Immediate window, as shown in Figure 3-8 on the following page.

Once you have reset the variable, you can press F11 to step through the application again, testing another condition. You can iterate through these steps until you have tested every condition of a *Select Case* or similar statement group.

Other Debug windows can be used with the Immediate window to understand what is happening with your application. Figure 3-8 on the following page shows the Immediate and Watch windows. The Locals window is also active in Figure 3-8 but is hidden behind the Immediate window. You can display hidden windows like this by clicking the tab for the window.

The Watch window is used to display the results of a Watch expression. After a variable or object is placed in the Watch window, the debugger will monitor that variable and continually display its value.

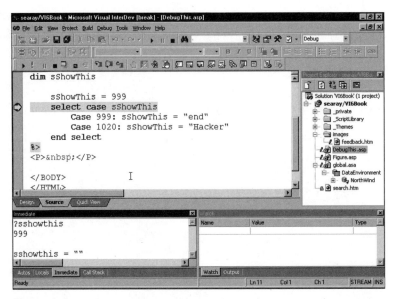

Figure 3-8. *The Immediate window can be used to execute almost any script command.*

You can drag and drop variables from the code window to either the Immediate window or the Watch window. You can also drag a variable from either window to the other. The Watch window allows you to double-click a variable and edit its value. This is a great feature for interactively debugging your applications.

The Watch window also allows you to monitor objects. If you place an object in the Watch window, you will see a plus (+) sign to the left of the object. Click the plus sign, and the object will expand to display its properties and other objects it contains. In the Value column, you will see the contents of each object's property.

You can display the Watch window by selecting Debug Windows from the View menu and then selecting Watch from the submenu. You can also use the Debug Windows menu item to display the other Debug windows, or you can use their shortcut keys.

Connecting to an Executing Application

The Running Documents window displays the documents that are currently executing. Figure 3-9 shows the Running Documents window with Page1.asp executing with several pages attached to it. Those attached pages are part of the Scripting Library and are providing support for the DTCs used in the page. If you aren't attached to any processes, the Running Documents window will be empty. To view the Running Documents window, select Debug Windows from the View menu, and then select Running Documents from the submenu.

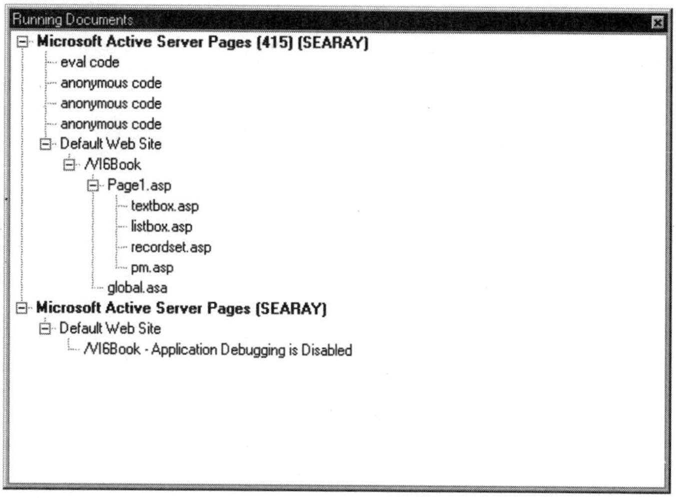

Figure 3-9. *The Running Documents window shows the debuggable documents that are currently running on a system.*

You can also enter break mode at run time when the application is idle (not processing an event). When you break into a running application, execution stops when the next line of code is executed. This allows you to start a debug session while the application is currently running. This is handy when you are testing and discover an anomaly or just want to observe what is currently happening in the application.

To break into a running application, select Break from the Debug menu.

You can select the Processes command on the Debug menu to use the Processes window to start debugging an active application. Before you can use this technique, you must have enabled debugging on the server for your site. This is handy when you detect an error while the application is running and need to attach the debugger to the application. For this to work, you must enable just-in-time debugging:

1. Select Options from the Tools menu.

2. Select Debugger in the Options dialog box.

3. Under the Script section, check Attach To Programs Running On This Machine.

This allows you to use Visual InterDev to debug any running ASP page that is part of a project that has debugging enabled. Now you can use the Processes window to attach Visual InterDev to the application.

To debug a running script:

1. Select Processes from the Debug menu.

2. In the Processes window, select Active Server Pages.

3. Click Attach.

4. Close the Processes window.

5. Display the Running Documents window (select Debug Windows from the View menu and then select Running Documents from the submenu, or press Ctrl+Alt+R).

6. In the Running Documents window, double-click the script you want to debug, and Visual InterDev will open that page in the source code editor.

7. Set breakpoints, and then choose Restart from the Debug menu or refresh the document in the browser.

Figure 3-10 shows the Processes window after we have attached to the Active Server Pages process. Now we can use the Running Documents window to obtain a list of the running pages and to open the page in the source code editor.

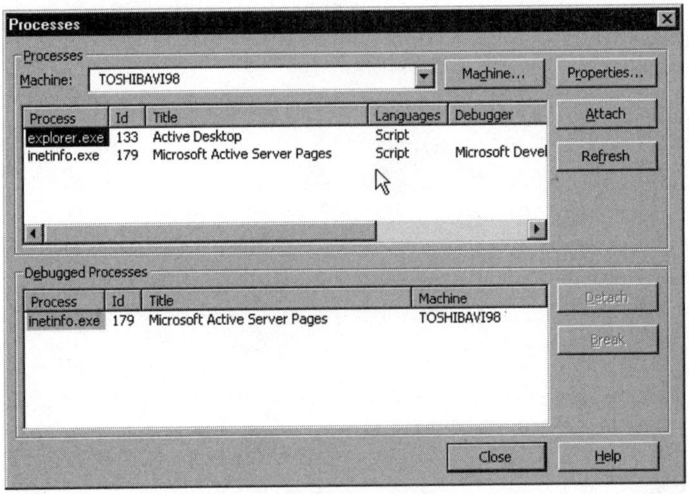

Figure 3-10. *The Processes window shows both the active processes and the ones that have been attached.*

Debugging Client Code

You can also use Visual InterDev 6 to debug client pages that execute in the browser. This process is similar to debugging server-side ASP code:

1.   Open Project Explorer.

2.   Right-click the .htm file you wish to start, and select Set As Start Page.

3.   Click the Start button on the toolbar, or select Start from the Debug menu.

The script will execute until Internet Explorer reaches the breakpoint. When Internet Explorer reaches the breakpoint, it stops and displays the source script in Source view.

Simultaneously Debugging Server and Client Code

You can debug both server and client code at the same time, as long as all the code is part of one Visual InterDev 6 project. The following is the normal process used when working with an ASP application:

1.   Open the project containing the server script you want to debug.

2.   Set the Start page for the application by right-clicking the page you wish to run first and choosing Set As Start Page from the context menu.

3.   Set breakpoints in the lines of client and server script that you want to debug.

4.   Click Start on the toolbar, or choose Start from the Debug menu. The server script will execute and stop at the first breakpoint.

Now you can step through the code line by line. The server code will execute and be sent to the browser. When the browser encounters a breakpoint, it will stop and display the code in Source view.

Of course, you must be careful when debugging client code. Much of the client code that is generated with ASP is dynamic in nature and exists only in the HTML stream to the client. In that case, you must look at the code as a result set only and try to determine what changes must be made to the ASP code to correct any problems.

Just-in-Time Debugging

Visual InterDev allows you to launch the debugger in response to an error in an application. You can do this only if just-in-time debugging is enabled and the application has debugging enabled.

You enable just-in-time debugging via the Options dialog box:

1. Select Options from the Tools menu.

2. In the Options dialog box, choose Debugger.

3. Under the Script section, check Just-In-Time Debugging.

Now when an error occurs or a Stop or Debugger statement appears, a dialog box will ask whether you want to debug the application, as shown in Figure 3-11.

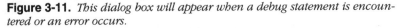

Figure 3-11. *This dialog box will appear when a debug statement is encountered or an error occurs.*

When you answer Yes to the dialog box shown in Figure 3-11, a new instance of Visual InterDev will be launched and you will be prompted to open a project. If Visual InterDev is already running, a second instance is launched. Open the project containing the file you wish to debug. If the project is already open in another instance of Visual InterDev, you cannot open it again and must create a new solution and project instead. Once you have the page to debug loaded into the editor, you can debug it like any other page.

Debugging Visual Basic Components

You can use Visual InterDev to debug your Visual Basic components directly from an ASP page. You must take a couple of steps to make this work, but the process is pretty simple.

First, the Visual Basic IDE and debugger work similarly to Visual InterDev and its debugger, and the look and feel of each are also similar. Consequently, it's easy for developers to use both tools and to work back and forth between them. The commands are the same, the windows are the same, and even the command keys are almost the same, including our old friend F5 (Run). (One exception is the Step Into command, which is F8 in Visual Basic and F11 in Visual InterDev.) If you use the toolbars, you'll find they also work the same way.

To debug a Visual Basic component, you must execute the component inside the Visual Basic IDE. This is the same technique you use to debug components in Visual Basic 4. To do this, follow these steps:

1. On the machine where the ASP application is running, load the source for the Visual Basic component.

2. Set breakpoints in the component.

3. Execute the component.

These steps will execute the component in the Visual Basic IDE. Executing a component starts the executable and keeps it active. This lets other applications use the component while the component is running in the IDE, with all its Visual Basic resources available. Figure 3-12 demonstrates a component that is loaded in the Visual Basic IDE and executing. Notice that the IDE is in Run mode—the Visual Basic title bar indicates this with the word Run.

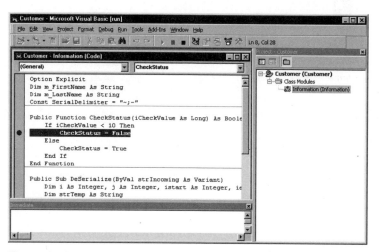

Figure 3-12. *This component has a breakpoint set and is executing within the Visual Basic IDE.*

Now start the debug process with the page that contains the code for executing the component. Figure 3-13 on the following page demonstrates a page that is using the component executing in Figure 3-12.

When you debug the page shown in Figure 3-13 and the line accessing the component executes—that is, *objCustInfo.CheckStatus(1)*—the Visual Basic IDE will become the current window and you will be debugging the component. Figure 3-14 demonstrates the component during the Visual Basic debug process.

```
<BODY>
<%
dim objCustInfo
dim retVal

    set objCustInfo = server.CreateObject("Customer.Informatio

    retVal = objCustInfo.CheckStatus(1)

    if retVal then
        txtStatus.value = "Value is ok"
    else
        txtStatus.value = "Value is too low"
    end if
%>
<P> </P>
```

Figure 3-13. *This page is using the component running in the Visual Basic IDE.*

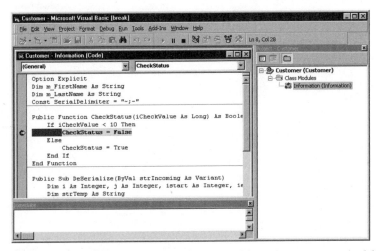

Figure 3-14. *The Visual Basic debugger can be used to interactively debug the component, complete with the data passed to it from the ASP page.*

REMOTE DEBUGGING

The Visual InterDev debugger allows you to debug ASP scripts on remote IIS servers using a feature known as *remote debugging*. This feature is useful in several situations, for example when:

■ Debugging applications running on development servers.

■ Getting assistance from another developer to debug an application running on your system.

■ Debugging an application on an ISP's system before it goes to production.

■ Debugging a production application that has exposed an error.

Normally, you will debug server script in an ASP page by installing Visual InterDev and the Web server on the same system and debugging scripts locally on that system. This is how we recommend you approach debugging, as we outlined earlier in this chapter.

However, with remote debugging, you can attach the debugger running on your computer to a script running on the Web server and issue debugging commands across the network. This is certainly useful in the situations we mentioned above. The material in this section is not meant to suggest that you do all of your debugging remotely, only that you know how to set up remote debugging and to use it when it's appropriate for the task.

Remote debugging is similar to debugging locally, except for these two differences:

■ You must perform some extra setup steps before you can use remote debugging.

■ Only one user can utilize remote debugging on a server at a time.

Before you can use remote debugging, you set up the server running IIS. The first step is to be sure that the proper debugging components have been installed on the server. A full server installation of Visual InterDev will normally load the proper components. If you did not perform a full server installation, or if you are not sure that you did, you can follow these steps to update the server:

1. On the IIS system, start the Visual Studio 6.0 (Enterprise Edition or Pro Edition) setup program.

2. Click Add/Remove, and select Server Applications And Tools.

3. On the next page, select Launch BackOffice Installation Wizard and then choose Install.

4. When the BackOffice Business Solutions wizard is displayed, choose Custom and then choose Next.

5. Proceed until you see the page displaying a list of components to install. Uncheck all components except Remote Machine Debugging and Visual InterDev Server.

6. Complete the installation.

Remote debugging requires that anyone using this facility must have a valid Windows NT administration account. This account must be a member of the Administrators or Domain Admins groups. You can set this up with the NT User

Manager utility. This step alone will give you pause about using Remote Debugging on a production server. If you either do not want to or cannot use this level of security, you can use a tool like PCAnyWhere32 on Windows NT to allow certain users to remotely access a copy of Visual InterDev running on the IIS server. This will not require the same security levels that remote debugging does.

The remote debugging process uses Distributed COM (DCOM) to communicate between the client and server computers. You must configure DCOM on the IIS server to allow a remote user to attach the debugger process on that server:

1. Log in as an administrator on the server running IIS.

2. From the Start menu, select the Run command.

3. In the Open box, type Dcomcnfg.exe, and click OK to start the DCOM Configuration Manager.

4. In the Distributed COM Configuration Properties window, select Machine Debug Manager.

5. Click Properties to display the Machine Debug Manager Properties dialog box.

6. Click Security to display the Security tab.

7. Click the Use Custom Access Permissions radio button.

8. Click the Edit button to display the Registry Value Permissions dialog box.

9. Verify that Allow Access is selected in the Type Of Access list.

10. Click the Add button to display the Add Users And Groups dialog box.

11. Select the server's name from the List Names From list. The server name typically is in the form \\server and appears at the top of the list.

12. Under Names, choose Administrators, click Add, and then click OK.

13. Click OK once more to return to the Security tab.

14. Click the Use Custom Launch Permissions radio button.

15. Click the Edit button.

16. Click the Add button to display the Add Users And Groups dialog box.

17. Select the server's name from the List Names From list. Again, the server name typically is in the form \\server and appears at the top of the list.

18. Under Names, choose Administrators, choose Add, and then choose OK.

19. Click OK once more to return to the Security tab.

20. Click OK to Return to the Distributed COM Configuration Properties window.

21. Select MTS Client Export.

22. Click the Properties button. Add the same custom access permissions that we did for the Machine Debug Manager.

23. Return to the Distributed COM Configuration Properties window.

24. Select the MTS Catalog 1.0 Object.

25. Click the Properties button. Add the same custom access permissions that we did for the Machine Debug Manager.

Now you can debug the application remotely using Visual InterDev just as you would if Visual InterDev and IIS were running on the same system.

Running the Debugger Remotely

After the server has been configured for remote debugging, you can debug on the server in much the same way you do locally. You can launch a remote debugging session in the same way that you launch a normal debugging session:

1. Launch a project using the debugger.

2. Attach to a process that is already running on the server.

The debug process runs on the server the ASP application runs on. For instance, if your ASP application is running locally, your debug session will also run locally. If the ASP application is running on another server, the debug session will run on that server.

> **NOTE** Because remote debugging ties up process threads on the server, it is recommended that while a remote debugging session is in progress, other users avoid using the server.

ERROR CODES

It's possible you'll see many different error codes show up in applications that you are developing. To find the descriptions for the error codes, you can check the Microsoft Developer Network Web site (*http://msdn.microsoft.com/developer*) and Table 3-4 on the following page.

Visual InterDev uses the data environment object model, based on the Microsoft ActiveX Data Objects (ADO) object model, for accessing and processing database records. Table 3-4 lists the error numbers and descriptions that are returned by the ADO object model. You might also receive error messages that are generated from the database driver or from the database engine your application uses.

Error Number	Description
3001	The application is using arguments that are of the wrong type, are out of acceptable range, or are in conflict with one another.
3021	Either BOF or EOF is True, or the current record has been deleted; the operation requested by the application requires a current record.
3219	The operation requested by the application is not allowed in this context.
3246	The application cannot explicitly close a *Connection* object while in the middle of a transaction.
3251	The operation requested by the application is not supported by the provider.
3265	ADO cannot find the object in the collection corresponding to the name or ordinal reference requested by the application.
3367	Can't append. Object already in collection.
3420	The object referenced by the application no longer points to a valid object.
3421	The application is using a value of the wrong type for the current operation.
3704	The operation requested by the application is not allowed if the object is closed.
3705	The operation requested by the application is not allowed if the object is open.
3706	ADO could not find the specified provider.
3707	The application cannot change the *ActiveConnection* property of a *Recordset* object with a *Command* object as its source.
3708	The application has improperly defined a *Parameter* object.
3709	The application requested an operation on an object with a reference to a closed or invalid *Connection* object.

Table 3-4. *A partial list of ADO error codes.*

> **NOTE** You can find more information about WinInet error codes at *http://support.microsoft.com/support/kb/articles/q193/6/25.asp.*

Part II

Creating Applications

Chapter 4

Using the Scripting Object Model

Microsoft Visual InterDev 6 introduces the Scripting Object Model (SOM). The Scripting Object Model provides a development framework that is similar to the one used in Microsoft Visual Basic. The SOM lets you use ASP files and features of those pages the same way you use forms and components in Visual Basic. This makes building your applications much easier and the process of maintaining them a more manageable task.

OVERVIEW

The Scripting Object Model provides an object-oriented development environment that forms the foundation for design-time controls (DTCs), DHTML, and the various run-time features. Specifically, the SOM provides:

- An object-oriented abstraction for building Web applications

- A consistent programming model for scripting with DHTML and ASP

- Support for building applications with broad reach

- A run-time layer that creates an ASP execution model similar to DHTML

- Event and method dispatching

- State management for the client and the server

The SOM's script objects provide a single abstraction for ASP and DHTML applications. The script objects support data binding, asynchronous remote execution of server-script functions, and more.

In addition to abstracting the code in the development environment, the SOM also provides a rich run-time architecture. For instance, the SOM provides the run-time support for each DTC. Each DTC is backed up by one or more SOM objects on the server.

HOW IT WORKS

Before you can use any feature (such as a DTC) that depends upon the Scripting Object Model, you must enable the SOM. If you try to insert an object in a page that requires the Scripting Object Model but have not yet enabled the SOM, Visual InterDev will warn you that you need to enable the SOM first and will prompt you to enable it.

You can directly enable the Scripting Object Model with these steps:

1. Display the properties for the ASP Web page by right-clicking the page and selecting Properties from the context menu.

2. Check the Enable Scripting Object Model check box under ASP Settings.

This will add the SOM code to your page, enabling you to use DTCs and other features that require the Scripting Object Model. This process is illustrated in Figure 4-1, which shows the Enable Scripting Object Model check box checked and the Apply button clicked. At the top of the page, the following code has been inserted:

```
<%@ Language=VBScript %>
<% ' VI 6.0 Scripting Object Model Enabled %>
<!--#include file="_ScriptLibrary/pm.asp"-->
<% if StartPageProcessing() Then Response.End() %>
<FORM name=thisForm METHOD=post>
```

This code will be inserted at the end of the file:

```
<% ' VI 6.0 Scripting Object Model Enabled %>
<% EndPageProcessing() %>
</FORM>
```

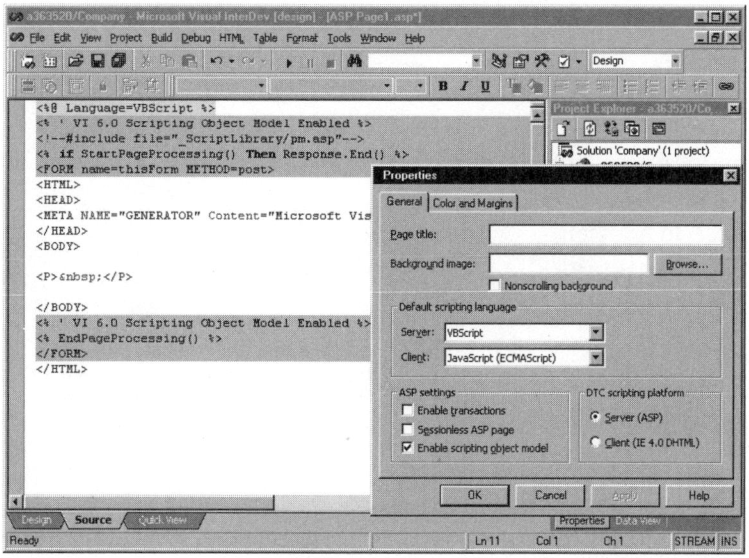

Figure 4-1. *The Properties dialog box for an ASP Web page allows you to enable the SOM.*

These two sections of code do several things. First, the pm.asp file is included in the project. This file contains numerous functions that will be called by DTCs and possibly by your code. Next, the *StartPageProcessing* function is called to initiate the SOM for this page. Then, an HTML form named *thisForm* is created. The form is used by DTCs and other objects as well as your own code. Lastly, the code at the end of the page executes the *EndPageProcessing* function and terminates *thisForm*.

The run-time properties of the Scripting Object Model do not appear in the Properties window. These properties and methods are available in the Microsoft IntelliSense statement completion features of Visual InterDev 6.

HOW THE SCRIPTING OBJECT MODEL WORKS

The files for the Scripting Object Model are contained in the _ScriptLibrary folder that Visual InterDev 6 inserts in your Web project when you create a project. (See Figure 4-2 on the following page.) You should never change anything in one of the _ScriptLibrary files or delete any of these files.

Microsoft is going to replace the JScript files that make up the SOM with a set of components written in C++ using the Active Template Library (ATL). The new Scripting Object Model components should provide faster execution, a more stable environment, and a true black-box architecture for the server. In the interim, you should treat the Scripting Object Model as a black box (that is, you should not be concerned about how it accomplishes its tasks).

Figure 4-2. *The _ScriptLibrary folder contains the Scripting Object Model files.*

ASP files execute in a linear manner as indicated by Figure 4-3. When a user visits an ASP file, the page starts executing at the first line of code and continues to execute sequentially top to bottom. Once the code in a page is executed, the HTML generated is sent to the browser via HTTP. The only changes to the linear flow of execution are governed by the logic in the page that might call procedures or redirect the flow of execution directly.

```
ASP        <HTML>
execution   <HEAD>
            <META NAME="GENERATOR" Content="Microsoft Visual Studio 6.0">
            </HEAD>
            <BODY>

            <P align=center>
            <IMG align=bottom src="images/32x.jpg" alt="32x logo" border=0 height

            <%
            Dim CurrentTime
            CurrentTime = TimeValue(Time)

            If CurrentTime > TimeValue("12:00:00 AM") And CurrentTime < TimeValue
                Response.Write "<P align=center>Good Morning. Welcome to</P>"
            Else
                If CurrentTime < TimeValue("6:00:00 PM") Then
                    Response.Write "<P align=center>Good Afternoon. Welcome to</P
                Else
                    Response.Write "<P align=center>Good Evening. Welcome to</P>"
                End If
            End If
            %>
```

Figure 4-3. *The ASP execution model is sequential from top to bottom.*

DHTML pages, on the other hand, execute in an event-driven manner just as Visual Basic applications do. Figure 4-4 demonstrates how this can look when a page executes.

```
                              <SCRIPT id=clientEventHandlersJS language=javascript>
                              <!--
Opening page in ─────────▶ function window_onload() {
browser triggers                  Textbox1.value = ""
                              }

Clicking Button1 ────────▶ function Button1_onclick() {
     triggers                     Textbox1.value = "Hello"
                              }

                              //-->
                              </SCRIPT>
                              <BODY>

                              [Textbox1            ]

                              [ Button1 ]

                              <P> </P>

                              </BODY>
```

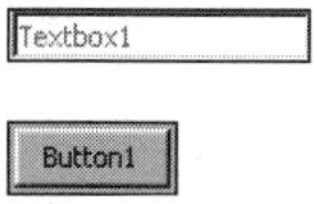

Figure 4-4. *The DHTML execution model is event-driven.*

In Figure 4-4, when a user clicks a hyperlink to this page, the *onload* event will execute when the page loads. The *onclick* event will not execute until the user clicks the command button. This execution model greatly simplifies the way you build Web applications and reduces the long-term maintenance costs of the applications. You as the developer can control what happens when particular parts of the page execute. This allows you to isolate your code and execute code discretely when certain actions (events) occur in a page.

The Document Object Model of the browser exposes the page as an object hierarchy. The script in the page can execute against the Document Object Model, automating features of the page and making it dynamic. DHTML pages are typically event driven, with code that is contained in event procedures within the page. Of course, you must be using a browser that supports DHTML, such as Microsoft Internet Explorer 4, to use the DHTML features.

The Scripting Object Model works with both DHTML and ASP files. It provides the framework to allow both ASP and DHTML Web pages to execute in an object-oriented manner. Figure 4-5 on the following page demonstrates how ASP files have an object model when using the SOM.

You can see the event model of ASP files in Figure 4-5. This new event model is particularly interesting as it allows you to script events for DTCs in either the client or server. Whenever you use the Scripting Object Model, at run-time an object is created for each DTC and the current page. These objects are the mechanism that you use to have access to the features of the page and its DTCs. More on this in a moment.

The following is the text associated with the figure:

Opening ASP page → in browser triggers

Clicking Button1 → triggers

```
<!--#include file="_ScriptLibrary/pm.asp"-->
<% if StartPageProcessing() Then Response.End() %>
<FORM name=thisForm METHOD=post>
<HTML>
<HEAD>
<META NAME="GENERATOR" Content="Microsoft Visual Studio 6.0">
<TITLE>Display Project Description</TITLE>
<SCRIPT ID=serverEventHandlersVBS LANGUAGE=vbscript RUNAT=Server>
Sub DisplayProjectDescription_onenter()
    Textbox1.value = ""
End Sub

Sub Button1_onclick()
    Textbox1.value = "Hello"
End Sub
</SCRIPT>
</HEAD>
<BODY>
```

Textbox1

Button1

Page Object
Name: DisplayProject

Figure 4-5. *The Visual InterDev 6 Scripting Object Model provides ASP events.*

The DTCs' event model is implemented by the Scripting Object Model at run time. This allows you to build events in client or server code. Usage of the new DTCs is covered in detail in Chapter 6. The server events for pages are provided by the PageObject DTC, which is the foundation for page type events and other support for treating pages as objects. Its close relationship to the Scripting Object Model is the reason for covering it in this chapter.

USING PAGEOBJECT DTCS

The PageObject DTC allows you to designate a page in your application as a page object, an ASP Web page containing server script you can use in your application. It provides the server-side events *onenter* and *onexit*, and also the *onbeforeserverevent* client event. The PageObject DTC also allows a page to expose methods and properties. (A page utilizing the Scripting Object Model can also be treated as an object itself through the use of the *thisForm* HTML form.)

When a user navigates to the ASP file, the *onenter* event fires. This allows you to place code in an event handler that executes when the page is first entered. When the page finishes, the *onexit* event fires; you can place code in an event handler for this event to clean up the page.

The PageObject DTC and the Scripting Object Model provide us with an object-oriented programming environment in both ASP and DHTML pages. You can treat your ASP code as objects with methods and properties. Both ASP and DHTML pages now are event driven.

There are other page events you can use, such as placing an *onclick* event in your ASP file that is called by HTML in the browser. These events are provided by the run-time Scripting Object Model components and are implemented by using DTCs.

This new object model is tremendously powerful. You can see all this magic in action by running an ASP application that uses these events. First set breakpoints in the code to stop your application. Next debug the application starting with that page.

To use the PageObject DTC to implement an ASP file as a page object, all you need to do is insert the DTC in a page:

1. Open the ASP file in the code editor.

2. Enable the Scripting Object Model for this page.

3. Drag the PageObject DTC from the Design-Time Controls tab of the Toolbox onto the page and inside the Scripting Object Model code.

4. Enter the name for the PageObject DTC in its Name text box.

The page should look similar to the one shown in Figure 4-6.

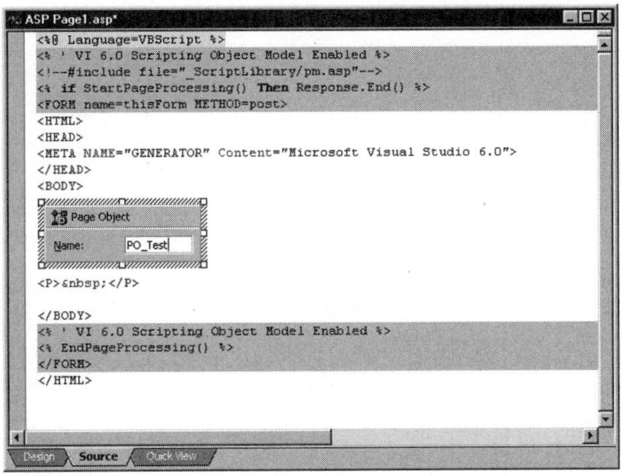

Figure 4-6. *The PageObject DTC's name is important because it is used to refer to items in the page.*

You can use the name you select for the page object when you want to refer to the page. The name is automatically registered in your Visual InterDev project and will remain the same, even if the page is moved. You can also move ASP files that are page objects into other projects.

Defining Page Methods

You can define methods on a page and expose them with the PageObject DTC. Once you have exposed a method using the PageObject DTC, you can execute the methods from either a client or server script. You do not need to do anything special for the methods that you create. The PageObject DTC will allow you to expose both function and procedure methods.

The PageObject DTC supports two types of methods. Navigate methods are used when a page needs to execute a procedure in an ASP file and then navigate to that or another page. Execute methods use remote scripting to execute ASP methods and return the data to the current page. Execute methods can be used from client script only. Navigate methods can be executed from either client or server script. To create a method of either of these types for a PageObject DTC, follow these steps:

1. Open the ASP file in the code editor. The page must contain the PageObject DTC and the script functions that you want to use.

2. Display the PageObject DTC's Properties dialog box by right-clicking the DTC and choosing Properties from the context menu.

3. Click the Methods tab.

4. Enter the name of your method in the Navigate Methods or Execute Methods section, depending upon which method type you want.

Once you enter the method name, the property page will display the method as shown in Figure 4-7. You can also enter method names that do not exist, but they will be shown in red until you create the method.

Once you enter the name of your method in the Navigate Methods or Execute Methods section, that method will be exposed to other pages. You can execute the method in your code by using this syntax:

```
<%
    MyProp.Execute.CheckInventory()
%>
```

or

```
<%
    MyProp.Navigate.CheckInventory()
%>
```

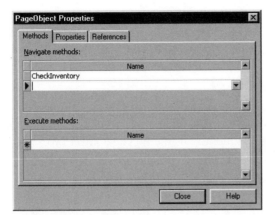

Figure 4-7. *This figure shows the PageObject Properties dialog box with one method that has been exposed..*

This syntax is similar to the *Execute* syntax you use with stored procedures. When you execute a method using *Execute*, the execution takes place either synchronously—that is, the current page waits on the method to execute—or asynchronously—the current page stays in the browser and the user can continue to work with it while the method executes. When you use *Execute* to asynchronously execute a method, you can pass a parameter containing the name of a callback procedure. The callback procedure will be executed when the method completes. The callback procedure name should be included as the last parameter in the parameter list:

```
<%
    MyProp.Execute.TotalInventory(ItemNumber, displayTotal)
%>
```

The callback procedure is simply a procedure or function in the client application. You can use the callback procedure to access the results of the function and display them or use them in some other manner. A callback procedure would look like this:

```
<script LANGUAGE="JavaScript">
function displayTotal(retObj)
{
    if (retObj.return_value == "OK")
        ProcessTotal(return_value);
}
</script>
```

This example uses the *retObj* variable to access the object returned from the executed procedure. The *return_value* property allows us to retrieve the return value of a function.

You can also use *Navigate* to execute methods. In fact, you must use *Navigate* to execute methods from ASP script. *Execute* can only be used by client script.

Defining Page Properties

You can use the PageObject DTC to define properties for an ASP file in the same manner you define methods. Page properties are global variables that you create in your code.

Page properties have three possible scopes:

- **Page** The property can be used anywhere on the page and is available until the user navigates to another page.

- **Session** The property is stored in a Session variable and is available anywhere in the user's session.

- **Application** The property is stored in an Application variable and is available anywhere in the application.

Storing values using the PageObject DTC is easier than using Session and Application variables. If you select Session as the variable scope, browsers visiting your site must support cookies. Browsers that do not support cookies will not be able to use Session level variables.

You define properties using the PageObject DTC using these steps:

1. Open the ASP file in the code editor. The page must contain the PageObject DTC and the script functions that you wish to use.

2. Display the PageObject DTC's Properties dialog box by right-clicking the DTC and choosing Properties from the context menu.

3. Click the Properties tab.

4. Enter the name of the property in the Name column.

5. Select the Lifetime value to set the property's scope.

6. Select the Client and Server access settings.

Figure 4-8 shows three properties in the PageObject Properties dialog box. *ItemNumber* and *ItemName* are both Page properties and are read-only for the client. This allows the user to see the property data, but the data cannot be changed. The *OrderNumber* property is read/write for the client and is a Session property. This allows the user to change the data in the property, and it allows the application to access the property throughout the user's session.

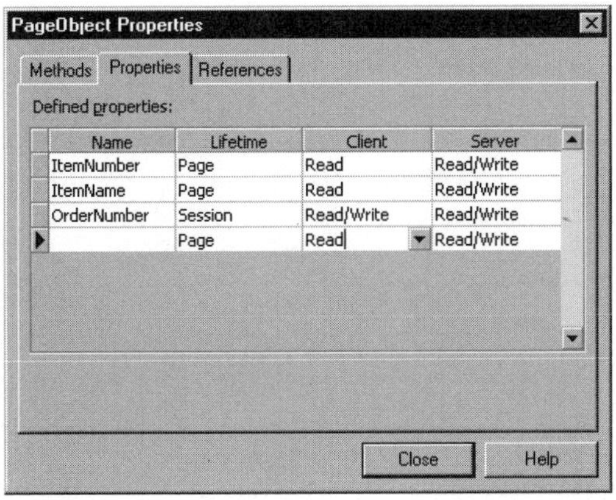

Figure 4-8. *Page properties are a useful way to store values in your application.*

You can access the properties in your script code by using IntelliSense. When the PageObject DTC creates the property procedures to use for accessing the properties, it builds them as *setxxx* and *getxxx*, where xxx is the name of a property. In other words, if we take the example shown in Figure 4-8, you would set these properties like this:

```
<%
    ProjectCallback.setItemName = "My Widget"
    ProjectCallback.setItemNumber = "101"
    ProjectCallback.setOrderNumber = "98-01001"
%>
```

The properties in this example can be referenced using these statements:

```
<%
    Response.Write ProjectCallback.getItemName
    Response.Write ProjectCallback.getItemNumber
    Response.Write ProjectCallback.getOrderNumber
%>
```

Figure 4-9 on the following page shows IntelliSense with these properties' *get* procedures displayed.

It might seem strange using *get* and *set* as the prefix to page property procedures. The PageObject DTC builds the property procedures similar to the way Visual Basic classes use *Property Get* and *Property Set* procedures. This ensures that your property names do not clash with the names of other objects or items in a project and make debugging the project a nightmare. This also prevents you from overriding a built-in property or method with one of your properties.

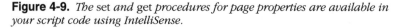

```
Sub GetIt()
    Response.Write ProjectCallback
    Response.Write ProjectCallback
    Response.Write ProjectCallback

    ProjectCallback.g|
End Sub                    advise
                           createDE
</SCRIPT>                  endPageContent
                           firstEntered
<script LANGUAGE=          getItemName
function displayR          getItemNumber
                           getOrderNumber
ign   Source   Quic        getState
                           location
ource   Design   So        navigate
```

Figure 4-9. *The* set *and* get *procedures for page properties are available in your script code using IntelliSense.*

ACCESSING METHODS AND PROPERTIES ON OTHER PAGES

Now that we have created page methods and properties by using the PageObject DTC, we can access those methods and properties from another page, either in server script or client script. To use the properties or methods of another page, you must create a reference from the current page to the page that contains the PageObject DTC and the methods and properties that we want to use. This process is similar to creating a reference to a Microsoft ActiveX component—we are telling the application where the other component/page is located. The following steps show you how to create a reference to another page containing a PageObject DTC:

1. Open the ASP file that will use properties or methods of another page in the code editor. The page must contain a PageObject DTC.

2. Display the PageObject DTC's Properties dialog box by right-clicking the DTC and selecting Properties from the context menu.

3. Click the References tab. This will display the property page shown in Figure 4-10.

4. Enter the name of the PageObject DTC you want to reference in the Name column. You can click the … button beside the Name space to display the Create URL dialog box shown in Figure 4-11. Using this dialog box, you can point to the page you want to reference, and Visual InterDev will insert the PageObject DTC name.

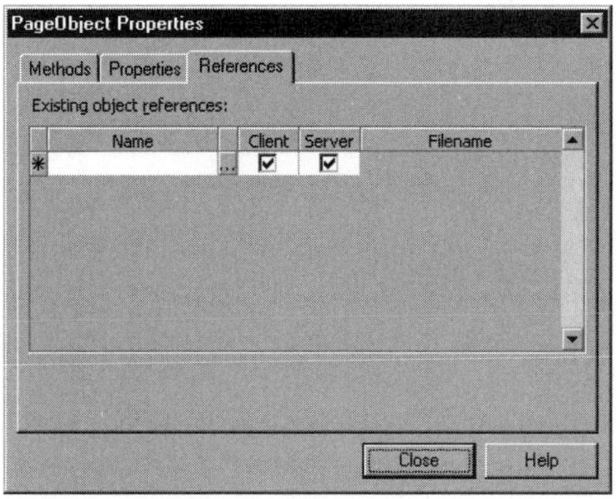

Figure 4-10. *The PageObject DTC must have a reference to other pages that your application will use as objects.*

The Client and Server columns in Figure 4-10 control whether the page properties and methods can be accessed from either client or server script. The default is to allow access by both. You can also set these properties per page, allowing you to have certain pages that can be used by client and server script and others that can be used by only one or the other.

The Create URL dialog box shown in Figure 4-11 assists you in preparing the reference to the correct PageObject DTC.

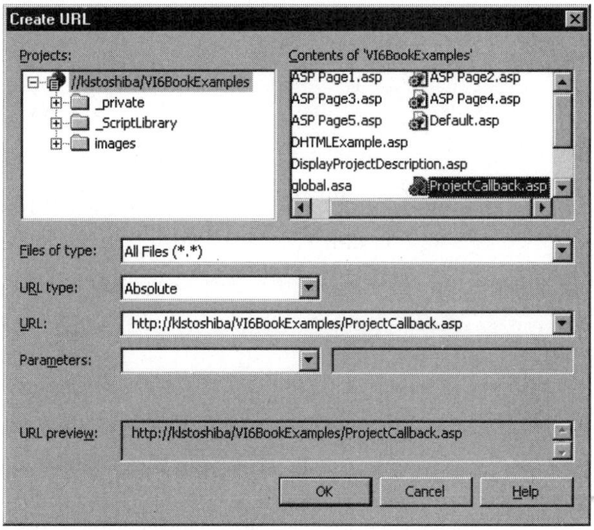

Figure 4-11. *You can use the Create URL dialog box to search for the page and create the reference.*

You can set other properties on the Create URL dialog box to control what happens when a property or method on the page is fired or when the page is navigated to. These properties are useful for controlling the various actions you take in the referenced page. For instance, you can use the Parameters field to add parameters to the URL that is generated for the page.

Now that you have a reference to the page containing the methods and properties, you can use them in your application. For this example, the following code is contained in the file ASP Page7.asp. The *OrderNumber* property and the *TotalInventory* method are contained in the ASP Page4.asp file. You can access both the property and the method by using the following syntax:

```
<%
    ASP_Page4.setOrderNumber = "98-001"
    ASP_Page4.navigate.TotalInventory("10")
%>
```

I used the *navigate* method in this example because the method I want to use (that is, *TotalInventory*) is exported as a Navigate method. Figure 4-12 shows a portion of the editor with this code and the IntelliSense display for the remote page. To use either the *navigate* or *execute* method, you should use IntelliSense to display the object and methods for you. Then you can type either *navigate* or *execute* and then select the appropriate method from the IntelliSense list. This will ensure that you have both the correct method of execution and the correct syntax.

```
<%
    ASP_Page4.setOrderNumber = "98-001"
    ASP_Page4.navigate.TotalInventory("10")
    ASP_Page4.navigate.|
%>
<P> </P>
                        ⊞ show
                        ⊞ TotalInventory
```

Figure 4-12. *The IntelliSense list for the ASP Page4.asp page.*

PageObject Methods and Properties

The PageObject run-time scripting object that underlies the PageObject DTC has several methods and properties that are useful in applications. These properties and methods can be used for various purposes in your application.

What's going on behind the scenes when you use the Scripting Object Model? When you insert a DTC on a page or enable the SOM for a page, Visual InterDev inserts the following code at the start of the file:

```
<%@ Language=VBScript %>
<% ' VI 6.0 Scripting Object Model Enabled %>
<!--#include file="_ScriptLibrary/pm.asp"-->
<% if StartPageProcessing() Then Response.End() %>
<FORM name=thisForm METHOD=post>
```

This code calls the *StartPageProcessing* routine in the pm.asp file. *StartPage-Processing* performs the startup activities for the page, including the creation of the page object *thisPage*. You can access *thisPage*'s events, methods, and properties for your own purposes. For instance, later in the chapter when we cancel the server processing, we'll cancel the action with *thisPage.cancelEvent = True*.

The *thisPage* page object also contains the *firstEntered* property, which can be used to determine whether a user is visiting a page with a browser or whether the page is being executed as the result of some type of posting action. This is handy when you are referencing a page repeatedly and want to determine when the user is coming to the page for the first time so that you can set the initial state of the page by setting its variables and properties. You do not need to do this with your own code by setting Session variables; instead, you can check the *firstEntered* property, and if it is True, the user has just entered that page via a browser.

The startup code also creates an HTML form and names it *thisForm*. You can access this form directly in your code. When you want to access an HTML field on a page that is in another form, you can use this syntax: *document.thisForm.fieldname*.

Figure 4-13 shows the Script Outline window and the file ASP Page6.asp with an empty *thisPage_onenter* event handler. I created this event handler by opening the Server Objects & Events folder in the Script Outline window, clicking the plus sign beside *thisPage* to open it, and then double-clicking onenter to insert an empty *thisPage_onenter* event in ASP Page6.asp.

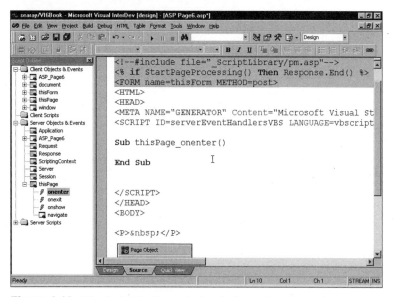

Figure 4-13. *The Script Outline window is the easiest way to insert any type of script events into a file.*

Now that we have the *onenter* event handler, we can use the PageObject object to determine how the user entered the page. Figure 4-14 demonstrates how *onenter* and the *firstEntered* property work. I added the code shown in Figure 4-14 to the *onenter* event from Figure 4-13. Then I started the page in debug mode to track the execution of the code. You can see how the cursor has stopped on the *Company* = "" line. This is the section of code that is executed when the user first enters the page.

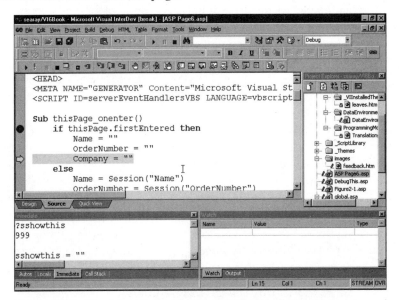

Figure 4-14. *The debug features of Visual InterDev 6 make it easy to understand how the various parts of your application are executing. This figure demonstrates how the* firstEntered *property is used.*

You can also use the *location* property to obtain the URL of the current page:

```
<%
    Response.Write "URL: " & thisPage.location
%>
```

The *thisPage* object also provides the *onbeforeserverevent* event, which is fired before posting a page for server processing. You can use this event to check values and other tasks that must occur before the page is sent back to the server. The *onbeforeserverevent* event is fired in the client before the server event executes. You can take advantage of your client script to check values and such before allowing the server event to execute.

```
<SCRIPT ID=clientEventHandlersJS LANGUAGE=javascript>
<!--

function ASP_Page9_onbeforeserverevent() {
    alert(document.thisForm.txtNumber.value)
    if (document.thisForm.txtNumber.value == "")
        thisPage.cancelEvent = true;
}

//-->
</SCRIPT>
```

This JScript code runs in the client browser and executes before any server events. The first line in the event code displays the value from the HTML text box *txtNumber*. Then the *if* statement checks the value—if it is zero, it cancels the server processing by setting the *cancelEvent* property of *thisPage*. The result is the cancellation of a needless round-trip to the server.

Working with the Scripting Object Model

As you have seen in this chapter, the Scripting Object Model adds a powerful set of capabilities to the Web development environment. You can perform all types of tasks, work with objects, and use object syntax with pages.

The Script Outline window is a key feature of this object environment: it shows a list of all the scriptable objects on the page along with the events that you can use to script against. The Script Outline window displays the objects in a page only when you have a page containing script open in the code editor.

The Script Outline window contains both client and server objects. You can see some objects that show up in both categories. For instance, *thisPage* will show as both a server object and a client object. Although it shows up in both client and server, the events that are available for *thisPage* are specific to one or the other. You saw this earlier when we used the *onenter* event in server script and the *onbeforeserverevent* event for client script. You should use the Script Outline window and the IntelliSense command completion feature wherever possible to cut down on the introduction of possible bugs in your applications.

You can now use command completion in script in HTML and ASP files as mentioned in the last paragraph. To use command completion, type the first part of the name for an object and press Ctrl+Space. This will drop the IntelliSense list. You can also display the IntelliSense list at any time by pressing Ctrl+J.

Chapter 5

Introduction to the Data Environment

The Data Environment (DE) in Microsoft Visual InterDev 6.0 collects your data connection and data manipulation code in one place. The Data Environment provides a standard interface for creating data-related objects and for placing them on Web pages. It also provides a layer of abstraction, allowing you to create and modify objects that represent your data independently of the database.

The Data Environment is a new object-based wrapper around ActiveX Data Objects (ADO) and is used in both Visual InterDev 6.0 and Microsoft Visual Basic 6.0. The consistency of using the Data Environment in both Visual InterDev and Visual Basic makes developing applications in either environment easy. Moving from Visual InterDev to Visual Basic, and vice versa, also becomes easier. This integration is likely to increase as we see new versions of Microsoft development tools in Visual Studio.

The Visual InterDev 6.0 Data Environment is created automatically when a data connection is added to a project. The DataEnvironment folder is displayed beneath the global.asa file in Project Explorer. Any data connections you add are displayed in the DataEnvironment folder.

Using the Data Environment is the easiest way to create data-driven web pages. You can create data command objects that live at the DE level in your project and can be used by any ASP file in the project. You don't have to continually re-create a Recordset control on different ASP Web pages for the same set of records as we did in Visual InterDev 1.0. Now you can create a data command object once and use it to quickly create Recordset controls by dropping them into an ASP file in the editor.

Data-bound design-time controls (DTCs) are the basic building blocks for connecting to databases and displaying data on your Web pages. The Data Environment allows you to create and manage all your DTCs in one location. You don't need to create new controls for each Web page, and you need to create controls for the same set of records only once. Because your database code can be used repeatedly, building, debugging, and maintaining applications is much easier.

A useful feature of the DE is the variety of drag-and-drop options. You can:

- Drag objects from the Data Environment and drop them into an ASP file to automatically create data-bound DTCs

- Drag the fields from a data command object's recordset and drop them onto an ASP Web page to automatically create data-bound DTCs

- Drag a table from Data View and drop it into an ASP file under a Recordset DTC created from dragging and dropping a data command object onto the page

Figure 5-1 shows the Data Environment as it looks in Project Explorer with one data connection and one data command. You can see how the DE is attached to global.asa.

Figure 5-1. *The Data Environment as displayed in Project Explorer under global.asa.*

Figure 5-1 shows the Northwind data connection and the GetCustomers data command. You can also see the fields in the GetCustomers recordset displayed beneath it. Each of these fields has a default data-bound DTC. The default is based upon the field's data type. You can right-click a field and assign it a specific DTC. That DTC will be used every time you drag the field from the recordset and drop it onto a page. We will discuss DTCs in more detail in Chapter 6 and throughout the remainder of the book.

WORKING WITH DATABASE CONNECTIONS

There are a number of steps you must take to work with databases from within Visual InterDev 6.0. The first step is to create a data connection and link it to a data source. If you do not have a data source definition before you create the data connection, you can add one at the time. The steps in this process are very similar to those in Visual InterDev 1.0.

Define a data connection to an existing data source by following these steps:

1. Right-click the Project name or global.asa in Project Explorer, and select Add Data Connection from the context menu. You will see the Select Data Source dialog box shown in Figure 5-2.

2. Click the File Data Source tab or the Machine Data Source tab to select the type of data source you want to select. Figure 5-2 shows the Machine Data Source tab.

3. Select the data source name, and click OK. A dialog box showing parameters for the data connection is displayed based upon the driver for the data source you select. (Setting these parameters is discussed in the following section.)

4. Enter the data connection parameters.

5. Click OK to add the data connection.

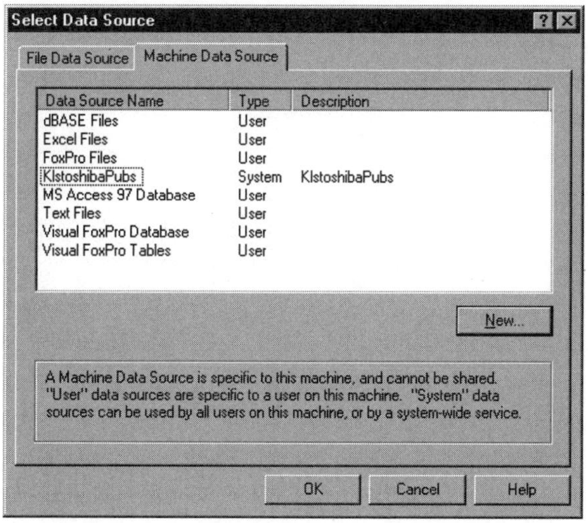

Figure 5-2. *The Select Data Source dialog box shows the existing data sources on a system.*

The data connection is displayed under the Data Environment icon in Project Explorer. You can also browse and edit the data from the database in the Data View window.

Setting Data Connection Parameters

After you select a data source for your data connection, you will see the data connection Properties dialog box shown in Figure 5-3. The dialog box is displayed as "Connection1 Properties" because Connection1 is the default name for a new data connection when it is the first in a project. Figure 5-3 also shows the new name I have assigned the data connection—cnPubs. This will become the name of the dialog box once I apply the change.

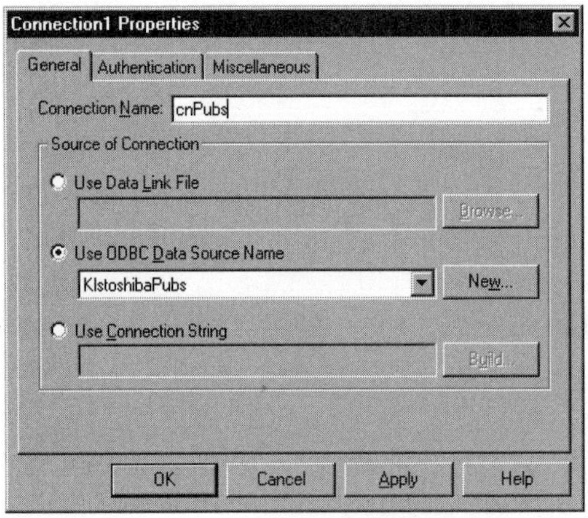

Figure 5-3. *The data connection Properties dialog box lets you name the data connection and set various design-time and run-time properties.*

You can use the data connection Properties dialog box to change the configuration of a data connection. You can:

- Change the data source

- Change the authentication properties used at both run time and design time

- Change other properties, such as cursor type

If you change the data source to a connection string, you can use the Build button to select the driver for the connection and then configure its properties. This option is not available for an ODBC data source or a data link file.

Figure 5-4 shows the Authentication tab of the data connection Properties dialog box. Notice that you can specify both user name and password strings for the run-time and design-time connections. You can choose whether to allow the Visual InterDev environment to prompt you at design time for any required connection information. You can also choose to allow a user prompt for connection information during design time.

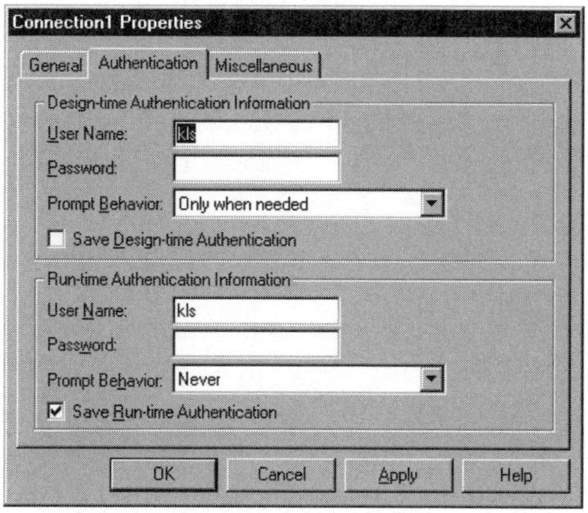

Figure 5-4. *The Authentication tab provides a design-time interface for changing both design-time and run-time authentication for the data connection.*

The run-time prompt must always be set to Never. The data connection cannot prompt the user for the connection information when the application executes because the data connection will be running on the server, not the client. Even if you set the run-time environment for DTCs to client, the prompting behavior will not work in Web applications. You can, of course, override these defaults by passing the security credentials in to the data connection when the application is executing.

Creating a New Data Source

Visual InterDev 6.0 will let you create a new data source when you add a data connection. The steps are similar to the ones used in Visual InterDev 1.0.

1. Right-click the Project name or global.asa in Project Explorer, and select Add Data Connection from the context menu. You will see the Select Data Source dialog box, shown in Figure 5-2.

2. Click the File Data Source tab or the Machine Data Source tab to select the type of data source. Figure 5-2 shows the Machine Data Source tab.

3. Click the New button.

4. Select the database driver for your database, and choose Next.

5. Type the name for the data source, and choose Next. The extension .dsn is automatically added to the name for a file data source.

6. Choose Finish. The database driver will be invoked and will display dialog boxes to complete the setup process. Enter driver-specific information, such as the name of the database.

Be careful when using data sources. Observe the guidelines listed below:

- When you specify the path for a file database such as Access, use the relative path to the database, not its location on your development computer. For example, if the database is located on a Web server, use the URL path to the database. This ensures that the database will be available from your Web server.

- Often it is best to use a system data source rather than a file data source. The reasons are twofold: First, using a system data source allows you to create the same data source name on all the developer systems and on the production server. Then you can move the application from one system to the other without any database issues. Second, the application will run faster, since system data sources are faster than file data sources.

- Be careful when using system and user data sources. System data sources are available to all users on the system. User data sources are only available to the user who creates them. For Web servers, always define the data sources as system, unless you want to define them explicitly for the run-time user only. Figure 5-5 shows this step in the Create New Data Source Wizard.

The step shown in Figure 5-5 will display only if you select the Machine Data Source tab in the Select Data Source dialog box before you click the New button in step 3 above.

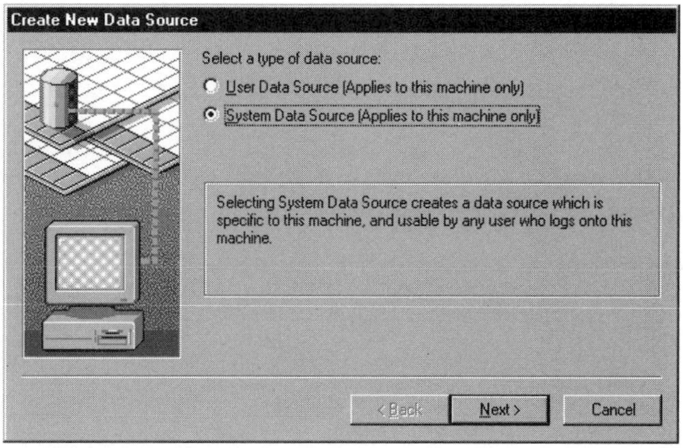

Figure 5-5. *The Create New Data Source Wizard steps you through the process of creating a new data source.*

When you reach the last step of the Create New Data Source Wizard, you will see a summary of the data source information you specified. An example of a SQL Server data source is shown in Figure 5-6. At the bottom of this dialog box you will see the Test Data Source button. Click this button, and the data source connection will be tested for you. This ensures that the data source information is valid and that the data connection will work.

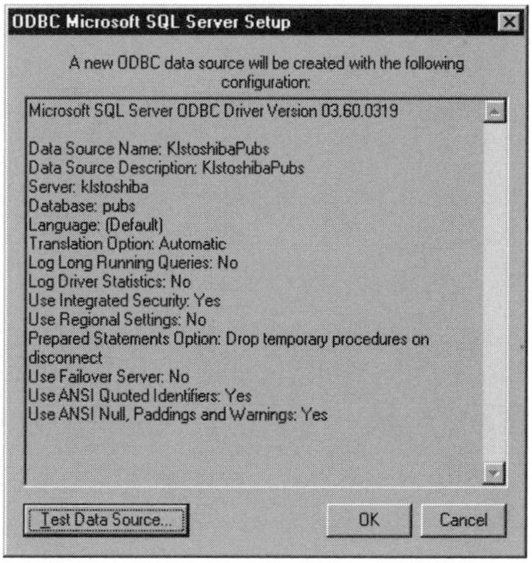

Figure 5-6. *You can test your data source during the creation stage by clicking the Test Data Source button.*

Once you have completed the steps to set up the data source, you are returned to the Select Data Source dialog box shown in Figure 5-2 and the data source name you created is displayed in the list. Select this name and click OK. This will add the data source to your project.

WORKING WITH DATA COMMAND OBJECTS

Once you add a data connection to a project, you are ready to start manipulating the database. To accomplish this, you will usually add a data command object to your connection. A data command object provides the link between the data connection and a recordset.

A data command object is a named object living under a data connection. Where the data connection points to a database or some other source of data, a data command object contains some type of connection information that works against the target of the data connection. For example, suppose we create a data connection that points to the Pubs sample database that ships with SQL Server. We could create a data command object under this data connection that extracts all the authors from the Pubs database. Any type of command that can be executed by the database can be used with a data command object.

A nice feature of data command objects is the way they work within a project. When you create a data command object, an ASP file in the project can use it. The properties of the data command object can be changed once and will be reflected in every ASP file that uses the object, making maintenance of your database objects much easier.

You can create a data command object by following these steps:

1. Right-click DataEnvironment in Project Explorer, and select Add Data Command from the context menu. This will display the data command Properties dialog box.

2. Enter a name for this data command object in the Command Name text box.

3. Select the data connection to use from the Connection drop-down list.

4. Select the database object to use from the Database Object and Object Name drop-down lists, or enter the SQL to use for the command. Figure 5-7 shows the data command Properties dialog box with a SQL statement to select all of the records in the Authors table from the database.

5. Click OK to close the dialog box.

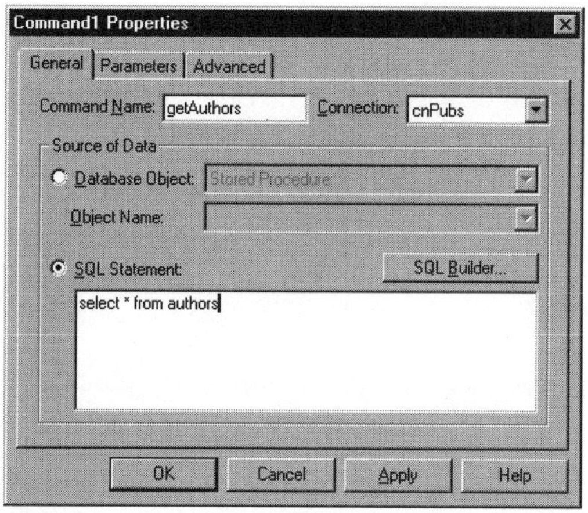

Figure 5-7. *The data command Properties dialog box can be used to build a data command object's properties or modify them for an existing data command object.*

Once you have created a data command object, it will be added to Project Explorer under the corresponding data connection. Figure 5-8 shows the new getAuthors data command object in Project Explorer.

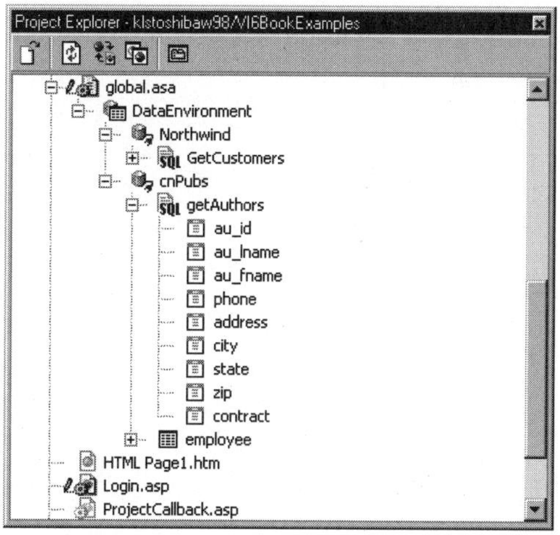

Figure 5-8. *Project Explorer exposes the fields in a data command object.*

Figure 5-8 also shows how your multiple data command objects will look in Project Explorer. In this case we only have one data command object for each data connection, but we can easily create many data command objects for one data connection, as you will see in later examples.

If you want to create a data command object that contains the complete set of records in a table, query, view, stored procedure, or other type of database object, you can add the data command object by dragging the object from Data View and then dropping it on a data connection.

You can also add a data command object by copying the object and pasting it onto a data connection:

1. Right-click the object name in Data View.

2. Select Copy from the context menu.

3. Right-click the data connection you want to add the object to, and select Paste from the context menu.

This creates a new data command object based upon the database object you selected.

If you want to use an explicit SQL statement to select a set of records, select the SQL Statement option in the data command Properties dialog box and then click the SQL Builder button to start the Query Designer or enter the SQL statement in the SQL Statement text box. Later in this chapter, we will introduce the Query Designer. Chapter 12 also covers the Query Designer in more depth.

Working with Recordsets

Now that you have created a data connection and added data command objects to it, you are ready to use them in your project. The easiest way to use a data command object in your project is to add a recordset to an ASP file. This recordset object will work with the database through the data command object and use DTCs to display or change the data.

You can add a Recordset DTC to an ASP file by following these steps:

1. Open the ASP file you want to use in the editor.

2. Drag the data command you want to use from Project Explorer, and drop it in the Body section of the page.

You can also drag a Recordset DTC from the Toolbox and manually set its properties to point to a data command object.

Now that you have placed a Recordset DTC in the file, you can add DTCs for the fields you want to display. The easiest way to accomplish this with a data command object is by using drag and drop from Project Explorer:

1. Expand the data command you dropped on the page in Project Explorer. You should see the fields in the recordset, as shown in Figure 5-8.

2. Drag the fields you want to display from the data command object, and drop them on the page just after the Recordset DTC. For each field you drag onto the page, Visual InterDev creates a data-bound Textbox DTC to display the field. The page should look similar to the one shown in Figure 5-9.

3. Right-click each Textbox DTC, and change its properties to adjust the control's display. You can also add HTML formatting around the DTCs.

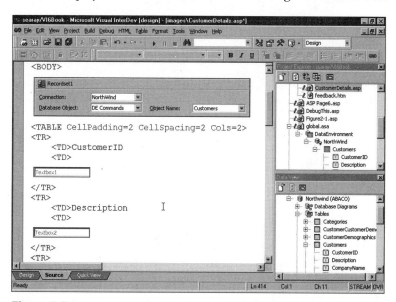

Figure 5-9. *You can display data command fields by dragging them from Project Explorer and dropping them onto an ASP Web page.*

Figure 5-9 shows a sample page after a data command object and its fields have been dropped onto it as described in the preceding steps. When you drag and drop multiple fields onto an ASP Web page, Visual InterDev creates an HTML table and inserts a Textbox DTC for each field into that table. Each of these Textbox DTCs is bound (linked) to the Recordset DTC. Figure 5-10 on the following page shows the Textbox Properties dialog box for one of the DTCs.

The *Recordset* property of the Textbox DTC in Figure 5-10 is set to Recordset1, the default name of our Recordset DTC. The *Field* property has been set to au_lname, the name of the database column linked to this DTC.

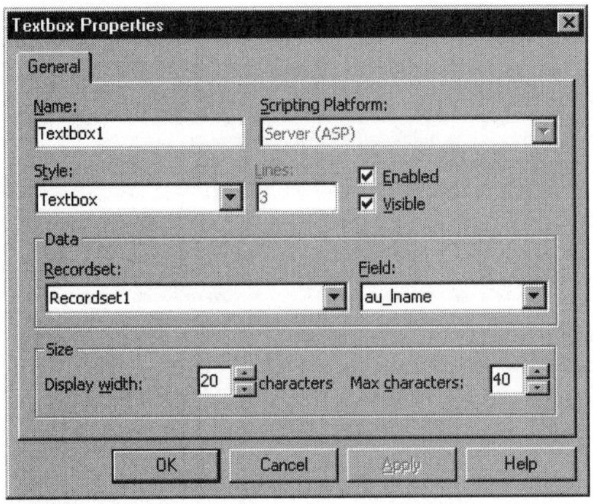

Figure 5-10. *The Textbox Properties dialog box for a data-bound Textbox DTC.*

Figure 5-11 shows the Recordset Properties dialog box for the Recordset DTC. You can see that the *Name* property is set to Recordset1. The *Database Object* property is set to DE Commands, while the *Object Name* property is set to getAuthors.

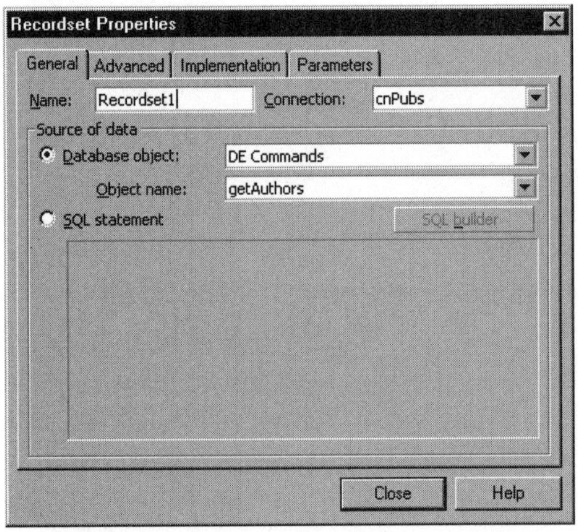

Figure 5-11. *The Recordset Properties dialog box allows you to change the configuration of the Recordset DTC.*

You can, of course, set the Recordset DTC to use a SQL query, stored procedure, or view. These items will be explored in much more detail in Chapter 14, where you'll learn how to use the Recordset DTC's events and how to set other properties.

Visual InterDev 6.0 provides the RecordsetNavbar DTC, which controls navigation between database records. This control provides the buttons with which a user navigates through the records in a recordset. You can insert the RecordsetNavbar DTC in a page by following these steps:

1. Open the ASP file in the editor.

2. Drag the RecordsetNavbar DTC from the Toolbox, and drop it onto the page.

3. Right-click the control, and select Properties from the context menu. This will open the RecordsetNavbar Properties dialog box, as shown in Figure 5-12.

4. Select the Recordset DTC to use from the Recordset drop-down list. In Figure 5-12, this is set to Recordset1.

The RecordsetNavbar DTC provides First, Next, Previous, and Last buttons. You can use these buttons to move among the records displayed on the page. You can also customize the functionality of these buttons by modifying the script that they create or by changing certain properties in the RecordsetNavbar Properties dialog box.

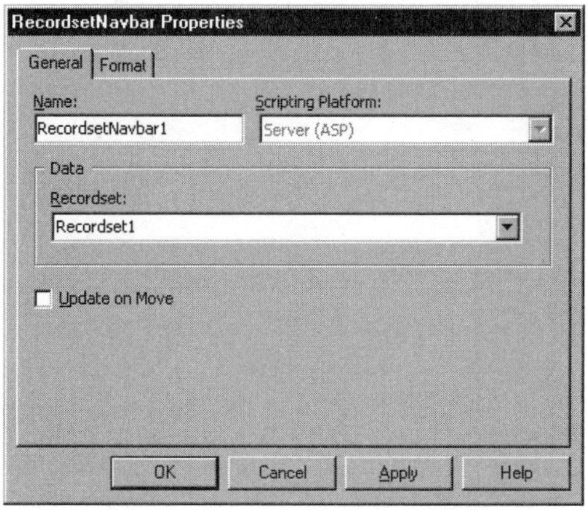

Figure 5-12. *The RecordsetNavbar Properties dialog box is used to bind the RecordsetNavbar DTC to the Recordset DTC.*

If the recordset is updatable and you want users to be able to change the data, you might want to set the *Update On Move* property to True by checking the Update On Move check box. If *Update On Move* is True, the fields in the recordset will be updated with the new data in the data-bound DTCs whenever the user moves to another record. If *Update On Move* is False, the data in the data-bound DTCs will be discarded when the user moves to a new record.

The RecordsetNavbar's *Scripting Platform* property defaults to Inherit From Page and should reflect the value set for the page's *Scripting Platform* property. Figure 5-12 shows this property set to Server (ASP), which is the page's setting. Once you have selected a Recordset DTC in the *Recordset* property, the *Scripting Platform* property becomes read-only. If you want to change the *Scripting Platform* property after you have selected a Recordset DTC, highlight and delete the Recordset DTC name and then change the *Scripting Platform* property. Once you have changed the *Scripting Platform* property, you can reselect the Recordset DTC.

Figure 5-13 demonstrates how the RecordsetNavbar DTC works in the browser. I created a new page and placed four fields from the GetCustomers data command object on the page. Then I added the RecordsetNavbar DTC as we did in the previous steps. Next I saved the page and displayed it in the browser. You can see the results in Figure 5-13.

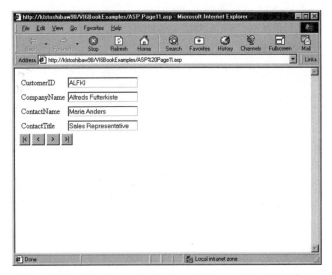

Figure 5-13. *The RecordsetNavbar DTC provides HTML buttons for navigation between records.*

Chapter 14 covers the Recordset DTC in detail, including its methods, properties, and events, as well as building complete applications with it and other controls.

Working with the Data Command Object Controls

You can adjust the way the data command objects work with the DTCs that are dropped onto a page. The Field Properties dialog box, shown in Figure 5-14, can be used to configure the properties of the fields within a data command object. You can change the DTC used when you drop the field onto a page and change the caption used in the HTML for the field.

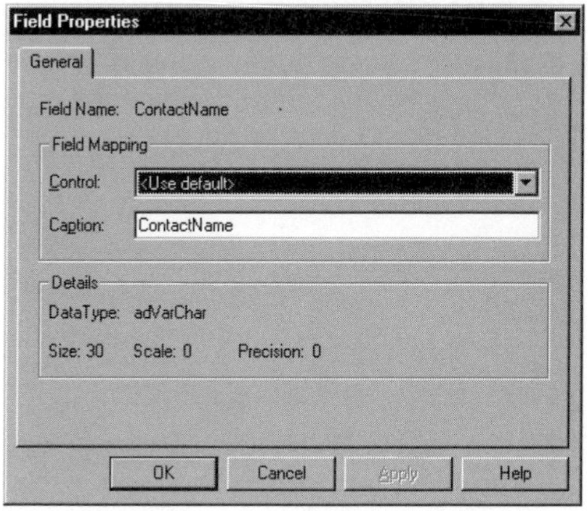

Figure 5-14. *The Field Properties dialog box is used to set the characteristics of a data command object's fields and how they behave when dropped onto a page.*

You change the default DTC for a field by following these steps:

1. Right-click the field in Project Explorer.

2. Select Properties from the context menu.

3. Select the DTC to use from the Control drop-down list.

You change the default caption for a field by following these steps:

1. Right-click the field in Project Explorer.

2. Select Properties from the context menu.

3. Enter the new caption in the Caption text box.

To see how these properties work, I changed the properties for the GetCustomers data command object and then created a new page with them. You can see the results in Figure 5-15 on the following page.

The captions for each field were changed. (Compare Figure 5-15 with Figure 5-13.) For example, you can see that Customer ID contains a space, while the field name does not (CustomerID). The CustomerID field is also displayed in a Label DTC, while the default control would have been the Textbox DTC, which is used for the other fields.

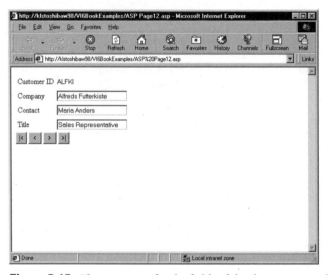

Figure 5-15. *The properties for the fields of the data command object used in this page have been changed.*

USING CLIENT DATABASE FEATURES

One beneficial feature of Visual InterDev 6.0 is the new support for DHTML clients. The Data Environment and DTCs can support DHTML clients such as Microsoft Internet Explorer 4.

By default, the DTC scripting platform is set to Server (ASP) for every new project. You can change this setting for all new pages in the project by displaying the Project Properties dialog box, clicking the Editor Defaults tab, and then selecting the Client (IE 4.0 DHTML) option. Changing this setting for the project after you have created data-driven pages does not affect the existing pages.

You can, however, change this setting for each page and for each DTC. Figure 5-16 shows the Properties dialog box for an ASP Web page. Notice that I have changed the DTC Scripting Platform setting to Client (IE 4.0 DHTML). As soon as this page is saved, the DTCs on the page inherit the change in the scripting platform. The inheritance from the page is the default action. You can override these settings for each DTC.

Now you are in for a surprise. Running pages with DTCs executing on the client does several things:

- The DTCs are implemented as objects on the client.

- The page is not redisplayed each time the user moves between records.

- The application's demands on the server decrease.

When you use DTCs and implement them as client objects, the database features are implemented using Remote Data Services (RDS). Using RDS pushes the database recordset down to the client and lets the client do most of the work. The load placed on both the network server and the network also decrease.

Client database features are covered in detail in Chapter 16.

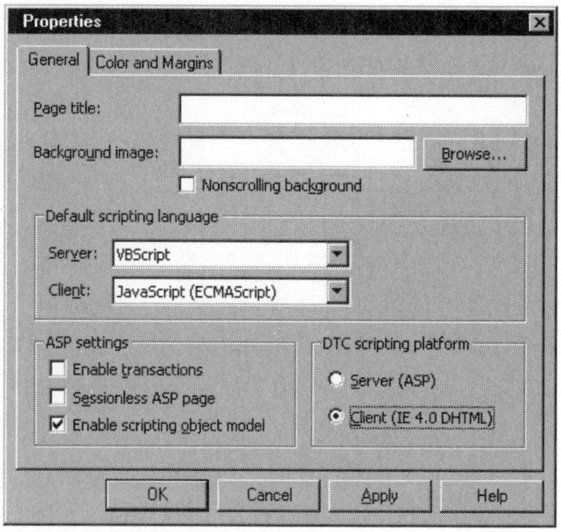

Figure 5-16. *The Page Properties dialog box allows you to change the scripting platform for DTCs on the page.*

USING THE QUERY DESIGNER

The Query Designer—a SQL Builder add-in for Visual InterDev—is a member of the Microsoft Visual Database Tools product family and is a key companion to the Data Environment in both Visual InterDev and Visual Basic. The Query Designer provides visual design tools to create SQL statements for performing queries, updates, and other tasks on any ODBC-compliant database. The Query Designer lets you perform the following tasks:

- Create queries to retrieve, update, insert, and delete data from any ODBC-compliant database

- Select tables, views, and columns for a query

- Specify how to order query results

- Build Where clauses that specify what values to search for

- Preview query results in the Results pane

- Join tables to create multitable queries

- Edit databases by inserting, updating, or deleting rows

- Create special-purpose queries, such as parameter queries in which search values are provided when the query is executed

- Enter SQL statements directly or edit the SQL statements created by the Query Designer

- Create back-end-specific SQL statements to take advantage of a particular database's features

- Execute Microsoft SQL Server stored procedures

The Query Designer Interface

The Query Designer interface is built around four panes, or windows, as described in Table 5-1.

You can control which panes are currently displayed by using the buttons on the Query toolbar, shown in Figure 5-17. The buttons are toggles that turn a pane's display on or off. Figure 5-17 shows the Query Designer with the SQL statement for the GetCustomers data command object.

The Query Designer supports drag-and-drop and cut-and-paste operations to the Clipboard. For example, the interactive interface lets you drag a column from the Diagram pane and drop it onto the Grid pane.

Query Designer Pane	*Description*
Diagram	Displays the input sources (tables or views) that you are querying
Grid	Contains a spreadsheet-like grid in which you specify query options, such as which data columns to display, how to order the results, which rows to select, and how to group rows
SQL	Displays the SQL statement for the current query and lets you create your own SQL statements
Results	Shows a grid with the results of the most recently executed query

Table 5-1. *The graphical panes of the Query Designer interface.*

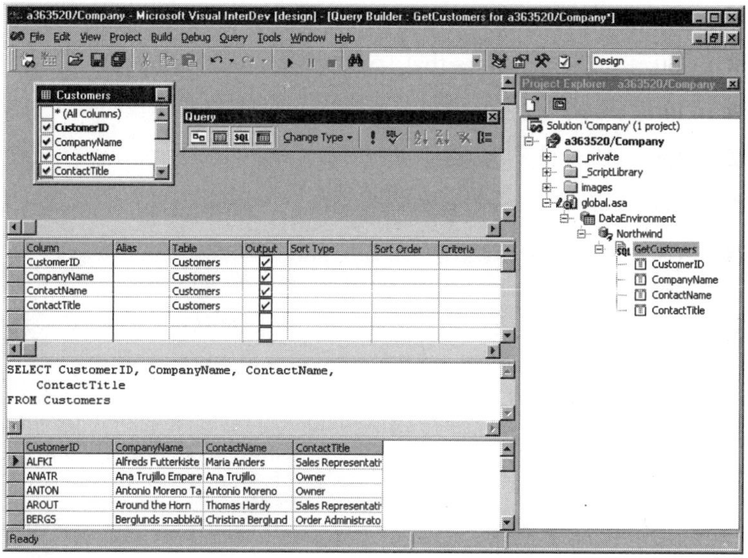

Figure 5-17. *The Query Designer interface is based upon four windows (from top to bottom): Diagram, Grid, SQL, and Results.*

Creating Queries with the Query Designer

You can create a query and/or display the Query Designer interface in several ways. You can open the Query Designer for an existing table or you can view it in Data View.

To open the Query Designer for a table or a view, take the following steps:

1.   Display the tables or views in the Data View window.

2.   Double-click a table or a view to open the Query Designer for that object.

These two steps open the Results pane for the selected table or view and display the data from the query. The Results pane lets you edit and delete the data returned by the query. You cannot access the Query Designer's other features because they are not useful for a table or a view. You can, however, use the Query toolbar to open the other panes.

If you open the Diagram or SQL pane, you can create an entirely new query. After you change the query definition, the query is no longer based on the table with which you opened the Query Designer. You can save the query to a file by clicking the Standard toolbar's Save button. The resulting .dtq file is an ASCII description of the query that you can add to a database project.

To open the Query Designer for the Recordset DTC, follow these steps:

1. Display the properties for the Recordset DTC by right-clicking the DTC and choosing Properties from the context menu.

2. Click the General tab of the Recordset Properties dialog box.

3. Select the SQL Statement option, and then click the SQL Builder button.

To open the Query Designer for a data command object, do the following:

- Right-click the data command in Project Explorer, and select SQL Builder from the context menu.

You can also open the Query Designer for a data command object by clicking the SQL Builder button on the data command Properties dialog box.

The query you create for a Recordset DTC or a data command object automatically updates the SQL for the object when you save or close the query.

To add input sources (tables and views) to the Query Designer, follow these steps:

1. Display the Data View window of the Project Workspace.

2. Drag the table or view, and drop it onto the Query Designer Diagram pane.

You can also drag a database diagram from the Database Designer and drop it onto the Query Designer. This step inserts all the tables in the diagram into the Query Designer. This is a quick way to get several tables into the Query Designer when you already have a database diagram containing the tables you need.

Once the Query Designer is open, you can quickly create a query. Just add the tables from which you want to retrieve the data, and then follow these steps:

1. Select the columns to use in the query by dragging them to the Grid pane or by selecting the check box next to the column name.

2. Enter any criteria for the query, such as filters or expressions.

3. Test the query by clicking the Run Query button on the Query toolbar.

Chapter 6

Using Design-Time Controls

INTRODUCTION

Design-time controls (DTCs) offer you a more functional and aesthetically pleasing interface for creating data-enriched pages than do standard HTML controls. The data-bound DTCs simplify incorporating data in your ASP Web pages or HTML pages to talk to a database (as you saw in the last chapter). The DTCs included with Microsoft Visual InterDev 6 allow you to target a wide range of browsers or to narrow the focus of the application to take advantage of the unique features of Microsoft Internet Explorer 4.

This chapter focuses on the features and uses of DTCs in applications. Chapter 8 will focus on how to use server and client script with DTCs.

DTCs have two components:

■ The control that runs in Visual InterDev to provide you with property pages and automated design features

■ The run-time scripting objects that implement the control

These two components work together to provide the developer with a powerful set of controls for use in Visual InterDev's integrated development environment (IDE).

Visual InterDev 6 includes a number of DTCs that automatically generate much of the server-side and client-side scripting required for applications. This includes traditional HTML, Microsoft VBScript (Visual Basic, Scripting Edition), Microsoft JScript, and ADO (ActiveX Data Objects) code. Many DTCs generate all the logic necessary to establish database connections within a Web site, perform queries, and display results.

Visual InterDev 6 builds upon the rich DTC foundation laid by Visual InterDev 1. The new DTC features not only work to automate ADO functions but also provide data-bound features that automatically link components such as Textbox DTCs with a Recordset DTC. This new functionality makes it extremely easy to build a Web page with fields linked to a database on the server.

Insert a DTC into a page by following these steps:

1. Select the Design-Time Controls tab of the Toolbox.

2. Drag the DTC you wish to insert from the Toolbox, and drop it on the ASP file in the editor.

   Edit the properties of a DTC by following these steps:

3. Right-click the DTC in the editor, and select Properties.

4. Make your changes in the Properties dialog box, and click Apply.

The new DTCs do not display the code for the implementation of the control in the editor as they did in Visual InterDev 1. Instead, the controls are represented graphically in both the Source View and Design View editors. Figure 6-1 shows the Design View editor with a Textbox DTC and a Label DTC on a page.

You can see how the two fields are represented graphically in the Design View editor. The label is a large text site and appears to be standard HTML text typed into the page. The string "Inventory Solutions" is actually text that is entered in the *DataField* property of the DTC. The other control on the page is the Textbox DTC containing the text "txtItemNumber." This text is the *ID* property of the DTC.

If you switch to Source view, the DTCs will still be graphically displayed. The display you see there is the same display that we have used in most of the figures in this book so far. Figure 6-2 shows the same page that is shown in Figure 6-1.

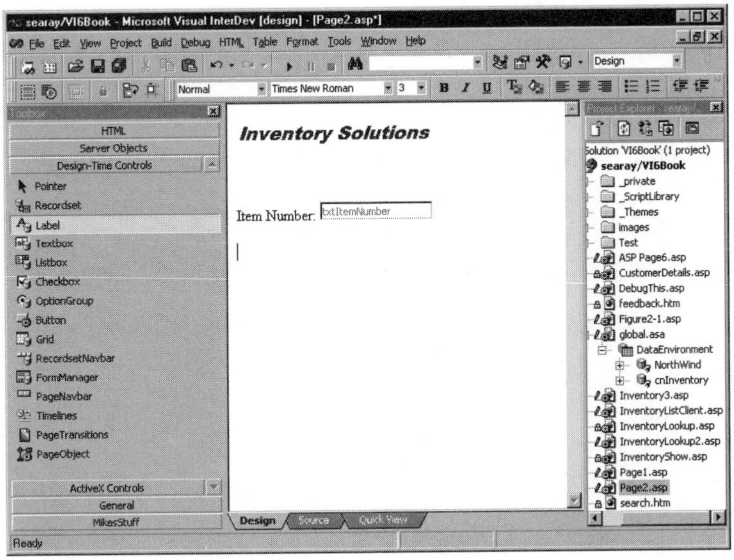

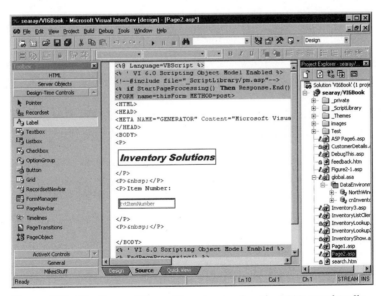

Figure 6-1. *The Visual InterDev 6 editors show a graphical version of the DTCs by default.*

Figure 6-2. *The Source View editor also renders the DTCs graphically.*

Often you will see the Source View editor when it is in the process of rendering the graphical display for a DTC. This occurs when you switch to Source view from another view or when you scroll along a page quickly. This is quite normal. When it happens, you might see Visual InterDev with a display similar to that in Figure 6-3.

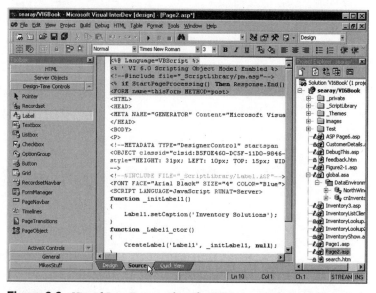

Figure 6-3. *Visual InterDev renders the DTCs in a page each time it must redisplay the portion of the page viewable in the editor.*

The display in Figure 6-3 shows some of the static text used to store the DTC properties in the page. For instance, you can see the text displayed in the Textbox DTC is set to "Inventory Solutions," just as we set it in the DTC properties.

You can also display the code for a DTC by changing a setting for the control in the editor. Follow these steps:

1. Display the page containing the DTC in Source view.

2. Right-click the DTC.

3. Select Show Run-Time Text.

Displaying the run-time text of a DTC will result in a display similar to Figure 6-4. You can see how the DTC relies on server-side code in the Script Library and also uses client-side Java code to implement the control. Examining this code will give you a good understanding of how a particular DTC is implemented.

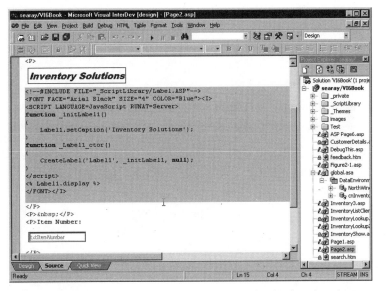

Figure 6-4. *The run-time text for a control can be displayed in the Source View editor.*

You can quickly hide the DTC's run-time code once you have finished reviewing it by selecting View Controls Graphically from the View menu.

You can view controls (that is, DTCs, Java applets, and other controls) in Source view as text. This is useful for viewing the exact contents of a page and for quickly making changes to a series of controls. You can choose to view a control always as text in the Source View editor. This shows the control in the same fashion as a Visual InterDev 1 DTC, shown in Figure 6-5 on the following page.

Viewing a control as text applies only in Source view. Design view and Quick view always render the graphical view of a control (if possible). You can set the default view for DTCs by selecting Options from the Tools menu and using the HTML section of the Options dialog box.

You can view a control as text by following these steps:

1. Right-click the DTC in the Source View editor.

2. Select Always View As Text.

These steps set the VIEWASTEXT attribute in the DTC's <OBJECT> tag.

You can also view all DTCs as text by selecting View Controls As Text on the View menu. When you select this option, all DTCs on the page will be displayed as text until you switch to Design view or Quick view and back. You can also use the View Controls Graphically command on the View menu to redisplay DTCs graphically. Any DTCs for which you have selected the Always View As Text option will continue to be viewed as text.

Selecting Refresh from the View menu will cause the editor to display all DTCs in the current default view except those whose <OBJECT> tag contains the VIEWASTEXT attribute.

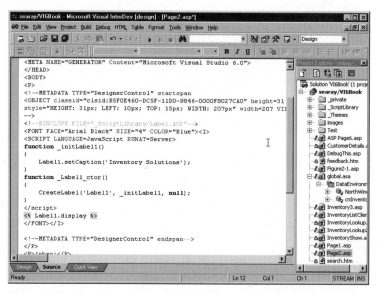

Figure 6-5. *DTCs can also be displayed as text in the Source View editor.*

Displaying DTCs as text can affect how DTCs function on a page. DTCs do not function properly if they are displayed as text, because they cannot communicate with the Scripting Object Model framework. You must make sure the options are set to view DTCs graphically before you add a DTC to a page. If you inadvertently add a DTC to the page while the view controls as text option is set, the HTML editor cannot create an instance of the DTC and will display only the HTML <OBJECT> tag for the DTC, not the DTC itself.

You can permanently convert a DTC's code to text by following these steps:

1. Display the page containing the DTC in Source view.

2. Right-click the DTC, and select Convert To Run-Time Text from the popup menu.

3. Visual InterDev will display a confirmation message warning you that this action cannot be undone and that you will experience a loss in functionality. (See Figure 6-6.) Click Yes to convert the DTC to text.

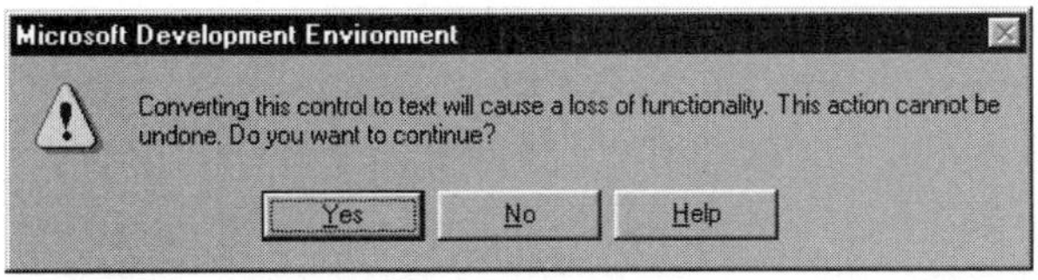

Figure 6-6. *This message warns you that the Convert To Run-Time Text action cannot be undone and that the DTC will experience a loss in functionality.*

Once you have converted a DTC to run-time text, the run-time code for the DTC will appear in the Source View editor. For example, the run-time code for the Textbox DTC looks like this:

```
<script language="JavaScript"
    src="_ScriptLibrary/TextBox.HTM"></script>
<SCRIPT LANGUAGE=JavaScript>
function _inittxtItemNumber()
{
    txtItemNumber.setStyle(TXT_TEXTBOX);
    txtItemNumber.setMaxLength(30);
    txtItemNumber.setColumnCount(30);
}
CreateTextbox('txtItemNumber', _inittxtItemNumber, null);
</script>
```

This code is now editable and can be changed to suit your purposes.

> **WARNING** Microsoft is going to replace the Scripting Object Model JScript code with COM objects in early 1999. It is quite likely that some or all of the run-time code for the DTCs will change at that point. For this reason, you should treat the code that a DTC generates as a black box. As with all black-box code, do not change it directly since you might render the code unusable in future versions. *Caveat emptor.*

DTC Properties Window and Property Pages

Visual InterDev now includes the Properties window that lists the properties for selected objects such as DTCs. The Properties window lists the property name and the current settings, as shown in Figure 6-7 on the following page.

As you work with objects, the Properties window will continually update to display the properties for the current object. Each time you select another object, the Properties window will update for that object. As you change properties, the changes are applied immediately. You can also use the drop-down list at the top of the Properties window to display the properties for another object.

You can display the Properties window at any time by pressing the F4 key.

Many objects will display a Custom property with an ellipsis button (a button with three periods on it). Clicking the ellipsis will display the property pages for that object.

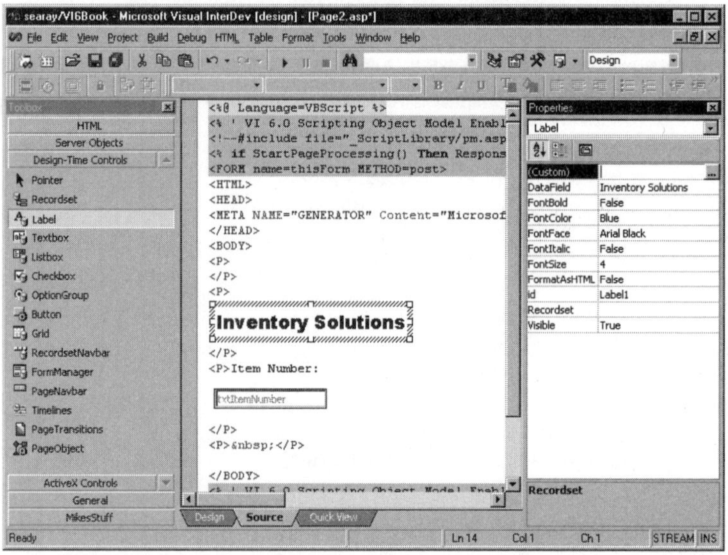

Figure 6-7. *The Properties window updates automatically as you select objects in the editors.*

The first property shown in Figure 6-7 is Custom. You can click the ellipsis to the right of the Custom property or double-click Custom and Visual InterDev 6 will display the custom property pages for the object. Figure 6-8 shows the custom property pages for the Label DTC.

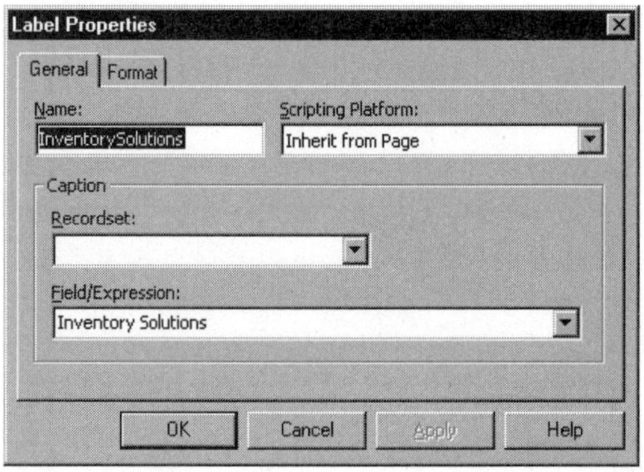

Figure 6-8. *Most DTCs have custom property pages.*

Like the Properties window, the custom property pages will display properties for the currently selected object in the editor. Just click a different object in the editor and the custom property pages will display for the new object.

Each DTC will display its own set of properties. Some controls have similar properties. For example, all the DTCs use the *ID* property to name the control. This is the property you use in your script code to refer to the control. The *ID* property is shown as ID in the Properties window and as Name on property pages.

USING DTCS

You have seen several examples of using DTCs earlier in the book. Those examples were created using the drag-and-drop features of the Data Environment to hook up the DTCs to a data command object. In this section, we will explore how to use DTCs in our applications and either set their properties or manually link them to a database.

You can use DTCs in any ASP or HTML application. Like any HTML control, DTCs have properties and they can be driven by scripting exactly like HTML controls can. However, DTCs are quite different from HTML controls because they expose an event model that allows you to script activities for them on both the client and the server.

To use a DTC, simply place it on a page. The easiest way to do this is to drag the control from the Toolbox and drop it onto a page, as illustrated by the following steps:

1. Open the file you wish to work on in the editor.

2. Drag the DTC from the Toolbox.

3. Drop the DTC onto the page.

The DTC will be added into the location where you drop it. If the page contains HTML tags, you can insert the DTC into a specific tag. For example, if your page contains an HTML table, you can place DTCs in the table. To demonstrate how to work with DTCs in production applications, I created a simple page that contains an HTML table and a few DTCs. The HTML table is used for formatting. The DTCs will contain the data. Figure 6-9 on the following page shows the page with a title and a subtitle. I typed both of these elements directly into the page using Design view. Then I highlighted each element and formatted its text with the HTML toolbar (the one containing the word Normal and showing the other style buttons).

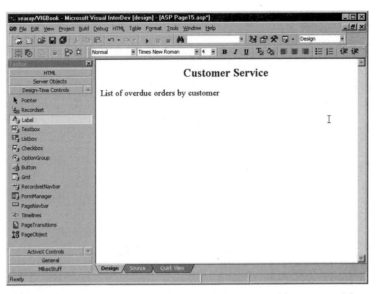

Figure 6-9. *Using Design view is the easiest way to add new visual features to a page.*

Next I selected Insert Table from the Table menu. This command displayed the dialog box shown in Figure 6-10.

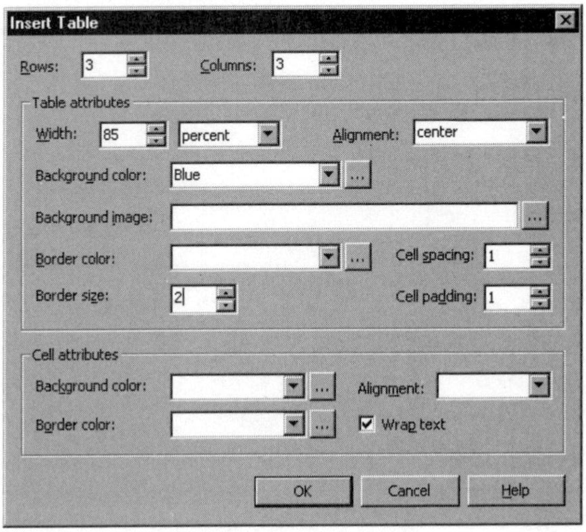

Figure 6-10. *The Insert Table dialog box allows you to quickly insert an HTML table or change an existing HTML table's properties.*

Then I clicked OK to close the dialog box and insert the table. This resulted in the following code being inserted into the file:

```
<TABLE align=center border=2 cellPadding=1 cellSpacing=1
    width=85%>
    <TR>
        <TD></TD>
        <TD></TD>
        <TD></TD></TR>
    <TR>
        <TD></TD>
        <TD></TD>
        <TD></TD></TR>
    <TR>
        <TD></TD>
        <TD></TD>
        <TD></TD></TR></TABLE>
```

Using the HTML toolbar and other features—such as the Table menu—simplifies many of the standard procedures for building a Web application with Visual InterDev.

Now that we have a table in the page, we can add DTCs to it.

1. Drag a DTC from the Toolbox.

2. Drop it into the appropriate cell in the table.

The results of this operation are shown in Figure 6-11.

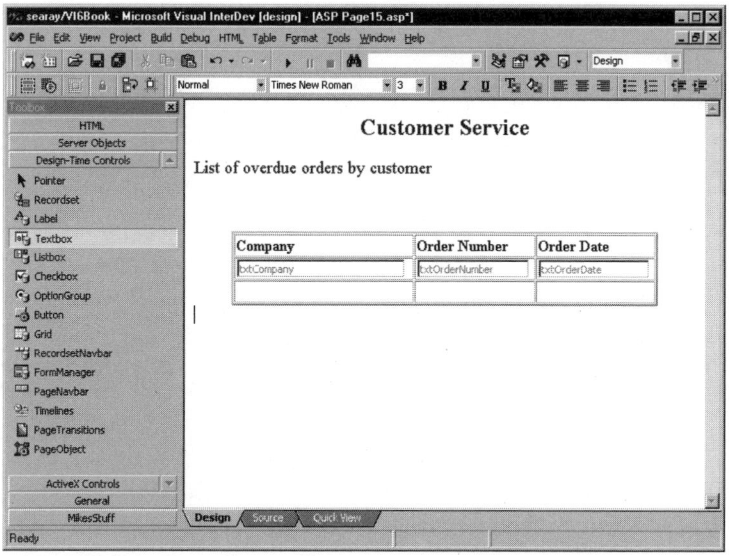

Figure 6-11. *DTCs can be used with other HTML elements.*

To complete the interface settings, I changed the widths of the Textbox DTCs from 20 characters to 30 characters. This also adjusted the DTCs' widths in the table.

Working with Data-Bound Controls

Now let's look at how to wire up DTCs to a page without dragging and dropping them from the Data Environment and a data command object. First you must place a Recordset DTC onto the page.

1. Open an ASP file in the editor.

2. Drag a Recordset DTC from the Toolbox.

3. Drop the Recordset DTC onto the page.

4. Right-click the Recordset DTC, and select Properties from the context menu.

5. Change the properties for the Recordset DTC. To do so, you can enter the SQL for the command directly into the DTC, you can select a data command object, or you can use the SQL Builder button to start the Query Designer and build the query graphically. When you have finished updating the Recordset DTC's properties, click Close.

Now that you have a Recordset DTC on the page, you can add your other DTCs and bind them to the Recordset DTC.

1. Drag a DTC from the Toolbox, and drop it onto the page.

2. Right-click the DTC, and choose Properties.

3. In the Recordset drop-down list, select the name of the Recordset DTC that will supply the data to this DTC.

4. In the Field drop-down list, select the name of the recordset field that the data-bound DTC will display.

The above steps link the new DTC to the Recordset DTC. Figure 6-12 shows the *txtCompany* Textbox DTC. The Properties window shows the *Recordset* property set to Recordset1 and the *DataField* property set to CompanyName.

To complete the page shown in Figure 6-12, I added two more Textbox DTCs and the RecordsetNavbar DTC. The Textbox DTCs are wired to Recordset1, and their *DataField* property is set to the appropriate field from the recordset. The RecordsetNavbar DTC has its *Recordset* property set to Recordset1.

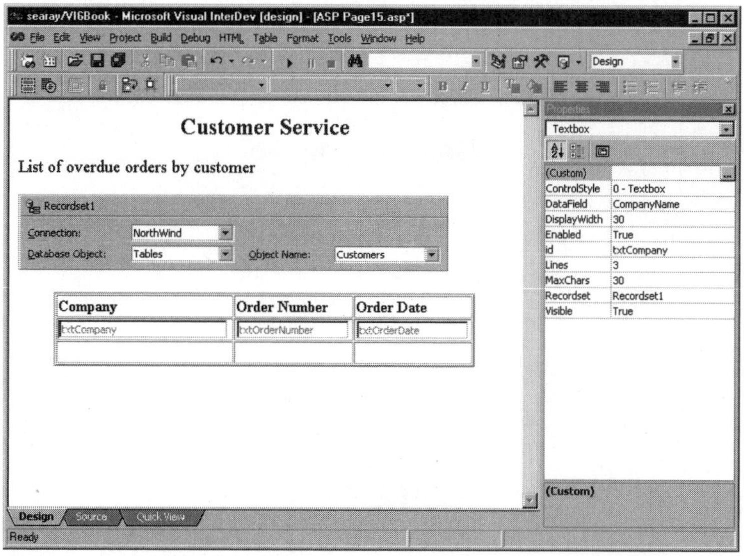

Figure 6-12. *You can use the data-binding features of certain DTCs to wire the DTCs to a recordset.*

If you change the *Update On Move* property of the RecordsetNavbar DTC to True, this DTC will let any user update the records displayed in the page. For example, to change the company name, you just make the change in the *txtCompany* Textbox and then click one of the RecordsetNavbar scroll buttons. The completed page is shown in the browser in Figure 6-13 on the following page.

The following DTCs can be bound to data sources:

■ Textbox

■ Listbox

■ Checkbox

■ OptionGroup (radio buttons)

■ Label

■ Grid

■ Recordset

■ RecordsetNavbar

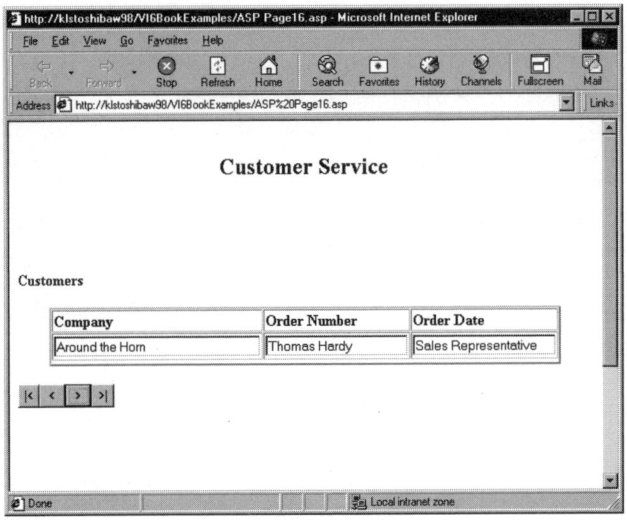

Figure 6-13. *A Recordset DTC, a RecordsetNavbar DTC, and data-bound Textbox DTCs combine to produce a simple database-driven Web page.*

When working with the Recordset DTC, you might see an error pop up. Figure 6-14 shows the error message you might receive when you drop a Recordset DTC on a page and the DTC cannot find the data connection it attempts to default to. The Recordset DTC tries to set itself to the first data connection (in alphabetical order) it finds. If it cannot find the first connection, it retries for several seconds and finally shows the message in Figure 6-14.

Figure 6-14. *The Recordset DTC generates this error when it cannot find the default data connection.*

Adding Other DTC Features

A number of DTCs included with Visual InterDev 6 allow you to better control both the appearance and the usability of a page.

Using the Textbox DTC

To demonstrate the Textbox DTC (and the rest of the DTCs in this chapter), the remaining examples will use a new ASP file. This file will start with the Recordset DTC and the Textbox DTC and then be modified to include other DTCs as well.

The first version of the page (CustomerInformation.asp) is shown in Figure 6-15.

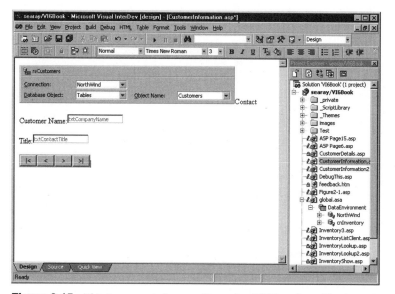

Figure 6-15. *This page contains one Recordset DTC and two Textbox DTCs that are linked to the Recordset DTC.*

The first thing you notice is that the two Textbox DTCs do not line up. We will fix this in the next version when we add the Label DTC.

Let's take a look at the Textbox DTCs and their properties. Figure 6-16 shows the Properties dialog box for one of the Textbox DTCs. You can see that we have changed the name of the DTC to *txtName*. The *Display Width* and *Max Characters* properties have been changed to 30. You can change one of these properties without changing the other, so be careful when modifying these properties.

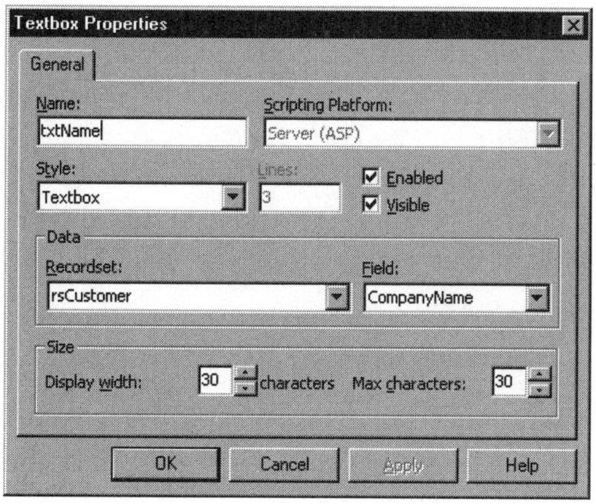

Figure 6-16. *The Properties dialog box for the* txtName *Textbox DTC.*

You can set the *Style* property to one of these options:

- **Textbox** Standard single-line text box
- **Text Area** Provides a multiline text box
- **Password** Provides an HTML password field for password data

The default for the *Style* property is Textbox. If you set *Style* to Text Area, the *Lines* property is enabled, allowing you to specify how many lines of display are allowed in the DTC.

If you want to hide the DTC when the page displays, you can uncheck the *Visible* property. This property can be set to True via script at run time.

The *Enabled* property allows users to edit data in the DTC. If you uncheck *Enabled*, the DTC will be read-only.

Using the Label DTC

The Label DTC can be used to insert read-only text onto a page. For example, let's say you want to retrieve a field such as CustomerName from the database, display it on an editable page, but restrict users from editing the field. The Label DTC is perfect for this task because it is always read-only. The text can be stored in the DTC or retrieved from a database by binding the Label DTC to a recordset.

Figure 6-17 shows the second version of the CustomerInformation.asp page. First I added an HTML table and placed the DTCs in it to align them. Then I replaced the first Textbox DTC with a Label DTC. Now the CustomerName field is read-only.

The data-binding properties for the Label DTC are set to the same settings as the Textbox DTC in the first version of the page. You cannot see the table in this example because the table has a border size of zero and is used merely to align the fields. By following the steps below, you can set Design view to display a border on tables (and other elements that have a zero border), making them easier to work with.

1. Select Options from the Tools menu.

2. Expand the HTML branch.

3. Click the HTML Editor node.

4. Check the *Borders* property in the Design View Display section.

The Format tab of the Label Properties dialog box is shown in Figure 6-18. The properties have been changed to specify a particular font and font size.

If you do not specify any properties on the Format tab, the Label DTC will use the properties currently in use in the page where the Label DTC is located. If you want to place the Label DTC on a page but not have it show, uncheck the Visible check box.

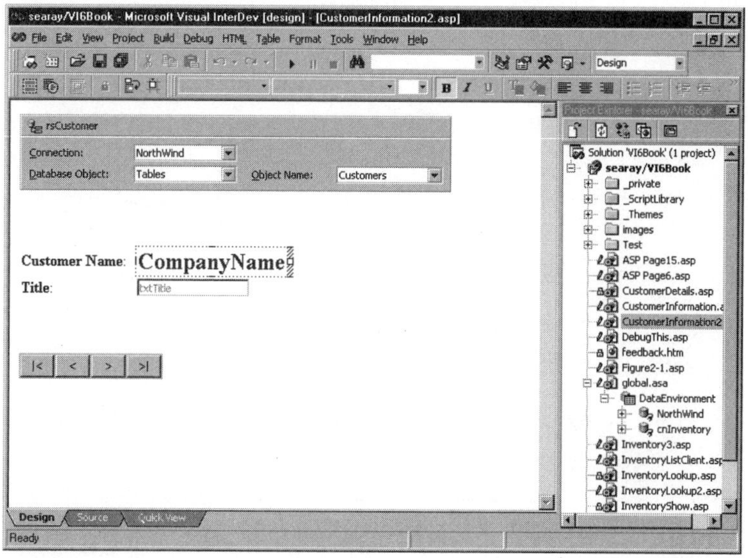

Figure 6-17. *The Label DTC provides an easy way to display read-only information.*

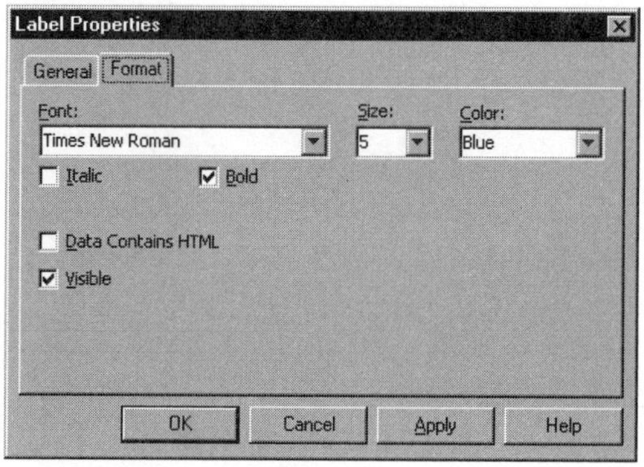

Figure 6-18. *The Format tab of the Label Properties dialog box allows you to control the appearance of the Label DTC.*

The Data Contains HTML check box should be checked when the field contains HTML coding. When you check this box, the field will be output with *Response.HTMLEncode* to ensure users that the HTML code is properly handled. If the field contains HTML and this option is not checked, the Label will display the field and HTML codes. If the option is checked, the Label will correctly display the field.

Using the Listbox DTC

The Listbox DTC can be used to display data from a database, look up data from a database, and display values from a static list. It works similarly to the Listbox control in Visual Basic.

Figure 6-19 shows the CustomerInformation3.asp file in Design view. The page now contains a Listbox DTC that displays the contact's title. The Listbox DTC is live in Design view—click the Listbox's arrow, and the options in the list will display. Figure 6-19 shows President (the first item in the list) as the first setting.

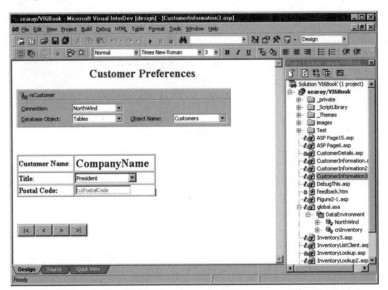

Figure 6-19. *The Listbox DTC provides an easy way to set up user-selectable lists in a Web page.*

Like the other DTCs, the Listbox is linked to the recordset using the data-binding properties, as shown in Figure 6-20. The *Style* property sets the type of list to display—this example uses a drop-down list. The other option is to set *Style* to ListBox, which will display a multirow list. If you select the ListBox option, you can control the number of lines that appear in the list by using the *Lines* property.

Also like most other DTCs, the Listbox DTC contains the *Visible* and *Enabled* properties.

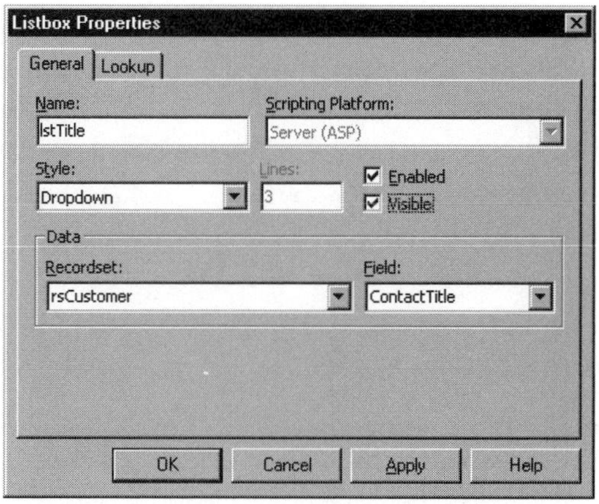

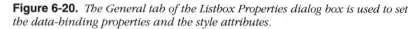

Figure 6-20. *The General tab of the Listbox Properties dialog box is used to set the data-binding properties and the style attributes.*

The values in the list are static and are set using the Lookup tab of the Listbox Properties dialog box, shown in Figure 6-21.

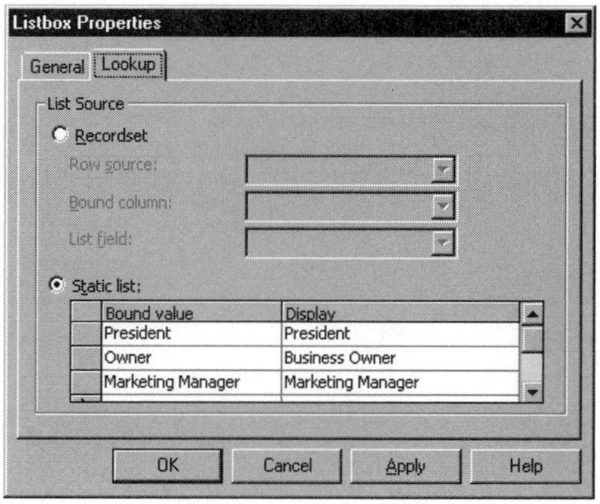

Figure 6-21. *The Lookup tab of the Listbox Properties dialog box lets you specify how the list will be populated.*

You set the static list's values by following these steps:

1. Click the Static List option button.

2. Click the first Bound Value cell, and enter the value of the first item in the list.

3. Click the Display cell, and enter the name to display in the list.

4. Repeat steps 2 and 3, as necessary, to populate the rest of the list.

When the application executes, the Listbox DTC will display the first item from the Display column of the static list. The value of the Listbox DTC is the item from the corresponding Bound Value column of the static list. When the user clicks the arrow for the list, he or she can select a new item. The DTC will update its display and value to match the entry selected from the list. For instance, if the user selects "Business Owner" from the list shown in Figure 6-21, the Listbox DTC displays "Business Owner" and its value is set to "Owner."

The Listbox DTC uses an intrinsic HTML Select list to display the list and provide the interaction for the user. Below is the list code inserted in the HTML stream for this example:

```
<SELECT name=lstTitle id=lstTitle size=1>
<OPTION value="President">President</OPTION>
<OPTION value="Owner">Business Owner</OPTION>
<OPTION value="Marketing Manager">Marketing Manager</OPTION>
</SELECT>
```

The Listbox DTC automates the process of binding the Select list to the database for both retrieval and update operations.

You can also set the properties on the Lookup tab to populate the list from a database. Populating the list from a database will be covered in later chapters.

Using the Checkbox DTC

The Checkbox DTC creates a Checkbox for a page. The DTC uses the intrinsic HTML check box but makes it bindable to a recordset, like the Listbox and other DTCs.

Figure 6-22 shows CustomerInformation4.asp with a Checkbox DTC in Design view. To create this page, I added a couple of rows to the existing table. To insert a row into a table, you must click a cell of the table and then select Insert Row from the Table menu. The new row is inserted just before the row of the cell you clicked.

Next I dropped a Checkbox DTC into the table, as shown in Figure 6-22. In the figure, the Checkbox DTC is bound to the rsCustomer recordset. The *Field* property of the Checkbox DTC is set to the MailBrochures field of the recordset. The MailBrochures field has an Access Yes/No data type. If you check the Checkbox DTC, its value will be set to 1, while unchecking the DTC sets its value to 0. The *Name* and *Caption* properties were changed to reflect the data contained in the DTC.

Table 6-1 (taken from the Visual InterDev documentation) lists the various values for a particular data type that will result in a checked or cleared Checkbox DTC. The MailBrochures field used in our example is an Access Yes/No field and results in 1 showing checked and 0 showing cleared. Make sure you understand the various options before you bind the Checkbox to a recordset field.

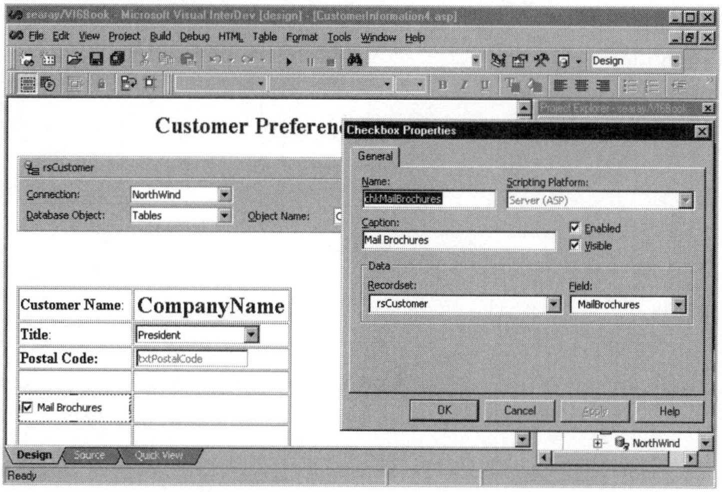

Figure 6-22. *The Checkbox DTC can be bound to a database column.*

Data Type of DataField	Displays Checked	Displays Cleared
Boolean	True	False
Bit	1	0
String, Char	"True"	""
Integer	Nonzero	0
Floating-point	Nonzero	0
Currency	Nonzero	0
Date/Time	N/A	N/A
All other data types	N/A	N/A

Table 6-1.

The value that is written to the recordset depends on the field's data type and the Checkbox DTC's state. Table 6-2 on the following page (also taken from the Visual InterDev documentation) lists the various values for a particular data type that will be stored in the recordset when the user checks or clears the check box.

Data Type	Checked	Cleared
Boolean	True	False
Bit	1	0
String, Char	"True"	""
Integer	-1	0
Floating-point	-1.0	0.0
Currency	-1	00.0
Date/Time	N/A	N/A
All other data types	N/A	N/A

Table 6-2.

Using the OptionGroup DTC

The OptionGroup DTC uses the intrinsic HTML radio buttons to create a group of buttons the user can choose from. Unlike a group of Checkbox DTCs, the user can choose only one button from the OptionGroup DTC. This allows you to create a group of mutually-exclusive items and let the user select one without your having to check the user's actions with script.

Figure 6-23 shows CustomerInformation4.asp with an OptionGroup DTC in Design view. To create this page, I added a new table with one row. Next I dropped the OptionGroup DTC into the table. Then I configured the DTC using the Properties dialog box.

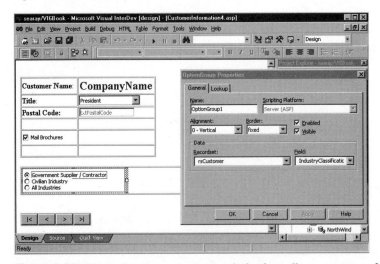

Figure 6-23. *The OptionGroup Properties dialog box allows you to configure the OptionGroup DTC and bind it to a database.*

Figure 6-23 shows the configuration of the properties to bind the Option-Group DTC to a database table and to set the border for the control. The other properties on the General tab are set at their default values.

The OptionGroup buttons can be set from either a static list or from a database table. The values in the list are static and, as was the case with the Listbox DTC, are set using the Lookup tab of the OptionGroup Properties dialog box. You enter the list by following these steps:

1. Click the Static List option button.

2. Click the first Bound Value cell, and enter the value of the first option button.

3. Click the corresponding Display cell, and enter the label that will appear next to the option button.

4. Repeat steps 2 and 3 as necessary.

You can set the OptionGroup buttons from a database by binding the DTC to a field. The steps to accomplish this are:

1. Display the OptionGroup Properties dialog box.

2. Click the Lookup tab.

3. Click the Recordset option button in the List Source section of the page.

4. Select the Recordset DTC to use from the Row Source drop-down list.

5. Select the field that will represent the values for the option buttons from the Bound Column drop-down list.

6. Select the field that will provide the labels for the option buttons from the List Field drop-down list.

Using the Grid DTC

The Grid DTC allows you to build a page that displays data from a database and lets the user navigate through the rows in the recordset. The Grid Properties dialog box lets you easily set the properties that control the Grid DTC's run-time characteristics.

Figure 6-24 on the following page shows the Grid DTC just after being dropped onto the CustomerList.asp file in Design view and having its properties displayed. The General tab allows you to select from a number of preset Autoformat styles for the Grid DTC. In this example, the Autoformat style is set to Basic Navy. The Autoformat style controls the appearance of the Grid DTC.

The Preview box shows a sample of what the Grid DTC will look like at run time. If you select an Autoformat style and then change any formatting properties, Preview is disabled.

You can also uncheck the Display Header Row check box to turn off the header.

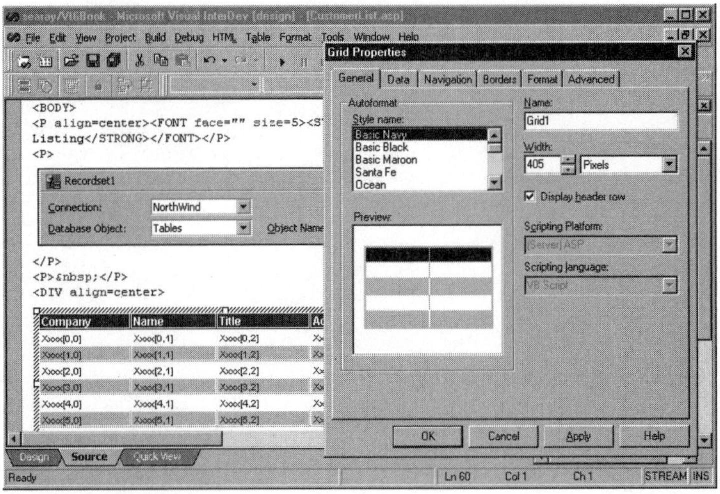

Figure 6-24. *The General property page is used to change the layout and style of the Grid DTC.*

Figure 6-25 shows the Data property page, which is used to bind the Grid DTC to a Recordset DTC. First, select the appropriate Recordset DTC from the Recordset drop-down list. Then, to add a field to the Grid DTC, check the check box to the left of the field's name in the Available Fields list. You can remove a field from the Grid DTC by unchecking this field.

You can also format the titles used for the header row on this page. Figure 6-25 shows the page after the titles have been reformatted:

■   CompanyName becomes Company

■   ContactName becomes Name

■   ContactTitle becomes Title

To reformat a header caption, select the field to reformat in the Grid Columns list, change the caption for it in the *Header* property in the Edit Columns section, and then click the Update button.

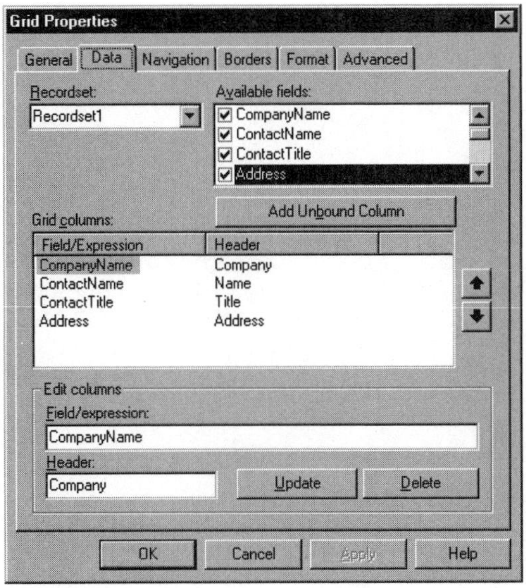

Figure 6-25. *The Data property page is used to bind the Grid DTC to a Recordset DTC and to set the Grid DTC's related data-bound properties.*

The *Field/Expression* property can contain expressions to reformat the data in the column. The following expression can be used to create an anchor tag that allows the user to link to another page based upon the company's name:

```
="<a href=www." + [CompanyName] + ".com>" +
    [CompanyName] + "</a>"
```

For example, the line above will output the following HTML if the Company-Name field contains the string "32X":

```
<a href=www.32X.com>32X</a>
```

You can use this technique with a Web address to format the data in any way you need to, such as creating an FTP link or an email link. You can also use HTML formatting and JScript functions in the *Field/Expression* property.

The Navigation page shown in Figure 6-26 on the following page sets the properties that control how users navigate through the data in the Grid DTC. If you want to let users scroll through the data one page at a time, set this functionality by checking the Enable Paging check box and setting the *Records/Page* property. The default is 20, but it is often best to set it to 5 or 10, depending upon the length of the fields you are displaying.

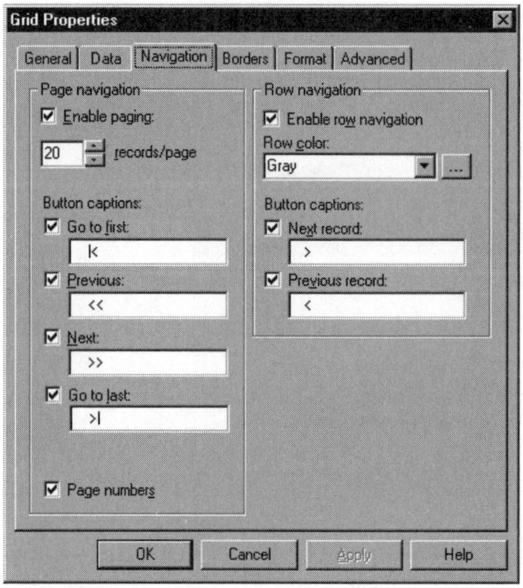

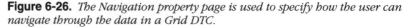

Figure 6-26. *The Navigation property page is used to specify how the user can navigate through the data in a Grid DTC.*

If you enable paging, the following default buttons are used to navigate through the pages in the recordset:

- |<   Goes to the first page

- <<   Goes back one page

- >>   Goes forward one page

- >| Goes to the last page

Checking the Enable Row Navigation check box allows the user to navigate through the page one row at a time. If you enable this option, the < and > buttons will move the highlight bar one row at a time.

You can also control exactly how the Grid DTC looks at run time by using the Borders page and the Format page, shown in Figures 6-27 and 6-28. The Borders page controls the style of borders used for the Grid DTC. Figure 6-27 shows the 3D border selected and a gray background color selected in the *Grid Background* property.

The Format property page controls the formatting of the Grid DTC. This page will override the default properties of one of the Autoformat styles. If you change a property here, the Preview box on the General tab will no longer work.

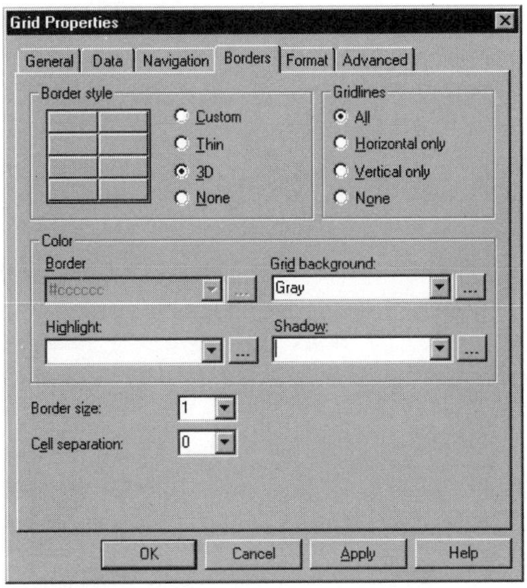

Figure 6-27. *The Borders property page is used to set the border properties of the Grid DTC.*

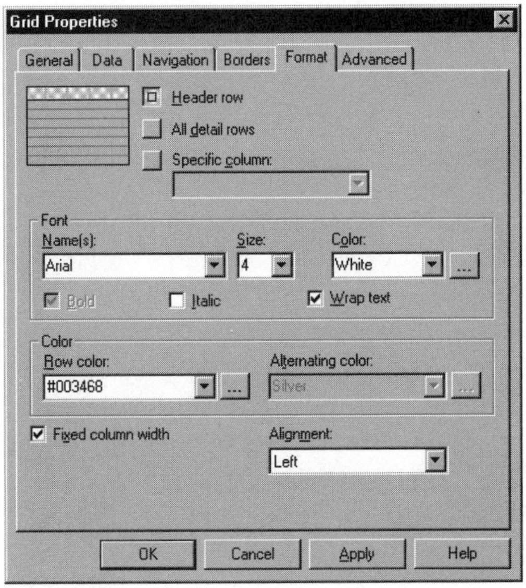

Figure 6-28. *The Format property page is used to change the formatting of the Grid DTC.*

The Format property page is useful for explicitly controlling the format of the Grid DTC. You can change the format for the header, the detail rows, or any particular column. First click the corresponding button at the top of the property page to select the area to change. Then make your changes, and click the Apply button when you are finished. You must click the Apply button before you move to the next section.

You can change the size of the columns directly by using the mouse. First click the Grid DTC to select it, then move the mouse over the border between two columns until you see it turn into a pointer with an arrow on each end. Now click the border and drag the mouse to change the size of the column. You can also change the size of the Grid DTC by dragging the sizing handles on either side to the right or left.

Figure 6-29 shows the Grid DTC in the CustomerList.asp page in Internet Explorer. You can see the formatting that was applied with the Grid DTC property pages.

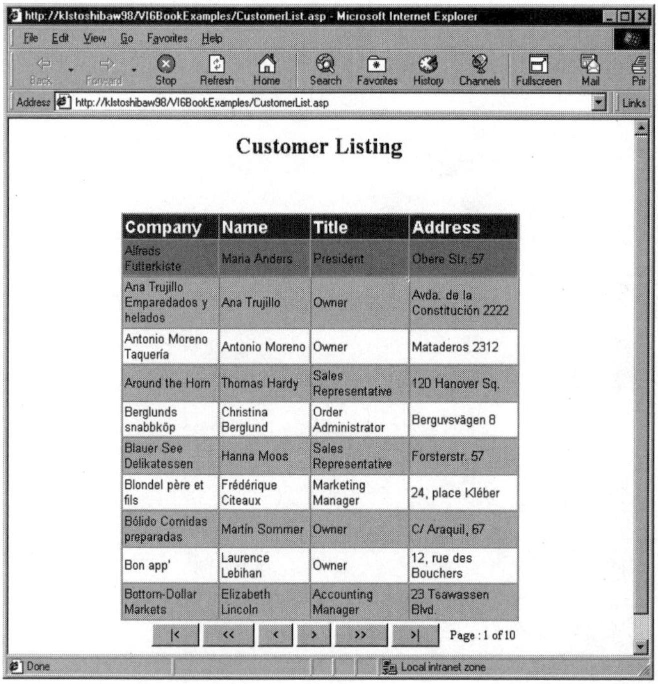

Figure 6-29. *The finished Grid DTC in action.*

The first row in the data area has a darker background than the others because it is the current row. If you click the < or > buttons, the highlight moves down one record at a time.

Chapter 7

Using Dynamic HTML

One of the fastest ways to become familiar with Dynamic HTML (DHTML) is to think of it as a mechanism that allows you to encapsulate HTML elements and then script those elements using Microsoft VBScript or JScript. Almost every aspect of a rendered document is alterable at run time, with the added advantage that it is not necessary to download the entire document again just to change its appearance. Every element in the document becomes an individually addressable object at run time. The browser is capable of changing the look of one object while dynamically rearranging the other objects around it. This means that the objects in a DHTML document are simple, consistent, run-time-programmable entities.

DHTML consists of several components and technologies that work together to provide dynamic features. These components and technologies are:

- **Document Object Model** The Document Object Model refers to the elements in the document that expose properties, methods, and events that we can program against. Every element in the document is an object with these characteristics. The big learning curve is getting a handle on these objects and their interfaces.

- **Dynamic styles**   You can dynamically change the style of any HTML element in a document. You can change colors, typefaces, spacing, indentation, position, and even the visibility of text. Because the Dynamic HTML Object Model makes every HTML element and attribute accessible, it is easy to use scripts to dynamically read and change styles.

- **Dynamic positioning**   Microsoft Internet Explorer 4.0 supports positioning and animation of elements even after a document has been loaded. Because the Dynamic HTML Object Model gives you access to styles and style sheets, you can set and change the position of an element as simply as you set and change its color. This makes it especially easy to change the position of elements based on how the user is viewing the document and even to animate the elements.

- **Dynamic content**   With Dynamic HTML, you can change the content of a document after it is loaded. Internet Explorer gives you a rich set of properties and methods to dynamically construct and alter documents, from inserting and deleting elements to modifying the text and attributes in individual elements.

- **Data binding**   Several core HTML elements, together with "traditional" data-bound controls, combine to form a very flexible data-oriented architecture. Chapter 16 demonstrates how to use the data-binding features of DHTML.

DYNAMIC HTML OBJECT MODEL

The DHTML Object Model is the cornerstone for all work in DHTML. Using the object model, you can access and manipulate virtually anything in the document. You can read and set properties of elements, call their methods, and intercept and process events. Figure 7-1 shows the DHTML Object Model supported in the Internet Explorer 4.0 browser.

The DHTML Object Model represents an evolution from the earlier object models seen in Netscape Navigator 2.x and 3.x and in Internet Explorer 3.x. If you have written client-side scripts for these browsers, you'll be able to pick up DHTML very quickly.

Having a rich object model available to script against for thin-client applications allows them to become more interactive and responsive to your end users. This goes a long way in helping you achieve the same type of look and feel that end users typically experience from client/server applications. In planning any migrations of existing client/server applications to Web-enabled versions, it's well worth exploring what you can do with DHTML to preserve the user experience.

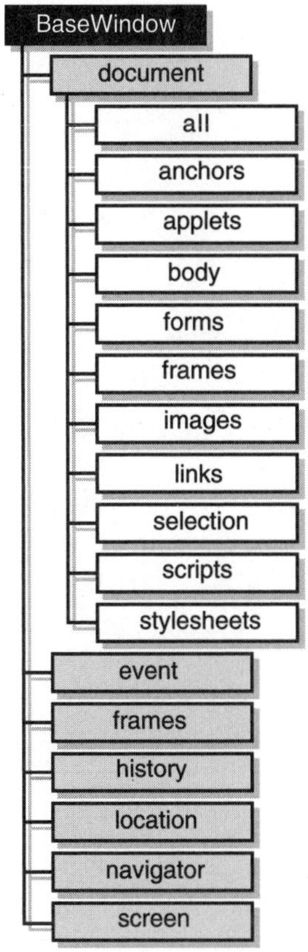

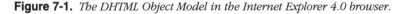

Figure 7-1. *The DHTML Object Model in the Internet Explorer 4.0 browser.*

As a simple example of what can be done with DHTML, take a look at the code in Figure 7-2. This code comes from the DynamicHTML.htm document in the Chap07 folder on the CD-ROM.

```
<HTML>
<HEAD>
<META NAME="GENERATOR" Content="Microsoft Visual Studio 6.0">
<TITLE>Dynamic HTML</TITLE>
```

Figure 7-2. *DHTML code that traps a mouse click event and changes various elements on the page.* *(continued)*

```
<SCRIPT LANGUAGE=javascript>
<!--
function ChangeText() {
    document.all.MyHeading.style.color = "red";
    document.all.MyText.innerText =
        "DHTML gives you total control over your document!";
}
//-->
</SCRIPT>

</HEAD>
<BODY onclick="ChangeText()">

<H3 ID=MyHeading>Welcome to Dynamic HTML!</H3>
<HR>
<P ID=MyText>Click anywhere in this document.</P>

</BODY>
</HTML>
```

When you run this DHTML code in your Internet Explorer 4.0 browser and click anywhere within the document, you'll see the heading change to red and the text change. You can also test out the code in the Quick View tab within Microsoft Visual InterDev 6.0. The main sections of code to notice within Figure 7-2 are the <SCRIPT> section and the <H3> and <P> tags. You'll notice that both the heading and the text element have been assigned IDs. This allows the script in the *ChangeText* function to reference the elements by name and change their properties.

DYNAMIC STYLES

Dynamic styles allow you to dynamically change the style of any HTML element in a document. You can change colors, typefaces, spacing, indentation, position, and even the visibility of text.

As a simple example of what can be done with dynamic styles, take a look at the code in Figure 7-3. This code comes from the DynamicStyles.htm document in the Chap07 folder on the CD-ROM.

```
<HTML>
<HEAD>
<META NAME="GENERATOR" Content="Microsoft Visual Studio 6.0">
<TITLE>Dynamic Styles</TITLE>
```

Figure 7-3. *DHTML code that changes the font size and color of a text element as the mouse moves over it.*   *(continued)*

```
<SCRIPT LANGUAGE="JScript">
function doChanges() {
    window.event.srcElement.style.color = "green";
    window.event.srcElement.style.fontSize = "20px";
}
</SCRIPT>

</HEAD>
<BODY>

<H3 ID=heading onmouseover="doChanges()"
    STYLE="color:black;font-size:18">
    Dynamic HTML - Dynamic Styles Example</H3>
<HR>
<P>This sample changes the font size and color when
    you move the mouse over the heading.

</BODY>
</HTML>
```

When you run this code example within Visual InterDev 6.0, you'll see that the font size and the color of the text element changes as you move the mouse over it. The text element has been given an ID of *heading*, and the mouse movement is trapped using the *onmouseover* event.

For another example, consider the code shown in Figure 7-4. This code is named DynamicStyles2.htm in the Chap07 folder on the CD-ROM.

```
<HTML>
<HEAD>
<META NAME="GENERATOR" Content="Microsoft Visual Studio 6.0">
<TITLE>Dynamic Styles</TITLE>

<SCRIPT LANGUAGE="JScript">
function doChanges() {
    window.event.srcElement.style.color = "red";
}
</SCRIPT>

<SCRIPT LANGUAGE="JScript">
function undoChanges() {
    window.event.srcElement.style.color = "black";
}
</SCRIPT>
```

Figure 7-4. *DHTML code that changes the color of a text element as the mouse moves over it.*   *(continued)*

```
</HEAD>
<BODY>

<H3 ID=heading onmouseout="undoChanges()"
    onmouseover="doChanges()" STYLE="color:black;font-size:18">
    Dynamic HTML - Dynamic Styles Example</H3>
<HR>
<P>This sample changes the font color when you move the mouse
    over the heading.

</BODY>
</HTML>
```

This example is similar to that shown in Figure 7-3, but it uses the *onmouseout* event to change the text color back to the original color. By trapping both the *onmouseover* and *onmouseout* events, the text appears highlighted when the mouse is moved over it. Using dynamic styles, you can achieve many special effects within the browser with just a small amount of scripting.

DYNAMIC POSITIONING

Dynamic positioning gives you the ability to move elements around on the page within the browser without having to take any round trips back to the server. This means you can create specialized animation effects and manipulate all elements in the browser as required. This can be especially useful for advertisements or for changing the screen appearance based upon user input. For instance, you may want to give users a way to arrange the layout of the screen to suit their individual preferences.

As an example, take a look at the code shown in Figure 7-5. This code comes from DynamicPositioning.htm in the Chap07 folder on the CD-ROM.

```
<HTML>
<HEAD>
<META NAME="GENERATOR" Content="Microsoft Visual Studio 6.0">
<HEAD>
<TITLE>Dynamic Positioning</TITLE>
<SCRIPT LANGUAGE="JScript">

var id;

function StartGlide()
{
```

Figure 7-5. *A dynamic positioning example showing how to move an image from right to left across the browser window.*   *(continued)*

```
        document.all.Banner.style.pixelLeft =
            document.body.offsetWidth;
        document.all.Banner.style.visibility = "visible";
        id = window.setInterval("Glide()",50);
}

function Glide()
{
    document.all.Banner.style.pixelLeft -= 10;
    if (document.all.Banner.style.pixelLeft<=0) {
        document.all.Banner.style.pixelLeft=0;
        window.clearInterval(id);
    }
}
</SCRIPT>
</HEAD>
<BODY onload="StartGlide()">
<BR>
<H3>Dynamic HTML - Dynamic Positioning Example</H3>
<HR>
<P>With dynamic positioning, you can move images anywhere in the
document even while the user views the document.
<IMG ID="Banner"
STYLE="visibility:hidden;position:absolute;top:0;left:0;z-index:-1"
SRC="images/msft.gif">
</BODY>
</HTML>
```

The code takes the Microsoft logo, msft.gif, and moves it from right to left across the top of the screen. The speed and direction of the animation can be exactly controlled. The *pixelLeft* property sets or retrieves the left position of the element, in pixels. The *Glide* function decrements the value of the *pixelLeft* property by 10 each time it is called by the *StartGlide* function. The *StartGlide* function uses the *window.setInterval* method to repeatedly call the *Glide* function every 50 milliseconds.

DYNAMIC CONTENT

Now that we've seen some code examples that change the style and position of elements on the screen, let's take a look at some examples that change the actual content that is displayed on the screen. Obviously, when dealing with content, we need to be able to change both the text that appears on the screen and its formatting. We therefore need to be able to change not only text itself but also the HTML tags that control the formatting of the text.

The following example shows how to change the text and HTML formatting of various textual elements on the screen. Figure 7-6 comes from the DynamicContent.htm file in the Chap07 folder on the CD-ROM.

```
<HTML>
<HEAD>
<META NAME="GENERATOR" Content="Microsoft Visual Studio 6.0">
<TITLE>Dynamic Content</TITLE>
<SCRIPT LANGUAGE="JScript">

function changeMe() {
    document.all.MyHeading.outerHTML =
        "<H1 ID=MyHeading>Dynamic HTML!</H1>";
    document.all.MyHeading.style.color = "red";
    document.all.MyText.innerText =
        "This text was altered using the innerText property.";
    document.all.MyText.align = "center";
    document.body.insertAdjacentHTML("BeforeEnd",
        "<P ALIGN=\"center\">This text was added using the
        insertAdjacentHTML property!</P>");
}

</SCRIPT>
</HEAD>
<BODY TOPMARGIN=0 BGPROPERTIES="FIXED" BGCOLOR="#FFFFFF"
    LINK="#000000" VLINK="#808080" ALINK="#000000"
    onclick="changeMe()">

<H2 ID=MyHeading>Dynamic HTML - Dynamic Content Example</H2>
<HR>
<P ID=MyText>Click anywhere on this page.</P>

</BODY>
</HTML>
```

Figure 7-6. *DHTML code showing how to change the text and formatting of several elements on a page.*

When this code is executed in the browser, you'll notice that the heading is changed in several ways. The color, text, and formatting are changed using the *style.color* property and the *outerHTML* property. Also, the alignment of text is changed by using the *align* property and some new text is added to the document by using the *insertAdjacentHTML* method.

The *insertAdjacentHTML* method has the following syntax:

```
object.insertAdjacentText(where, text)
```

Table 7-1 lists the *where* parameters for this method and their effects.

Parameter	Description
BeforeBegin	Inserts the text immediately before the element
AfterBegin	Inserts the text after the start of the element but before all other content in the element
BeforeEnd	Inserts the text immediately before the end of the element but after all other content in the element
AfterEnd	Inserts the text immediately after the end of the element

Table 7-1. *Parameters for the* insertAdjacentHTML *method.*

The next example, shown in Figure 7-7, is intended to demonstrate some of the differences between the following properties: *innerText, outerText, innerHTML,* and *outerHTML.* The following list describes how each of these properties can be applied:

- **■   *innerText***   Sets or retrieves the text between the start and end tags of the current element

- **■   *outerText***   Sets or retrieves the text of the current element

- **■   *innerHTML***   Sets or retrieves the HTML between the start and end tags of the current element

- **■   *outerHTML***   Sets or retrieves the current element and its content in HTML

These properties are useful in manipulating content within a document.

```
<HTML>
<HEAD>

<META NAME="GENERATOR" Content="Microsoft Visual Studio 6.0">
<TITLE>Dynamic Content</TITLE>

<SCRIPT ID=clientEventHandlersJS LANGUAGE=javascript>
<!--

function submit1_onclick()
{
    document.all.MyText.innerText = "Changed using innerText";
}
```

Figure 7-7. *DHTML code illustrating the differences between the* innerText, outerText, innerHTML, *and* outerHTML *properties for manipulating content within the browser.*   *(continued)*

```
function submit2_onclick()
{
    document.all.MyText.outerText = "Changed using outerText";
    alert("You'll need to click Refresh to get the ID property
        back or you'll get an error!");
}

function submit3_onclick()
{
    document.all.MyText.innerHTML =
        "<B><I>Changed using innerHTML</B></I>";
}

function submit4_onclick()
{
    document.all.MyText.outerHTML =
        "<H4 ID=MyText><U>Changed using outerHTML</U></H4>";
}

//-->
</SCRIPT>

</HEAD>
<BODY TOPMARGIN=0 BGPROPERTIES="FIXED" BGCOLOR="#FFFFFF"
    LINK="#000000" VLINK="#808080" ALINK="#000000">

<H2>Dynamic HTML - Dynamic Content Example</H2>
<HR>
<H3 ID=MyText>Example showing functionality of innerText,
    outerText, innerHTML, and outerHTML.</H3>

<HR>
<INPUT type="submit" value="innerText" id=submit1 name=submit1
    LANGUAGE=javascript onclick="return submit1_onclick()">
    Changes the text only
<P>
<INPUT type="submit" value="outerText" id=submit2 name=submit2
    LANGUAGE=javascript onclick="return submit2_onclick()">
    Changes the HTML and text and replaces with just text
<P>
<INPUT type="submit" value="innerHTML" id=submit3 name=submit3
    LANGUAGE=javascript onclick="return submit3_onclick()">
```

```
        Changes the text and adds HTML tags; does not change
            current HTML tags
<P>
<INPUT type="submit" value="outerHTML" id=submit4 name=submit4
    LANGUAGE=javascript onclick="return submit4_onclick()">
    Changes the text and the HTML
<HR>

</BODY>
</HTML>
```

Figure 7-7 allows you to experiment with these various properties and see how the text within the browser is altered. The code comes from the DynamicContent2.htm file in the Chap07 folder on the CD-ROM. Note that if you choose the *outerText* property you'll lose the ID of the text element and you'll need to refresh the page to be able to continue applying various properties. The reason for this is that the *outerText* property replaces both the text of the element and its surrounding HTML so that the ID attribute is replaced along with all the rest of the HTML formatting.

Figure 7-8 shows the view within Visual InterDev 6.0 when running this code sample.

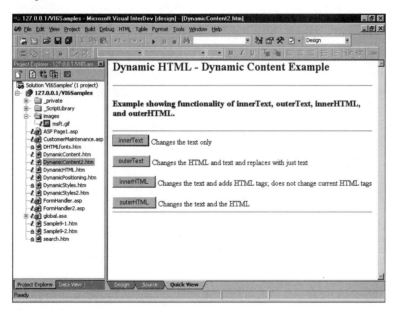

Figure 7-8. *The output of DynamicContent2.htm.*

NOTE The *innerText*, *outerText*, *innerHTML*, and *outerHTML* properties do not apply to text elements only. For example, the *outerText* property applies to the following HTML elements: A, ACRONYM, ADDRESS, APPLET, AREA, B, BGSOUND, BIG, BLOCKQUOTE, BR, BUTTON, CENTER, CITE, CODE, COMMENT, DD, DEL, DFN, DIR, DIV, DL, DT, EM, EMBED, FIELDSET, FONT, FORM, H1, H2, H3, H4, H5, H6, HR, I, IFRAME, IMG, INPUT, INS, KBD, LABEL, LEGEND, LI, LISTING, MAP, MARQUEE, MENU, OBJECT, OL, P, PLAINTEXT, PRE, Q, S, SAMP, SELECT, SMALL, SPAN, STRIKE, STRONG, SUB, SUP, TABLE, TEXTAREA, TT, U, UL, VAR, XMP. See the Visual InterDev online documentation for complete details of which property supports which HTML elements.

Using Design View with DHTML

Visual InterDev 6.0 supports DHTML in Microsoft Internet Explorer 4 (or any other DHTML-capable browser). The Visual InterDev 6.0 editor helps you create script for DHTML objects and events by presenting statement-completion options for the object model, and also by displaying the object model hierarchy in the Script Outline window. As well as scripting directly to the Internet Explorer 4 object model, you can choose to have your design-time controls (DTCs) create client-side data-binding script.

There are two ways to place controls on the page from the Toolbox: either drag them from the Toolbox or double-click them (placing the control in the upper left corner of the page).

One of the nicest features of DHTML is the ability to absolutely position elements on a page. Once a control is on the page, it can be absolutely positioned by dragging it to a new location. However, you need to turn this capability on before it will work. The Design toolbar, shown in Figure 7-9, contains the key. By first selecting the control you are interested in, and then clicking the Absolute Positioning button on the toolbar, you can position the control anywhere on the page.

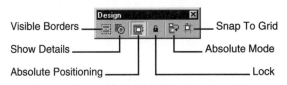

Figure 7-9. *The Design toolbar.*

Remember that the Design toolbar is active only while you are viewing the Design tab. (It's easy to Quick View the page and then wonder why the toolbar isn't active.) Also, the control you wish to place absolutely needs to be selected with the four-headed arrow (by moving the pointer over the control border) before the Absolute Positioning button will be active.

Here's a little shortcut that can save you time when you are adding a lot of controls to a page. Activate Absolute Mode by clicking the Absolute Mode button on the Design toolbar. In Absolute Mode, if you place controls on a page by double-clicking, it won't have any effect—the controls will still appear in the upper left corner of the page. However, if you drag them from the Toolbox, they'll stay right where you drop them.

Want to see where breaks and other nonvisual HTML elements are placed? No problem. Use the Show Details button on the Design toolbar and glyphs for nonvisual elements will appear.

Unfortunately, DTCs cannot be absolutely positioned (as evidenced by the fact that none of the Design toolbar buttons are enabled when working with DTCs). In order to absolutely position DTCs you'll need to resort to the old HTML table tricks.

CASCADING STYLE SHEETS

In developing standards for the World Wide Web, the W3C (World Wide Web Consortium) has proven, in their rejection of several submissions, to be aware of the need to separate content from presentation. In particular, "formatting" tags such as <FONT>, <LAYER>, and <MARQUEE> have failed to gain approval in favor of well-developed support for the Cascading Style Sheets (CSS) specification. CSS has become the accepted way to define page appearance.

While Internet Explorer 3 provided a "reference implementation" of the original CSS specification, including support for approximately 80 percent of the nonpositional CSS attributes, Internet Explorer 4 improves upon this, resulting in roughly 99 percent compliance. There are just a few attributes of the CSS specification unimplemented in Internet Explorer 4. Among these unsupported attributes are some of the CSS pseudoclasses (first-line and first-character), and interword spacing. You can specify these attributes, pseudoclasses, and values; however, Internet Explorer 4 will ignore them. Oddly enough, there are technically unsupportable attributes in the specification. For example, how would one implement a vertical alignment of center when parsers are not allowed to "look ahead" to see where the next element might be?

Controlling Page Appearance

DHTML provides a number of ways to control the appearance of a page. You can position the page, use filters on text elements, and take advantage of many other features to enhance the user's experience.

It's a big deal in the HTML world to be able to specify absolute positioning. However, application designers have been able to do this for years. Absolute positioning, however, goes beyond the traditional *x* and *y* placement. There are also positioning modes that allow relative location on the page as well as allowing reflow, floats, and keeps (taken from the document-oriented nature of HTML).

The Visibility, Display, and Z-index attributes are three useful positioning characteristics. The Visibility attribute determines whether an element is visible. The Display attribute controls whether the item still takes up space in the document according to its actual (though invisible) size. When set to "none," it removes the item and its allotted space from the document, causing all items later in the document to reflow to fill the item's space. The Z-index attribute specifies the relative depth of elements on the page. This is particularly useful with absolutely positioned items.

Using Microsoft WEFT (Web Embedding Fonts Tool), which is available from Microsoft's typography group, we can create "font objects" that we can download with our pages. These font objects are installed privately: only Internet Explorer can use them, and then only in the context of the site for which they were defined. See *http://www.microsoft.com/opentype/free.htm* for more information and to download WEFT and other utilities.

We can specify typeface, size, family, color, and special treatments (small caps, for example). Using filters, we can also rotate, illuminate, and make masks from our text elements.

Maintenance and Performance

One of the simple advantages of using style sheets is the fact that, since style information is separate from the document (in most cases, anyway) we can use the style information in many contexts. This is great, because developing a good style sheet is no trivial task, and it is important to be able to gain as much reusability as possible. As the shared style sheet changes, documents that use the style sheet do not need to be changed. Hits to the client documents of a style sheet will reflect the changed styles—no recompilation or relinking required.

There are thousands upon thousands of graphics that are simply words formatted in a pretty way. The capabilities introduced with style sheets allow many of those graphics to be replaced with smaller, faster-to-download text.

A side benefit of using a global style sheet for many pages in an application is that the style information goes down to the client machine once. This cached style sheet will be referenced on all client pages, further reducing the download costs of using style sheets.

There's just a whole lot less coding when using style sheets than there is with one-off formatting of each and every paragraph. Within a document, many paragraphs will typically receive common treatment. By using style definitions, you simply point to a rule and your information is formatted by that rule. If you want an exception to the rule—no problem.

In a well-designed document, all of the style information is moved out to the style sheet. This substantially reduces clutter, leaving only content. You will rarely need to mix style information with content.

When working in multiple media, you can use different styles for each medium. For example, you might make the printable set of styles active when you want to print a document designed primarily for online presentation. By removing the formatting from the content, you can more easily repurpose the information.

No more pesky font tags or tables in tables in tables—or any of those weird tagging arrangements once used to get a special effect on the page. All has been reduced to declarative "put-it-right-here, just-like-this" language.

Linked-In Style Sheets

Linked-in style sheets form the most reusable style information you can get. The style sheet is a stand-alone document of MIME-type text that can be referenced by multitudes of individual pages.

There are two ways to reference external style sheets—using the <LINK> tag or using the *@import* statement inside a <STYLE></STYLE> block. Generally, you link the primary style sheet in, and *@import* other supporting style sheets from within that linked-in main style sheet.

Whether you use <LINK> or *@import*, you can give each style block a separate name. Why would you bother to do this? Because at run time you can turn whole style sheets on or off with a single statement. That's a pretty powerful tool. For example, with external style sheets, we can implement separate online and print versions of a document within a single file. To print the document, we simply turn off the online styles and turn on the styles suitable for printing.

You can import a style sheet by using *@import*:

```
<STYLE>
    @import url(http://www.32x.com/ie4sem/styles/primary.asp);
</STYLE>
```

The next example uses the <LINK> tag:

```
<HTML>
<HEAD><LINK REL="stylesheet" TYPE="text/css"
     HREF="_Themes/expeditn/COLOR0.CSS" VI6.0THEME="Expedition">
</HEAD>
```

Embedded Style Sheets

While you're experimenting with presentation, it might be easier to have the style information in a style block right there in your test document. You can move the information into a separate style sheet at any time. The advent of the CSS editor in Visual InterDev 6.0 makes working with separate style sheets easier.

Suppose all your documents share a global style sheet. Usually the definitions in the global style sheet satisfy 95 percent of each document's requirements. You can satisfy the other 5 percent by defining an embedded style sheet, which is a style block local to the document. An embedded style sheet fits the bill until the global style sheet can incorporate the needed additions.

You might find that some styles are too document-specific to include in the global style sheet. In these cases, an embedded style sheet might be the trick. However, remember that you can reference multiple style sheets. The last one overrides the earlier ones, so at some point it still might be advantageous to separate the embedded style sheet out into a separate file.

To add an embedded style sheet, simply add a <STYLE></STYLE> pair inside the <HEAD> section of your document. Technically, you could add an embedded style sheet to the <BODY> section as well, but the recommendation is to add it in the <HEAD>. Place your style definitions, one to a line, inside the <STYLE> block.

Using the CSS Editor

The CSS Editor allows you to edit style sheets by selecting properties in a set of property pages. This graphical interface makes it easy to create and modify style sheets. Figure 7-10 shows the CSS Editor in the center of the Visual InterDev development environment. To add a style sheet to your Web project and invoke the CSS Editor, simply select Add Item from the Project menu and then double-click Style Sheet in the Add Item dialog box. In the left part of the CSS Editor window, you can see the style sheet outline, which displays the tags and classes in the style sheet. You can use this outline view to move around in the style sheet. When you click a tag or a class in the outline, the CSS Editor updates the display of the property pages to reflect the current settings of the item you selected.

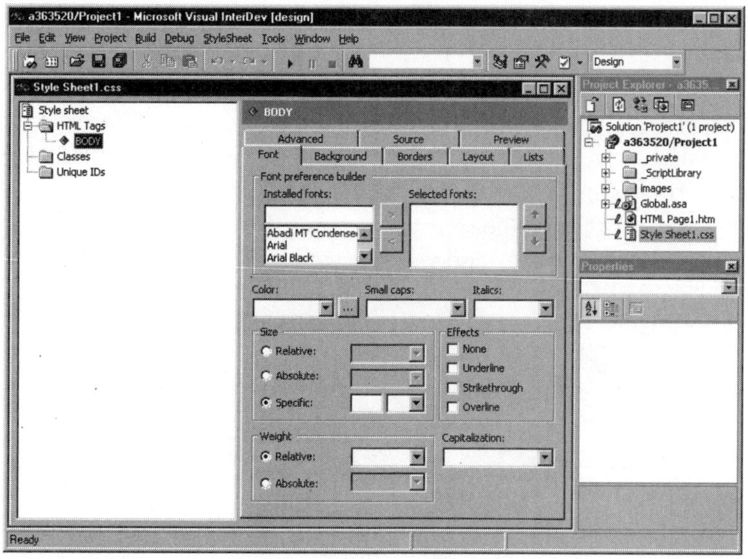

Figure 7-10. *The CSS Editor.*

Table 7-2 contains descriptions of the CSS Editor property pages.

Page	Description
Font	Controls the font aspects of the current style or class.
Background	Changes background properties. This is handy when you need to use an image for the page background. You can set the image file name, specify how to tile the image, and in general control the image's formatting. This is much easier than trying to remember the individual attributes to make these changes.
Borders	Changes border properties. The Borders page makes setting borders a quick and easy process. You can choose the border style, set the margins and padding, and control the border's color.
Layout	Changes layout properties. This page is useful for controlling layout features such as spacing between characters or page breaks.
Lists	Controls list characteristics. This page makes setting up list features a snap. You can control the type of list, the type of bullets used for the list, and the location of the bullets.
Advanced	Controls positioning and other advanced properties. You can control the clipping rectangle and you can control whether the item is visible.
Source	Displays the source for the style sheet.
Preview	Previews the style sheet.

Table 7-2. *CSS Editor property pages.*

The Preview page demonstrates how a page will look when rendered with your style sheet. Figure 7-11 shows the Preview page.

The Preview page simplifies style testing by providing on-demand previews. You can use this page at the click of a button to display almost any feature of the style sheet you are working on. You can also change the page that is used for the preview.

By unchecking the Style Sheet Applied check box, you can toggle between viewing the page with and without your style sheet.

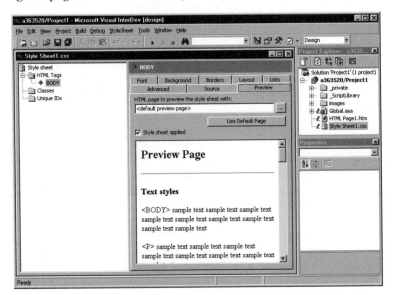

Figure 7-11. *The CSS Editor Preview page.*

Style Information on the Tag

Most of the time, positioning information is one-off. That is, you want a particular element placed in a particular location, and you don't want to make any general rules about the placement. In such cases, it's perfectly appropriate to specify style information directly on the tag.

In fact, certain attributes don't work unless they're directly on the tag. For example, the Background-image attribute no longer works in the style definition. It must be specified on the tag! As it turns out, this is true of every style attribute that implicitly creates a multimedia object to control the attribute, such as background image characteristics and filter attributes.

Style information attached to a tag is also appropriate for any "ad hoc" style data. Again, at the times when you need very specific one-off control, this method allows for that fine-grained control.

Just as the embedded style sheet overrode the linked-in style, the on-tag style information overrides both the embedded and the linked-in style definitions. However, there is an exception. If a style rule is declared as important (we'll see this later when we talk about style rules), it can override even in-tag style information regardless of where it is defined.

Don't get carried away with in-tag styles! They'll wreak havoc on your attempts to define more global style information later. In-tag styles also muddy up the well-separated relationship between style sheets and the content, potentially rendering your document less portable.

It's easy to define style information on the tag: just put a Style attribute on the tag. Every Visible tag supports the Style attribute.

Defining Style Rules

Rules specified in linked-in style sheets or in embedded style sheets have the same syntax. There is a rule scope followed by the rule itself, which looks like this:

```
rule-scope   {attribute:value;attribute:value;...}
```

You can specify as many attribute-value pairs as you want in a style rule. The braces, colons, and semicolons are required. (Technically, the last semicolon isn't required, but it does make cutting and pasting attribute-value pairs less error-prone.)

Rules specified on tags do not require a scope because the rule is implicitly the duration of the tag itself. This can, depending on the inheritance of the specified rule, also apply to any elements coded within the bounds of block elements. So, in-tag rules look like this:

```
<SOMETAG STYLE="attribute:value;attribute:value;...">
```

Any visual tag can have a Style attribute, although not all rules are valid for all tags.

Specifying the rule's scope

Rules that are more specific have precedence over less specific rules. That's why the in-tag styles override the style-sheet-defined rules. When we define style rules we can define various scopes. For example, we can define how all text in the document looks, and then we can make specific exceptions based on tag, class, or on an individual basis. This is a typical way to work—first define general rules, and then the finer scope defines exceptions to those rules.

You can define a single set of rules that applies to as many scopes as you want. Just separate the scopes with commas:

```
s1, s2, s3  {attribute:value;attribute:value;...}
```

The tag scope is the most general, least specific scope, and can therefore be easily overridden or augmented in later style rules. Some tags have broader scope than others do. For example, the <BODY> tag contains all other visible tags in a document, and therefore has the broadest style scope. Consider the following:

```
body       {font-family:arial;font-size:10;}
p          {font-size:9;}
```

In the example above, the <P> tag inherits its font family from the <BODY> tag's rule but overrides the font size rule.

You can define rules that apply to a broad range of elements. Rules defined by class can even span different tags, since the same class can be applied to many different elements regardless of tag. You use a period (.) to indicate a class rule:

```
.error     {font-color:red;}
```

Specifying a rule by class is convenient but implies that many tags in the document can end up with Class attributes on them. While not a huge maintenance burden, this can be tedious. There is a way to specify how things will look when they're contained inside another scope. For example, the following rule indicates how a paragraph will look when it is inside a <DIV> of class *Error*:

```
div.error p {font-color:red}
```

Now all the paragraphs inside an Error section will share this characteristic without requiring individual Class attributes specified.

You can define a rule for all elements that share an ID. Technically, IDs are supposed to be unique, which implies that the rule applies to a single item. This might sound like a ridiculous scope, but it's actually quite valuable.

Setting Style Attributes

Attribute-value pairs don't all need to be specified on the same line. CSS uses curly braces ({ }) to determine where a rule starts and ends, and the semicolon (;) to separate attribute-value pairs. So use as much space as is helpful to make your style sheets readable.

Font size, family, weight, and style

A large portion of a typical style specification concerns itself with the fonts of various elements in the document. You can control the significant characteristics of the font using the following properties:

```
font-family
font-size
font-weight
font-style
font-variant
@font-face
```

A couple of notes on these attributes:

- When specifying the family name, use quotes around the name. It's required if the name has embedded blanks (and it's a good idea anyway).

- The @font-face attribute is used to name a "font object" that you've defined with the font-object creation tool.

Margins, spacing, and positions

You can also control the relative spacing of elements as they appear on the page. The most commonly used attributes are:

```
margin derivatives (margin, margin-left, etc.)
left
top
width
height
position
display
```

With Internet Explorer 4.0, we now have *onresize* events. We can use *onresize* to implement a layout policy for items on the page. This is the standard procedure in application environments such as Microsoft Visual Basic. However, a more robust and easier to develop approach is to use percentage-based values for the placement attributes.

Colors, borders, and special effects

We have a rich set of attributes to control the colors, border styles, and special-effect filters for each element. Note, however, that filters and borders only work for block elements (those elements that essentially form their own separate paragraphs). Block elements imply a line break at the beginning and end of the element.

Miscellaneous page characteristics

With HTML-only browsers, we had the attributes on the <BODY> tag to control the background color and image displayed behind the document. For DHTML browsers you can still do this, but the preferred method is to use the background-management attributes on the Style attribute of the <BODY> tag. In fact, you can do this for any block element.

Differences in Netscape Navigator and Internet Explorer

Netscape Navigator and Communicator versions 4.0 through 4.03 implement cascading style sheets in a different manner than Internet Explorer. Navigator and Communicator treat relative URLs in style sheets as relative to the document they are referenced in, instead of relative to the linked-in style sheet. You should edit the CSS files and change the relative links to absolute links to work around this problem.

Part III

Scripting the Scripting Object Model

Chapter 8

Scripting Design-Time Controls

The design-time controls (DTCs) included with Microsoft Visual InterDev 6 each contain properties, events, and methods that developers can use to work with the DTCs in an application. These features provide a way of working with the DTC to receive data (by using properties), to track what users do with the DTC (by using events), and to cause the DTC to take certain actions (by using methods).

When you use a DTC in a page, the DTC uses the Script Library to create an instance of a scripting object at run time. These underlying scripting objects implement the run-time behavior of the DTC. The interface and client-side actions of the DTC are usually implemented with a standard intrinsic HTML control, such as the Textbox or Button controls. Some DTCs, such as Recordset, are implemented with run-time features only, as there is no intrinsic HTML control for the client. This chapter deals with scripting DTCs in particular and does not explore using the database DTCs such as the Recordset. Those DTCs are covered in detail in Chapters 12, 13, and 14.

CHOOSING THE SCRIPTING PLATFORM

You should exercise care in choosing the scripting platform for DTCs. If you set the scripting platform as Server, each time an event occurs in a DTC the event is processed on the server, resulting in a complete roundtrip from the browser to the server and back. This occurs because the Scripting Object Model wraps each page in an HTML form. When an event occurs, the form is posted to the server, processed, and then sent back to the browser. This processing takes time and should be carefully controlled.

If you set the scripting platform as Client, the events for a DTC are processed in the page completely in the browser. The result is faster response time, less network traffic, and less load on the server.

Often the best approach to choosing the scripting platform is to use both Server and Client modes for different DTCs. For example, you can have a page with a Textbox DTC and a Button DTC. If your database connections are all server-based, it might make sense to have the Textbox DTC use the Client scripting platform and the Button DTC use the Server scripting platform. This will allow the page to quickly process client events related to the Textbox, but let the server process any button-click events.

THE BASICS

To demonstrate how to script the DTCs, I created a simple Inventory database. This database contains the structure shown in Figure 8-1.

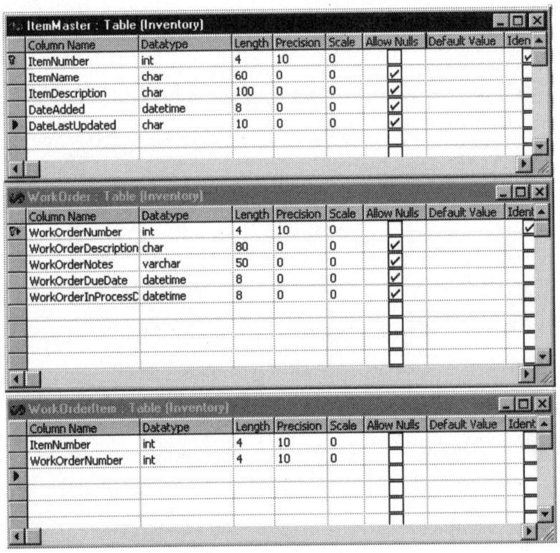

Figure 8-1. *The Inventory database contains information for producing and maintaining inventory items and work orders.*

I used Microsoft SQL Server for the database engine, but you can use Oracle, Microsoft Access, or any other database supported by Visual InterDev. The database access in this chapter will be simple. It will demonstrate how to script DTCs—not how to use the database features. You can learn more about scripting database features in Chapters 13 and 14.

A number of properties, methods, and events are shared across multiple DTCs. For example, almost every DTC will have *show* and *hide* methods that can be used to show or hide the DTC at run time. Some DTCs have a *value* property that you can use to extract data from the DTC or to place data in the DTC at run time.

Other DTCs have properties, methods, and events that are specific only to them. For instance, the Listbox and OptionGroup DTCs have an *addItem* method for adding items to the DTC at run time.

You can access the properties and methods of a DTC at run time by using the dot syntax. For example, to load a Listbox DTC that has an ID of *ItemName*, you might use the following code:

```
ItemName.addItem "Widget A"
ItemName.addItem "Widget B"
ItemName.addItem "Widget C"
ItemName.addItem "Widget D"
```

These commands add the Widget item names to *ItemName*.

You must call the methods for a DTC from the scripting platform it uses. For example, if you define a DTC and specify that it uses the Client scripting platform, the DTC's properties, methods, and events are available only in script code on the client. Conversely, if you define a DTC and specify that it uses the Server scripting platform, the DTC's properties, methods, and events are available only in ASP code running on the server.

To demonstrate how to call a method in the correct scripting platform, let's look at the following sample code:

```
<SCRIPT ID=serverEventHandlersVBS LANGUAGE=vbscript RUNAT=Server>
Sub thisPage_onenter()
    if thisPage.firstEntered then
        Listbox1.addItem "Widget A"
        Listbox1.addItem "Widget B"
        Listbox1.addItem "Widget C"
        Listbox1.addItem "Widget D"
    end if
End Sub
</SCRIPT>
```

This code runs whenever the page loads, whether the page is being accessed by a browser navigating to it or it is being entered by processing an HTML form. If the *thisPage.firstEntered* property is true, the user has navigated to the page and this code loads *Listbox1* with data. The results are shown in Figure 8-2 on the following page.

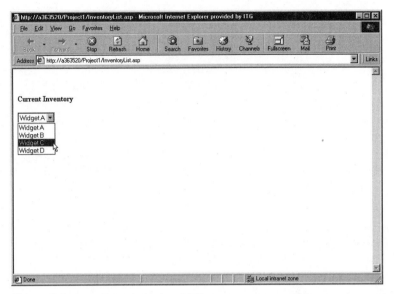

Figure 8-2. *A server-side Listbox DTC.*

You can also implement this code on the client, but you must change the event that contains the code to an event that will be fired in the browser. This code executes the same *addItem* statements, but this time they execute in the *window_onload* event in the browser.

```
<SCRIPT ID=clientEventHandlersVBS LANGUAGE=vbscript>
<!--
Sub window_onload
    ListBox1.addItem "Widget A"
    ListBox1.addItem "Widget B"
    ListBox1.addItem "Widget C"
    ListBox1.addItem "Widget D"
End Sub
-->
</SCRIPT>
```

Another issue you must correctly deal with involves the syntax of the various commands. Visual InterDev 6.0 implements the DTCs using the Script Library, which is composed of JScript routines. Service Pack 1 for Microsoft Visual Studio 6 will offer the option of using a set of COM components on the server in place of the JScript Script Library.

At least until Service Pack 1 is released, you must get used to using the correct case in your programming. JScript is case-sensitive while Microsoft Visual

Basic is not. Since the DTCs are implemented using the JScript Script Library, the run-time executes all your code in JScript. This is true even if you are developing in VBScript (Visual Basic, Scripting Edition). For example, the following line of code will work:

```
if thisPage.firstEntered then
```

This line of code will fail:

```
if thispage.firstEntered then
```

If you execute this last line of code, the following message will appear in the browser:

```
Microsoft VBScript runtime error '800a01a8'
Object required: 'thispage'
/VI6BookExamples/InventoryList.asp, line 13
```

This error is generated because the "*p*" in '*thispage*' is not capitalized. Capitalize the *P*, and the script works fine.

USING THE USER INTERFACE DTCS

The standard User Interface (UI) DTCs are:

- Button
- Textbox
- Listbox
- Label
- Grid
- Checkbox
- OptionGroup
- RecordsetNavbar

These DTCs allow you to bind to a database and construct an event-driven interface. With these DTCs, you can build an interface with the same functionality of a traditional application written in Visual Basic but design the interface in a traditional Web style.

You can use the events and methods of the DTCs to control their actions at run time. The next bit of code takes the value in the Listbox DTC and places it in the Textbox DTC. Then it hides the list box and displays the text box.

```
<SCRIPT ID=clientEventHandlersVBS LANGUAGE=vbscript>
<!--

Sub window_onload
    Listbox1.addItem "Widget A"
    Listbox1.addItem "Widget B"
    Listbox1.addItem "Widget C"
    Listbox1.addItem "Widget D"
    txtItemName.hide
End Sub

Sub Listbox1_onchange()
    if Listbox1.getValue() > "" then
        MsgBox "list is: " & Listbox1.getText()
        txtItemName.value = Listbox1.getValue()
        Listbox1.hide
        txtItemName.show
    end if
End Sub
-->
</SCRIPT>
```

The above code comes from the InventoryListClient.asp file.

The *if* statement checks the value of the list box to determine whether the user has selected a valid entry. This expression must include the empty parentheses at the end of *getValue*:

```
Listbox1.getValue()
```

The *()* must be included because *getValue* is a function. If you do not include them, this expression will evaluate to the JScript code that implements *getValue*. This is *not* the desired effect!

The events for the DTCs are also handy for setting up database operations. You can use the *onchange* event to determine when a user has completed an action in a DTC, and then take the value of that DTC and perform some database action with it. To demonstrate this, we created InventoryLookup.asp and InventoryShow.asp.

InventoryLookup.asp displays a list of item names in a list box. When a user selects an item, the *onchange* event navigates to InventoryShow.asp and displays the record which corresponds to that item. The InventoryLookup.asp file is shown in the Source Editor in Figure 8-3.

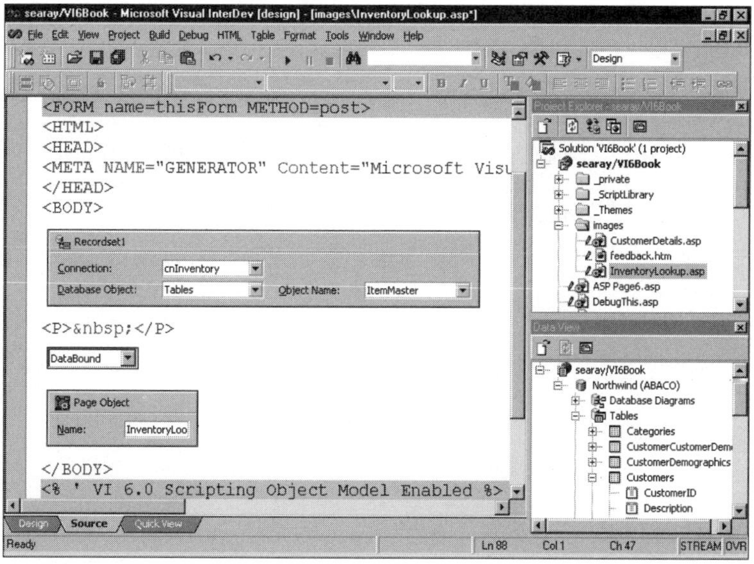

Figure 8-3. *The InventoryLookup.asp page contains Listbox, Recordset, and RecordsetNavbar DTCs.*

The Recordset DTC uses the following SQL statement to extract all the records in the ItemMaster table:

```
Select * from ItemMaster
```

The Listbox DTC's properties are shown in Figure 8-4.

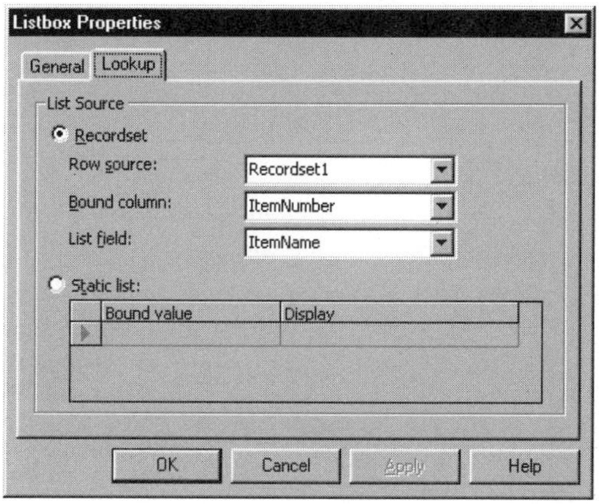

Figure 8-4. *The Lookup tab of the Listbox Properties dialog box sets the parameters for the lookup operation of the Listbox DTC, not the binding of the DTC.*

You can see in Figure 8-4 that the Recordset option is chosen in the List Source group on the Lookup tab. (There are no data settings for this DTC on the General tab because we are only using the DTC to populate the list, not to update a field in the recordset.) The Row Source drop-down list corresponds to the Listbox DTC's *RowSource* property, and is set to Recordset1. The Bound Column drop-down list corresponds to the *BoundColumn* property, and is set to ItemNumber—the field that should be returned from the list box when the user selects an entry. The List Field drop-down list corresponds to the *ListField* property, and is set to ItemName. When the page is displayed in the browser, the user will see a list of ItemName entries, which is more descriptive than ItemNumber entries. When the user selects an ItemName entry from the list, the corresponding ItemNumber is returned from the DTC. You will see how this works in the code in just a moment.

In addition to the Recordset and Listbox DTCs, we added a PageObject DTC named *InventoryLookup*. The PageObject DTC will be used to store the ItemNumber in a property and to navigate to the page that will display the details for the item. To set the properties for the PageObject DTC, follow these steps:

1. Right-click the PageObject DTC, and select Properties.

2. Click the Properties tab in the PageObject Properties dialog box.

3. Create a property with the name *ItemNumber*.

4. Set the Lifetime for *ItemNumber* to Session.

This creates a variable that we can use across the entire session.

The Listbox DTC's *onchange* event is used to determine when the user selects an ItemName entry from the list. The code in the *onchange* event is shown below:

```
<SCRIPT ID=serverEventHandlersVBS LANGUAGE=vbscript RUNAT=Server>
Sub Listbox1_onchange()
    if Listbox1.getValue() then
        InventoryLookup.setItemNumber(Listbox1.getValue())
        InventoryLookup.navigateURL("InventoryShow.asp")
    end if
End Sub
</SCRIPT>
```

The first line checks the value of the list box to make sure it is not blank. The second line sets the PageObject DTC's *ItemNumber* property to the value contained in the list box. Pay particular attention to the parentheses on the methods such as *getValue*. It is important to note that the *set* and *get* methods for the PageObject DTC's properties are methods, not properties. To use them, you must pass the value in as a parameter to the method, as shown in the previous code. You cannot set the property using an equal sign (=), as you can in Visual Basic.

The second line of code in the *onchange* event navigates to Inventory-Show.asp.

Figure 8-5 shows InventoryShow.asp in Design view.

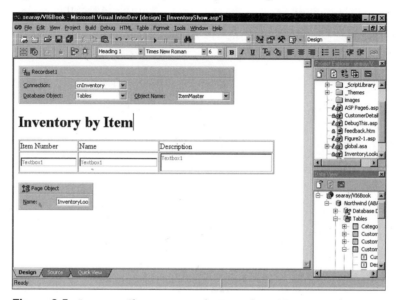

Figure 8-5. *InventoryShow.asp uses the Recordset DTC to open the ItemMaster table.*

This page contains the following DTCs:

DTC	Name
Recordset	Recordset1
Textbox	Textbox1 (displays ItemNumber)
Textbox	Textbox2 (displays ItemName)
Textbox	Textbox3 (displays ItemDescription)
PageObject	InventoryShow

The Textbox DTCs are each bound to Recordset1. The SQL statement for Recordset1 is

```
Select * from itemmaster
```

This SQL is used to preset the Recordset DTC so that we can bind the Textbox DTCs to it. When the page executes, we reset the SQL. The field that each Textbox DTC is bound to is shown after its name in the table on page 189.

After you add the Recordset DTC to the page, right-click the DTC, select Properties to display the Recordset Properties dialog box, and then click the Implementation tab. (See Figure 8-6.) Uncheck the Automatically Open The Recordset option, and then click Close to apply the change.

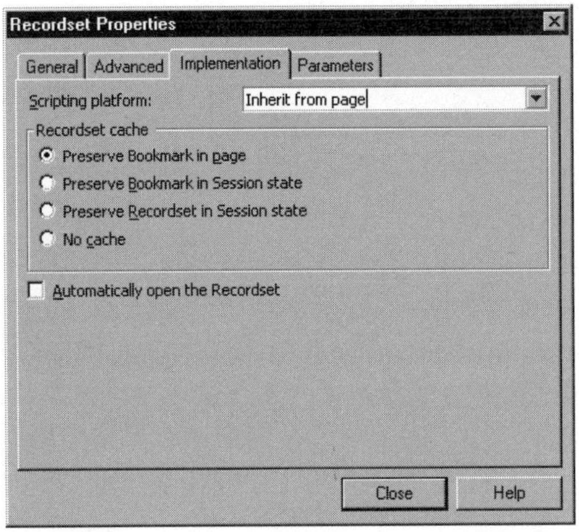

Figure 8-6. *You can change the implementation properties of a Recordset DTC by using the Recordset Properties dialog box.*

The Automatically Open The Recordset option is checked by default, which results in the recordset opening when the page loads. Unchecking this value allows you to control when the recordset opens.

Add the PageObject DTC and set a reference to InventoryLookup.asp:

1. Right-click the PageObject DTC, and select Properties.

2. Click the References tab in the PageObject Properties dialog box.

3. Click Browse (…), and select InventoryLookup.asp.

Now you can add the code used in InventoryShow.asp just after the <HEAD> tag:

```
<%
    dim ItemNumber
    ItemNumber = InventoryLookup.getItemNumber()
    Recordset1.setSQLText _
```

```
    ("Select * from itemmaster where itemnumber = " & _
    ItemNumber)
  Recordset1.open
%>
```

The next line extracts the value from the *ItemNumber* property of the PageObject DTC in InventoryLookup.asp and places it in the *ItemNumber* variable using the *getItemNumber* method:

```
ItemNumber = InventoryLookup.getItemNumber()
```

Then set the SQL for the recordset by concatenating the string using a Select statement and the *ItemNumber* variable. Now open the recordset using the *open* method.

We can also provide this functionality in a single page without using the PageObject DTC. The page shown in Figure 8-7 is a single page. The user simply selects an item from the list box and the page redisplays with the correct information. The code for the page is also straightforward.

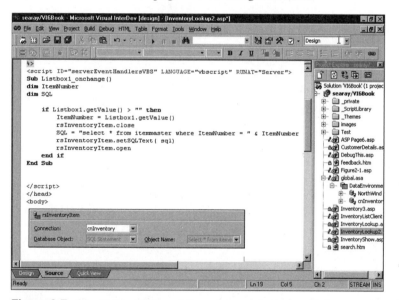

Figure 8-7. *The Listbox DTC and its* onchange *event control the operation of this page.*

Below, the code for InventoryLookup2.asp is shown from the beginning of the page through the </HEAD> tag. The section of code on the following page contains all the script that I added to the page.

```
<%@ Language=VBScript %>
<% ' VI 6.0 Scripting Object Model Enabled %>
<!--#include file="_ScriptLibrary/pm.asp"-->
<% if StartPageProcessing() Then Response.End() %>
<FORM name=thisForm METHOD=post>
<HTML>
<HEAD>
<META NAME="GENERATOR" Content="Microsoft Visual Studio 6.0">
<%
    if thisPage.firstEntered then
        Listbox1.addItem "","",0
    end if
%>
<SCRIPT ID=serverEventHandlersVBS LANGUAGE=vbscript RUNAT=Server>
Sub Listbox1_onchange()
    dim ItemNumber
    dim SQL

    if Listbox1.getValue() > "" then
        ItemNumber = Listbox1.getValue()
        rsInventoryItem.close
        SQL = "Select * from itemmaster where " & _
            "ItemNumber = " & ItemNumber
        rsInventoryItem.setSQLText(SQL)
        rsInventoryItem.open
    end if
End Sub
</SCRIPT>
</HEAD>
```

This code runs when the page is executed:

```
<%
    if thisPage.firstEntered then
        Listbox1.addItem "","",0
    end if
%>
```

If the page is executed as a result of a user navigating to it, *firstEntered* is True and the *addItem* method fires. This method is used to add a blank entry to the list. The 0 at the end of the parameters puts the blank entry at the top of the list. This code was added to present a blank to the user when the page first starts. If you do not use this code, the user cannot select the first item in the list without selecting another item in the list. Why, you might ask? When the page is loaded for the first time, the first entry in the list would be the first item in the recordset. If the user selects that item, the data the user selects and the data in the bound field are the same, and the *onchange* event does not fire. The blank entry solves this problem and gives the application a cleaner look.

The code in the *onchange* event works similarly to the code we might use in a Visual Basic application containing a list box. The *if* statement makes sure we have a nonblank item in the list:

```
if Listbox1.getValue() > "" then
```

The next line extracts the current value from the list box and stores it in *ItemNumber*:

```
ItemNumber = Listbox1.getValue()
```

The next line might seem out of place. This line makes sure the recordset is closed before you try to open it. If you use *open* and the recordset is already open, it is not refreshed. Since we are changing the SQL for the recordset, it should be reopened anyway.

```
rsInventoryItem.close
```

This statement sets the variable *SQL* to the new query. The query is built in the same manner as the last page, except that we are now storing it in a variable:

```
SQL = "Select * from itemmaster where " & _
    "ItemNumber = " & ItemNumber
```

This line sets the *SQLText* property of the recordset object:

```
rsInventoryItem.setSQLText(SQL)
```

The next line opens the recordset, and then we terminate the *if* statement:

```
    rsInventoryItem.open
end if
```

We created one more version of this page to demonstrate the flexibility of using the DTCs. This one is Inventory3.asp and uses the same list box and logic but replaces the Textbox DTCs with the Grid DTC. This page also allows you to choose between seeing one record or all records in the table by selecting the various items in the list.

Figure 8-8 on the following page shows the page when the user has selected All Items from the list.

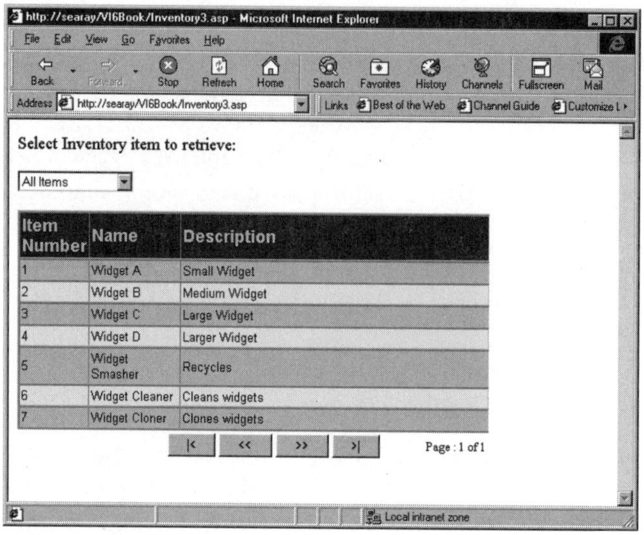

Figure 8-8. *The list contains the All Items entry to allow users to select all records from the table.*

Notice that Figure 8-8 shows the Grid DTC displaying several rows. Figure 8-9 shows the same page when we have selected Widget A from the list. Notice how the display changes to show only that record.

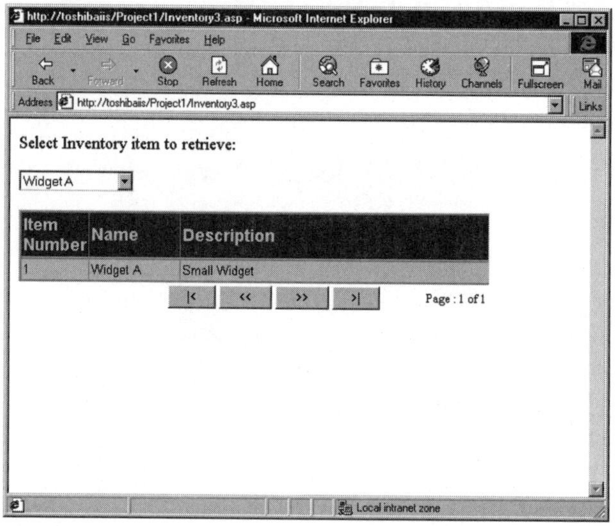

Figure 8-9. *The Grid DTC automatically adjusts its output, depending upon the number of records in the recordset.*

You can see how the grid adjusts itself to the number of records in the recordset. Setting up the page to use the grid is quite simple:

1. Delete the Textbox controls from the original page.

2. Add the Grid DTC.

3. Right-click the Grid DTC, and select Properties.

4. Click the Data tab in the Grid Properties dialog box.

5. Select the Recordset DTC to use from the Recordset drop-down list.

6. Select the fields to use from the Available Fields list.

Figure 8-10 shows the Data tab with the data-binding settings. Those are all the setting changes you must make to wire the control up and make it functional. In our sample, we also changed the layout and the number of records per page. You can see in Figure 8-10 that we also modified the headings.

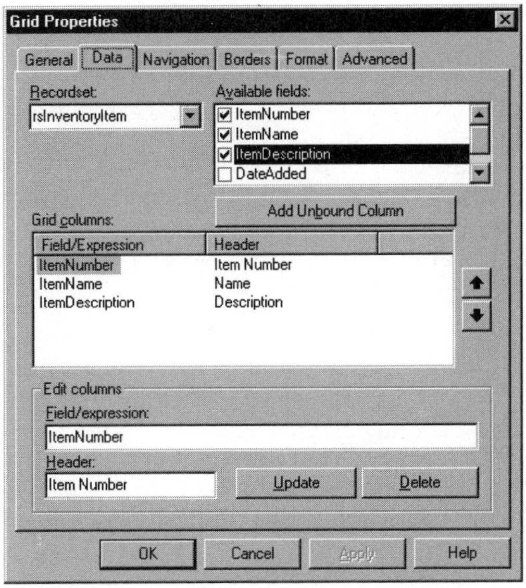

Figure 8-10. *The Data tab of the Grid Properties dialog box contains the settings to bind the Grid DTC to the Recordset DTC.*

The code that controls this page is shown below:

```
<%@ Language=VBScript %>
<% ' VI 6.0 Scripting Object Model Enabled %>
<!--#include file="_ScriptLibrary/pm.asp"-->
```

(continued)

```
<% if StartPageProcessing() Then Response.End() %>
<FORM name=thisForm METHOD=post>
<HTML>
<HEAD>
<META NAME="GENERATOR" Content="Microsoft Visual Studio 6.0">
<%
    dim qFlag
    if thisPage.firstEntered then
        Listbox1.addItem "All Items","*",0
        Listbox1.addItem "","",0
    end if


%>
<SCRIPT ID=serverEventHandlersVBS LANGUAGE=vbscript RUNAT=Server>
Sub Listbox1_onchange()
    dim ItemNumber
    dim SQL
    if Listbox1.getValue() > "" then
        ItemNumber = Listbox1.getValue()
        rsInventoryItem.close
        select Case ItemNumber
            case "*": SQL = "Select * from itemmaster"
            case else:
                SQL = "Select * from itemmaster " & _
                    " where ItemNumber = " & ItemNumber
        end select
        rsInventoryItem.setSQLText( sql)
        rsInventoryItem.open
    end if
End Sub
</SCRIPT>
```

The first bit of script code has the following line added:

```
Listbox1.addItem "All Items","*",0
```

This line adds the All Items entry in the list and places it just after the blank entry. The placement occurs because the line to add the blank entry follows this one. Also notice the * parameter. This sets the bound field of the control which is returned as the value field when we call *getValue*. So, when the user clicks the All Items entry, a * is returned so that we can correctly set the SQL statement.

Next I added this code to set the SQL statement:

```
select Case ItemNumber
    case "*": SQL = "select * from itemmaster"
    case else:
        SQL = "Select * from itemmaster " & _
            " where ItemNumber = " & ItemNumber
end select
```

This code checks for an *ItemNumber* that is equal to *, and if it finds one, sets the SQL statement to retrieve all records from the database. If the value is not *, it sets the SQL statement as we did in the first two pages.

Those are all the changes required to set up the Grid DTC as opposed to the Textbox DTCs. In fact, the first version of the Grid DTC page was made with no code changes whatsoever. We added the other features to enhance the page, but they were not required. This is one of the advantages of using the data-binding features. You can make changes quickly without having to do a lot of recoding.

MOVING ON

There are many ways that you can use the new DTCs in your applications. These ways will be covered in the remaining chapters of this book.

Chapter 9

Creating Forms

There are two ways you can build forms with Microsoft Visual InterDev. The first is to create HTML forms and then use Active Server Pages (ASP) to process them. The second is to use the FormManager design-time control (DTC) and the Scripting Object Model to create easy-to-maintain forms. This chapter covers both approaches.

USING THE FORMMANAGER DTC

The FormManager DTC is designed to automate much of the coding required to construct a mode-based data-entry form. For instance, if you want a four-button form (Display, New, Modify, and Delete, for example) to control the form's mode, you can hook this form up with the FormManager DTC without writing any code.

Let's look at an example of the FormManager DTC. This form has two actions:

- **New** Clears the form and lets you enter a new record
- **Modify** Lets you modify the current record

You can scroll around the form in either mode. Figure 9-1 on the following page shows the form in Modify mode. Notice that the Modify button is disabled.

This form uses the RecordsetNavbar DTC to navigate through the recordset. The RecordsetNavbar DTC is located at the bottom of the form. You can change any one of the fields. After you have changed a field, you can save it by moving

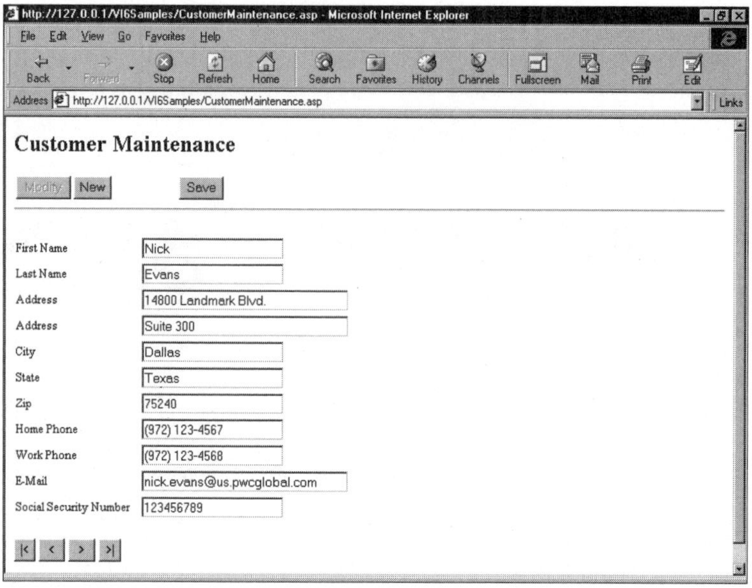

Figure 9-1. *Data Entry form in Modify mode.*

to the next record with the RecordsetNavbar DTC or clicking the Save button. Figure 9-2 shows the same form in New mode, immediately after a new record has been entered and saved.

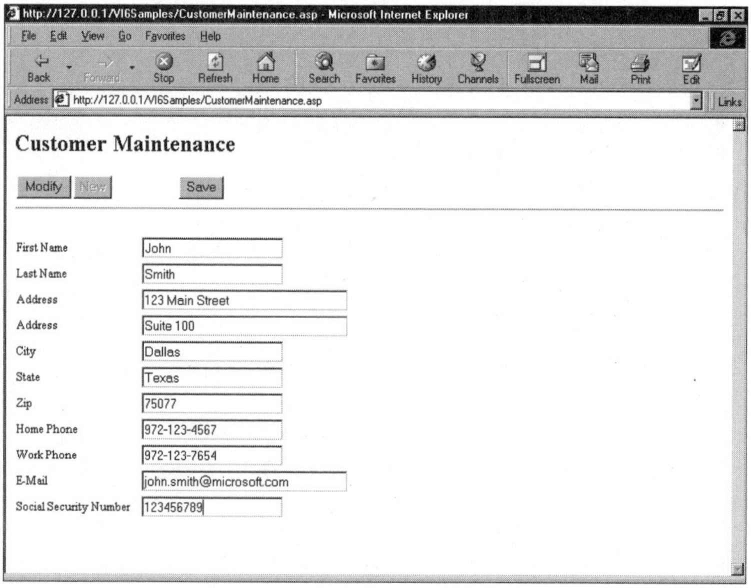

Figure 9-2. *Data Entry form in New mode.*

The FormManager DTC is a type of "super DTC"—it works with the other DTCs on the page to map and control functional changes during mode switches. Here's how to use it:

1. Create an ASP Web page.

2. Insert the DTCs you will use for your data form. This normally includes a Recordset DTC, DTCs for each field you will display, a RecordsetNavbar DTC to control navigation, and buttons that will control switching from one mode to the next.

3. Insert a FormManager DTC. This FormManager interface wires the various modes and actions together.

The first step in creating the data entry form is easy—you can use the standard techniques we have already covered to build the form and bind it to a recordset. Figure 9-3 shows the sample page in Design view. You can see the Recordset DTC at the top of the page. Next are the Button DTCs that will switch from one mode to the next. Next come the Textbox DTCs for the fields on the form. Finally the RecordsetNavbar DTC and the FormManager DTC come below the last Textbox DTC (off the screen).

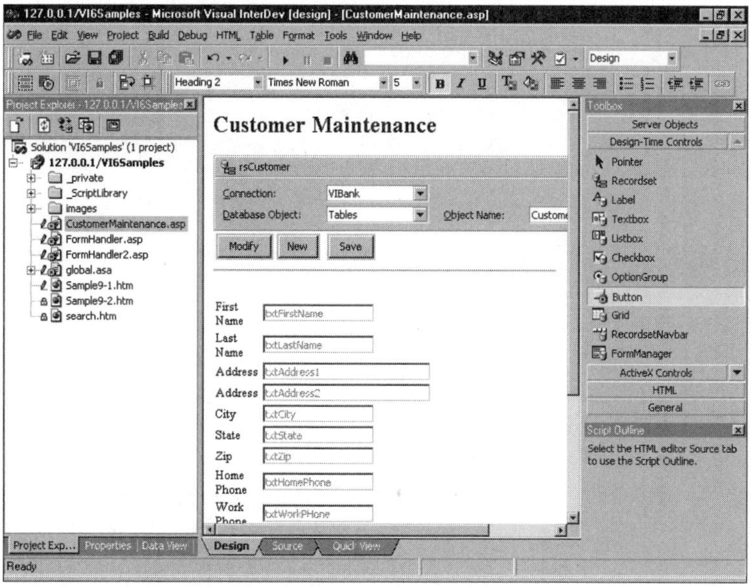

Figure 9-3. *Data Entry form in Design view.*

After building the basic layout of the page with the controls just mentioned, your next step is to test it in the browser. Finally, you'll want to edit the FormManager DTC on the page and set its properties. Let's look at how to wire up the FormManager DTC with a few lines of ASP code.

Defining Modes, Actions, and Transitions in the FormManager DTC

First a few terms used in conjunction with the FormManager DTC need to be defined:

Term	Description
Form Mode	Defines an operational setting for the form. For instance, in New mode the user should be able to enter a new record but not delete a record. In Modify mode, the user can make changes to a record but not enter a new record or delete a record.
Action	Determines what happens at an execution point between modes. Actions occur when the form switches from one mode to another. For instance, when the user clicks the New button, we set the *disabled* property of the cmdNew button to True to turn off that button, and we set the *disabled* property of cmdModify to False to turn it on.
Transition	The period between one mode and another. Transitions occur when the form changes from one mode to another. For instance, when the user clicks the New button, the transition period occurs between the time the New button is clicked and the New mode becomes active.

Table 9-1. *FormManager modes.*

Defining modes for the FormManager DTC

Defining modes for the form is the first step in setting up the FormManager DTC. Figure 9-4 shows the Form Mode tab of the FormManager Properties dialog box. This figure shows two modes defined for our form: Modify and New.

To define a mode:

1. Right-click the FormMode DTC and select Properties.

2. Click the Form Mode tab in the FormManager Properties dialog box.

3. Enter the new mode name in the New Mode text box.

4. Click the > button to create the mode and add it to the Form Mode list.

Figure 9-4 also shows the Default Mode set to Modify. The form will start in this mode.

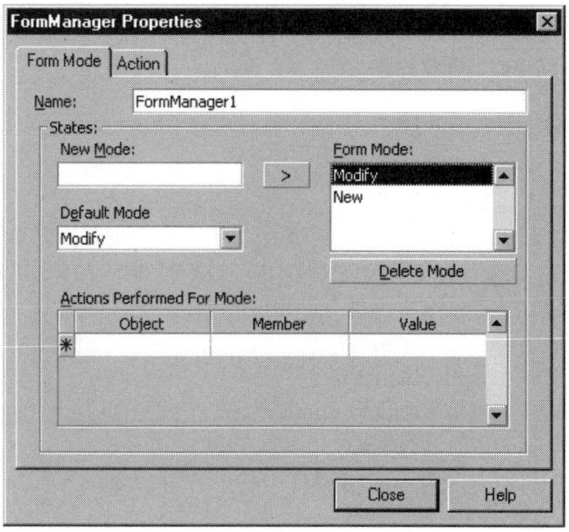

Figure 9-4. *The Form Mode tab of the FormManager Properties dialog box.*

Defining actions for the FormManager DTC

Now that we have defined our modes, we can define the actions for them. Figure 9-5 shows the Form Mode tab of the FormManager Properties dialog box with actions defined for the Modify mode. You can display the actions for a mode by selecting the mode in the Form Mode list. The actions will display in the Actions Performed For Mode grid.

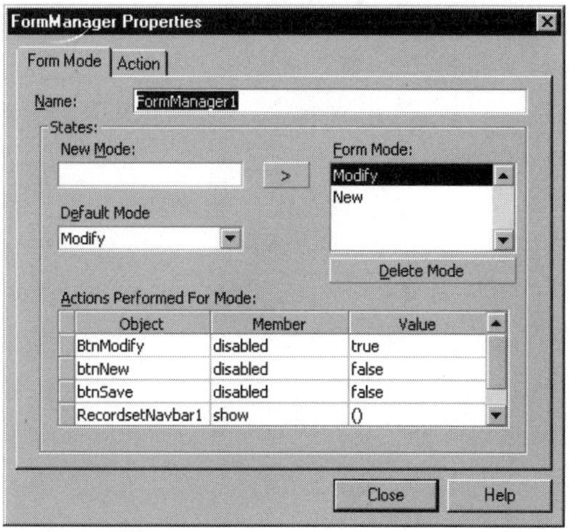

Figure 9-5. *The FormMode tab of the FormManager Properties dialog box with actions defined.*

The actions occur when the mode becomes active. For instance, when the Modify mode becomes active, the properties shown in Figure 9-5 are set.

To define actions for a mode:

1. Select the mode in the Form Mode list.

2. Click in the first Object cell to activate it, and then select the object you wish to use from the drop-down list.

3. Tab to the Member cell.

4. Select the member (method or property) to use from the drop-down list.

5. Tab to the Value cell.

6. Enter the value for the property or method.

Defining transition actions for the FormManager DTC

When our mode actions have been defined, we can define the transition actions. Your transition actions can do several things. First you will define a Form Mode Transition for each mode that performs the change to the new mode. For instance, Figure 9-6 shows the Action tab of the FormManager Properties dialog box for the FormManager DTC in our sample. You can see that we have a Form Mode Transition defined for each of our modes (New and Modify). In addition, we have a third and fourth transition defined for Modify and New mode when the user clicks the Save button.

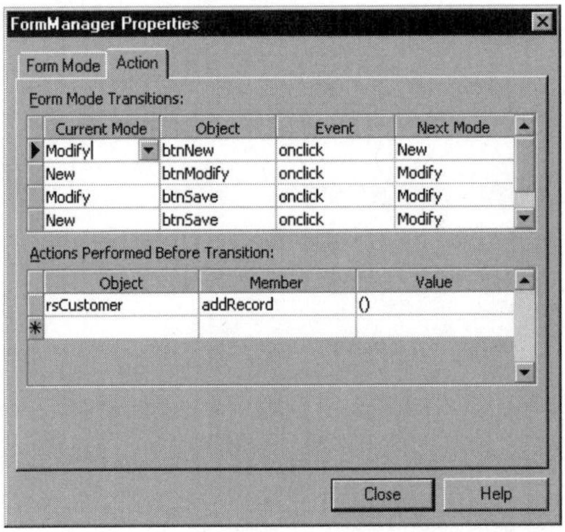

Figure 9-6. *The Action tab of the FormManager Properties dialog box.*

You can also define actions that take place before the transition occurs. This is extremely useful in database operations. In Figure 9-6, notice that we have selected the first Modify mode line in the Form Mode Transitions grid. This displays the corresponding actions that occur before that transition occurs in the Actions Performed Before Transition grid. In this example, the *rsCustomer-.addRecord* method will execute when the user clicks the New button. Clicking the second Modify mode line in the top grid would show that the *rsCustomer-.updateRecord* method is executed when the user clicks the Save button. The same is true for the New mode line in the top grid when the user clicks the Save button.

This example demonstrates the power of the FormManager DTC. No code actually has to be written on the page to achieve this type of functionality. Everything has been accomplished using the Recordset, Button, Textbox, RecordsetNavbar and FormManager DTCs. Of course, you can also add your own custom code to the ASP Web page to extend the functionality by adding data validation checks and so on. The FormManager DTC allows you to create the basic wiring for your dynamic, data-driven forms automatically and to concentrate on the specific business rules for your applications—thus increasing your productivity.

INTERACTING WITH HTML FORMS AND PAGES

After looking at the new method for working with forms to collect and edit data via the FormManager DTC, we'll now cover the original Visual InterDev 1 method which is still supported in Visual InterDev 6. This older technique is still important because it can often be simpler to program and gives you more manual control over the code that you write. The FormManager DTC is typically used for more complex data entry and editing routines that involve multiple modes. The HTML form technique is used for simpler data capture requirements. An example might be where there is no need for multiple modes and where there is no need for navigation through a Recordset DTC.

This section describes the primary way to get user information with the *Form* collection. We'll also briefly touch on the *QueryString* and *ServerVariables* collections. These are just three of the collections available in the *Request* object in the Active Server Framework. For more information on the other collections, namely the *ClientCertificate* and *Cookies* collections, see Chapter 10 or the online documentation that comes with Visual InterDev.

The *Form* Collection

One of the most common ways to obtain input for a server-side application is from an HTML form. Forms are part of standard HTML, and virtually all modern browsers support them. Forms let users of your HTML page enter information using text boxes, check boxes, radio buttons, and list boxes. Users can then submit this data by clicking a command button on the form. The form then embeds the information within an HTTP request string and sends the string back to the server.

Traditionally, the return string has been passed to a CGI application (an .exe file running on the server). The CGI application then parses the string and interprets the results. Many aspects of this technique make it cumbersome. The CGI application is often written in C. This means you must be familiar with an additional language, use a separate set of tools, use a complex debugging process involving unintegrated components, and then interpret the HTTP request. You may have seen the strange text that your browser adds to the URL when sending a request to the server after you click the Submit button on a form. For instance, the following text is sent to the Microsoft search site when you try to search for "Space Exploration near mars" and select Excite as the search engine:

```
http://www.excite.com/search.gw?searchType=Concept&category=
    default&mode=relevance&showqbe=1&display=msn,hb&search=
    %22Space+Exploration%22+near+mars
```

The CGI programmer must know the rules of HTTP requests and be able to parse the data out of a string such as that shown above. This can be a tedious process.

The *Request* object in Active Server Script lets you circumvent all these complications. First, it lets you access the data from within the ASP Web page and keep the entire process inside Visual InterDev. Second, it parses the HTTP request for you, making the data readily available and easy to use.

Processing Forms with ASP Files

An ASP file lets you collect or process HTML form values in three ways:

- A static .htm file can contain a formCX that posts its values to an ASP file.

- An ASP file can create a form that posts information to another ASP file.

- An ASP file can create a form that posts information to itself—that is, to the ASP file that contains the form.

The first two methods operate the same way as forms that interact with other gateway programs, but with ASP you can include commands that read and respond to user choices. The third method is more complicated, requiring logic to handle different states within the file. Creating an ASP file that contains a form definition that posts information to itself is a slightly more complicated but powerful means of working with forms.

> **NOTE** If you are considering writing a self-posting ASP Web page, you might want to consider using the FormManager DTC instead since your page is most likely multimodal (that is, having multiple entry paths).

The first step in processing forms with ASP is to create the appropriate HTML form (which can itself be an HTML or ASP file) and tell the form to send its data to the form handler ASP file. You do this in the HTML <FORM> tag by specifying the path of the ASP file that handles the processing, as shown here:

```
<HTML>
<HEAD>
<META NAME="GENERATOR" Content="Microsoft Visual Studio 6.0">
<TITLE>Favorite Car</TITLE>
</HEAD>
<BODY BGCOLOR="#ffffff">

<FORM METHOD=POST ACTION="FormHandler.asp">
<P>
First Name: <INPUT NAME="FName" SIZE=30>
<P>
Last Name: <INPUT NAME="LName" SIZE=30>
<P>
Which car do you like best?
<SELECT NAME="Car">
<OPTION>Porsche
<OPTION>BMW
<OPTION>Ferrari
<OPTION>Chrysler
<OPTION>Lamborghini
</SELECT>
<P>
<INPUT TYPE=Submit>
</FORM>

</BODY>
</HTML>
```

This form produces the page shown in Figure 9-7 on the following page (which is in Quick view mode in Visual InterDev).

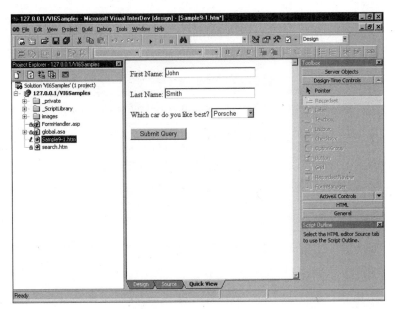

Figure 9-7. *A simple HTML form.*

The <FORM> tag tells the browser to collect the data the user enters on the form and package it in an HTTP request. If you weren't using ASP, a CGI program would be specified in the ACTION attribute. The following syntax specifies the ASP file named FormHandler.asp:

```
<FORM METHOD=POST ACTION="FormHandler.asp">
```

When the user clicks the Submit button on the form, control is transferred to FormHandler.asp. (See Figures 9-8 and 9-9.)

The HTML form has three inputs: the text box named FName, the text box named LName, and a list box named Car. When the user clicks the Submit button, the names of all the form's inputs are passed to the target specified in the form tag's *Action* qualifier, as are the values in the form's controls. Figure 9-8 shows how to retrieve the first and last name from the form, as well as the name of the car that the user selects as his or her favorite. The code shows how you can use this information to make a decision about what output to send to the user.

```
<%@ Language=VBScript %>
<HTML>
<HEAD>
<META NAME="GENERATOR" Content="Microsoft Visual Studio 6.0">
<TITLE>Form Handler</TITLE>
</HEAD>
<BODY BGCOLOR="#FFFFFF">
```

Figure 9-8. *Retrieving information from a form by using the* Request *object is a straightforward process.* *(continued)*

```
Welcome,

<% = Request.Form("FName") & " " & Request.Form("LName") %>.
<P>
Your favorite car is a
<%
DIM favcar
favcar = Request.Form("Car")
If favcar = "Chrysler" Then
    Response.Write("... wait a minute... there must be an error.")
    Response.Write("<P>A <B>Chrysler</B>?")
Else
    Response.Write(favcar & ".<P>That's cool.")
End If
%>


</BODY>
</HTML>
```

In the ASP Web page, you can reference the values the user enters by using the *Form* collection of the *Request* object.

The syntax for retrieving the variables from the *Form* collection is

```
Request.Form(parameter)[(index)|.Count]
```

You retrieve the first name and last name values using the following syntax, which outputs the form's variables to the HTML stream with a space between them:

```
<% = Request.Form("FName") & " " & Request.Form("LName") %>
```

The *Car* form variable is retrieved in the same fashion:

```
favcar = Request.Form("Car")
```

If the HTTP request contains more than one parameter with the same name, it forms a collection that you can index by a number. For instance, if the HTML form has two first name text boxes named FName, you can access them in your script like this:

```
The first FName is <% = Request.Form("FName")(1) %>
And the second FName is <% = Request.Form("FName")(2) %>
```

If you do not use the index on such a parameter, you get a string with both values separated by commas. You can use the *Count* property to determine how many form variables with a particular name are in the Request's *Form* collection. For instance, if the HTML form has two FName variables, the value of the following is 2.

```
Request.Form("FName").Count
```

Self-posting pages

You can easily create an ASP Web page with a form that posts the input values back to itself. The user can then fill in the form variables and submit the form. The values are sent along with the request to reload the ASP file. The ASP file simply uses the *Request* object to access the form variables. The ASP file can check the results and update the form with a message if necessary. Also, self-posting forms are great for pages that progressively build as the user completes the form. For instance, when a user selects a type of car from the list, the page redisplays with a list of submodels. If the user then selects one of the submodels, the page redisplays with another list of features for the submodel. You can handle each step of the page in the same ASP file to give the user a seamless view of the application.

Self-posting pages work much more seamlessly than separate pages that are sent back to users with some type of message—separate pages require users to move back to the previous page. Self-posting forms can display the message and let users continue.

Self-posting pages require only one type of special logic—the logic to handle the different states the page might take. The page must be able to distinguish between each mode it might take. For instance, a page typically has one mode to display one section of the page and another mode to process the section.

The GetEmail.asp page from the online Visual InterDev documentation is a simple implementation of a self-posting page. This page checks the *Email* variable for several things. If *Email* is blank, the resulting page asks the user for his or her e-mail address. If *Email* does not contain the @ character, the user sees the same message with a note on the proper syntax. If *Email* does not meet one of the last two criteria, it's probably OK and the final message appears. Figure 9-9 shows the code for GetEmail.asp.

```
<HTML>
<BODY>
<!-- GetEmail.asp -->

<%
    If IsEmpty(Request("Email")) Then
        Msg = "Please enter your email address."
    ElseIf InStr(Request("Email"), "@") = 0 Then
        Msg = "Please enter an email address" & _
            " in the form username@location."
    Else
        ' In a real application, the following message
        ' would be replaced by actual processing.
        Msg = "This script could process the " & _
            "valid Email address now."
    End If
```

Figure 9-9. *An example of a self-posting page.* (continued)

```
%>
<FORM METHOD="POST" ACTION="GetEmail.asp">
<PRE>
Email: <INPUT TYPE="TEXT" NAME="Email" SIZE=30
    VALUE="<%= Request("Email")%>">
<%= Msg %><P>
<INPUT TYPE="Submit" VALUE="Submit">
</PRE>
</FORM>
</BODY>
</HTML>
```

THE *QUERYSTRING* COLLECTION

The *QueryString* collection creates a parsed version of the *QUERY_STRING* server variable. This information is the part of an HTTP request that comes after the question mark. This collection provides the same easy access to the *Request* variables that the *Form* collection provides to *Form* variables.

The syntax for using the *QueryString* collection is

```
Request.QueryString(variable)[(index)|.Count]
```

The most common way to extract the contents of an HTTP request is to use the *Form* collection of the *Request* object. But you can get an HTTP request that is not from a form. In that case, you use the *QueryString* collection to pull the individual variables from the query string.

Each variable in a query string has a name associated with it. The following example has two variables, *Name* and *Age*:

```
http://www.hypothetical.com/nameinfo.asp?name=fred&age=22
```

To access the *Name* and *Age* variables, you use the following syntax:

```
TheName = Request.QueryString("name")    ' value is "fred"
TheAge = Request.QueryString("age")      ' value is 22
```

As with the *Form* collection, the *QueryString* collection can contain the same variable name more than once. If two values are sent with the same name, you can access the different values by using an index. In the following example, *QueryString* has two values for the *name* variable:

```
http://www.old.com/nameinfo.asp?name=Tony+Orlando&name=Dawn&age=22
```

You can get the values by using a numeric index after specifying the variable:

```
Name1 = Request.QueryString("name")(1) ' Value is "Tony Orlando"
Name2 = Request.QueryString("name")(2) ' Value is "Dawn"
```

You can also determine the number of values in the *name* variable by calling the following:

```
Request.QueryString("name").Count
```

To print out all the values in the *name* variable, you use a looping structure, as follows:

```
<%
    For I = 1 To Request.QueryString("name").Count
        Response.Write Request.QueryString("name")(I) & "<BR>"
    Next
%>
```

USING SERVER VARIABLES WITH FORMS

One example of a useful server variable is *REQUEST_METHOD*. If you check it in an ASP Web page, it has a value of POST when the page is referenced by a form, and it has a value of GET when the user has referenced a page either directly or by using the Refresh feature of the browser. This is useful because if the user refreshes the ASP Web page that was used to respond to a form, the values are not set in the *Request* object and your page does not display correctly.

> **NOTE** The problem of a user refreshing an ASP Web page that was used to respond to an HTML form is not so significant if your users are using Microsoft Internet Explorer 4.0. During a refresh, this browser will display a message box ("Repost form data?") so that the end user has the option of reposting the data. Checking for GET or POST in your ASP code is still useful, however, because it covers the scenario in which the page might be accessed directly.

Figure 9-10 shows how to modify the Favorite Car form's corresponding ASP Web page, FormHandler.asp. The modified file is named FormHandler2.asp. This example tests *REQUEST_METHOD* and displays a message when the user clicks the Refresh button.

```
<%@ Language=VBScript %>
<HTML>
<HEAD>
<META NAME="GENERATOR" Content="Microsoft Visual Studio 6.0">
<TITLE>Form Processor</TITLE>
```

Figure 9-10. *An example that tests the* REQUEST_METHOD *server variable.*

(continued)

```
</HEAD>
<BODY BGCOLOR="#FFFFFF">
<%
Dim RequestMethod
' reference 1
RequestMethod = Request.ServerVariables("REQUEST_METHOD")
' reference 2
If RequestMethod = "GET" Then
' This means the user refreshed FormHandler2.asp

' reference 3
%>
<H1>
<C>Sorry!</C>
</H1>
You can't use Refresh to view this screen. Use your Back button to go
to the form, change the data if need be, and press the Submit button
to get back to this point.
<P>
Thanks!
<%
Else   ' The user pressed submit on the form
%>
Welcome,
<% = Request.Form("FName") & " " & Request.Form("LName") %>.
<P>
Your favorite car is a
<%
DIM favcar
favcar = Request.Form("Car")
If favcar = "Chrysler" Then
    Response.Write("... wait a minute... there must be an error.")
    Response.Write("<P>A <B>Chrysler</B>?")
Else
    Response.Write(favcar & ".<P>That's cool.")
End If
%>

<%
End If
%>
</BODY>
</HTML>
```

The statement after the reference 1 comment gets the value of *REQUEST_METHOD* and stores it in a local variable. *REQUEST_METHOD*'s value is POST when the ASP Web page is called by a <FORM> tag's ACTION attribute. Any other time the ASP Web page is called—when the user types the Web address directly into the browser, refreshes the page, or clicks on a link that is connected to the page—the value of *REQUEST_METHOD* is GET.

The script then checks the value of *REQUEST_METHOD* (the statement after the reference 2 comment). As in Visual Basic, the *If* construct in VBScript contains a block of code that is executed if the condition being evaluated is True; and an optional *Else* block that, when included, executes if the condition is False. One technique you can use in this VBScript is to place a chunk of HTML in between the VBScript *If*, *Else*, and *End If* statements. Even though the VBScript section is closed after the reference 3 comment, the code that follows is still part of the *If* block. The HTML between the *If* block and the VBScript section with the *Else* statement is executed only when the condition in the *If* is true, even though it is not between the <% and %> symbols. Although this technique can be slightly confusing at first, it is important and is often used in ASP Web pages.

Chapter 10

Using Active Server Pages

Microsoft Active Server Pages (ASP), a feature of Microsoft Internet Information Server (IIS) (in versions 3 and later) provides an application framework for developing powerful, server-based functionality for a Web site. Because the logic for ASP runs on the Web server, applications built using ASP can be accessed from a variety of Web browsers running across different platforms.

ASP provides the following core functionality:

- **Server-side scripting** You can embed scripting such as Microsoft VBScript (Visual Basic, Scripting Edition), Microsoft JScript, Perl, or other language syntax directly in an HTML page for execution on the Web server as opposed to the Web browser.

- **Flexible Web-to-database connectivity** Through server-side scripting and Microsoft ActiveX Data Objects (ADO), you can easily build rich database functionality into your Web sites.

- **State management** You can track and manage application state on a per-user, per-application, and per-server basis using built-in objects. Using the built-in objects helps you overcome the limitations of the stateless Hypertext Transfer Protocol (HTTP) for building rich Web applications.

- **Active Server components**   Perhaps most important, you can instantiate and use programmable components. You can create these components using tools such as Microsoft Visual Basic, Microsoft Visual C++, Microsoft Visual J++, Borland Delphi, and Powersoft PowerBuilder. This lets you integrate Web applications with existing client/server systems.

ASP works with the following Microsoft Web servers:

- IIS 3 on Microsoft Windows NT Server 4
- IIS 4 on Windows NT Server 4
- Microsoft Peer Web Services on Windows NT Workstation 4
- Microsoft Personal Web Server on Microsoft Windows 95, Windows 98, or Windows NT Workstation 4

IIS 4 and the Personal Web Server for Windows 95, Windows 98, and Windows NT Workstation 4 are included in the Windows NT Option Pack that can be downloaded or purchased from Microsoft. The Option Pack is the easiest way to install IIS or the Personal Web Server and its related applications, such as Microsoft Transaction Server (MTS).

You can use server-side scripting to easily create dynamic content—content that responds to circumstances such as user-supplied information requests, personal profiles, or conditional logic. With server-side scripting, the same physical Web page can be customized differently every time it is downloaded. You can also use server-side scripting to dynamically generate client-side interactivity. For instance, you can detect whether the browser being used supports Java, and you can then decide whether to include a Java applet within the Web page before sending it to the browser.

To date, Common Gateway Interface (CGI) programming has typically been used to provide server-based intelligence within Web applications. However, CGI programs are typically complex and inflexible. With server-side scripting and ASP, you can leverage Visual Basic or JScript programming experience and more quickly create rich applications for the Web.

WHAT IS AN ASP WEB PAGE?

An ASP Web page consists of an HTML document with embedded server-side script logic. The script logic, such as VBScript or JScript, is dynamically executed on the Web server and then stripped out of the document so that only HTML is sent to the browser. Figure 10-1 shows how an ASP Web page is used.

Since an ASP Web page is an HTML document, all HTML tags are allowed in the ASP file and can be used normally. ASP files let you dynamically generate HTML tags within the source ASP Web page before it is sent to the browser. You can freely include server-side script anywhere in the ASP file and intermingle it with HTML.

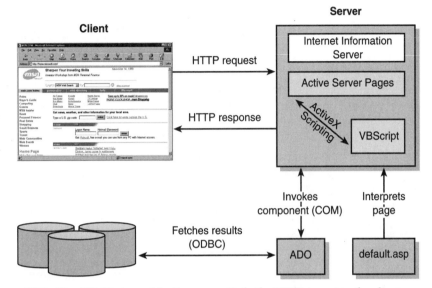

Figure 10-1. *The ASP file is read by the server. Only the HTML is sent to the client browser.*

THE BASIC ELEMENTS OF ASP

ASP processes scripts that you can incorporate into HTML pages. ASP is not a scripting language; it contains language-specific syntax required for operations, based on the scripting engine being used.

VBScript and JScript scripting languages are contained within ASP. The default scripting language is VBScript, but you can easily change it by following these steps:

1. Display the properties for the project.

2. Display the Editor Defaults page.

3. Select either JavaScript (ECMAScript) or VBScript for the default Server and Client scripting languages.

Scripts are written in languages that have specific rules. A user must employ the correct syntax to successfully access your Web page. To use another scripting language, the server must run the scripting engine that understands the language. For more information on changing the primary scripting language default or using VBScript, JScript, or other scripting languages with ASP, look under Platform SDK/Internet/Intranet/Extranet Services in the MSDN online documentation. This section of the documentation contains a wealth of information on platform technologies such as VBScript, JScript, ASP, and more.

SCRIPT TAGS AND DELIMITERS

A script delimiter is a character or sequence of characters that marks the beginning or end of a unit. Delimiters differentiate HTML tags from text. In the case of HTML, these delimiters are the less than (<) and greater than (>) symbols (also known as angle brackets).

Similarly, delimiters differentiate ASP script commands and output expressions from both text and HTML tags. ASP uses the shorthand delimiters <% and %> to enclose script commands. For instance, the command

```
<% sport = "climbing" %>
```

assigns the string "climbing" to the variable *sport*.

ASP also uses the delimiters <%= and %> to enclose output expressions. For instance, the output expression

```
<%= sport %>
```

sends the current value of the variable to the browser.

You can include any valid primary scripting language expression within ASP delimiters. For instance, the following line produces text ending with the current server time:

```
This page was last refreshed at <%= Now %>.
```

In this case, the Web server returns the value of the VBScript function *Now* to the browser along with the text.

The statements, expressions, commands, and procedures that are used within script delimiters must be valid for the default primary scripting language. ASP comes with the default primary scripting language set to VBScript. However, ASP lets you use other scripting languages. You can use the HTML script tags <SCRIPT> and </SCRIPT>, together with the Language and Runat attributes, to enclose complete procedures written in any language for which you have the scripting engine.

For instance, the following .asp file processes the JScript procedure *MyFunction*:

```
<HTML>
<BODY>
<% Call MyFunction %>
</BODY>
</HTML>
<SCRIPT RUNAT=SERVER LANGUAGE=JAVASCRIPT>
    function  MyFunction ()
    {
        Response.Write("MyFunction Called")
    }
</SCRIPT>
```

Do not include any output expressions or script commands that are not part of complete procedures within <SCRIPT> tags.

You can include procedures written in your default primary scripting language within ASP delimiters.

STATEMENTS

A statement is a syntactically complete unit that performs some task. It expresses one kind of action, declaration, or definition. The following statements are typical of a Visual Basic program or VBScript program:

```
If I = 10 Then
    ...
End If
```

The following conditional *If...Then...Else* statement is a common VBScript statement:

```
<%
If Time < #12:00:00 PM#  Then
    greeting = "Good Morning!"
Else
    greeting = "Hello!"
End If
%>
```

A user running this script before 12:00 noon by the Web server's system clock sees

Good Morning!

A user running the script at or after 12:00 noon sees

Hello!

This statement stores either the value "Good Morning!" or the value "Hello!" in the variable *greeting*. It does not send any values to the client browser.

The following lines send the value, displayed in green, to the client browser:

```
<FONT COLOR="GREEN">
<%= greeting %>
</FONT>
```

You can include HTML text between the sections of a statement. For example, the following script produces the same result as the script in the previous section:

```
<FONT COLOR="GREEN">
<% If Time <#12:00:00 PM#  Then %>
    Good Morning!
<% Else %>
    Hello!
<% End If %>
</FONT>
```

This script mixes HTML within an *If...Then...Else* statement. If the condition is True—that is, if the time is before noon—the Web server sends the HTML that follows the *If* condition ("Good Morning!") to the browser; otherwise, it sends the HTML that follows *Else* ("Hello!") to the browser.

INTRODUCING VBSCRIPT AND JSCRIPT

Microsoft Visual InterDev offers two scripting languages for Web page development: VBScript and JScript. Both are secure and safe. Script writers cannot perform any actions that will harm another user's system without using some additional type of application or component.

VBScript is a subset of the Visual Basic programming language. It is stripped down so that you can implement it without a large set of support files and so that it can be secure. VBScript programs run on a Web browser, with the VBScript code itself embedded as part of a Web page. This means that you can unknowingly download and execute VBScript programs as you browse the Web. To make browsing safe, Microsoft has removed everything from Visual Basic that might interact with the computer in any kind of dangerous way.

You can use VBScript to generate a Web page dynamically, and you can use it to validate data on a form before you send it to the server. These features reduce the amount of traffic that has to be sent over the Internet and reduces the load on your Web server. In this sense, VBScript makes Web technology increasingly client-server—part of the load is handled by the Web server and part of it is handled by the browser.

Anatomy of VBScript

VBScript is embedded on a Web page between <SCRIPT> tags, as shown below:

```
<SCRIPT LANGUAGE = VBScript>
<!--
Function Cube(num)
    Cube = num * num * num
End Function
-->
</SCRIPT>
```

These tags mark the beginning and end of a VBScript. The VBScript code itself is also embedded between comment tags if it is sent as part of the HTML stream to the browser. Therefore, if you send your page to a browser that cannot understand VBScript, the code is simply ignored and not displayed. Server-side scripting does not require the comment tags.

Comments

You can place comments within your VBScript code by using either the remark keyword (*REM*) or an apostrophe ('), as follows:

```
REM This is a comment
' This is another comment
```

Variables

A variable is a temporary storage area for data. You can create variables in one of two ways with VBScript. You can declare a variable using a *Dim* statement or you can declare more than one variable in the *Dim* statement by separating the variables with commas, as shown here:

```
Dim age, height, weight
```

You can also implicitly create a variable by referring to it in your code. If the variable has not been created when you first refer to it, it is created at that point in the code. This might seem like a convenient way to create variables, but it is not good programming practice. If you make a habit of not using the *Dim* statement to declare variables, you increase the chance of accidentally creating a new variable by misspelling the name of an existing one.

VBScript's *Option Explicit* command forces you to declare variables using the *Dim* statement. The *Option Explicit* command should be the first command in your VBScript. *Option Explicit* disables implicit variable declaration, so if you use a variable without first declaring it, a Variable Is Undefined error is generated. This message contains the variable name and the line number of the statement that has the undefined variable.

Arrays

A variable that holds a single value is said to be *scalar*. The following example creates the variable *Name*:

```
Dim Name
```

Name can hold any value, but it can hold only one value at a time. Any value you place in *Name* will replace the existing value.

You can also dimension an array variable:

```
Dim  Names(10), Addresses(10,3)
```

In this example, *Names* has space for 11 values, from 0 through 10. All arrays in VBScript are zero-based, so the first element is always 0. The *Addresses* array is two-dimensional; it has 11 * 4 values. (Remember the zero-based arrays in VBScript.) You can dimension an array with up to 60 dimensions, but if you find yourself using more than two or three, you're probably using the array incorrectly. When you multiply the number of elements in each dimension, you get the total number of elements in the array. If you use several dimensions, you'll quickly allocate space for huge numbers of values—more values than you probably need.

You can also declare *dynamic* arrays. In a dynamic array, the size is not determined in the *Dim* statement:

```
Dim Scores()
```

Before you use a dynamic array in code, you must redimension it using the *Redim* statement to hold as many values as you need. This is useful because you might not know how many values your array needs to hold until run time.

```
Redim Scores(NumOfStudents)
```

You can redimension a dynamic array any number of times in your code. If you want to change the size of the array without losing its contents, you must include the *Preserve* keyword:

```
Redim Preserve Scores(NumOfStudents)
```

If you redimension the array to a smaller size, you lose the values beyond the end of your array.

Operators

VBScript includes a range of operators for arithmetic, comparison, concatenation, and logical operations on data. Table 10-1 describes the available operators. For comparison operations on data, you can use combinations of the greater than (>), less than (<), and equals (=) operators.

Operator	Description	Type
+	Addition	Arithmetic
And	Conjunction	Logical
&	String concatenation	Concatenation
/	Division	Arithmetic
Eqv	Equivalence	Logical
^	Exponentiation	Arithmetic
Imp	Implication	Logical
\	Integer division	Arithmetic
Is	Object equivalence	Comparison
Mod	Modulus	Arithmetic
*	Multiplication	Arithmetic
-	Negation	Arithmetic
Not	Negation	Logical
Or	Disjunction	Logical
-	Subtraction	Arithmetic
Xor	Exclusion	Logical

Table 10-1. *VBScript operators.*

Data types

Visual Basic has several data types, but VBScript has only one—Variant. When you dimension a variable using *Dim*, the variable is a Variant. The Variant data type can hold any value that you assign to it, so you don't need to use separate data types for dates, strings, numbers, and so on. When you assign a value to a variable, VBScript stores the type of data in that variable along with its value. You can use the *VarType* function to return the data type in the Variant variable. This can be useful if you need to ensure, for instance, that a user entered a number. The following code snippet shows how to use *VarType* to determine whether a variable is an integer from 0 through 100:

```
<SCRIPT>
Function ValidScore(num)

    Dim IntegerType

    IntegerType = 2
```

(continued)

```
If VarType(num) = IntegerType Then
    If num >= 0 and num <= 100 Then
        ValidScore = True
    Else
        ValidScore = False
    End If
Else
    ValidScore = False
End If

End Function
</SCRIPT>
```

The *VarType* function returns a number that represents the type of data the Variant holds. Table 10-2 shows the value returned by *VarType* for different types of data.

VarType	*Type of Variant*
0	Empty (uninitialized)
1	Null (no valid data)
2	Integer
3	Long integer
4	Single-precision floating-point number
5	Double-precision floating-point number
6	Currency
7	Date
8	String
9	Automation object
10	Error
11	Boolean
12	Variant (used only with arrays of Variants)
13	Data-access object
17	Byte
8192	Array

Table 10-2. *The value of* VarType *for data types.*

Most programming languages support constants, and Visual Basic is no exception. But the VBScript version of Visual Basic has no constants. Even though there is no explicit mechanism for defining constants in VBScript, it is still good programming practice to use a symbol in your code instead of a number. In VBScript, you need to use a variable. In the above example, in which you check the number to see whether it was an acceptable score, the *IntegerType* variable is assigned the value of 2 and uses the variable in the *If...Then* statement. You should use this technique in VBScript where you'd normally use constants in Visual Basic.

Flow control

When a procedure or script starts running, it starts at the beginning and runs through to the end. You can change this flow either by using a decision construct or by looping. In this section, we'll cover some of the basic flow control statements, such as *If...Then...Else*, *For...Next*, and *Do...Loop*. Flow control statements not discussed here include the following:

- **While...Wend**   For executing a series of statements as long as a given condition is True

- **Select Case**   For executing one of several groups of statements, depending on the value of an expression

- **For Each...Next**   For repeating a group of statements for each element in an array or collection

If...Then...Else statement

The decision construct is known as the *If...Then...Else* statement. It lets you test a condition and take one action if the condition is True and take another if the condition is False. It comes in two forms. The first form is the single-line form used for short, simple tests:

```
If condition Then statements [Else elsestatements ]
```

The square brackets surrounding the *Else* block indicate that the *Else* clause is optional.

The second form is the block form, which provides more structure and flexibility than the single-line form and which is usually easier to read, maintain, and debug:

```
If condition Then
    [statements]
[ElseIf condition Then
    [elseifstatements]]
[Else
    [elsestatements]]
End If
```

The condition is a logical statement that evaluates to either True or False. The condition can be a comparison, such as the one shown below, or it can be a function that returns a Boolean value (True or False).

```
If score > 70 Then
```

For example, VBScript has a function called *IsDate* that returns True if the value you pass it is a date, and False otherwise. The function can serve as the condition in your *If...Then...Else* statement:

```
If IsDate(MyVariable) Then
```

It isn't necessary to have an *Else* block in your *If...Then* statement. In fact, you should include an *Else* block only if you need to do two separate tasks— one if the condition is True, and one if it is False. The following code snippet is a complete *If...Then...Else* statement:

```
If IsDate(MyVariable) Then
    ' Report back that the variable is a good date
Else
    ' Report back that we still need a date
End If
```

If you need to take action only when the condition is True, do not include the *Else* block:

```
If username = "Eric" Then
    ' Write a welcome statement for Mr. Vincent
End If
```

It is bad practice not to include any code in the *If...Then* block and then to include code in the *Else* block:

```
If Grade >= 70 Then
Else
    ' Write a message saying they failed!
End If
```

If you find yourself writing code like the previous *If...Then...Else* statement, you need to invert the condition so that you have an *If* block without an *Else* block. The above code uses a poor technique and makes for hard-to-read code. Here is the corrected code:

```
If Grade < 70 Then
    ' Write a message saying they failed!
End If
```

In addition to using *If...Then...Else* statements to control program flow, you can use looping constructs. A loop is a section of code that executes more than once.

For...Next statement

Use the *For...Next* loop when you want to execute a block of code a fixed number of times. The syntax for the *For...Next* loop is as follows:

```
For counter = start To end [Step step]
    [statements]
    [Exit For]
    [statements]
Next
```

It uses a variable you supply as a counter to count the number of times through the loop.

You specify the counter's starting and ending values, as shown below:

```
For MyCounter = 1 To 5
    Sum = Sum + Counter
Next
```

The counter is incremented by one each time the loop gets to the *Next* keyword.

To increment or decrement the counter by a different value, you can use the *Step* keyword:

```
For MyCounter = 5 To 1 Step -1
    DisplayCountdown(MyCounter)
Next
```

Do...Loop statement

For...Next loops are useful if you know how many times you need to execute a block of code. However, in some situations you won't know how many times the loop needs to be executed.

Using the *While* keyword, the *Do* loop executes a block of code while a condition is True. Here's the complete syntax:

```
Do [{While | Until} condition]
    [statements]
    [Exit Do]
    [statements]
Loop
```

The following code executes the loop as long as the *MoreData* function returns True:

```
Do While MoreData(variable)
    ProcessData
Loop
```

You can use the *While* keyword either at the beginning or the end of the loop. If you place the keyword and the condition at the beginning of the loop, the condition is checked before the first time through the loop. If the *While* condition is False when it is first evaluated, the contents of the loop never execute.

If you put the *While* keyword at the end of the loop, the condition is not evaluated until after the first time through the loop. In this case, your code is executed at least once. Here's the complete syntax:

```
Do
    [statements]
    [Exit Do]
    [statements]
Loop [{While | Until} condition]
```

And here's an example:

```
Do
    AskUserForAnswer(answer)
Loop While DontHaveAnswer(answer)
```

The *AskUserForAnswer* subroutine executes at least once, and it continues to execute as long as the *DontHaveAnswer* function returns True. The type of loop you use will depend on the problem you're trying to solve; neither one is more correct than the other. The first example requires that you check to see if there's any data to process; if there is, you can try to process the data and then continue to process it as long as there is more data to process. In the second example, you have to ask the user for the answer at least once and continue to ask for the answer only as long as you don't have an acceptable answer.

You can also use the *Do* loop with the *Until* keyword. With this keyword, the loop executes as long as the condition is *not* True. *Until* is the inverse of *While*. You can also use the *Until* keyword at the beginning or end of the loop just as you can with the *While* keyword. This gives you the same flexibility over the loop block's first execution:

```
Do
    AskUserForAnswer(answer)
Loop Until HaveAnswer(answer)
```

Procedures

Procedures are the building blocks of VBScript programs. A procedure is a named block of code that is grouped together to perform a job. VBScript has two types of procedures: functions and subroutines. A function can return a value, and a subroutine performs its task without returning a value.

You declare a subroutine by enclosing the block of code that it comprises between the *Sub* and *End Sub* keywords. The declaration itself must be enclosed in <SCRIPT> tags. Procedure declarations must come before the procedure is used, so it's good practice to declare your procedures in the Head section of the HTML page. In this way, all of your subroutines and functions are defined before they are used, and all the definitions are located in the same place on the page. In addition to enclosing procedure declarations in <SCRIPT> tags, they should also be within HTML comment tags so that the code is not displayed in a browser that doesn't understand VBScript.

Here's the formal syntax for declaring a subroutine:

```
[Public | Private] Sub name [(arglist)]
    [statements]
    [Exit Sub]
    [statements]
End Sub
```

Here's an example that shows the use of the <SCRIPT> tags and HTML comment tags:

```
<SCRIPT LANGUAGE=VBScript>
<!--
Sub Warning
    MsgBox "Hey, this is dangerous!"
End Sub
-->
</SCRIPT>
```

MsgBox is a VBScript function that displays a dialog box with the message you specify. *MsgBox* can also display buttons and icons. For more information on *MsgBox*, see the VBScript Language Reference for the *MsgBox* function in Visual InterDev's online Help. You can use *MsgBox* only in client-side script.

You can also declare a procedure with arguments. An argument is a variable that your procedure expects as input. You can have any number of arguments. When a procedure is used, it expects values to be passed in as arguments. Since VBScript has only Variant types of variables, you cannot specify what kind of data you want the procedure to use. You have two options: make sure you pass the right type of data to the procedure, or write code in the procedure to verify the data types before the data is used. One common error is a *type mismatch*. This occurs when you try to use data of one type (such as a string) as data of another type (such as a date). VBScript is considered a weakly typed language because it doesn't do a lot of type checking automatically. The following is an example of a procedure with arguments:

```
<SCRIPT LANGUAGE=VBScript>
<!--
Sub DisplayMessage(Message, HowManyTimes)
    Dim Count

    For Count = 1 to HowManyTimes
        MsgBox Message
    Next
End Sub
-->
</SCRIPT>
```

You declare functions in much the same way that you declare subroutines, except you use *Function* and *End Function* keywords. Functions return values; you return a value by assigning a value to the function name as if it were a variable within the function.

Here's the formal syntax for declaring a function:

```
[Public | Private] Function name [(arglist)]
    [statements]
    [name = expression]
    [Exit Function]
    [statements]
    [name = expression]
End Function
```

Here's a function that takes a number and raises it to the third power using the exponentiation operator (^):

```
<SCRIPT LANGUAGE=VBScript>
<!--
Function Cube(number)
    Cube = number ^ 3
End Function
-->
</SCRIPT>
```

Using a function or a subroutine

Once the procedure is declared, you can use it by referring to it in VBScript code. Since a subroutine does not return any values—you simply name it in code and pass it values (separated by commas) for any arguments it might have.

```
' Call the DisplayMessage subroutine
DisplayMessage "Hello there", 3
```

Functions return a value, so you should be ready to use the value being returned. You can use the function name as if it were a variable and use it in an expression:

```
' Use the Cube function to calculate a new variable
Dim Num1, Num2

Num1 = 10
Num2 = Cube(Num1)
```

You can also design a function that returns either True or False, and then use the function as a condition in a *Do* loop or an *If...Then* statement. The functions *HaveAnswer* and *DontHaveAnswer* from earlier in the chapter are examples of functions that return Boolean values.

Built-in VBScript functions

VBScript makes many intrinsic functions available. See Visual InterDev's online Help for more information on all of them, including math functions such as sine and cosine. You can derive the trigonometric functions not supplied in VBScript from the mathematical functions that are available.

VBScript comes with a set of functions that help you determine the type of data stored in a variable. Table 10-3 describes these functions.

Function	*Description*
IsArray	True if variable is an array of values
IsDate	True if variable is a date value
IsEmpty	True if variable has been initialized
IsNull	True if variable is the Null value
IsNumeric	True if variable is recognized as a number
IsObject	True if variable refers to an Automation object

Table 10-3. *VBScript functions.*

Objects

VBScript includes several Automation objects that can be accessed via scripting. The objects are as follows:

- *Dictionary*
- *Err*

- *FileSystemObject*

- *TextStream*

Using VBScript with ASP

When using VBScript on the server with ASP, two VBScript features are disabled:

- Statements that present UI elements, such as *InputBox* and *MsgBox*

- The VBScript function *GetObject*

Use of these statements will cause an error.

When you use *CreateObject*, you are actually using the default method of the *Server* object. *CreateObject* lets you integrate ActiveX Server components within your Web application.

All ASP script processing is performed on the server side. There is no need to include HTML comment tags to hide the scripts from browsers that do not support scripting, as is often done with client-side scripts. All ASP commands are processed before content is sent to the browser and stripped out of the document before the document is sent to the browser.

VBScript supports basic *REM* and apostrophe style comments. Unlike HTML comments, these are removed when the script is processed. They are not sent to the client.

Anatomy of JScript

While VBScript is a powerful client-side and server-side scripting language, other scripting languages are also available to Visual InterDev developers. JScript is Microsoft's implementation of the ECMAScript language, which is the Web's only standard scripting language. While you might think that JScript is a derivative of Java, it is actually an independently conceived, object-based programming language. JScript has similarities to Java, as well as to C++. Developers comfortable with these programming languages will find many of JScript's constructs familiar.

JScript code is embedded in the HTML or ASP Web page with the <SCRIPT> tag. Use the Language attribute to specify that the script block is JScript, as opposed to VBScript, like this,

```
<SCRIPT LANGUAGE=JAVASCRIPT>
//
// JScript code
//
</SCRIPT>
```

or like this,

```
<SCRIPT LANGUAGE=JSCRIPT>
//
// JScript code
//
</SCRIPT>
```

Statements and comments

A statement in JScript consists of a line of code, much like VBScript. Although a new line indicates a new statement, you can also end a statement with a semicolon. This construct is testimony to JScript's heritage in Java and C++, and it is optional. Unlike the following example, however, it is good programming practice either to use the semicolon statement delimiter throughout all code or not to use it at all.

```
// These are all legal JScript statements
energy = mass * (Speed_of_light * Speed_of_light);
paycheck = rate * hour
sum = num1 + num2;
```

JScript supports a block construct that is defined by a series of statements delimited by curly braces. You use blocks of statements to define functions, as well as in conditional and other flow control operations.

Comments in JScript also follow Java and C++ convention. Two forward slashes (//) begin a comment when all characters after it on the current line are to be ignored. For multiple-line comments, you can use the /* and */ characters to delimit the comment block.

Variables

You do not have to declare variables in JScript, but it is good programming practice to do so using the *var* statement. JScript variables are case-sensitive, so the following two variables (*MyName* and *myName*) are different, even though they have the same name:

```
var MyName

MyName = "Eric"
window.document.write(myName)
```

Inspection of this code reveals a flaw. Assuming that *window.document .write* is a method that sends its arguments to the HTML stream, what does this code segment print? Nothing! *MyName* is a different variable from *myName*. Because JScript does not *require* that new variables be declared, when it sees *myName* it assumes that a new, empty variable should be created, which is probably not the author's intention. Developers familiar with case-insensitive languages should beware—mistakes in case are a leading cause of troublesome bugs that are difficult to spot when you browse over source code. Good discipline in coding techniques is more important than ever in this situation.

Operators

JScript includes a range of operators for arithmetic, assignment, bitwise, and logical operations on data. Table 10-4 summarizes the available operators.

Operator	Description	Type
-	Unary negation	Arithmetic
++	Increment	Arithmetic
- -	Decrement	Arithmetic
*	Multiplication	Arithmetic
/	Division	Arithmetic
%	Modulus	Arithmetic
+	Addition	Arithmetic
-	Subtraction	Arithmetic
!	Not	Logical
==	Equality	Logical
!=	Inequality	Logical
&&	And	Logical
||	Or	Logical
?:	Conditional	Logical
,	Comma	Logical
~	Not	Bitwise
<<	Shift left	Bitwise
>>	Shift right	Bitwise
>>>	Unsigned shift right	Bitwise
&	And	Bitwise
^	Xor	Bitwise
|	Or	Bitwise
=	Assignment	Assignment

Table 10-4. *JScript operators.*

As with VBScript, you can use combinations of the greater than (>), less than (<), and equals (=) operators for comparison operations on data.

Data types

The basic data types in JScript are numbers, strings, and Booleans. The other data types are functions, methods, arrays, and objects.

Numbers can be either integer or floating point and can be represented in decimal (base 10), octal (base 8), and hexadecimal (base 16) notations. Octal and hexadecimal representations cannot, however, represent the decimal part of a number. Here are a few examples:

```
128.83    // Base 10 representation of a float
221       // Base 10 integer
0xFF92    // Hex notation. Note the leading "0x"
02265     // Octal notation. Note the leading zero
```

JScript's Boolean variables are the familiar True and False. However, unlike in some other programming languages, True and False are not equal to 1 and 0; each is an actual, separate data type.

Arrays and objects

You handle arrays and objects almost identically in JScript. At times, it seems that there is no difference between them. An object is an entity that has properties and methods. A property can be a simple data type or another object. A method is a function that belongs to the object.

For example, JScript has a built-in object called *Math*. *Math* has, among others, the properties *LN10* and *PI*. This means that *Math* can supply the values for the natural logarithm of 10 and pi.

```
var x
var y

x = Math.PI;
y = Math.LN10;
```

The *Math* object also has methods, such as *max* and *round*. The *max* method returns the larger of two numbers, and the *round* method returns a number rounded to the nearest integer.

```
var num1
var num2
var biggest
var my_integer

...
biggest = Math.max(num1, num2);
my_integer = Math.round(12.84521);
```

JScript also provides other intrinsic (built-in) objects, such as *Date*, *String*, and *Array*.

Strings

You can delimit a string literal in JScript using either single or double quotes. This is handy if you need to represent a single or double quote as part of the string. For instance, to represent the text "JScript's string literals," you can use the following string literal:

```
"JScript's string literals"
```

But to represent the following text,

The cop said "STOP," so he did.

you can use single quotes:

```
'The cop said "STOP," so he did.'
```

String variables in JScript are actually objects. Although you can implicitly create them by assigning a variable name to a string literal, string variables also have methods that make them a powerful and intuitive string manipulation tool:

```
myName = "Eric F. Vincent";    // Implicitly creates string
myName.toUpperCase();          // Value is now 'ERIC F. VINCENT'
```

Flow control

JScript uses similar constructs to control the flow of a script, as does VBScript and most other popular languages. The *if* construct is the primary decision-making mechanism. *for* and *while* implement loops. For the most part, the difference is in the syntax.

if...else statement

The JScript syntax for the *if...else* statement is as follows:

```
if (condition)
{
    // block of code
}
[else
{
    // block of code
}]
```

In this example, *condition* is a Boolean expression that evaluates to either True or False. The square brackets surrounding the *else* block indicate that the *else* clause is optional, like the *Else* clause in VBScript. JScript uses curly braces to indicate a block of code.

Curly braces are unnecessary if the block has only one statement:

```
if (current < top)
{
    next = next + 1;
    TakeAction(current);
}
else
    Finalize(current);
```

In this example, the two statements following the *if* statement are grouped together. When the condition is True, both statements are executed because the *if* statement considers the statements in a block of code to be a unit.

The *else* clause has no block of code; it has only one statement. When the condition is False, the one statement is executed and program flow continues. There is no need for an *End If* construct because the curly braces delimit blocks of code.

for statement

Again, the concept of the *for* statement is similar to the *For* loop in VBScript but is implemented a little bit differently. JScript's syntax for a *for* loop is

```
for (initializer ; condition ; increment )
{
    // block of code
}
```

The loop has three parts: The first is the *initializer*, a statement that is executed only once before the first time through the loop. You typically use it to initialize a variable that will count as the loop progresses. The second is the *condition*, a Boolean expression that evaluates to True or False. The condition is evaluated before the first time through the loop, and again each time through the loop until it returns False. The condition typically tests a counter to see if it has reached a certain number. The block of code won't execute if the condition is False the first time through the loop. The third part—the *increment*—is a statement that is executed at the end of each loop. You typically use it to increment a counter by one each time through the loop. When you use these three parts together, they can behave the same as the *For...Next* loop in VBScript.

The following is a *for* loop in which *x* varies from 1 through 10 in increments of one. Each time though the loop, *x* is added to a variable called *total*. This example introduces two new operators. The first is used in the increment part of the loop.

```
for (x = 1; x <= 10; x++)
    total += x;
```

The increment operator, x++, is the third part of the loop. It adds one to its operand (in this case, *x*). There is also a decrement operator (--) that subtracts one from its operand, as well as a compound assignment.

The compound assignment operator is little more than a shortcut. The statement

```
total += x;
```

is equivalent to

```
total = total + x;
```

while statement

The *while* statement is also straightforward:

```
while (condition)
{
    // block of code
}
```

Again, the condition is a Boolean expression, and the block of code can be either several lines of code surrounded by curly braces or a single line of code. The condition is checked before the first time through the loop, so if it starts off as False, the block or statement never executes.

```
while (theTime == right)
{
    DisplayAds();
    Feed(theHungry);
}
```

INCLUDING OTHER FILES: THE SERVER-SIDE INCLUDE

One of the handiest features of ASP is the server-side include. This feature lets you dynamically include arbitrary files within an ASP Web page at run time. This feature is extremely useful for creating global functions, headers, footers, or other elements that need to be reused on multiple pages. If you need to change these functions or HTML fragments, you can do so once and the change will be automatically reflected in all pages that reference the file using a server-side include. One trade-off associated with server-side includes is that they add a small amount of overhead to the server-side processing because the Web server has to find the file to be included and merge it into the ASP Web page. Note that include files can be used from regular HTML pages as well as ASP Web pages.

The *#INCLUDE* directive inserts the content of another file into an .asp file before ASP processes it, as shown in the following syntax:

```
<!--#INCLUDE VIRTUAL|FILE="filename"-->
```

Included files do not need a special filename extension; however, we recommend giving included files an .inc filename extension to distinguish them from other types of files.

Use the *VIRTUAL* keyword to indicate a path beginning with a virtual directory. For information on using virtual directories, see the Microsoft Web server's online documentation. For instance, if a file named footer.inc resides in a virtual directory named /Myapp, the following line inserts the contents of footer.inc into the file containing the line:

```
<!--#INCLUDE VIRTUAL="/myapp/footer.inc"-->
```

The *FILE* keyword indicates a relative path. A relative path begins with the directory that contains the including file. For instance, if the file is in the same directory as Myapp and the file header1.inc is in Myapp/Headers, the following line inserts header1.inc in your file:

```
<!--#INCLUDE FILE="headers/header1.inc"-->
```

The *FILE* parameter with the ../ syntax is used to include a file from a parent directory. Script commands and procedures must be contained within the script delimiters <% and %>, the HTML tags <SCRIPT> and </SCRIPT>, or the HTML tags <OBJECT> and </OBJECT>. That is, a user cannot open a script delimiter in an including .asp file and then close the delimiter in an included file. The script or script command must be a complete unit.

The Include design-time control (DTC) is the most convenient way to add a server-side include to your project. (The Include DTC that ships with Visual InterDev 6 is the same Include DTC that shipped with Visual InterDev 1.) You can add the Include DTC to your Toolbox and use it to include files into a page. This DTC lets you choose from a graphical, tree view of all the elements in your Web site, and it automatically generates the appropriate include syntax.

USER-DEFINED PROCEDURES AND FUNCTIONS

As you saw earlier in this chapter, a procedure is a group of script commands that performs a specific task. Specific procedures can be defined and called repeatedly in the scripts. Procedure definitions can appear within <SCRIPT> and

</SCRIPT> tags and must follow the rules for the declared scripting language. You can define a procedure within the scripting delimiters <% and %> as long as the procedure is in the same scripting language as the primary script.

You can place procedure definitions in the same .asp file that calls the procedures. You can place commonly used procedures in a shared .asp file and use them with the server-side include statement <!--#INCLUDE FILE= ...--> to include the statement in other .asp files that call the procedures.

Calling Procedures

To call a procedure, include the name of the procedure in a command. For VBScript, use the *Call* keyword when calling a procedure, or just use the name of the procedure. The several methods that follow address conditions for calling a procedure:

- If the procedure that is called requires any arguments, you must enclose the argument list in parentheses.

- If you omit the *Call* keyword, you must also omit the parentheses around the argument list.

- If you use the *Call* syntax to call any built-in or user-defined function, the function's return value is discarded.

- If JScript procedures are called from VBScript, you must use parentheses after the procedure name.

- If a JScript procedure has no arguments, use empty parentheses.

You can call procedures by simply using the procedure name inside a script block. For example, to call a procedure named *PrintDate*, simply code the following:

```
PrintDate
```

You can use the following syntax to call the same procedure inside HTML:

```
<% PrintDate %>
```

To continue the example, the proper syntax for passing parameters when you call a procedure is

```
PrintFact "IBM"
```

Functions are a special type of procedure that return a value. You can call functions using this type of syntax:

```
OrderedQuantity = CalculateOrders("All")
```

The following example illustrates creating and calling procedures using two different scripting languages, VBScript and JScript.

```
<HTML>
<BODY>
<TABLE>
<% Call Echo %>
</TABLE>
<% Call PrintDate %>
</BODY>
</HTML>
<SCRIPT LANGUAGE=VBScript RUNAT=Server>
Sub Echo
    Response.Write _
        "<TR><TD>Name</TD><TD>Value</TD></TR>"
    Set Params = Request.QueryString
    For Each p in Params
        Response.Write "<TR><TD>" & p & "</TD><TD>" & _
            Params(p) & "</TD></TR>"
    Next
End Sub
</SCRIPT>
<SCRIPT LANGUAGE=JavaScript RUNAT=Server>
function PrintDate()
{
    var x
    x = new Date()
    Response.Write(x.toString())
}
</SCRIPT>
```

To pass an entire array to a procedure in VBScript, use the array name followed by empty parentheses. In JScript, enclose the array name in square brackets.

SERVER OBJECTS

The ASP framework provides objects (and associated methods, events, and properties) that give information about the Web server and its environment, make processing forms easy and manageable, and provide a flexible system of data storage. You can roll all these abilities into a well-rounded, robust Web application that is easy to develop and maintain and is more extensible than you might have thought possible.

The five built-in objects in the ASP framework are as follows:

- *Application*
- *Request*
- *Response*
- *Server*
- *Session*

These objects are an essential part of the ASP framework, and as such they occur frequently in Visual InterDev development and throughout this book. In the following sections we'll cover the basics of these objects with particular focus on the *Request* and *Response* objects.

Throughout the discussion you'll find that these objects have typical object-oriented features of methods, events, and properties. When a group of related properties for an object can be classified as a single unit, they are termed a *collection*. The *Application*, *Response*, and *Request* objects have collections, whereas the other objects have properties.

The *Application* Object

The *Application* object can be used to share information among all users of your application. The application is defined as all the .asp files within the virtual directory and its subdirectories.

The *Application* object has two methods named *Lock* and *Unlock*. Since the data is shared among users, these methods allow you to effectively lock and unlock access to the application object while you apply changes to its variables.

The events that relate to the *Application* object are *Application_OnStart* and *Application_OnEnd*. These events are declared in the global.asa file, which is part of a Visual InterDev Web project.

The syntax for setting a variable within the *Application* object is as follows:

```
Application("variable_name") = value
```

You can then reference the value of the variable as follows:

```
MyVariable = Application("variable_name")
```

The *Application* object also has two collections named *Contents* and *StaticObjects*. The *Contents* collection contains all of the variables that you've set within the *Application* object. The *StaticObjects* collection contains all of the application-level objects that have been declared with the <OBJECT> tag.

The *Response* Object

The *Response* object is used to send information to the browser. It has collections, properties, and methods. In fact, the only collection it has is the *Cookies* collection, which can be used to set cookie values. This is the opposite of the *Cookies* collection in the *Request* object, which is used to read cookie values. (We'll discuss cookies later in this chapter.) The *Response* object has several properties and methods that are fully detailed in Appendix E. In this section, we'll just take at look at some of the more common properties and methods such as the *Buffer*, *Expires*, and *ExpiresAbsolute* properties and the *Clear*, *End*, *Flush*, *Redirect*, and *Write* methods.

The most common application of the *Response* object is to send string output for display in the browser. This can be done by simply using an equal sign (=) in front of the information to be sent or by using the *Response.Write* syntax, as you'll see in the following examples.

In the first example, variables and values have been inserted into the HTML stream by starting the VBScript line with an equal sign:

```
MyName = "Ken Spencer"
= "Hello, my name is " & MyName
```

The preceding syntax sends the following string to the browser:

```
Hello, my name is Ken Spencer
```

If you are familiar with Visual Basic, you might find this syntax a bit strange. It is unusual to start a line with an equal sign—it's an exception to the otherwise simple rules about how to use equal signs in Visual Basic. However, it isn't quite as strange as it seems. In the above example, starting the line with an equal sign is shorthand for

```
MyName = "Ken Spencer"
Response.Write("Hello, my name is" & MyName)
```

The above code uses the *Response* object and a method named *Write*. The *Write* method takes a string as an argument and writes it to the HTML stream, effectively writing it to the browser. That is exactly what is happening, and it makes perfect sense in the context of Visual Basic syntax. Because you often type *Response.Write*, VBScript just made it a little easier for you.

The *Response* object sends output to the client. You will most often use the *Write* method and its associated "equal sign first" shorthand, but it's important to remember that the *Response* object has additional methods and properties as well.

Controlling the *Response* object's properties

The *Response* object has a set of properties that you can use to adjust how ASP sends output to browsers. When the *Buffer* property is set to True, IIS collects or buffers all output destined for the browser. It holds on to it until all the server script code on the page finishes processing, at which time all the HTML is sent at once. This is useful because you might have code in your ASP that cancels output to the browser or that redirects the browser to a different page. Having IIS buffer the output to the browser saves time in these situations. If HTML were sent to the browser while your script is executing and you come to a point where you want to jump to another page, all the time it took to send the HTML across the Internet to that point would be wasted.

After you decide to set buffering on the *Response* object to True, you can use the *Redirect* and *End* methods. *Redirect* lets you send a command to the browser that causes it to connect to a different URL. A good use of this is to direct users to a certain page on your Web site based on their input on a form, as shown in the following syntax:

```
<%
If Request.Form("age") > 21 Then
    Response.Redirect "http://www.mysite.com/GrownUps.asp"
Else
    Response.Redirect "http://www.mysite.com/Children.asp"
End If
%>
```

The *End* method does just what it says. When you reach a *Response.End* statement in your script, script processing stops and whatever is in the buffer is sent to the browser. If you want to end the script and not send the output to the browser, you must first use the *Clear* method of the *Response* object to clear the buffer and then use the *End* method to end the script:

```
<%
If Request.Form("Attitude") = "bad" Then
    ' If the user has a bad attitude, then
    ' stop processing the script and clear
    ' the output that has been buffered to this point
    Response.Clear
    Response.End
End If
%>
```

When a page is sent to the browser, the page is usually cached on that machine so that the browser doesn't have to download the page the next time it's visited. Using the *Expires* property of the *Response* object, you can control how long a page is valid in the cache. If the user revisits the page in less than the number of minutes you set in the *Expires* property, the cached version is used; otherwise, a new version is downloaded.

```
<%
' This page is good only for one hour. After that,
' be sure to reload this page
Response.Expires = 60
%>
```

Sometimes you want to let a page be cached until a certain date or time. The *ExpiresAbsolute* property takes a date or a time value, at which time the cached version of the page expires.

```
<%
' Cache this page until the fourth of July, 2:00pm
Response.ExpiresAbsolute = #July 4, 1999 14:00#
%>
```

The date that *ExpiresAbsolute* takes is a standard VBScript date and/or time (hence the pound signs). You must have the correct time zone information set on your server because the time is converted to Greenwich Mean Time (GMT) before it is sent to the browser, ensuring that the time is accurate regardless of the client's location.

Saving data with cookies

A cookie is a variable that you store on the user's machine so that it's available the next time the user logs onto your application. This is often advantageous. Cookies are a great way to maintain application information and preferences that are specific to a particular user. An example of this is the customizable Web site. Some Web sites let you set preferences according to your tastes. The Microsoft Network (MSN) has a home page that lets you set your favorite sites, the types of information you're interested in, and so forth. The site saves a cookie on your machine and then retrieves this cookie each time you hit the MSN site. MSN then has a way of knowing who you are, that you've visited the site before, and what your preferences are.

The user is usually unaware that cookies are in use, and cookies have no adverse effect on the user's machine. In fact, hundreds of Web sites already use cookies, and most people who spend time browsing the Web have cookies stored on their machines. However, some browsers can be set to notify users that a cookie is being sent so the user can cancel cookie reception.

To get cookies from the user, you use the *Cookies* collection in the *Request* object. Conversely, the *Response* object's *Cookies* collection allows you to set the cookie's properties. If the cookie does not exist, it is created. If it already exists, it takes the new value that is assigned to it.

Here is the syntax for setting a cookie using the *Response* object:

```
Response.Cookies(cookie)[(key)|.attribute] = value
```

The *attribute* parameter specifies information about the cookie, such as its expiration date and whether it is secure. A secure cookie is encrypted when it is stored on the user's machine. Table 10-5 lists the available cookie attributes:

Cookie Attribute	Description
Expires	Write-only. The date on which the cookie expires.
Domain	Write-only. If specified, the cookie is sent only to requests to this domain.
Path	Write-only. If specified, the cookie is sent only to requests to this path.
Secure	Write-only. Specifies whether the cookie is secure.
HasKeys	Read-only. Specifies whether the cookie contains keys.

Table 10-5. *Cookie attributes.*

You can create two types of cookie. The first is a single-value cookie: one cookie, one value. For example, you can write a single value to the cookie *Username* using the following code:

```
<%
' Simple cookie named Username, with
' only one value, "Smith"
Response.Cookies("Username") = "Smith"
%>
```

You can also specify a key when assigning the value. This creates the second type of cookie—a dictionary. A dictionary is a cookie with an array of keys in which each key has a unique value. The following code writes multiple values to the dictionary *CarAttributes*:

```
<%
' Cookie Dictionary called CarAttributes, with keys
' named "color", "style", and "brand"
Response.Cookies("CarAttributes")("color") = "Red"
Response.Cookies("CarAttributes")("style") = "Sports"
Response.Cookies("CarAttributes")("brand") = "ACME"
%>
```

As mentioned earlier, if a cookie exists, the value is discarded when you assign a new value. If you assign a value to a cookie dictionary, you lose all the keys in that dictionary. If you assign a key value to a simple one-value cookie, you lose the cookie value. It is important to know what type of cookie you're using before you set its value. Often you'll know the type because you set the value of the cookie in the same application. But if you're not sure of the type, you can check the *HasKeys* attribute. The *HasKeys* attribute is True for a dictionary and False for a single-value cookie.

The *Request* Object

One of the ways information can be passed from a browser to the server is via an HTTP request. The *Request* object retrieves information sent via an HTTP request from the browser. Five types of variables can be passed to your application through the *Request* object. Each type has its own collection in the *Request* object. They are:

- **QueryString** The values of variables in the HTTP query string

- **Form** The values of form elements in the HTTP request body

- **Cookies** The values of cookies sent in the HTTP request

- **ServerVariables** The values of predetermined environment variables

- **ClientCertificate** The values of fields stored in the client certificate that is sent in the HTTP request

You can access variables by referring to the *Request* object, then the collection, and then the particular variable you're trying to access. When retrieving a variable, naming the collection is optional. If you don't include the collection, all the collections are searched for the variable that you're looking for, in the above order. The syntax is:

```
Request[.Collection](variable)
```

It's good practice to use the name of the collection even when it's optional. There is less chance for confusion when someone else reads your code or when you return to the code after not visiting it for a long time.

QueryString and Form

The *QueryString* and *Form* collections of the *Request* object allow you to access the values of variables in the HTTP query string and the values of form elements in the HTTP request body, respectively.

Reading data from cookies

Cookies are written to the client machine using the *Response* object. The *Cookies* collection of the *Request* object lets you retrieve the cookies from the client machine. The syntax for using the *Cookies* collection is:

```
Request.Cookies(cookie)[(key)|.attribute]
```

As the syntax implies, each cookie can be an array, or more appropriately, a collection of values. Each value has a name called a key.

ServerVariables

This collection consists of several predefined server environment variables that can prove handy in your ASP code. You generally use this collection to read information about the server or the user's browser. The variables shown in Table 10-6 are read-only.

HTTP Variable	Description
ALL_HTTP	All HTTP headers sent by the client.
ALL_RAW	Retrieves all headers in the raw form. The difference between *ALL_RAW* and *ALL_HTTP* is that *ALL_HTTP* places an HTTP_ prefix before the header name and the header name is always capitalized. In *ALL_RAW*, the header name and values appear as the client sets them.
APPL_MD_PATH	Retrieves the metabase path of the Web Application Manager (WAM) for the ISAPI DLL.
APPL_PHYSICAL_ PATH	Retrieves the physical path corresponding to the metabase path. IIS converts the *APPL_MD_PATH* to the physical (directory) path to return this value.
AUTH_ PASSWORD	The value entered in the client's authentication dialog box. This variable is only available if Basic authentication is used.

Table 10-6. *Server environment variables.*   *(continued)*

HTTP Variable	Description
AUTH_TYPE	The authentication method the server uses to validate users when they try to access a protected script.
AUTH_USER	Raw authenticated user name.
CERT_COOKIE	Unique ID for client certificate, returned as a string. Can be used as a signature for the whole client certificate.
CERT_FLAGS	bit0 is set to 1 if the client certificate is present.
	bit1 is set to 1 if the Certifying Authority of the client certificate is invalid (not in the list of recognized CA on the server).
CERT_ISSUER	Issuer field of the client certificate (O=MS, OU=IAS, CN=user name, C=USA).
CERT_KEYSIZE	Number of bits in Secure Sockets Layer connection key size. For example, 128.
CERT_SECRETKEYSIZE	Number of bits in server certificate private key. For example, 1024.
CERT_SERIALNUMBER	Serial number field of the client certificate.
CERT_SERVER_ISSUER	Issuer field of the server certificate.
CERT_SERVER_SUBJECT	Subject field of the server certificate.
CERT_SUBJECT	Subject field of the client certificate.
CONTENT_LENGTH	The length of the content as given by the client.
CONTENT_TYPE	The data type of the content. Used with queries that have attached information, such as HTTP POST and PUT.
GATEWAY_INTERFACE	The revision of the CGI specification used by the server. Format: CGI/revision.
HTTP_<HeaderName>	The value stored in the header HeaderName. Any header other than those listed in this table must be prefixed by HTTP_ in order for Request.ServerVariables to retrieve its value.
HTTPS	Returns ON if the request came in through secure channel (SSL) or it returns OFF if the request is for a nonsecure channel.

(continued)

Table 10-6 *continued*

HTTP Variable	Description
HTTPS_KEYSIZE	Number of bits in Secure Sockets Layer connection key size. For example, 128.
HTTPS_SECRETKEYSIZE	Number of bits in server certificate private key. For example, 1024.
HTTPS_SERVER_ISSUER	Issuer field of the server certificate.
HTTPS_SERVER_SUBJECT	Subject field of the server certificate.
INSTANCE_ID	The ID for the IIS instance in textual format. If the instance ID is 1, it appears as a string. You can use this variable to retrieve the ID of the Web-server instance (in the metabase) to which the request belongs.
INSTANCE_META_PATH	The metabase path for the instance of IIS that responds to the request.
LOCAL_ADDR	Returns the Server Address on which the request came in. This is important on multihomed machines where there can be multiple IP addresses bound to a machine and you want to find out which address the request used.
LOGON_USER	The Windows NT account that the user is logged into.
PATH_INFO	Extra path information as given by the client. You can access scripts by using their virtual path and the *PATH_INFO* server variable. If this information comes from a URL, the server decodes it before passing it to the CGI script.
PATH_TRANSLATED	A translated version of *PATH_INFO* that takes the path and performs any necessary virtual-to-physical mapping.
QUERY_STRING	Query information stored in the string following the question mark in the HTTP request.
REMOTE_ADDR	The IP address of the remote host making the request.
REMOTE_HOST	The name of the host making the request. If the server does not have this information, it sets *REMOTE_ADDR* and leaves this empty.

HTTP Variable	Description
REMOTE_USER	Unmapped user-name string sent in by the user. This is the name that is really sent by the user as opposed to the ones that are modified by any authentication filter installed on the server.
REQUEST_METHOD	The method used to make the request. For HTTP, this is GET, HEAD, POST, and so on.
SCRIPT_NAME	A virtual path to the script being executed. This is used for self-referencing URLs.
SERVER_NAME	The server's host name, DNS alias, or IP address as it would appear in a self-referencing URL.
SERVER_PORT	The port number to which the request was sent.
SERVER_PORT_SECURE	A string that contains either 0 or 1. If the request is being handled on the secure port, this is 1; otherwise, it is 0.
SERVER_PROTOCOL	The name and revision of the request information protocol. Format: protocol/revision.
SERVER_SOFTWARE	The name and version of the server software answering the request (and running the gateway). Format: name/version.
URL	Gives the base portion of the URL.

The following code loops through the entire collection of variables and outputs them into an HTML table:

```
<TABLE>
    <TR>
        <TD><B>Server Variable</B></TD>
        <TD><B>Value</B></TD>
    </TR>
<% For Each name In Request.ServerVariables %>
    <TR>
        <TD><%= name %> </TD>
        <TD><%= Request.ServerVariables(name) %> </TD>
    </TR>
<% Next %>
</TABLE>
```

This code is similar to the code in the ASP documentation, except the </TABLE> tag has been moved after the *Next* statement so the code works correctly. This code demonstrates how you can walk through a collection using *For Each* and provides a good example of how to retrieve all the server variables.

ClientCertificate

If the Web browser is using Secure Sockets Layer (SSL) to connect to your Web server and the server requests certification, a series of client certificate objects in this collection will contain information about the client's certification. You can tell when an SSL connection is being used because the address in the browser begins with *https://* instead of *http://*.

The syntax for retrieving these certificates is

```
Request.ClientCertificate( Key[Subfield] )
```

Table 10-7 lists the possible key values, along with their uses.

Key	*Use*
Subject	A list of values that contain information about the subject of the certificate. Subfields are used with this key to extract the individual values from the list.
Issuer	A list of values that contain information about the issuer of the certificate. Subfields are used with this key to extract the individual values from the list.
ValidFrom	A valid date that indicates when the certificate becomes active.
ValidUntil	A valid date that indicates when the certificate expires.
SerialNumber	A string that represents the serial number. This string is a series of hexadecimal bytes separated by hyphens.
Certificate	The entire certificate (all the previous keys). It is represented in a binary format, so it's best to use the other keys to attain the values.
Flags	A set of flags that provide additional client certificate information. The following flags can be set: *ceCertPresent*—A client certificate is present. *ceUnrecognizedIssuer*—The last certification in this chain is from an unknown issuer.

Table 10-7. *Client certificate key values.*

A variety of SubField values are available to extract specific information from the Subject and Issuer keys. A complete description of SubField values is available in the Object Reference in the ASP online documentation.

Retrieving data with cookies: the *Request* object

The *Cookies* collection of the *Request* object lets you retrieve the cookies from the client machine. The *Cookies* collection is a collection of the cookie values stored on the user's machine.

The syntax for using the *Cookies* collection of the *Request* object is

```
Request.Cookies(cookie)[(key)|.attribute]
```

As the syntax implies, each cookie can be an array, or more appropriately, a collection of values. Each value has a name, called a *key*. You can check a cookie to see if it has simply one value or if it has more than one key—each of which has a value—by checking the cookie's *HasKeys* property. *HasKeys* will be either True or False, so you can use it in an *If...Then...Else* statement:

```
<% If Request.Cookies("MyCookie").HasKeys Then %>
MyCookie has the following values:
<P>
<% For Each key in Request.Cookies("MyCookie") %>
<% = key %> has the value
<% = Request.Cookies("MyCookie")(key) %>
<P>
<% Next %>
<% Else %>
My Cookie's value is
<% = Request.Cookies("MyCookie") %>
<% End If %>
```

First you use the cookie's *HasKeys* property in the *If* statement. If there are keys in the cookie, you use the *For Each* statement to iterate through the collection of keys and print the value of each one. You can then use the *For Each* statement to loop through all the collections in the *Request* object, not just the cookies. This technique is useful if you don't know how many objects are in a collection.

If you do know what you're looking for in a collection, you might be better off referring to the exact item that you need in the collection rather than looping though them all with the *For Each* statement.

The *Server* Object

The *Server* object is exactly what its name implies. It provides methods and properties that let you interact with the actual machine that your application is running on—namely, the Web server.

The *Server* object has a *ScriptTimeout* property and the following four methods: *CreateObject*, *HTMLEncode*, *MapPath*, and *URLEncode*.

While only a few methods and properties are available in the *Server* object, they are extremely useful. The *Server* object opens the door to using server-side ActiveX components within your Web applications. It lets you instantiate components in your Web application that you've written in Visual Basic, Visual C++, or any other development environment that can create COM components.

The *CreateObject* method of the *Server* object is probably the most important method of any built-in ASP object. By passing it the Programmatic ID (ProgID) of a server component, you create an instance of that component and assign an object variable to it.

You can create objects for any COM component on your system, but you cannot create instances of the objects that are built into ASP. For instance, you can't create a *Session* object using this syntax. You can, however, take advantage of the five server-side ActiveX components that are supplied with ASP:

- Ad Rotator
- Browser Capabilities
- Database Access
- Content Linking
- TextStream

The *Session* Object

The *Session* object is similar to the *Application* object in that it also contains events within the global.asa file. Unlike the *Application* object, however, the *Session* object stores information for a particular user session. The *Session* object persists for the entire session and thus provides a very elegant solution to the common persistence-of-state problem—when you need to keep track of a user from one web page to the next, as in a "shopping cart" type of application. This is difficult to do given the stateless nature of the HTTP protocol.

The syntax for setting a variable within the *Session* object is as follows:

```
Session("variable_name") = value
```

You can then reference the value of the variable as follows:

```
MyVariable = Session("variable_name")
```

MANAGING APPLICATION STATE

One of the most difficult tasks that a Web developer faces is how to manage state-of-the-session information for an application. This problem surfaces when you want to track information from users who log onto your site. For example, if users go from page to page selecting items to buy, you need to be able to store that information somewhere so that you can display a list of all the items ordered and the total cost. You might store that information in a database, but you need a temporary storage method while users are accessing your Web page.

This is exactly what Active Server Pages lets you do with its *Server*, *Application*, and *Session* objects. These objects let you interact with ASP. You can use the objects to do certain tasks, such as send cookies to the client's browser or store information in the object for later reuse.

The Active Server Application

Just as a Web site is actually a collection of HTML files in a directory on your Web server, the Active Server application (also known as an ASA or ASP application) is actually a set of .asp and .htm files. Of course, you can use .htm files only, but if you want to use server-side scripting, you need to use at least some ASP files because the server won't even try to execute server-side script code in an .htm file.

One particular file in the ASP application is used to declare objects and define event procedures: the global.asa file.

The Application as a Unit

An ASP application is a collection of all the .asp, .htm, and other pages and documents that comprise the Web site. A Web site in the context of an application is defined as a virtual root that contains a global.asa file, including all the files and directories down to any subdirectory that contains a global.asa file. When a subdirectory contains a global.asa file, that subdirectory and all of its children are part of another application.

Think of an ASP application in the same way that you think of other familiar applications. For instance, a traditional Visual Basic application might consist of many different .dll and .exe files, among others. The files from one application can also be shared among applications. An ASP application works the same way. Files in one ASP application can be used by another ASP application.

You store global information within one application using the *Application* object as a global storage container. To share information between two or more applications, you must use a file or some other persistent storage mechanism, such as a database.

The global.asa File

The global.asa file is included automatically when you create a new Web project in Visual InterDev, unless you have disabled this feature. Instead of having the .asp extension that the rest of the ASP files have, it has an .asa extension. This file defines event procedures that are triggered by events when the application or session starts or ends. The application begins when the first user accesses the application, and it ends when the last user's session times out. (In IIS 3, the application does not end until the Web service is stopped.) Each user visit to your Web site counts as a session.

The *Application_OnStart* event occurs when the first user starts a session in your application. For example, the event occurs when someone visits your Web site for the first time. The user session is identified by the session ID created automatically in global.asa. If that person is still at your site (still has an active session) when another person visits, the *Application_OnStart* event does not occur. In other words, one instance of the application serves all sessions. You can write code (event procedures) that is triggered when the application starts and ends. The *Application_OnEnd* event does not occur when the last user leaves the application or the last user's session times out, but rather when the Web service stops.

The *Session_OnStart* event procedure is a good place for the application's startup code, which is similar to the *OnLoad* event of a Visual Basic application's main form. You can write event procedures that are triggered every time someone new comes to or leaves your site. This *Session_OnStart* event is often used to record the number of visits to a site. There can thus be many *Session* objects in existence simultaneously—one for each person using your site.

By default, as soon as a user hits the first ASP Web page of a Visual InterDev project, the global.asa page is executed. During this execution, the request from the browser is checked to see if there is a valid session cookie being sent. If so, global.asa is not executed, since the user is in an already-active session for that application, but the ASP Web page is executed.

If a valid session cookie is not coming from the browser for that application, a new session is started and the following actions are performed:

- Global.asa is executed.

- A unique session identifier (SessionID) is created for that user.

■ A cookie is created and sent to the browser so subsequent requests can be recognized as part of an existing session.

■ If this is the first session for an application, the *Application_OnStart* event occurs.

■ The *Session_OnStart* event occurs.

Session and Application Scope

Just as a normal procedural program has scope, so does the ASP application. But the ASP application has two types of variable scope, and two types of objects hold the variables for each scope.

Each ASP application has a single *Application* object, which is shared among all users who are running the application. Other ASP applications can refer to the *Application* object and will all refer to the same object.

The *Session* object has a smaller scope. Each person that visits your application gets his or her own session. The user's *Session* object is shared among all of the ASP Web pages in your site, but other people visiting your application have their own sessions.

If you have a variable named *FavoriteTeam* that you fill in from a form in your application, you can store it in one of several places. One way is to store it on the ASP Web page that handles the form by declaring it as a variable, as shown here:

```
Dim FavoriteTeam
FavoriteTeam = "Oakland Raiders"
```

In this case, the variable loses its value when the user leaves the page, so if you're not storing it (in a database or elsewhere), it disappears.

You can also store the variable in the *Session* object:

```
Session("FavoriteTeam") = "Oakland Raiders"
```

This way, even as the user moves from page to page, the value remains. However, other people who log onto your Web site cannot see what the first user's favorite team is because each user has his or her own session.

You can also store the variable in the *Application* object:

```
Application("FavoriteTeam") = "Oakland Raiders"
```

This *FavoriteTeam* variable has the same value on every page within the application. Other people also see this value when they visit your Web site. In fact, someone else can visit the site, load the form that sets the value of *FavoriteTeam*, and enter a new value. After everyone leaves the site, the application still keeps this value. The value persists until the Web service stops or is changed by another user.

You can turn off session-state management by checking the *Sessionless ASP Pages* property on the Editor Defaults page in the Project Properties dialog box. If you check this property, Visual InterDev inserts this line as the first line in each new ASP file you create:

```
<%@ Language=VBScript EnableSessionState=False%>
```

This line turns off session management in each page. You can selectively turn it back on by changing the line to true in each page:

```
<%@ Language=VBScript EnableSessionState=True%>
```

The *Application* Object

In an ASP application it is important to be able to store application-related information, such as the number of visits made to the application. If you plan to sell advertising space on your Web site, for example, you'll want to know how many hits the site gets because the value of the space will be directly related to the number of hits.

The *Application* object is a kind of storage area in which you can place variables and make them available not only to any script in your application but also across all instances of your application. If 100 people visit your Web site and you store a value in the *Application* object, all 100 "copies" of your site can reference the *Application* object and access that value.

The *Application* object is therefore a great place to store simple values that apply to the entire application, such as the number of hits your Web site gets. Unfortunately, it is not a good place to store large, complex values, such as the inventory of your warehouse.

An application variable is created when you assign it a value, as in this example:

```
Application("NumOfHits") = Application("NumOfHits") + 1
```

The first time this line is executed, the *NumOfHits* application variable is created and stored in the *Application* object. Like all numeric variables in VBScript, it starts off with a value of 0. Every subsequent time the line is executed, the same value is updated, regardless of how many users are on the Web page simultaneously.

The ability to share this number between different running Web sessions raises an interesting question: What happens when two people are on your Web server at once and they both hit that statement at exactly the same time? A couple of methods of the *Application* object handle this scenario: *Lock* and *Unlock*. The *Lock* method puts a lock on the *Application* object so that no other instance of the application can perform any operation on it. *Unlock* reverses the process so that the other copies have access to the *Application* object again. You can modify your hit counter to take advantage of this:

```
Application.Lock
Application("NumOfHits") = Application("NumOfHits") + 1
Application.Unlock
```

When this code is executed, the application is temporarily locked, the *NumOfHits* variable of the *Application* object is modified, and the *Application* object is unlocked. In this way, no two copies can ever simultaneously modify the *Application* object. If a client tries to modify the *Application* object when it is locked, the client must wait until the copy holding the lock unlocks it or until the Web page times out.

You must keep the application locked for as little time as possible because other clients might be waiting. In the previous example, the application is locked only for as long as it takes to update the hit counter, and then it is released.

The *NumOfHits* variable in this example disappears when the application ends. If you want to use an application variable to count the number of Web site hits, you have to save its value when the application ends and retrieve its value when the application restarts.

Application events

In addition to running scripting code in a page that's being loaded, an ASP application can also respond to events. Unlike forms and controls in Visual Basic that have dozens of events, the *Application* object has only two events: *Application_OnStart* and *Application_OnEnd*. The *Application* object's events are caused by actions from outside the application. You can write code that you want to execute when these events occur.

The *Application_OnStart* event occurs the first time someone starts a new session of your Web application. For instance, let's say that no one is visiting your Web site. Then users A, B, and C visit your site, in that order. Your *Application_OnStart* event occurs only when user A hits the site. When users B and C arrive a fraction of a second later, the application is already running because of user A; therefore, *Application_OnStart* does not occur again.

On the flip side, you have the *Application_OnEnd* event, which occurs only when the IIS's Web service shuts down.

Application_OnStart

The *Application_OnStart* event code is placed in the global.asa file. The following is an example of a global.asa file that contains event procedures for the *OnStart* and *OnEnd* event procedures of both the *Application* and the *Session* objects:

```
<SCRIPT LANGUAGE="VBScript" RUNAT="Server">
```

```
Sub Session_OnStart
    'Insert script to be executed when
    'a session starts
End Sub

Sub Session_OnEnd
    'Insert script to be executed when
    'a session ends
End Sub

Sub Application_OnStart
    'Insert script to be executed when
    'the application starts
End Sub

Sub Application_OnEnd
    'Insert script to be executed when
    'the application ends
End Sub

</SCRIPT>
```

The global.asa file created by the Web Project Wizard has comments that tell you how to create these event handlers. You can use the application's events to count the number of visitors to your Web site. The AdventureWorks sample application (available from Microsoft's web site at *www.microsoft.com,* and also as part of the ASP software) uses *Application_OnStart* to get information from a text file on the system and save it in the *Application* object. A portion of the sample's code is shown below.

```
<SCRIPT LANGUAGE="VBScript" RUNAT="Server">
SUB Application_OnStart
    ' This script executes when the first user comes to the site.
    ' Open file and read the number of visitors so far
    VisitorCountFilename = Server.MapPath("/AdvWorks") + _
        "\visitors.txt"
    Set FileObject = _
        Server.CreateObject("Scripting.FileSystemObject")
    Set Out = _
        FileObject.OpenTextFile _
            (VisitorCountFilename, 1, FALSE, FALSE)
    ' Initialize soft visitor counter here
    Application("visitors") = Out.ReadLine
    ' Store physical filename of file containing the
    ' visitor count
    Application("VisitorCountFilename") = VisitorCountFilename
END SUB
</SCRIPT>
```

This script creates a reference to an object using the *Set FileObject = Server.CreateObject("Scripting.FileSystemObject")* syntax. The *FileObject* object is used to read and write the number of visitors to a text file. The script uses the *FileSystemObject* object named *FileObject* to open a text file. The *Visitors* variable in the *Application* object is then set to the value read from the text file. This technique retrieves the number of visitors. While the application is running, the value of *Visitors* is incremented when the session starts. (The script for the *Application_OnEnd* event for the same application is shown below.)

```
<SCRIPT LANGUAGE="VBScript" RUNAT="Server">
SUB Application_OnEnd
    ' This script executes when the server shuts down or when
    ' global.asa changes.
    ' Overwrites the existing visitors.txt file
    Set FileObject = _
        Server.CreateObject("Scripting.FileSystemObject")
    Set Out = FileObject.CreateTextFile _
        (Application("VisitorCountFilename"), TRUE, FALSE)
    Out.WriteLine(Application("visitors"))
END SUB
</SCRIPT>
```

The *Application_OnEnd* event procedure again creates a *FileSystemObject* object named *FileObject* that is used to create a text file named visitors.txt. This file overwrites the file you read in *OnStart* and writes the new number of visitors to the file. Writing the number of users to the file is one way to save the number of visits to this site between application sessions.

The *Session* Object

The *Session* object is similar to the *Application* object in that it also provides scope for variables. The variables are available to all pages in your application, but the *Session* object has a more limited scope. The same object is not available to all users of the site (for example, the *Application* object); instead, each user has his or her own *Session* object. Any variables stored in the *Session* object are for that session only.

Session variables are analogous to global variables in a traditional program. They are available throughout the program, but if you start another copy of the program, that other copy has its own global variables.

The *Session* object also has *Session_OnStart* and *Session_OnEnd* events, similar to those of the *Application* object. In the previous examples, the application read the number of visitors from a text file when it started and saved this number to the text file when it ended. The application needs to increment that number each time someone enters the site. The *Session_OnStart* event procedure is the perfect place for that code, as shown on the following page.

```
<SCRIPT LANGUAGE="VBScript" RUNAT="Server">
SUB Session_OnStart
...
    ' Increase the visitor counter
    Application.Lock
    Application("visitors")= Application("visitors") + 1
    t_visitors = Application("visitors")
    Application.UnLock
    Session("VisitorID") = t_visitors

    ' Periodically, save to file
    If t_visitors MOD 15 = 0 Then
        Set FileObject = Server.CreateObject( _
            "Scripting.FileSystemObject")
        Set Out= FileObject.CreateTextFile _
            (Application("VisitorCountFilename"), TRUE, FALSE)
        Application.Lock
        Out.WriteLine(t_visitors)
        Application.UnLock
    End If
...
END SUB
</SCRIPT>
```

You'll also notice that the visitor count is periodically saved to disk. This is because the *Application_OnEnd* event only fires when the Web service stops gracefully. Saving the visitor count every 15 visitors or so within the *Session_OnStart* event procedure keeps the visitor count more accurate even if the Web service stops abnormally.

The *OnStart* and *OnEnd* events for the *Session* object are located in the global.asa file along with the *Application* object's events. With this code in place, the *Visitors* application variable is incremented anytime someone visits the site. Remember to lock the application before you change the value to make sure only one client can execute that statement at a time.

The *Session* object also has two properties: *SessionID* and *Timeout*. *SessionID* has a data type of LONG. It uniquely identifies the session on the server. Don't use this value as the primary key of a database because the same *SessionID* might be used again after the server is shut down and restarted.

Timeout specifies the number of minutes the session stays active if the user does not refresh or request a page from your application. At the end of the period defined by *Timeout*, the session is destroyed and all its resources are returned to the server. By default, session *Timeout* is 20 minutes. This default is set in the registry, under the *SessionTimeout* entry.

You can also force a session to be destroyed by calling its *Abandon* method. This ends the session at the end of the current VBScript. Further references to the *Session* object will create a new session.

Sessions and cookies

You might wonder how ASP knows that a browser requesting a page is already a member of a session. After all, when a browser requests a page, it is simply asking that a file be downloaded. How can the server know that this is the same person who has been browsing around your system for the last hour and a half? The answer is in the cookie.

When the user first accesses a page in your application, the server scans the request's HTTP header for a SessionID. If the user is hitting your site for the first time, there is no SessionID, so the server generates an ID and asks the browser to create a cookie with this ID. Of course, this cookie will not last forever. The server specifies that this cookie should disappear in a certain amount of time. The next time the user asks for a page, the server will be able to find the cookie with the SessionID and know what session the user is associated with, and therefore what session variables the ASP Web page should use.

You can also set the Timeout value for a session. The Timeout value is how long the session lasts before it is terminated. This is done with the *Timeout* property of the *Session* object. The server takes the *Timeout* property of the *Session* object and sets the SessionID cookie to expire in that much time. Every time the user requests a page from your server, the server resets the cookie's expiration timer.

Chapter 11

Integrating Client-Side ActiveX Controls and Java Applets

Microsoft Visual InterDev provides tools for inserting Microsoft ActiveX controls and Java applets into Web pages. You can drag them from the Toolbox and drop them into a page, or you can manually code them in an HTML or Active Server Pages (ASP) Web page. You can script them using any scripting language that the page's target platform supports, such as Microsoft VBScript or Microsoft JScript. The client-side script is sent from the page down the HTML stream to the client browser. The Web server (such as Internet Information Server [IIS]) does not interpret or interact with the client-side script unless it is script that has been dynamically created.

An ActiveX control or Java applet is often a user interface element, such as a command button, a text box, or a list box. But ActiveX controls and Java applets are not restricted to the mundane—they can be any piece of software imaginable. They can include audiovisual movie player controls, grids, graphs, treeviews, listviews, toolbars, calendars, progress bars, spreadsheets, video games, and even entire applications.

You can find many ActiveX controls and Java applets on the Web and from various vendors. Microsoft Internet Explorer 4.0 comes with several ActiveX controls, and many others are available for free from Microsoft's Web site and other Web sites.

In this chapter, we'll look at how to incorporate ActiveX controls and Java applets into your Visual InterDev applications. By using these types of controls within your applications, you can enhance the client-side interactivity and performance of your applications and provide end users with a richer experience similar to that of client/server applications. Combined with client-side scripting and Dynamic HTML (DHTML), ActiveX controls and Java applets give you complete programmatic control over the objects contained in the browser window.

INTEGRATING CLIENT-SIDE ACTIVEX CONTROLS

ActiveX controls do everything from providing a simple text label to creating full-function spreadsheetlike grids. Many types of ActiveX controls are available.

The operating system and the browser running on that operating system must support ActiveX controls in order for them to run in the browser. Most ActiveX controls in use today are for 32-bit Windows-based systems—Microsoft Windows 95, Windows 98, and Microsoft Windows NT. These controls can be written in a number of languages, including Microsoft Visual Basic, Delphi, PowerBuilder, and C++.

The Macintosh version of Internet Explorer supports ActiveX controls specifically compiled for the Macintosh with MetroWorks CodeWarrior. You can use the Browser Capabilities component, discussed in Chapter 17 and included with ASP, to detect which browser is making requests. This lets you determine whether the browser supports ActiveX controls and which control to send (Macintosh or Windows, for example).

ActiveX controls provide building blocks and an easy development model because they come with visual property sheets for easy customization. Thousands of controls are available commercially that you can use not only in Web pages, but with Visual Basic, Microsoft Visual C++, Microsoft Office, Lotus Notes, Delphi, PowerBuilder, and many other applications.

Inserting ActiveX Controls in HTML and ASP Files

You insert ActiveX controls into HTML and ASP files with the <OBJECT> tag, an HTML tag that specifies the class ID (CLASSID) of the object to insert. You use the class ID to identify the control in a system's registry.

The CLASSID attribute is possibly the most important attribute within the <OBJECT> tag; it specifies the object's class identifier, a long hexadecimal number that refers to the ActiveX control. Every class ID is unique. In fact, the number itself is called a *globally unique identifier (GUID)* because it is generated by an algorithm that combines the time (to the millisecond) and information about the current machine to create a number that's guaranteed to be unique. When you install an ActiveX control on your machine, the GUID is written to the registry along with other information that you need to create the control. The GUID travels with the control, so whether you upload it to a friend or someone reading your Web site downloads it, the GUID in your <OBJECT> tag always matches the right control.

You can insert ActiveX controls in a page with both Visual InterDev and the Microsoft FrontPage editor. Both automate the insertion of ActiveX controls with special features. Both of these tools insert the <OBJECT> tag in the target page automatically. The <OBJECT> tag has many options, as shown in the following code example:

```
<OBJECT classid="clsid:8E27C92B-1264-101C-8A2F-040224009C02"
    id=Calendar1 style="LEFT: 0px; TOP: 0px" VIEWASTEXT>
    <PARAM NAME="_Version" VALUE="524288">
    <PARAM NAME="_ExtentX" VALUE="7620">
    <PARAM NAME="_ExtentY" VALUE="5080">
    <PARAM NAME="_StockProps" VALUE="1">
    <PARAM NAME="BackColor" VALUE="-2147483633">
    <PARAM NAME="Year" VALUE="1998">
    <PARAM NAME="Month" VALUE="10">
    <PARAM NAME="Day" VALUE="31">
    <PARAM NAME="DayLength" VALUE="1">
    <PARAM NAME="MonthLength" VALUE="2">
    <PARAM NAME="DayFontColor" VALUE="0">
    <PARAM NAME="FirstDay" VALUE="1">
    <PARAM NAME="GridCellEffect" VALUE="1">
    <PARAM NAME="GridFontColor" VALUE="10485760">
    <PARAM NAME="GridLinesColor" VALUE="-2147483632">
    <PARAM NAME="ShowDateSelectors" VALUE="-1">
    <PARAM NAME="ShowDays" VALUE="-1">
    <PARAM NAME="ShowHorizontalGrid" VALUE="-1">
    <PARAM NAME="ShowTitle" VALUE="-1">
    <PARAM NAME="ShowVerticalGrid" VALUE="-1">
    <PARAM NAME="TitleFontColor" VALUE="10485760">
    <PARAM NAME="ValueIsNull" VALUE="0">
</OBJECT>
```

The qualifiers for the <OBJECT> tag specify the items on the next page.

- The object or ActiveX control placed on the Web page

- The name used to reference the control

- The initial parameters that control the ActiveX control's characteristics

The various parameters contain enough information for the browser to find the control and load it for display on the Web page.

The *ID* attribute specifies the name by which you can refer to the control. The following code sets the control's name to *Calendar1*:

```
<OBJECT classid="clsid:8E27C92B-1264-101C-8A2F-040224009C02"
    id=Calendar1 style="LEFT: 0px; TOP: 0px" VIEWASTEXT>
```

Property settings are also required to determine how the control functions. You can use the <PARAM> tags within the <OBJECT> tag to specify parameters that are required by the ActiveX control, as in the following example:

```
<PARAM NAME="Year" VALUE="1998">
<PARAM NAME="Month" VALUE="10">
<PARAM NAME="Day" VALUE="31">
```

In this example, the parameters set the opening values of the day, month, and year for the ActiveX Calendar control that you'll find in the Visual InterDev Toolbox. Like Java applets, <PARAM> tags set the ActiveX control's properties. These parameters are optional; you do not have to enter them on the Web page. While some properties are common and found in many controls, such as caption and size, other properties are specific to a given control, as illustrated in the example above.

If you do not use a <PARAM> tag to set a control's properties, the control sets those properties with the defaults. Web pages support persistent properties in ActiveX controls unless you set them with a <PARAM> tag. The other option is to set a property with some type of script code.

ActiveX controls in ASP Web pages

An interesting application of ASP server-side scripting is to dynamically generate parameters for ActiveX controls before you send the Web page to the browser. For instance, you can use a Grid control and set the control's values to correspond to the values coming from a database. You simply use the *<%=varname%>* expression or a similar expression within the appropriate <PARAM> tags for the ASP Web page's control. Your server-side script code can write any parameter that you see for an <OBJECT> tag, including the tag itself. An ASP Web page can contain any number of ActiveX controls. We'll see an example of dynamically building the parameters for a Java applet using server-side scripting later in this chapter.

Adding an ActiveX control from the Toolbox

Visual InterDev conveniently inserts the <OBJECT> tag in HTML or ASP code and <PARAM> tags for properties that you can visually set in the Visual InterDev Properties window. You don't have to determine the GUID and manually set the initial properties; Visual InterDev does it automatically. To insert an ActiveX control into a Web page, take the following steps:

1. Open the HTML or ASP Web page in which you want to place the control.

2. Select the ActiveX control from the ActiveX Controls tab on the Toolbox, and drag it onto the page. (See Figure 11-1.)

3. Make any necessary changes to the control's properties in the Properties window, and make the control the size you want it to be in the Web page.

Figure 11-1 shows an ActiveX Calendar control on an ASP Web page. You can also see the Toolbox to the right and the Properties window to the left. You'll notice that the Properties window displays the properties for the Calendar control. These properties are predefined when you drag the ActiveX control onto the Web page. You can change these properties either within the Properties window or via scripting within the Web page.

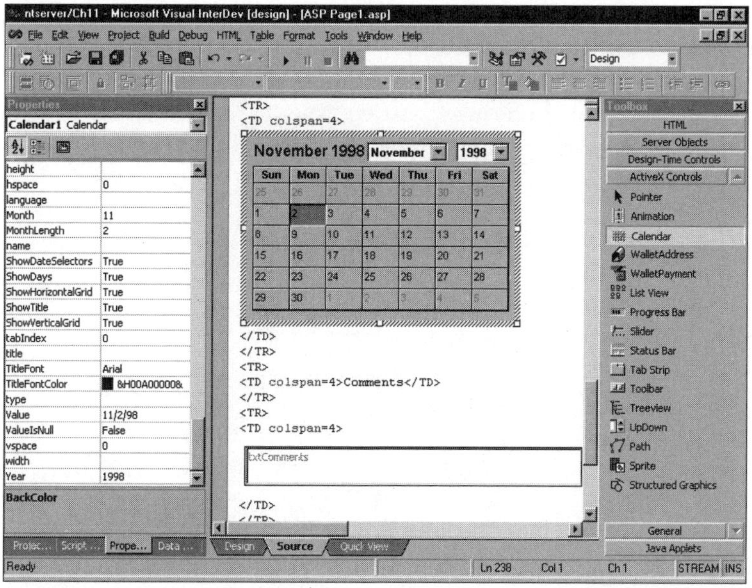

Figure 11-1. *Visual InterDev showing an ActiveX Calendar control that was dragged onto the page from the Toolbox.*

Adding an ActiveX control to the Toolbox

If the ActiveX control you want to place on your Web page is not shown on the ActiveX Controls tab of the Toolbox, you can use the following steps to add a new control to the Toolbox:

1. Right-click within the Toolbox, and choose Customize Toolbox from the context menu.

2. Click the ActiveX Controls tab in the Customize Toolbox dialog box. (See Figure 11-2.)

3. Select the required ActiveX control by checking the check box within the listing of available controls, or select another control by clicking the Browse button and locating the relevant .ocx file within your file system.

4. Click OK to add the new control to the ActiveX Controls tab in the Toolbox.

You'll notice that the ActiveX Controls tab on the Customize Toolbox dialog box presents you with the name of the ActiveX controls available, plus their path on your file system and the date they were last modified. After you have added a control to the Toolbox, you can add it to your Web page in the same manner as before by simply dragging and dropping it onto the page.

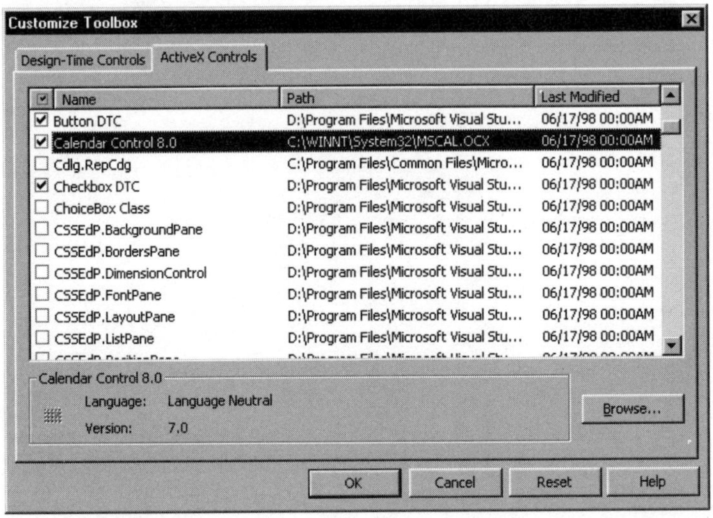

Figure 11-2. *The Customize Toolbox dialog box showing the ActiveX Controls tab where you can select ActiveX controls to add to the Toolbox.*

Customizing the Toolbox

You can further customize the Toolbox in several ways:

- By adding, renaming, or deleting tabs
- By renaming or deleting items on the tabs

To add, rename, or delete tabs from the Toolbox, simply right-click a tab and choose the relevant menu item from the context menu. You can also move tabs up or down to change their respective ordering.

To rename or delete items from the Toolbox, right-click over the item you want to change and choose the relevant menu item from the context menu.

Setting properties for an ActiveX control

Once you've added the ActiveX control to your Web page, you'll most likely want to change some of its properties. As mentioned earlier, you can do this in one of several ways:

- By entering values in the Properties window
- By accessing the ActiveX control's Properties dialog box
- By entering values in the <PARAM> tag within the source code

To enter values in the Properties window, simply scroll through the properties listed until you find the item you want to change. Then directly change the value of the property in the relevant cell. Notice that you can sort the properties either alphabetically or in a categorized fashion by clicking one of the buttons at the top of the Properties window.

To access the ActiveX control's Properties dialog box, either click the Property Pages button at the top of the Properties window or right-click the control and choose Properties from the context menu. Figure 11-3 on the following page shows the Properties dialog box for the ActiveX Calendar control.

The third way to modify a control's properties is within the source code. First you'll need to convert the control from a graphical representation to a textual one. You can do this by right-clicking the control and choosing Always View As Text from the context menu. Now that the <PARAM> tags are available for editing, you can add new tags or edit existing ones within the Visual InterDev Source View editor.

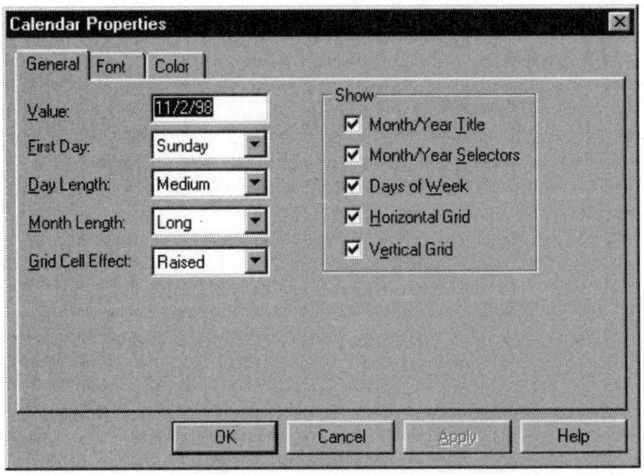

Figure 11-3. *The Properties dialog box for the ActiveX Calendar control.*

Using the Codebase property to download a control

To specify the location of a control for downloading, use the *Codebase* property. The location can be either a relative or full URL. You can edit the CODEBASE attribute in the HTML or ASP Web page, or you can use the Properties window. In the Properties window, enter the control's URL as the *Codebase* property. This tells the browser where it can download the control if the user's machine does not have that control installed.

Internet Explorer automatically installs the control on users' machines as required. Once it is installed and registered, a user does not have to download it again. You can also specify version information in the *Codebase* property; this lets you make sure a newer version is downloaded to users' machines if you create one.

Using the Package & Deployment Wizard

You can use Visual Basic 6.0 to build ActiveX controls and then use the Package & Deployment Wizard to package your control for easy deployment. You can access the Package & Deployment Wizard by choosing Start | Programs | Visual Studio 6.0 | Microsoft Visual Studio 6.0 Tools | Package & Deployment Wizard. You can also access the Wizard from Visual Basic 6.0 if you have installed it as an add-in.

To install the Package & Deployment Wizard as an add-in to Visual Basic 6.0, follow these steps:

1. Start Visual Basic 6.0, and choose Add-In Manager from the Add-Ins menu.

2. Choose Package And Deployment Wizard from the Add-In Manager dialog box.

3. Check the Load On Startup check box, and click OK.

4. Restart Visual Basic 6.0.

The Package & Deployment Wizard will now be available as a menu item on the Add-Ins menu.

Figure 11-4 shows the opening window for the Package & Deployment Wizard. From here you select the appropriate Visual Basic 6.0 project and then select Package. The Wizard then guides you through the rest of the steps needed to deploy your ActiveX control as a CAB file (that is, a cabinet file that uses Microsoft's file compression and storage technology and that can hold several files).

Figure 11-4. *The Package & Deployment Wizard's main screen.*

When you use the Package & Deployment Wizard to package a control for Internet downloads by choosing the Internet Package type, it creates a sample HTML file that contains an <OBJECT> tag for the control, as in the following example:

```
<HTML>
<HEAD>
<TITLE>Nick.CAB</TITLE>
</HEAD>
<BODY>
<!--    If any of the controls on this page require licensing,
    you must create a license package file. Run LPK_TOOL.EXE to
    create the required LPK file. LPK_TOOL.EXE can be found on
```

(continued)

the ActiveX SDK, http://www.microsoft.com/intdev/sdk/sdk.htm.
If you have the Visual Basic 6.0 CD, it can also be found in
the \Tools\LPK_TOOL directory.

The following is an example of the Object tag:

```
<OBJECT CLASSID="clsid:5220cb21-c88d-11cf-b347-00aa00a28331">
    <PARAM NAME="LPKPath" VALUE="LPKfilename.LPK">
</OBJECT>
-->

<OBJECT ID="UserControl1"
    CLASSID="CLSID:FCAED242-72C2-11D2-B8A0-0040051F31F4"
    CODEBASE="Nick.CAB#version=1,0,0,0">
</OBJECT>
</BODY>
</HTML>
```

The example above was created using the Package & Deployment Wizard, which creates the minimum <OBJECT> tag needed to download a control. The CODEBASE attribute specifies the filename of the CAB file. The example created by the Wizard does not include a URL, so you might need to modify the CODEBASE attribute to include the full URL, as shown in the following example:

```
CODEBASE="http://www.nevans.com/vi/nick.CAB#version=1,0,0,0"
```

After these items are in place and a Web page has the <OBJECT> tag defined, users can download the component. When a browser links to the page containing an ActiveX control, it invisibly downloads the control and all the files needed to support it. You can package all these files together into a single autoinstall CAB file.

When a user browses the Web page, the browser interprets the <OBJECT> tag, which has a URL indicating the CAB file's location. The browser then downloads the CAB file and decompresses it. The CAB file contains all the information the browser needs to automatically download the control, along with the support files the control needs.

The browser first looks for the additional support files on the user's system. If the files are already there, the installation is complete. If they're not, the files are downloaded from the site specified in the URL.

Component safety

VBScript and JScript are benign scripting languages that do not pose any safety threats, because access to system components are disabled. (For instance, you cannot write to the file system.) Java applets run inside the Java virtual machine and likewise cannot access system components. ActiveX controls, however, are a different matter. You can write a control that does just about anything to the user's machine. This has significant advantages as well as disadvantages. An ActiveX control, like almost all commercial software, can be very powerful, offer high performance, and take unique advantage of the operating system. However, on the Internet, a hacker can write a control that harms a user's computer.

ActiveX controls come with a mechanism called Authenticode to reduce the risk of downloading a dangerous ActiveX control from an unknown source. With Authenticode, controls can be digitally signed so that users know the component's exact source. When the Web browser begins downloading the ActiveX control, it checks to see whether the control has a certificate. The browser then presents the user with the certificate information so that the user can decide whether to let the control be downloaded and installed on the local machine.

Microsoft's Web site has information on how to get custom controls signed by third-party signing authorities such as VeriSign.

Scripting ActiveX Controls

As an example of how to script ActiveX controls within Visual InterDev, we'll use a sample ASP Web page that allows a user to schedule an appointment. The page is named Appointment.asp and is included on the CD-ROM under the CHAP11 folder.

The example uses an ActiveX Calendar control so that the end user can easily select a day for the appointment. The start time and end time of the appointment are specified by using Listbox DTCs. Textbox DTCs are used to capture the Subject, Location, and Comments regarding the appointment. Finally, a Button DTC is used to submit the captured information. Rather than complicate this example with a database update, the Button simply displays a message box confirming the details of the appointment.

Figure 11-5 on the following page shows the Appointment.asp page as it appears in the Internet Explorer 4.0 browser after an end user has entered information and has clicked the Save button. You can see the message box displaying the details of the appointment.

Another important thing about this example is that it uses a client-side scripting model so that all feedback regarding input validation and so on is immediately returned to the user without a round-trip to the server.

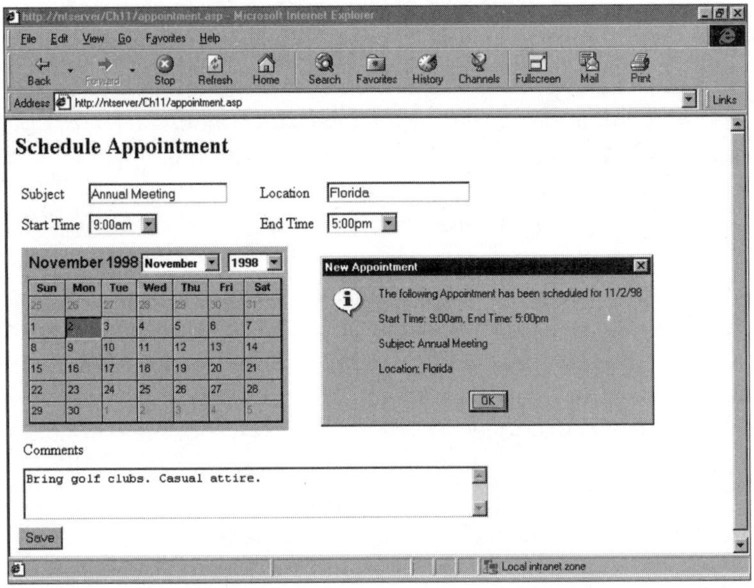

Figure 11-5. *The Appointment.asp page demonstrating the integration of an ActiveX Calendar control into an ASP Web page with client-side scripting.*

Let's take a look at some of the client-side scripting for the Calendar control within this sample code. The first piece of script ensures that, when the user selects a date, the date selected is greater than or equal to the current date. The code is as follows:

```
<SCRIPT ID=clientEventHandlersVBS LANGUAGE=vbscript>
<!--
Sub Calendar1_Click
    If CDate(thisForm.Calendar1.Value) < Date() Then
        MsgBox("Please select today's date or a future date.")
    End If
End Sub
-->
</SCRIPT>
```

The code uses the *Click* event for the Calendar control and compares the current date with the date the user selected. To find out what events are available for this control, you can view the Script Outline window within Visual InterDev. Figure 11-6 shows the Script Outline window and the Calendar control events. The Calendar control is actually found within the *thisForm* object under the Client Objects & Events node in the Script Outline window.

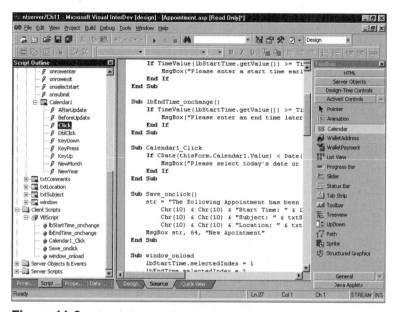

Figure 11-6. *The* Click *event for the Calendar control shown within the Script Outline window.*

The Script Outline window

The Script Outline window is a powerful tool to aid you in your client-side or server-side scripting. If you do not see the Script Outline window within Visual InterDev, you can add it by choosing View | Other Windows | Script Outline. The Script Outline window displays both client objects and events and server objects and events. You can also use it to navigate to client-side and server-side scripts that you have already written for your page. By expanding the Client Scripts or the Server Scripts nodes, you'll see a list of all your current scripts within your page. By double-clicking a script name, you can move the cursor to that script within the Source View editor. Figure 11-6 also shows the client scripts for the Appointment.asp page.

Completing the Appointment sample application

We've already seen how the Calendar control is scripted to check that the date selected is greater than or equal to the current date. The other areas in the Appointment.asp page where the Calendar control is scripted are the *window_onload* event and the *Save_onclick* event.

The code on the following page shows the full client-side script for the Appointment.asp example.

```
<SCRIPT ID=clientEventHandlersVBS LANGUAGE=vbscript>
<!--
Sub lbStartTime_onchange()
    If TimeValue(lbStartTime.getValue()) >= _
        TimeValue(lbEndTime.getValue()) Then
        MsgBox("Please enter a start time earlier than the end time.")
    End If
End Sub

Sub lbEndTime_onchange()
    If TimeValue(lbStartTime.getValue()) >= _
        TimeValue(lbEndTime.getValue()) Then
        MsgBox("Please enter an end time later than the start time.")
    End If
End Sub

Sub Calendar1_Click
    If CDate(thisForm.Calendar1.Value) < Date() Then
        MsgBox("Please select today's date or a future date.")
    End If
End Sub

Sub Save_onclick()
    str = "The following Appointment has been scheduled for " _
        & thisForm.Calendar1.Value & _
        Chr(10) & Chr(10) & _
        "Start Time: " & lbStartTime.getValue() & _
        ", End Time: " & lbEndTime.getValue() & _
        Chr(10) & Chr(10) & "Subject: " & txtSubject.value & _
        Chr(10) & Chr(10) & "Location: " & txtLocation.value
        MsgBox str, 64, "New Appointment"
End Sub

Sub window_onload
    lbStartTime.selectedIndex = 1
    lbEndTime.selectedIndex = 2
    thisForm.Calendar1.Value = Date()
End Sub
-->
</SCRIPT>
```

The *window_onload* event is used to set the date displayed in the calendar to the current date according to the system clock. This is achieved by setting the *Value* property of the Calendar control equal to *Date*. The *Save_onclick* event is used to print out the value selected in the Calendar control to a message box displayed to the user. Again, the *Value* property is used to retrieve the current date that the user has selected. In the *Save_onclick* event, the *MsgBox* VBScript function is called with both a prompt and a title caption. The number 64 passed to the function is used to display an information message icon as opposed to the normal message box that has no icons displayed.

From this example, you'll see that scripting ActiveX controls is really no different from scripting other elements (such as design-time controls) within the page. Both offer a rich set of events, methods, and properties for you to script against. When writing your script, you can also take advantage of statement completion to assist you with finding the required properties and methods for your ActiveX controls.

INTEGRATING CLIENT-SIDE JAVA APPLETS

Java applets are commonly used for user interface elements such as scrolling tickers, advertisement animations, charts, and so forth. The advantage of Java applets over ActiveX controls is their breadth of deployment. In theory, you can write a Java applet once and deploy it anywhere. In practice, Java applets that are intended to run in multiple types of browser require a lot of testing to ensure consistent functionality across all browser platforms. It is therefore up to you as a developer to understand the trade-offs involved in choosing to go with ActiveX controls or Java applets.

ActiveX controls are generally easier to write but are restricted somewhat in their browser support. Java applets, on the other hand, take a little longer to develop (arguably) and require more testing but can run on a wider variety of browsers and platforms.

Ultimately, the decision rests upon the target audience for your applications. If you are developing for the Internet, where the client-side is unknown, it's often best to go with Java applets or even plain HTML. If you are developing for an intranet or extranet, where the client-side is known or can be controlled more easily, it's often best to go with ActiveX controls or plain HTML. In recent years, there has been somewhat of a push-back on both ActiveX controls and Java applets, and organizations are often opting for the more straightforward HTML deployment option, especially for their Internet and extranet applications. For intranet applications, ActiveX controls and Java applets can give your end users the interactivity they need without causing too much stress for developers since the client platform is known and controlled.

Inserting Java Applets into HTML and ASP Files

The easiest way to integrate a Java applet into an HTML or ASP Web page is to manually code the <APPLET> tag directly into the Visual InterDev Source View editor. If you plan to reuse the <APPLET> code, you can highlight the code in the Source View editor and drag it onto the Toolbox to create a new item. You might also want to create a new tab named Java Applets prior to dragging the applet code onto the Toolbox so that you have a way to organize your applets and keep them separate from your ActiveX controls.

If you add a Java applet to the Toolbox, be sure to rename the item so that it is more meaningful. By default, applets are given the name *HTML Fragment*, so you'll want to change the name to reference your specific applet. Figure 11-7 shows an applet in the Source View editor and its corresponding item in the Toolbox. The item was named *ChartGear Sample* after the name of the Java applet.

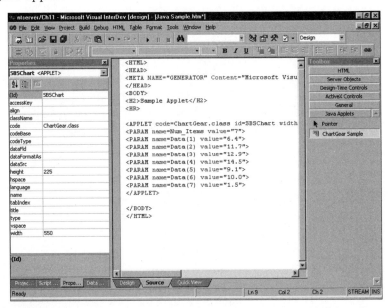

Figure 11-7. *A Java applet in the Source View editor and shown in the Java Applets tab in the Toolbox.*

NOTE The ChartGear applet is available from Solstice Inc. on their Web site at *http://www.solsticeinc.net*. This applet can be used for creating graphs and has been rated in the top five percent of applets on the Web by the Java Applet Rating Service (JARS).

Applets are similar to ActiveX controls in that they also use <PARAM> tags to specify additional properties. The following code shows an example applet within an HTML page:

```
<HTML>
<HEAD>
<META NAME="GENERATOR" Content="Microsoft Visual Studio 6.0">
</HEAD>
<BODY>

<H2>Sample Applet</H2>
<HR>

<APPLET code=ChartGear.class id=SBSChart width="550"
    height="225" VIEWASTEXT>
    <PARAM name=Num_Items value="7">
    <PARAM name=Data(1) value="6.4">
    <PARAM name=Data(2) value="11.7">
    <PARAM name=Data(3) value="12.9">
    <PARAM name=Data(4) value="14.5">
    <PARAM name=Data(5) value="9.1">
    <PARAM name=Data(6) value="10.0">
    <PARAM name=Data(7) value="1.5">
</APPLET>

</BODY>
</HTML>
```

This code is taken from the Java Sample.htm page in the CHAP11 folder on the CD-ROM. The code displays the ChartGear applet, as shown in Figure 11-8.

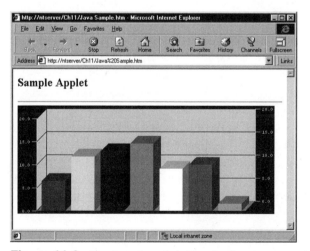

Figure 11-8. *The Java Sample.htm page showing a graphing applet.*

When deploying applets, you might also need files that the applet depends on. The applet may have a number of additional .class files that you need to include on your Web server and in your development environment. Class files are the machine-independent byte code generated from .java files by the javac compiler in the JDK or by another compiler in a visual Java development environment such as Microsoft Visual J++. When deploying Java applets, you must be aware of the applet's requirements in terms of required files and make sure you meet them.

As with ActiveX controls, you can switch to viewing the graphical representation of your Java applets within the Source View editor by right-clicking the applet section of the code and unchecking Always View As Text on the context menu.

Scripting Java Applets

One of the interesting uses of ASP server-side scripting is to dynamically generate parameters for Java applets before you send the Web page to the browser. For instance, using ASP, you can query a database and then dynamically map the returned results into client-side <PARAM> tags for the applet so that the variables are sent down to the client with the applet. You can use a Chart applet that charts data in this manner—by setting the chart values to equal values coming from a database. This is easy to do; you simply use the *<%=varname%>* expression or a similar expression within the appropriate <PARAM> tags for the applet in the ASP Web page. An ASP Web page can contain any number of Java applets.

As an example of how to script Java applets within Visual InterDev, we'll use a sample ASP Web page that builds a dynamically created graph, as described earlier. The page is named Funds.asp and is included on the CD-ROM under the CHAP11 folder.

The example uses a graphing applet so that the end user can see his or her 401K investment fund performance by twelve-month period and by two-week period. The data is pulled from the database for that specific user and is output both as <PARAM> tags for the Java applet and as an HTML table below the applet. The user is also given the option of being able to change the chart display type and the periods to be graphed. In addition to supplying the data for the fund performance graph, the database query also supplies the data for some of the graph labels, such as the period ending date. A Recordset DTC is used to perform the query within the ASP Web page.

Figure 11-9 shows the Funds.asp page as it appears in the Netscape Communicator 4.01 browser. This browser was chosen to illustrate that the code is functional both within Internet Explorer and within Communicator.

The code below shows the source code for the Funds.asp page. The code for the Recordset DTC has been edited so that it shows the SQL query only. Also, the code that displays the HTML table with all the fund performance values at the bottom of the Web page has also been removed for the sake of brevity. As you can see from the code, the <PARAM> tags for the applet are created using a loop over each record in the recordset. This allows the resulting graph to contain however many rows are returned from the query. In the query, you'll see that there are six funds selected.

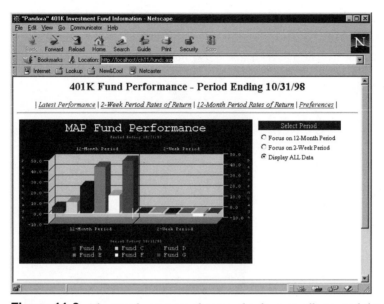

Figure 11-9. *The Funds.asp page showing the dynamically created data displayed in the Fund Performance graph. The graph uses the ChartGear Java applet.*

```
<%@ LANGUAGE="VBSCRIPT" %>
<% ' VI 6.0 Scripting Object Model Enabled %>
<!--#include file="_ScriptLibrary/pm.asp"-->
<% if StartPageProcessing() Then Response.End() %>
<FORM name=thisForm METHOD=post>

<HTML>
<HEAD>
<TITLE>&quot;Pandora&quot; 401K Investment Fund Information</TITLE>
</HEAD>
<BODY>

<!--METADATA TYPE="DesignerControl" startspan
...
<Recordset DTC>
...
cmdTmp.CommandText = 'SELECT id, Date_start, Date_end, fund_a,
    fund_c, fund_d, fund_e, fund_f, fund_g FROM FundPerformance
    WHERE Date_End IN (SELECT Max(Date_End) FROM FundPerformance)
```

(continued)

```
        ORDER BY id, Date_end'
...
<!--METADATA TYPE="DesignerControl" endspan-->


<CENTER>
<% DataCommand1.MoveLast %>
<H2>401K Fund Performance - Period Ending <% =
    CStr(DataCommand1.fields.getValue("Date_End")) %></h2>
<% DataCommand1.MoveFirst %>
 | <i><a HREF="funds.asp">Latest Performance</a></i>
 |
<i><a HREF="funds_history_2wk.asp">2-Week Period Rates of Return</a></
i>
 |
<i><a HREF="funds_history.asp">12-Month Period Rates of Return</a></i>
 |
 <i><a HREF="preferences.asp">Preferences</a></i>
 |
</CENTER>

<HR>

<TABLE>
<TR>
<TD>

<APPLET code="ChartGear.class" align="baseline" width="500"
    height="300" id="graph1" VIEWASTEXT>

<%
counter = 1
DO WHILE NOT DataCommand1.EOF
cnt = 1
%>

<PARAM name="Data(<% = counter %>,<% = cnt %>)"
    value="<% = DataCommand1.fields.getValue("Fund_A") %>">
<% cnt = cnt + 1 %>
<PARAM name="Data(<% = counter %>,<% = cnt %>)"
    value="<% = DataCommand1.fields.getValue("Fund_C") %>">
<% cnt = cnt + 1 %>
<PARAM name="Data(<% = counter %>,<% = cnt %>)"
    value="<% = DataCommand1.fields.getValue("Fund_D") %>">
<% cnt = cnt + 1 %>
<PARAM name="Data(<% = counter %>,<% = cnt %>)"
    value="<% = DataCommand1.fields.getValue("Fund_E") %>">
```

(continued)

```
<% cnt = cnt + 1 %>
<PARAM name="Data(<% = counter %>,<% = cnt %>)"
    value="<% = DataCommand1.fields.getValue("Fund_F") %>">
<% cnt = cnt + 1 %>
<PARAM name="Data(<% = counter %>,<% = cnt %>)"
    value="<% = DataCommand1.fields.getValue("Fund_G") %>">
<% cnt = cnt + 1 %>

<% counter = counter + 1 %>
<% DataCommand1.MoveNext %>
<%
LOOP
%>

<PARAM name="Num_Items" value="<% = cnt - 1 %>">
<% num_sets = counter - 1 %>
<PARAM name="Num_Sets" value="<% = counter - 1 %>">

<% DataCommand1.MoveFirst %>

<PARAM name="Set_Name(1)" value="12-Month Period">
<PARAM name="Set_Name(2)" value="2-Week Period">

<% cnt = 1 %>
<PARAM name="Item_Name(<% = cnt %>)" value="Fund A">
<% cnt = cnt + 1 %>
<PARAM name="Item_Name(<% = cnt %>)" value="Fund C">
<% cnt = cnt + 1 %>
<PARAM name="Item_Name(<% = cnt %>)" value="Fund D">
<% cnt = cnt + 1 %>
<PARAM name="Item_Name(<% = cnt %>)" value="Fund E">
<% cnt = cnt + 1 %>
<PARAM name="Item_Name(<% = cnt %>)" value="Fund F">
<% cnt = cnt + 1 %>
<PARAM name="Item_Name(<% = cnt %>)" value="Fund G">

<PARAM name="Legend_Color" value="white">
<PARAM name="Legend_BG_Color" value="black">
<PARAM name="Legend_Location" value="Bottom">

<PARAM name="Title" value="MAP Fund Performance">
<% DataCommand1.MoveLast %>
<PARAM name="Set_Label" value="Period Ending <% =
    CStr(DataCommand1.fields.getValue("Date_End")) %>">
<PARAM name="Mag_Label" value="Percentage">

</APPLET>
```

(continued)

```
</TD>
<TD valign=top>

<TABLE>
<TR>
<TD align="center" bgcolor="#0000FF">
    <FONT color="#FFFFFF">Select Period</FONT>
</TD>
</TR>

<TR>
<TD valign="top" width="175"><FONT size="2">
<INPUT type="radio" name="Set" value="Set2"
    onclick="if(document.graph1 != null) {
        document.graph1.set_Area_Of_Interest(1,1);
        document.graph1.refresh();
    }">Focus on 12-Month Period<BR>

<INPUT type="radio" name="Set" value="Set1"
    onclick="if(document.graph1 != null) {
        x = 2
        y = 3
        document.graph1.set_Area_Of_Interest(2,2);
        document.graph1.refresh();
    }">Focus on 2-Week Period

<INPUT type="radio" name="Set" value="SetAll"
    onclick="if(document.graph1 != null) {
        document.graph1.set_Area_Of_Interest(1,2);
        document.graph1.refresh();
    }">Display ALL Data</FONT>
</TD>
</TR>
</TABLE>

</TD>
</TR>
</TABLE>

<BR>
</P>

<HR>
...
<Code to display the HTML table>
...
<HR>
Be sure to visit the rest of our site!
```

(continued)

```
<%
DataCommand1.Close
%>

</BODY>
<% ' VI 6.0 Scripting Object Model Enabled %>
<% EndPageProcessing() %>
</FORM>
</HTML>
```

The page also contains some code that allows the graph to be changed dynamically by the end user. A series of radio buttons allow the end user to select the area of interest to graph. This can be fund performance for the two-week period, the twelve-month period, or both periods.

While there is quite a lot of code within this sample, once you have developed such a page you have a very flexible and powerful way of graphing data dynamically from the database. This single ASP Web page can provide customized graphs to end users and can even be customized further to display only those fund types that the user wants to see. One way to achieve this customization is via conditional logic in the ASP Web page and the use of cookies to store user preferences.

The trick to sucessfully integrating Java applets into your ASP Web pages is in learning all the events, methods, and properties that are available to you within the applet itself. Once you know how it can be manipulated and what parameters it requires, it's relatively easy to write the ASP code or other script code for your applications. Be sure to use the Script Outline window within Visual InterDev to assist you in your scripting. Also, when working with Java applets, you'll want to be sure to test the applet in whatever browsers you need to support.

Part IV

Advanced Database Development

Chapter 12

Exploring the Data Environment

Within Microsoft Visual InterDev 6.0, you have access to the Microsoft Visual Database Tools for creating and managing your data-driven applications. The Visual Database Tools are available in Visual InterDev 6.0, Microsoft Visual J++ 6.0, Microsoft Visual C++ 6.0, and Microsoft Visual Basic 6.0, Enterprise Editions. To start using the Visual Database Tools, all you need to do is create a Web project or a database project within Visual InterDev and add a data connection to the project.

There are four main components to the Visual Database Tools. They are listed and defined below. This chapter will cover all of them, as well as database projects.

■ **Data View**   The Data View allows you to view live connections to the databases in your Web projects and to work with the objects within each database. Objects available include database diagrams, tables, views, stored procedures, and triggers.

■ **Database Designer**   The Database Designer allows you to create, edit, or delete database objects. You can also create database diagrams to visualize the structure of your database tables and their relationships.

■ **Query Designer** The Query Designer allows you to create SQL commands using a visual interface and to view and edit the results of your queries.

■ **Source Code Editor** The source code editor allows you to edit stored procedures and triggers. It also allows you to execute, debug, and view stored procedure results.

The combination of these four Visual Database Tools enables you to create and manage your entire database environment within the familiar Visual Inter-Dev IDE. With the Visual Database Tools, you can:

■ Connect to and explore any ODBC-compliant database

■ Create and modify Microsoft SQL Server databases by using database diagrams

■ Design, execute, and save complex queries

■ Add, update, and delete data stored in database tables

■ Design objects—such as tables, triggers, and stored procedures— in SQL Server and Oracle databases

■ Drag database objects onto a design surface—such as an HTML template form—and then drop to bind controls to those objects

An excellent feature of the Visual Database Tools is that they provide a consistent visual interface that allows you to work with all ODBC-compliant databases in the same way. Thus, for the most part you don't need to be aware of any differences from one database to another. There are some special considerations, however, when you are working with SQL Server and Oracle databases. The Visual Database Tools provide extended functionality for these databases, and in some areas you need to be aware of the differences when working with one database or another. Examples include the differences in the data types supported by each database (noticeable when working with Database Designer), and the slight differences in the SQL syntax (noticeable when working with the Query Designer).

Table 12-1 describes the Visual InterDev features that work for different databases. Most Visual Database Tools support any database that is supported by an ODBC 3 driver. The last three features work only with SQL Server 6.5 (or later) or Oracle 7 (or later).

NOTE To work with Visual InterDev's Database Designer on SQL Server 6.5 databases, you need to apply SQL Server Service Pack 1 to the database.

Feature	Supporting Databases
Creating, editing, and executing stored procedures	Any database supported by an ODBC 3 driver. The database must support stored procedures.
Creating and executing views	Any database supported by an ODBC 3 driver. The database must support views or a similar feature.
Creating queries and other Database Manipulation Language (DML) statements, such as Select, Insert, Update, and Delete	Any database supported by an ODBC 3 driver. The database and ODBC driver must support the specific DML features that you are trying to use.
Using the Query Designer	Any database supported by an ODBC 3 driver. The database and ODBC driver must support the specific DML features that you are trying to use.
Data View features	Any database supported by an ODBC 3 driver. The database and ODBC driver must support the specific features that you are trying to use. Features that a database does not support do not show up in Data View menus and toolbars.
Creating and editing triggers	Any database supported by an ODBC 3 driver. The database and ODBC driver must support triggers and the functions you use in them.
Creating database diagrams	SQL Server and Oracle databases only.
Creating and modifying tables in a database	SQL Server and Oracle databases only.
Creating a new database	SQL Server and Oracle databases only.

Table 12-1. *Visual InterDev features and the databases that support them.*

In Visual InterDev 1.0, extended functionality—such as the ability to create databases, to create and modify tables, and to create database diagrams—was only provided for SQL Server databases. In Visual InterDev 6.0, this functionality is also provided for Oracle databases. This is an important enhancement to Visual InterDev, since many Web-enabled corporate applications are being created with extant Oracle systems for the back-end database.

DATA VIEW

Data View allows you to view live connections to the databases in your Web projects and to work with the objects within each database. Objects available include database diagrams, tables, views, stored procedures, and triggers. For each database connection, the Data View provides a node under which you can drill down into more detail on the various database objects within your particular database.

Figure 12-1 shows how each database object—such as a table or a stored procedure—is treated like a folder. To expand a folder, you click the plus sign (+) next to it. Figure 12-1 shows Data View with both the Database Diagrams and Tables folders expanded to show their contents. You can also expand folders such as Stored Procedures to show their contents.

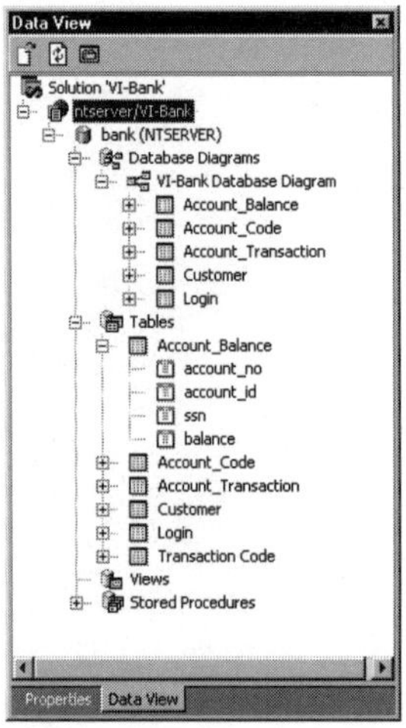

Figure 12-1. *Data View provides a hierarchical view of your database connections.*

Data View also supports various popup menus for the different objects it displays. For instance, you can right-click a SQL Server table to create a new table. To create a new stored procedure, you can also right-click a stored-procedure from any database that supports stored procedures. You can open a table to edit its data, open a stored procedure to edit the SQL definition, and so forth. The features supported by your database and database driver show up as available commands on the submenu; the commands that are not available are grayed out.

Another way you can create new database objects is to use the Project menu. From here you can choose Add Database Item and then select the appropriate item from the cascading menu.

NOTE To create triggers, you'll need to select a table within the Data View, access the context menu by right-clicking the selected table, and then choose the New Trigger menu item. This menu item is only available when you have selected a table.

Data View serves as the launching pad for moving into the other components of the Visual Database Tools. For example, the Tables folder allows you to access the Database Designer or the Query Designer, whereas the Stored Procedures folder allows you to access the source code editor.

DATABASE DESIGNER

The Database Designer allows you to create, edit, or delete database objects. You can also create database diagrams to visualize the structure of your database tables and their relationships.

Creating and Modifying Database Diagrams

Database Diagrams graphically represent the tables in your database. They also show the relationships between the tables and their indexes and constraints. To create a Database Diagram, you right-click the Database Diagrams folder in Data View and then choose New Diagram. Figure 12-2 shows a Database Diagram within Visual InterDev.

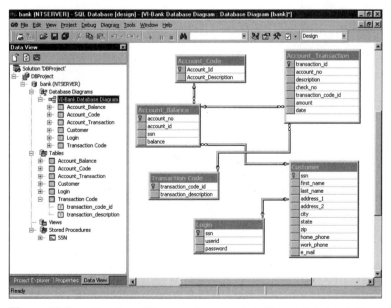

Figure 12-2. *A Database Diagram showing six tables and their relationships.*

You can use Database Diagrams to:

- Manipulate database objects without having to write SQL code
- Visualize the structure of your database tables and their relationships
- Provide different visualizations of complex databases
- Experiment with database changes without modifying the underlying database
- Create new tables, indexes, relationships, and other constraints
- Alter the structure of your database

You can place tables onto your Database Diagram by dragging them from the Data View. You can also create new tables by right-clicking within the Database Diagram and choosing New Table from the context menu. Tables can be dragged around within the Database Diagram to help you better visualize your database schema.

The Database Diagram has extensive context menus for working with tables, allowing you to perform a variety of tasks. Any changes you make to your tables are not saved to the database until you save the diagram. Figure 12-3 shows the context menu that appears if you right-click a particular table.

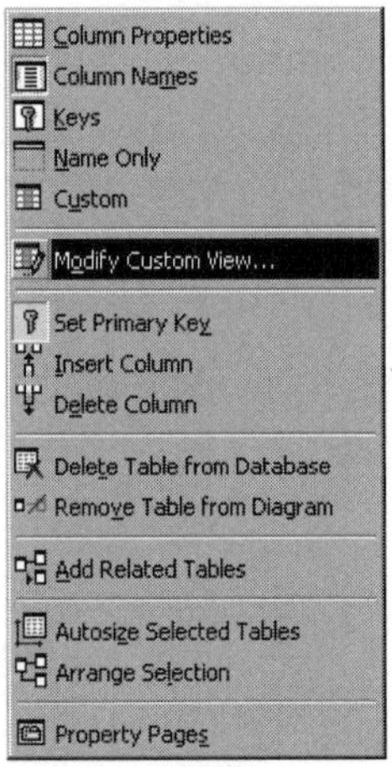

Figure 12-3. *The Database Diagram context menu that appears when a table is selected.*

In Figure 12-3, the top six menu items allow you to set and modify your view of the tables within the Database Diagram. You have the following choices:

- Column Properties
- Column Names
- Keys
- Name Only
- Custom
- Modify Custom View

If you choose Column Properties, you'll see the tables with all their column properties displayed. For SQL Server, this includes Column Name, Datatype, Length, Precision, Scale, Allow Nulls, Default Value, Identity, Identity Seed, and Identity Increment. If you choose Column Names, you'll see only the column names associated with each table, as shown in Figure 12-2. If you choose Keys, you'll see only those columns associated with a primary or foreign key. If you choose Name Only, only the table name is displayed. If you choose Custom, you can view a custom set of table properties. The default custom view shows all column names with their associated data types and nullability, as shown in Figure 12-4.

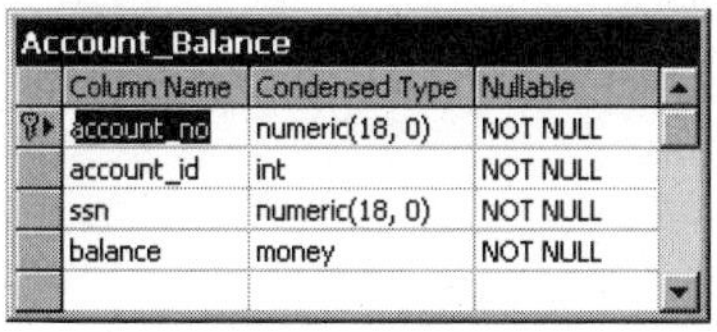

Account_Balance		
Column Name	Condensed Type	Nullable
account_no	numeric(18, 0)	NOT NULL
account_id	int	NOT NULL
ssn	numeric(18, 0)	NOT NULL
balance	money	NOT NULL

Figure 12-4. *A custom view of a table within the Database Diagram showing column names, data types, and nullability.*

Finally, you can choose Modify Custom View from the context menu to create your own custom view for the tables within the Database Diagram. Figure 12-5 on the following page shows the resulting dialog box. Here you can choose from a set of available columns. You can also sort the columns in any order you choose and save your changes as the default custom view.

Other menu items on the context menu shown in Figure 12-3 allow you to define primary keys, insert or delete columns, remove tables from the diagram, delete tables from the database, arrange the size and location of the tables on the diagram, and view table property pages.

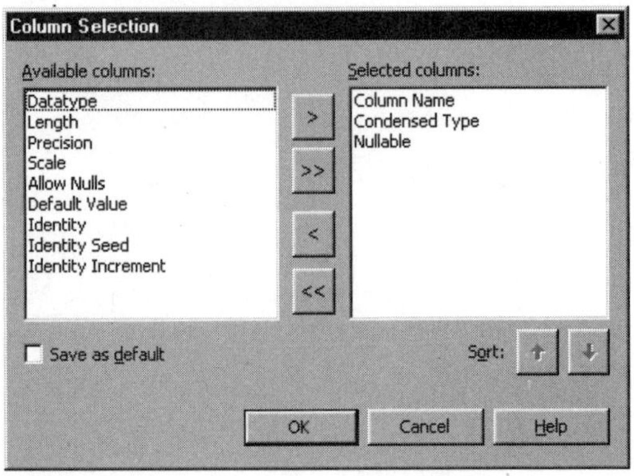

Figure 12-5. *The Column Selection dialog box for modifying a custom view of a table.*

By right-clicking outside of any table in the Database Diagram, you can pull up another context menu that allows you to manipulate your diagram. For example, you can zoom the diagram from 10 percent to 200 percent, arrange the layout of tables on the diagram, view page breaks (useful when printing), and create text annotations to place on the diagram.

Printing the Database Diagram is useful when you are developing your applications since it gives you a handy reference to the column names and data types within each of your tables.

Creating and Modifying Database Objects

For SQL Server and Oracle databases, you can use the Database Designer to exercise complete control over your database objects. You can create tables, relationships, indexes, keys, and constraints.

Tables

To create a new table, follow these steps:

1.   Expand the Tables folder in Data View.

2.   Right-click a table name, or right-click the Tables folder.

3.   Choose New Table from the context menu.

4.   Enter the table name in the Choose Name dialog box. The new table definition appears in a window, as shown in Figure 12-6.

5. Define the name of a column for the new table in the Column Name field.

6. Tab to the Datatype field, and select the column's data type.

7. Select or deselect the Allow Nulls option, depending on your project's requirements.

8. If desired, make the column a primary key (PK) by clicking the Primary Key button on the Table toolbar. A key symbol appears to indicate that the field is the primary key.

9. Enter the other column information. Your table definition window should resemble the one in Figure 12-7 on the following page.

10. Choose Save from the File menu or click the Save button on the toolbar to save your new table and update the database.

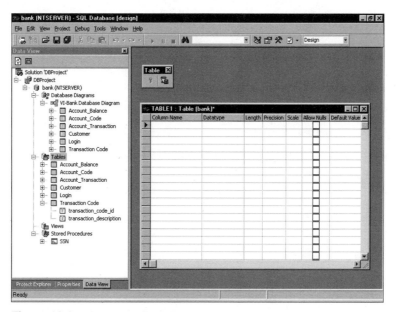

Figure 12-6. *The new table definition window is shown in the right pane.*

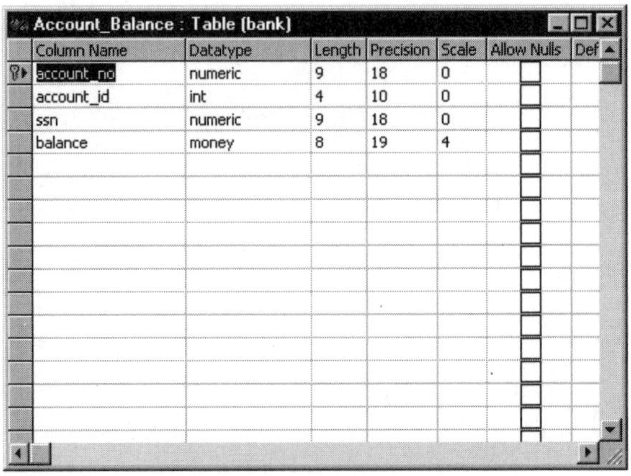

Figure 12-7. *The table definition window for the Account_Balance table.*

You can also easily modify any existing table using the Database Designer. Take the following steps:

1. Right-click a table name, or right-click the Tables folder.

2. Choose Design from the context menu to display the table definition window, like the one shown in Figure 12-7 above.

3. Modify the table definition as desired.

4. Save the table definition by clicking the Save button on the toolbar.

You can also create a new table by right-clicking an open space on the Database Designer and then choosing New Table from the context menu.

Now that you have a new table, you can easily create related tables. You can copy the table definition to the Clipboard to copy information from one table to another. This is useful for creating other tables with related columns.

The Clipboard is extremely useful when you need to create a one-to-many relationship between two tables—such as a Customer table that must be linked to an Account_Balance table. Create the Customer and Account_Balance tables, and then copy the primary key from the Customer table and paste it into the new Account_Balance table. Copy and paste assures that you have no misspelled words in the Account_Balance table's new foreign key.

To use the Clipboard in this manner, simply select the row that defines the column you want to copy. Choose Copy from the Edit menu, and then select the other table and choose Paste from the Edit menu to paste the column definition into the other table.

Relationships

You can create relationships between tables within a Database Diagram. A typical relationship between two tables is a one-to-many relationship: one record in a table can have one or many related records in another table.

The relationship lines indicate the current relationships defined in the database. You can edit a relationship by right-clicking the line and choosing the Property Pages command from the context menu or by right-clicking the relevant table and choosing the Property Pages command from its context menu. Figure 12-8 shows the Relationships tab on the Property Pages dialog box.

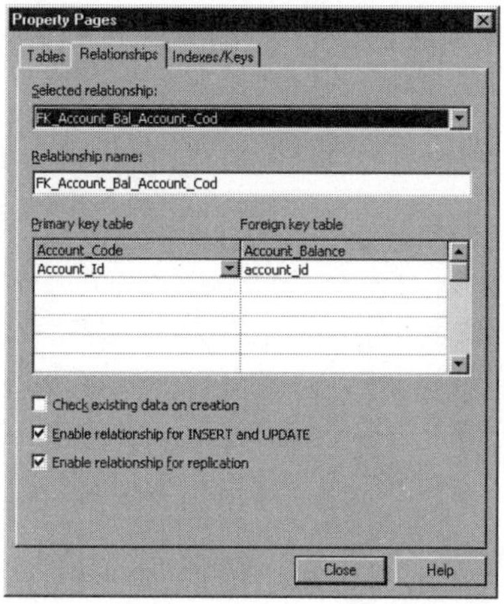

Figure 12-8. *The Relationships tab on the Property Pages dialog box showing a relationship between the Account_Balance and Account_Code tables.*

You can reposition the relationship lines between tables by moving line segments with the mouse. You can also add segments by grabbing the corner of a line and moving it diagonally.

You can create a reflexive relationship on a table by dragging a column and then dropping it back onto the same table. For instance, if you have an Employees table with a Manager ID field that also represents an Employee ID, you can create a reflexive relationship. First make Employee ID the primary key, and then drag a relationship out from Manager ID and drop it back onto the Employees table.

When you drag relationships from one table to another, the Database Designer keeps track of which columns you drag and which you drop on. For instance, if you drag a nonprimary key column into another table, the Database

Designer assumes that you want to link on that table's PK column. If you drag a PK column to another table, it assumes that the column you drop on is the foreign key (FK) column for a one-to-many relationship.

You can also change the keys on a table as well as change the data type across FK relationships. This feature lets you change either the data type or the length of a PK or FK column and then change all the related tables. The Database Designer monitors your changes, alerting you before applying them to the database.

Indexes and keys

The primary key for a table is a column or combination of columns that uniquely identifies a row in a table. It cannot allow null values and must always have a unique index. A primary key is used to relate a table to foreign keys in other tables. You can add a primary key to a table within a Database Diagram by right-clicking the appropriate column in the table and choosing Set Primary Key from the context menu or by using the Indexes/Keys tab in the Property Pages dialog box.

Figure 12-9 shows the Indexes/Keys tab for the Account_Balance table. You can see that the index is named PK_Account_Balance and that it is a primary key. The key is based upon the account_no column in the Account-_Balance table.

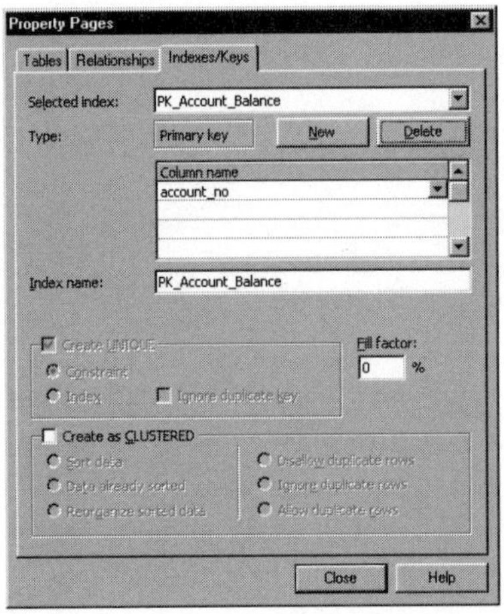

Figure 12-9. *The Indexes/Keys tab on the Property Pages dialog box showing the primary key for the Account_Balance table.*

From this Indexes/Keys tab, you can create additional indexes by clicking the New button. You can then select one or more columns to include in the index and specify various properties of the index, such as whether it is unique and whether it is clustered. A unique index can uniquely identify a row in a table. In a clustered index, the physical order of the rows in the table is the same as the logical (indexed) order of the key values. Clustered indexes are useful for several purposes, including speeding up UPDATE and DELETE SQL statements and for queries that return large resultsets.

Constraints

Constraints are business rules that you can apply to the data within your tables. In SQL Server, there are two types of constraints: check constraints and unique constraints. Check constraints apply certain business rules to your data, such as ensuring the data is within a certain range of values. You can apply check constraints to multiple columns and you can apply multiple check constraints to a single column. Unique constraints ensure that the data entered is unique for that specific column in a table. NULL values are allowed in a unique constraint as long as rows are unique in the table.

You define unique constraints using the Indexes/Keys tab in the Property Pages dialog box, as shown in Figure 12-9.

To create a unique constraint:

1. Select the appropriate table from the Database Diagram, and access its Property Pages dialog box.

2. Select the Indexes/Keys tab.

3. Click the New button.

4. Select the column name for the constraint.

5. Check the Create Unique check box.

6. Ensure the Constraint radio button is selected.

7. Click the Close button to save your new constraint but not immediately apply it to the database, or choose File | Save to save your new constraint.

You define check constraints using the Tables tab in the Property Pages dialog box, as shown in Figure 12-10 on the following page.

To create a check constraint:

1.   Select the appropriate table from the Database Diagram, and access its Property Pages dialog box.

2.   Select the Tables tab.

3.   Click the New button.

4.   Enter the constraint expression.

5.   Enter the name for the constraint.

6.   Click the Close button to save your new constraint but not immediately apply it to the database, or choose File | Save to save your new constraint.

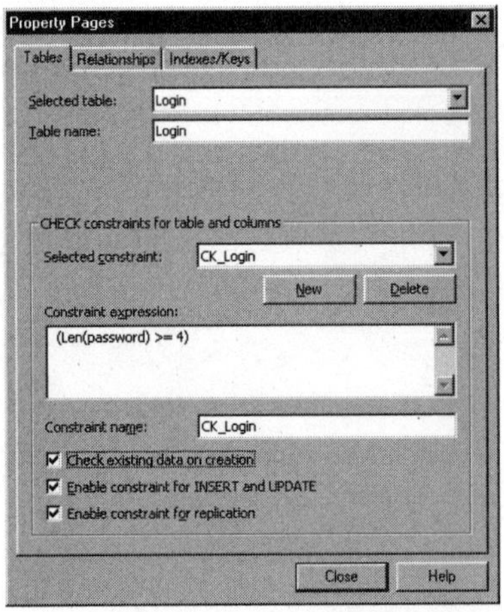

Figure 12-10. *The Tables tab showing a check constraint for the password column in the Login table.*

In Figure 12-10, you'll also notice the check boxes at the bottom of the dialog box that allow you to specify whether the constraint should check existing data upon creation and whether it should be enabled for INSERTs, UPDATEs, and replication. Once a constraint has been created (assuming the constraint is enabled for INSERTs), if any new data that is entered into the table violates the constraint you'll see an error message similar to the one shown in Figure 12-11.

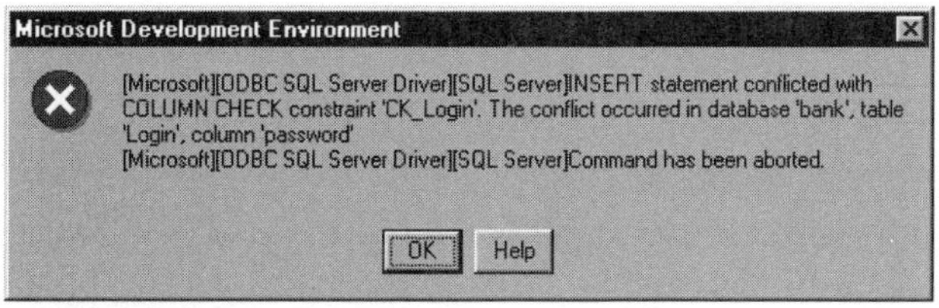

Figure 12-11. *A sample error message that is displayed when a check constraint is violated upon an INSERT statement.*

Creating Scripts

Whenever you make changes to your database schema within the Database Diagram, the changes are not applied to the database until you choose the Save command from the File menu. At this point, you'll be prompted with the Save dialog box, which will inform you which tables will be saved to the database and give you the option either to continue or to cancel the save operation. If you choose Yes to save your changes to the database, you'll see a Save Change Script dialog box, as shown in Figure 12-12 on the following page.

This dialog box gives you the option to view your change script and to save it to a text file. The change script is a SQL script (for your SQL Server or Oracle database) that contains all the Data Definition Language (DDL) syntax necessary to apply your changes to the database. These changes can include creation, modification, or deletion of tables, columns, constraints, relationships, indexes, and so on. The change scripts are useful for a number of purposes, including:

- Keeping a record of changes that you've made to your database for version control

- Passing along to a database administrator for review/approval and for changes to the production database

- Applying to other databases such as test databases so that the database schemas are kept in sync

Another way to save your change script is to click the Save Change Script button on the Database Diagram toolbar. If you don't see the Database Diagram toolbar on your screen, you can access it by choosing View | Toolbars | Database Diagram from the menu.

When you save your change script the name of the file is DbDgmN.sql, where N is the number of the change script you generate. N starts at 1 and increments each time you save a script. You can execute the script against a database at any time using the Query Designer within Visual InterDev or a tool such as ISQL/W, which comes as part of SQL Server. Oracle databases provide similar tools for applying SQL scripts to the database.

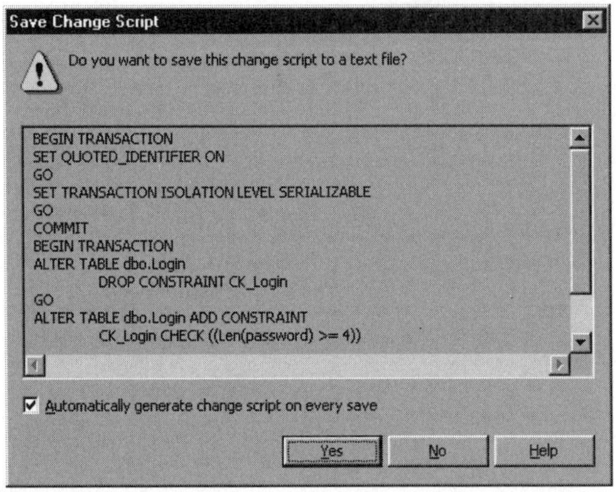

Figure 12-12. *The Save Change Script dialog box allows you to view and save your database changes as a SQL script for later use.*

THE QUERY DESIGNER

The Query Designer allows you to create SQL commands using a visual interface and to view and edit the results of your queries. We had an introduction to the Query Designer in Chapter 5. In this section, we'll look at creating insert, update, and delete queries. We'll also examine parameter queries. All of these queries can be constructed in the Query Designer and saved in your data command objects or Recordset DTCs for use within your Visual InterDev applications. To launch the Query Designer from your data command object or Recordset DTC, specify SQL Statement as the source of the data and then click the SQL Builder button.

Creating Update Queries

To create an update query, take the following steps:

1. Add the table you want to update to the Diagram pane.

2. Click the Change Type button, and select Update from the Query toolbar.

3. Add the columns you want to update to the Grid pane.

4. Add your update values.

5. In the Criteria column, set the criteria to use for selecting the rows to update.

6. Verify the SQL syntax by clicking the Verify SQL Syntax button on the Query toolbar.

7. Execute or save your query.

Figure 12-13 shows the Query Designer with an update query. The update statement in the figure changes the account_no field to 123401 for each row that is currently set to 123402.

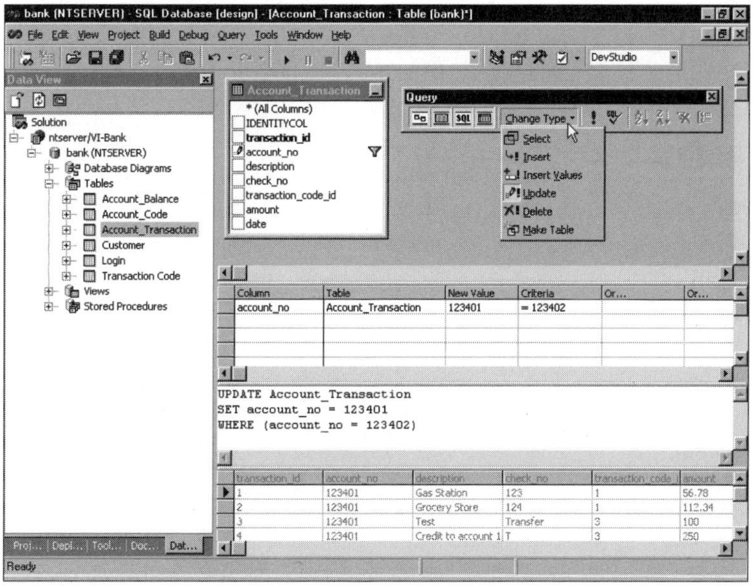

Figure 12-13. *The SQL pane shows the update query that the Query Designer generates from the information in the Grid pane.*

Creating Insert Queries

There are two types of insert queries you can define: insert and insert values. The insert query uses a SELECT statement to gather the result set for insertion into the table. It can therefore be a multirow insert statement. The following code shows a sample insert query:

```
INSERT INTO "Account_Code"
    (Account_Id, Account_Description)
SELECT Account_Id, Account_Description
FROM Account_Code_Tmp
```

The insert values query does not use a SELECT statement and inserts specific values into a single new record. The following code shows a sample insert values query:

```
INSERT INTO Account_Code
    (Account_Id, Account_Description)
VALUES (5, 'Personal Loan')
```

To create an insert query, take the following steps:

1. Add the table you want to insert in the Diagram pane.

2. Click the Change Type button, and select Insert or Insert Values from the Query toolbar.

3. If you have selected Insert, select the table name from the Insert Into Table dialog box and click OK. The table you selected in step 1 becomes the source table for the insert query.

4. Add the columns you want to insert in the Grid pane.

5. Add your update values.

6. Verify the SQL syntax by using the Verify SQL Syntax button on the Query toolbar.

7. Execute or save your query.

Figure 12-14 shows the Query Designer with an insert values query.

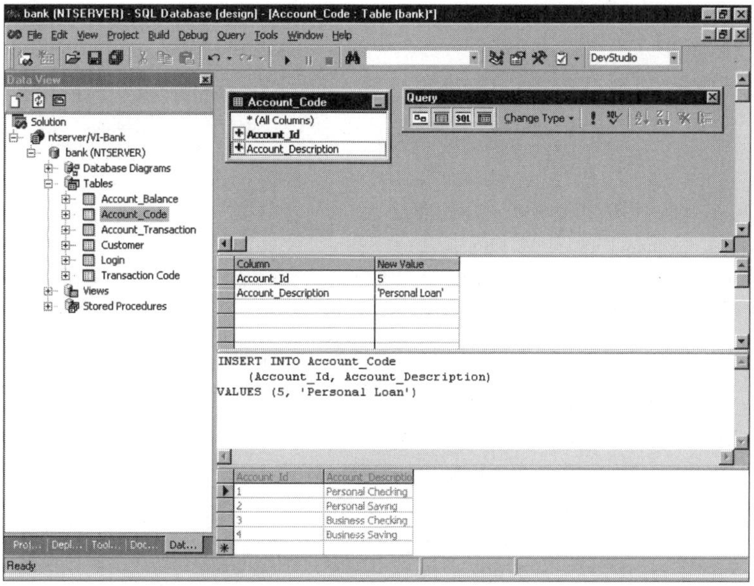

Figure 12-14. *The SQL pane shows the insert values query that the Query Designer generates from the information in the Grid pane.*

Creating Delete Queries

To create a delete query, take the following steps:

1.   Add the table in which you want to delete records to the Diagram pane.

2.   Click the Change Type button on the Query toolbar, and select Delete.

3.   In the Criteria column, set the criteria to use for selecting the rows to delete.

4.   Verify the SQL syntax by clicking the Verify SQL Syntax button on the Query toolbar.

5.   Execute or save your query.

SQL delete queries do not use columns; they use only the name of the table to delete the row from, and they use a WHERE clause to determine which rows to delete. You can delete the row inserted by the earlier insert values query with this statement:

```
DELETE FROM Account_Code
WHERE (Account_Id = 5)
```

This delete query deletes all rows in which the Account_Id field is equal to 5.

Parameterized Queries

Parameterized queries will be the most typical queries that you create for your Web applications. These queries take input from the application during run time in the form of a variable or number of variables and build the SQL statement from these input parameters. Input parameters are typically used to supply values for the WHERE clause of a SELECT, UPDATE, or DELETE statement or are used as input parameters for stored procedures.

To build a parameterized query, you simply use the Query Designer. Use a question mark (?) to indicate parameters within your query. Figure 12-15 shows the Properties dialog box of a data command object named Customer, with a parameterized query entered as a SQL statement.

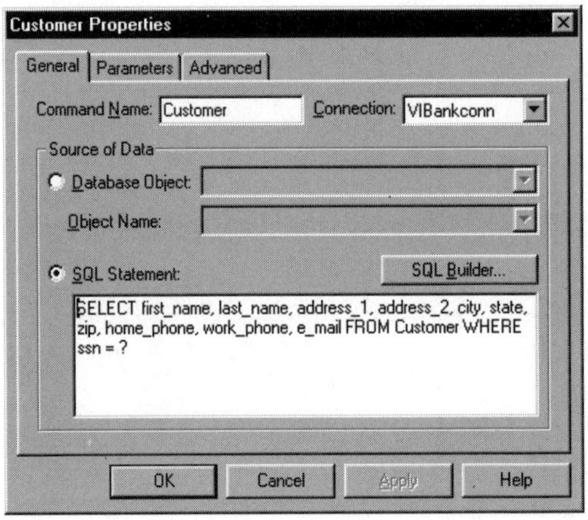

Figure 12-15. *A parameterized query for a data command object named Customer.*

Once you have entered the SQL statement with the question mark, you can further define the type of parameter you want to supply to the query by moving to the Parameters tab of the Properties dialog box, as shown in Figure 12-16.

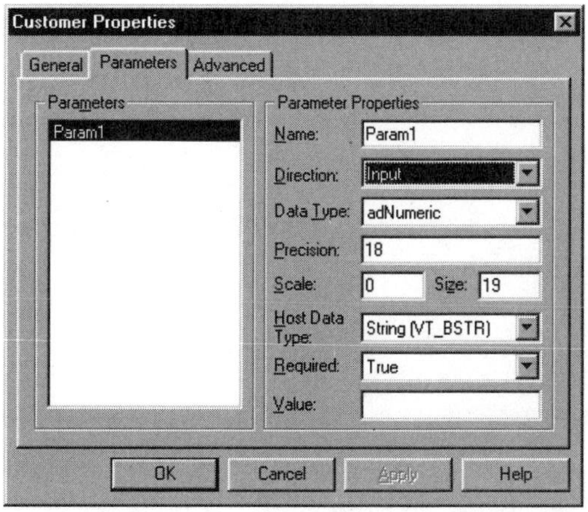

Figure 12-16. *The Parameters tab of a data command object's Properties dialog box. Here you can further define your parameters.*

Within this tab you can define the data types for your parameters and specify whether they are input, output, or input/output parameters. For SQL statements these parameters can only be input parameters. For stored procedures, however, you can choose any of the options. In Figure 12-16, you'll also notice that there is a Value textbox. Here you can enter any of the following:

- **Literals** Character values in single quotes or numeric values without quotes.

- **Variables** Name of a variable defined in server code that will contain the value you want to pass.

- **Object References** An object reference and property value such as *Textbox1.value*. The object must be available in server script. Also, note that the expression will be evaluated as a JScript expression.

- **Expressions** The expression is evaluated as a JScript expression and can be any combination of literals, variables, object references, and function calls.

If you enter expressions into the Value text box, be sure to use correct capitalization—the expressions are evaluated as JScript expressions and are therefore case sensitive. Use a plus sign (+) for concatenation and single quotation marks for string literals. You can also leave the Value text box blank and supply it later via a *Recordset* scripting object (that uses the data command object as its data source) and the *setParameter* method.

In addition to data command objects, you can also create parameterized queries within *Recordset* scripting objects. The Recordset DTC also includes a Parameters tab in its Properties dialog box where you can enter a value for your parameter.

> **NOTE** To pass parameters into a *Recordset* scripting object, you want to be sure that the parameter is specified before the underlying recordset opens. You do this either by using the *onenter* event for the page or the *onbeforeopen* event for the *Recordset* scripting object or by marking the recordset not to open automatically and then programmatically setting the parameter and opening the recordset. Chapter 14 goes into more detail on the various *Recordset* scripting object methods, properties, and events.

Figure 12-17 shows a parameterized query within the Query Designer. Creating these types of queries is easy: simply add a question mark to the criteria column in the SQL grid pane for the specific column or columns you want to work with.

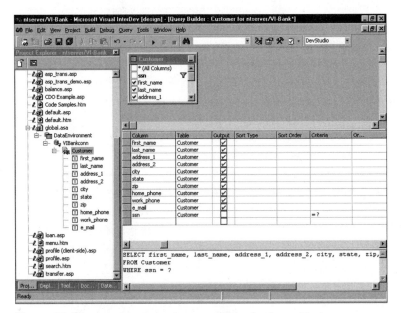

Figure 12-17. *A parameterized query within the Query Designer.*

When you execute a parameterized query from within the Query Designer, you'll see a dialog box like the one shown in Figure 12-18. This dialog box asks you to define the query parameters prior to executing the query. After you have entered the relevant parameters, the results of the query are displayed as usual in the results pane within the Query Designer.

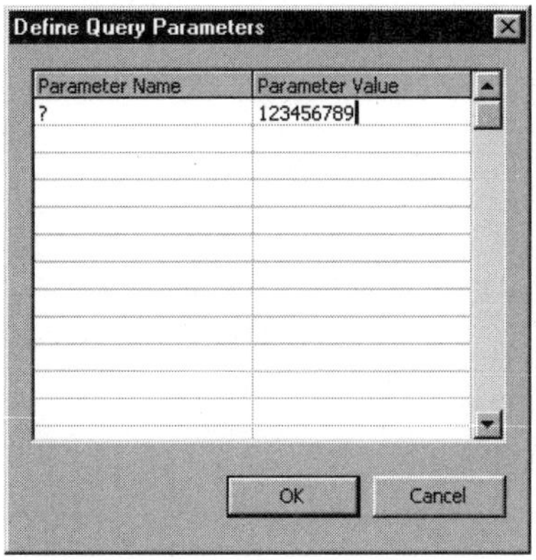

Figure 12-18. *The Define Query Parameters dialog box that appears when you execute a parameterized query from within the Query Designer.*

SOURCE CODE EDITOR

The source code editor enables you to edit stored procedures and triggers and to execute and debug stored procedures and view their results. The source code editor is launched from within Visual InterDev when you create or edit a stored procedure or trigger within Data View.

To create a new stored procedure:

1. Select the Stored Procedures folder in Data View.

2. Right-click, and select New Stored Procedure from the context menu.

To create a new trigger:

1. Select the relevant table in Data View.

2. Right-click, and select New Trigger from the context menu.

When you create a new stored procedure or trigger, the source code editor will open and will include the basic syntax for the CREATE PROCEDURE or CREATE TRIGGER statement. Figure 12-19 on the following page shows the source code editor after a new trigger has been created for the Customer table.

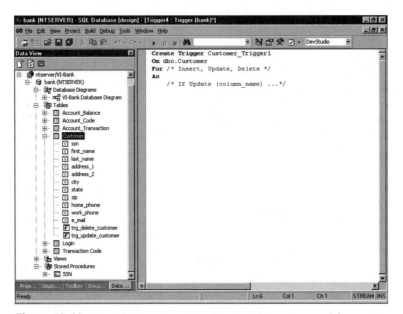

Figure 12-19. *The source code editor showing the syntax used for creating a new trigger.*

DATABASE PROJECTS

Database projects are collections of one or more data connections that enable you to access your server database from within Visual InterDev. Database projects are also available within Visual C++ and Visual J++. Using database projects in addition to Web projects gives you the following benefits:

- Data connections aren't required in a database project until you want to run a SQL script against a database. In addition, you can rename data connections in a database project.

- You can use source control to ensure that the database and its structure are under the administrator's control.

- You can easily deploy the database to other projects.

One of the main benefits of working with database projects is that you can create and manage database objects using SQL scripts. You can also put these files under Microsoft Visual SourceSafe control.

To create a database project:

1. Choose File|New Project from the main menu.

2. Select the Database Projects folder in the New Project dialog box, as shown in Figure 12-20.

3. Enter the name of the new database project, and click Open.

4. Select the data source from the Select Data Source dialog box, and click OK.

5. If connecting to SQL Server, enter the Login ID and Password for the data connection and click OK.

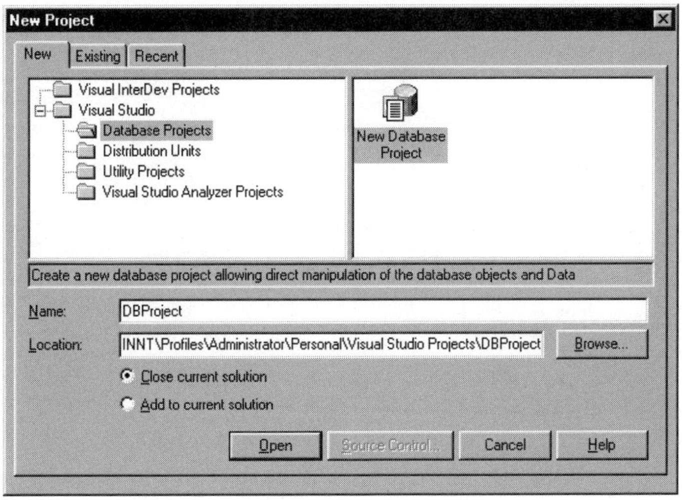

Figure 12-20. *The New Project dialog box showing the New Database Project icon.*

Once you have created a database project, you can use SQL script files to create and manage your database objects and store other frequently used SQL commands.

To create a new SQL script file and add it to a project in Visual InterDev:

1. Expand the database project folder in the Project Explorer.

2. Right-click the data connection, and choose Add SQL Script from the context menu. The Add Item dialog box is displayed, as shown in Figure 12-21 on the following page.

3. Select the SQL Script icon in the right pane. Enter a name for the SQL script in the Name text box, and click Open. The SQL Editor window is displayed, and the SQL script is added to the Project Explorer under the data connection node.

4. In the SQL Editor window, enter SQL statements that define the database objects you want to add to the database project.

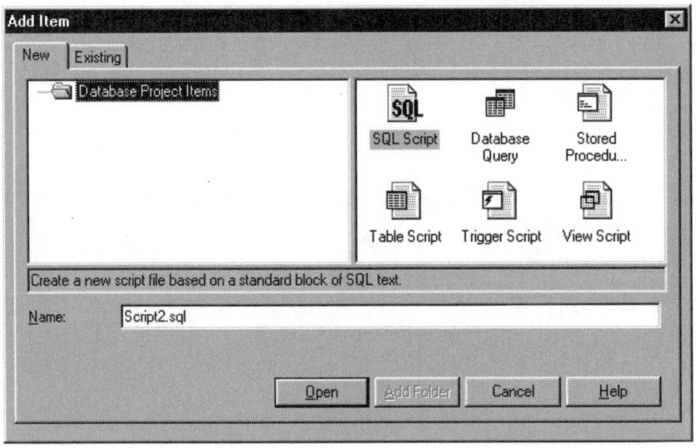

Figure 12-21. *The Add Item dialog box, where you can create a new SQL script or choose from an existing SQL template.*

As you can see in Figure 12-21, you can use the SQL templates already supplied in addition to creating new SQL script files. You can select a SQL script file that creates a table, view, stored procedure, trigger, or query. If you select the Database Query option, Visual InterDev will launch the Query Designer. If you select any of the other options, Visual InterDev will launch the source code editor with the template SQL code ready for you to customize. Figure 12-22 shows the template code for creating a new table.

Visual InterDev makes it easy for you to generate SQL scripts for any existing database objects within your database project. You can select a single database object from within Data View or select multiple database objects.

To create a SQL script for creating a database object:

1. Within Data View, select one or more database objects for which you want to generate a SQL script to create the objects.

2. Once you have selected the database objects, simply right-click them and choose the Copy SQL Script command from the context menu.

3. From within Project Explorer, right-click the data connection object and choose Paste.

Your SQL script will now be added to the project. If you are using source control, you'll be prompted about whether you want to add the SQL file to source control on the server. The prompt is shown in Figure 12-23.

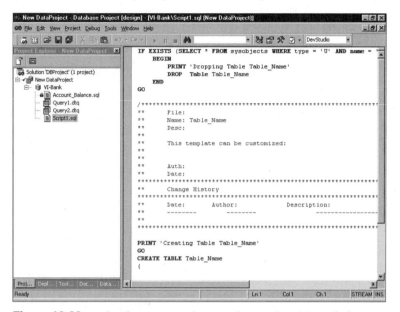

Figure 12-22. *A database project showing the template SQL code for creating a new table.*

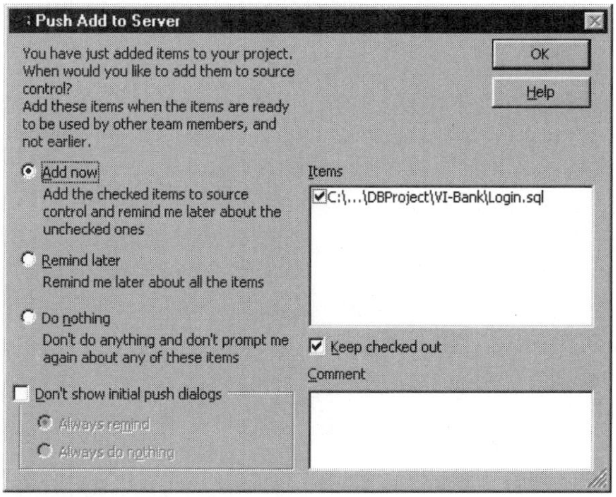

Figure 12-23. *The Push Add To Server dialog box asks you whether you want to add your SQL script to source control.*

The following code shows an example of a SQL script that is generated for the Login table in the VI-Bank project. You can see that the script includes not only the CREATE TABLE statement but also the appropriate SQL syntax to add various constraints such as primary and foreign key constraints and check constraints.

```
If Exists (Select * From sysobjects Where
    name = 'Login' And user_name(uid) = 'dbo')
    Drop Table dbo.Login
Go

Create Table dbo.Login
    (
    ssn numeric(18, 0) Not Null,
    userid varchar(8) Not Null,
    password varchar(8) Not Null
    )
Go
Alter Table dbo.Login Add Constraint
    PK_Login Primary Key Nonclustered
    (
    ssn
    )
Go
Alter Table dbo.Login Add Constraint
    CK_Login Check (len(password) >= 4)
Go
Alter Table dbo.Login Add Constraint
    FK_Login_Customer Foreign Key
    (
    ssn
    ) References dbo.Customer
    (
    ssn
    )
Go
```

In addition to SQL Server database objects, the Copy SQL Script command also works with Oracle views, triggers, stored procedures, and functions, but not with Oracle tables and synonyms.

To execute a SQL script:

1. Within Project Explorer, select the script or scripts you want to execute. You can select more than one script at a time.

2. Right-click, and choose Execute from the popup menu.

Adding a Database Project to Source Control

Database projects consist of folders and SQL script files. You can add these files and folders to source control just as you do with other files, such as HTML and Active Server Pages Web pages.

To add a database project to source control:

1. In Project Explorer, right-click the database project name and choose Add To Source Control from the context menu.

2. Login to Visual SourceSafe by entering your Username and Password, as shown in Figure 12-24.

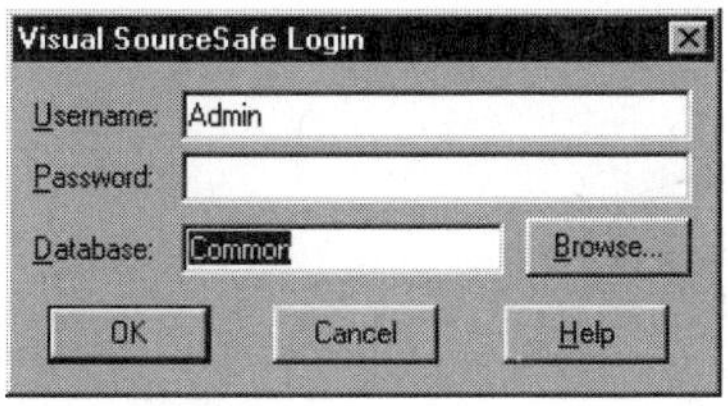

Figure 12-24. *The Visual SourceSafe Login dialog box.*

3. Enter a project name in the Add To SourceSafe Project dialog box, and click OK.

4. Click OK on the Add To Source Control dialog box to add any existing files within the database project to source control.

Once you have placed your project under source control, you can check files in and out by selecting the file you want to work with, right-clicking to access the context menu, and then choosing the relevant menu option. In addition to being able to check files in and out, you can also undo the check-out status of any file. When a file is checked out for modification within your database project, you'll see a red check mark alongside the file within Project Explorer. When a file is checked in to Visual SourceSafe, you'll see a blue padlock icon alongside the file.

In addition to the right-click menu, you can access even more source control functionality by choosing Project|Source Control from the main menu. Figure 12-25 on the following page shows the available options on the Source Control menu.

In Figure 12-25, you'll see that the highlighted menu item is labeled Source-Safe. This menu item allows you to launch the Visual SourceSafe Explorer if you have it installed on your workstation. The Visual SourceSafe Explorer is a client tool that interacts with a Visual SourceSafe database in much the same way as a database project does. You do not need to have this tool installed on your workstation to place scripts under source control, but it can provide you with another interface for working with your Visual SourceSafe database. Figure 12-26 shows the Visual SourceSafe Explorer after it has been launched from Visual InterDev. You can see that the Account_Balance.sql script is currently checked out to user Admin under a check-out folder on the user's workstation.

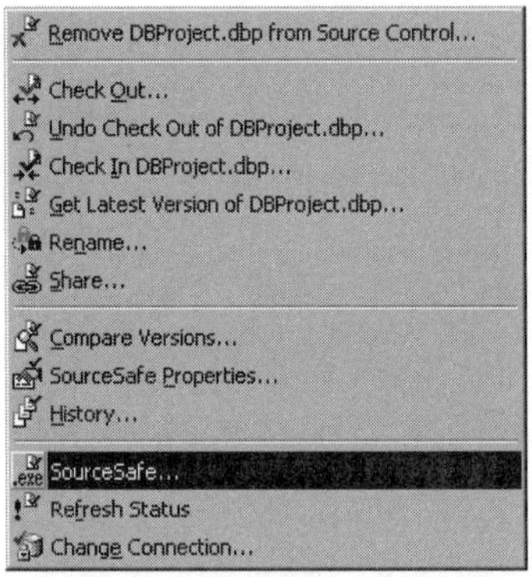

Figure 12-25. *The menu options displayed after choosing Project | Source Control within a database project.*

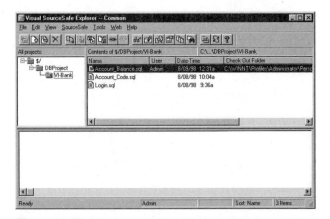

Figure 12-26. *Visual SourceSafe Explorer showing a SQL script named Account_Balance.sql that is checked out to the Admin user.*

Chapter 13

Scripting the Data Environment

The Data Environment allows you to use a variety of techniques to create your dynamic, data-driven applications. The easiest technique is to use the Recordset design-time control (DTC) and data-bound controls and to work with their object model. This way you can often access database functionality without having to write a single line of code. Another technique is to create your own script that accesses the database more directly. Here the advantage is that your Web page is smaller than if it had DTCs placed on it. You also have more flexibility in terms of the user interface. In this chapter, we'll look at examples of both techniques. Often the best approach is to use a combination of Recordset DTCs, data-bound controls, and manual scripting to gain the necessary functionality and flexibility.

SCRIPTING THE DE OBJECT

The Data Environment provides a special object that you can use to script server-based database access: the *DE* object. This object exposes an object model that you can use to execute database commands and manage their recordsets. The *DE* object is a simplified version of the ActiveX Data Objects (ADO) model.

Before starting to script the *DE* object, you'll need to add a data connection to your Web project within Microsoft Visual InterDev. Once you have done this, Visual InterDev adds script to the global.asa file to create a *DE* object for you to work with. The Visual InterDev–generated script also specifies the connection information for the *DE* object. Figure 13-1 shows a sample global.asa file. You can see that the *DE* object is created using the *Server.CreateObject* syntax and is then stored in an Application-level variable named *DE*. All of this code was generated automatically when the data connection was created.

```
<SCRIPT LANGUAGE=VBScript RUNAT=Server>

'You can add special event handlers in this file that will get
'run automatically when special Active Server Pages events occur.
'To create these handlers, just create a subroutine with a name
'from the list below that corresponds to the event you want to
'use. For example, to create an event handler for Session_OnStart,
'you would put the following code into this file (without the
'comments):

'Sub Session_OnStart
'**Put your code here **
'End Sub

'EventName                Description
'Session_OnStart          Runs the first time a user runs any page
'                         in your application
'Session_OnEnd            Runs when a user's session times out or
'                         quits your application

'Application_OnStart      Runs once when the first page of your
'                         application is run for the first time by
'                         any user

'Application_OnEnd        Runs once when the Web server shuts down

</SCRIPT>

<SCRIPT LANGUAGE=VBScript RUNAT=Server>
Sub Application_OnStart
    '==Visual InterDev Generated - startspan==
    '--Project Data Connection
    Application("VIBankconn_ConnectionString") = "DRIVER=SQL
        Server;SERVER=ntserver;UID=sa;APP=Microsoft(R)
        Windows NT(TM) Operating System;WSID=NTSERVER;
        DATABASE=bank;User Id=sa;"
```

Figure 13-1. *A global.asa file showing how the* DE *object is created in the* Application_OnStart *event.*

(continued)

```
     Application("VIBankconn_ConnectionTimeout") = 15
     Application("VIBankconn_CommandTimeout") = 30
     Application("VIBankconn_CursorLocation") = 3
     Application("VIBankconn_RuntimeUserName") = "sa"
     Application("VIBankconn_RuntimePassword") = ""
     '-- Project Data Environment
     Set DE = Server.CreateObject("DERuntime.DERuntime")
     Application("DE") = DE.Load(Server.MapPath("Global.ASA"),
          "_private/DataEnvironment/DataEnvironment.asa")
     '==Visual InterDev Generated - endspan==
End Sub
</SCRIPT>
```

By scripting the *DE* object, you can achieve many of the same end results as when you use Recordset DTCs and data-bound controls. For example, you can execute database commands (including SQL queries, parameterized queries, and stored procedures associated with command objects) and work with recordsets.

Executing Database Commands

To execute a database command using the *DE* object, you first create an instance of the *DE* object on your Web page. You can then execute any data command object associated with the *DE* object. This means any data command that you have created and placed under your data connection within the Visual InterDev Data Environment.

Creating a *DE* object

If you have the Scripting Object Model enabled, use the following syntax to create a *DE* object for your Web page:

```
<%
thisPage.createDE()
%>
```

If you do not have the Scripting Object Model enabled, use the syntax shown here:

```
<%
Set DE = Server.CreateObject("DERuntime.DERuntime")
DE.Init(Application("DE"))
%>
```

Executing a SQL query

To execute a SQL query associated with a data command object, use the following syntax:

```
<% DE.commandObjectName %>
```

If the command takes parameters, use the syntax shown here:

```
<% DE.commandObjectName (parameter1, parameter2, […]) %>
```

If the command returns a value, use the this syntax:

```
<% RetValue = DE.commandObjectName (parameter1, parameter2, […]) %>
```

Working with Recordsets

After you have executed a data command using the *DE* object, you can access the recordset and navigate through it with *Recordset* objects. To give you access to the recordset, the DE object creates a *Recordset* object named after the data command object but with an "rs" prefix. Here is the syntax for accessing the *Recordset* object:

```
<% DE.rscommandObjectName %>
```

For example, if your data command object is named *AccountCode,* the *Recordset* object is named *rsAccountCode.*

Extracting values within a recordset

Follow these steps to extract values within a recordset:

1. Create the recordset, and set a variable to point to the DE *Recordset* object, as shown here:

    ```
    <%
    DE.AccountCode
    Set rs = DE.rsAccountCode
    %>
    ```

2. Extract individual values from the *Fields* collection of the *Recordset* object, as shown here:

    ```
    <%
    DE.AccountCode
    Set rs = DE.rsAccountCode
    Account_Id = rs.Fields("Account_Id")
    Account_Description = rs.Fields("Account_Description)
    %>
    ```

Navigating a recordset

Follow these steps to navigate a recordset:

1. Use the *moveNext*, *movePrevious*, *moveFirst*, or *moveLast* methods of the *Recordset* object.

2. Use the *EOF* or *BOF* properties to determine whether you are at the end or the beginning of the *Recordset* object.

DE Object Scripting Examples

Figure 13-2 shows an example of scripting the *DE* object to display a list of account descriptions on a Web page. This example is taken from the AccountCodeDE.asp page within the VI-Bank Web project on the companion CD-ROM.

> **NOTE** The VI-Bank Web project is a sample Internet Banking application that we'll be using throughout this chapter and many of the following chapters —especially chapters on three-tier transactional applications. VI-Bank is primarily a Microsoft SQL Server 6.5–based application. However, several of its Web pages—including the examples in this chapter—can be run against the Microsoft Access database that is also supplied with the application.

```
<%@ Language=VBScript %>
<% ' VI 6.0 Scripting Object Model Enabled %>
<!--#include file="_ScriptLibrary/pm.asp"-->
<% if StartPageProcessing() Then Response.End() %>
<FORM name=thisForm METHOD=post>
<HTML>
<HEAD>
<META NAME="GENERATOR" Content="Microsoft Visual Studio 6.0">
<TITLE>Vi-Bank - Account Code Listing</TITLE>

<LINK REL="stylesheet" TYPE="text/css"
    HREF="_Themes/blueprnt/THEME.CSS"
    VI6.0THEME="Blueprint">
<LINK REL="stylesheet" TYPE="text/css"
    HREF="_Themes/blueprnt/GRAPH0.CSS"
    VI6.0THEME="Blueprint">
<LINK REL="stylesheet" TYPE="text/css"
    HREF="_Themes/blueprnt/COLOR0.CSS"
    VI6.0THEME="Blueprint">
```

Figure 13-2. *Source code for the AccountCodeDE.asp Web page showing how the DE object can be scripted to query and display data from a relational database.*

(continued)

```
<LINK REL="stylesheet" TYPE="text/css"
    HREF="_Themes/blueprnt/CUSTOM.CSS"
    VI6.0THEME="Blueprint"></HEAD>
<BODY>

<TABLE>
<TR valign=top>
<TD width=125>
<!--#INCLUDE FILE="maintmenu.htm"-->
</TD>
<TD>

<H2><FONT COLOR="navy"><I>VI-Bank - Account Code Listing</I></FONT>
</H2>
<HR style="COLOR: navy">
<P>

<%
thisPage.createDE()
DE.AccountCode
Set rs = DE.rsAccountCode
Response.Write "<TABLE BORDER=1 CELLSPACING=2 CELLPADDING=2>" + _
    "<TR><TH>Account Code</TH><TH>Account Description</TH></TR>"
Do While Not rs.EOF
    Response.Write "<TR><TD>" + CStr(rs.Fields("account_id")) + _
        "</TD>" + "<TD>" + rs.Fields("account_description") + _
        "</TD></TR>"
    rs.MoveNext
Loop
Response.Write "</TABLE>"
%>

</TD>
</TR>
</TABLE>

</BODY>
<% ' VI 6.0 Scripting Object Model Enabled %>
<% EndPageProcessing() %>
</FORM>
</HTML>
```

Figure 13-3 shows the resulting output from the AccountCodeDE.asp page. In just nine lines of code, the *DE* object has been used to query the Account_Code table and then present the results in an HTML table on screen.

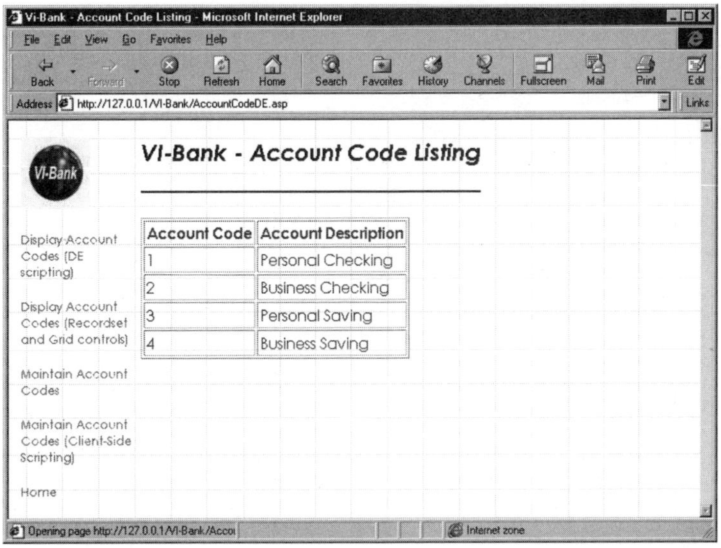

Figure 13-3. *Output from the AccountCodeDE.asp Web page, showing the contents of the Account_Code table.*

The *DE* object accesses the AccountCode data command object within the VI-Bank Web project for the source of the query. The query is a simple SQL SELECT statement, as shown here:

```
SELECT account_id, account_description
FROM account_code
ORDER BY account_id
```

> **NOTE** When working with data command objects, it is often preferable to select *SQL Statement* as the source of the data. You then write the SQL code yourself within the Properties dialog box, as opposed to simply selecting a *Database Object* data source and selecting a table from the drop-down list box. By using hand-coded SQL, you can specify the sort order for your recordset and have more control over the result.

This example simply outputs the records for viewing within your browser. This type of multirow output is often combined with the ability to select a specific record and then edit that record on another Web page. This was achieved within Visual InterDev 1.0 by using the Data Form Wizard, which generated both form views and list views. To enable individual records within your output HTML table to be selected and launch another Web page, you might add some code, as in the following example:

```
<%
thisPage.createDE()
DE.AccountCode
Set rs = DE.rsAccountCode
Response.Write "<TABLE BORDER=1 CELLSPACING=2 CELLPADDING=2>" + _
    "<TR><TH>Account Code</TH><TH>Account Description</TH></TR>"
Do While Not rs.EOF
    Response.Write _
        "<TR><TD><A HREF=accountcodemaint.asp?account_id=" + _
        CStr(rs.Fields("account_id")) + ">" + _
        CStr(rs.Fields("account_id")) + "</A></TD>" + _
        "<TD>" + rs.Fields("account_description") + "</TD></TR>"
    rs.MoveNext
Loop
Response.Write "</TABLE>"
%>
```

In this example, a hyperlink is added to the output of the first column within the HTML table. This way the accountcodemaint.asp page is called and is passed the value of the account_id for editing. The accountcodemaint.asp page can use this value as a record locator so that it knows which record to query.

From these examples, you can see how easy it is to script the Data Environment and to output resultsets to the Web page. In situations where you want to be able to navigate a lengthy recordset, perhaps ten rows at a time, it's more convenient to use some of Visual InterDev's DTCs to simplify the process, as we'll see in the following section.

SCRIPTING USING DTCS AND DATA-BOUND CONTROLS

Now that we've seen how to script the Data Environment using 100 percent manual coding, let's see how to incorporate the Recordset DTC and data-bound controls to achieve the same results. We'll look at several examples, including simple SQL queries using the Recordset and Grid DTCs. We'll also spend time on more advanced examples that use the Recordset, FormManager, and several other DTCs together.

Writing Database Queries

Besides scripting the *DE* object, another way to execute a query and display the resulting output on screen is to use a Recordset DTC to perform the query and to use a Grid DTC to display the output. Figure 13-4 shows the output of the AccountCodeGrid.asp file (part of the VI-Bank Web project on the CD-ROM). This file performs the same operation as our earlier example—it queries a database table named Account_Code and presents the resulting records in an HTML table on screen.

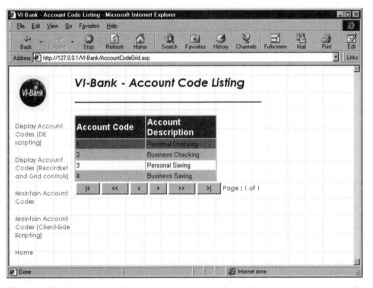

Figure 13-4. *Output from the AccountCodeGrid.asp page, showing the records in the Account_Code table.*

What is the advantage of using the Recordset DTC plus the Grid DTC rather than the pure scripting approach? The Grid DTC can give you some additional functionality—it provides navigation buttons for moving through the recordset. These buttons can be useful, especially for large recordsets that cannot be displayed on a single Web page. You can specify your exact navigation requirements for page or row navigation via the Navigation tab on the Grid Properties dialog box, as shown in Figure 13-5 on the following page. Here you can specify the button captions and the number of records displayed per page. You can also specify the color used for the current row.

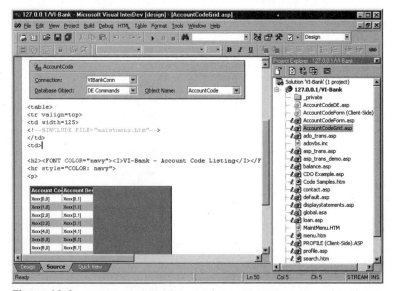

Figure 13-5. *The Grid Properties dialog box for the Grid DTC allows you to specify various navigation options for your recordset.*

Figure 13-6 shows the AccountCodeGrid.asp page. The Recordset DTC uses a data command object named AccountCode as the source for its data. This is the same data command object that we used for our *DE* script object example earlier in this chapter. This is an example of how data command objects can be reused across many pages within your Web applications.

Figure 13-6. *AccountCodeGrid.asp Web page as it appears within the Visual InterDev IDE.*

The Data tab of the Grid Properties dialog box is where you specify the fields to be output on your Web page. Figure 13-7 shows the Data tab for the Grid DTC on AccountCodeGrid.asp. The two output fields are the account_id and account-_description columns. The headers for these columns have been named Account Code and Account Description. You can see that the Grid DTC is bound to the AccountCode data command object.

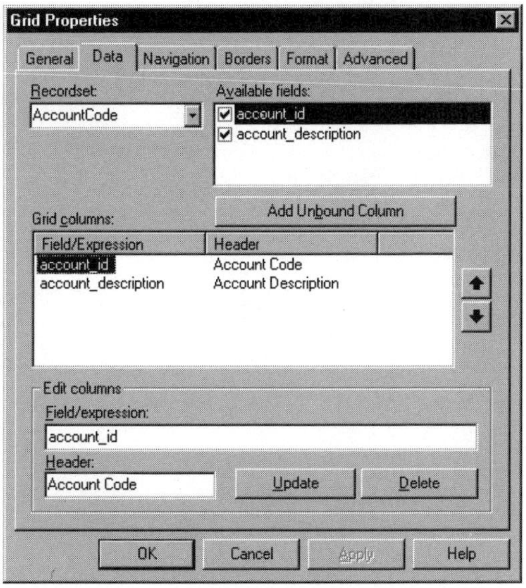

Figure 13-7. *The Data tab of the Grid Properties dialog box.*

As another example of using the Recordset DTC along with a Grid DTC, we'll take a look at the balance.asp page in the VI-Bank Web project. This page displays a user's bank balance for both checking and saving accounts. What is interesting is that the results of the query are displayed via the Grid DTC in an HTML table and also via manual scripting for display on the Web page outside the Grid DTC's HTML table. The Recordset DTC executes a parameterized query as follows:

```
SELECT Customer.first_name, Customer.last_name,
    Account_Code.Account_Description, Account_Balance.balance,
    Account_Balance.balance - 100 AS Available
FROM Account_Code
INNER JOIN Account_Balance ON Account_Code.Account_Id =
    Account_Balance.account_id
INNER JOIN Customer ON Account_Balance.ssn = Customer.ssn
WHERE (Customer.ssn = ?)
```

Since the Recordset DTC is expecting a parameter in order to execute the query, it is marked to not open the recordset at run time. The following code is placed just below the Recordset DTC to set the input parameter and to execute the query:

```
<%
rsAccountBalance.setParameter 0, "123456789"
rsAccountBalance.Open()
%>
```

> **NOTE** You can learn more about the *setParameter* and *Open* methods for *Recordset* objects in Chapter 14.

The customer's first and last names are displayed via the following script code within the balance.asp page:

```
<%
Response.Write "Account Balance for " + _
    rsAccountBalance.fields.getValue("First_Name")
Response.Write " " + rsAccountBalance.fields.getValue("Last_Name") + _
    "<P>"
%>
```

The remaining columns from the query are displayed in the Grid DTC. These are the Account_Description and Balance columns from the Account_Code and Account_Balance tables. Another column—Available Balance—is a calculated field from the Balance column. Figure 13-8 shows the output from the Balance.asp page. In this example, the page-navigation and row-navigation features available within the Grid DTC were turned off since they are not required.

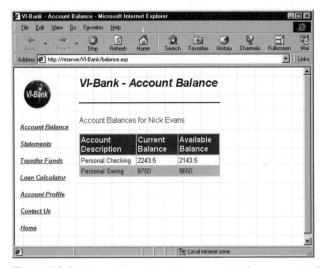

Figure 13-8. *Output from the Balance.asp Web page created using a Recordset DTC and a Grid DTC.*

Using the FormManager DTC

In the previous section, we saw how to use the Recordset and Grid DTCs to display the results of SQL queries to the end user. By using the FormManager DTC along with the Recordset and other DTCs, you can provide your users with complete control over their data. This DTC provides the ability to insert, update, and delete records from the database.

As an example, we'll again look at some of the code in the VI-Bank Web project on the companion CD-ROM. The code we'll look at is the Profile.asp page. This page allows a bank customer to update his or her profile information, including address, home and work phone numbers, and e-mail address. The page uses a Recordset DTC to provide the SQL query, a number of Textbox and Button DTCs to display and manipulate the data, and a FormManager DTC to coordinate the various modes and actions available on the page.

This example requires that, given the customer's social security number, the Recordset DTC will query the Customer table for a specific customer and retrieve all the necessary fields. These include fields for the first name, last name, address, city, state, ZIP code, home phone, work phone, and e-mail address of the customer. The following code shows the query:

```
SELECT first_name, last_name, address_1, address_2,
    city, state, zip, home_phone, work_phone, e-mail
FROM Customer
WHERE ssn = ?
```

The customer should be able to click an Edit button and edit all fields except the first name and last name fields. After clicking the Edit button, the customer should have access to the Save and Cancel buttons. A Display button should also be available to enable viewing of the data in display-only mode—this should be the starting mode for the Web page. Figure 13-9 on the following page shows the profile.asp page within the browser.

The starting point for this Web page is a data command object named *Customer*. This command object contains the SQL code listed above. The next step is to create the profile.asp page. First a Recordset DTC is dragged onto a new ASP Web page and associated with the *Customer* data command object. Next the Textbox and Button DTCs are dragged onto the page. Each Textbox DTC is associated with one of the fields in the recordset by accessing the Textbox Properties page and selecting the appropriate field from the drop-down selection list. When you lay out the Textbox fields, use the Design tab within Visual InterDev—it's the most efficient way to control the positioning of the elements on the page. An HTML table can be used to align the Textbox fields horizontally.

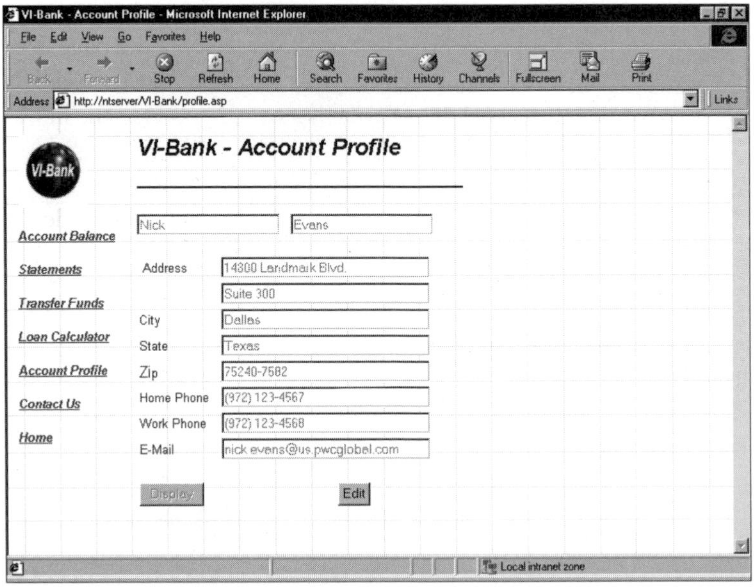

Figure 13-9. *The profile.asp page showing the Account Profile page for the VI-Bank sample Internet Banking application.*

The buttons required for this page are Display, Edit, Save, and Cancel. Finally, a FormManager DTC is used to specify the modes and actions for the page. Figure 13-10 shows the profile.asp page in Design view within Visual InterDev.

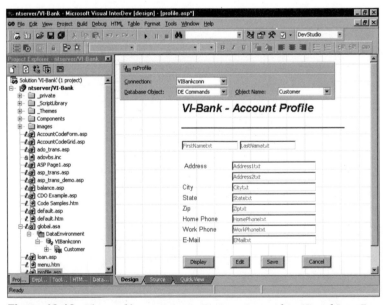

Figure 13-10. *The profile.asp page in Design view within Visual InterDev. An HTML table is used to align the text and Textbox DTCs on the page.*

The FormManager DTC is given two modes: Edit and Display. In Display mode, only the Display and Edit buttons are visible on the page and all the fields are grayed out. In Edit mode, the Display, Edit, Save, and Cancel buttons are all visible on the page and the fields, with the exception of the first and last name fields, are enabled and visible.

Table 13-1 shows the actions performed for Display mode. Table 13-2 on the following page shows the actions performed for Edit mode. These actions are specified in the Form Mode tab of the FormManager Properties dialog box.

Object	*Member*	*Value*
Displaybtn	Disabled	True
Displaybtn	Show	()
Editbtn	Disabled	False
Editbtn	Show	()
Savebtn	Disabled	True
Savebtn	Hide	()
Cancelbtn	Disabled	True
Cancelbtn	Hide	()
FirstNametxt, LastNametxt	Disabled	True
FirstNametxt, LastNametxt	Show	()
Address1txt, Address2txt, Citytxt, Statetxt, Ziptxt, HomePhonetxt, WorkPhonetxt, Emailtxt	Disabled	True
Address1txt, Address2txt, Citytxt, Statetxt, Ziptxt, HomePhonetxt, WorkPhonetxt, Emailtxt	Show	()

Table 13-1. *The actions performed for the Display mode of the profile.asp page.*

Object	Member	Value
Displaybtn	Disabled	False
Displaybtn	Show	()
Editbtn	Disabled	True
Editbtn	Show	()
Savebtn	Disabled	False
Savebtn	Show	()
Cancelbtn	Disabled	False
Cancelbtn	Show	()
FirstNametxt, LastNametxt	Disabled	True
FirstNametxt, LastNametxt	Show	()
Address1txt, Address2txt, Citytxt, Statetxt, Ziptxt, HomePhonetxt, WorkPhonetxt, Emailtxt	Disabled	False
Address1txt, Address2txt, Citytxt, Statetxt, Ziptxt, HomePhonetxt, WorkPhonetxt, Emailtxt	Show	()

Table 13-2. *The actions performed for the Edit mode of the Profile.asp page.*

Now that the status of the buttons and Textbox DTCs on the page have been defined for both the Display and Edit modes, the final step is to specify the actions to take when each of the buttons are clicked. To do this, enter data into the Action tab of the FormManager Properties dialog box. Table 13-3 summarizes the actions to take for each button's *onclick* event.

Current Mode	Object	Event	Next Mode	Action
Display	*Editbtn*	*Onclick*	Edit	N/A
Edit	*Displaybtn*	*Onclick*	Display	N/A
Edit	*Savebtn*	*Onclick*	Edit	rsProfile.updateRecord()
Edit	*Cancelbtn*	*Onclick*	Edit	rsProfile.cancelUpdate()

Table 13-3. *The actions performed for the* onclick *events for the four buttons on the profile.asp page.*

Figure 13-11 shows the profile.asp page in Edit mode. Compare this figure with Figure 13-9, which shows the same page in Display mode. One way to improve the experience of this Web page for the end user is to change the scripting platform from the server to the client. This way, the buttons react immediately to being clicked, as opposed to having to perform a round-trip (to the server and back) to perform the required action. Changing the scripting platform can be accomplished easily: simply access the Properties dialog box for the ASP page and change the DTC Scripting Platform radio button from Server (ASP) to Client (IE 4.0 DHTML). One drawback to this is that the recordset can be moved to the client side for processing only if your end users are running Microsoft Internet Explorer 4.0 or later. If you do not know or cannot enforce the browser types of your end users, you are probably better off keeping the scripting platform on the server side for breadth of deployment.

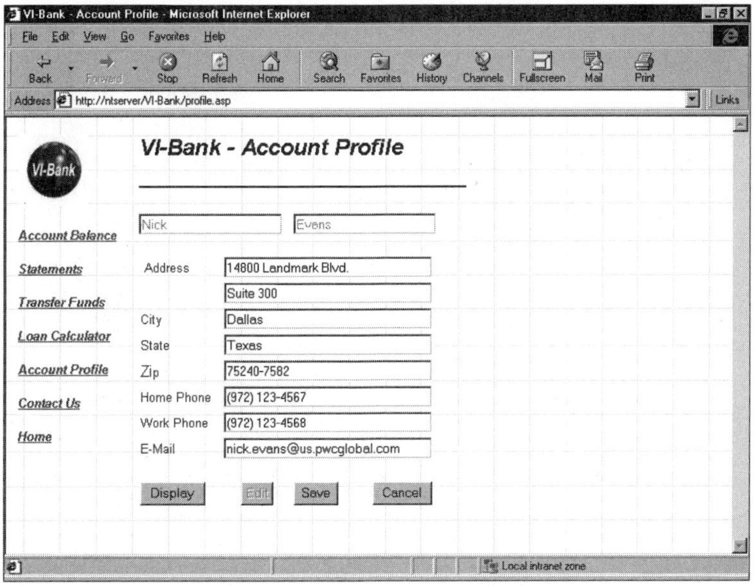

Figure 13-11. *The profile.asp page showing the Account Profile page for the VI-Bank sample Internet Banking application. The page is shown in Edit mode.*

What if you do decide to make the change to the client-side scripting platform? After you have applied the change to your Web page, all the DTCs will inherit the change and will run under the client-scripting platform. Be sure to move any manual code that you have added for the Recordset DTC—or for any of the Textbox DTCs—from the server side to the client side. These objects no longer exist on the server, so you can script them using only client-side Microsoft JScript or Microsoft VBScript (Visual Basic, Scripting Edition).

Another advantage of moving the scripting platform from the server side to the client side is that you can perform validation of user-entered data more easily on the client. In the next chapter, we'll see how this can be accomplished via *Recordset* events.

Chapter 14

Using Recordset Events

The *Recordset* object is one of the key components within the Microsoft Visual InterDev Data Environment. It acts as a cache for your data and can be accessed using methods, properties, or events to give you complete control of your data-driven Web applications—either on the server side or the client side. In this chapter, we'll take a look at the *Recordset* object in detail with special emphasis on *Recordset* events.

THE *RECORDSET* OBJECT

As we have seen in previous chapters, you can use the Recordset design-time control (DTC) at design time to place a *Recordset* object onto your Web pages. After you have placed the Recordset DTC on your page, you can script the object in whatever manner necessary. The *Recordset* object has a rich set of properties, methods, and events for you to take advantage of in your applications.

Recordset Properties

The *Recordset* object has seven properties, as listed in Table 14-1 on the following page.

Property	Description
absolutePosition	Absolute position of the current record in the *Recordset* object
BOF	Cursor is positioned before the first record in the *Recordset* object
EOF	Cursor is positioned after the last record in the *Recordset* object
fields	Enables you to return names and values of fields that are related to the *Recordset* object's fields
id	*Recordset* object's ID
maintainState	Maintains the state of the *Recordset* object during server processing
name	*Recordset* object's name

Table 14-1. Recordset *object properties.*

absolutePosition

The *absolutePosition* property specifies the absolute position of the current record in the *Recordset* object. The syntax for the *absolutePosition* property is as follows,

```
Recordset.absolutePosition
```

where *Recordset* is the name of your *Recordset* script object. The index returned is 1-based, so the first record is 1, the second record is 2, and so on. This can be useful for keeping track of the cursor location as the recordset is traversed. For example, you could use this property to print out the row number on a Web page, as shown here:

```
Row <% =rsAccountCode.absolutePosition %> of
<% =rsAccountCode.getCount() %>
```

BOF and EOF

The *BOF* and *EOF* properties indicate when you are at the beginning and the end of the recordset data. These properties are quite useful when you are iterating through the recordset and displaying the results on screen. By checking the *EOF* property, you can determine when to end your loop, as in the following example:

```
Do While not MyRecordset.EOF
    Response.write MyRecordset.fields.getValue("myfield")
    MyRecordset.moveNext
Loop
```

A more elaborate example using the <TABLE> syntax for formatting the resulting output might look like this:

```
<TABLE BORDER=1>
<TR>
<TH>Account Id</TH>
<TH>Account Description</TH>
</TR>
<%
Do While NOT rsAccountCode.EOF
    Response.Write "<TR><TD>" + _
        CStr(rsAccountCode.fields.getValue("account_id")) + _
        "</TD>"
    Response.Write "<TD>" + _
        rsAccountCode.fields.getValue("account_description") + _
        "</TD></TR>"
    rsAccountCode.MoveNext
Loop
%>
</TABLE>
```

Note that the *EOF* property tells you when the cursor is positioned *after* the last record in the recordset and the *BOF* property tells you when the cursor is positioned *before* the first record in the recordset. Both of these properties are read-only and available only at run time.

fields

The *fields* property of the *Recordset* object is actually an object in itself. It contains the *fields* collection, which enables you to return names and values of fields that are related to the *Recordset* object's fields.

The *fields* object has four methods: *getCount*, *getName*, *getValue*, and *setValue*, as shown in Table 14-2.

Method	*Description*
getCount	Returns the number of items in the object
getName	Returns the name of a field from the fields collection
getValue	Returns a value from an object
setValue	Sets a value of an object

Table 14-2. *Methods for the* fields *object.*

You can use *getCount* to determine the number of columns in the *Recordset* object, as in the following example:

```
Number of columns = <% =rsAccountCode.fields.getCount() %>
```

You can use *getName* to determine the column name for each column in the *Recordset* object, as shown here:

```
<%
For i = 0 to rsAccountCode.fields.getCount() - 1
    Response.Write "Field " + Cstr(i) + " = " + _
        rsAccountCode.fields.getName(i) + "<BR>"
Next
%>
```

Notice that when you use the *getName* method the index is zero-based. Therefore, *getName(0)* returns the column name for the first column, *getName(1)* returns the column name for the second column, and so on.

You can use *getValue* to determine the values of the data in the *Recordset* object, as in the following example:

```
Account Id = <% =rsAccountCode.fields.getValue("account_id") %>
```

This gets the value for the account_id column in the currently selected row. In addition to using the actual field name as the parameter for the *getValue* method, you can also use an index number. The index number is zero-based and indicates which column you are interested in. Assuming the account_id column is the first column in the *Recordset* object, the following code produces the same result as above by using an index instead of the column name.

```
Account Id = <% =rsAccountCode.fields.getValue(0) %>
```

You can use *setValue* to update the values of the data in the *Recordset* object, as in the following example:

```
rsAccountCode.fields.setValue "account_id", 1
```

This example updates the value of the account_id column to 1 for the currently selected record in the *Recordset* object. Changes are applied to the database directly using this method, eliminating the need to call the *updateRecord* method. When making these types of updates, be sure to check for errors arising from the database update because of primary or foreign key constraints.

id and *name*

The *id* and *name* properties specify a unique identifier and the name of the *Recordset* object. These are often identical. The name is taken from the name given to the *Recordset* object on the General tab of the Recordset Properties dialog box. By default this name is Recordset#, where # is a sequential number. Both the *id* and *name* properties are read-only at run time.

maintainState

The *maintainState* property specifies whether the object state is maintained through server processing. The object state default setting is set to True. This means that the object maintains its properties and values during server processing. The object state can be turned off using the following syntax,

```
ObjRS.maintainState = False
```

where *ObjRS* is the name of the *Recordset* object.

Recordset Object Methods

Table 14-3 lists the *Recordset* object's many methods.

Method	Description
addRecord	Creates a new record in the *Recordset* object
advise	Registers an object to be notified and a function to be called when a specific event occurs
cancelUpdate	Cancels the changes being made to the current record
close	Closes a *Recordset* object
deleteRecord	Deletes the current record from the *Recordset* object
getBookmark	Returns a bookmark for the current record
getConnectString	Returns a text string or object that determines the data connection
getCount	Returns the number of items in the *Recordset* object
getDHTMLDataSourceID	Returns a text string from the ID of the DHTML data source; available only in client script
getParameter	Gets a parameter from a stored procedure or parameterized query
getRecordSource	Returns the ActiveX Data Objects (ADO) *Recordset* object
getSQLText	Returns the SQL statement that queries the database for the *Recordset* object
isOpen	Returns a Boolean value that indicates whether a *Recordset* object is open

Table 14-3. Recordset *object methods.* *(continued)*

Table 14-3 *continued*

Method	Description
move	Moves the cursor, relative to its current position, within a *Recordset* object
moveAbsolute	Moves the cursor to a specific index within a *Recordset* object
moveFirst	Moves the cursor to the first record of the *Recordset* object
moveLast	Moves the cursor to the last record of the *Recordset* object
moveNext	Moves the cursor forward by one record within the *Recordset* object
movePrevious	Moves the cursor backward by one record within the *Recordset* object
open	Opens a *Recordset* object
requery	Refreshes the current recordset by requerying the database
setBookmark	Sets the bookmark for pointing to a particular record
setParameter	Sets a parameter for a stored procedure or parameterized query that is referenced by the *Recordset* object
setRecordSource	Sets the connection properties for opening a *Recordset* object
setSQLText	Sets the SQL statement that is used to query the database for the recordset
unadvise	Cancels the registration of an object that was registered by the *advise* method
updateRecord	Updates the *Recordset* object with changes to the current record

addRecord, deleteRecord, updateRecord, and cancelUpdate

The *addRecord*, *deleteRecord*, *updateRecord*, and *cancelUpdate* methods allow you to modify the *Recordset* object or cancel the update. The *addRecord* method adds a new record to the *Recordset* object, the *deleteRecord* method deletes a record, and the *updateRecord* updates the *Recordset* object with updates to the current record. Updates have to be made on a record-by-record basis.

The *cancelUpdate* method cancels the changes that are currently being made to the current record. This method is typically called from a cancel button that the user can click on to undo any pending changes to the data. The *cancelUpdate* method will replace the values on the form with their previous values prior to the user's changes.

advise and unadvise

The *advise* method allows you to register an object to be notified and a function to be called when a specific event occurs. The syntax for the *advise* method is as follows:

```
[id = ]object.advise(strEvent, CallFunction)
```

Here, *object* can be any script object, not just a *Recordset* object; *id* is an identifier that can be used by the *unadvise* method to unregister the object. The *strEvent* event causes the object to be notified; *CallFunction* is the function that the object should call when the event occurs.

The *advise* method is needed only for events that are not implicit to the particular object in question.

The *unadvise* method cancels the registration of the object with the particular event. The syntax is as follows:

```
object.unadvise(strEvent, id)
```

close, open, and isOpen

The *close*, *open*, and *isOpen* methods are useful when you want to use the same recordset but make a few programmatic modifications. For example, you might want to allow an end user to build his or her own queries and then view the results. After the results have been displayed, you might want to give the user the ability to create a new, different query using the same recordset behind the scenes. To do this, you'll need to close the recordset, modify the SQL statement, and then reopen the recordset. The following code shows an example:

```
If rsQuery.isOpen() Then
    rsQuery.close()
    ...
    // Build your custom SQL statement here.
    ...
    rsQuery.setSQLText(strSQL)
    rsQuery.open()
End If
```

getBookmark and setBookmark

The *getBookmark* and *setBookmark* methods allow you to set a bookmark for the current record in the recordset and then to return to that specific record even if the recordset has been closed and then reopened. The bookmarks also work if you have added or deleted records from the recordset between the time you get the bookmark and the time you set the bookmark.

The syntax for using the *getBookmark* method is as follows,

```
strBookmark = Recordset.getBookmark()
```

where *strBookmark* is a string representing the value of the bookmark.

The syntax for using the *setBookmark* method is shown here:

```
Recordset.setBookmark(strBookmark)
```

You might use these methods in your applications when you want to add bookmarking capability to an online catalog. This way you can allow your users to bookmark an item of interest and then to return to it later on. To do this, you would call the *getBookmark* and *setBookmark* methods from a couple of buttons that you'd place on screen. The following code shows an example:

```
<SCRIPT ID=serverEventHandlersVBS LANGUAGE=vbscript RUNAT=Server>
Sub getBookmark_onclick()
    Session("tmpBookmark") = rsCustomer.getBookmark()
    Response.Write Session("tmpBookmark")
End Sub

Sub setBookmark_onclick()
    rsCustomer.setBookmark(Session("tmpBookmark"))
End Sub
</SCRIPT>
```

In this example, the scripting platform is server-side. The Web page for this example contains two buttons, as shown in Figure 14-1. The Bookmark This Record button is used to create the bookmark; the Return To Bookmark button is used to return to the bookmark. Since the bookmark must be persisted between calls to the ASP Web page, it is stored in a *Session* object variable. The code for this example is contained on the CD-ROM in the DBSamples Web project in a file named Bookmark.asp. To illustrate the actual text contained in a bookmark, the *onclick* event of the *getBookmark* button prints out the value of the bookmark. You can see from Figure 14-1 that the bookmark string contains the absolute number of the row plus the primary key value for the *Recordset* object.

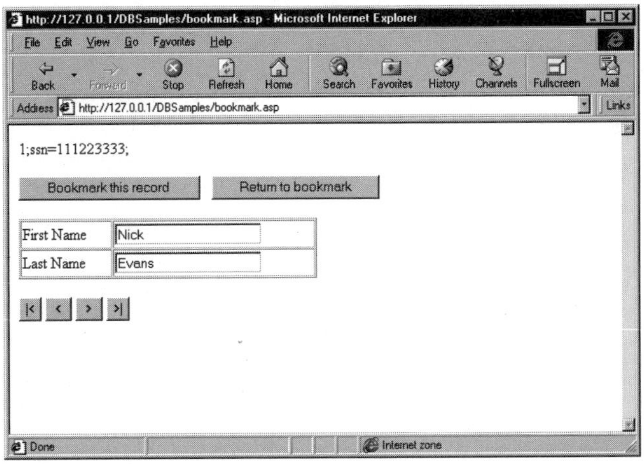

Figure 14-1. *Sample Web page with bookmarking functionality.*

When the user creates the bookmark and then clicks the Return To Bookmark button, the ASP Web page reloads and displays the bookmarked record.

getConnectString

The *getConnectString* method returns a text string that shows the data connection string for the *Recordset* object. The following code shows an example:

```
Connection String = <% =rsAccountCode.getConnectString() %>
```

A typical connection string output from the above statement would be:

```
Connection String = Provider=MSDASQL.1;User ID=admin;
    Connect Timeout=15;Extended Properties="DBQ=C:\database\bank.mdb;
    DefaultDir=C:\database;Driver={Microsoft Access Driver
    (*.mdb)};DriverId=25;FIL=MS Access;ImplicitCommitSync=Yes;
    MaxBufferSize=512;MaxScanRows=8;PageTimeout=5;
    SafeTransactions=0;Threads=3;UID=admin;UserCommitSync=Yes;";
    Locale Identifier=1033
```

getCount

The *getCount* method can be used to determine the number of records present in the *Recordset* object, as shown in the following example:

```
Number of records = <% =rsAccountCode.getCount() %>
```

This is useful if you wish to inform the user of the total record count—perhaps at the bottom of a Web page that shows 10 records at a time. The *getCount* method can be applied to other scripting objects, such as list boxes, as well as to *Recordset* objects.

getDHTMLDataSourceID

The *getDHTMLDataSourceID* method returns a text string that represents the ID of the DHTML data source. This method is available only in client script. The method must be placed in client side, and the *Recordset* object must be set for the client (IE 4.0 DHTML) scripting platform.

```
<SCRIPT ID=clientEventHandlersVB LANGUAGE=VBSCRIPT>
<!--
Sub rsAccountCode_ondatasetcomplete()
    MsgBox(rsAccountCode.getDHTMLDataSourceID())
End Sub
//-->
</SCRIPT>
```

The example above would return an ID such as rsAccountCode_RDS. This ID can be used to bind the *Recordset* object with intrinsic HTML.

getParameter and setParameter

The *getParameter* method gets a parameter from a stored procedure or a parameterized query. The syntax is as follows:

```
Recordset.getParameter(n)
```

Here, *n*—which is zero-based—is the index that specifies the particular parameter to return.

The *setParameter* method sets a parameter for a stored procedure or a parameterized query. The syntax is as follows:

```
Recordset.setParameter(nIndex, strParameter)
```

Here, *nIndex* is the zero-based parameter number to set, and *strParameter* is a string value that you want to assign to the parameter. You could use the *setParameter* method to pass a parameter to a *Recordset* object, as follows:

```
<%
rsAccountCode.setParameter 0, 4
rsAccountCode.open()
%>
```

Notice that the Automatically Open The Recordset check box in the Implementation tab of the Recordset Properties dialog box must not be set, as shown in Figure 14-2. This is because the *setParameter* method must be called prior to opening the recordset. In the sample code listed above, a parameter value of 4 is passed into the first parameter of the *Recordset* object. In the following example, the *Recordset* object is actually a parameterized query:

```
SELECT account_id, account_description FROM Account_Code
    WHERE (account_id = ?) ORDER BY account_id
```

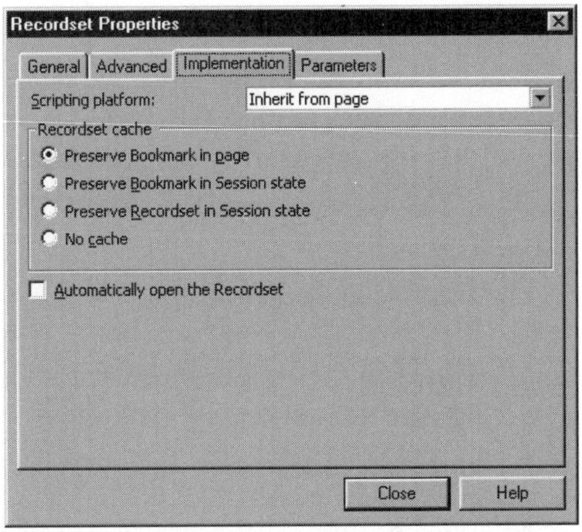

Figure 14-2. *The Implementation tab of the Recordset Properties dialog box showing the Automatically Open The Recordset check box.*

NOTE If the *Recordset* object represents a stored procedure, as opposed to a parameterized query, the 0 index refers to the return value from the stored procedure and the 1 index and above refer to the actual parameters that are passed to the stored procedure.

getRecordSource and *setRecordSource*

The *getRecordSource* method returns the ADO *Recordset* object. This object can then be used to access properties and methods supported by ADO that are not exposed in the *Recordset* script object.

The *setRecordSource* method sets the connection properties for opening a *Recordset* object. You can pass the *setRecordSource* method either an ADO *Recordset* object or a data connection string plus a SQL statement.

An interesting application of the *setRecordSource* method is to assign a recordset returned from a middle-tier COM component to a *Recordset* script object within your Web page. This way you can pass rich data types such as *Recordset* objects between two tiers of your Web applications, and you don't have to worry, for example, about programmatically parsing through strings with delimiters to separate variables. The following code shows an example of how you would take a recordset returned from a server-side component and load it into a *Recordset* script object within your Web page:

```
Sub rsData_onbeforeopen()
    Set obj = Server.CreateObject("COMObject.Class")
    rsData.setRecordSource( obj.recordsetfunction )
End Sub
```

In this example, VBScript running on the server side within an ASP Web page creates an instance of a server-side component named *COMObject.Class* and then executes its *recordsetfunction* method. The recordset returned from the function is assigned to the *rsData* recordset using the *setRecordSource* method.

getSQLText and setSQLText

The *getSQLText* and *setSQLText* methods are useful if you want to display the SQL statement to the user or if you wish to adjust the SQL statement. The following example shows how to determine the SQL statement and present it to the user:

```
SQL = <% =rsAccountCode.getSQLText() %>
```

> **NOTE** If you use *getSQLText* to get the SQL statement for a *Recordset* object containing a parameterized query, you will get the placeholder for the parameter along with the SQL statement, not the actual value of the parameter. This is true even if you have already used the *setParameter* method to specify the parameter. To get the parameter value, use the *getParameter* method.

To set the SQL statement for the *Recordset* object, use the *setSQLText* method and pass it the relevant SQL statement, as in the following example:

```
Recordset.setSQLText("select * from account_code order by account_id")
```

The *setSQLText* method can be used for custom queries, as mentioned in the earlier section on the *open* and *close* methods. The following code shows an example:

```
Sub Search_onclick()
    rsSearch.close()
    sql = "SELECT * FROM Customer WHERE first_name like '%" + _
        txtFirst.value + "%' AND last_name like '%" + _
        txtLast.value + "%' AND city like '%" + _
        txtCity.value + "%' ORDER BY " + _
        txtOrder.getValue(txtOrder.selectedIndex)
    rsSearch.setSQLText(sql)
    rsSearch.open()
End Sub
```

In this example, the SQL statement is built by using the values that the end user has entered into text boxes for the search criteria: first name, last name, and city. The SQL statement also includes an ORDER BY clause that is determined by the end user's selection from a drop-down list box named *txtOrder*. The complete Web page for this sample search is on the companion CD-ROM under the DBSamples Web project. It includes a *Recordset* object, *rsSearch*, which takes the custom SQL statement, a search button for building the query and performing the search, and a Grid DTC for displaying the output results. Figure 14-3 shows how this page—named setSQLText.asp—appears within Visual InterDev 6.0.

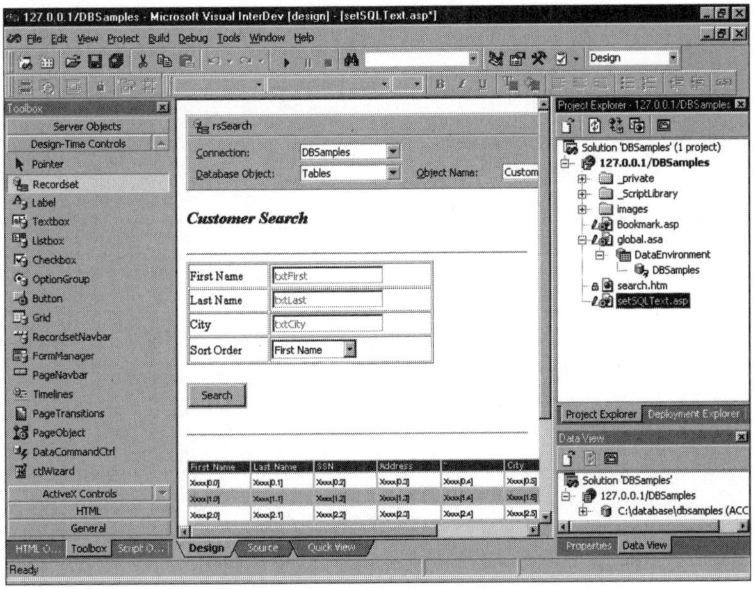

Figure 14-3. *setSQLText.asp is a sample Web page that uses the* setSQLText *method to provide a custom query capability.*

Navigation methods

Six methods can be used for *Recordset* navigation: *move, moveAbsolute, move-First, moveLast, moveNext,* and *movePrevious.* The latter four are by far the most common and are fairly self-explanatory. The *move* method moves the cursor a certain number of records—either forward or backward—from its current position. The syntax for the *move* method is as follows:

```
Recordset.move(nRecords)
```

Here *nRecords* is an integer that determines the number of records to move either forward or backward. If the integer is positive, the cursor moves forward. If it is negative, the cursor moves backward. The method returns a Boolean value indicating the success or failure of the operation.

The *moveAbsolute* method allows you to move the cursor to a specific record in the *Recordset* object. The syntax is as follows:

```
Recordset.moveAbsolute(n)
```

Here *n* is an index that specifies the number of the record to move to. The index is 1-based, so if *n* is 1 the cursor moves to the first record, and so on.

Recordset Events

At run time, the *Recordset* object exposes several events (via the Scripting Object Model) that can be handled either on the server side within Active Server Pages or on the client side using Dynamic HTML. These events give Web developers precise control over their data-driven applications at all stages of recordset processing. *Recordset* object events are triggered as a response to certain user actions or changes that occur in the recordset itself.

Table 14-4 lists the seven events available within the *Recordset* object.

Event	*Description*
onafterupdate	Fires after the *UpdateRecord* method has been called successfully on the *Recordset* object
onbeforeopen	Occurs right before a *Recordset* object is opened (either automatically or through the *open* method)
onbeforeupdate	Fires after the *UpdateRecord* method has been called, but before the actual update occurs on the *Recordset* object
ondatasetchanged	Occurs whenever there is a change made to the *Recordset* object
ondatasetcomplete	Occurs when the *Recordset* object has finished being downloaded from the server
onrowenter	Occurs when the cursor position moves to another record in the *Recordset* object
onrowexit	Occurs when the cursor position moves from a record in the *Recordset* object

Table 14-4. Recordset *object events.*

Each event fires at a certain point during recordset processing. For example, during a simple select operation where data is queried and then loaded into the recordset, the following events are triggered: *onbeforeopen, onrowenter, onrowexit, onrowenter, ondatasetchanged,* and *ondatasetcomplete.* An update operation triggers *onbeforeupdate* and *onafterupdate.* Record navigation triggers *onrowexit* and *onrowenter.*

An easy way to determine the sequence of event firing is to display a message within your event handlers indicating which event has fired. This can be achieved by using the *MsgBox* function for client-side scripting or by using the *Response.Write* syntax for server-side scripting. Be aware of the sequence of event firing so that you can place validation code and other types of code in the appropriate events.

The *onafterupdate* event

The *onafterupdate* event fires after the record has been updated via the *Update-Record* method. This event can be used to notify the end user that changes have been successfully saved to the database. The following code shows an example:

```
<SCRIPT ID=clientEventHandlersVB LANGUAGE=vbscript>
<!--
Sub rsProfile_onafterupdate()
    MsgBox "Your changes have been saved.", 0, "VI-Bank"
End Sub
//-->
</SCRIPT>
```

This code would be placed within the <HEAD> section of your HTML code and would be appropriate for Internet Explorer browsers since the scripting language is VBScript.

The *onbeforeopen* event

The *onbeforeopen* event fires before the recordset is opened either automatically or via the *open* method. It is useful if you want to change the SQL statement for the recordset or set some parameters.

The *onbeforeupdate* event

The *onbeforeupdate* event fires after the *UpdateRecord* method has been called but before the actual update occurs within the data source. This event is extremely useful for data validation. Within the *onbeforeupdate* event, data fields that have been input by the user can be validated against certain criteria. If they meet the criteria, the update can be allowed to proceed; if they do not meet the criteria, you can call the *CancelUpdate* method within the event to cancel the update and prompt the user to retry the input with some different values.

Here's an example:

```
<SCRIPT ID=clientEventHandlersVB LANGUAGE=vbscript>
<!--
Sub rsProfile_onbeforeupdate()
    If trim(rsProfile.fields.getValue("e_mail")) = "" Then
        MsgBox "E-Mail is a required field.", 0, "VI-Bank"
        rsProfile.CancelUpdate()
    End If
End Sub
//-->
</SCRIPT>
```

This example checks the value of the e_mail field within the *rsProfile Recordset* object. If there is no entry in the field, a message box appears to the user and reminds the user that this is a required field. Finally, the *CancelUpdate* method is used to cancel the update of the recordset. If you were writing the same procedure for server-side execution, you might take advantage of a label field for displaying the message, like this:

```
Sub rsProfile_onbeforeupdate()
    If trim(rsProfile.fields.getValue("e_mail")) = "" Then
        lblStatus.setCaption("E-Mail is a required field.")
        rsProfile.CancelUpdate()
    End If
End Sub
```

The *ondatasetchanged* event

The *ondatasetchanged* event fires whenever there is a change made to the *Recordset* object. The event is fired under two circumstances: after a new data set is requested or when the existing data set is altered via the *addRecord*, *deleteRecord*, or *updateRecord* methods.

The *ondatasetcomplete* event

The *ondatasetcomplete* event fires when the *Recordset* object has finished being downloaded from the server. When the scripting platform is Internet Explorer 4.0, this means that the *Recordset* object has cached all its data on the client. When the scripting platform is ASP, this means that the *Recordset* object is completely available to the ASP code. In either case, all the requested data is available in the *Recordset* object once the *ondatasetcomplete* event has fired (assuming the query was valid and returned some rows).

This event is particularly useful when performing client-side scripting because the data transfer is asynchronous. The *ondatasetcomplete* event can be used to tell you when the entire transfer of data from the server to the client has completed.

The *onrowenter* event

The *onrowenter* event fires when the cursor position moves to another record in the *Recordset* object. Methods that can trigger this event include the *move*, *moveAbsolute*, *moveFirst*, *moveLast*, *movePrevious*, and *moveNext* methods. The event is also fired when data is first populated into the *Recordset* object.

An interesting thing happens at the first or last row of the *Recordset* object. If the cursor is on the first row and the *movePrevious* method is called, the cursor moves to the BOF record and then back to the first row again. This causes the *onrowenter* event to fire twice. If the cursor is on the first row and the *moveFirst* method is called, the cursor simply moves to the first row and the *onrowenter* event fires once. Something similar happens when the cursor is located on the last row of the *Recordset* object. The *moveNext* method causes the *onrowenter* event to fire twice, whereas the *moveLast* method causes the *onrowenter* event to fire just once.

The *onrowexit* event

The *onrowexit* event fires when the cursor position moves from a record in the *Recordset* object. Methods that can trigger this event include the *move*, *moveAbsolute*, *moveFirst*, *moveLast*, *movePrevious*, and *moveNext* methods. The event is also fired when data is first populated into the *Recordset* object.

If you are using the client-side scripting platform, the *onrowexit* event also fires when you move away from the Web page within your browser—perhaps by using the browser's Back button, Refresh button, Home button, or bookmarks. You can't use this event to determine whether the user is leaving the page, however, because it also fires when the user first retrieves the record and then whenever the user navigates through the *Recordset* object.

If you want to know when the user is leaving the page, you should use another event—the *onbeforeunload* event for the window object. The window object *onbeforeunload* event can therefore be used to warn users that their changes (if any have been made) will be lost if they continue with the operation and they have not yet saved the changes. You can present the user with a message box and then allow the user to decide whether to continue and thereby lose any changes or to go back to the page and save any changes.

```
Function window_onbeforeunload()
    window_onbeforeunload = "If you have made changes and have " + _
        "not yet saved them, they will be lost."
End Function
```

Figure 14-4 on the following page shows the dialog box that appears given the sample code above.

Figure 14-4. *A message box that asks users if they want to navigate away from the current page.*

Chapter 15

Using Stored Procedures

In Chapter 12, we saw that within Microsoft Visual InterDev 6.0 you have access to the Microsoft Visual Database Tools for creating and managing your data-driven applications. When working with more advanced databases such as Microsoft SQL Server or Oracle, as opposed to Access and other desktop-style databases, you can take advantage of Visual InterDev's support for the creation, editing, debugging, and execution of stored procedures.

In this chapter, we'll take a look at stored procedures in detail. We'll start by looking at the benefits of stored procedures over other techniques, and then we'll go into detail on how to incorporate stored procedures into your Visual InterDev 6.0 applications. We'll look at all aspects of stored procedure development from the initial creation of the database and the various stored procedures, through editing and debugging, and finally to execution of stored procedures both within the run-time environment and in the deployment environment. The database we'll use for our example will be SQL Server 6.5, but these examples could easily apply to SQL Server 7.0 or Oracle 7.x or later with a few minor syntax changes where necessary.

STORED PROCEDURE BASICS

A stored procedure is a precompiled collection of SQL statements that can take and/or return user-supplied parameters. You can place any number of SQL statements into a stored procedure. Also, stored procedures can be nested, up to 16 levels deep, so that one procedure can call another. Stored procedures are also available to triggers within your database.

Benefits of Stored Procedures

The main benefit of stored procedures is their performance. Stored procedures are simply the fastest way to execute your data-driven code. This is because the SQL statements are precompiled and stored in memory on the database server. It's much faster to encompass all your database processing logic into a stored procedure and have a single round-trip from the browser to the server and back than to have lots of database calls that place traffic on the network. In the client/ server days, there was typically much traffic between the client machine and the database. In the Web world, this traffic is more often seen between the Web server (perhaps executing Web pages) and the database.

Stored procedures can be used as a form of security. For example, users can be given access to the data via stored procedures only and not directly to the tables in the database. This helps ensure that users cannot perform restricted operations on the data. All their database access has to go through the stored procedures, which have predefined operations.

Stored procedures are also objects. In this way, you can consider them components that you can use to package some of your business logic. Other applications can then reuse this business logic, which can help speed development and promote reuse across an organization.

Stored Procedure Syntax

Stored procedures can be created using the *CREATE PROCEDURE* syntax in SQL Server. The full syntax is

```
CREATE PROCEDURE [owner.]procedure_name[;number]
    [(parameter1 [, parameter2]…[parameter255])]
[{FOR REPLICATION} | {WITH RECOMPILE}
    [{[WITH] | [,]} ENCRYPTION]]
AS sql_statements
```

where

- *procedure_name* is the name of the new stored procedure

- *;number* is an optional integer used to group procedures of the same name so that they can be dropped together with a single DROP PROCEDURE statement

- *parameter* has the form

    @parameter_name datatype [= *default*] [OUTPUT]

where

❑   *parameter* specifies a parameter in the procedure

❑   *datatype* specifies the datatype of the parameter

❑   *default* specifies a default value for the parameter

❑   OUTPUT indicates the parameter is a return parameter

■ *sql_statements* specifies the actions that the procedure is to take. Any number and type of SQL statements can be included in the procedure

In addition to creating stored procedures, you might also want to rename them or drop them from the database. To rename a stored procedure within SQL Server, use the *sp_rename* system stored procedure as follows:

```
sp_rename old_procedure_name, new_procedure_name
```

To drop a stored procedure within SQL Server, you use the DROP PROCEDURE statement as follows:

```
DROP PROCEDURE procedure_name
```

Both of these commands can be executed either from the SQL Enterprise Manager (part of SQL Server) or from the SQL pane within Visual InterDev. If you are using the SQL Enterprise Manager, you can choose the SQL Query Tool by choosing SQL Query Tool from the Tools menu.

Another system stored procedure within SQL Server that you might find useful is the *sp_help* stored procedure. This procedure will give you a report on a stored procedure, including the name and owner of the stored procedure along with the parameter names, data types, lengths, and precisions of any parameters that the stored procedure has defined. You call the *sp_help* stored procedure as follows:

```
sp_help procedure_name
```

> **NOTE**   Within Visual InterDev, you can find most of this information by simply expanding the plus sign (+) next to the stored procedure in the Data View window. This will open up a listing of all the parameters, including resultset columns, that are contained in the stored procedure. You can then view the properties of these parameters by right-clicking the relevant parameter and choosing Properties from the context menu.

Here's a few rules to bear in mind when creating stored procedures. These rules apply to SQL Server 6.5 databases only.

- The CREATE PROCEDURE definition can include any number and type of SQL statements, with the exception of the following: CREATE VIEW, CREATE DEFAULT, CREATE RULE, CREATE TRIGGER, and CREATE PROCEDURE.

- You can create other database objects within a stored procedure as long as they are created before they are referenced in the procedure.

- The maximum number of parameters in a stored procedure is 255.

- The maximum number of local and global variables in a procedure is limited only by available memory.

- You can reference temporary tables within a stored procedure.

PREPARING THE DATABASE

Obviously, before you can start working with stored procedures, you'll want to set up a database that enables you to create them.

Creating the Database in SQL Server

In this example, we'll use SQL Server 6.5. To create a new database within SQL Server, you first create a new database device and then create the database itself and assign it to the database device.

> **NOTE** A database device is one of two types of files in which databases are stored; backup devices are the other type. More than one database can be stored on a device.

Take these steps to create a new database device within SQL Server:

1. Choose Start | Microsoft SQL Server 6.5 | SQL Enterprise Manager.

2. Select the server you want to work with from within the Server Manager window, and expand the node.

3. Right-click Database Devices, and choose New Device from the context menu.

4. Enter a name for the new device in the New Database Device dialog box, and specify the location for the device and the device size in MB.

5. Click the Create Now button to create the new device.

Once you have created the new database device, it will appear under the Database Devices node within the Server Manager window. You can later edit the device properties by right-clicking the device and choosing Edit from the context menu. You can edit the size of the device and also specify whether the device is mirrored. Mirroring makes a continuous copy of the information in the device to another device. This can help recovery in the event of a media failure.

Take the following steps to create a new database within SQL Server:

1. Choose Start|Microsoft SQL Server 6.5|SQL Enterprise Manager.

2. Select the server you want to work with from within the Server Manager window, and expand the node.

3. Right-click Databases, and choose New Database from the context menu.

4. Enter a name for the new database in the New Database dialog box, and specify the data device name and log device name for the database.

5. Click the Create Now button to create the new database.

Figure 15-1 shows the SQL Server Enterprise Manager with the New Database dialog box ready to create a new database named VI6Samples. Note that the database device has already been created and is displayed under the Database Devices node.

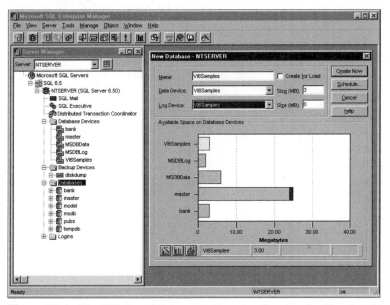

Figure 15-1. *The SQL Server Enterprise Manager showing the New Database dialog box.*

Creating the ODBC Connection in Visual InterDev

After you have created the database within SQL Server, the next step is to start Visual InterDev, create your web project, and add a data connection to the database. After opening the Web project you want to work with, right-click the global.asa file within the Project Explorer and choose Add Data Connection from the context menu. This will launch the Select Data Source dialog box, which will allow you to create a new File DSN (data source name) for your database.

To configure the ODBC connection to your SQL Server database, take the following steps:

1. Click the New button in the Select Data Source dialog box.

2. Choose SQL Server as the driver name, and click Next in the Create New Data Source dialog box.

3. Type the name of the File DSN you want to save this connection to, and click Next. Click Finish on the next screen.

4. In the Create A New Data Source To SQL Server dialog box, enter a description for the data source and specify the name of the server that you wish to connect to. (See Figure 15-2.)

Figure 15-2. *The Create A New Data Source To SQL Server dialog box, in which you specify the name of the server to connect to.*

5. On the next screen, specify how SQL Server should verify the authenticity of the login ID. Choose With SQL Server Authentication Using A Login ID And Password Entered By The User, enter *sa* as the login ID, and click Next. (See Figure 15-3.)

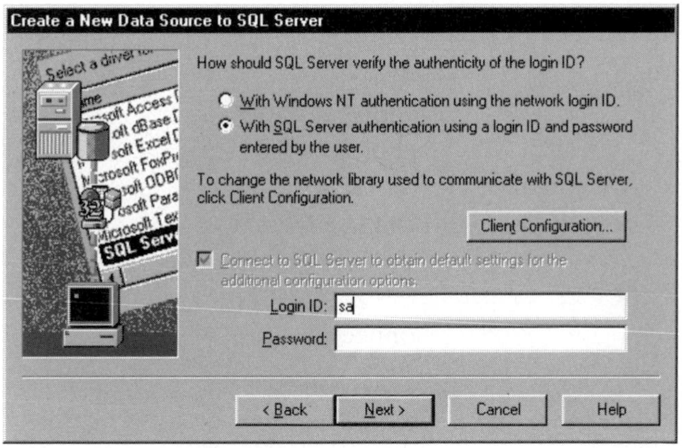

Figure 15-3. *The dialog box in which you specify how SQL Server should verify the authenticity of the login ID.*

6. On the next screen, check the Change The Default Database To check box, and select your database name in the drop-down list box. Click Next.

7. Click Next and then Finish to get to the final screen. This screen allows you to test the connection. Click the Test Data Source button, and verify that the connection succeeds. Click OK to complete the ODBC Microsoft SQL Server Setup.

After following the steps outlined above, you have created a File DSN for your SQL Server data source. You can now select this File DSN and click OK to begin establishing the data connection within Visual InterDev. Now click OK in the SQL Server Login dialog box to log in to the database. The next step is to specify a name for the data connection and to specify the authentication information for the data connection both in the design-time and run-time environment.

Follow these steps to complete your definition of the database connection:

1. In the General tab of the Connection Properties dialog box, enter a name for the data connection and choose Use Connection String for the source of the connection.

2. Select the Authentication tab, and enter *sa* for both the design-time and run-time user name. Check both the Save Design-time Authentication and the Save Run-time Authentication check boxes. (See Figure 15-4 on the following page.)

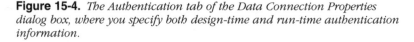

Figure 15-4. *The Authentication tab of the Data Connection Properties dialog box, where you specify both design-time and run-time authentication information.*

CREATING STORED PROCEDURES

Once you've created your data connection within Visual InterDev, you're all set to create stored procedures. To create a stored procedure, follow these steps:

1. Right-click Stored Procedures in the Data View window, and choose New Stored Procedure from the context menu. Visual InterDev will create a template stored procedure, as shown in the code following step 2. (See also Figure 15-5.)

2. Enter the code for your stored procedure into the source code editor, and click the Save button on the toolbar when you are ready to save the stored procedure.

```
Create Procedure StoredProcedure1
/*
    (
        @parameter1 datatype = default value,
        @parameter2 datatype OUTPUT
    )
*/
As
    /* set nocount on */
    return
```

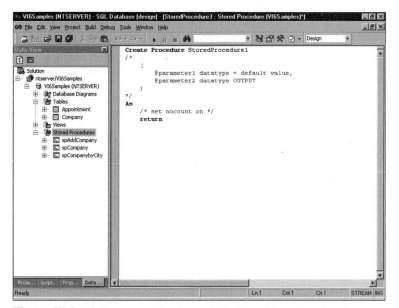

Figure 15-5. *The source code editor within Visual InterDev showing a new stored procedure.*

Stored procedures can be as simple as a single SQL SELECT statement, or they can be hundreds of lines of SQL code. Here is an example stored procedure that performs a simple SQL SELECT statement:

```
Create Procedure spCompany
As
    SELECT * FROM Company
    return
```

Here is another example stored procedure that performs a SQL SELECT statement. This procedure takes an input parameter for the City name and returns only those rows from the Company table that exactly match the search criteria:

```
Create Procedure spCompanybyCity
    (
    @city varchar(50)
    )
As
    SELECT *
    FROM Company
    WHERE city = @city

    return
```

If you want to return some information in addition to the resultset from the stored procedure to the calling program, you can use the OUTPUT option when you declare your parameters. The output parameter is passed by reference, so you pass the stored procedure a variable name that can point to the value of the output parameter. The following example returns the number of rows contained in the resultset:

```
Create Procedure spCompanybyCity2
    (
    @city varchar(50) = 'Dallas',
    @num_rows int OUTPUT
    )
As
    SELECT *
    FROM Company
    WHERE city = @city

    SELECT @num_rows = @@ROWCOUNT

    return
```

The *@@ROWCOUNT* global variable has been used to determine the number of rows in the resultset. The value of *@@ROWCOUNT* refers to the last statement executed, which was the SELECT statement for the Company table. You'll also note that a default value has been used for the *@city* parameter so that the input defaults to 'Dallas' if there is no user input specified for this parameter.

As another example, the stored procedure shown in the following code performs an INSERT statement into a table given some parameters as input.

```
Create Procedure spAddCompany
    (
        @company_name varchar(50),
        @address1 varchar(50) = Null,
        @address2 varchar(50) = Null,
        @city varchar(50) = Null,
        @state varchar(50) = Null,
        @zip varchar(10) = Null,
        @phone varchar(12) = Null,
        @fax varchar(12) = Null,
        @error_msg varchar(255) OUTPUT
    )
As
    If Len(@phone) < 10
        BEGIN
        SELECT @error_msg = 'Please include the area code in the phone
            number.'
```

(continued)

```
        return -100
        END
Else
    BEGIN
    INSERT INTO Company(company_name, address1, address2,
        city, state, zip, phone, fax)
    VALUES (@company_name, @address1, @address2,
        @city, @state, @zip, @phone, @fax)
    END

return
```

The calling program can use the return code to check the success of the stored procedure. In this example, if a code of -100 is returned, the calling program can display an error message to the user. Of course, another way to handle data validation is via client-side scripting so that a round-trip to the server is not required and the user receives instantaneous feedback. Inspecting return codes from a stored procedure is useful, however, to ensure that the procedure executed successfully and that no unexpected errors were obtained during processing.

> **NOTE** SQL Server has several reserved return status values. These range in value from -1 through -99 to indicate various reasons for failure. When returning a user-generated return value, be sure to pick a number outside of this range. Zero is also reserved by SQL Server for successful completion of the stored procedure.

In the spAddCo*mpany* stored procedure example, the Company table uses an IDENTITY property for the company_id column (the table's primary key). Columns that have the IDENTITY property set contain system-generated values that uniquely identify each row within the table. The values typically start at 1 and increment by 1 for each row that is added. To determine the latest value of an IDENTITY column after an INSERT statement, you can use the *@@IDENTITY* global variable. In the *spAddCompany* stored procedure, we would simply add the following code after the INSERT statement:

```
SELECT @company_id = @@IDENTITY
```

The *@company_id* variable can be defined as an output parameter in the stored procedure definition to return the value to the calling program. This value can then be used when performing INSERT statements on other tables which contain the company_id column as a secondary key.

DEBUGGING AND EXECUTING STORED PROCEDURES

After you have entered your stored procedure into the source code editor and have saved it, you'll see the new stored procedure name appear in the Data View window under the Stored Procedures icon.

To execute the stored procedure from within Visual InterDev, follow these steps:

1.   Right-click the name of your stored procedure from the list of procedures under the Stored Procedures icon in the Data View window.

2.   Select Execute from the context menu. An Output window will appear showing the results of the stored procedure execution.

Figure 15-6 shows the Output window after execution of the *spCompany* procedure.

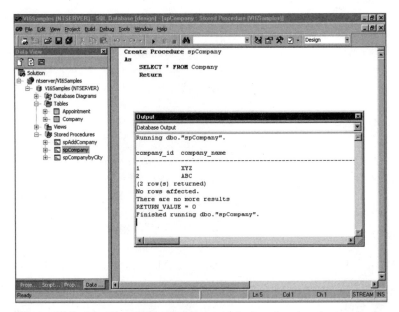

Figure 15-6. *The Visual InterDev Output window showing the result of executing the* spCompany *stored procedure.*

If you execute a stored procedure that requires input parameters, you'll see a dialog box as shown in Figure 15-7. This Execute dialog box prompts you to enter the values for all parameters that the stored procedure requires. In Figure 15-7, the Execute dialog box is prompting for the *City* parameter for use by the *spCompanybyCity* stored procedure. Notice that the Execute dialog box also displays the data type and name of the required parameters.

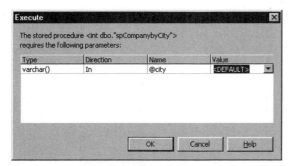

Figure 15-7. *The Execute dialog box, in which you enter the value of the required parameters for a stored procedure.*

In addition to choosing the Execute option from the context menu, there's another way you can execute stored procedures within Visual InterDev. You can use the SQL pane in the Query Designer. To execute a stored procedure in this manner, carry out the following steps:

1. Open up the SQL pane within the Query Designer.

2. Enter your SQL code to execute the stored procedure using the *EXEC procedure_name* syntax. If you need to pass parameters along to the stored procedure, include them after the procedure name using the following syntax:

```
EXEC procedure_name parameter1, parameter2, …parameter n
```

3. Choose Run Query from the Query toolbar to execute the query.

Figure 15-8 shows the output after having executed the *spCompanybyCity* stored procedure from within the SQL pane and passing it the parameter 'Dallas' for the city name.

If you use the EXEC statement to call a stored procedure from within the SQL pane and you omit some required parameters, you'll get a warning message. For example, if you execute the *spCompanybyCity* stored procedure without supplying the city name to search for, you'll see a warning message like the one shown in Figure 15-9. You'll also get a similar message if you click the Verify SQL Syntax button on the Query toolbar prior to executing the same command.

> **NOTE** If you can't remember the parameters that need to be passed to your stored procedure, it's best to choose the first method of execution using the Execute menu item from the context menu. This way the Execute dialog box will prompt you to fill out all the required parameters. On the other hand, if you know which parameters need to be passed to your stored procedure and you want to be able to more easily read the resulting output from the procedure, use the EXEC statement in the SQL pane. This way you can see the results in the Results Pane, which is easier to read than the Output window.

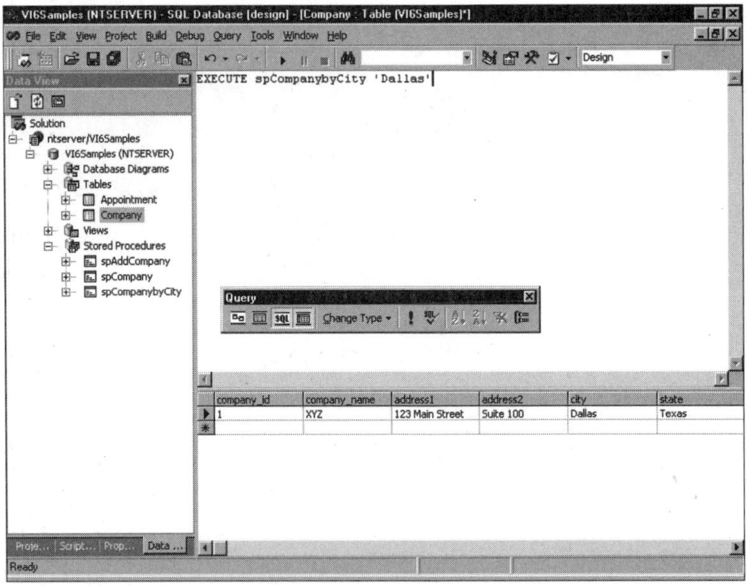

Figure 15-8. *Stored procedure output shown in the Results pane of the Query Designer.*

Figure 15-9. *A warning message displayed by Visual InterDev when a stored procedure is missing a required parameter.*

Debugging SQL Server Stored Procedures

If you have the Enterprise edition of Microsoft Visual Studio, Visual InterDev includes a SQL debugger that you can use to debug SQL Server stored procedures and triggers in much the same way that you debug other kinds of scripts or programs.

To run the SQL Debugger, you must have the following components installed:

- Visual Studio, Enterprise Edition

- SQL Server 6.5 with Service Pack 2

- Microsoft Windows NT 4.0 or later

- Workstation running Microsoft Windows 95 or Windows NT 4.0 or later

In addition, you must have installed the SQL Server Debugging components onto your server from the Visual Studio, Enterprise Edition CD-ROM. You must also have set up Distributed COM (DCOM) for SQL Debugging. For more details about the installation and configuration of these components, please see the online Visual Studio documentation.

To debug a stored procedure within Visual InterDev, follow these steps:

1. In the Data View window, right-click the stored procedure and choose Debug from the context menu. The source code editor window will open with the stored procedure code in it.

2. Now you can add breakpoints by clicking to the left of the code in the gray vertical border or by right-clicking and choosing Insert Breakpoint from the context menu.

The options on the Debug menu allow you to control the debugging process.

Figure 15-10 shows a stored procedure within the source code editor with some breakpoints applied. You can also see the context menu showing the Insert Breakpoint command.

The Locals window allows you to view the values of variables and parameters. You can also drag an expression from the stored procedure code and drop it into the Watch window. You can open up the Locals window and the Watch window by clicking the appropriate buttons on the Debug toolbar.

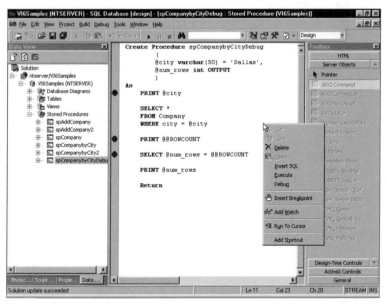

Figure 15-10. *Debugging a stored procedure from within the source code editor.*

CALLING STORED PROCEDURES FROM ACTIVE SERVER PAGES

You can execute a stored procedure from within your Active Server Pages (ASP) code in your Visual InterDev web projects. The two main techniques for doing so are as follows:

- Via data command objects and scripting the Data Environment

- Via *Recordset* objects and literals, variables, object references, or expressions

We'll now take a look at both of these techniques. The first technique gives you more control over the stored procedure call since the code is written manually with the exception of the data command object that contains the stored procedure. The second technique provides a fast way to call stored procedures but is sometimes harder to code for more advanced stored procedures calls that involve a lot of input and output parameters and that might or might not return a resultset. The authors preference is for the first technique: scripting the Data Environment.

Calling Stored Procedures via Data Command Objects and Data Environment Scripting

In this section, we'll continue with the example stored procedure named *spAddCompany* and see how to call it from within ASP code. You'll remember that this stored procedure takes a number of input parameters and performs a SQL INSERT into the Company table.

First, we'll create an HTML file named AddCompanyScript.htm. This file, and the rest of this example, is included on the CD-ROM under the VI6Samples folder. The htm file is used to capture user input for the Company information. It consists of a simple HTML form, as shown in Figure 15-11.

Second, we need to create a data command object that can reference the *spAddCompany* stored procedure. You can create this object as follows:

1. In the Project Explorer, right-click the data connection and choose Add Data Command.

2. Enter *AddCo* for the Command Name, and set the connection to VI6Samplesconn (or whatever connection name you have created).

3. For the source of the data, choose Stored Procedure from the Database Object drop-down list and then select the *dbo.spAddCompany* stored procedure from the Object Name drop-down list.

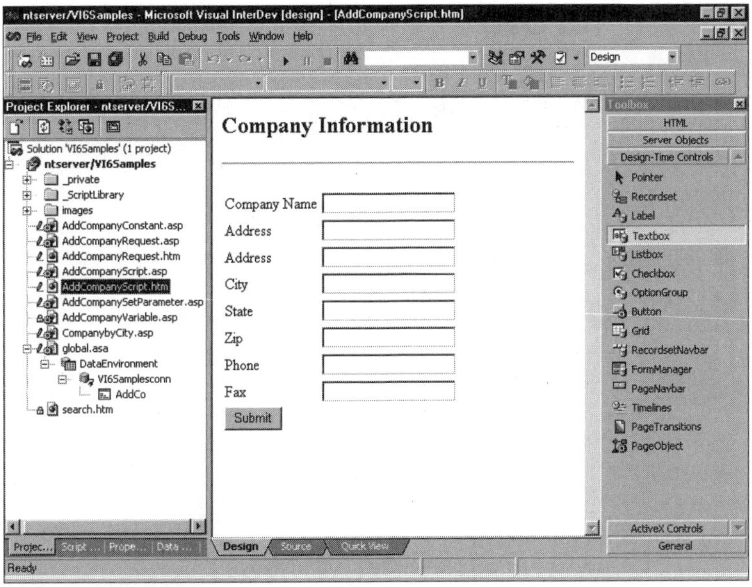

Figure 15-11. *An HTML form for capturing the user input for the* spAddCompany *stored procedure.*

Figure 15-12 shows the Properties dialog box for the data command object we have created.

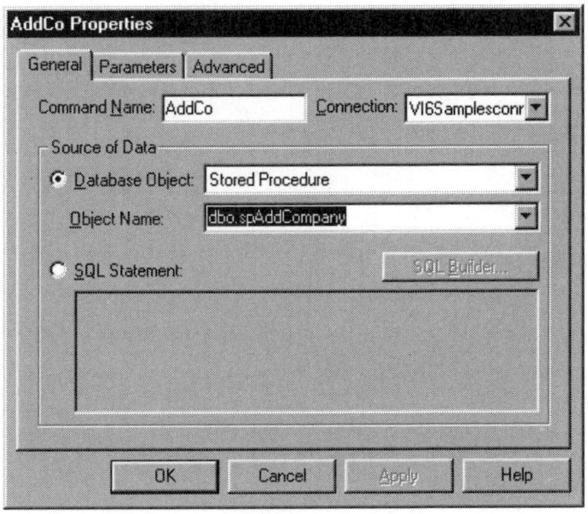

Figure 15-12 *The Properties dialog for the data command object showing stored procedure named* spAddCompany *as the data source.*

Within the Properties dialog box for the data command object that we've created, you'll also notice a Parameters tab. Here you can inspect the list of parameters that the stored procedure is expecting. Figure 15-13 on the following page shows the Parameters tab. On this tab, you can inspect the names of the parameters and their associated direction (that is, input, output, or input/output), data type, and size.

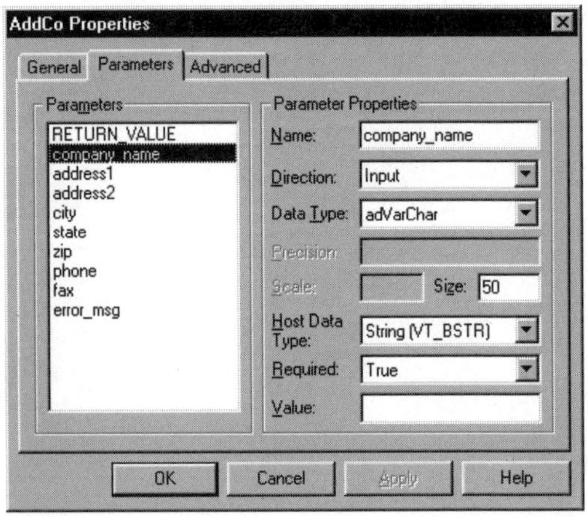

Figure 15-13 *The Properties dialog box for the data command object showing the parameters required by the stored procedure.*

After having created the HTML file to capture user input and the data command object to reference the stored procedure, next you create an ASP Web page that can call the data command object and pass it the user-supplied input values. The code below does just this. As you can see, there are no visual controls on the page at all—just Data Environment scripting.

```
<%@ Language=VBScript %>
<% ' VI 6.0 Scripting Object Model Enabled %>
<!--#include file="_ScriptLibrary/pm.asp"-->
<% if StartPageProcessing() Then Response.End() %>
<FORM name=thisForm METHOD=post>
<HTML>
<HEAD>
<META NAME="GENERATOR" Content="Microsoft Visual Studio 6.0">
</HEAD>
<BODY>

<%
' Initialize parameters
a = Request.Form("company_name")
b = Request.Form("address1")
c = Request.Form("address2")
d = Request.Form("city")
e = Request.Form("state")
f = Request.Form("zip")
g = Request.Form("phone")
h = Request.Form("fax")
error_msg = ""
```

(continued)

```
' Call the stored procedure
thisPage.createDE()
rtnVal = DE.AddCo (a, b, c, d, e, f, g, h, error_msg)

' Display the return status
If rtnVal = 0 Then
    Response.Write "Company information sucessfully captured."
Else
    Response.Write "Error: " + CStr(rtnVal) + "<BR>"
    Response.Write "Description: " + error_msg + "<P>"
    Response.Write "Please try again."
End If
%>


</BODY>
<% ' VI 6.0 Scripting Object Model Enabled %>
<% EndPageProcessing() %>
</FORM>
</HTML>
```

There are basically three steps to follow in the AddCompanyScript.asp page. First, the parameters to be passed to the stored procedure are collected from the *Request* object and stored into variables. Second, the stored procedure is executed using the following syntax:

```
thisPage.createDE()
rtnVal = DE.AddCo (a, b, c, d, e, f, g, h, error_msg)
```

Finally, the results of the procedure call are displayed on the screen. If the return value is 0, the procedure executed successfully and the new record was inserted into the Company table. If the return value was -100 or any other value other than 0, an error message is printed on the screen. Notice that the error_msg variable is an input/output parameter, so it is assigned a new value should the stored procedure encounter an error condition.

As you can see from this example, using scripting in the Data Environment makes it easy to work with stored procedures. Only a couple of lines of code are needed, and you have access to all the necessary output parameters and return values you need to track the completion status of the stored procedure execution.

Calling Stored Procedures Using *Recordset* Objects

In this section, we'll use the example stored procedure named *spCompanybyCity* and see how to call it from ASP code using a *Recordset* object. You'll remember that this stored procedure takes a single input parameter (the name of a city) and performs a SQL SELECT statement against the Company table.

First create an ASP file named CompanybyCity.asp. This file is included on the CD-ROM under the VI6Samples folder. The next step is to place a *Recordset* object onto the ASP Web page. You can do this by dragging a Recordset design-time control (DTC) from the Toolbox. Next, name the Recordset DTC *rsCompanybyCity*. Display the Recordset Properties dialog box, choose the General tab, and then choose Stored Procedures from the Database Object drop-down list. Choose *spCompanybyCity* from the Object Name drop-down list. This is the name of the stored procedure we want to call from the *Recordset* object.

Since a Recordset DTC executes its query when the ASP Web page is first loaded, we'll need to specify the value of any parameters early on. Typically, we cannot gather or evaluate the value of the parameter after the page has been displayed. You can therefore specify the value of the parameter in one of these two events prior to the opening of the *Recordset* object:

- The *onenter* event for the page
- The *onbeforeopen* event for the *Recordset* object

In this example, however, we'll use another technique. We'll uncheck the Automatically Open The Recordset check box. This check box is found on the Implementation tab of the Recordset Properties dialog box. By unchecking this option, you can now specify your parameters and then programmatically open the *Recordset* object after the parameters have been defined. The following code shows an example:

```
<%
rsCompanybyCity.setParameter 1, "Dallas"
rsCompanybyCity.open
%>
```

NOTE   You can pass parameters to *Recordset* objects in several ways. These include specifying the following types of values in the Parameters tab of the Recordset Properties dialog box:

Literals   Character values in single quotes and numeric values without quotes.

Variables   Names of variables defined in server code that contain the value you want to pass.

Object References   References to objects such as the *Request* object or a Textbox DTC and their associated property values.

Expressions   Any combination of literals, variables, and object references. The expression is evaluated as a Microsoft JScript expression, so be sure to use single quotes for character literals and the plus sign (+) for concatenation.

The code below shows the full code for the CompanybyCity.asp page minus the code that is generated by the Recordset DTC and the Grid DTC. You'll notice that there is very little code that needed to be manually scripted.

```
<%@ Language=VBScript %>
<% ' VI 6.0 Scripting Object Model Enabled %>
<!--#include file="_ScriptLibrary/pm.asp"-->
<% if StartPageProcessing() Then Response.End() %>
<FORM name=thisForm METHOD=post>
<HTML>
<HEAD>
<META name=VI60_DTCScriptingPlatform content="Server (ASP)">
<META NAME="GENERATOR" Content="Microsoft Visual Studio 6.0">
</HEAD>
<BODY>
<H2>Company List</H2>
<HR>

<!--METADATA TYPE="DesignerControl" startspan
...

<Recordset design-time control>
...
<!--METADATA TYPE="DesignerControl" endspan-->

<%
rsCompanybyCity.setParameter 1, "Dallas"
rsCompanybyCity.open
%>

<!--METADATA TYPE="DesignerControl" startspan
...
<Grid design-time control>
...
<!--METADATA TYPE="DesignerControl" endspan-->

</BODY>
<% ' VI 6.0 Scripting Object Model Enabled %>
<% EndPageProcessing() %>
</FORM>
</HTML>
```

Notice also that a Grid DTC has been used to display the output from the Recordset DTC. Figure 15-14 on the following page shows the output as it appears in the browser window.

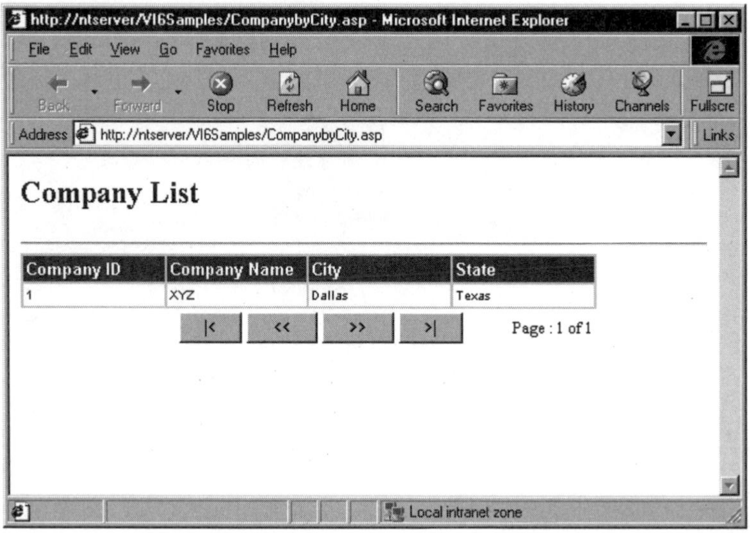

Figure 15-14. *Output from the CompanybyCity.asp page. This page uses a Recordset DTC to call a stored procedure named* spCompanybyCity. *The results are displayed in a Grid DTC.*

Using either the Data Environment scripting technique or the *Recordset* object technique allows you to work with stored procedures easily. By trying out both techniques, you'll be able to find out which one works best for you and gives you the right level of programmatic control versus speed of development that you need. As mentioned earlier, the authors' preference is for scripting the Data Environment. This technique seems to provide the most dependable results no matter the nature of the stored procedure. We found the *Recordset* object technique provided unusual results when we were attempting to work with stored procedures that did not return a recordset.

Overall, using stored procedures is an excellent way for both improving the performance of your Visual InterDev applications and for separating the business logic from the presentation layer within your applications. Performing this separation will allow you to write code that can be easily maintained in the future by other developers. One drawback to stored procedures, however, is that they are proprietary. A stored procedure written for a SQL Server database will require a few changes before you can place it into an Oracle database.

Chapter 16

Using Client Database Features

As we saw in Chapter 7, Dynamic HTML (DHTML) is basically HTML with additions that allow scriptable changes to a document at run time. You can change nearly everything about the document content at run time by using a scripting language such as Microsoft VBScript (Visual Basic, Scripting Edition) or Microsoft JScript to access the HTML objects. Every element in the document becomes an individually addressable object at run time. Objects are very simple, consistent, run-time–programmable entities. In Chapter 7, we looked at several elements of DHTML, including the DHTML object model, dynamic styles, dynamic positioning, and dynamic content. In this chapter, we'll take a look at another key feature of DHTML provided by Microsoft Internet Explorer 4.0—data binding.

In Chapter 13, we saw how the scripting platform can be changed from server side to client side, thus moving the data to the client side for greater user interactivity and performance. Users are able to filter and sort data on the client side without having to take round-trips to the server. Additionally, users can page through a form displaying a single record at a time without having to take a round-trip to the server each time. Not only does this work for viewing and navigating through data, it also works for recordsets that need to be updatable so that the user can add, edit, and delete records where necessary.

All this actually occurs through data binding. Microsoft Visual InterDev 6.0 makes it easy to incorporate data binding into your applications via the development environment using the Scripting Object Model, *Recordset* objects, design-time controls, and DHTML so that you don't have to be concerned with the internals of how data binding is implemented.

In this chapter, we'll take a look at data binding both in theory and in practice. We'll look at how to use this technique within and outside the Visual InterDev environment—meaning with or without *Recordset* objects and design-time controls. Exploring the internals of data binding will give you more insight into how this mechanism works and into the endless possibilities for using it within your business applications. We'll start with the theory and then get into some code samples that illustrate how to apply data binding in your applications.

DATA-BINDING ARCHITECTURE

There are four fundamental components to the Dynamic HTML data-binding architecture:

- Data source objects
- Data consumers
- Data binding agent
- Table repetition agent

Data source objects (DSOs) provide the data to the page, data consumers display the data on the page, and the data binding and table repetition agents ensure that the DSOs and the data consumers are synchronized. Figure 16-1 shows the data-binding architecture.

Notice in Figure 16-1 that all four of these components must be present within the HTML page in Internet Explorer 4.0. Even the DSO is an object that needs to be placed on the page, usually as a Microsoft ActiveX control or Java applet.

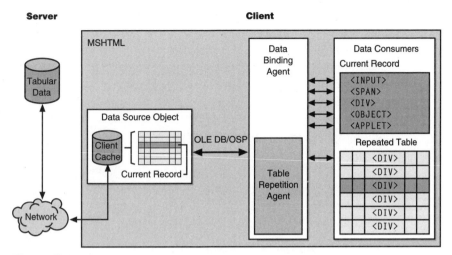

Figure 16-1. *Data-binding architecture.*

Data Source Objects

Data source objects are those entities that expose data from some server in a regular row-by-column orientation. Internet Explorer 4.0 ships with a number of DSOs, including the following:

- Tabular Data Control (TDC)
- Remote Data Service (formerly ADC)
- JDBC applet
- XML data source object
- MSHTML data source object

DSOs have several key responsibilities:

- Defining how the data is specified
- Transporting the data to the page
- Possibly manipulating the data
- Possibly relaying changes back to the server

Data can be transported to the page using any protocol desired by the DSO developer. Additionally, the data can be transferred either synchronously or asynchronously. Asynchronous transmission is the recommended method since this way the end user doesn't have to wait for data as it arrives on the page.

Depending on the provider and the nature of the data, updating the data might not be necessary. Many data providers support read-only data to the page. Note that the transport and manipulation of the data is at the provider's discretion. The only "real" requirement is that the provider exposes the data through one of two APIs:

- OLE DB
- OLE DB Simple Provider (OSP)

Following these minimal requirements allows Internet Explorer 4.0 to manage the binding of your source to the bindable data elements on a page.

We'll now look at three sample DSOs: the Tabular Data Control, the Remote Data Service, and the XML data source object.

The Tabular Data Control

The Tabular Data Control (TDC) is an ActiveX control provided with Internet Explorer 4.0 that takes its data from an input file. This file is normally a comma-delimited text file with carriage returns at the end of each record. However, if necessary you can instruct the TDC to parse on different delimiter characters of your choice. Note that the default format (commas and carriage returns) is the most common export option on most popular database tools. You can specify the TDC object within your HTML page, as in the following example:

```
<OBJECT id=TDC classid="clsid:333C7BC4-460F-11D0-BC04-0080C7055A83"
    height=0 width=0>
    <PARAM NAME="DataURL" VALUE="customers.csv ">
    <PARAM NAME="UseHeader" VALUE="True">
</OBJECT>
```

You can tell the TDC that the first record in the file is information about the rest of the records, or metadata. This is achieved by setting the *UseHeader* property to True in the <PARAM> tag. You can include field names and data type information in this first record. The delimiters used by the rest of the field separate each field description, but if there is both a field name and data type information, they are separated by a colon.

Having your data come from text files might not seem very interesting, but it's not as limiting as you might first suspect. You can bind the TDC to an ASP file, for example, and have the server dynamically generate the data for you. The minimum requirement is to have the ASP file return text appropriate for the client object by specifying the text/plain mime type as in the following example:

```
<%@ Language="JScript"%>
<%
Response.ContentType = "text/plain";
Response.Write("Example,Location,Type\n");
Response.Write(
    "Current record example,examples/CurrentRecord.ASP,data\n");
```

In this example, the text to be sent to the client is hardcoded, but we could have created an ActiveX Data Objects (ADO) recordset, retrieved data into the recordset, and then written out the recordset rows and columns instead.

The object model for the TDC includes several file properties for describing the location of the data file and its format, plus properties for filtering and sorting the data. A *reset* method is used to apply the new filter or the new sort order so that it refreshes the HTML elements on the page. Table 16-1 shows the properties and methods for the TDC control.

Property/Method Name	Type	Description
CharSet	Property	Identifies the character set used by the data file. The default character set is latin1.
DataURL	Property	Specifies the location of the data file as a URL.
EscapeChar	Property	Identifies the character to be used as an escape character in the data file. There is no default escape character.
FieldDelim	Property	Identifies the character that is used to mark the end of a field in the data file. The default character is the comma (,).
Language	Property	Specifies the language used to generate the data file. (This specifier uses the HTML standard code based on ISO 369.) The default specifier is eng-us.
TextQualifier	Property	Specifies the optional character that surrounds a field.
RowDelim	Property	Identifies the character used to mark the end of each row of data. The default character is the newline (NL) character.

Table 16-1. *Properties and methods for the Tabular Data Control.* (*continued*)

Table 16-1. *continued*

Property/Method Name	Type	Description
UseHeader	Property	Specifies whether the first line of the data file contains header information. The default value is FALSE.
Sort	Property	Sorts the data. Specified using a semicolon-delimited list of column names. Prefix with a plus (+) symbol for ascending order or a minus (-) symbol for descending order.
Filter	Property	Filters the data.
Reset	Method	Sorts and/or filters the data and refreshes the contents of the HTML elements bound to the data supplied by the TDC.

You can find the source code for the TDC on the Internet Client SDK. There is also plenty of reference information and sample code on the Microsoft Web site. The section "Using the Tabular Data Control" later in this chapter also gives some examples of how to use this control within your applications.

Remote Data Service

Remote Data Service (RDS—formerly known as ADC) is a bit more robust and complex than the TDC. RDS provides bindable recordsets to the client much as the TDC does but relies on a connection to some "real" back-end database and permits updates as well.

RDS is a data-marshaling technology. The client-side component, called the *RDS.DataControl* object, interacts with a server-side component to move the records from server to client and back. Nominally, the server-side component is called the *RDS.DataFactory* object, but you can replace this object with one (or more) of your own creation.

The *RDS.DataControl* object is the client-side component responsible for interacting with the Web page. Under most circumstances, you simply create the object on the page with an <OBJECT> tag and allow it to manage all the interactions with the server:

```
<OBJECT id=rowData
    classid="clsid:BD96C556-65A3-11D0-983A-00C04FC29E33">
    <PARAM name="Server" value="http://www.myserver.com">
    <PARAM name="Connect" value="DSN=mydsn">
    <PARAM name="SQL" value="select * from products">
</OBJECT>
```

Of course, you can specify these values at run time, too. Once you've made changes that you want to keep, you call the *RDS.DataControl* object's *Submit-Changes* method and only the modified records are returned to the server.

The *RDS.DataFactory* object is the default middle-tier component in RDS. It's the workhorse of the relationship, responsible for interacting with the client-side *RDS.DataControl* object, retrieving data from the ODBC database, and updating that database with the modified records returned by the *RDS.DataControl* object. However, the *RDS.DataFactory* object is relatively simple. It cannot reconcile update conflicts, for example, or negotiate with the data server in any but the simplest way. If it is unsuitable for your needs, you can replace it with a business server of your own design.

The *RDS.DataControl* and *RDS.DataFactory* objects communicate across one of four protocols:

■   HTTP

■   HTTPS

■   DCOM

■   In-process COM

You specify which protocol to use with the *Server* property on the *RDS.DataControl* object. The recordset exchanged between the *RDS.Data-Control* object and the *RDS.DataFactory* object is marshaled (in the case of Web servers) into a special MIME format called table datagrams. This marshaling is transparent to the applications using the RDS objects.

XML Data Source object

The XML data source object allows you to display data from an XML file within your Web pages. XML stands for eXtensible Markup Language. One of the key features of XML is that is describes the format of data. In fact, it is the universal format for data on the Web. Being extensible means that you can create whatever tags you want within your XML code—you are not limited by the predefined tags of HTML. Rather than replacing HTML, XML is a complementary format that has many areas of application. The following is an example of an XML file:

```
<?XML VERSION="1.0" RMD="NONE"?>
<VALUES>
<ITEM>
    <FIRST>1</FIRST>
    <SECOND>2</SECOND>
</ITEM>
```

(continued)

```
<ITEM>
    <FIRST>3</FIRST>
    <SECOND>4</SECOND>
</ITEM>
</VALUES>
</XML>
```

The XML data source object is particularly useful for displaying hierarchical data on your Web pages. The XML data source object is implemented as a Java applet and can be obtained from the Microsoft Web site by downloading the XML Parser in Java. The class file that implements the XML data source object is named XMLDSO.class.

The Microsoft Web site has plenty of information on XML, including information about XML support in Internet Explorer 4.0 and in Internet Explorer 5.0 Beta. Later in this chapter, we'll take a look at how to use the XML data source object in a sample HTML page.

Data Consumers

Data Consumers are elements on an HTML page that render the data supplied by the DSO. Elements can be intrinsic HTML elements or custom Java applets and ActiveX controls.

HTML data-binding attributes

To enable intrinsic HTML elements to render data from a DSO, Microsoft has introduced four attributes that make up the entire HTML interface to data binding. Table 16-2 lists the four attributes.

Attribute	Description
DATASRC	Specifies which element on the page (by ID) contains the data you want the element bound to.
DATAFLD	Specifies which field (by name) in the data you want the element bound to.
DATAFORMATAS	Specifies the format you want the data rendered in. This can be "text" for plain text or numeric data or "html" if the data contains HTML markup in it. The data will be dynamically parsed and rendered on the page for each record displayed.
DATAPAGESIZE	For use with tables, specifies how many rows of data to display at once. Two additional methods, *nextPage* and *previousPage*, allow you to page through the records at run time.

Table 16-2. *HTML data-binding attributes.*

Data-Consuming HTML elements

Most elements that we'll look at are bound to the "current row" in the data source. Some specialized components, like grids and tables, know how to use the entire recordset. Presently, the only "native" HTML element that uses the entire recordset is the TABLE element. All the other elements bind to the current record only. The data-consuming HTML elements are shown in the following list of items.

- **INPUT, TEXTAREA, and LABEL elements**   The simplest data-bound elements are the INPUT, TEXTAREA, and LABEL elements. Note that you do not have to code these elements inside a FORM to use them. Each element identifies its own DATASRC and DATA-FLD attributes, which identify the data source and the data field, respectively. As the current record changes, the text in these elements changes accordingly. The INPUT and TEXTAREA elements can update data as well.

- **DIV and SPAN elements**   These two elements, while read-only, provide novel functionality in that they both support the DATA-FORMATAS=HTML property assignment, which causes the bound text to be parsed and presented as HTML text. This provides a mechanism for having parts of the presentation itself stored in a database and displayed in multiple contexts.

- **A and IMG Elements**   The A and IMG elements are "indirect" in that the bound data is a URL. That is, the data is expected to point to a valid HREF (in the case of the A element) or a valid image file (in the case of the IMG element). If you want to bind the text of the A element, you can use a bound SPAN element. Note that the IMG element does not support "blob" image data from the database.

- **SELECT and INPUT TYPE=RADIO binding**   In the previous elements, the interface of the control changed with each record. In SELECT and INPUT TYPE=RADIO controls, the interface is static as you scroll from record to record. What changes is which item in the list is selected for each record. Each OPTION element within a SELECT or each INPUT TYPE=RADIO sharing a NAME attribute has a VALUE attribute which corresponds to legal values in the data. If a given record has no corresponding VALUE in an element, no element is shown as selected.

- **TABLE binding**   We can bind the TABLE element to a recordset and get a complete picture of the contents of that recordset. We have a lot of control over how that table displays the data. Basically, you define your header and a "template" row that describes the way you want the data represented. When Internet Explorer 4.0 displays this table, it repeats the template row for each record in the recordset.

You don't have to stop at a single template row. Internet Explorer 4.0 will repeat everything in the TBODY (explicitly or implicitly defined) for each record. When a recordset has lots of rows, it is sometimes appropriate to show the data in chunks rather than having one long scrolling view. You can specify the size of the chunk to display with the DATAPAGESIZE attribute on the TABLE element.

In addition to the HTML elements listed above, there are many more that can be bound to a recordset. Table 16-3 lists the complete set of bindable elements, describes whether they are updatable and whether they can render HTML, and gives a description of the bound property of the element.

Element	Updatable	Renders HTML	Bound Property
A	False	False	href
APPLET	True	False	property value via PARAM
BUTTON	False	True	innerText, innerHTML
DIV	False	True	innerText, innerHTML
FRAME	False	False	src
IFRAME	False	False	src
IMG	False	False	src
INPUT TYPE=CHECKBOX	True	False	checked
INPUT TYPE=CHECKBOX	True	False	checked
INPUT TYPE=HIDDEN	True	False	value
INPUT TYPE=LABEL	True	False	value
INPUT TYPE=PASSWORD	True	False	value
INPUT TYPE=RADIO	True	False	checked
INPUT TYPE=TEXT	True	False	value
LABEL	False	True	innerText, innerHTML
MARQUEE	False	True	innerText, innerHTML
SELECT	True	False	obj.options(obj.selectedIndex).text
SPAN	False	True	innerText, innerHTML
TEXTAREA	True	False	value

Table 16-3. *Bindable HTML elements.*

Binding Agent

The part of the DHTML data-binding architecture that glues the HTML elements to the data sources is the binding agent in Internet Explorer 4.0. It is implemented by mshtml.dll, which is the HTML viewer for Internet Explorer. The binding agent is responsible for managing the relationship between the DSOs and data consumers to ensure that they are always synchronized.

The binding agent actually fires scriptable events that the Web author can take advantage of. These signal various changes in the state of the data between the DSOs and their data consumers.

Table Repetition Agent

The table repetition agent works with data consumers that present tabular data such as the HTML TABLE element. It ensures that the entire data set is repeated properly by the data consumer. For individual elements, it relies on the data binding agent to ensure synchronization.

USING THE TABULAR DATA CONTROL

Now that we've covered some of the theory involved in DHTML data binding, let's take a look at some real examples. For the TDC, we'll look at two code samples—a simple example and then a more advanced example.

Sorting a Simple HTML Table

The code below shows the source code for TDC.htm. This file, along with all the other related files, is included on the CD-ROM under the CHAP16 folder.

```
<HTML>
<HEAD>
<META name=VI60_defaultClientScript content=VBScript>
<META NAME="GENERATOR" Content="Microsoft Visual Studio 6.0">
<SCRIPT ID=clientEventHandlersVBS LANGUAGE=vbscript>
<!--
Sub Col1_onclick
    CTDCCtl1.Sort = "A"
    CTDCCtl1.Reset
End Sub

Sub Col2_onclick
    CTDCCtl1.Sort = "B"
    CTDCCtl1.Reset
End Sub
```

(continued)

```
Sub Col3_onclick
    CTDCCtl1.Sort = "C"
    CTDCCtl1.Reset
End Sub

Sub btnFilt_onclick
    CTDCCtl1.Filter = "A=1"
    CTDCCtl1.Reset
End Sub

Sub btnReset_onclick
    CTDCCtl1.Filter = "A=*"
    CTDCCtl1.Reset
End Sub
-->
</SCRIPT>
</HEAD>
<BODY>
<H2>Simple Table (Using the Tabular Data Control)</H2>
<HR>

<OBJECT CLASSID="clsid:333C7BC4-460F-11D0-BC04-0080C7055A83"
id=CTDCCtl1 VIEWASTEXT>
<PARAM NAME="DataURL" VALUE="TDC.csv">
<PARAM NAME="UseHeader" VALUE="True">
</OBJECT>

<TABLE BORDER=1 DATASRC="#CTDCCtl1">
<THEAD>
<TR>
<TH ID="Col1">1st<TH ID="Col2">2nd<TH ID="Col3">3rd
<TBODY>
<TR>
<TD><SPAN DATAFLD=A></SPAN>
<TD><SPAN DATAFLD=B></SPAN>
<TD><SPAN DATAFLD=C></SPAN>
</TABLE>
<P>
<INPUT type="button" value="Filter" id="btnFilt" name="filter">
 
<INPUT type="button" value="Reset" id="btnReset" name="reset">
<P>
<FONT face="" size=2>
Click a column heading to sort the table by that column
</FONT>
</BODY>
</HTML>
```

The TDC.htm file demonstrates how to use the TDC to retrieve data from a comma-delimited text file named TDC.csv and display it within the browser in the form of an HTML table. Notice that the code consists of the <OBJECT> tag for the TDC, plus an HTML table for the display. Also notice the DATASRC and DATAFLD attributes that are used to bind the data to the HTML table. And that each column within the HTML table has been given an ID. This allows us to reference the various columns in our script. Finally, client-side VBScript has been used to trap several events: the *onclick* event for the column headers is used to sort the data by the values in that column. Also, the Filter and Reset buttons are used to demonstrate how to filter the data and reset the data back to its original setting.

Figure 16-2 shows how this page appears within the Internet Explorer 4.0 browser. When you click the column headers, you'll see that the table is sorted so that the numbers appear in ascending order for that particular column. This is done on the client side with no round-trip back to the TDC.csv file.

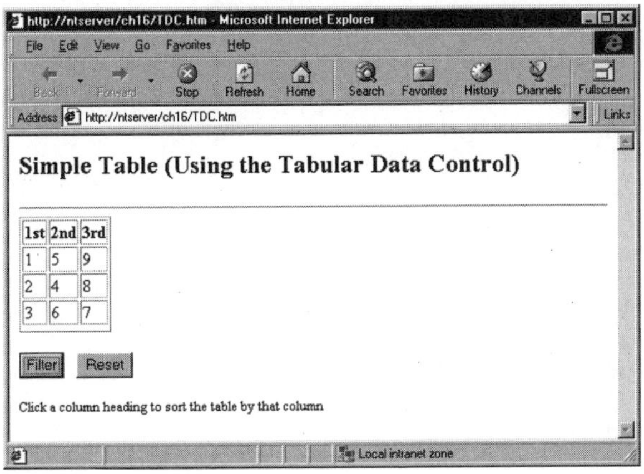

Figure 16-2. *The TDC.htm file within the Internet Explorer 4.0 browser.*

Sorting and Searching Using an HTML Table

The next example takes the functionality of the TDC a little further. We'll use the TDC to retrieve information about customers and use an HTML table to navigate through the resultset and to search for data by customer ID, company name, or contact name.

> **NOTE** If you want to add the TDC ActiveX control onto your Visual InterDev Toolbox just bring up the Customize Toolbox dialog box and then browse through the list of ActiveX controls until you find the control with the name *Tabular Data Control*. This control is named tdc.ocx and is usually installed in the C:\WINNT\System32 folder if you are running

Windows NT. Having the TDC in your Toolbox makes it easy to add it to your Web pages instead of having to manually code the <OBJECT> tag and the CLASSID attribute.

The code below shows the source code for TDC_Customer_List.htm. This file, along with all the other related files, is included on the CD-ROM under the CHAP16 folder.

```
<HTML>
<HEAD>
<META name=VI60_defaultClientScript content=VBScript>
<META NAME="GENERATOR" Content="Microsoft Visual Studio 6.0">
<SCRIPT ID=clientEventHandlersVBS LANGUAGE=vbscript>
<!--
Sub Col1_onclick
    CTDCCtl1.Sort = "CustomerID"
    CTDCCtl1.Reset
End Sub
Sub Col2_onclick
    CTDCCtl1.Sort = "CompanyName"
    CTDCCtl1.Reset
End Sub
Sub Col3_onclick
    CTDCCtl1.Sort = "ContactName"
    CTDCCtl1.Reset
End Sub
Sub search_onclick
    If listbox.selectedIndex = 0 Then
        col = "CustomerID"
    Elseif listbox.selectedIndex = 1 Then
        col = "CompanyName"
    Else
        col = "ContactName"
    End If
    str = col & "=" & CStr(find.value)
    MsgBox(str)
    CTDCCtl1.Filter = str
    CTDCCtl1.Reset
End Sub
Sub reset_onclick
    CTDCCtl1.Filter = "CustomerID=*"
    CTDCCtl1.Reset
End Sub
Sub next_onclick
    datatbl.nextPage
End Sub
Sub previous_onclick
    datatbl.previousPage
```

(continued)

```
End Sub
-->
</SCRIPT>
</HEAD>
<BODY>
<H3>Customer List (Using the Tabular Data Control)</H3>
<HR>
<TABLE cellpadding=3>
<TR>
<TD>Find</TD>
<TD><INPUT id=find name=find></TD>
<TD>In Column</TD>
<TD>
<SELECT id=listbox name=listbox>
<OPTION selected>Customer ID</OPTION>
<OPTION>Company Name</OPTION>
<OPTION>Contact Name</OPTION>
</SELECT>
</TD>
</TR>
</TABLE>
<OBJECT classid=clsid:333C7BC4-460F-11D0-BC04-0080C7055A83
    id=CTDCCtl1 VIEWASTEXT>
    <PARAM NAME="UseHeader" VALUE="1">
    <PARAM NAME="DataURL" VALUE="Customers.csv">
</OBJECT>
<TABLE id=datatbl BORDER=1 DATASRC="#CTDCCtl1" DATAPAGESIZE="8">
<THEAD>
<TR>
<TH ID="Col1">CustomerID
<TH ID="Col2">CompanyName
<TH ID="Col3">ContactName</TR>
<TBODY>
<TR>
<TD><SPAN DATAFLD=CustomerID></SPAN>
<TD><SPAN DATAFLD=CompanyName></SPAN>
<TD><SPAN DATAFLD=ContactName></SPAN></TR></TBODY>
</TABLE>
<TABLE cellpadding=3>
<TR>
<TD>
<INPUT type="button" value=" <- " id=previous name=previous>
</TD>
<TD>
<INPUT type="button" value=" -> " id=next name=next>
</TD>
</TR>
```

(continued)

```
</TABLE>
<HR>
<TABLE cellpadding=3>
<TR>
<TD>
<INPUT type="button" value="Search" id=search name=search>
</TD><TD>
<INPUT type="button" value="Reset" id=reset name=reset>
</TD>
</TR>
</TABLE>
<P>
<FONT face="" size=2 style="BACKGROUND-COLOR: #ffffff">
    Click a column heading to sort the table by that column</FONT>
</BODY>
</HTML>
```

Figure 16-3 shows the resulting screen when viewed within Internet Explorer. You'll notice that the table displays eight rows of data. This was accomplished by setting the DATAPAGESIZE attribute within the <TABLE> tag as follows:

```
<TABLE id=datatbl BORDER=1 DATASRC="#CTDCCtl1" DATAPAGESIZE="8">
```

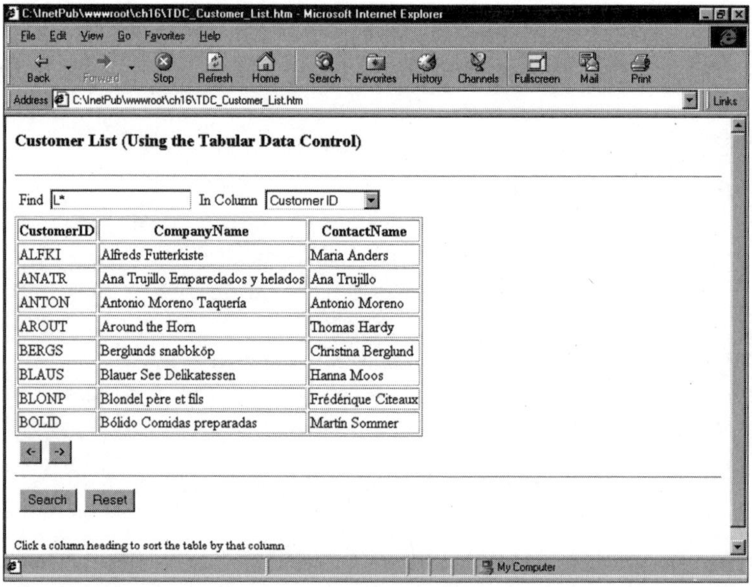

Figure 16-3. *The TDC_Customer_List.htm file showing how the TDC together with the HTML TABLE element can be used to navigate, search, and sort a client-side recordset.*

The previous and next buttons shown in Figure 16-3 allow the end user to page through the recordset. This is accomplished by calling the *previousPage* and *nextPage* methods on the table object. Note that we are not calling methods on the TDC here. The methods are executed against the table object by referencing its ID, which in this case is *datatbl*.

Search functionality is provided via a text box and a drop-down list box. The drop-down list box allows the user to specify the column on which to perform the search. When the Search button is clicked, the *search_onclick* event fires and the TDC is filtered using the *filter* property. Wildcards also work in this type of search. The Reset button simply resets the filter to include all customer IDs by using a wildcard and retrieves all the data back into the HTML table.

When you run this code sample, you'll notice how quickly the page responds to your input. Using an HTML table is a way to keep the page size light and ensure fast download plus fast navigation, searching, and sorting. One minor drawback to loading the data on the client side is that there might be some delay in loading the page because of the amount of data being retrieved. To minimize this effect, you should load only the data you need for your particular Web page to carry out the required functionality.

USING THE XML DATA SOURCE OBJECT

To use the XML data source object, you'll need to ensure that you have the XMLDSO.class file installed on your Web server. You can obtain this class file by downloading the Microsoft XML Parser in Java from the Microsoft Web site. After installation, the class file should be located in the following folder: c:\msxml\classes\com\ms\xml\dso.

Now all we need to do is to create an XML file to use as our data file, an HTML file that contains the XML data source applet, plus some data-bound HTML elements to display the data. The code below shows the source code for xml.htm. This file is included on the CD-ROM under the CHAP16 folder along with the other relevant files.

```
<HTML>
<HEAD>
<META NAME="GENERATOR" Content="Microsoft Visual Studio 6.0">
<TITLE></TITLE>
</HEAD>
<BODY>
<H2>Simple Table (Using XML Data Source Object)</H2>
<HR>
<APPLET CODE=com.ms.xml.dso.XMLDSO.class
```

(continued)

```
        ID="xmldso"
        WIDTH="0"
        HEIGHT="0"
        MAYSCRIPT="true">
        <PARAM NAME="url" VALUE="xml.xml">
</APPLET>

<TABLE ID=table border=2 width="50%" datasrc=#xmldso cellpadding=5>
<THEAD>
<TH>1st</TH>
<TH>2nd</TH>
</THEAD>
<TR>
<TD><SPAN datafld="FIRST" dataformatas="HTML"></SPAN></TD>
<TD><SPAN datafld="SECOND" dataformatas="HTML"></SPAN></TD>
</TR>
</TABLE>

</BODY>
</HTML>
```

You'll notice in the code that the <APPLET> tag is used to define the XML data source object. The URL attribute in the <PARAM> tag is used to specify the URL location of the XML file to read. In this case, the file is named xml.xml and the contents are the same as the sample XML file listed earlier in this chapter. The width and height of the applet are set to 0 so that the applet does not display on screen.

Notice that an HTML table is used to display the data from the XML file. The DATASRC attribute of the table element is set to #XMLDSO, which is the name assigned to this XML data source applet. The DATAFLD attributes for the table cells are set to FIRST and SECOND. These are the names of the tags that were defined in the XML file. The DATAFORMATAS attribute has been set to HTML.

Figure 16-4 shows the HMTL page as it appears in the Internet Explorer 4.0 browser.

As you can see from this sample, it is very easy to write HTML code that can read an XML file and display the data on screen. The powerful part of this technique is that it is extensible. The XML file can use whatever tags are necessary to represent the data structures involved.

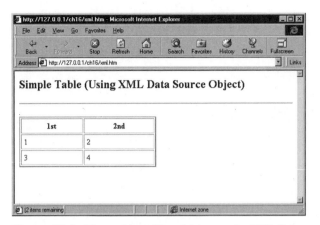

Figure 16-4. *The xml.htm file, which uses the XML data source object to display the data from an XML file.*

USING DESIGN-TIME CONTROLS

By using Visual InterDev, you can create applications that easily use client database features. As we have seen in earlier chapters, all you need to do is move the scripting platform from the server side to the client side. Remember that this can be accomplished by right-clicking within the white space in your ASP Web page and choosing Properties from the context menu. You then set the DTC Scripting Platform to Client (IE 4.0 DHTML) in the General tab of the Properties dialog box. Changing the scripting platform for the page will change the scripting platform for all components on your page since by default they inherit their scripting platform from the page.

Figure 16-5 on the following page shows the design-time control equivalent of the earlier TDC_Customer_List.htm example. This file is named DTC_Customer_List.asp. Instead of using a TDC, we are using the built-in client database features of Visual InterDev implemented behind the scenes using Remote Data Service.

The Search button performs a similar search to that applied in the TDC sample. In this case, it builds a SQL string and then uses it to requery the data source. The code for this section is as follows:

```
Sub btnSearch_onclick()
    If txtSearch.value = "" Then
        str = "SELECT * FROM Customers"
    Else
        str = "SELECT * FROM Customers WHERE " + lstColumn.value + _
            " LIKE '" + txtSearch.value + "'"
```

(continued)

```
    End If
    MsgBox(str)
    Recordset1.setSQLText(str)
    Recordset1.requery()
End Sub
```

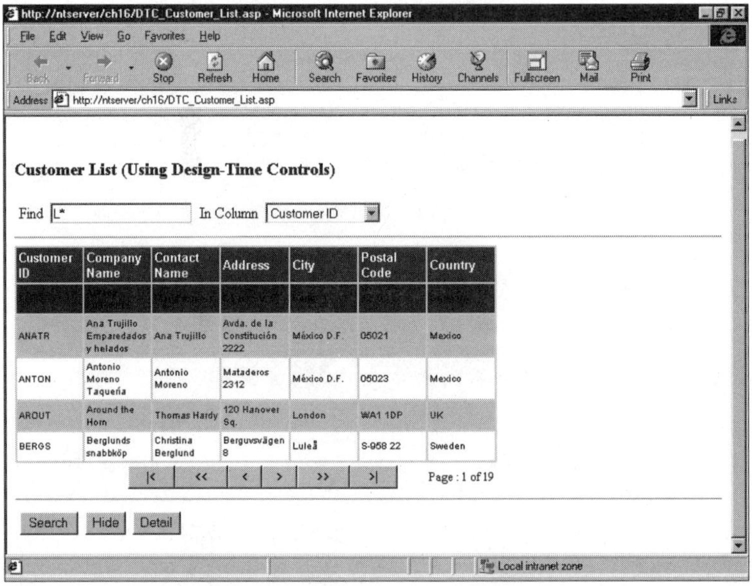

Figure 16-5. *Internet Explorer 4.0 showing an ASP Web page that uses client database features.*

CHOOSING YOUR SCRIPTING PLATFORM

As with all development topics, there is a trade-off to be made between using client-side database features and server-side database features. If you go with server-side recordsets, you get faster processing when the page is first loaded but you have to take round-trips to the server each time you need to carry out some action on the data. If you go with client-side recordsets, you often get a slower download but faster response time when working with your data on the page. Using the Scripting Object Model does involve some overhead in terms of additional files that need to be processed. Therefore, if you want to squeeze the most out of your applications, you might even want to forgo the Scripting Object Model entirely, which means doing without design-time controls. The trade-off is speed of development versus speed of execution.

Part V

Developing n-Tier Applications

Chapter 17

Using Server Components

In this section of the book, we'll be covering how to develop n-tier architectures using Microsoft Visual InterDev 6.0 and other products in the Microsoft Visual Studio 6.0 and Microsoft BackOffice Server 4.0 product suite. Over the next six chapters, we'll take a look at:

■ The prebuilt, server-side components available in the Visual InterDev Toolbox

■ How to use Microsoft Visual Basic 6.0 to construct your own server-side components

■ How to work with transactional Active Server Pages (ASP) Web pages

■ How to use Visual Basic 6.0 to construct transactional server-side components

■ How to use Microsoft Message Queue (MSMQ) within your Web applications

Of course, we'll also be taking a look at how to use Microsoft Transaction Server (MTS) for managing the transactional components that we create with Visual Basic 6.0.

We'll start off this section by covering some of the basics regarding Microsoft's framework for the development of n-tier applications. When we say "building n-tier applications," we really mean creating distributed, component-based applications that extend the scalability, performance, security, reliability, manageability, and maintainability of personal computer–based client/server and Internet applications. As Microsoft Windows NT makes significant advances into enterprise computing and is used as a strategic platform for business-critical applications, these types of architecture become increasingly important. This distributed computing architecture also enables Microsoft technologies to compete effectively. Of course, in the rapidly moving business and technology landscape, the products that deliver the simplest approach, the fastest results, the best interoperability and integration, and the lowest total cost of ownership often win. It's far more productive for developers to be able to concentrate on the business specifics of their applications than to have to become systems integrators and learn the complexities of object models and the like. Microsoft development tools and products do an excellent job of shielding developers from these types of complexities so that they can concentrate on what's important—delivering timely and highly functional applications to support their organizations' business objectives.

One advantage of an n-tier architecture is that the business logic is separated from the presentation layer. This simplifies application maintenance because business rules can be changed more easily without having to rework the presentation layer. It also means that business rules are encapsulated within server-side components instead of being scattered (often redundantly) throughout the presentation layer. By moving the business rules to a middle tier, they can also be reused across multiple applications and often across multiple delivery channels, including browser, personal computer, hand-held PC, WebTV, kiosk, and others.

Windows DNA

Windows Distributed interNet Applications Architecture (Windows DNA) is Microsoft's framework for building a new generation of computing solutions that brings together personal computing and the Internet. This framework is the basis for Microsoft's Web architecture for the next three to five years. Microsoft is delivering on this framework in three phases over this time frame. The first phase is available now in products such as Visual Studio 6.0, Windows NT 4.0 Server and Workstation, Microsoft Internet Information Server (IIS) 4.0, and Microsoft Internet Explorer 4.0. Windows NT 5.0 and then COM+ will take developers and end users into the next generation of Windows DNA by making it even easier to create and manage distributed applications.

These guiding principles outline the goal of Windows DNA:

- Web computing without compromise
- Interoperability
- True integration
- Lower cost of ownership
- Faster time to market

Once again, these principles make sound business sense. Developers are empowered to focus their efforts on delivering applications without worrying about the system integration aspects.

Windows DNA is comprised of a standard set of Microsoft Windows–based services that support user interface and navigation, business processes, and data storage. These services are distributed application services, distributed infrastructure services, and common interfaces. Table 17-1 shows the services supported by Windows DNA and the product mappings.

Service	Interface	Product Mapping
Application services		
Web server	HTML	Internet Information Server (IIS)
Web browser	HTML	Internet Explorer
Scripting	VBScript, JScript™	"Denali," Dynamic HTML
Transaction service	OLE Transactions	MTS
Message queuing service	"Falcon" API	MMQS
Database	ODBC, OLE DB	Microsoft SQL Server
Mail and collaboration Server	MAPI, POP3	Microsoft Outlook, Microsoft Exchange
Java virtual machine	Java	Microsoft Java virtual machine
Universal data access	ADO, OLE DB, ODBC	Various
Infrastructure services		
Directory	ADSI	Active Directory, Windows NT Server
Security	SSL	Windows NT Server, Internet Explorer

Table 17-1. *Windows DNA services and product mappings.*   *(continued)*

Table 17-1 *continued*

Service	*Interface*	*Product Mapping*
Network	TCP/IP, pipes, WinSock, etc.	Windows family
Remote file and print	CIFS, SMB	Windows family
Components	COM, DCOM, Microsoft ActiveX	Windows family

Figure 17-1 shows the Windows DNA services and how they fit in with COM.

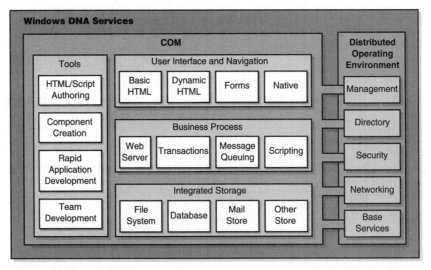

Figure 17-1. *Windows DNA services.*

Windows DNA's support for legacy integration allows organizations to leverage existing infrastructure investments. Microsoft's Cedar technology allows bidirectional access to transaction systems such as CICS, as well as legacy data sources, including DB2/MVS, IMS, and VSAM. Cedar also enables legacy applications to be Web-enabled via IIS. Visual InterDev developers can therefore create Web applications that can truly reach into the organization and pull out data wherever it may reside.

COM+

COM+ will arrive in the third phase of the Windows DNA evolution. COM+ makes it even easier for developers to build and reuse components. It preserves the investments in code and skill sets that organizations have made in COM, and places more of the infrastructure into the system. Thus developers can concentrate on higher-level business functionality rather than the low-level services to support that functionality.

COM+ defines a simpler and more robust model for registering, installing, and versioning components than its predecessor. It also introduces a new extensibility mechanism called "interception." Interceptors can receive and process events related to instance creation, calls and returns, errors, and instance deletion.

You can expect to hear a lot more about COM+ in the coming months as Windows DNA evolves.

WEB ARCHITECTURES

Prior to diving into the details of building n-tier applications using Visual InterDev 6.0, Visual Basic 6.0, and other tools, let's take a quick look from the 30,000-foot level at how these various n-tier applications can be wired together.

Within a large corporation, you can utilize several different models for your Web architectures based upon the demands placed upon each specific application. For example, you can use a three-tier architecture with server-side components and MTS for part of your external Internet site. However, you might use a simpler two-tier architecture on your Intranet site to speed the development process and reduce the application complexity. When deciding upon the appropriate technical architectures to use for your applications, keep in mind the application requirements: functionality, scalability, performance, security, reliability, manageability, and maintainability.

Two-Tier Architectures

The basic two-tier architecture for a Microsoft Web solution involves the browser, the Web server, and the database. This may well involve Internet Explorer, IIS, and SQL Server. On the browser end, you are free to deliver plain HTML or Dynamic HTML (DHTML) for breadth of deployment and Java applets and/or ActiveX controls for depth of functionality. Of course, this is a trade-off and depends upon your target audience and the required sophistication of your user interface. If you are trying to reach the largest audience possible (with a variety of browser types) on an Internet or extranet site, you might want to deliver plain HTML. If you know your target audience, perhaps on an intranet site, or are in the position to dictate browser requirements and you need a richer GUI than HTML allows, you might want to take advantage of DHTML, Java applets, or ActiveX controls.

On the server side, the only real stake in the ground is that you must be running Windows NT 4.0 and IIS 4.0 to execute the ASP Web pages you have generated from Visual InterDev. This is changing somewhat, however, as vendors such as Chili!Soft produce software that can run ASP code on UNIX platforms such as Sun Solaris. The database that you interface with can be any ODBC-compliant database. Figure 17-2 shows the typical two-tier Web architecture.

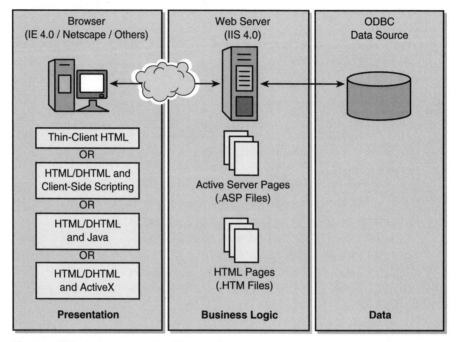

Figure 17-2. *Microsoft two-tier Web architecture.*

Three-Tier Architectures

The three-tier architecture for a Microsoft Web solution takes the basic two-tier architecture and extends it by adding server-side components. These server-side components are COM components that contain nonvisual business logic. They can be either nontransactional or transactional. Transactional components are placed under MTS, which manages the transactions and handles multithreading, security, database connection pooling, and so on.

Three-tier architectures generally take longer to develop and test than two-tier architectures, but they provide a more robust infrastructure for running business-critical Web applications. As noted earlier, middle-tier components can also be reused across different applications or even across different channels. Application maintenance is also simplified since the business logic is more likely to be contained within a single component. Figure 17-3 shows the typical three-tier Web architecture.

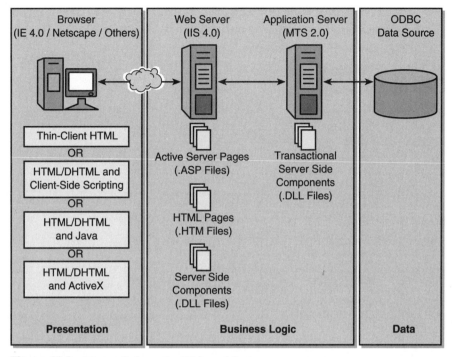

Figure 17-3. *Microsoft three-tier Web architecture.*

The Visual InterDev 6.0 Toolbox allows you to access several prebuilt components that extend ASP to make an enormous impact. As we shall see in the following chapters, you can also write your own components using Visual Basic, Microsoft Visual C++, Microsoft Visual J++, or any other development tool that supports creating Active Server components. Also, just as ActiveX controls are proliferating all over the Web, many Active Server components are now available for purchase from third-party software vendors. These software vendors are incorporating functionality that pushes the extremely flexible architecture of Active Server components to the limit.

USING SERVER OBJECTS FROM THE TOOLBOX

Some interesting server-side ActiveX components are available to the Visual InterDev developer via the Server Objects tab of the Visual InterDev 6.0 Toolbox. Figure 17-4 on the following page shows the available components. These components address common challenges facing Web developers, such as determining the type of browser that is requesting a page, sending e-mail from within

ASP code, or reading and writing text files. These components can save you many hours of development time while they increase the functionality and interactivity of your applications.

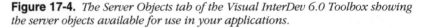

Figure 17-4. *The Server Objects tab of the Visual InterDev 6.0 Toolbox showing the server objects available for use in your applications.*

To access the server objects on the Toolbox, all you need to do is open a new or existing ASP Web page within the Visual InterDev environment. This will enable all of the server object icons on the Server Objects tab so that you can drag them from the Toolbox onto your Web page.

> **NOTE**   The list of objects on the Server Objects tab is predefined. This means that the list is the same no matter what workstation or server you are on. There is a chance that a server object that is displayed on the Toolbox might not actually be installed on your server. Always be sure to test your pages to ensure they are running correctly and the relevant server objects are installed on your server. The server objects are part of the IIS 4.0 installation, so if they are missing you'll want to install them from the Windows NT 4.0 Option Pack.

When you drag an object from the Server Object tab of the Toolbox onto your ASP Web page, the editor will create an <OBJECT> block for you with the correct RUNAT and PROGID attributes. After specifying the id that you would like to use for the object, you can reference it in your script. For example, if you drag a Collaboration Data Objects for Windows NT Server (CDONTS) Library *NewMail* object onto your Web page, the <OBJECT> block looks like this:

```
<OBJECT RUNAT=server PROGID=CDONTS.NewMail id=OBJECT1></OBJECT>
```

First you'll want to rename the id for the *NewMail* object to something more meaningful, such as *oNewMail*:

```
<OBJECT RUNAT=server PROGID=CDONTS.NewMail id=oNewMail></OBJECT>
```

Now you can reference the *NewMail* object in your script, as shown here:

```
<%
oNewMail.From = nick.evans@us.pwcglobal.com
oNewMail.To = nick.evans@us.pwcglobal.com
oNewMail.Subject = "CDONTS"
oNewMail.Body = "This NewMail object makes sending e-mail simple!"
oNewMail.Send
Set oNewMail = Nothing
%>
```

The complete ASP code for this example would look like this:

```
<@ Language=VBScript %>
<HTML>
<HEAD>
<META NAME="GENERATOR" Content="Microsoft Visual Studio 6.0">
</HEAD>
<BODY>

<OBJECT RUNAT=server PROGID=CDONTS.NewMail id=oNewMail></OBJECT>

<%
oNewMail.From = nick.evans@us.pwcglobal.com
oNewMail.To = nick.evans@us.pwcglobal.com
oNewMail.Subject = "CDONTS"
oNewMail.Body = "This NewMail object makes sending e-mail simple!"
oNewMail.Send
Set oNewMail = Nothing
%>

<P> </P>

</BODY>
</HTML>
```

In this listing, you'll notice that the <OBJECT> block lies within the HTML source code and not within the ASP script blocks. We'll be learning more about the CDONTS objects for working with e-mail later in this chapter.

Returning to the Toolbox, you'll see that the components listed on the Server Objects tab are as follows:

- **ADO Command**   ActiveX Data Objects *Command* object for specifying the parameters necessary to execute a database command such as a SQL statement

- **ADO Connection**   ActiveX Data Objects *Connection* object for specifying the parameters necessary to make a database connection

- **ADO Recordset**   ActiveX Data Objects *Recordset* object that stores the resultset from a database command

- **Ad Rotator**   Automatically rotates advertisements displayed on a page according to a specified schedule

- **Browser Capabilities**   Determines the capabilities, type, and version of each browser that accesses your site

- **Content Linking**   Creates tables of contents for Web pages and links them sequentially, like pages in a book

- **My Info**   Creates a *MyInfo* object that keeps track of the site administrator's name, address, and so on

- **Dictionary**   VBScript object that stores data key and item pairs

- **Filesystem Object**   VBScript object that provides access to file input and output

- **CDONTS NewMail**   *NewMail* object for sending e-mail message; part of the Microsoft CDONTS Library

- **CDONTS Session**   *Session* object for storing session-wide settings and options; part of the Microsoft CDONTS Library

- **Index Server Query**   Object for writing customized queries against Index Server

- **Index Server Utility**   Object that provides various utilities for developers who are using the Index Server *Query* object

- **MSMQ Query**   Microsoft Message Queue *Query* object

- **MSMQ QueueInfo**   Microsoft Message Queue *QueueInfo* object

- **MSMQ Message**   Microsoft Message Queue *Message* object

- **MSMQ MailEMail**   Microsoft Message Queue *MailEMail* object

In addition to these components, IIS 4.0 also provides the following components that are not shown on the Toolbox but can be used nonetheless:

- **Content Rotator**   Similar to the Ad Rotator above but can work with any type of content—including text, images, or hyperlinks

- **Counters**   Creates a *Counters* object that can create, store, increment, and retrieve any number of individual counters

- **Page Counter**   Creates a *PageCounter* object that counts and displays the number of times a Web page has been opened

- **Permission Checker**   Creates a *PermissionChecker* object that uses the password authentication protocols in IIS to determine whether a Web user has been granted permissions to read a file

- **Status**   Creates a *Status* object that contains server status information; currently only available on Personal Web Server for Macintosh

- **Tools**   Creates a *Tools* object that has a variety of utilities

For more information on these additional components, please see the online Internet Information Server documentation within the Windows NT 4.0 Option Pack documentation. This documentation can be found by choosing Start | Programs | Windows NT 4.0 Option Pack | Product Documentation.

In this chapter, we'll take a look at some of the above components in greater detail. Since the ADO components have been covered in earlier chapters, and the MSMQ components have their own chapter, we'll concentrate on the following components:

- Ad Rotator
- Browser Capabilities
- Content Linking
- Dictionary
- Filesystem Object
- CDONTS NewMail
- CDONTS Session
- Index Server Query
- Index Server Utility
- Permission Checker

Sample code for all of these components is contained on the CD-ROM under the Components Web project. There's a main page named default.htm that gives you links to all of the examples. Figure 17-5 shows the main Component Samples page.

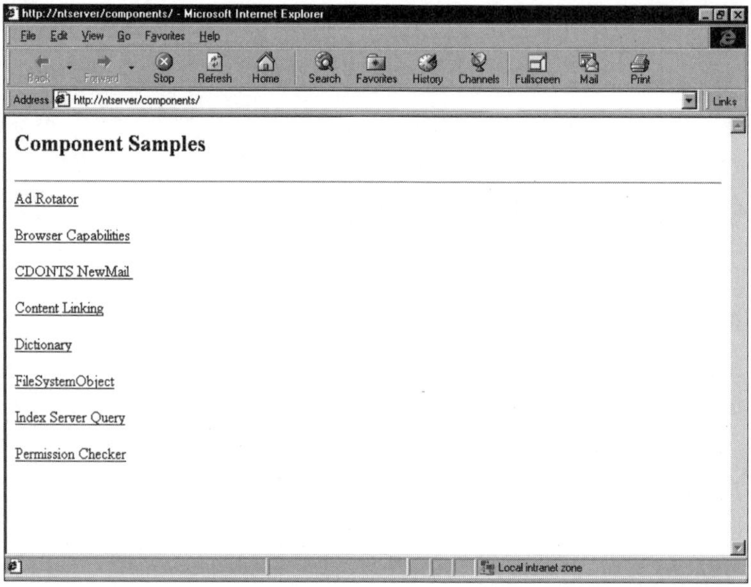

Figure 17-5. *The Component Samples page from the Components Web project on the companion CD-ROM has hyperlinks to all the code samples.*

THE AD ROTATOR COMPONENT

The Ad Rotator component displays advertisements on your Web page. You configure a data file called a Rotator Schedule file with information about the different ads you want to display. The Ad Rotator displays a graphic image with your ad and creates a hyperlink to a Web site associated with your ad. Each time the Web page is downloaded or refreshed, the Ad Rotator determines which ad in the data file should appear and then inserts the appropriate HTML. You do not have to change the ads yourself; simply update the Rotator Schedule file. The Ad Rotator also has a mechanism for recording the number of times a visitor jumps to a site that your ad points to.

You can implement an Active Server component in either an EXE or DLL; the Ad Rotator is implemented in the DLL named adrot.dll. If you are running IIS, the file is in the C:\WINNT\SYSTEM32\INETSRV folder.

In general, components that are implemented as DLLs perform better. When a component is implemented as an EXE, it must run as its own process. When the component and IIS pass data between them, the interprocess communication that must occur is relatively expensive. The same component written as a DLL is loaded as part of IIS's processes—there is no interprocess communication, so performance is better. All the components that come with Visual InterDev are implemented as DLLs.

The Rotator Schedule File

The Rotator Schedule file holds the information about the ads you display. The default filename is adrot.txt, and it is in the C:\InetPub\iissamples\sdk\asp-\components folder if you are using IIS.

The file holds four pieces of information about each ad:

- **adURL**   The path to the image file

- **adHomePageURL**   The URL of the advertiser's home page

- **Text**   Text to be displayed if the browser does not support graphics

- **Impressions**   A priority for the ad

The priority for the ad is a number that can range from 0 through 4,294,967,295. This number determines what percentage of time the ad is shown compared to the other ads in the Rotator Schedule file. To figure the percentage, total all the priorities for all the ads in the Rotator Schedule file and compare the ad's priority to that total. For instance, if you have ads with priorities set at 100, 300, 400, and 200, they are shown 10, 30, 40, and 20 percent of the time, respectively.

The Rotator Schedule file also contains header information that you specify only once for the entire file:

- **Redirect**   The URL for a redirector page. This page counts the number of hits that each ad gets.

- **Width**   The width of the ad image, in pixels. The default is 440.

- **Height**   The height of the ad image, in pixels. The default is 60. You'll notice that 440 x 60 is a common size for ads on Web pages.

- **Border**   The thickness of the border around the image, in pixels. The default is 1. This parameter can be set to 0 for no border.

Below is a sample Rotator Schedule file layout that contains three ads. An asterisk marks the beginning of the actual ad settings; the four items in each setting contain no keywords.

```
-- ADROT.TXT --
REDIRECT AdCounter.asp
WIDTH 440
HEIGHT 60
BORDER 1
*
images/ads/vi-bank/vi-bank.jpg
http://www.vi-bank.com/
Welcome to the premier Internet Bank!
10
images/ads/cau/logo.jpg
-
Consultants Are Us
20
images/ads/cc/freecomponents.gif
http://www.coolcomponents.com/
Free Server-Side Components
70
```

This schedule file contains three ads. The header section specifies that AdCounter.asp is to be called each time a user clicks on one of the ads on this page. The height, width, and border settings are the same as the default settings, so you can omit these lines. Lines beginning with a hyphen in the header section are ignored; they simply describe what's happening in the header. An asterisk indicates that the ad information is beginning. You cannot put any comments in this section—this is why it's important to put all your descriptive text in the header. The position of the lines in this section determines their meaning, so you have to be careful. For instance, the first line is the path to the image, and the second is the URL for the advertiser's Web site. If the advertiser doesn't have a Web site, you must hold the position with a hyphen. The Consultants Are Us ad, for instance, doesn't include a Web site address for Consultants Are Us.

Using the Ad Rotator in an ASP Web Page

To use the Ad Rotator in an ASP Web page, simply drag the component onto your page from the Server Objects tab on the Toolbox. You can also use the following syntax:

```
Set oAdRotator = Server.CreateObject("MSWC.AdRotator")
```

In this case, the *Server* object's *CreateObject* method instantiates the *AdRotator* object. This means that it loads the DLL into memory and creates an instance of the object. The *Set* keyword assigns the object to a variable. Here, a variable named *oAdRotator* refers to the new *AdRotator* object you created. Table 17-2 describes the properties available in the *AdRotator* object.

Property	Description
Border	Sets the size of the border around the image. If you set this property in your VBScript code, it overrides the same property set in your Rotator Schedule file.
Clickable	When this property is set to False, the user cannot jump to the advertiser's Web site by clicking on the image. This overrides the advertiser's URL setting that might or might not be set in the Rotator Schedule file.
TargetFrame	When used on a Web page that has multiple frames, the property specifies the frame in which the ad will be displayed. The HTML frame tag has a name attribute so that you can name your frames. It's good practice to put your ads in a frame so that users can browse your site in one frame without disturbing the ad in another frame.

Table 17-2. *Properties in the* AdRotator *object.*

The *GetAdvertisement* method, shown below, does the work for the *AdRotator* object:

```
Output = oAdRotator.GetAdvertisement("schedule file")
```

When called, the *GetAdvertisement* method generates the HTML image tag appropriate for the ad, including hyperlink information. You pass a path to a Rotator Schedule file as an argument to this method. You typically pass the result of this method to the browser using the *Response.Write* method or using the leading equal sign syntax.

Pulling it all together

To use the *AdRotator* object, you need to create a Rotator Schedule file, a redirector ASP file, the Web page that will display the actual ad, and some images to display. The Components Web project in the Components/VIntDev98 folder on the companion CD-ROM contains all the source code for this exercise.

The code below assumes that the images can be found in a directory named /images/ads in your Web project. The Rotator Schedule file in the code below lists three ads, which are scheduled at 40, 20, and 40 percent, respectively. It also specifies an ASP Web page named AdCounter.asp to act as your redirector page. The rotator schedule file, adrot.txt, is located in the root directory of the Components Web project.

```
--
-- Advertisement Schedule
--
-- Contains three ads to be shown 40%, 20%, and 40%
-- of the time, respectively
--
REDIRECT AdCounter.asp
WIDTH 88
HEIGHT 31
BORDER 1
*
images/ads/vi-bank.jpg
http://www.vi-bank.com
VI-Bank
40
images/ads/nts_iis.gif
http://www.microsoft.com/iis
Microsoft Internet Information Server
20
images/ads/ie.gif
-
Microsoft Internet Explorer
40
```

The third ad, for Internet Explorer, doesn't have a URL to go to. The hyphen holds the place of the URL.

The sample redirector page, AdCounter.asp, does a couple of things. First, it records when users visit one of your advertisers' Web pages. Second (and most obvious), it helps send users to the advertiser's Web site. The *AdRotator* object does not do this automatically; when a user clicks on the image of the ad, the *AdRotator* object calls your redirector page and the advertiser's URL is sent in the query string. Therefore, in your redirector page, you have to check the *Request.QueryString* object and see which URL to redirect to.

```
<%@ Language=VBScript %>
<%
    TargetURL = Request.QueryString("URL")
    HitCount = Session("ADCNT" & TargetURL)
    Session("ADCNT" & TargetURL) = HitCount + 1

    Response.Redirect TargetURL
%>
```

The redirector page has Active Server Script code that saves the URL that you need to go to. The URL is passed to this page in a variable named *URL* in the *QueryString* object. A counter is then used to determine the number of times this URL has been jumped to during this session. Look for a variable in the *Session* object named *ADCNT* with the URL appended. The *Session* variable name might look like this:

```
ADCNThttp://www.vi-bank.com
```

If the URL has not been jumped to during the current session, referring to this variable creates a new session variable and initializes its value to 0. The code then saves the previous number of hits plus one in the *Session* object. This updates the number of times the URL has been jumped to during this session. Moreover, the *Redirect* method of the *Response* object is used to jump to the target URL.

This process saves the number of hits to the URL in the *Session* object. At the end of the session, you must save this information more permanently. The best place to store this information is in a database.

Putting the ad on a Web page

Now that the images are in place, a redirector ASP file is built, and a schedule file is ready to go, all you need to do is put the ad on a page. You create an *AdRotator* object and then call its *GetAdvertisement* method. You can do both of these tasks on the same page. However, you probably want to use the same set of ads in more than one page in your site. So it's better programming practice not to create an *AdRotator* object on each page but rather to create one *AdRotator* object for the session and use it on each page necessary.

To create the *AdRotator* object once for the session, create it in the *Session_OnStart* event procedure in the global.asa file as shown below:

```
<SCRIPT LANGUAGE=VBScript RUNAT=Server>

Sub Session_OnStart
    ' Create an AdRotator object to be
    ' used in this session
    Set Session("oAdRotator") = _
        Server.CreateObject("MSWC.AdRotator")
End Sub

' Session_OnEnd
' Application_OnStart
' Application_OnEnd

</SCRIPT>
```

Notice that since the code needs to reside within a <SCRIPT> block, we cannot use the <OBJECT> block to define the Ad Rotator component. We therefore have to use the *Server.CreateObject* syntax.

Use the *Set* keyword to create an *AdRotator* object named *oAdRotator*. The *Server.CreateObject("MSWC.AdRotator")* command creates the object for you. The value *MSWC.AdRotator* is the programmatic ID of the object you want to create. If you are not using the Server Objects tab of the Toolbox, you must know the programmatic ID of any component that you need to use from your ASP Web page.

After the object is created, you can use it from any page in your application without having to create the object each time. The code below, AdRotator.asp, shows how to actually put the ad on a page:

```
<@ Language=VBScript %>
<HTML>
<HEAD>
<META NAME="GENERATOR" Content="Microsoft Visual Studio 6.0">
</HEAD>
<BODY>

<H2>Ad Rotator Sample</H2>
<HR>

<%
Output = Session("oAdRotator").GetAdvertisement("adrot.txt")
Response.Write Output
%>

<P>
<A HREF="AdRotator.asp">Reload Page</A>
<P>
<A HREF="AdCounterDisplay.asp">Check number of image clicks</A>

</BODY>
</HTML>
```

You need only one line—the call to the *GetAdvertisement* method of the *AdRotator* object. You pass the path to the schedule file you created earlier. The object itself stays in the *Session* object—you created it in the *Session_OnStart* procedure in the global.asa file when the session started.

When the Web browser hits this page, it sees the source code shown below:

```
<@ Language=VBScript %>
<HTML>
<HEAD>
<META NAME="GENERATOR" Content="Microsoft Visual Studio 6.0">
</HEAD>
<BODY>
```

(continued)

```
<H2>Ad Rotator Sample</H2>
<HR>

<A HREF="AdCounter.asp?url=http://www.vi-bank.com
    &image=images/ads/vi-bank.jpg">
    <IMG SRC="images/ads/vi-bank.jpg"
    ALT="VI-Bank" WIDTH=88 HEIGHT=31 BORDER=1></A>
<P>
<A HREF="AdRotator.asp">Reload Page</A>
<P>
<A HREF="AdCounterDisplay.asp">Check number of image clicks</A>

</BODY>
</HTML>
```

The *AdRotator* object places a reference (using the HTML <A> tag) to your redirector page and passes it two variables in the query string. The first is the URL for the ad, and the second is the URL for the image file. It also inserts the image file with the appropriate size and border. When users click on the image, the query string is sent to your redirector. In the example on the CD-ROM, you can access the AdCounterDisplay.asp page to query the current values of the session values that track the number of hits to the various images.

THE BROWSER CAPABILITIES COMPONENT

The recent plethora of new Web technologies has created a dilemma for Web authors. Which technologies do you use to design your Web pages? VBScript (Visual Basic, Scripting Edition), ActiveX controls, Java applets, frames, and cascading style sheets are each supported in some browsers but not in others. So do you write applications that only the most technically capable browsers can use? Or do you write for the lowest common denominator?

The Browser Capabilities component helps you solve this problem. You can check a browser's capabilities and send HTML that you know the browser can handle.

When a browser requests a page from your Web server, it sends some information about itself in the HTTP user agent header of the request. The Browser Capabilities component compares this information to a list of browsers that it keeps in a file named browscap.ini. This file also has information about each browser's abilities. The Browser Capabilities component can then return information from the browscap.ini file for your use.

This component doesn't actually know anything more about a browser than you tell it in the browscap.ini file. It is strictly an engine for looking up already recorded capabilities. The more robust you make your browscap.ini file, the more information you'll have available in your application. Thankfully, Microsoft has provided a fairly extensive browscap.ini file. It covers browsers produced by Microsoft, Netscape, and Oracle. It is installed in different directories based on whether you're using Microsoft Windows 95 or Microsoft Windows NT and where your installation is. Therefore, do a search (Start | Find | Files or Folders) for browscap.ini.

The browscap.ini File

The browscap.ini file's layout is like any other .ini file, and it must be in the same directory as the component itself (the browscap.dll file). The default location for these files in IIS is C:\WINNT\system32\inetsrv.

Within the browscap.ini file, each browser definition has its own section and each section has any number of properties that you can set. You can also insert comments in the browscap.ini file, which are indicated by a semicolon (;). You can use comments anywhere in the file.

The HTTP user agent header within browscap.ini defines a browser's section. It must be enclosed in brackets, as shown here:

```
[IE 4.0]
```

You can use an asterisk as a wildcard in the HTTP user agent header. If the Browser Capabilities component cannot find the exact HTTP header, it tries to find the header by substituting any wildcards in the header. If more than one header matches the user agent header sent by the browser, the first matching header is used. For example,

```
[Mozilla/2.0 *]
```

matches

```
[Mozilla/2.0 (compatible; MSIE 3.0; AK; Windows 95)]
```

and

```
[Mozilla/2.0 (compatible; MSIE 3.0B; Windows 95;1600,1280)]
```

but it does not match

```
[Mozilla/3.01b1 (Macintosh; I; PPC)]
```

Within a section, you define any number of properties and their values. A property name must begin with a letter and cannot be longer than 255 characters. Below is a section from the browscap.ini file that comes with IIS 4.0.

```
[IE 4.0]
browser=IE
Version=4.0
```

(continued)

```
majorver=4
minorver=0
frames=TRUE
tables=TRUE
cookies=TRUE
backgroundsounds=TRUE
vbscript=TRUE
javascript=TRUE
javaapplets=TRUE
ActiveXControls=TRUE
Win16=False
beta=False
AK=False
SK=False
AOL=False
crawler=False
cdf=True
```

A property can have three types of values. By default, a value is a string. You can make it an integer by prefacing it with a number sign (#). The *majorver* and *minorver* properties of Internet Explorer 4.0 are set to integers. You can set a property to a Boolean value by assigning it True or False.

There is one special property named *parent* whose value is the HTTP user agent header of another section from which you want to inherit properties, as shown here:

```
;;ie 4 beta 1
[Mozilla/4.0 (compatible; MSIE 4.0b1; Windows 95)]
parent=IE 4.0
platform=Win95
beta=True
cdf=False
```

In this section, the *parent* property is set to *IE 4.0*. This section inherits all the properties from the IE 4.0 section. It also sets the *platform* property (which is not defined in its parent), sets the *beta* property to True, and sets the *cdf* property to False. The *beta* property is set to False in the IE 4.0 section, but the value is overridden in this section, as is the *cdf* value.

The browscap.ini file also supports a section for a default browser, shown below. You can use this to define what you consider the minimum base capabilities that you want to define in your application.

```
[Default Browser Capability Settings]
browser=Default
Version=0.0
```

(continued)

```
majorver=#0
minorver=#0
frames=False
tables=True
cookies=False
backgroundsounds=False
vbscript=False
javascript=False
javaapplets=False
activexcontrols=False
AK=False
SK=False
AOL=False
beta=False
Win16=False
Crawler=False
cdf=False
AuthenticodeUpdate=
```

The programmatic ID of the *BrowserType* object is *MSWC.BrowserType*, and the DLL that implements the component is named browscap.dll. The syntax for creating the object is

```
<OBJECT RUNAT=server PROGID=MSWC.BrowserType id=oBrowsCap></OBJECT>
```

This instantiates the *BrowserType* object and assigns it to the variable *oBrowsCap*.

The properties in the browscap.ini file define the properties for the *Browser-Type* object. To add another property, you simply add the property to the .ini file. If the property is not found for a particular browser, it has a value of *Unknown*. If the browser itself is not found in the .ini file and no default browser section is defined, all the properties have a value of *Unknown*.

The *BrowserType* object has no methods.

Using the Browser Capabilities Component in an ASP Web page

The following code example displays the capabilities of the browser on an ASP Web page. The code is taken from the BrowserCapabilities.asp file in the Components Web project on the CD-ROM. Figure 17-6, on page 424, shows the page's output.

```
<%@ Language=VBScript %>
<HTML>
<HEAD>
<META NAME="GENERATOR" Content="Microsoft Visual Studio 6.0">
```

(continued)

```
</HEAD>
<BODY>

<H2>Browser Capabilities Sample</H2>
<HR>

<OBJECT RUNAT=server PROGID=MSWC.BrowserType id=oBrowsCap> </OBJECT>

<Table border=1>
<tr>
<td>Browser Name</td>
<td> <%=oBrowsCap.Browser %> </td>
<tr>
<td>Browser Version</td>
<td> <%=oBrowsCap.Version %> </td>
<tr>
<td>Major Version</td>
<td> <%=oBrowsCap.Majorver %> </td>
<tr>
<td>Minor Version</td>
<td> <%=oBrowsCap.Minorver %> </td>
<tr>
<td>Frame Support</td>
<td> <%=oBrowsCap.Frames %> </td>
<tr>
<td>Table Support</td>
<td> <%=oBrowsCap.Tables %> </td>
<tr>
<td>Cookie Support</td>
<td> <%=oBrowsCap.Cookies %> </td>
<tr>
<td>Background Sound Support</td>
<td> <%=oBrowsCap.BackgroundSounds %> </td>
<tr>
<td>VBScript Support</td>
<td> <%=oBrowsCap.VBScript %> </td>
<tr>
<td>JavaScript Support</td>
<td> <%=oBrowsCap.JavaScript %> </td>
</table>

</BODY>
</HTML>
```

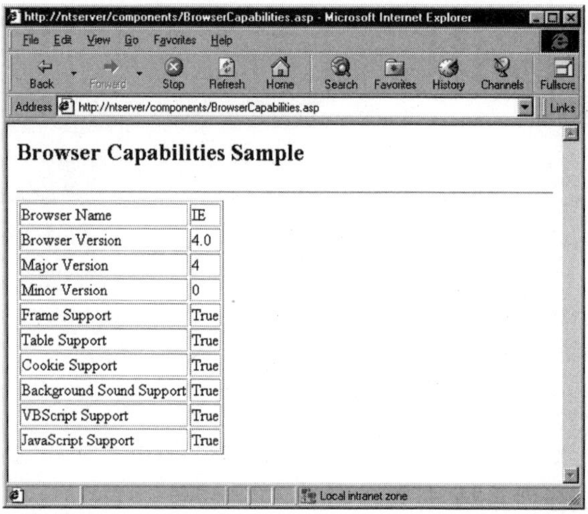

Figure 17-6. *Output from the BrowserCapabilities.asp page.*

There are many potential uses for the Browser Capabilities component. For example, if you want to play a background sound in your default or application home page and the browser is capable, you simply include an *If...Then* statement to check the browser's ability, as shown below:

```
<HTML>
<HEAD>
<META NAME="GENERATOR" Content="Microsoft Visual Studio 6.0">
<TITLE>Document Title</TITLE>
</HEAD>

<BODY>
<%
If Session("oBrowsCap").Backgroundsounds Then
%>
    <BGSOUND SRC="sounds/jingle.wav">
<%
End If
%>

<!-- Page Content Here -->

</BODY>
</HTML>
```

Of course, this is not a particularly dramatic example of what you can do with this component. You can, for example, have an application written twice— once for frame-compatible browsers and once for browsers that are not frame-compatible. You can also use the *Redirect* method of the *Response* object to jump to the correct point from the default page based on the Browser Capabilities component.

THE FILESYSTEM OBJECT COMPONENT

The Filesystem Object component makes available two objects for manipulating text files from ASP Web pages. The *FileSystemObject* object opens or creates text files, and the *TextStream* object reads and writes to the text file once it's opened.

The *FileSystemObject* Object

The syntax for creating an instance of the *FileSystemObject* object is

```
<OBJECT RUNAT=server PROGID=Scripting.FileSystemObject
    id=objFileSys>
</OBJECT>
```

This statement instantiates a *FileSystemObject* object, and it adds a reference to the new object in the *objFileSys* variable. After the object is created, you can use it to access files. The *FileSystemObject* object has no properties. Its sole purpose is to create or open text files.

The *FileSystemObject* object has two methods, one for creating files and one for opening text files. The *CreateTextFile* method takes the filename you specify and creates the file for you. It returns a *TextStream* object that you can use to manipulate the file after it's been created. The syntax, explained further in Table 17-3, is

```
Set objTextStream = objFileSys.CreateTextFile(FileName,
    [Overwrite], [Unicode])
```

Argument	Description
objTextStream	The variable that contains the *TextStream* object created by this function.
objFileSys	A variable referencing an existing *FileSystemObject* object.
FileName	A string that contains the path to a file. This can be the fully qualified path, including the drive letter and directory, or just the filename. If it's just the filename, the file is created in the root directory of the site.

Table 17-3. *Arguments in the* CreateTextFile *method of the* FileSystemObject *object.*

(continued)

Table 17-3 *continued*

Argument	Description
Overwrite	This Boolean value can be set to False to keep the *FileSystemObject* object from deleting an existing file when you create a new file. This parameter is optional; if you don't specify a value, it defaults to True, and an existing file with the same name is deleted.
Unicode	Set this argument to True to write in Unicode format. This is an optional argument, and it defaults to False if omitted.

The *OpenTextFile* method takes the filename you specify and opens the file. It has arguments that specify in which mode to open the file and what to do if the file is not there. Like *CreateTextFile*, *OpenTextFile* returns a *TextStream* object that you can use to manipulate the file once it's open. The following syntax is explained further in Table 17-4.

```
Set objTextStream = objFileSys.OpenTextFile(FileName, [IOMode],
    [Create], [Format])
```

Argument	Description
FileName	This required variable is the path and filename of the file you're trying to open. If you don't include the full path, the *FileSystemObject* object looks in the root directory.
IOMode	This optional constant is either *ForReading* or *ForAppending*, indicating that the file is open for either reading or appending.
Create	This optional Boolean argument specifies what happens if the file you're trying to open doesn't exist. When set to True, it creates an empty file if the file is not found. When set to False, it generates an error if the file is not found. The default is False if you omit this argument. If you set it to True, you can avoid having to open the file, check for an error, and create the file if the open operation failed.
Format	This optional value is one of three *Tristate* values (*TristateTrue* for Unicode, *TristateFalse* for ASCII, and *TristateUseDefault* for the system default) used to indicate the format of the opened file. If this value is omitted, the file is opened as ASCII.

Table 17-4. *Arguments in the* OpenTextFile *method of the* FileSystemObject *object.*

The *TextStream* Object

After you open or create the text file, you have a *TextStream* object. This object represents the file on disk. It has a cursor that, like the cursor in your word processor, indicates where the next typed characters will appear. The *TextStream* cursor also indicates where characters that you write to the stream will go, and where characters that you read will come from.

You cannot create a *TextStream* object using the *Server.CreateObject* method. The only way to get a *TextStream* object is to open an existing text file or create a new one using the *FileSystemObject* object as discussed earlier. Table 17-5 lists the properties of the *TextStream* object, while Table 17-6 lists its methods.

Property	Description
AtEndOfLine	A read-only Boolean value. It is True if the cursor is at the end of the current line, False if otherwise.
AtEndOfStream	A read-only Boolean value. It is True if the cursor is at the end of the stream, False if otherwise.
Column	A read-only integer that indicates the number of characters from the beginning of the line to where the cursor is located.
Line	A read-only integer value that indicates the line number in the file where the cursor is located.

Table 17-5. *Properties of the* TextStream *object.*

Method	Description
Close	Closes the stream and its text file.
Read(NumCharacters)	Reads the number of characters from the text file starting at the current cursor position. *NumCharacters* is an integer value. The characters are returned in a string.
ReadAll	Reads the entire stream into a string.
ReadLine	Reads an entire line into a string.
OSkip(NumCharacters)	Moves the cursor a number of characters in the stream.
SkipLines(NumLines)	Moves the cursor a number of lines in the stream.

Table 17-6. *Methods of the* TextStream *object.* (continued)

Table 17-6 *continued*

Method	Description
Write(Text)	Writes a string to the stream.
WriteLine([Text])	Writes a text string to the stream and appends an end-of-line character to it. This string is optional.
WriteBlankLines(NumLines)	Writes a number of blank lines to the stream.

Implementing a Simple Text-Based Data File

You can do many different things with a *FileSystemObject* object and a *Text-Stream* object. To illustrate some of these uses, we'll look at a sample application that uses a text file to record the names and addresses of people who leave that information at your Web site. The code for this sample is located in the Components Web project on the companion CD-ROM.

You want to store everyone's name and address in the same text file. This text file will be opened for write access. Since a file can be opened for write access by only one application at a time, you have to ensure that you try to open the file only once for write access. One way to do this is to execute the *Application* object's *Lock* method before you try to write to the file. If the application is already locked when you try to lock it, your session waits until the application is unlocked before proceeding. The downside of using *Application-.Lock* is that you might tie up the *Application* object for a long time while the operation is pending. Another way to control opening the file only once is to store a reference to the open file in the *Application* object. If the reference to the file shows that the file is open, don't try to open it; if the reference shows it's not open, you can open it.

Next you build a sample page that lets you obtain a user's name and address, and then you save that information to a text file. The first thing you need is the data to write to the file. A simple HTML form does the trick. The sample HTML form, named FileSystemObject.htm and shown in Figure 17-7, has seven text boxes—two for the user's first and last name and five for the address fields. It calls an ASP file named FileSystemObjectHandler.asp that does the actual work of writing the file.

```
<%@ Language=VBScript %>
<HTML>
<HEAD>
```

Figure 17-7. *The source code for FileSystemObject.htm captures user input and passes it to FileSystemObjectHandler.asp to create a text file.*   *(continued)*

```
<META NAME="GENERATOR" Content="Microsoft Visual Studio 6.0">
</HEAD>
<BODY>

<H2>FileSystemObject Sample</H2>
<HR>

<FORM METHOD="POST" ACTION="FileSystemObjectHandler.asp">
<TABLE border=0 cellPadding=1 cellSpacing=1 width=50%>

    <TR>
        <TD>First Name</TD>
        <TD>
            <INPUT id=firstname name=firstname></TD></TR>
    <TR>
        <TD>Last Name</TD>
        <TD>
            <INPUT id=lastname name=lastname></TD></TR>
    <TR>
        <TD>Address</TD>
        <TD>
            <INPUT id=address1 name=address1></TD></TR>
    <TR>
        <TD>Address</TD>
        <TD>
            <INPUT id=address2 name=address2></TD></TR>
    <TR>
        <TD>City</TD>
        <TD>
            <INPUT id=city name=city></TD></TR>
    <TR>
        <TD>State</TD>
        <TD>
            <INPUT id=state name=state></TD></TR>
    <TR>
        <TD>Zip</TD>
        <TD>
            <INPUT id=zip name=zip></TD></TR></TABLE>
<P><INPUT id=submit name=submit type=submit value=submit></P>
</FORM>

</BODY>
</HTML>
```

The FileSystemObjectHandler.asp file creates the text stream and writes the data to the file, as shown in Figure 17-8 below:

```
<%@ Language=VBScript %>
<HTML>
<HEAD>
<META NAME="GENERATOR" Content="Microsoft Visual Studio 6.0">
</HEAD>
<BODY>

<%
On Error Resume Next

' Lock the application so only one update is allowed at a time
Application.Lock
%>

<OBJECT RUNAT="server" PROGID="Scripting.FileSystemObject"
    id="objFileSys">
</OBJECT>

<%
' Define the filename and path
fname = Server.MapPath("\components\names.txt")

' Create a text stream object and open the file
Set MyFile = objFileSys.OpenTextFile(fname, 8)

If Err.number <> 0 Then
    Set MyFile = objFileSys.CreateTextFile(fname)
    Err.Clear
End If

' Prepare the output string
OutString = Request.Form("firstname") & "|" & _
    Request.Form("lastname") & "|" & _
    Request.Form("address1") & "|" & _
    Request.Form("address2") & "|" & _
    Request.Form("city") & "|" & Request.Form("state") & "|" & _
    Request.Form("zip")

' Write the string to the text file
MyFile.WriteLine(OutString)

' Close the file
MyFile.Close
```

Figure 17-8. *Source code for the FileSystemObjectHandler.asp file.*   *(continued)*

```
' Display a success or failure message
If Err.number = 0 Then
    Response.Write "<H2>FileSystem Object Sample</H2><HR>"
    Response.Write "<P>Data written successfully to " + fname
    Response.Write "<P><A HREF=" + fname + ">View the file.</A>"
Else
    Response.Write "<H2>FileSystem Object Sample</H2><HR>"
    Response.Write "<P>An error occurred while writing the " + _
        "data to " + fname
End If

' Unlock the application
Application.UnLock
%>

</BODY>
</HTML>
```

You have to do a couple of things before you create the main logic portion of the file. The first line in this script is *On Error Resume Next.* This means that if the script has an error, the script ignores it and continues executing on the next line. You must have this error trapping in place when you try to open the file. If the file is not there and any script statement has a problem, you get a scripting error. Rather than ending the script, you should continue and try to create a new file. You must expect that the file might not exist and be prepared to handle this possibility. One way to handle the problem of a file not found is to set the *Create* argument of the *OpenTextFile* method to True. When set to True, the argument creates an empty file if the file is not found. (See Table 17-4 on page 426 for more details.)

After setting up error trapping, the script tries to lock the *Application* object. If it is already locked, the script pauses at that line and waits for the *Application* object to unlock until the time-out period expires. In this example, you needn't worry about this, but in a larger-scale production environment it might be an issue.

To open a file, you first create a *FileSystemObject* object by dragging the object onto your ASP Web page from the Toolbox. You also need a filename for the text file you'll write to. The *MapPath* method of the *Server* object translates the text file's virtual path—the path within your Web site—to a fully qualified path on a device on your Web server. *MapPath* returns that path, which is stored in the *fname* variable.

Next, try to open the file with the *OpenTextFile* method of the *FileSystem-Object* object. If you can open the file, a *TextStream* object is created and is assigned to the variable *objTextStream.* If you cannot open the file, an error is generated. Because of the *On Error Resume Next* statement, the script continues to run. The next line checks to see if the value of the error object, *Err*, is not 0. If no error occurred, the value is 0. If the value is anything other than 0, there was a problem opening the file, so try using the *CreateTextFile* method instead. In a production system, you can determine the exact error by checking the value of the *Err* object's *Number* property, but in this example assume that the problem results from a file not being found.

You should now have a *TextStream* object, whether you had to create a file or open an existing one. Next you use the *Request* object to get the name and address information that the user typed into the system. The strings are combined with the pipe character between them. This is the string you write to the text file using the *WriteLine* method. After writing the data, all you have to do is close the text file.

To provide the user with some constructive feedback, check the *Err* object again. If an error occurred while writing the data, use the *Description* property of the *Err* object to relay the error to the user. Otherwise, just thank the user for the input. Either way, you will unlock the *Application* object before the script ends. You must leave the *Application* object unlocked or other sessions will get stuck when they try to write data.

THE DICTIONARY COMPONENT

The *Dictionary* object of the Dictionary component is used for storage and is very much like an array. The *Dictionary* object has properties that make it more flexible—and in some cases much more usable—than an array. Unlike an array, a *Dictionary* object does not have to be declared to hold a certain number of elements; it is always dynamic. When you add an element to a *Dictionary* object, it grows to hold the element; when you remove an element, it shrinks. While you can do the same thing with a dynamic array, you have to manually manage the growing and shrinking of the array by using the *Redim Preserve* command.

A *Dictionary* object also lets you remove elements from any position within it. For instance, you can remove the first element and the *Dictionary* object will take care of freeing up that space. The element that was at position 2 is now at position 1, and so on.

The last significant advantage of using a *Dictionary* object is that, just like with a printed dictionary, you don't have to refer to the elements in the dictionary by a number; instead, you look them up using a key. When you add something to a dictionary, you not only add the actual value, you also add a string that will be used to look up the value later.

In the following statement, *objDictionary* is the variable that will hold a reference to the new *Dictionary* object. The methods and properties are described in Table 17-7 and Table 17-8.

```
<OBJECT RUNAT=server PROGID=Scripting.Dictionary id=objDictionary>
</OBJECT>
```

Method	Description
Add(Key, Item)	Adds an item to the dictionary with the specified key. An item can be a variable containing any type of data— dates, strings, integers, or other objects.
Exists(key)	Checks to see if the key exists in the dictionary. Returns True if the specified key exists in the *Dictionary* object, False if it does not.
Items	Returns an array of all the items in the dictionary.
Keys	Returns an array of all the keys in the dictionary. Each string in the resulting array is a key in the dictionary.
Remove(Key)	Removes a key and item pair from the dictionary. The *Dictionary* object automatically frees up the space used by the key item pair.
RemoveAll	Empties the dictionary. The *Dictionary* object frees up all the space used by key item pairs in the dictionary.

Table 17-7. *Methods in the* Dictionary *object.*

Property	Description
CompareMode[= compare]	Sets and returns the comparison mode for comparing string keys in a *Dictionary* object (See Table 17-9 on the following page.)
Count	Returns the number of items in the dictionary
Item(key)[= newitem]	Sets or returns an item for a specified key in a *Dictionary* object
Key(key) = newkey	Sets or returns a key in a *Dictionary* object

Table 17-8. *Properties in the* Dictionary *object.*

Table 17-9 shows the possible values for the *CompareMode* property described earlier.

Value	Dictionary *Lookup Type*
0	Binary
1	Text
2	Database
>2	Values greater than 2 can be used to refer to comparisons using specific Locale IDs (LCID)

Table 17-9. *The* CompareMode *property values.*

A Sample Dictionary Lookup

To illustrate the use of the *Dictionary* object, you can, for example, create a Web page that supplies information about some books. The code for this example is on the CD-ROM in the Components Web project. An HTML form collects the ISBN for a book that the user is interested in, and the response looks up that book in the dictionary and returns a string that describes the book. The code in Figure 17-9 shows the dictionary being loaded in the script itself, with only three books. In a production environment, you should probably load a dictionary from either a data file or a database. The HTML form simply prompts the user for the book he or she is interested in.

```
<HTML>
<HEAD>
<META NAME="GENERATOR" Content="Microsoft Visual Studio 6.0">
<TITLE>Dictionary Sample</TITLE>
</HEAD>
<BODY>

<H2>Dictionary Sample</H2>
<HR>

This page searches the dictionary for book information
<BR>based upon the ISBN.
<P>
Currently, the following three books are available:

<UL>
<LI>Inside Visual InterDev (1-57231-583-0)
<LI>Running IIS 4.0 (2)
```

Figure 17-9. *Source code for the Dictionary.htm page that captures an ISBN for a search using the* Dictionary *object.*   *(continued)*

```
<LI>Programming Visual InterDev 6.0 (3)
</UL>
<P>

<FORM Action="DictionaryHandler.asp" METHOD=POST>
Please enter an ISBN:
<INPUT TYPE=TEXT NAME=ISBN>
<P>
<INPUT TYPE=SUBMIT>
</FORM>

<HR>
</BODY>
</HTML>
```

When the user clicks the Submit button, data is passed to the Dictionary-Handler.asp page, as shown in Figure 17-10. This page creates the dictionary and enters information about three books.

```
<HTML>
<HEAD>
<META NAME="GENERATOR" Content="Microsoft Visual Studio 6.0">
<TITLE>Dictionary Sample</TITLE>
</HEAD>
<BODY>

<H2>Dictionary Sample</H2>
<HR>

<OBJECT RUNAT=server PROGID=Scripting.Dictionary id=objDictionary>
</OBJECT>

<%
' Enter three books in the dictionary

' VI 1.0
objDictionary.Add "1-57231-583-0", "Inside Visual InterDev by " & _
    "Miller, Spencer, Vincent, and Evans"

' IIS 4.0
objDictionary.Add "2", "Running IIS 4.0"

' VI 6.0
objDictionary.Add "3", "Programming Visual InterDev 6.0 by " & _
    "Miller, Spencer, and Evans"
%>
```

Figure 17-10. *Source code for the DictionaryHandler.asp page that loads a dictionary with book information and performs a search given a key of the ISBN.* *(continued)*

Figure 17-10 *continued*

```
Your entry was ISBN <%=Request.Form("ISBN") %>
<p>

<%
key = Request.Form("ISBN")
If Not objDictionary.Exists(key) Then
%>
ISBN <%=key %> was not found in the dictionary!
<%
Else
%>
The book that corresponds with ISBN <%=Key %> is
<P>
<B><I><%=objDictionary.Item(key) %></I></B>
<%
End If
%>

</BODY>
</HTML>
```

The first thing you do is create the *Dictionary* object and assign it to the *objDictionary* variable. Using the *Add* method, you add entries for the three different books into the dictionary. In production, you can use a *TextStream* object that contains the books and then load this object at the *Session_OnStart* event. This is a good approach, especially if the data will be used in more than one page and as long as there is not too much data for the *Session* object to carry around.

After loading the dictionary, the code checks that the user's input is in the dictionary with the *Exists* method. If it is False, it lets the user know that his or her entry was not found. If it does find it, it displays the information from the dictionary. Figure 17-11 shows the resulting output from the DictionaryHandler-.asp page.

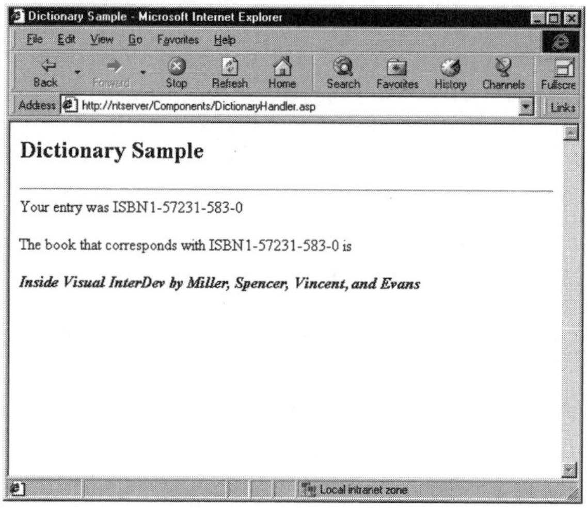

Figure 17-11. *Output from the DictionaryHandler.asp page.*

THE CONTENT LINKING COMPONENT

The Content Linking component lets you organize the pages of your Web site like the pages of a book. It constructs a table of contents and maintains previous and next page links in your Web pages. This allows you to change the order of pages, insert pages, or delete pages without having to do much maintenance work on the pages themselves. Content linking has two parts: a Content Linking List and a *NextLink* object.

The Content Linking List

The Content Linking component needs to know which pages are to be included in the table of contents. This information is maintained in the Content Linking List, which is a text file. Each URL is listed on one line in the file—along with a description and a comment—in the order that it will appear in a table of contents. This syntax, shown below, is described in Table 17-10 on the following page.

```
URL [Description] [Comment]
```

A tab character separates the URL from the description and the comment. The description and comment are optional. The comment is for your use only; the component does not use it.

Item	Description
URL	The URL for the page. It must be a virtual or relative URL. The Content Linking component will not use an absolute URL (one that begins with *http*).
Description	A textual description of the URL.
Comment	A textual comment, which the component will not process.

Table 17-10. *The format of the Content Linking List file.*

The *NextLink* Object

The *NextLink* object is implemented in the NextLink.dll file. It contains several methods for managing a list of URLs. For IIS, the file is located by default in the C:\WINNT\system32\inetsrv folder.

The syntax to instantiate the *NextLink* object is as follows, where *objNextLink* refers to the new *NextLink* object.

```
<OBJECT RUNAT=server PROGID=MSWC.NextLink id=objNextLink>
</OBJECT>
```

The methods within the *NextLink* object all require the Content Linking List file as a parameter, as shown in Table 17-11. The *NextLink* object has no properties.

Method	Description
GetNextURL(ContentLinkFile) *GetPreviousURL(ContentLinkFile)* *GetNextDescription(ContentLinkFile)* *GetPreviousDescription(ContentLinkFile)*	Returns a string that is the next or previous URL or description. These calls are valid only from a page that is in the Content Linking List file.
GetListCount(ContentLinkFile)	Returns the number of pages in the Content Linking List file.
GetListIndex(ContentLinkFile)	Returns the index number of the current URL in the Content Linking List file.
GetNthDescription (ContentLinkFile, index)GetNthURL (ContentLinkFile, index)	Returns the page's URL or description, as specified by the index in the Content Linking List file.

Table 17-11. *Methods in the* NextLink *object.*

A Sample Table of Contents

The Content Linking List file is fairly easy to use because it has only one purpose—to provide the list of URLs and their descriptions. You must create a Content Linking List file and some Active Server Script code to build the table of contents and the links to other pages. The following example is a table of contents for an online book and is included on the CD-ROM in the Components Web project. The code below shows the Content Linking List file, toc.txt:

```
ch1.asp    Chapter 1 - Introduction
ch2.asp    Chapter 2 - Active Server Pages
ch3.asp    Chapter 3 - Database Access
ch4.asp    Chapter 4 - N-Tier Architectures
```

In this file, tabs are used to separate the URL from the descriptions.

To keep your table of contents easy to maintain, you can store all your files in the same virtual directory on your Web server. This includes the Content Linking List file (toc.txt), the Table of Contents page (ContentLinking.asp), and the pages of the book (ch1.asp etc.).

One of the Content Linking component's most useful features is its ability to automatically create the table of contents. The Active Server script used in the ContentLinking.asp page, shown below, is generic enough for you to use in any of your tables of contents.

```
<HTML>
<HEAD>
<META NAME="GENERATOR" Content="Microsoft Visual Studio 6.0">
<TITLE>Content Linking Sample</TITLE>
</HEAD>

<BODY>

<H2>Content Linking Sample</H2>
<HR>

<OBJECT RUNAT=server PROGID=MSWC.NextLink id=objNextLink>
</OBJECT>

<B>Table of Contents</B>

<%
count = NextLink.GetListCount("toc.txt")
Response.Write "<UL><ul>
For i = 1 to count
    Response.Write "<LI><A HREF=" + _
```

(continued)

```
            objNextLink.GetNthURL("toc.txt", i) + _
            ">" + objNextLink.GetNthDescription("toc.txt", i) + "</A>"
Next
%>
</UL>

</BODY>
</HTML>
```

Figure 17-12 shows the output from this script. This script uses *GetListCount* to find the number of pages. It then uses *GetNthURL* and *GetNthDescription* in a *For...Next* loop to build a bulleted list of the table of contents.

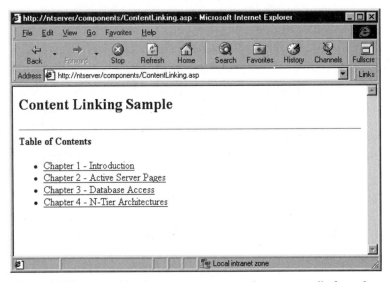

Figure 17-12. *The table of contents is generated automatically from the contents in the text file that defines the pages.*

Each page in the book needs links to the previous and next pages. Using the Content Linking component, you can include the same standard boilerplate code in each page. In this way, you don't have to make any changes if you rearrange the order or the number of pages.

You include parts of the following script at the end of each page of the report. You can, of course, place the relevant sections of this file in an Include file and use the server-side include to pull this file into each page. This makes code maintenance much easier.

```
<%@ Language=VBScript %>
<HTML>
<HEAD>
```

(continued)

```
<META NAME="GENERATOR" Content="Microsoft Visual Studio 6.0">
</HEAD>
<BODY>

<H2>Content Linking Sample - Chapter 2</H2>
<HR>

<OBJECT RUNAT=server PROGID=MSWC.NextLink id=objNextLink>
</OBJECT>

<B>Chapter 2</B>
<P>
<%
last = objNextLink.GetListCount("toc.txt")
current = objNextLink.GetListIndex("toc.txt")

If current > 1 Then
    Response.Write "<A HREF=" + _
        objNextLink.GetPreviousURL("toc.txt") + _
        ">Previous Page</A>"
End If
%>
 
<%
If current < last Then
    Response.Write "<A HREF=" + _
        objNextLink.GetNextURL("toc.txt") + _
        ">Next Page</A>"
End If
%>
<P>
<A HREF="ContentLinking.asp">Table of Contents</A>

</BODY>
</HTML>
```

This code automatically generates the links in the bottom part of the page, as shown in Figure 17-13 on the following page. The Next Page and Previous Page links move users forward and backward in the pages listed in the Content Linking List file.

Since you will use this same code for each page in your situation report, you need to check which page you're on and include next and previous links only when necessary. The script's first job is to create a *NextLink* object and get the number of pages and the current page.

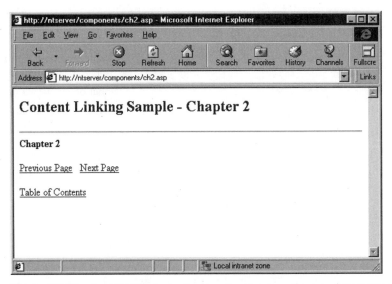

Figure 17-13. *An ASP Web page showing the Previous Page and Next Page hyperlinks created using the Content Linking component.*

Two *If...Then* statements make comparisons on the current page. The first statement determines whether the current page is greater than one; if it is, you need to include a link back to the previous page. The second checks whether the current page is the last page; if it is not, you need a next-page link.

Each page of your online book will have the correct links, both backward and forward. All you have to do is edit the toc.txt file to change the order of the pages.

THE CDONTS NEWMAILOBJECT

The Microsoft CDO for NTS Library version 1.2 exposes messaging objects for use by Visual Basic, C/C++, Visual C++, and VBScript applications. The library makes it easy to add mail functionality (both sending and receiving) into the server-side of your Visual InterDev 6.0 applications via ASP scripting. There is no user interface supported by the library, and you must be running on Windows NT 4.0. The nice thing about the CDONTS Library is that you don't even need to be running Exchange—all you need is the SMTP server component of IIS 4.0 installed.

The *NewMail* object is just one object in the CDONTS Library. Other objects are shown in Table 17-12.

Object	Description
AddressEntry	Specifies addressing information for an individual messaging user
Attachment	Associates an additional object with a message
Attachments collection	Accesses all attachments on a message; creates new attachments
Folder	Opens the default Inbox or Outbox folder in a message store
Message	Composes, populates, sends, and receives an e-mail document
Messages collection	Accesses all messages in a folder; creates new messages
Recipient	Specifies information for a messaging user intended to receive a message
Recipients collection	Accesses all recipients of a message; creates new recipients
Session	Establishes a connection between an application and a messaging system

Table 17-12. *Objects in the CDONTS Library.*

The *NewMail* object is specifically designed to give developers a quick way to send an automated message with little coding required. All that's needed is to create the object, set some properties, send the message, and then set the object to *Nothing* to clean up. You can even send file attachments or send attachments with an associated URL.

The following code shows an example of how to create the *NewMail* object and then send an e-mail message:

```
<@ Language=VBScript %>
<HTML>
<HEAD>
<META NAME="GENERATOR" Content="Microsoft Visual Studio 6.0">
</HEAD>
<BODY>

<OBJECT RUNAT=server PROGID=CDONTS.NewMail id=oNewMail></OBJECT>

<%
oNewMail.From = "nick.evans@us.pwcglobal.com"
oNewMail.To = "nick.evans@us.pwcglobal.com"
oNewMail.Subject = "CDONTS"
```

(continued)

```
oNewMail.Body = "This NewMail object makes sending e-mail simple!"
oNewMail.Send
Set oNewMail = Nothing
%>

</BODY>
</HTML>
```

The code below shows an example of how to create the *NewMail* object and then send a file attachment within an e-mail message:

```
<OBJECT RUNAT=server PROGID=CDONTS.NewMail id=objNewMail>
</OBJECT>

objNewMail.AttachFile("\\ntserver\reports\1998q1.xls", "1998Q1.XLS")
objNewMail.Send("Automated Report Generator", "manager@xyz.com", _
    "1998 Sales Report - 1st Quarter", _
    "Here's the latest sales report for the 1st quarter 1998", 0)
objNewMail = Nothing
```

In this code example, the parameters included within the *Send* method specify the sender, recipient, subject line, body, and importance of the e-mail message, as the following syntax shows:

```
ObjNewMail.Send ( [From] [, To] [, Subject] [, Body] [, Importance] )
```

These parameters correspond to the *From, To, Subject, Body*, and *Importance* properties of the *NewMail* object. The *AttachFile* method takes the full path and filename of the file plus the file name to appear in the attachment's placeholder in the message as arguments.

In your applications, you could easily create an HTML form to capture user input in a feedback form and then pass those values as the parameters for the e-mail message. This is a great way to automate the capture of input and the creation and routing of e-mail messages. In addition to forwarding the e-mail messages to the appropriate parties (perhaps based upon a selection from a drop-down list), you can also store the e-mail responses in a relational database. This way you have both a workflow process—so that the e-mails get routed—and a storage area for the e-mail information for analysis at a later date. For example, in an Internet Banking application you might have a loan application form for your users to complete. The message body in the completed form could be e-mailed to the loan processing department and the rest of the data could be captured in a relational database table so that the loan processors can access it later on. The CDONTS Library extends the possibilities for your Visual InterDev applications so that you can move from relational database access into the world of e-mail and workflow.

THE CDONTS *SESSION* OBJECT

The *Session* object is a top-level component used to establish a session with the SMTP server component of IIS. The *LogonSMTP* method is used to establish a session. This method must be called prior to using any of the other CDONTS Library objects (other than *NewMail*). Sessions can be terminated using the *Logoff* method. The following code shows the syntax for logging on to an SMTP session:

```
<OBJECT RUNAT=server PROGID=CDONTS.Session id=objSession>
</OBJECT>

<%
objSession.LogonSMTP "Nicholas D. Evans", _
    "nick.evans@us.pwcglobal.com"
%>
```

The advantage of using the *Session* object over the *NewMail* object is that you have access to richer functionality. The *NewMail* object is used to send e-mail messages with very few commands. The *Session* object allows you to gain access to folders, messages, attachments, and recipients within your mail application. This way you have fuller access to the mail within your application. For example, you can delete or send mail, delete attachments, navigate through messages, add or delete recipients, and so on.

The *Session* object has several properties that you can access within your scripts, including *Inbox, Outbox, Application, MessageFormat, Version,* and so on. These are all read-only properties except *MessageFormat*. The *Inbox* and *Outbox* properties return *Folder* objects that represent the current user's Inbox folder and Outbox folder.

THE INDEX SERVER *QUERY* OBJECT

Index Server 2.0 is the latest version of Microsoft's search engine that is integrated with IIS 4.0 and the Windows NT Server 4.0 operating system. Index Server allows you to use any Web browser to perform full text searching of HTML, text, and Microsoft Office documents. This includes documents in Microsoft Word, Microsoft Excel, and Microsoft PowerPoint. This is a powerful feature of Index Server —you don't need to convert all your content to HTML! Just place your documents out on the Web server—Index Server can do all the work for you and return detailed summaries and hyperlinks to the actual documents.

The Index Server *Query* object allows you to customize your interaction with Index Server through ASP scripting. This is a new feature introduced with Index Server 2.0 and IIS 4.0.

NOTE   Prior to the introduction of Index Server 2.0, developers had to use the HTML/IDQ/HTX technique to customize Index Server. This technique consists of using three separate files for the various operations that need to take place: the HTML file is used for the query form, the IDQ file is used to process the search, and the HTX file is used to format the results. It remains a good option when compared to the other techniques such as SQL and ASP scripting because of its fast performance.

The syntax to instantiate the Index Server *Query* object is as follows, where *objQuery* refers to the new object.

```
<OBJECT RUNAT=server PROGID=IXSSO.Query id=objQuery>
</OBJECT>
```

The following code in Figure 17-14, taken from the IndexServerQuery.asp file within the Components project on the CD-ROM, shows an example of how to use the *Query* object. First it builds a simple query using the *SetQueryFromURL* method. The query contains a search on the word "Sample" with the maximum number of hits to be returned specified as 25. These types of values could easily be obtained via an HTML form that allows end users to specify their own queries. There are also many other properties that can be queried, including metaproperties such as author name, filename, and file size.

```
<%@ Language=VBScript %>
<HTML>
<HEAD>
<META NAME="GENERATOR" Content="Microsoft Visual Studio 6.0">
</HEAD>
<BODY>

<H2>Index Server Query Sample</H2>
<HR>

<OBJECT RUNAT=server PROGID=IXSSO.Query id=objQuery>
</OBJECT>

<%
If IsObject(objQuery) = False Then
    Response.Write "Index Server Query object not installed."
Else
    ' Build the query string
    ' Set the search to "Sample" and the maximum hits to 25
    iRequest = "qu='Sample'&mh=25"
    objQuery.SetQueryFromURL(iRequest)
```

Figure 17-14. *Source code for the IndexServerQuery.asp file, which queries Index Server and returns a recordset to the browser.*   *(continued)*

```
    ' Define the columns for the recordset
    objQuery.Columns = "filename, vpath, size, write"

    Set rs = objQuery.CreateRecordset("sequential")
End If
%>

<FONT SIZE="2">
<TABLE BORDER=1>
<TR>
<TH>Record</TH>
<TH>File name</TH>
<TH>Path</TH>
<TH>Size</TH>
<TH>Write</TH>
</TR>

<%
' Loop over the recordset
NextRecordNumber = 1
Do While NOT Rs.EOF
%>
<TR>
<TD><%=NextRecordNumber %></TD>
<TD><%=rs("Filename") %></TD>
<TD><A HREF="<%=rs("vpath") %>"><%=rs("vpath") %></A></TD>
<TD><%=rs("Size") %></TD>
<TD><%=rs("Write") %></TD>
</TR>
<%
rs.MoveNext
NextRecordNumber = NextRecordNumber + 1
Loop
%>
</TABLE>
</FONT>

</BODY>
</HTML>
```

Next the code defines the columns that are required for the recordset using the *Columns* property of the *Query* object. These columns include the filename, the file size, the virtual path to the file, and the time stamp of the file. After defining the columns to be returned by the recordset, the *CreateRecordset* method is called for the *Query* object and the results are stored in the *rs* recordset.

Now that the query portion is complete, all that's left is for the code to loop over the recordset and display the results in the browser. This is done using a standard Do Loop syntax and by using an HTML table to control the formatting of the resulting output. Figure 17-15 shows an example of the resulting output in the browser.

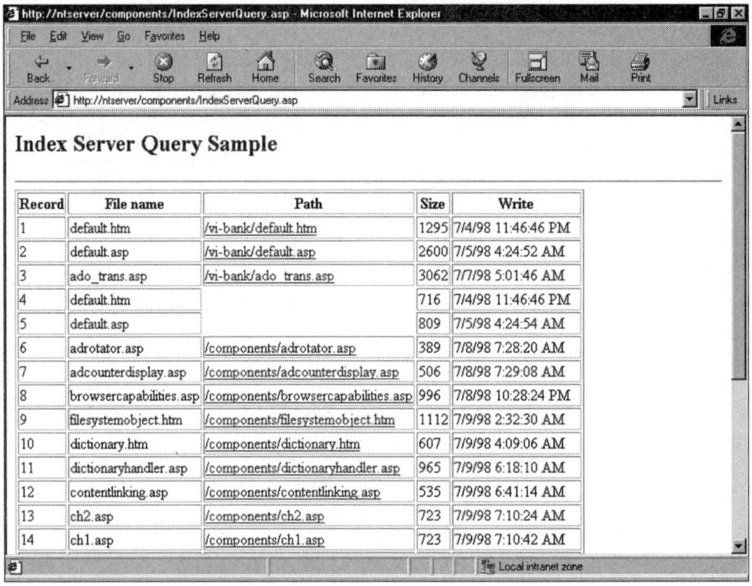

Record	File name	Path	Size	Write
1	default.htm	/vi-bank/default.htm	1295	7/4/98 11:46:46 PM
2	default.asp	/vi-bank/default.asp	2600	7/5/98 4:24:52 AM
3	ado_trans.asp	/vi-bank/ado_trans.asp	3062	7/7/98 5:01:46 AM
4	default.htm		716	7/4/98 11:46:46 PM
5	default.asp		809	7/5/98 4:24:54 AM
6	adrotator.asp	/components/adrotator.asp	389	7/8/98 7:28:20 AM
7	adcounterdisplay.asp	/components/adcounterdisplay.asp	506	7/8/98 7:29:08 AM
8	browsercapabilities.asp	/components/browsercapabilities.asp	996	7/8/98 10:28:24 PM
9	filesystemobject.htm	/components/filesystemobject.htm	1112	7/9/98 2:32:30 AM
10	dictionary.htm	/components/dictionary.htm	607	7/9/98 4:09:06 AM
11	dictionaryhandler.asp	/components/dictionaryhandler.asp	965	7/9/98 6:18:10 AM
12	contentlinking.asp	/components/contentlinking.asp	535	7/9/98 6:41:14 AM
13	ch2.asp	/components/ch2.asp	723	7/9/98 7:10:24 AM
14	ch1.asp	/components/ch1.asp	723	7/9/98 7:10:42 AM

Figure 17-15. *Output from the IndexServerQuery.asp page, which performs a simple search and formats the results in an HTML table.*

THE INDEX SERVER *UTILITY* OBJECT

The Index Server *Utility* object has five methods that Visual InterDev developers can use when working with the Index Server *Query* object:

- *AddScopeToQuery*
- *GetArrayElement*
- *ISOToLocaleID*
- *LocaleIDToISO*
- *TruncateToWhitespace*

The *AddScopeToQuery* method adds a scope restriction to a query. This restricts a search to a particular virtual or physical path within the Index Server catalog. The syntax is

```
AddScopeToQuery QueryObj, Path[ , Depth]
```

An example might be

```
ObjUtil.AddScopeToQuery objQuery, "/extranet", "deep"
```

The depth specifies whether the search includes subdirectories (deep) or not (shallow).

Another useful method of the *Utility* object is the *TruncateToWhitespace* method. This is useful when you are displaying a lengthy property such as a description. By using the *TruncateToWhitespace* method you can truncate the string without cutting off any characters. The following example shows how this is achieved:

```
<%
Response.Write _
    objUtil.TruncateToWhitespace(RS("Characterization"), 200)
%>
```

THE PERMISSION CHECKER COMPONENT

The Permission Checker component implements the *PermissionChecker* object, which uses the password authentication protocols in IIS to determine whether a Web user has permission to read a file.

A typical use of the *PermissionChecker* object is to test whether the user has permission to read a particular Web page (by clicking a hyperlink to that page). If the *PermissionChecker* object determines that the user does not have permission to read the page, ASP script can be used to disable the hyperlink, or better yet, not to show the hyperlink at all. The *PermissionChecker* object has one method, named *HasAccess*.

The example in Figure 17-16 shows how to test whether a user has access to a Web page.

```
<%@ Language=VBScript %>
<HTML>
<HEAD>
<META NAME="GENERATOR" Content="Microsoft Visual Studio 6.0">
</HEAD>
<BODY>

<H2>Permission Checker Sample</H2>
<HR>

<OBJECT RUNAT=server PROGID=MSWC.PermissionChecker id=oPermChk>
</OBJECT>
```

Figure 17-16. *Permission Checker sample code, PermissionChecker.asp, showing how to read whether a user has access to a particular Web page using either a physical or a virtual path.* *(continued)*

Figure 17-16 *continued*

```
The following code checks to see if the current user has
access to the PermissionChecker.asp file
<P>
Physical Path = <%=oPermChk.HasAccess(".\PermissionChecker.asp") %>
<P>
Virtual Path =
    <%=oPermChk.HasAccess("/Components/PermissionChecker.asp") %>

</BODY>
</HTML>
```

You can use physical paths, such as .\PermissionChecker.asp, as well as virtual paths, such as /Components/PermissionChecker.asp, when checking permissions using this component. Figure 17-17 shows the resulting output from the PermissionChecker.asp page.

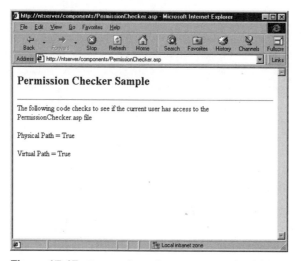

Figure 17-17. *Output from the PermissionChecker.asp page.*

Chapter 18

Creating ActiveX Components with Visual Basic 6.0

INTRODUCTION

In the last chapter, we saw the various types of architectures that can be designed using Microsoft Web technologies. We also took a look at the server objects provided with Microsoft Internet Information Server (IIS) 4.0 that developers for Microsoft Visual InterDev can take advantage of in their applications.

In this chapter, we'll see how we can create our own Microsoft ActiveX components, how they can be staged on the Web server, and how they can be called from within Active Server Pages (ASP) Web pages. We'll use Microsoft Visual Basic 6.0 to develop these ActiveX components.

This type of n-tier application architecture is often employed to create more reusable and component-based Web applications. It employs a browser-based client for the presentation layer, components in the middle tier for the business rules layer, and a relational database management system (RDBMS) for the data layer. Rather than having ASP communicate directly with the database via the Data Environment or the ActiveX Data Objects (ADO) model, the ASP Web pages call methods within COM components, which then communicate with the database. These COM components can also use ADO for their database access. ADO has a simpler object model than either Data Access Objects (DAO) or Remote Data Objects (RDO), some of the earlier database access techniques.

This application architecture is also a nice way to create more object-oriented and componentized code. Instead of having your business logic embedded within ASP Web pages (and often intermingled with the presentation logic), it resides in components. These components are compiled so that they can execute faster than interpreted ASP code.

CREATING ACTIVEX COMPONENTS

In this section, we'll create an ActiveX server-side component using Visual Basic 6.0 and then create an ASP Web page to call the component. The example component that we'll create will be used for the Loan Calculator in our VI-Bank sample application. The Loan Calculator calculates the monthly payment on a loan given the annual percentage rate, the principal amount of the loan, and the term of the loan in number of months.

Creating an ActiveX Component

First run Visual Basic 6.0 and choose to create an ActiveX DLL project from the New Project dialog box, as shown in Figure 18-1. Next enter the code in Figure 18-2 into the class module.

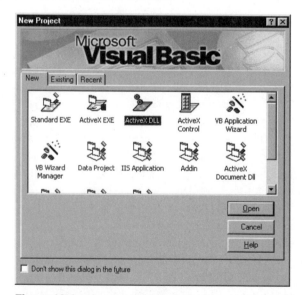

Figure 18-1. *The New Project dialog box within Visual Basic 6.0 showing an ActiveX DLL project.*

```
' Filename: Financial.cls (VI-Bank.vbp)
'
' Description: Financial Class
'
' This file is provided as part of the "Programming Visual
' InterDev 6.0" CD-ROM
'
' THIS CODE AND INFORMATION IS PROVIDED "AS IS" WITHOUT
' WARRANTY OF ANY KIND, EITHER EXPRESSED OR IMPLIED,
' INCLUDING BUT NOT LIMITED TO THE IMPLIED WARRANTIES
' OF MERCHANTABILITY AND/OR FITNESS FOR A PARTICULAR
' PURPOSE.
'
' Copyright (C) 1998 Microsoft Corporation, All rights reserved

Option Explicit

Private Const APP_ERROR = -2147467008

Public Function Payment(ByVal NumMonths As Integer, _
    APR As Double, Principal As Double)

    Dim strResult As String

    On Error GoTo ErrorHandler

    ' Check for zeros
    If NumMonths = 0 Then
       Err.Raise Number:=APP_ERROR, Description:= _
           "Please enter a non-zero value for the number of months"
    End If
    If APR = 0 Then
       Err.Raise Number:=APP_ERROR, Description:= _
           "Please enter a non-zero value for the APR."
    End If
    If Principal = 0 Then
       Err.Raise Number:=APP_ERROR, Description:= _
           "Please enter a non-zero value for principal."
    End If

    ' Convert APR from a percentage to a decimal
    APR = APR / 100#

    ' Convert APR to a monthly percentage rate
    APR = APR / 12#
```

Figure 18-2. *The financial.cls class module within the VI-Bank.vbp project. The Payment method determines the monthly payment on a loan.* *(continued)*

Figure 18-2 *continued*

```
' Check that we don't divide by zero
If (((1 + APR) ^ NumMonths) - 1) = 0 Then
    Err.Raise Number:=APP_ERROR, Description:= _
        "Division by zero. Please retry with different inputs."
Else
    Payment = Principal * (APR * ((1 + APR) ^ NumMonths)) / _
        (((1 + APR) ^ NumMonths) - 1)
End If
```

```
Exit Function
```

```
ErrorHandler:
```

```
    Payment = -1 ' indicate that an error occurred
```

```
    Err.Raise Err.Number, "VIBank.Financial.Payment", _
        Err.Description
```

```
End Function
```

Alternatively, you can access the code for this example on the CD-ROM under the VI-Bank/VB98 folder in a Visual Basic 6.0 project named VI-Bank.vbp. After opening this project file and selecting the Financial class module, you should see a screen similar to that shown in Figure 18-3.

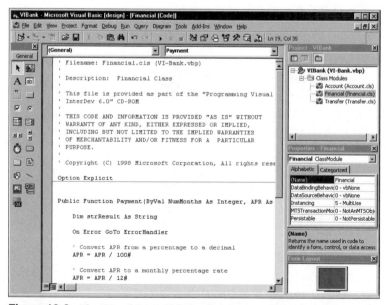

Figure 18-3. *The Visual Basic 6.0 development environment showing the financial.cls class module within the VI-Bank.vbp project.*

The code in the financial.cls class module shown in Figure 18-2 defines a function called *Payment*. *Payment* is a simple function that takes three parameters as input (the principal, the APR, and the term of the loan) and calculates the monthly payment on the loan. This is a simple example that could easily be extended by adding more functions into the same class module. By doing this, you would have a powerful financial component with a variety of functions that can be reused across multiple applications.

If you are creating your own Visual Basic 6.0 ActiveX DLL project, you'll also want to go into the Project Properties dialog box (by choosing Properties from the Project menu) and mark the project for Unattended Execution, as shown in Figure 18-4. In the case of our example project, this setting is already stored in the project file on the CD-ROM. To compile an ActiveX DLL for your project, simply choose Make from the File menu.

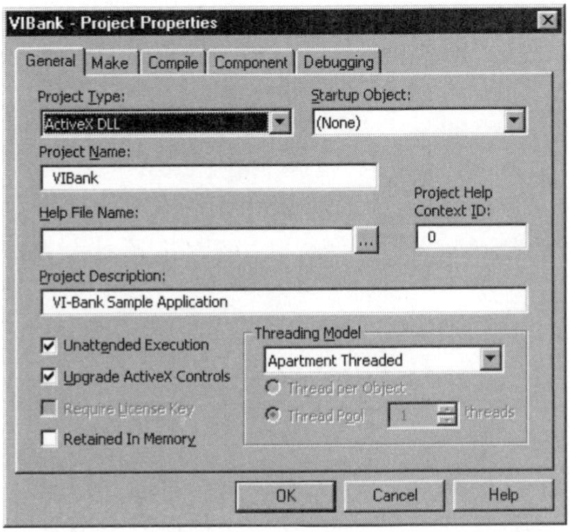

Figure 18-4. *The Project Properties dialog box within Visual Basic 6.0 showing the Unattended Execution check box.*

After compiling the project to make an ActiveX DLL (vibank.dll), you'll want to stage it on your Web server. If you are simply developing on a single machine and your copy of Visual Basic is on the same machine as your Web server, you won't need to stage the component—having compiled the component inside Visual Basic will have already registered the component on your machine for you. If you want to stage the component on another machine, see the "Deploying ActiveX Components" section later in this chapter.

Calling the ActiveX Component from ASP

To call an ActiveX component from an ASP Web page, simply use the *Server.CreateObject* syntax to instantiate the object and then reference its methods. Here is an example:

```
<%
Dim oFinancial
Set oFinancial = Server.CreateObject("VIBank.Financial")
MonthlyPayment = oFinancial.Payment(36, 7.5, 10000)
Response.Write "Monthly Payment is '" + _
    FormatCurrency(MonthlyPayment) + "'.<p>"
%>
```

This code instantiates the *Financial* object of the VIBank component and then executes the *Payment* method. The resulting value from the method is stored in the *MonthlyPayment* variable. Finally, the value of the *MonthlyPayment* variable is converted to currency format using the *FormatCurrency* function and is then output to the browser using the *Response.Write* syntax.

Instead of using *Server.CreateObject*, you can also use an <OBJECT> tag in which you specify the attribute RUNAT=SERVER. Creating an <OBJECT> tag allows you to reference the object in any server script on the page and adds the object and its members to the Microsoft IntelliSense statement completion drop-down list. For example, the following creates an object reference to the *Financial* object:

```
<OBJECT RUNAT="Server" ID=oFinancial
    PROGID="VIBank.Financial">
</OBJECT>
```

In your script, you can reference this object by using the name you assigned in the ID attribute. The following statement uses the object defined in the <OBJECT> block:

```
MonthlyPayment = oFinancial.Payment(36, 7.5, 10000)
```

Figure 18-5 shows the IntelliSense statement completion drop-down list for the *Payment* method.

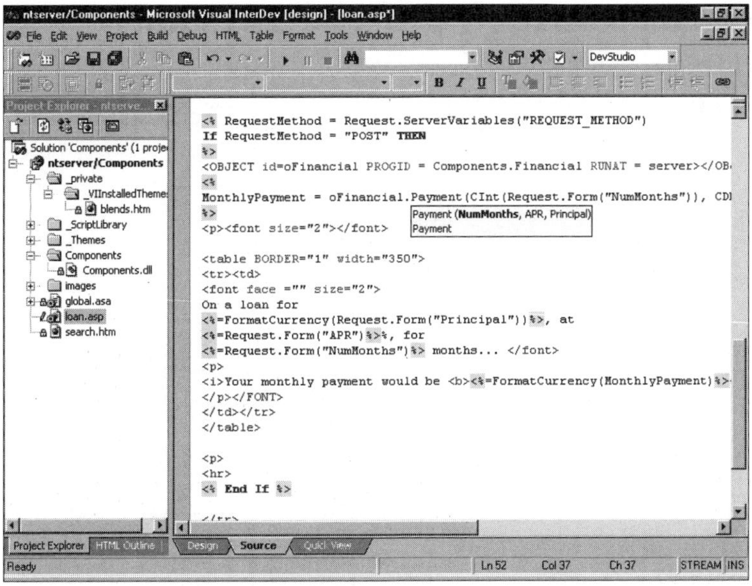

Figure 18-5. *The Visual InterDev 6.0 IDE showing an ASP Web page with IntelliSense statement completion for the* Payment *method of the* Financial *object.*

To continue our ActiveX component example, we'll look at the entire ASP Web page that calls the *Payment* method. The ASP Web page presents the user with a form for entering three values for principal, annual percentage rate, and number of months for a loan. It is also a self-posting ASP Web page so that when the user clicks the Calculate button, the page is reloaded, the monthly loan payment amount is calculated (by calling the component), and the results are presented to the user on the same page. The code in Figure 18-6 shows the relevant page, named loan.asp, which is in the VI-Bank/VIntDev98 folder on the CD-ROM.

```
<html>
<head>
<meta NAME="GENERATOR" Content="Microsoft Visual Studio 6.0">
<title>VI-Bank - Loan Calculator</title>

<LINK REL="stylesheet" TYPE="text/css"
    HREF="_Themes/blueprnt/THEME.CSS"
    VI6.0THEME="Blueprint">
```

Figure 18-6. *The loan.asp page, which calls the* Payment *method of the* Financial *object. The page is a self-posting ASP Web page that both captures input values and displays results.* *(continued)*

Figure 18-6 *continued*

```
<LINK REL="stylesheet" TYPE="text/css"
    HREF="_Themes/blueprnt/GRAPH0.CSS"
    VI6.0THEME="Blueprint">
<LINK REL="stylesheet" TYPE="text/css"
    HREF="_Themes/blueprnt/COLOR0.CSS"
    VI6.0THEME="Blueprint">
<LINK REL="stylesheet" TYPE="text/css"
    HREF="_Themes/blueprnt/CUSTOM.CSS"
    VI6.0THEME="Blueprint"></head>
<body>

<table>
<tr valign=top>
<td width=125>
<!--#INCLUDE FILE="menu.htm"-->
</td>
<td>

<h2><FONT COLOR="navy">
    <I>VI-Bank - Loan Calculator</I>
</FONT></h2>
<hr color=navy>
<p>
<form METHOD="post" ACTION="loan.asp">

<table border="1" cellPadding="3" cellSpacing="1" width="350">
<tr>
<td><font face ="" size="2">Number of Months:</font></td>
<td><font face ="" size="2">
    <input id="NumMonths" name="NumMonths" size="15">
</font></td>
</tr>
<tr>
<td><font face ="" size="2">Annual Percentage Rate (APR):
</font></td>
<td><font face ="" size="2">
    <input id="APR" name="APR" size="15">
</font></td>
</tr>
<tr>
<td><font face ="" size="2">Principal:</font></td>
<td>><font face ="" size="2">
    <input id="Principal" name="Principal" size="15">
</font></td>
</tr>
```

(continued)

```
</table>
<P>

<table width="350">
<tr><td>
<div align="center"><input id="submit" name="submit"
    type="submit" value="Calculate"></div>
</td></tr>
</table>

</form>
<hr>

<%
RequestMethod = Request.ServerVariables("REQUEST_METHOD")
If RequestMethod = "POST" THEN
%>

<OBJECT id=oFinancial RUNAT=server PROGID=VIBank.Financial>
</OBJECT>

<%
MonthlyPayment = oFinancial.Payment(CInt(Request.Form("NumMonths")),
    CDbl(Request.Form("APR")), CDbl(Request.Form("Principal")))
%>
<p>

<table BORDER="1" width="350">
<tr><td>
<font face ="" size="2">
On a loan for <%=FormatCurrency(Request.Form("Principal"))%>
, at <%=Request.Form("APR")%>
%, for <%=Request.Form("NumMonths")%> months...
</font>
<p>

<i>Your monthly payment would be <b>
<%=FormatCurrency(MonthlyPayment)%></b></i>
</p></FONT>
</td></tr>
</table>

<p>
<hr>
    <% End If %>
```

(continued)

Figure 18-6 *continued*

```
</td>
</tr>
</table>

</body>
</html>
```

Figure 18-7 shows the loan.asp page when it is first loaded into the browser. The REQUEST_METHOD HTTP environment variable is used to determine whether the page has been submitted. The value of this variable is stored in the *RequestMethod* variable. At this stage, the form has not been posted, so the ASP and HTML code enclosed within the *If* statement is not executed.

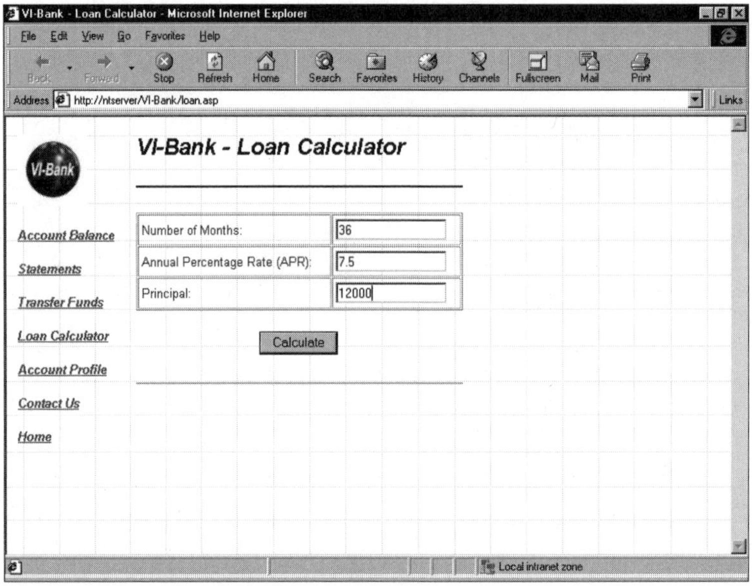

Figure 18-7. *The loan.asp page shown within the browser prior to the Calculate button being clicked.*

After the Calculate button has been clicked, the page calls itself and the *RequestMethod* variable evaluates to POST. Now the *Financial* object is instantiated, its *Payment* method is passed the values collected in the HTML form, and the results are output to the screen. Figure 18-8 shows the resulting output. Notice that HTML tables have been used to format the elements on the page and a theme has been applied to the page to give it more visual appeal. More important, notice that the values collected on the HTML form have been converted to the appropriate data types prior to being passed to the *Payment* method. The *Payment* method takes the *NumMonths* variable as an Integer and the *APR* and *Principal* variables as Doubles. The Microsoft VBScript (Visual Basic, Scripting Edition) functions *CInt* and *CDbl* have been used to perform this data type conversion. The *FormatCurrency* VBScript function has been used to present the resulting output from the *Payment* method to the user.

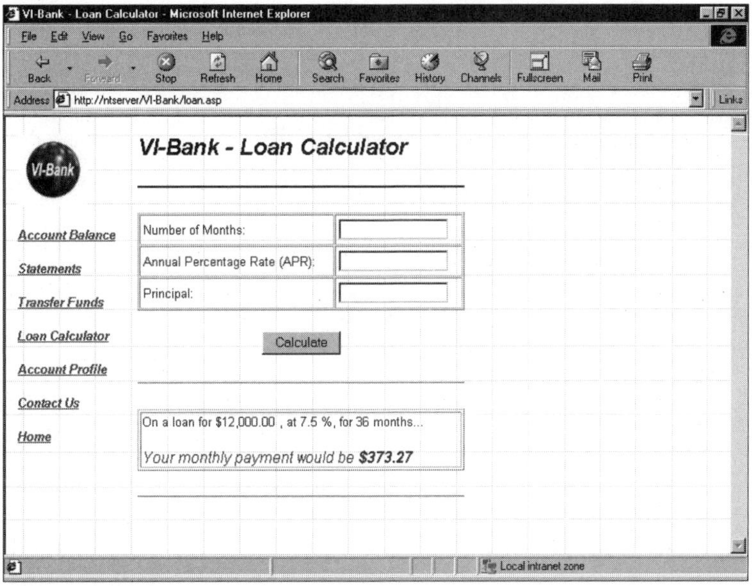

Figure 18-8. *The loan.asp page shown within the browser after the Calculate button has been clicked.*

As you can see from the code in Figure 18-6, the amount of code necessary to instantiate a server-side component and execute its methods is just a couple of lines. Most of the code in the listing is used to collect the input values from the end user and to format the results. Additional code could be added to this example to provide more robust error handling. Specifically, client-side scripting could be used to ensure that the input values are of the correct data type and range.

DEPLOYING ACTIVEX COMPONENTS

There are two methods of deploying ActiveX components: you can either deploy them using Regsvr32 or you can deploy them in a more automated fashion using Visual InterDev 6.0. The remote deployment capabilities for middle-tier COM server components is one of the exciting new features in Visual InterDev 6.0. In this section, we'll see how both of these procedures are performed.

Using Regsvr32

Regsvr32 is a program that allows you to register components from the command line. You can launch Regsvr32 either from within the Run dialog by choosing Start|Run or from within the DOS Command Prompt by choosing Start|Programs|MS-DOS Prompt. Regsvr32 has the following syntax:

```
Regsvr32 [/u] [/s] [/n] [/i[:cmdline]] dllname

Where

dllname - Component to register
cmdline - Optional command line parameters
/u - Unregister server
/s - Silent; display no message boxes
/c - Console output
/i - Call dllinstall passing it an optional [cmdline];
    when used with /u calls dlluninstall
/n - Do not call dllregisterserver;
    this option must be used with /i
```

The most common usage of Regsvr32 is simply to call it and pass it the name of the component that you want to register, as shown in the following example.

```
C:\regsvr32 vibank.dll
```

Of course, Regsvr32 has to be run locally on the machine on which you want to register the component. You also have to manually copy the component DLL file to the machine prior to registration. Figure 18-9 shows the output message box after the component has been successfully registered.

Figure 18-9. *The message box displayed after a component has been successfully registered using Regsvr32.*

Using Visual InterDev 6.0 to remotely deploy the component can be much more convenient as we'll see in the next section.

Using Visual InterDev 6

Now that we've seen how to deploy a component using Regsvr32, let's take a look at the equivalent operation within Visual InterDev 6.0. For developers, this is a much more straightforward approach—you develop your component on a workstation along with your Web project and then deploy the component to the server remotely.

> **NOTE** To register components through Visual InterDev on a remote Web server, the Web server must have IIS installed with the Visual InterDev RAD Remote Deployment Support option selected during custom installation.

The first step is to add your component to a Web project:

1. Open up your Web project.

2. Create a folder named Components under your Web project. This step is not required but is good practice so that your middle-tier components are kept separate from your HTML and ASP code.

3. Prepare to add the component to the Components folder by right-clicking the folder and choosing Add|Add Item.

4. In the Add Item dialog box, choose the Existing tab.

5. Locate your ActiveX DLL file, and then click Open.

Your component will now be added to your Web project.

Figure 18-10 shows the Project Explorer with an ActiveX DLL named vibank.dll added to the Components folder within the VI-Bank Web project.

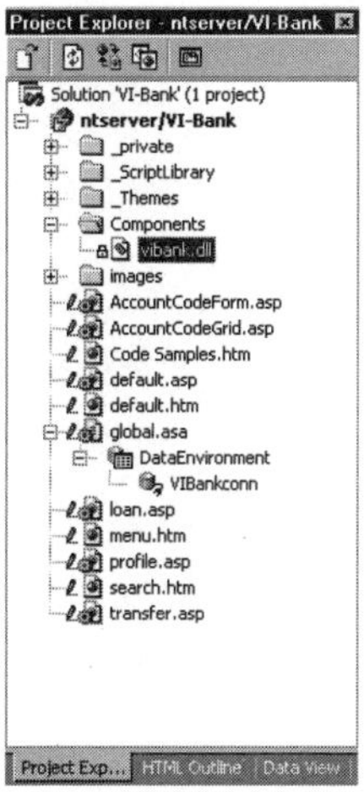

Figure 18-10. *The Project Explorer within Visual InterDev 6.0 showing a component that has been registered remotely.*

Now that the component has been added to your Web project, you are ready to register it on the server. You can do this as follows:

1. Right-click the component, and choose Properties from the context menu.

2. Choose the Component Installation tab on the Properties dialog box.

3. Check the Register On Server box. (See Figure 18-11.)

4. Click OK.

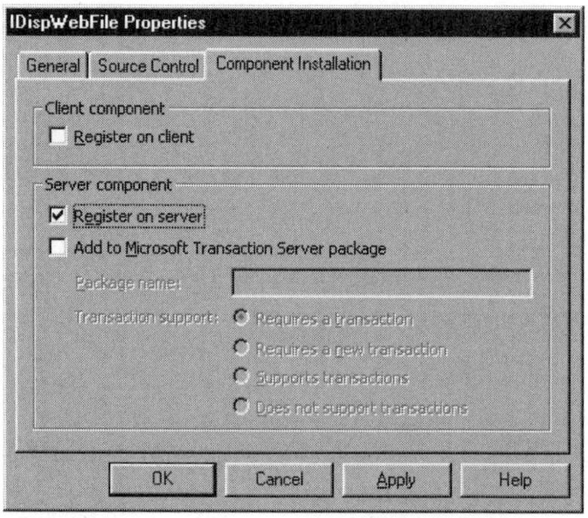

Figure 18-11. *The Component Installation tab of the component Properties dialog box.*

After you select OK, the component will be registered on the server. You'll be able to see the sequence of events by watching the status bar in the lower left corner of the screen.

NOTE   If your master Web server and local project are on the same computer, the registry for that machine notes the component only once, not once each for the master and local version. If you remove the local copy, the registry entry for the component is also removed, even though the component is marked as a server component in the project.

If you want to deploy your entire Web project, including components, to another destination Web server (that is, not your local or master Web server), you can use Visual InterDev to register the components. You can do this as follows:

1. In the Project Explorer, select the Web project that you want to deploy.

2. Choose Web Project|Copy Web Application from the Project menu.

3. In the Copy Project dialog box, choose which copy of your application you want to deploy (local or master copy), enter the name

of the Web server to which you want to deploy, and enter a name for the Web project.

4. Select the Register Server Components check box to register your components on the new Web server. (See Figure 18-12.)

Figure 18-12 shows the Copy Project dialog box with the Register Server Components check box marked. In this example, the VI-Bank Web project is being copied to a Web server named testserver.

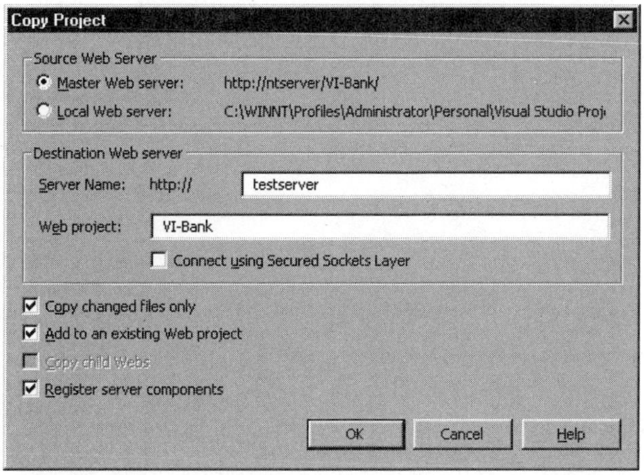

Figure 18-12. *The Copy Project dialog box showing the Register Server Components check box. This dialog box is used to copy a Web project, including components, from one server to another.*

SUMMARY

In this chapter, we've studied how to create ActiveX components using Visual Basic 6.0. Component creation is often simple since there is no presentation layer to be concerned with—the components just contain nonvisual business logic that performs various functions and that perhaps interfaces with the database. Components are created by choosing the ActiveX DLL project type within Visual Basic 6.0.

We've also seen how to deploy these ActiveX components either by using Regsvr32 or by using the remote deployment features of Visual InterDev 6.0. ASP Web pages can call ActiveX components either by using the *Server.CreateObject* syntax or by using the <OBJECT> tag. When calling ActiveX components from your ASP Web pages, be sure to match the data types by using the VBScript conversion functions, if necessary.

Chapter 19

Creating Transactional ASP Web Pages

In this chapter, we'll look at how you can create transactional applications using Active Server Pages (ASP). Therefore, in addition to Microsoft Visual InterDev 6.0, we'll be looking at Internet Information Server (IIS) 4.0 and Microsoft Transaction Server (MTS) 2.0 and how the two can be leveraged to create transactional, browser-based applications. MTS 2.0 must be installed and the Microsoft Distributed Transaction Coordinator (DTC) service must be running for your transactional ASP Web pages to work. You can run MTS 2.0 either with IIS 4.0 or with Personal Web Server (PWS) 4.0, although IIS 4.0 is the recommended approach. It's worth noting that transactional ASP is just one way that you can write a transactional client-side application. Of course, you can also write transactional applications by using Microsoft Visual Basic, Microsoft Visual C++, or Microsoft Visual J++ for your client-side presentation layer.

As we learned in Chapter 17, one nice thing about Microsoft technology is that it gives you a number of options. For example, you can leverage the same server-side components in MTS by calling them both from Visual Basic clients and from a browser-based client using ASP. You might do this in a situation where you want to make the MTS components available to both Web-based users (perhaps mobile workers) and LAN-based users.

Before you begin dealing with transactions, it's worthwhile to review some of the basic theory surrounding Microsoft Transaction Server. Specifically, you need to know the definitions of the following:

- A transaction

- Transaction attributes

- MTS packages and components

- The context object

This knowledge will prove useful not only for the work that we perform in this chapter but also for the subsequent chapter, which covers creating transactional components with Visual Basic 6.0. Once you've learned the basics about transactions and MTS, you'll be well equipped to start writing transactional applications—either two-tiered or n-tiered.

TRANSACTIONS

Those of you familiar with client/server applications should be accustomed to dealing with transactions. A transaction can be defined as a logical unit of work. It is performed as an atomic operation in that it either succeeds or fails as a whole. A simple example is that of transferring money from a savings account to a checking account. The transaction includes both the withdrawal of money from savings and the addition of the same amount of money into the checking account. If one of these steps fails, the transaction fails. Likewise, if the transaction fails, any step that had succeeded must be rolled back.

MTS simplifies the task of developing application components by allowing you to perform work with transactions. This protects applications from anomalies caused by concurrent updates or system failures.

Transactions maintain what are known as the *ACID* properties, as follows:

- *Atomicity* ensures that all the updates completed under a specific transaction are either committed and made durable, or aborted and rolled back to their previous state.

- *Consistency* means that a transaction is a correct transformation of the system state, preserving the state invariants.

■ *Isolation* protects concurrent transactions from seeing each other's partial and uncommitted results, which might create inconsistencies in the application state. Resource managers use transaction-based synchronization protocols to isolate the uncommitted work of active transactions.

■ *Durability* means that committed updates to managed resources—such as a database record—survive failures, including communication failures, process failures, and server system failures. Transactional logging even allows you to recover the durable state after disk media failures.

The intermediate states of a transaction are not visible outside the transaction, and either all the work happens or none of it does. This allows you to develop application components as if each transaction executes sequentially and without regard to concurrency. This simplifies the lives of application developers: they can develop code without having to worry about multiple users executing the same code. They can simply write the code as if it's intended for a single user.

MICROSOFT TRANSACTION SERVER

The Microsoft Windows NT 4.0 Option Pack includes Microsoft Transaction Server, a transaction processing system for developing, deploying, and managing distributed server applications. MTS takes care of all the server-side plumbing issues, such as automatic management of processes and threads, object instance management, and a distributed security service, so that developers can concentrate on writing the business logic specific to their applications. MTS brings a higher level of scalability to Web applications running on IIS by conserving server resources. As we have seen above, MTS also provides transactional behavior for applications so operations either succeed or fail as a whole.

Once you have installed MTS, take a few minutes to familiarize yourself with the Transaction Server Explorer, shown in Figure 19-1 on the following page. You can access the Transaction Server Explorer by choosing Start|Programs|Windows NT 4.0 Option Pack|Microsoft Transaction Server|Transaction Server Explorer, or by choosing Start|Programs|Windows NT 4.0 Option Pack|Microsoft Internet Information Server|Internet Service Manager. Both of these options will launch the Microsoft Management Console, which contains the Transaction Server Explorer.

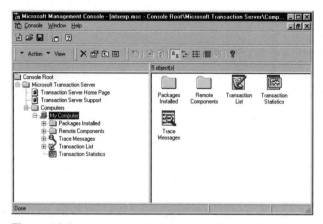

Figure 19-1. *The Transaction Server Explorer within the Microsoft Management Console.*

In the right-hand pane of the Transaction Server Explorer, you'll see the Packages Installed folder. This folder is where you can install, deploy, and maintain your packages and components. We'll now look at some of the MTS terminology: packages, components, roles, interfaces, and methods.

Packages

All components need to belong to a *package*. A package is a set of components that perform related application functions. While packages are simple to create—using the Transaction Server Explorer—the components that are added to the package should be selected carefully. Packages can define process boundaries, so you want to carefully consider your component design and deployment strategy. For performance reasons, you'll want to minimize the number of process boundaries that are crossed. The following design issues should be considered when defining packages:

- Activation
- Shared Resources
- Fault Isolation
- Security Isolation

A package can be activated either as a Library Package or as a Server Package. A Library Package runs in the same process as the client that created it and offers no component tracking, role checking, or process isolation. A Server Package runs in its own process. It supports role-based security—see the section on roles below—resource sharing, process isolation, and process management.

Components that are in the same package are able to share expensive resources, such as database connections, via database pooling. Sharing of resources allows applications to scale more easily and can also improve performance. This design consideration favors placing components in the same package.

Fault isolation means that components in different packages are protected from each other. If the process for one package dies for some reason, this does not affect the other package, which is running a separate process. This is one design consideration that tends to favor placing components in separate packages. This can be especially relevant during development and testing phases when components are still being verified for correct functionality. A similar consideration applies when deciding whether to run Web projects in a separate memory space from the Web server to avoid crashing the Web server if the application crashes.

Packages also define security boundaries, so by placing components in separate packages you can isolate them from one another. When a component calls another component in a different package, the MTS security model will check the authorization of the calling client. No authorization checking between components within the same package occurs unless it is done at a programmatic level.

Components

A *component* is an ActiveX DLL that you create and install into MTS. They can be written in any language that supports the creation of COM components. Components provide the objects that clients request at run time.

There are several advantages of running your component under MTS, including simplified management of components via the Transaction Server Explorer, location transparency, thread management, and database connection pooling.

Roles

A *role* is a symbolic name that defines a class of users for a set of components. Roles are applied at the package, component, or interface level. They are defined within the Transaction Server Explorer and are similar to Windows NT groups. After creating a role, you typically assign Windows NT users and/or groups to that particular role. This tells MTS which users have authorization to access methods within components in packages.

MTS offers two types of security: programmatic security and declarative security. Role assignments are a form of declarative security and are typically handled by an MTS administrator.

Interfaces

An *interface* is defined as a group of logically related operations or methods that provides access to a component. Within the Transaction Server Explorer, the Interfaces folder shows the methods and role membership for a component.

Methods

Methods are those functions exposed by your components. In the Transaction Server Explorer, the Methods folder contains all the methods defined in a selected interface. The Methods folder is a useful way of browsing a component to see what methods it exposes.

THE *OBJECTCONTEXT* OBJECT

An MTS object is an instance of an MTS component. Remember that an MTS component is a COM component that is installed into MTS. On disk it is a Microsoft ActiveX DLL. The component can contain any number of methods and usually provides a certain category of service. For example, a finance component might contain many different types of financial methods and is therefore a bundling of a particular category of business logic.

MTS maintains context for each object. This context, which is implicitly associated with the object, contains information about the object's execution environment, such as the identity of the object's creator and, optionally, the transaction encompassing the work of the object. The object context is similar in concept to the process context that an operating system maintains for an executing program.

An MTS object and its associated context object have corresponding lifetimes. MTS creates the context before it creates the MTS object. MTS destroys the context after it destroys the MTS object.

The *ObjectContext* Object and ASP

In Internet Information Server 3.0, the ASP framework provided five built-in objects: *Application*, *Session*, *Request*, *Response*, and *Server*. The built-in objects are special because they are built into ASP Web pages and do not need to be created before you can use them in scripts. For example, to send output to the browser you use the *Write* method of the *Response* object. You simply call *Response.Write* and pass it a string. You don't have to create an instance of this object before using its methods.

In IIS 4.0, there is now a sixth built-in object: the *ObjectContext* object. You can use the *ObjectContext* object either to commit or to abort a transaction managed by MTS that has been initiated by a script contained in an ASP Web page.

When an ASP Web page contains the @TRANSACTION directive, the page runs in a transaction and does not finish processing until the transaction either succeeds completely or fails. We'll find out more about the @TRANSACTION directive later on in this chapter.

Methods

The *ObjectContext* object has 11 methods that can be called from your applications. These methods allow you to carry out a number of tasks, including:

- Declaring that the object's work is complete

- Preventing a transaction from being committed

- Instantiating other MTS objects

- Finding out if a caller is in a particular role

- Finding out if security is enabled

- Finding out if the object is executing within a transaction

- Retrieving IIS built-in objects

Table 19-1 lists the methods that can be found in the *ObjectContext* object.

Method	*Description*
Count	Returns the number of context object properties.
CreateInstance	Instantiates another MTS object.
DisableCommit	Declares that the object hasn't finished its work and that its transactional updates are in an inconsistent state. The object retains its state across method calls, and any attempts to commit the transaction before the object calls *EnableCommit* or *SetComplete* will result in the transaction being aborted.
EnableCommit	Declares that the object's work isn't necessarily finished, but its transactional updates are in a consistent state. This method allows the transaction to be committed, but the object retains its state across method calls until it calls *SetComplete* or *SetAbort*, or until the transaction is completed.

Table 19-1. *Methods of the* ObjectContext *object.*   *(continued)*

Table 19-1. *continued*

Method	Description
IsCallerInRole	Indicates whether the object's direct caller is in a specified role (either directly or as part of a group).
IsInTransaction	Indicates whether the object is executing within a transaction.
IsSecurityEnabled	Indicates whether security is enabled. MTS security is enabled unless the object is running in the client's process.
Item	Returns a context object property.
Security	Returns a reference to an object's *SecurityProperty* object.
SetAbort	Declares that the object has completed its work and can be deactivated on returning from the currently executing method, but that its transactional updates are in an inconsistent state or that an unrecoverable error occurred. This means that the transaction in which the object was executing must be aborted. If any object executing within a transaction returns to its client after calling *SetAbort*, the entire transaction is doomed to abort.
SetComplete	Declares that the object has completed its work and can be deactivated on returning from the currently executing method. For objects that are executing within the scope of a transaction, it also indicates that the object's transactional updates can be committed. When an object that is the root of a transaction calls *SetComplete*, MTS attempts to commit the transaction on return from the current method.

Not all of these methods are available to all Microsoft Visual Studio development tools. Table 19-1 actually lists the methods available to Visual Basic. Visual C++ and Visual J++ gain access to the current object's context through the *IObjectContext* interface, as we shall see later on. Active Server Pages has access to only two of the methods above: *SetComplete* and *SetAbort*.

Events

Two events can occur after an *ObjectContext* method has executed: *OnTransactionAbort* and *OnTransactionCommit*.

The *OnTransactionAbort* event occurs if the transaction is aborted. When the *OnTransactionAbort* event occurs, IIS will process the script's *OnTransactionAbort* subroutine, if it exists.

As you might expect, the *OnTransactionCommit* event occurs after a transacted script's transaction commits. When the *OnTransactionCommit* event occurs, IIS will process the script's *OnTransactionCommit* subroutine, if it exists.

We'll see some examples of how to use these events within your ASP script later on in this chapter.

ASP TRANSACTION BASICS

As mentioned earlier, to have ASP take advantage of the reliability provided by MTS services, you need to include only the @TRANSACTION directive in your script. This directive tells MTS that any changes that occur in that page—such as database manipulation or Microsoft Message Queue Server (MSMQ) message transmission—should be considered transactions. A change that is being managed by transaction services can be either committed, making it more or less permanent, or aborted, which would result in rolling back to the state of the database or queue before the changes were made.

The code in Figure 19-2 shows a simple example of how to add transactional behavior to your ASP Web pages. The code starts with the @TRANSACTION directive. This must be the first line of code within the ASP Web page or an error will be generated. The transaction attributes that are available are shown in Table 19-2 on the following page.

```
<% @TRANSACTION=Required LANGUAGE="VBScript" %>

<HTML>
<HEAD>
<META NAME="GENERATOR" Content="Microsoft Visual Studio 6.0"
<TITLE>Simple Transactional ASP Page</TITLE>
</HEAD>

<BODY BGCOLOR="White" topmargin="10" leftmargin="10">

<h2><font color="navy">Simple Transactional ASP Page</font></h2>
<hr>

This is a simple example demonstrating the basic
structure of a transactional ASP Page.

</BODY>
</HTML>
```

Figure19-2. *ASP code showing the @TRANSACTION directive to declare an ASP script as transactional.* *(continued)*

Figure 19-2. *continued*

```
<%
' The Transacted Script Commit Handler. This sub-routine
' will be called if the transacted script commits.
' Note that in the example above, there is no way for the
' script not to commit.

Sub OnTransactionCommit()
    Response.Write "<p><b>The Transaction just committed</b>."
    Response.Write "<br>This message came from the "
    Response.Write "OnTransactionCommit() event handler."
End Sub


' The Transacted Script Abort Handler. This sub-routine
' will be called if the transacted script aborts.
' Note that in the example above, there is no way for the
' script not to commit.

Sub OnTransactionAbort()
    Response.Write "<p><b>The Transaction just aborted</b>."
    Response.Write "<br>This message came from the "
    Response.Write "OnTransactionAbort() event handler."
End Sub
%>
```

Value	Meaning
Requires_New	Starts a new transaction
Required	Starts a new transaction
Supported	Does not start a transaction
Not_Supported	Does not start a transaction

Table 19-2. *Transaction attributes for the @TRANSACTION directive in ASP Web pages.*

The code in Figure 19-2 specifies that a transaction is required, so a new transaction is started for the page. You'll also notice two subroutines within the page. These are the event handlers for the *OnTransactionCommit* and *OnTransactionAbort* events for the *ObjectContext* object. They provide a way to trap the event and take an appropriate action. In this example, the event handlers merely print a message to the browser (standard output) stating the success or failure of the transaction. Of course, in this example, there is no way for the script not to commit. The listing is included on the companion CD-ROM as the asp_trans.asp file within the VI-Bank/VIntDev98 folder of the VI-Bank sample Web project. Figure 19-3 shows the resulting output after the code has been run within the browser.

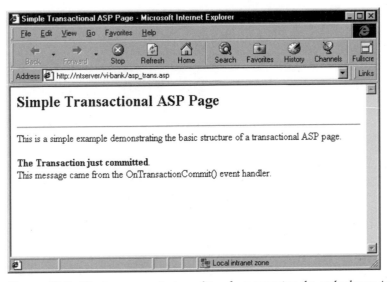

Figure 19-3. *The browser output resulting from running the code shown in Figure 19-2.*

Just to prove to yourself that the ASP Web page listed above was truly included as a transaction, try pulling up the Transaction Server Explorer application. Access this program group by choosing Start | Programs | Windows NT 4.0 Option Pack | Microsoft Transaction Server | Transaction Server Explorer from the task bar. After you have started Transaction Server Explorer, choose Transaction Statistics from the left pane. Each time you run the ASP example, you'll see the Committed and Total counters in the Aggregate section increase by one. Figure 19-4 on the following page shows the Transaction Server Explorer window.

You'll notice in Figure 19-4 that the Transaction Server Explorer also shows you the minimum, average, and maximum response times for the transactions. The response time is the duration of the transaction in milliseconds from the moment it begins to the moment when it is committed. It does not count transactions that are aborted. Looking at the transaction statistics is a good way to monitor how quickly your transactions are executing. It's worth allowing as many transactions to occur as possible before you start looking at the response times in order to determine performance data. This will give you better statistical results. After 50 to 100 transactions, you should start to get a clear picture of the average MTS performance for your particular applications.

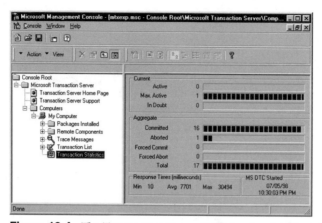

Figure 19-4. *The Transaction Server Explorer showing the total number of committed and aborted transactions.*

To give an example of how you might use the event handlers in real life, suppose your transaction aborted for some reason. Now MTS is capable of only rolling back changes made to the database. It does not roll back changes to files on your hard disk, ASP session and application variables, and so on. The *OnTransactionAbort* event handler would be an ideal place to roll back these types of changes.

You can also explicitly commit or roll back transactions using the *SetCommit* or *SetAbort* methods of the *ObjectContext* object. Therefore, a transaction is committed when either the script has successfully completed or the *ObjectContext.SetComplete* method has been called. Likewise, the transaction is aborted when the script either encounters some kind of processing error, the script times out, or the *ObjectContext.SetAbort* method has been called. The code in Figure 19-5 illustrates all of these scenarios.

```
<%@ TRANSACTION=Required LANGUAGE="VBScript" %>
<% ' VI 6.0 Scripting Object Model Enabled %>
<!--#include file="_ScriptLibrary/pm.asp"-->
<% if StartPageProcessing() Then Response.End() %>
<FORM name=thisForm METHOD=post>

<HTML>
<HEAD>
<META NAME="GENERATOR" Content="Microsoft Visual Studio 6.0">
<TITLE>Simple Transactional Web Page using ASP</TITLE>
</HEAD>
<BODY BGCOLOR="white" topmargin="10" leftmargin="10" >

<h2><font color="navy">
```

Figure 19-5. *ASP code (asp_trans_demo.asp) illustrating four different processing scenarios for transactional ASP.*   *(continued)*

```
    Simple Transactional Web Page Using ASP
</font></h2>
<hr>

<FORM METHOD=post ACTION="asp_transaction.asp">
<table cellpadding="5", cellspacing="5">
<tr>
<td>

<!-- Radiobutton Design-Time Control -->
<!--METADATA TYPE="DesignerControl" startspan
<OBJECT classid="clsid:B5F0E45D-DC5F-11D0-9846-0000F8027CA0"
    height=39 id=TransactionGroup
    style="HEIGHT: 39px; LEFT: 0px; TOP: 0px;
    WIDTH: 102px" width=102>
    <PARAM NAME="_ExtentX" VALUE="3254">
    <PARAM NAME="_ExtentY" VALUE="1693">
    <PARAM NAME="id" VALUE="TransactionGroup">
    <PARAM NAME="DataSource" VALUE="">
    <PARAM NAME="DataField" VALUE="">
    <PARAM NAME="ControlStyle" VALUE="0">
    <PARAM NAME="BType" VALUE="0">
    <PARAM NAME="Enabled" VALUE="-1">
    <PARAM NAME="Visible" VALUE="-1">
    <PARAM NAME="Platform" VALUE="256">
    <PARAM NAME="UsesStaticList" VALUE="-1">
    <PARAM NAME="CLSize" VALUE="4">
    <PARAM NAME="CLED1" VALUE="Commit">
    <PARAM NAME="CLEV1" VALUE="1">
    <PARAM NAME="CLED2" VALUE="Forced Commit">
    <PARAM NAME="CLEV2" VALUE="2">
    <PARAM NAME="CLED3" VALUE="Forced Abort">
    <PARAM NAME="CLEV3" VALUE="3">
    <PARAM NAME="CLED4" VALUE="Syntax Error">
    <PARAM NAME="CLEV4" VALUE="4">
    <PARAM NAME="LocalPath" VALUE=""></OBJECT>
-->
<!--#INCLUDE FILE="_ScriptLibrary/OptionGrp.ASP"-->
<SCRIPT LANGUAGE=JavaScript RUNAT=Server>
function _initTransactionGroup()
{
    TransactionGroup.addItem('Commit', '1');
    TransactionGroup.addItem('Forced Commit', '2');
    TransactionGroup.addItem('Forced Abort', '3');
    TransactionGroup.addItem('Syntax Error', '4');
}
```

(continued)

Figure 19-5. *continued*

```
function _TransactionGroup_ctor()
{
    CreateOptionGroup('TransactionGroup',
        _initTransactionGroup, null);
}
</script>
<% TransactionGroup.display %>

<!--METADATA TYPE="DesignerControl" endspan-->

</td>
<td>
<font size="2">

This example shows four scenarios as follows:
<UL>
    <LI>Commit - The page commits automatically
    <LI>Forced Commit - A commit is forced using
    ObjectContext.SetComplete
    <LI>Forced Abort - An abort is forced using
    ObjectContext.SetAbort
    <LI>Syntax Error - A syntax error is used to trigger an
    abort</LI>
</UL>
</font>
</td>
</tr>
<tr>
<td align="center">
<INPUT type="submit" value="Submit" id=submit name=submit>
</FORM>
</td>
<td>
</td>
</tr>
</table>
<%
RequestMethod = Request.ServerVariables("REQUEST_METHOD")
If RequestMethod = "POST" Then
    Select Case Request.Form("TransactionGroup")
        Case 1
            ' Do nothing
        Case 2
            ' Force a commit
            ObjectContext.SetComplete
        Case 3
            ' Force an abort
```

(continued)

```
                    ObjectContext.SetAbort
            Case 4
                ' Force an abort via a syntax error
                Microsoft.Rules
        End Select
    End If
%>


</BODY>
<% ' VI 6.0 Scripting Object Model Enabled %>
<% EndPageProcessing() %>
</FORM>
</HTML>


<%
    ' The Transacted Script Commit Handler. This subroutine
    ' will be called if the transacted script commits.

    Sub OnTransactionCommit()
        If RequestMethod = "POST" Then
            Response.Write _
                "<p><b>The Transaction just committed</b>."
            Response.Write "<br>This message came from the "
            Response.Write "OnTransactionCommit() event handler."
        End If
    End Sub


    ' The Transacted Script Abort Handler. This subroutine
    ' will be called if the transacted script aborts.

    Sub OnTransactionAbort()
        If RequestMethod = "POST" Then
            Response.Write "<p><b>The Transaction just aborted</b>."
            Response.Write "<br>This message came from the "
            Response.Write "OnTransactionAbort() event handler."
        End If
    End Sub
%>
```

NOTE It's important to know that a transaction cannot span multiple ASP Web pages. If a transaction requires objects from several transactional components, you should group operations that use those objects into one ASP Web page.

In Figure 19-5, the code allows you to select a scenario using the radio buttons (created using an OptionGroup design-time control) and then to submit the page in order to have that scenario executed on the server. The event handlers report the resulting commit or abort back to the user. The four scenarios included are as follows:

- **Commit**   The page is allowed to commit automatically with no programmatic intervention.

- **Forced Commit**   A commit is forced using the *ObjectContext-.SetComplete* syntax within the ASP Web page.

- **Forced Abort**   An abort is forced using the *ObjectContext.SetAbort* syntax within the ASP page.

- **Syntax Error**   A syntax error within the ASP page is used to trigger an abort.

The code for Figure 19-5 is included on the CD-ROM as the asp_trans-_demo.asp file in the VI-Bank/VIntDev98 folder. Figure 19-6 shows the output from the page when the Forced Abort radio button has been chosen.

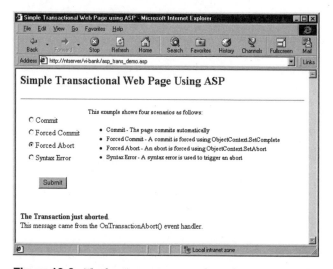

Figure 19-6. *The browser output resulting from running the code shown in Figure 19-5 and choosing a "Forced Abort" via the* ObjectContext.SetAbort *syntax.*

TRANSACTIONS USING ADO FROM ASP

In this section, we'll see how an ASP Web page can participate in a true database transaction. To start simply, we'll only use ActiveX Data Objects (ADO) to access the data—we won't employ MTS components. The ASP code will therefore go directly against the database. The same functionality in the code could also be written by using the Data Environment and data command objects. In this particular example, we'll simply use straight ADO so that you can more easily see the code in the listing and thus focus on the transactional nature of the page.

Figure 19-7 shows the code for this example. The code is included on the companion CD-ROM as the ado_trans.asp file within the VI-Bank/VIntDev98 folder. The example selects information from the customer table in the Microsoft SQL Server 6.5 "Bank" database, which is part of the VI-Bank sample Internet Banking application. It then updates the customer's e-mail address in the customer table as well as the customer's checking account in the account_balance table by a debit of $0.50 for this service. Of course, in real life you might not want to charge anything for this service or your customers might go elsewhere! There are two phases to this operation. Since they are both contained within this transactional ASP Web page, they must both succeed or the transaction will be rolled back.

```
<%@ TRANSACTION=Required LANGUAGE="VBScript" %>

<!--#include file="adovbs.inc"-->

<HTML>

<HEAD>
<META NAME="GENERATOR" Content="Microsoft Visual Studio 6.0">
<TITLE>Transactional Database Update</TITLE>
</HEAD>

<BODY BGCOLOR="White" topmargin="10" leftmargin="10">

<h2><font color="navy">Transactional Database Update</font></h2>

<hr>
This sample code shows how to transactionally update a SQL 6.5
database using ADO and Transacted ASP. The example SELECTS information
from the CUSTOMER table in the SQL 6.5 "Bank" database which is
part of the VI-BANK sample Internet Banking application.
It then UPDATES the customer's e-mail address in the CUSTOMER
```

Figure 19-7. *Sample code showing how to transactionally update a SQL Server 6.5 database using ADO and transactional ASP.*

(continued)

Figure 19-7. *continued*

table, as well as UPDATING the customer's checking account in the
ACCOUNT_BALANCE table by a debit of $.50 for this service.
<p>
Because the two database operations are wrapped within a shared ASP
Transaction, both will be automatically rolled back to their previous
state in the event of a failure.

```
<%
Dim oConn ' object for ADODB.Connection obj
Dim oRs   ' object for recordset object
Dim oRs2  ' object for recordset object

' Create Connection and Recordset components
Set oConn = Server.CreateObject("ADODB.Connection")
Set oRs = Server.CreateObject("ADODB.Recordset")
Set oRs2 = Server.CreateObject("ADODB.Recordset")

' Open ADO Connection using the VI-Bank file DSN
oConn.Open "FILEDSN=VI-Bank"
Set oRs.ActiveConnection = oConn
Set oRs2.ActiveConnection = oConn

' Get the customer record based on the ssn
oRs.Source = "SELECT * FROM customer WHERE ssn = 123456789"
oRs.CursorType = adOpenStatic ' use a cursor other than Forward Only
oRs.LockType = adLockOptimistic ' use a locktype permitting insertions
oRs.Open

' Change e-mail address
If (Not oRs.EOF) Then
    oRs("e_mail").Value = "nick.evans@us.pwcglobal.com"
    oRs.Update
End If

' Find the customer's account balance information
oRs2.Source = "SELECT * FROM account_balance " & _
    "where ssn = 123456789 and account_id = 1"
oRs2.CursorType = adOpenStatic    ' use a cursor other than
                                  ' Forward Only
oRs2.LockType = adLockOptimistic ' use a locktype
                                  ' permitting insertions

oRs2.Open

' Debit the checking account balance by $0.50
If (Not oRs2.EOF) Then
    oRs2("balance").Value = _
        CDbl(oRs2("balance").Value) - CDbl(0.5)
```

(continued)

```
      NewBalance = oRs2("balance").Value
      oRs2.Update
End If

' Clean up
oRs.Close
oRs2.Close
oConn.Close
%>

</BODY>
</HTML>

<%
' The Transacted Script Commit Handler. This subroutine
' will be called if the transacted script commits.

Sub OnTransactionCommit()
    Response.Write "<p><table border=1 width=350><tr><td>"
    Response.Write "<b>New account balance is " + _
        FormatCurrency(NewBalance)
    Response.Write "<p>The update was successful.</b>"
    Response.Write "</td></tr></table>"
End Sub

' The Transacted Script Abort Handler. This subroutine
' will be called if the transacted script aborts.

Sub OnTransactionAbort()
    Response.Write "<p><b>The update was not successful</b>."
End Sub
%>
```

Once again we start the ASP script with the @TRANSACTION directive. The script then proceeds to create one *Connection* object and two *Recordset* objects. It then uses a SELECT statement to obtain profile information from the customer table. The specific customer social security number is hard-coded in this example. Using the first *Recordset* object, the code changes the e-mail address for the customer and performs an update. Then, using the second *Recordset* object, the code uses a SELECT statement to obtain information about the customer's checking balance from the account_balance table. Finally, the customer's checking account balance is debited by $0.50 using the second *Recordset* object.

At the end of the ASP script, the event handlers are used to write a message to the browser to indicate whether the update was successful. If either the first or the second update failed (or both), the entire transaction is aborted automatically by MTS. This relieves the developer from having to write code to handle these scenarios. Because all the database operations have been placed into a single ASP Web page, they are made part of a single transaction. If both updates are successful, the transaction commits automatically when the script finishes execution. Figure 19-8 shows the resulting browser output after running the code.

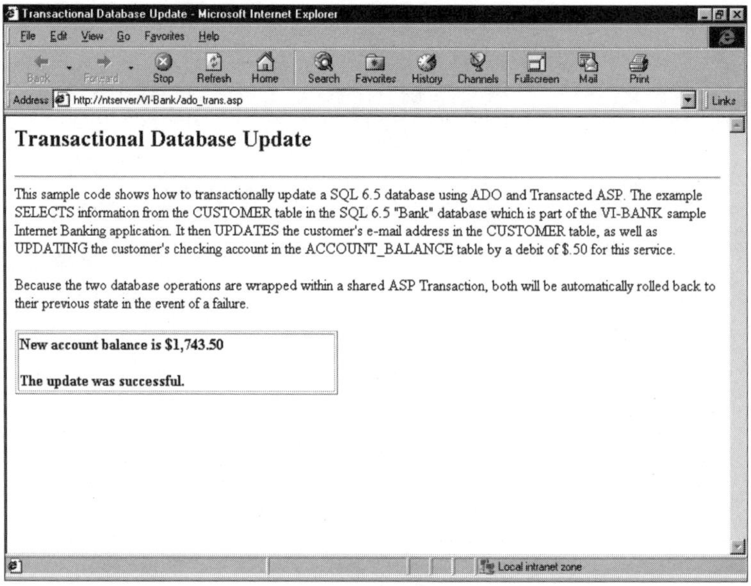

Figure 19-8. *Resulting browser output after running the code shown in Figure 19-7. This ASP Web page participates in a transaction using ADO against a SQL Server 6.5 database.*

SUMMARY

In this chapter, we've learned about transactional ASP Web pages and we've seen how an ASP Web page can be declared as transactional by using the @TRANSACTION directive at the top of the page. We've also covered several topics surrounding Microsoft Transaction Server, including transactions, packages, components, roles, interfaces, and methods. These are important topics that will help you in building n-tier, transactional applications. We've learned about the *ObjectContext* object and how it can be used from within ASP code to explicitly commit or abort a transaction. We've also seen how event handlers can be used in ASP code to automatically trap commits or aborts. Finally, we took another look at transactional ASP Web pages, this time using ADO and performing database operations against a SQL Server database. This chapter has set the groundwork for the next chapter, "Creating Transactional Components with Visual Basic 6.0," in which we'll be extending transactions from ASP Web pages into MTS components.

Chapter 20

Creating Transactional Components with Visual Basic 6.0

In Chapter 19, we learned about working with transactions within ASP Web pages. In this chapter, we'll see how to work with transactions within Microsoft Transaction Server (MTS) components that have been called from ASP Web pages. We'll use Microsoft Visual Basic 6.0 to develop these MTS components. We'll also take a quick look at transactional C/C++ components.

CREATING TRANSACTIONAL COMPONENTS

In this section, we'll create a server-side component using Visual Basic 6.0 and then place it under MTS control. We'll then create an ASP Web page to call the component, and we'll see how the ASP Web page and the component can work together in a single transaction.

Creating a Transactional Component

For our transactional component, we'll create an ActiveX dynamic-link library (DLL) project in Visual Basic 6.0 and define a class with one method—the *Transaction* class with the *CommitOrAbort* method—as shown in the following code.

```
' Filename: transaction.cls (mts_example.vbp)
'
' Description:  Transaction Class
'
' This file is provided as part of the "Programming Visual
' InterDev 6.0" CD-ROM.
'
' THIS CODE AND INFORMATION IS PROVIDED "AS IS" WITHOUT
' WARRANTY OF ANY KIND, EITHER EXPRESSED OR IMPLIED,
' INCLUDING BUT NOT LIMITED TO THE IMPLIED WARRANTIES
' OF MERCHANTABILITY AND/OR FITNESS FOR A PARTICULAR
' PURPOSE.
'
' Copyright (C) 1998 Microsoft Corporation. All rights reserved

Option Explicit

Public Function CommitOrAbort(ByVal TransType As Integer)

    Dim strResult As String

    On Error GoTo ErrorHandler

    Dim ctxObject As ObjectContext
    Set ctxObject = GetObjectContext()

    ' Take the appropriate action based on the TransType code.
    If TransType = 1 Then
        ' Commit
        ctxObject.SetComplete
        CommitOrAbort = "Committed"
    Else
        ' Abort
        ctxObject.SetAbort
        CommitOrAbort = "Aborted"
    End If

Exit Function

ErrorHandler:
```

(continued)

```
ctxObject.SetAbort

CommitOrAbort = "Aborted" ' Indicate that an error occurred.

Err.Raise Err.Number, "MtsExample.Transaction.CommitOrAbort", _
    Err.Description
```

End Function

The *CommitOrAbort* method takes an integer as input and then explicitly commits or aborts the transaction based on the input. If the value of the *TransType* variable is 1, it will commit; otherwise, it will abort. The method also returns a text string to the calling program describing the action that took place.

You'll notice that the method gets its current context by calling the *GetObjectContext* function. The context is stored in a *ContextObject* object variable named *ctxObject*. To commit the transaction, the method calls *ctxObject.SetComplete*, and to abort the transaction, it calls *ctxObject.SetAbort*.

The code for this example is contained on the CD-ROM under the transactions/VB98 folder in a Visual Basic 6.0 project named mts_example.vbp. After opening this project file, you should see a screen similar to that shown in Figure 20-1.

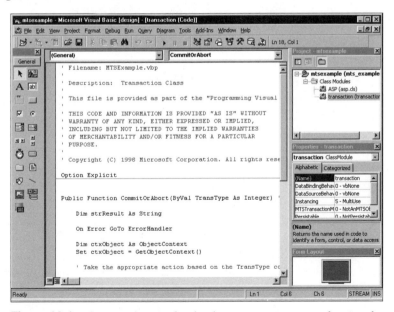

Figure 20-1. *The Visual Basic 6.0 development environment showing the transaction.cls class module within the mts_example.vbp project.*

If you are creating your own Visual Basic 6.0 ActiveX DLL project, make sure that the References dialog box includes a reference to the Microsoft Transaction Server Type Library, as shown in Figure 20-2. You'll also want to go into the Project Properties dialog box (by choosing Properties from the Project menu) and mark the project for Unattended Execution. In the case of our example project, both of these settings are already stored in the project file on the CD-ROM. To compile an ActiveX DLL for your project, simply choose Make from the File menu.

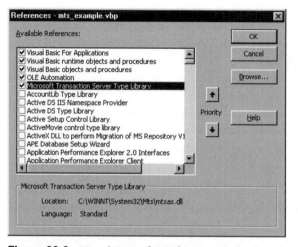

Figure 20-2. *Visual Basic 6.0 References dialog box showing the reference to the Microsoft Transaction Server Type Library.*

After compiling the project to make an ActiveX DLL (mts_example.dll), you'll need to install it within MTS. You can install it using the Transaction Server Explorer to create a package and then using the Component Wizard to import the already registered component. Alternatively, you can take the DLL that is supplied on the CD-ROM and choose the Install New Component option from the Component Wizard. Figure 20-3 shows the MTS Example package within the Transaction Server Explorer. For more detailed information on how to create packages and install components into MTS, see the section "Deploying Transactional Components," beginning on page 501.

For an MTS component to be transactional, it needs to have its transaction attribute defined within the Transaction Server Explorer. You can do this by right-clicking the component and choosing Properties. Next choose the Transaction tab, and select the Requires A Transaction radio button in the Transaction Support group box. Finally, choose OK and you're done—your transactional component has been installed into MTS.

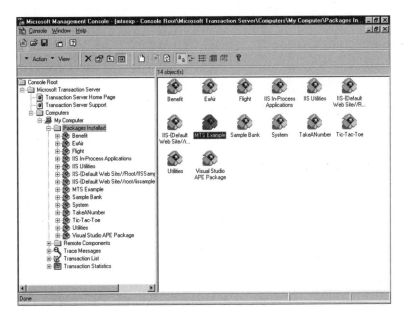

Figure 20-3. *The MTS Example package within the Transaction Server Explorer.*

Calling the Transactional Component from ASP

To call a transactional component from an ASP Web page, you simply use the *Server.CreateObject* syntax to instantiate the object and then you can reference its methods. Here is an example:

```
<%
Dim myObject
Set myObject = Server.CreateObject("mtsexample.transaction")
rtnString = myObject.CommitOrAbort(TransVal)
Response.Write "Return status is '" +  rtnString + "'.<p>"
%>
```

To continue our transactional component example, we'll look at an HTML page and an ASP Web page. The HTML page allows you to specify the action the component should take: whether it should commit or abort. The ASP Web page captures this input (sent via an HTML form) and sends the appropriate code to the *CommitOrAbort* method of the mtsexample.transaction component. The ASP Web page displays both the resulting status returned from the component and the final status of the entire transaction.

The code beginning on the following page shows the cmp_trans.htm page, which is in the transactions/VIntDev98 folder on the CD-ROM.

```
<HTML>
<HEAD>
<META NAME="GENERATOR" Content="Microsoft Visual Studio 6.0">
<TITLE>Simple Transactional Web Page Using ASP and Components</TITLE>
</HEAD>

<BODY BGCOLOR="White" topmargin="10" leftmargin="10">

<!-- Display Header -->

<font size="4" face="Arial, Helvetica">
<b>Simple Transactional Web Page Using ASP and Components</b>
</font><br>

<hr size="1" color="#000000">

<!-- Brief Description Blurb -->

This is a simple example demonstrating the basic
structure of a transacted Web page using ASP and components.
<p>
The ASP Web page calls the CommitOrAbort method in the
mtsexample.transaction component. You can make this
component either commit or abort by specifying the action
to take on the cmp_trans.htm page.
<p>

<!-- HTML Form so you can make the component either
commit or abort -->
Specify whether you would like the mtsexample.transaction
component to either commit or abort, and then click
the Submit button.
<FORM METHOD=POST ACTION="cmp_trans.asp">
<TABLE>
<TR>
<TD><input type="radio" checked name="TransFlg"
value="Commit">Commit</TD>
</TR>
<TR>
<TD><input type="radio" name="TransFlg" value="Abort">Abort</TD>
</TR>
<TR>
</TR>
<TR>
<TD>
<INPUT type="submit" name="Submit" value="Submit">
```

(continued)

```
</TD>
</TR>
</TABLE>
</FORM>

<p>

</BODY>
</HTML>
```

The cmp_trans.htm page simply sends the value of the currently selected radio button ("Commit" or "Abort") to the cmp_trans.asp page via an HTML form. The following code shows the cmp_trans.asp page.

```
<%@ TRANSACTION=Required LANGUAGE="VBScript" %>

<HTML>
<HEAD>
<META NAME="GENERATOR" Content="Microsoft Visual Studio 6.0">
<TITLE>Simple Transactional Web Page Using ASP and Components</TITLE>
</HEAD>

<BODY BGCOLOR="White" topmargin="10" leftmargin="10">

<!-- Display Header -->

<font size="4" face="Arial, Helvetica">
<b>Simple Transactional Web Page Using ASP and Components</b>
</font><br>

<hr size="1" color="#000000">

<!-- Brief Description Blurb -->
This is a simple example demonstrating the basic
structure of a transacted Web page using ASP and components.
<p>
The ASP Web page calls the CommitOrAbort method in the
mtsexample.transaction component. You can make this
component either commit or abort by specifying the action
to take on the cmp_trans.htm page.
<p>

<!-- Find out whether the users want to commit or abort. -->
<%
If Request.Form("TransFlg") = "Commit" Then
    TransVal = 1
```

(continued)

```
            Else
                TransVal = 0
            End If
        %>

        <!-- Instantiate the transaction component, and
            call the CommitOrAbort method. -->
        <%
        Dim myObject
        Set myObject = Server.CreateObject("mtsexample.transaction")
        rtnString = myObject.CommitOrAbort(TransVal)
        Response.Write "The component transaction status is '" + _
            rtnString + "'.<p>"
        %>

        </BODY>
        </HTML>

        <%
            ' The Transacted Script Commit Handler. This subroutine
            ' will be called if the transacted script commits.

            Sub OnTransactionCommit()
                Response.Write "<p><b>The transaction just committed</b>."
                Response.Write "This message came from the "
                Response.Write "OnTransactionCommit() event handler."
            End sub

            ' The Transacted Script Abort Handler. This subroutine
            ' will be called if the transacted script aborts.

            Sub OnTransactionAbort()
                Response.Write "<p><b>The transaction just aborted</b>."
                Response.Write "This message came from the "
                Response.Write "OnTransactionAbort() event handler."
            End sub
        %>
```

Notice in the code above that the value from the HTML form is obtained using the *Form* method of the *Request* object, as follows:

```
Request.Form("TransFlg")
```

The mtsexample.transaction component is instantiated using the *Server-.CreateObject* syntax, and the *CommitOrAbort* method is called with the *TransFlg* variable passed along as a parameter. Finally the ASP Web page prints out the return status from the *CommitOrAbort* method. When you run this page within your browser, after first choosing "Commit" from the HTML page, you'll see the resulting output, as shown in Figure 20-4.

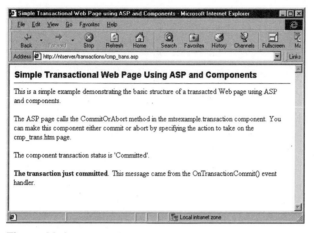

Figure 20-4. *Output from the cmp_trans.asp page after selecting to commit the transaction.*

You'll also notice from Figure 20-4 that the transaction as a whole completed successfully. Because the component's transaction was successful (that is, it fired the *SetComplete* method), the ASP Web page was able to capture the event in its *OnTransactionCommit* event handler. If you look at the Transaction Statistics within the Transaction Server Explorer, you'll see just one transaction for this entire process.

If you choose the Abort radio button from the HTML page, you see that the entire transaction aborts. The ASP Web page captures the event using the *OnTransactionAbort* event.

Using the Built-In ASP Objects from the Context Object

Within your Visual Basic server-side components, you can also use the context object to access the built-in ASP objects of Microsoft Internet Information Server (IIS). These are the *Request, Response, Server, Session,* and *Application* objects.

You can do this by using the *Item* method of the context object. The following example retrieves the value of the server name from the *ServerVariables* collection of the *Request* object. In the example on the following page, *oc* is the object variable for the context object.

```
Dim oc As ObjectContext
Set oc = GetObjectContext()
oc("Request").ServerVariables("SERVER_NAME")
```

The ability to access the built-in ASP objects from within a server-side Visual Basic component yields some interesting possibilities. For example, you can actually write output to the browser from your component—you don't have to return the output to your ASP code for processing. The following code shows you an example.

```
' Filename: asp.cls (mts_example.vbp)
'
' Description:  ASP Class
'
' This file is provided as part of the "Programming Visual
' InterDev 6.0" CD-ROM.
'
' THIS CODE AND INFORMATION IS PROVIDED "AS IS" WITHOUT
' WARRANTY OF ANY KIND, EITHER EXPRESSED OR IMPLIED,
' INCLUDING BUT NOT LIMITED TO THE IMPLIED WARRANTIES
' OF MERCHANTABILITY AND/OR FITNESS FOR A  PARTICULAR
' PURPOSE.
'
' Copyright (C) 1998 Microsoft Corporation. All rights reserved

Option Explicit

Public Function BuiltInAsp() As String

    Dim strResult As String

    On Error GoTo ErrorHandler

    ' Get the context object.
    Dim oc As ObjectContext
    Set oc = GetObjectContext()

    ' Print some text to the browser using the Response object.
    oc("Response").Write "<p>Here's some text from " & _
        "the Visual Basic component!</p>"

    ' Print the server name using the Request object.
    oc("Response").Write "<p>Server Name: " & _
        oc("Request").ServerVariables("SERVER_NAME") & "</p>"
```

(continued)

```
' Print the user's first name using the Request object.
oc("Response").Write "<p>First Name: " & _
    oc("Request").Form("FirstName") & "</p>"

oc.SetComplete

BuiltInAsp = "Committed"

Exit Function

ErrorHandler:

oc.SetAbort

BuiltInAsp = "Aborted" ' Indicate that an error occurred.

Err.Raise Err.Number, "MTSExample.ASP.BuiltInAsp", _
    Err.Description

End Function
```

The code for this example is contained on the CD-ROM under the transactions/VB98 folder in the Visual Basic 6.0 project named mts_example.vbp. This is the same project file that we looked at earlier in the chapter. The code is just stored in a class named *ASP* instead of in the previous class named *Transaction*.

You'll see from the code that there's a lot you can do by accessing the ASP built-in objects. The code uses the *Write* method of the *Response* object to send output to the browser. It prints a simple line of text, the server name from the *Request* object, and finally the value of the *FirstName* variable from an HTML form.

To run this example, you should choose the cmp_built-in.htm file from the transactions/VIntDev98 folder. This file captures the user's first name and then calls cmp_built-in.asp. The ASP file calls the *BuiltInAsp* method shown in the preceding code. You'll also want to install the mtsexample.asp component into MTS using the Transaction Server Explorer.

Notice that there's nothing significant about the names of these files or the names of the methods. They are just examples meant to demonstrate how to access the ASP built-in objects from within a server-side component. Figure 20-5 on the following page shows the output from this example as viewed within the browser. You'll notice that both the ASP Web page and the component are part of a transaction once again.

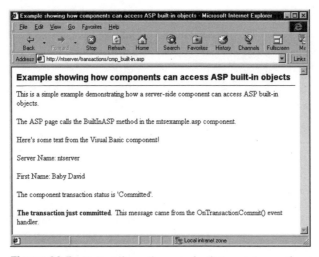

Figure 20-5. *Output from the cmp_built-in.asp page after entering "Baby David" for the user's first name in the cmp_built-in.htm page.*

An Overview of Transactional C/C++ Components

Working with transactions and the context object from C/C++ components is similar to Visual Basic—the syntax is just slightly different.

The *IObjectContext* interface provides access to the current object's context. You obtain a reference to the *IObjectContext* interface by calling the *GetObject-Context* function. As with any COM object, you must release an *ObjectContext* object when you're finished using it.

The *IObjectContext* interface exposes the following methods:

- *CreateInstance*

- *DisableCommit*

- *EnableCommit*

- *IsCallerInRole*

- *IsInTransaction*

- *IsSecurityEnabled*

- *SetAbort*

- *SetComplete*

These methods provide the same functionality as they do in Visual Basic. You'll notice that there is no *Item* method, as there is for Visual Basic. The *Item* method enabled us to access the ASP built-in objects and other context object properties. To do this within C/C++ components, you can use the *IGetContext-Properties* interface. This interface has a method called *GetProperty*.

The *IGetContextProperties* interface also has a method named *Count* that returns the number of context object properties and a method named *Enum-Names* that returns a reference to an enumerator that you can use to iterate through all the context object properties. You use the *EnumNames* method to obtain a reference to an enumerator object. The returned *IEnumNames* interface exposes several methods you can use to iterate through a list of BSTRs representing context object properties. Once you have a name, you can use the *GetProperty* method to obtain a reference to the context object property it represents.

DEPLOYING TRANSACTIONAL COMPONENTS

There are two methods of deploying transactional components: you can either deploy them using the Transaction Server Explorer or you can deploy them in a more automated fashion using Microsoft Visual InterDev 6.0. As we learned in Chapter 18, remote deployment for middle-tier COM server components is one of the exciting new features in Visual InterDev 6.0.

In this section, you'll learn how to perform both of these procedures. It's important to understand both techniques. Since Visual InterDev 6.0 allows you to remotely deploy these components from your workstation, you might want to modify some of the properties of your packages and components. These types of configuration operations can be performed only by using the Transaction Server Explorer.

Using the Transaction Server Explorer

Using the Transaction Server Explorer to deploy a transactional component requires that you first create a package and then install the component into that package. You'll also need to configure various properties of the package and its components.

First access the Transaction Server Explorer by choosing Start | Programs | Windows NT 4.0 Option Pack | Microsoft Transaction Server | Transaction Server Explorer or by choosing Start | Programs | Windows NT 4.0 Option Pack | Microsoft Internet Information Server | Internet Service Manager. Both of these options will launch the Microsoft Management Console. The following steps illustrate how to create a package:

1. Open the folder named Computers.

2. Open the icon named My Computer.

3. Right-click the Packages Installed folder, and select New | Package from the context menu.

4. In the Package Wizard, click the Create An Empty Package button. (See Figure 20-6.)

5. Enter a name for the new package.

6. Click Next.

7. On the Set Package Identity step, select Interactive User.

8. Click Finish.

You should now see an icon representing your new package under the Packages Installed folder.

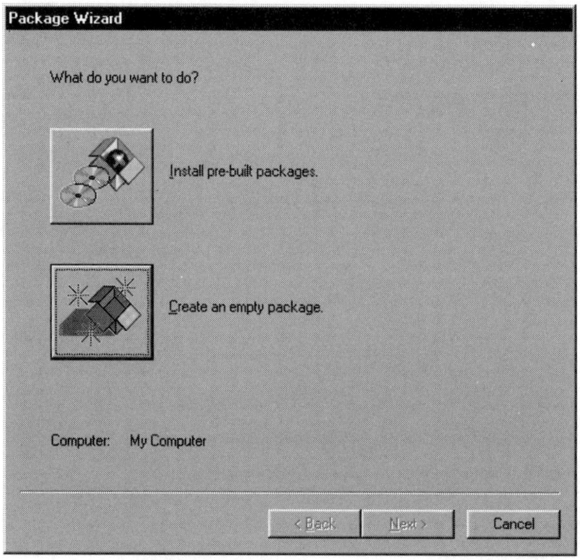

Figure 20-6. *The Package Wizard allows you either to create an empty package or to install prebuilt packages.*

If you want to adjust any of the properties of your package, simply right-click the package and choose Properties to bring up the Properties dialog box. This dialog box has five tab folders for configuring the general, security, advanced, identity, and activation properties.

On the General tab, you can change the name of the package and add a description. On the Security tab, you can enable authorization checking and specify the authentication level for calls. The Advanced tab allows you to specify how the server process should be shut down. You can either keep the process running when idle or have the process shut down after a certain number of minutes of inactivity.

> **NOTE** When developing and testing your components, it's worth setting the value on the Advanced tab to 1 minute so that the process is shut down quickly after execution. This will enable you to compile other versions of the component and stage them within MTS without having to wait as long for the process to shut down.

The Identity tab is used to specify which account the process will run under. This can either be the currently logged on user or another Microsoft Windows NT user account that you specify. Finally, the Activation tab allows you to choose the activation type for your package. This can either be a library package or a server package. Server packages are recommended because they allow the component to be activated in a dedicated server process.

Now that you have created your package, you can install your component. The following steps illustrate how to achieve this:

1. Start the Transaction Server Explorer.

2. Open the icon representing your new package.

3. Right-click the folder labeled Components in the left-hand pane, and select New Component from the context menu.

4. In the Component Wizard, click the Install New Component button.

5. In the Install Components dialog box, click Add Files.

6. Use the Select Files To Install dialog box to navigate to the folder holding your ActiveX DLL. Select the DLL and click Open. You can continue adding components to the package if you wish.

7. In the Install Components dialog box, click Finish. One or more icons, representing each of the various classes within your component, will appear beneath the folder labeled Components.

After installing the component, you'll need to configure the properties of the component. The following steps show how to achieve this:

1. Right-click the icon representing your new component, and select Properties from the context menu to display the Properties dialog box, shown in Figure 20-7 on the following page.

2. Select the Transaction tab of the Properties dialog box, as shown in Figure 20-8 on page 505.

3. Select Requires A Transaction, and click OK.

4. Right-click the folder labeled Roles underneath your package in the left-hand pane, and select New | Role from the context menu.

5. In the New Role dialog box, type in the word *Administrator*.

6. Open the Roles folder to display the icon representing your new role.

7. Open the Administrator role icon to display the folder labeled Users.

8. Right-click the Users folder, and select New | User from the context menu.

9. Use the Add Users And Groups To Role dialog box to assign permissions. For testing purposes, you can simply select the group named Everyone from the list.

10. Click Add, and then click OK. An icon representing the group will appear beneath the Users folder.

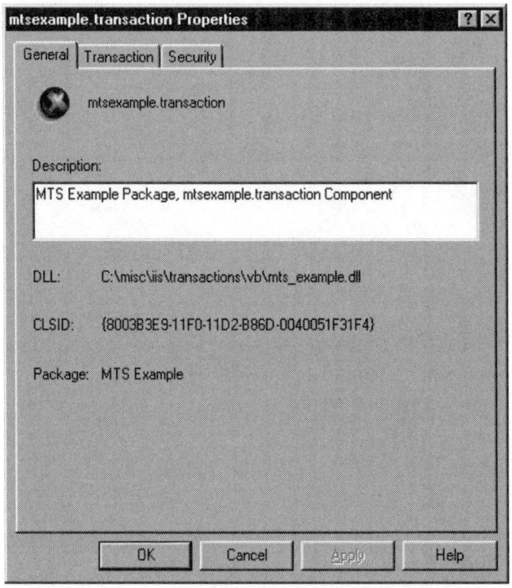

Figure 20-7. *The General tab of the Properties dialog box for a component within the Transaction Server Explorer.*

Your component is now ready for use! Figure 20-7 shows the General tab in the Properties dialog box. Here you'll notice the name of the DLL is listed as well as the CLSID and the package name. The CLSID is the component's class ID. This is the universally unique identifier (UUID) that identifies the component. The CLSID is stored in the Windows Registry. Figure 20-8 shows the Transaction tab of the Properties dialog box.

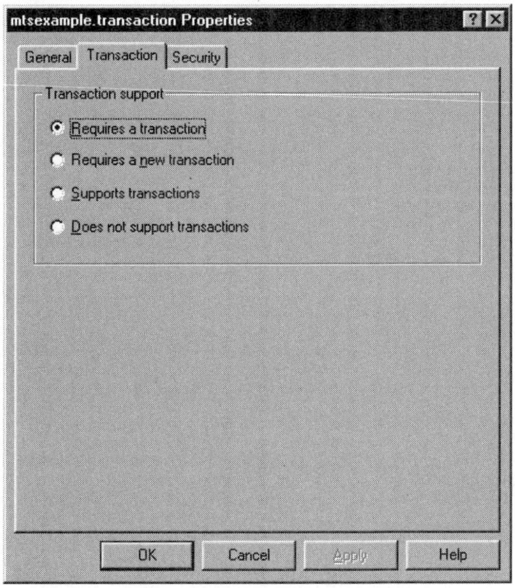

Figure 20-8. *The Transaction tab of the Properties dialog box for a component within the Transaction Server Explorer.*

Figure 20-9 on the following page shows the Transaction Server Explorer after we have created a package named MTS Example, installed components named mtsexample.ASP and mtsexample.transaction (both part of the mtsexample.dll ActiveX component that we created earlier), and added an Administrator role and associated users to the package.

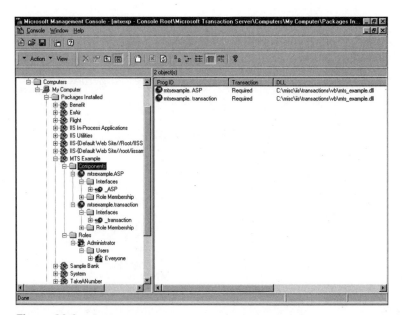

Figure 20-9. *The Transaction Server Explorer showing the components and roles that have been set up for the MTS Example package.*

Using Visual InterDev 6.0

Now that we've seen how to deploy a component using the Transaction Server Explorer, let's take a look at the equivalent operation within Visual InterDev 6.0. The first step is to add your component to a Web project. The following steps show how to achieve this:

1.   Open up your Web project.

2.   Create a folder named Components under your Web project. (This step is not required but is good practice so that your middle-tier components are kept separate from your HTML and ASP code.)

3.   Prepare to add the component to the Components folder by right-clicking the folder and choosing Add | Add Item from the context menu.

4.   In the Add Item dialog box, choose the Existing tab.

5.   Locate your ActiveX DLL file, and choose Open.

Your component will now be added to your Web project.

Now that the component has been added to your Web project, you are ready to install it in Microsoft Transaction Server. You can do so by following these steps:

1. Right-click the component, and choose Properties from the drop-down menu.

2. Choose the Component Installation tab of the Properties dialog box.

3. Check the Register On Server and Add To Microsoft Transaction Server Package check boxes, as shown in Figure 20-10.

4. In the Package Name text box, enter the name of the package to add the component to.

5. Select the transaction support option appropriate for your component, and choose OK.

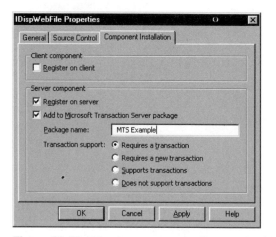

Figure 20-10. *The Component Installation tab of the component Properties dialog box within Visual InterDev 6.0.*

When you enter a package name, you can either enter the name of an existing package within MTS or you can specify a new package and have Visual InterDev request MTS to create it for you. You'll remember from the discussion of transactional ASP in Chapter 19 that there are four available options for specifying transaction support. Table 20-1 on the following page summarizes these options.

Option	Action
Requires A Transaction	Set the component's objects to execute within the scope of a transaction regardless of whether the client has a transaction.
Requires A New Transaction	Create a new transaction for the component's objects to execute within regardless of whether the client has a transaction.
Supports Transactions	Set the component's objects to execute within the scope of the client's transaction.
Does Not Support Transactions	Set the component's objects to run without a transaction regardless of whether the client has a transaction.

Table 20-1. *Transaction support options available on the Component Installation tab of the component Properties dialog box within Visual InterDev 6.0.*

After you select OK, the component will be registered on the server and will be added into MTS under the appropriate package with the appropriate transaction support option that you specified. You'll be able to see the sequence of events by watching the status bar in the lower left-hand corner of the screen.

THE INTERNET BANKING EXAMPLE

Throughout this chapter, we've seen several short examples of how to create transactional components and how to call them from within ASP Web pages. In this section, we'll consolidate what we've learned in this and earlier chapters by taking a look at an example that combines all of these techniques in a practical and fully functioning application.

We'll again use the VI-Bank sample application, which is located on the CD-ROM under the VI-Bank folder. Remember that the Visual Basic files are located under the VI-Bank/VB98 folder and the Visual InterDev files are located under the VI-Bank/VIntDev98 folder. The necessary Microsoft SQL Server 6.5 database for this example is also on the CD-ROM under the VI-Bank/SQL folder. Complete installation instructions are included on the CD-ROM.

The example that we'll look at is the part of the VI-Bank application that allows for the transfer of funds. A customer at the bank is able to transfer funds between any of his or her existing accounts. Figure 20-11 shows the initial screen.

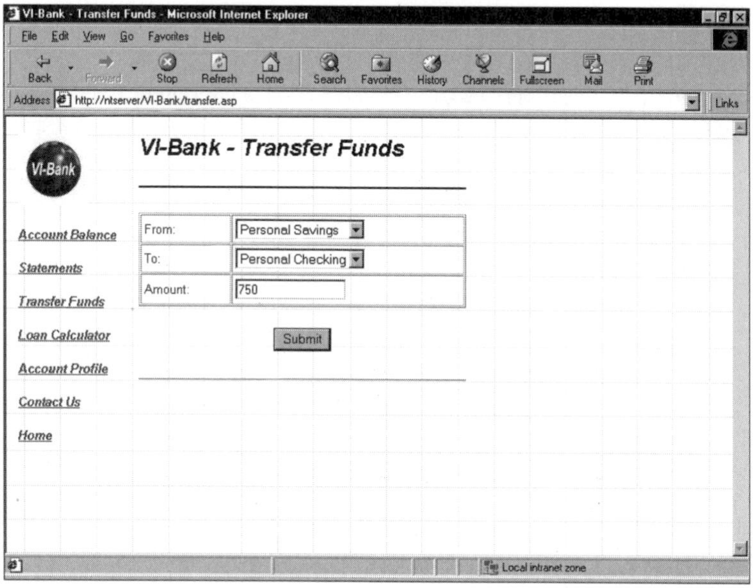

Figure 20-11. *The Transfer Funds page of the VI-Bank sample application.*

There are two parts to this application:

- **Server-side ActiveX components** These are installed into MTS and perform the actual transfer of funds and interact with the database.

- **The ASP presentation layer** This displays the names of the accounts available to the user, captures user input, and presents the results of the transaction to the user.

Visual Basic Components

The source code for the transfer.cls file appears below. This file is part of the VI-Bank.vbp project and has a method named *Transfer* that is called from within the ASP code.

```
' Filename: VI-Bank.vbp (Transfer.cls)
'
' Description:  Transfer Class
'
' This file is provided as part of the "Programming Visual
' InterDev 6.0" CD-ROM.
'
```

(continued)

```
' THIS CODE AND INFORMATION IS PROVIDED "AS IS" WITHOUT
' WARRANTY OF ANY KIND, EITHER EXPRESSED OR IMPLIED,
' INCLUDING BUT NOT LIMITED TO THE IMPLIED WARRANTIES
' OF MERCHANTABILITY AND/OR FITNESS FOR A PARTICULAR
' PURPOSE.
'
' Copyright (C) 1998 Microsoft Corporation. All rights reserved

Option Explicit

Private Const ERROR_NUMBER = vbObjectError + 0
Private Const APP_ERROR = -2147467008

Public Function Transfer(ByVal lngAmount As Long, _
    ByVal lngAccountTo As Long, ByVal lngAccountFrom As Long) _
    As String

    Dim strResult As String

    On Error GoTo ErrorHandler

    ' Check for security.
    If (lngAmount > 500 Or lngAmount < -500) Then
        If Not GetObjectContext.IsCallerInRole("Administrator") Then
            Err.Raise Number:=APP_ERROR, Description:= _
                "Need 'Administrator' role for amounts over $500"
        End If
    End If

    ' Create the account object using our context.
    Dim objAccount As VIBank.Account
    Set objAccount = GetObjectContext.CreateInstance("VIBank.Account")

    If objAccount Is Nothing Then
        Err.Raise ERROR_NUMBER, _
            Description:="Could not create account object"
    End If

    ' Call the Transaction function.
    Dim strCredit As String, strDebit As String

    ' Apply the credit to the "To" account.
    strCredit = objAccount.Transaction(lngAccountTo, lngAmount)

    If strCredit = "" Then
        Err.Raise ERROR_NUMBER, Description:=strCredit
```

(continued)

```
    Else
        ' Apply the debit to the "From" account.
        strDebit = objAccount.Transaction(lngAccountFrom, _
            0 - lngAmount)
        If strDebit = "" Then
            Err.Raise ERROR_NUMBER, _
                Description:=strDebit      ' Debit failed
        Else
            strResult = strCredit + "   " + strDebit
        End If
    End If
End If

GetObjectContext.SetComplete

' Return the results of the transfer.
Transfer = strResult

Exit Function

ErrorHandler:

GetObjectContext.SetAbort

Transfer = ""      ' Indicate that an error occurred.

Err.Raise Err.Number, "VIBank.Transfer.Transfer", _
    Err.Description

End Function
```

You can see from the above code that the *Transfer* method is passed the amount for the transfer and the relevant account numbers to credit and debit. The first thing the code does is ensure that the caller of the method is in the correct role. Only callers in the Administrator role are allowed to perform transfers of more than $500. This code is a great way to secure your server-side components and to make sure that only authorized callers can execute their methods. You'll remember that the roles can be set up from within the Transaction Server Explorer.

The next step for the code is to create an instance of the *Account* object. This object is used to perform the actual database access, as we shall see later in the chapter. After instantiating the *Account* object, the code calls its *Transaction* method twice: once for the credit and once for the debit. If all is successful, the code calls the *SetComplete* method to commit the transaction and returns a string to the calling application.

The source code for the account.cls file begins beneath the note below. This class contains the *Transaction* function. You'll notice within the code that the File DSN, VI-Bank, of the SQL Server database is set in the *strConnect* constant. The *Transaction* function takes an account number and a dollar amount as input. It again checks to see that the caller is in the appropriate role by using the *IsCallerInRole* method of the context object.

> **NOTE** If you want to make your code a little more flexible, you should externalize the role names so they are not hard-coded in your components. One way to externalize the role names is to place them in the database and have your code perform a query. This way you can make changes to the security of your components without having to rewrite and recompile your code.

```
' Filename: Account.cls (VI-Bank.vbp)
'
' Description:  Account Class
'
' This file is provided as part of the "Programming Visual
' InterDev 6.0" CD-ROM.
'
' THIS CODE AND INFORMATION IS PROVIDED "AS IS" WITHOUT
' WARRANTY OF ANY KIND, EITHER EXPRESSED OR IMPLIED,
' INCLUDING BUT NOT LIMITED TO THE IMPLIED WARRANTIES
' OF MERCHANTABILITY AND/OR FITNESS FOR A PARTICULAR
' PURPOSE.
'
' Copyright (C) 1998 Microsoft Corporation. All rights reserved

Option Explicit

Private Const ERROR_NUMBER = vbObjectError + 0
Private Const APP_ERROR = -2147467008
Private Const strConnect = "FILEDSN=VI-Bank"

Public Function Transaction(ByVal lngAccountNo As Long, _
    ByVal lngAmount As Long) As String

    Dim strResult As String

    On Error GoTo ErrorHandler

    ' Check for security.
    If (lngAmount > 500 Or lngAmount < -500) Then
        If Not GetObjectContext.IsCallerInRole("Administrator") Then
```

(continued)

```
          Err.Raise Number:=APP_ERROR, Description:= _
              "Need 'Administrator' role for amounts over $500"
        End If
    End If


    ' Obtain the ADO environment and connection.

    Dim adoConn As New ADODB.Connection
    Dim varRows As Variant

    adoConn.Open strConnect

    ' Update the Account_Balance table given the Account Number.
    Dim strSQL As String
    strSQL = "UPDATE Account_Balance SET Balance = Balance + " _
        + Str$(lngAmount) + " WHERE Account_No = " + _
        Str$(lngAccountNo)


TryAgain:

    adoConn.Execute strSQL, varRows

    ' If anything else happens,
    On Error GoTo ErrorHandler

    ' Get resulting balance.
    strSQL = "SELECT Balance FROM Account_Balance WHERE " + _
        "Account_No = " + Str$(lngAccountNo)

    Dim adoRS As ADODB.Recordset
    Set adoRS = adoConn.Execute(strSQL)
    If adoRS.EOF Then
        Err.Raise Number:=APP_ERROR, Description:= _
            "Error. Account " + Str$(lngAccountNo) + _
            " not on file."
    End If

    Dim lngBalance As Long
    lngBalance = adoRS.Fields("Balance").Value

    ' Check if account is overdrawn.
    If (lngBalance) < 0 Then
        Err.Raise Number:=APP_ERROR, Description:= _
            "Error. Account " + Str$(lngAccountNo) + _
            " would be overdrawn by " + _
```

(continued)

```
                          Str$(lngBalance) + ". Balance is still " + _
                          Str$(lngBalance - lngAmount) + "."
              Else
                  If lngAmount < 0 Then
                      strResult = strResult & "Debit from account " & _
                          lngAccountNo & ", "
                  Else
                      strResult = strResult & "Credit to account " & _
                          lngAccountNo & ", "
                  End If

                  ' Now insert the transaction into the Account_Transaction
                  ' table. Use the strResult variable as the entry for the
                  ' transaction description.

                  strSQL = "INSERT INTO Account_Transaction " + _
                      " (account_no, description, check_no, " + _
                      "transaction_code_id, amount, date) VALUES (" + _
                      Str$(lngAccountNo) + ", '" + strResult + _
                      "','T', 3," + Str$(lngAmount) + ", GETDATE())"
                  Set adoRS = adoConn.Execute(strSQL)

                  strResult = strResult + "balance is $" & _
                      Str$(lngBalance) & "."
              End If

          ' Clean up.
          Set adoRS = Nothing
          Set adoConn = Nothing

          GetObjectContext.SetComplete

          Transaction = strResult

      Exit Function

      ErrorHandler:

          ' Clean up.
          If Not adoRS Is Nothing Then
              Set adoRS = Nothing
          End If
          If Not adoConn Is Nothing Then
              Set adoConn = Nothing
          End If
```

(continued)

```
GetObjectContext.SetAbort

Transaction = ""        ' Indicate that an error occurred.

Err.Raise Err.Number, "VIBank.Account.Transaction", _
    Err.Description

End Function
```

Using ADO, the code first performs a SQL update to the Account_Balance table and then checks to ensure that the account is not overdrawn. Finally, it performs a SQL insert into the Account_Transaction table, which keeps a log of all account activity. It then calls the *SetComplete* method to commit the transaction and returns a result string to the calling component—in this case, the *Transfer* function in the *Transfer* object.

In a real-life banking application, you'd probably want to issue a receipt number to the end user to provide a way of tracing the transaction. For the sake of brevity, we omitted this step in our example.

Visual InterDev Components

We'll now turn our attention to the Visual InterDev portion of this application. We'll look at the ASP Web page that drives the entire transfer of funds process. You saw the initial screen in Figure 20-11. This ASP Web page is self-posting and has two states. The first state occurs when the page is first loaded into the browser. The second state occurs after the user has entered data and submitted the funds transfer. The state of the page is determined by using the *REQUEST_METHOD* environment variable. The entire source code for the ASP Web page named transfer.asp appears below. This page is part of the VI-Bank Web project.

```
<%@ TRANSACTION=Required Language=VBScript%>
<% ' VI 6.0 Scripting Object Model Enabled %>
<!--#include file="_ScriptLibrary/pm.asp"-->
<% if StartPageProcessing() Then Response.End() %>
<FORM name=thisForm METHOD=post>

<html>
<head>
<meta NAME="GENERATOR" Content="Microsoft Visual Studio 6.0">
<title>VI-Bank - Transfer Funds</title>
<LINK REL="stylesheet" TYPE="text/css"
    HREF="_Themes/blueprnt/THEME.CSS" VI6.0THEME="Blueprint">
```

(continued)

```
<LINK REL="stylesheet" TYPE="text/css"
    HREF="_Themes/blueprnt/GRAPH0.CSS" VI6.0THEME="Blueprint">
<LINK REL="stylesheet" TYPE="text/css"
    HREF="_Themes/blueprnt/COLOR0.CSS" VI6.0THEME="Blueprint">
<LINK REL="stylesheet" TYPE="text/css"
    HREF="_Themes/blueprnt/CUSTOM.CSS" VI6.0THEME="Blueprint">
</head>
<body>

<%
RequestMethod = Request.ServerVariables("REQUEST_METHOD")
%>

<!-- Recordset DTC Control (SQL shown below) -->
<!--METADATA TYPE="DesignerControl" startspan
<OBJECT classid="clsid:9CF5D7C2-EC10-11D0-9862-0000F8027CA0"
    id=rsAccountCode style="LEFT: 0px; TOP: 0px">
...
</OBJECT>
-->
...
cmdTmp.CommandText = 'SELECT Account_Code.Account_Description,
    Account_Balance.account_no, Customer.ssn FROM Account_Code
    INNER JOIN Account_Balance ON Account_Code.Account_Id =
    Account_Balance.account_id INNER JOIN Customer ON
    Account_Balance.ssn = Customer.ssn WHERE
    (Customer.ssn = 123456789)';
...
<!--METADATA TYPE="DesignerControl" endspan-->

<!-- Table used for general page formatting -->
<table>
<tr valign=top>
<td width=125>
<!--#INCLUDE FILE="menu.htm"-->
</td>
<td>

<h2><FONT COLOR="navy"><I>VI-Bank - Transfer Funds</I></FONT></h2>
<HR color=navy>
<p>
<form METHOD="post" ACTION="transfer.asp">

<table border="1" cellPadding="3" cellSpacing="1" width="350">
<tr>
```

(continued)

516

```
<td><font face ="" size="2">From:</font></td>
<td>

<!-- Data-Bound ListBox DTC Control (AccountFrom) -->
<!--METADATA TYPE="DesignerControl" startspan

<OBJECT classid="clsid:B5F0E450-DC5F-11D0-9846-0000F8027CA0"
    height=21 id=AccountFrom style="HEIGHT: 21px; LEFT: 0px; TOP:
    0px; WIDTH: 96px" width=96>
...
</OBJECT>
-->
...
<!--METADATA TYPE="DesignerControl" endspan-->

</td></tr>
<tr>
<td><font face ="" size="2">To:</font></td>
<td>

<!-- Data-Bound ListBox DTC Control (AccountTo) -->
<!--METADATA TYPE="DesignerControl" startspan

<OBJECT classid="clsid:B5F0E450-DC5F-11D0-9846-0000F8027CA0"
    height=21 id=AccountTo style=
    "HEIGHT: 21px; LEFT: 0px; TOP: 0px; WIDTH: 96px" width=96>
</OBJECT>
-->
...
<!--METADATA TYPE="DesignerControl" endspan-->

</td></tr>
<tr>
<td><font face ="" size="2">Amount:</font></td>
<td>
<% If RequestMethod = "POST" Then %>
    <!-- Show the previously entered amount. -->
    <input id="Amount" name="Amount" value=
        <%=Request.Form("Amount")%> size="15"></td></tr>
<% Else %>

    <input id="Amount" name="Amount" size="15"></td></tr>
<% End If %>
</table>
<p>
```

(continued)

```
<table width="350">
<tr><td>
<div align="center"><input id="submit" name="submit"
    type="submit" value="Submit"></div>
</td></tr>
</table>

</form>
<hr>

<%
' Ensure that this page has been submitted.
If RequestMethod = "POST" THEN
%>
<P>
<table BORDER="1" width="350">
<tr></tr>
<tr><td>
<I>
<font face ="" size="2">
<%
' Check that the From and the To accounts are different.
If AccountFrom.getText() = AccountTo.getText() Then
    Response.Write ("<P>")
    Response.Write ("Please choose different accounts " + _
        "to transfer money between.")
    Response.Write ("<P>")
Else
    ' Check that the user has entered a value in the Amount field.
    If Request.Form("Amount") <> "" Then
        ' Set a variable to indicate the transaction
        ' is taking place.
        Transaction_Flag = "Y"

        ' Write out some summary information about the transfer.
        Response.Write "<P>"
        Response.Write "Transfer " + _
            FormatCurrency(Request.Form("Amount"))
        Response.Write " from " + AccountFrom.getText() + _
            "(" + CStr(AccountFrom.getValue()) + ")"
        Response.Write " to " + AccountTo.getText() + _
            "(" + CStr(AccountTo.getValue()) + ")<P>"
        %>
        <OBJECT id=oTransfer PROGID =VIBank.Transfer RUNAT=Server>
        </OBJECT>
        <%
```

(continued)

```
        ' Call the Transfer method of the VIBank.Transfer component.
        strResult = _
            oTransfer.Transfer(CLng(Request.Form("Amount")), _
                CLng(AccountTo.getValue()), _
                CLng(AccountFrom.getValue()) )
        Response.Write strResult
    Else
        Response.Write ("<P>")
        Response.Write _
            ("Please enter a value for the amount of the transfer.")
        Response.Write ("<P>")
    End If
End If
%>

</I></FONT>
</td></tr>
<tr></tr>
</table>

<% End If %>

</td></td>

</tr>
</table>

</body>
<% ' VI 6.0 Scripting Object Model Enabled %>
<% EndPageProcessing() %>
</FORM>
</html>
<%
' The Transacted Script Commit Handler. This subroutine
' will be called if the transacted script commits.

Sub OnTransactionCommit()
    If RequestMethod = "POST" Then
        If Transaction_Flag = "Y" Then
            Response.Write "<p><center>Your transaction " + _
                was successfully completed.</center>"
        Else
            Response.Write "<p><center>Your transaction " + _
                was not completed.</center>"
```

(continued)

```
        End If
    End If
End Sub

' The Transacted Script Abort Handler. This subroutine
' will be called if the transacted script aborts.

Sub OnTransactionAbort()
    If RequestMethod = "POST" Then
        Response.Write "<p><center>Your transaction was " + _
            "not completed.</center>"
    End If
End Sub
%>
```

The transfer.asp page is interesting because there's so much going on. Not only does the page maintain its state, it also has to query the database, display the users' account descriptions in data-bound design-time controls (DTCs), call the *Transfer* function within MTS, and display the results of the transaction on screen. Note that the code for the DTCs has been trimmed down for clarity's sake. There's a *Recordset* DTC that performs the initial SQL select statement to get the users' account descriptions. There are also two data-bound Listbox DTCs that are used to display these account descriptions on screen. The dollar amount that the user wants to transfer is captured using a standard text box.

After the user presses the Submit button to submit the form, the selected account information is determined by using the *getValue* and *getText* methods of the list box DTCs. This information is then passed as parameters into the *Transfer* method to perform the transfer. The ASP code also includes some error checking to ensure that the user has entered a value in the Amount field and that the "From" and "To" accounts are different. In a production system, you might want to move some of this error checking to the client side and also trap for non-numeric input in the Amount field.

Finally, the transfer.asp page uses the familiar *OnTransactionCommit* and *OnTransactionAbort* event handlers to capture the success or failure of the transaction. This will be determined by the server-side components and by whether the database has been updated correctly. Figure 20-12 shows the results of a successful transaction, while Figure 20-13 shows the results of an unsuccessful transaction. In Figure 20-13, the transaction was rolled back because the transfer would have overdrawn the user's savings account.

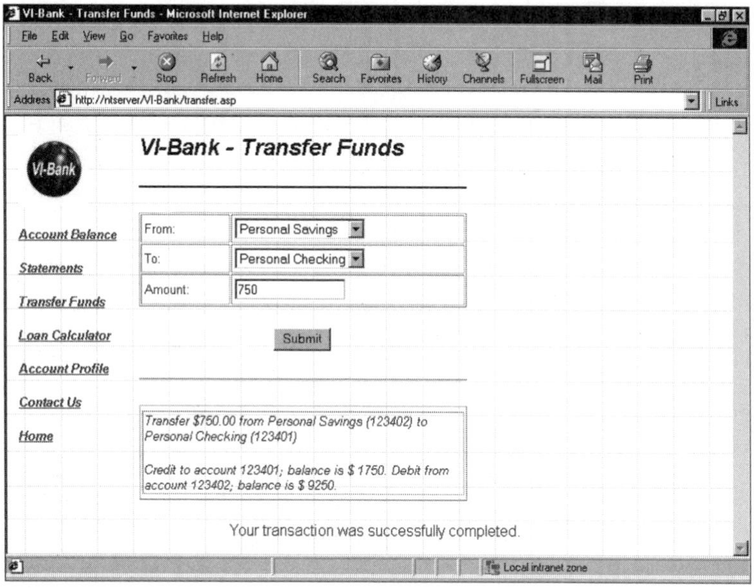

Figure 20-12. *The Transfer Funds page of the VI-Bank sample application after a successful transfer.*

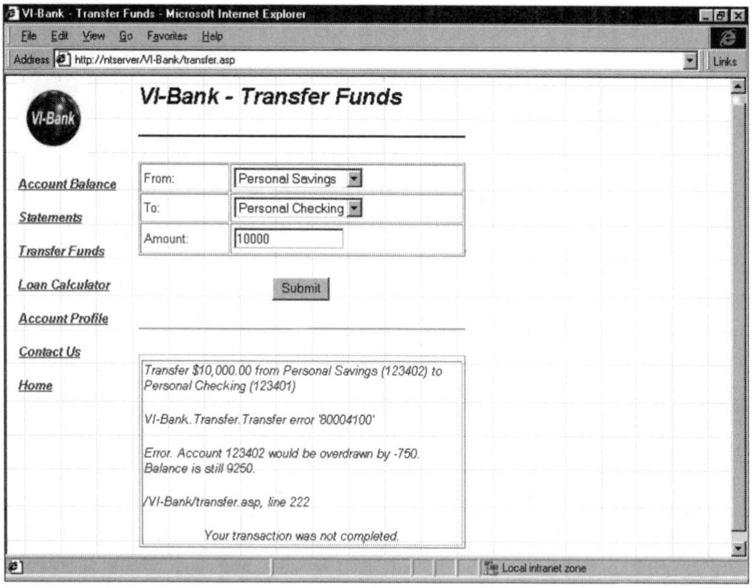

Figure 20-13. *The Transfer Funds page of the VI-Bank sample application after an unsuccessful transfer.*

SUMMARY

In this chapter, we've learned how to work with transactional components: how to create them, how to declare them as transactional, and how to deploy them by using the Transaction Server Explorer or Visual InterDev 6.0.

We've also seen how components can communicate via the context object to signal their completion status and how the context object can be used within a component to access the ASP built-in objects. The context object is a powerful mechanism for working with transactions—it provides a rich set of methods for you to perform the following actions:

- You can declare an object's work complete.

- You can prevent a transaction from being committed.

- You can instantiate other MTS objects and include their work within the scope of the current object's transaction.

- You can retrieve Internet Information Server built-in objects and other important methods.

There's a lot more to discover about Microsoft Transaction Server and the creation and deployment of transactional components within your Visual InterDev Web projects. One of the best ways to learn is to actually use all the products together and experiment with a variety of techniques. You can also run the many code examples included on the CD-ROM accompanying this book.

Chapter 21

Using Microsoft Message Queue Server in ASP

INTRODUCTION

In this chapter, we'll take a look at Microsoft Message Queue Server (MSMQ). First we'll take a look at its features, installation, and management; then we'll look at how you can communicate with MSMQ in your Microsoft Visual InterDev applications by using the MSMQ server-side components.

MICROSOFT MESSAGE QUEUE SERVER

MSMQ is provided as part of the Microsoft Windows NT 4.0 Option Pack. The purpose of MSMQ is to provide *loosely coupled* and *reliable* network communications services based on a messaging queuing model. MSMQ makes it easy to integrate applications, implement a push-style business-event delivery environment between applications, and build reliable applications that work over unreliable but cost-effective networks.

You can think of MSMQ as a type of automated e-mail system between computers. MSMQ is able to deliver messages from one application to another in an asynchronous manner. This means that messages are queued up for delivery and do not require the client application to wait for delivery to be completed. The client application—and the end user—are both free to move on to other activities. Once the message has been sent to the message queue, it is guaranteed to be delivered to its recipient.

MSMQ is important because there are many business situations that require an asynchronous message delivery model. For example, let's say a customer places an order. Once the customer has placed the order, the system needs to guarantee that the order is passed to fulfillment and then shipped to the customer. This process can take place asynchronously so that the customer on the telephone (or on the Web site) does not need to wait for all the relevant processing to occur. Another example might be that of an insurance agent. The agent could go to a customer's home with his or her laptop and take an order for an insurance policy. When the agent returns to the office and connects to the network, MSMQ will forward the order to headquarters for processing. MSMQ can also inform the agent via a confirmation message that prior policy orders have been placed.

MSMQ features include the following:

- Full COM support, dynamic directory service-based architecture, and centralized systems management.

- Comprehensive message queuing functionality, such as resilient message delivery, cost-based message routing, and full support for transactions. MSMQ also offers interoperability with other message queuing products, such as IBM's MQSeries, through products from Level 8 Systems, Inc.

- Complete integration with other Windows NT features, such as Microsoft Transaction Server (MTS), Microsoft Internet Information Server (IIS), Windows NT clustering services, and the Windows NT security environment.

Message Queue Concepts

Figure 21-1 shows the MSMQ message queuing model. When a message is sent from one application to another it is placed in a queue. This can be either a local queue (for example, on an independent client) or a queue on another message server. The queue can be considered a mail box that holds the messages. Once the message has been sent to the queue, it can be considered delivered. MSMQ will ensure that the message is routed from the queue to the receiving application.

Messages can be prioritized so that more important messages take precedence over lower priority messages. The priority can take a value anywhere from 0 to 7. The default priority is 3, and the highest priority is 7.

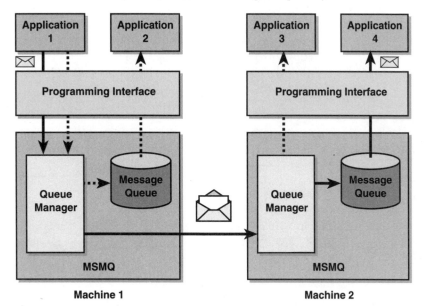

Figure 21-1. *MSMQ message queuing model.*

Public and private queues

MSMQ has two types of queues that you can use in your applications: public queues and private queues. A public queue is replicated throughout the MSMQ enterprise configuration using the MSMQ Information Server (MQIS). The queue can be searched for and queried by any applications using MSMQ. Private queues can be accessed only by applications that have access to the full path or format name of the queue. In the default view, the MSMQ Explorer does not display private queues.

Types of message queues

In addition to the public and private queues, there are several queues that MSMQ uses as part of the messaging process. These queues are listed below:

- Journal Queues
- Dead-Letter Queues
- Transaction Dead-Letter Queues

- Administration Queues
- Report Queues
- System Queues

Each of the above queues is simply a standard queue used for a particular purpose. These queues are used to separate out various types of messages that fall into the particular categories that are described below.

Journal queues

Journal queues are used to store a copy of a message in a process called journaling. There are two types of journaling available: source and target. Source journaling is the process of storing a copy of an outgoing message. Target journaling is the process of storing a copy of an incoming message.

Dead-letter queues

Messages that have expired or are undeliverable are stored in dead-letter queues. A nontransactional message that cannot reach the destination application is stored in a dead-letter queue on the computer on which the message expired (or failed).

Transaction dead-letter queues

A transactional message that cannot reach the destination application is stored in the transaction dead-letter queue on the source computer. Transaction dead-letter queues are created for each independent client and server on your MSMQ network when MSMQ is installed on that computer. The MSMQ Explorer displays these queues as Xact Dead Letter, under the computer.

Administration queues

Administration queues contain acknowledgment messages generated by MSMQ for messages you send. These messages indicate that the messages you sent either arrived (a positive acknowledgment) or that an error occurred before the message could be retrieved (a negative acknowledgment).

Report queues

Report queues contain report messages that indicate the message's route through your enterprise. Report queues can be used when sending test messages or when tracking message routes for a specific application.

System queues

MSMQ uses up to six system queues. All six are implemented as private queues and cannot be deleted. They are used for various MSMQ system purposes.

MSMQ Server Roles

MSMQ Servers can perform various roles within an enterprise configuration. These roles are as follows:

- **Primary Enterprise Controller (PEC)**   This is the main MSMQ server for the enterprise. There can be only one PEC and this must be installed prior to installing any other servers.

- **Primary Site Controller (PSC)**   Usually the main MSMQ server for a particular geographic site.

- **Backup Site Controller (BSC)**   A backup server in case the primary site controller goes down. The backup site controller holds a read-only copy of the PSC database.

- **Routing Server**   Used to route messages between sites.

- **Connector Server**   Used to communicate with other messaging schemes, such as Microsoft Exchange e-mail or IBM's MQSeries on the mainframe.

MSMQ Client Roles

As far as client machines go, MSMQ has two roles: dependent clients and independent clients.

MSMQ independent client software can be installed on computers running Microsoft Windows 95, Microsoft Windows 98, Windows NT Workstation version 4.0 or later, and Windows NT Server version 4.0 or later. MSMQ independent clients can create and modify queues locally, and can send and receive messages, just as MSMQ servers can. MSMQ independent clients can create queues and store messages on the local computer, without synchronous access to an MSMQ server. The primary differences between MSMQ independent clients and MSMQ servers are that independent clients do not have the intermediate store-and-forward capability of MSMQ servers, nor do they store information from the distributed MSMQ database.

An advantage of MSMQ independent clients is that they can send messages to public queues while disconnected from the network. The disconnect can be a brief interruption in a network server or the mobile use of a laptop or portable computer, as in the case of a mobile worker like an insurance agent.

MSMQ dependent clients function much like MSMQ independent clients; however, they cannot function without synchronous access to a PEC, PSC, BSC, or MSMQ routing server (referred to as the dependent client's *supporting server*). MSMQ dependent clients rely on their assigned server to perform all standard MSMQ functions on their behalf (such as creating queues, sending messages, and receiving messages).

INSTALLING MSMQ

MSMQ is provided as part of the Windows NT 4.0 Option Pack and can be installed on Windows NT 4.0 Server, Windows NT 4.0 Workstation, or Windows 95/Windows 98. When installing MSMQ from the Windows NT 4.0 Option Pack, you should choose the Microsoft Message Queue option from the Setup dialog box, as shown in Figure 21-2. For a Windows NT 4.0 Server installation, the entire MSMQ software including documentation is 41.3 MB. Figure 21-3 shows the subcomponents available for MSMQ. You can access these subcomponents by clicking the Show Subcomponents button on the Setup dialog box.

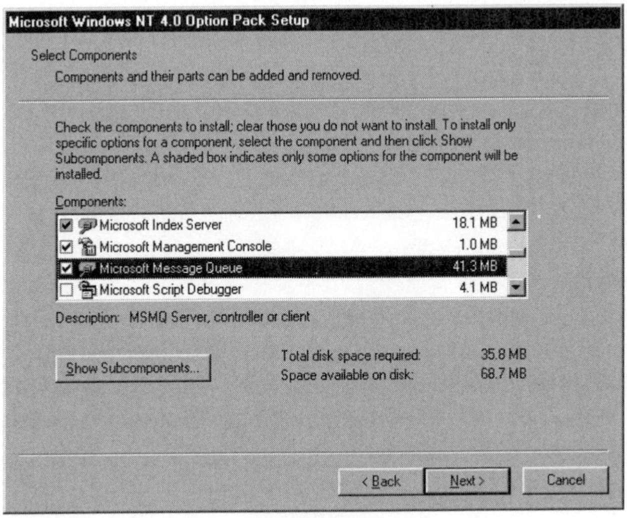

Figure 21-2. *The Windows NT 4.0 Option Pack Setup dialog box showing the MSMQ component.*

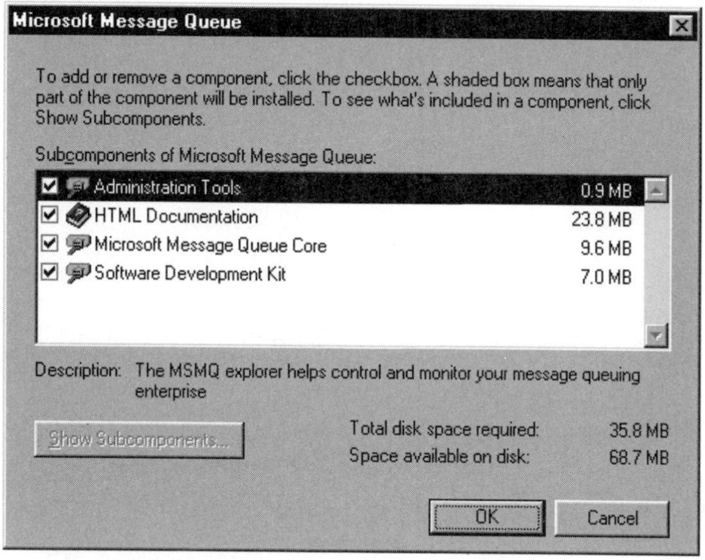

Figure 21-3. *The Microsoft Message Queue dialog box showing the subcomponents of MSMQ.*

The available MSMQ subcomponents are as follows:

- Administration Tools (0.9 MB)

- HTML Documentation (23.8 MB)

- Microsoft Message Queue Code (9.6 MB)

- Software Development Kit (7.0 MB)

The steps to install MSMQ onto Windows NT 4.0 Server are as follows:

1. Select the MSMQ client or server to install. For a new installation, you should choose the Primary Enterprise Controller (PEC) and then click the Next button, as shown in Figure 21-4 on the following page.

2. Enter the MSMQ Enterprise Name and MSMQ Site Name, and click Next.

3. Enter the MSMQ installation folder location, and click Next.

4. Enter the folder location for the Data Device and Log Device for the MSMQ Information Server database on SQL Server. The default size is 80 MB for the data device and 20 MB for the log device. Click the Continue button to have setup create the MQIS database.

5. Click the Add button on the MSMQ Connected Networks dialog box to enter the name of the new connected network and select its protocol. When completed, the screen should look similar to Figure 21-5.

6. Click the Finish button in the Windows NT 4.0 Option Pack Setup dialog box.

7. Restart the server for the changes to take effect.

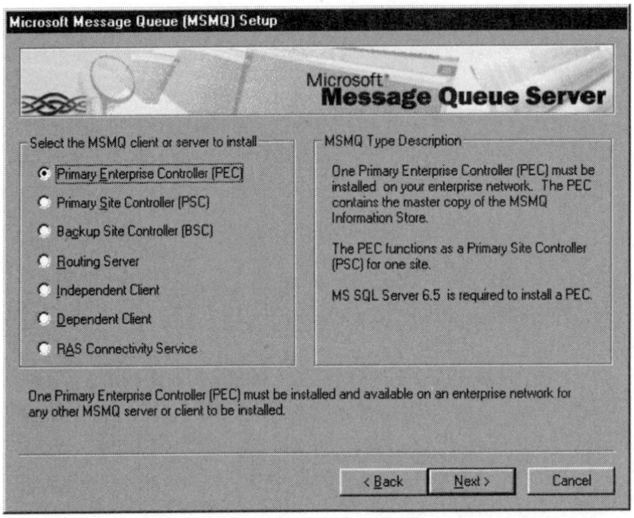

Figure 21-4. *The Microsoft Message Queue (MSMQ) Setup dialog box showing the available MSMQ clients and servers that can be installed.*

Note   Prior to installing the Primary Enterprise Controller (PEC) onto Windows NT 4.0 Server, you'll need to make sure you have Microsoft SQL Server 6.5 installed. MSMQ uses SQL Server 6.5 for the MQIS database. The MQIS is a distributed database that stores the following information:

❑ Enterprise topology (such as sites, CNs, and InRS/OutRS assignments)

❑ Enterprise settings (such as enterprise name, PEC name, and default-replication intervals)

❑ Computer information

❑ Queue information

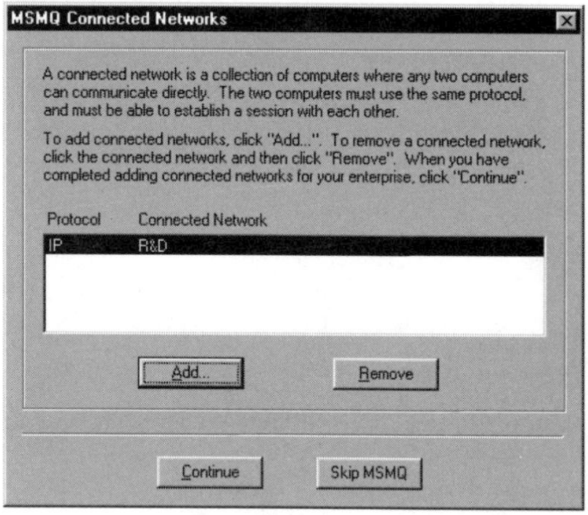

Figure 21-5. *The MSMQ Connected Networks dialog box showing an installed connected network and its protocol.*

When you have completed the installation of MSMQ on your Windows NT 4.0 Server, you will have a Microsoft Message Queue folder available from the Start menu on the taskbar. Under the Microsoft Message Queue folder, you will find samples, documentation, and the MSMQ Explorer.

MANAGING MSMQ

MSMQ can be managed via the MSMQ Explorer. You can launch the MSMQ Explorer by choosing Programs|Windows NT 4.0 Option Pack|Microsoft Message Queue|Explorer from the Start menu on the taskbar. Figure 21-6 shows the MSMQ Explorer window.

Figure 21-6. *The MSMQ Explorer.*

The MSMQ Explorer gives you a hierarchical view of the enterprise, sites, computers, queues, and messages within MSMQ. Figure 21-6 shows an enterprise named VI6; a site named VI6; a Primary Enterprise Controller named ntserver; and three queues, named Dead Letter, Journal, and Xact Dead Letter.

Creating a Queue

To create a new queue within the MSMQ Explorer, follow these steps:

1.   Right-click the computer name, and choose New|Queue from the context menu.

2.   Enter the name of the queue in the Queue Name dialog box.

3.   Mark the check box to declare the queue transactional, if required.

4.   Click OK.

The queue will now appear in the list of queues below the machine name. Figure 21-7 shows a queue named *myqueue* within the MSMQ Explorer.

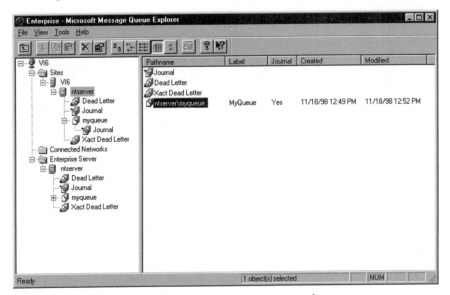

Figure 21-7. *The MSMQ Explorer showing a queue named myqueue.*

Property Windows

The MSMQ Explorer provides you with property windows for the enterprise, sites, computers, queues, and messages. Using these property windows, you can view existing properties and modify certain properties as well. The available property windows are as follows:

- Enterprise Properties Window

- Site Properties Window

- Computer Properties Window

- Queue Properties Window

- Message Properties Window

To access a property window, right-click the appropriate node within the MSMQ Explorer and choose Properties from the context menu.

The Enterprise Properties window

The Enterprise Properties window allows you to view the Enterprise Name and Enterprise Server. It also allows you to specify certain global defaults such as the default lifetime of a message within the network. Other tabs within this property window allow you to specify default settings for MQIS and to configure security in terms of permissions, auditing, and ownership. The security is tied back to the Windows NT security model.

The Site Properties window

The Site Properties window allows you to specify MQIS defaults and security on a finer granularity and to set the costs for various links between sites in your enterprise. By setting cost values, you can tell MSMQ about the relative costs of connecting to various sites in your enterprise in terms of bandwidth. For example, some sites might only be accessible via a slow WAN connection such as a dial-up line.

The Computer Properties window

The Computer Properties window presents you with several tabs for configuring MSMQ. These tabs include Dependent Clients, Tracking, Security, General, Network, Events, Status, and IS Status.

The Queue Properties window

The Queue Properties window presents four tabs: General, Advanced, Status, and Security. The General tab tells you the creation date of the queue, the queue label, and the queue ID. The Advanced tab includes options that allow you to specify whether journalling is enabled, the privacy level, and any limits in terms of message storage and journal storage. The Status tab provides a useful summary of the number of messages in the queue and the number of bytes in the queue. The Security tab again provides a finer level of granularity and ties back to the Windows NT 4.0 security model.

The Message Properties window

The Message Properties window provides you with information about particular messages in a queue. It tells you the date and time the message was sent, the date and time the message arrived, the message priority, the message label, the body of the message, the size of the message body in bytes, and information about the sender.

MSMQ COMPONENTS

MSMQ has several Microsoft ActiveX components that you can access within your Active Server Pages (ASP) code or other applications. These components support queue lookup, queue management, message management, queue administration, and transaction support. Four of these components can be found on the Server Objects tab in the Toolbox within Visual InterDev. The main four components in the Toolbox are:

- MSMQ Query
- MSMQ QueueInfo
- MSMQ Message
- MSMQ MailEMail

In addition to these components, MSMQ also contains other objects that provide most of the MSMQ API functionality. These include *MSMQQueue, MSMQQueueInfos, MSMQEvent, MSMQTransaction, MSMQTransactionDispenser, MSMQApplication,* and *MSMQCoordinatedTransactionDispenser.* There are also many other MSMQ Mail ActiveX objects available for you to script against. For complete details on these objects and their properties and methods, see the MSMQ online documentation.

> NOTE   MSMQ fires very few events. The only events fired are *Arrived* and *ArrivedError.* These are fired by the MSMQEvent component in response to a message or error arriving at a queue.

We'll now take a more in-depth look at MSMQ Query, MSMQ QueueInfo, MSMQ Message, and MSMQ MailEMail.

MSMQ Query

The *MSMQQuery* object allows you to query MSMQ for existing public queues. The *LookupQueue* method returns a collection of public queues based on the following queue properties: queue identifier, service type, label, create time, and modify time.

MSMQ QueueInfo

The *MSMQQueueInfo* object provides queue management. It allows you to create a queue (either a transaction or nontransaction queue), open an existing queue, change a queue's properties, and delete a queue.

MSMQQueueInfo objects are either returned by a query or created by you. There is a one-to-one relationship between each *MSMQQueueInfo* object and the queue it represents. However, there is also a one-to-many relationship between the queue's *MSMQQueueInfo* object and each open instance of the queue. (Each instance of a queue is referenced by an *MSMQQueue* object.)

MSMQ Message

The *MSMQMessage* object provides properties to define MSMQ messages, plus a single *Send* method for sending the message to its destination queue. This single method is used for transaction and nontransaction messages.

MSMQ MailEMail

The *MSMQMailEMail* object represents an e-mail message. The e-mail message can be a form with several fields, a text message with a single text body, a MAPI TNEF message, or a delivery or nondelivery report.

USING MSMQ IN ASP

By using the MSMQ server-side components that we discussed in the previous section, we can write ASP code that works with MSMQ to send messages, receive messages, and even perform transactional messaging.

As an example of transactional messaging, we might want to make an update to SQL Server and also send an MSMQ message all as part of one transaction. As we shall see in this section, MSMQ messages can be sent to queues that support transactions and are managed by MTS. We'll also see how easy it is to send and receive messages from MSMQ using ASP code.

Sending a Message

To send an MSMQ message using ASP code, we need to create two MSMQ objects: *MSMQQuery* and *MSMQMessage*. The *MSMQQuery* object allows you to query MSMQ for existing public queues. The *MSMQMessage* object allows you to send your message. The code on the following page shows how to search for an existing queue and send a message.

```
<%@ Language=VBScript %>
<HTML>
<HEAD>
<META NAME="GENERATOR" Content="Microsoft Visual Studio 6.0">
<TITLE>Send MSMQ Message</TITLE>
</HEAD>
<BODY>
<H2>Send MSMQ Message</H2>
<HR>

<%
Set Query = Server.CreateObject("MSMQ.MSMQQuery.1")
Set QInfos = Query.LookupQueue(,,"MyQueue")
QInfos.Reset
Set QInfo = QInfos.Next
Set Queue = QInfo.Open(2,0)

Set Message = Server.CreateObject("MSMQ.MSMQMessage.1")
Message.Label = "MSMQ Message"
Message.Body = "This message was sent by SendMessage.asp."
Message.Send Queue

Response.Write "Message Sent. Please check MSMQ Explorer."
%>

</BODY>
</HTML>
```

In the above code, we use the *Server.CreateObject* syntax to create both the *MSMQQuery* object and the *MSMQMessage* object. The *LookupQueue* method of the *MSMQQuery* object is used to locate the queue named MyQueue within MSMQ.

The message is sent by simply setting various properties of the *MSMQ-Message* object. These properties include the message label and the message body. Finally, the message is sent by calling the *Send* method of the *MSMQ-Message* object.

In this example, the ASP Web page displays a confirmation message to the browser indicating that the message was sent. In a real application, you would probably not notify the user that a message has been sent since this is typically back-end functionality that the end users do not need to be concerned with.

Figure 21-8 shows the resulting message within the MSMQ Explorer.

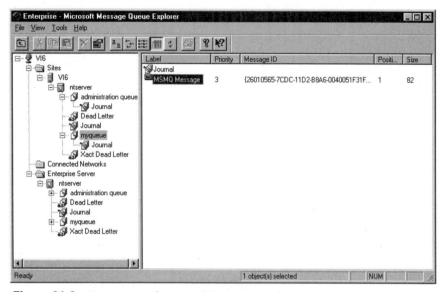

Figure 21-8. *Message sent from SendMessage.ASP shown within the MSMQ Explorer.*

In Figure 21-8, you can see some basic information about the message. You can see the message label, the priority, the message ID, the message position in the queue, and the size of the message in bytes.

For more information about the message, you can right-click the message and choose Properties from the context menu. By clicking the Body tab of the Message Properties dialog box, you can see the actual text within the body of the message. In this example, as shown in Figure 21-9 on the following page, the text reads "This message was sent by SendMessage.asp."

> **NOTE**   Another way to view the text within the body of the message is to choose Columns from the View menu of the MSMQ Explorer. Next choose Body from the list of available columns, and choose Add. This will add this particular column to the list of columns that are displayed within the MSMQ Explorer. There are many other available columns to choose from that allow you to customize your view of messages within the MSMQ Explorer. The Columns dialog box also allows you to customize your view of queues, computers, and sites within the MSMQ Explorer.

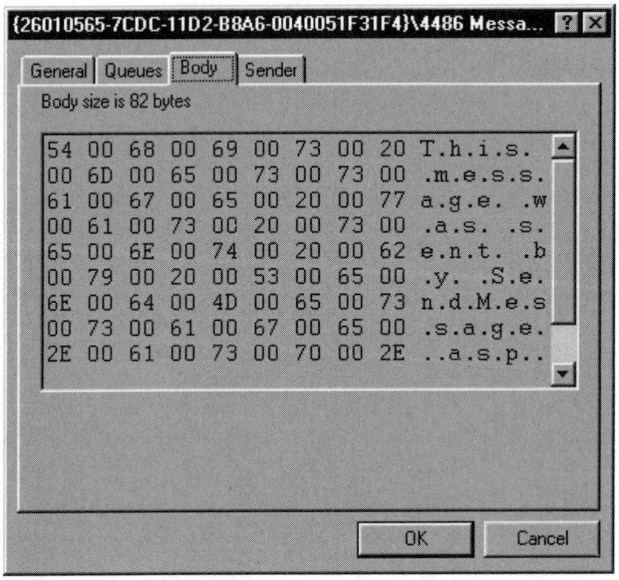

Figure 21-9. *The Body tab of the Message Properties dialog box showing the text within the body of the message.*

Receiving Messages

In addition to sending messages, you can also write ASP code to read and/or receive messages. The following code shows how this is achieved.

```
<%@ Language=VBScript %>
<HTML>
<HEAD>
<META NAME="GENERATOR" Content="Microsoft Visual Studio 6.0">
<TITLE>Read MSMQ Message</TITLE>
</HEAD>
<BODY>
<H2>Read MSMQ Message</H2>
<HR>

<%
Set Query = Server.CreateObject("MSMQ.MSMQQuery.1")
Set QInfos = Query.LookupQueue(,,"MyQueue")
QInfos.Reset
Set QInfo = QInfos.Next
Set Queue = QInfo.Open(1,0)
```

(continued)

```
Set Message = Queue.Receive

Response.Write "Message Detail<P>"
Response.Write "Message Label: " + Message.Label + "<BR>"
Response.Write "Message Body:  " + Message.Body
%>


</BODY>
</HTML>
```

The code is similar to our earlier code in which we sent a message. The main difference is that we call the *Receive* method of the *MSMQQueue* object instead of calling the *Send* method of the *MSMQMessage* object. Calling the *Receive* method actually creates a message object for us that we can then use to inspect the message properties. The code above prints the message label and the message body properties on screen. Also note that the *Open* method has been called using a parameter of 1. This value means that the queue is opened for read access instead of write access. Figure 21-10 shows the resulting browser output when running this sample code.

Figure 21-10. *Sample output from the ReadMessage.ASP file that opens up a queue in MSMQ and reads the first message.*

NOTE To read a message in a queue, you might need to alter the security permissions on the queue. You may well encounter a message such as "MSMQQueueInfo error 'c00e0025' - Access is denied". This is because by default only the queue owner has read access to messages in the queue. A simple way to open up the security during development of your code is to choose the Security tab from the Queue Properties dialog box and go into the Permissions section. Next change the permissions for Everyone from Send (SqGpPg) to Special Access (All). This setting is obviously not advised for production usage, but it is a simple way to be able to read the messages during your development and experimentation with MSMQ.

Transactional Messaging

To send a transactional message using ASP code, you simply follow the same basic procedure as on page 536 but add a few lines of code to declare the Web page as transactional and your message as transactional. The code listing below shows how to search for an existing transactional queue and send a message.

There are a number of differences here when compared to the code on page 536. First, the page is declared as transactional by using this syntax:

```
<%@TRANSACTION=Required LANGUAGE=VBScript%>
```

Next, the event handlers at the bottom of the code listing are used to trap either the *OnTransactionCommit* event or the *OnTransactionAbort* event and print out an appropriate message on screen.

The one change to the main code body in the code is that the *Send* method is called with an additional parameter. The parameter value of 1 after the *Send* method indicates that the call is part of the current MTS transaction. The value of 1 is equivalent to the MQ_MTS_TRANSACTION value.

```
<%@TRANSACTION=Required LANGUAGE=VBScript%>
<HTML>
<HEAD>
<META NAME="GENERATOR" Content="Microsoft Visual Studio 6.0">
<TITLE>Send Transactional MSMQ Message</TITLE>
</HEAD>
<BODY>
<H2>Send Transactional MSMQ Message</H2>
<HR>

<%
Set Query = Server.CreateObject("MSMQ.MSMQQuery.1")
Set QInfos = Query.LookupQueue(,,"mytransqueue")
QInfos.Reset
```

(continued)

```
Set QInfo = QInfos.Next
Set Queue = QInfo.Open(2,0)

Set Message = Server.CreateObject("MSMQ.MSMQMessage.1")
Message.Label = "Transactional MSMQ Message"
Message.Body = _
    "This message was sent by SendTransactionalMessage.asp."
Message.Send Queue, 1
Queue.Close
%>

</BODY>
</HTML>

<%
Sub OnTransactionCommit
    Response.Write _
        "Transactional MSMQ Message Sent and Committed."
End Sub
%>

<%
Sub OnTransactionAbort
    Response.Write "Transactional MSMQ Message Aborted."
End Sub
%>
```

> **NOTE** To send a transactional message, you must be sure to locate and use a transactional queue. If you have not yet set up a transactional queue within the MSMQ Explorer, you can do so by creating a new queue and marking the Transactional check box within the Queue Name dialog box at the time you create the queue. Once you have created a queue, you cannot change its transactional property from nontransactional to transactional or vice versa. You need to mark the queue as transactional during queue creation.

SUMMARY

Microsoft Message Queue is another advanced service that you can access from within your Visual InterDev 6.0 applications. It provides loosely coupled and reliable network communications services based on a message queuing model. The MSMQ objects such as *MSMQQuery* and *MSMQMessage* provide a rich API for integrating message queuing services into your applications. By taking advantage of the MSMQ server-side ActiveX components, you can easily send messages, read and receive messages, and send transactional messages using just a few lines of ASP code.

Part VI

SECURITY

Chapter 22

Adding Security

Security is extremely important. Placing a Web server on the Internet means that millions of people might have access to that server. Sensitive information must be protected from those who do not have the right to view it, yet it must still be made readily available for others. This is a fundamental challenge of Web server administration for those who deploy Internet applications, as well as those who manage intranet and extranet servers.

Consider, for example, a corporate Human Resources application. All employees probably have the right to view their own information and request changes. A much smaller number of employees, such as the Human Resources department, might need to view all employee information. An even smaller group will be able to change an employee's benefits based on an employee request or other circumstance such as a promotion. Another small group will be able to modify the application itself. In many cases, only the Web administrator has the right to create a new application.

Fortunately, several general mechanisms are available to address these and other security needs: access control, user authentication, and encryption. These mechanisms include but are not limited to

- IP Filtering
- Microsoft Windows NT User Access Rights
- Microsoft FrontPage Server Extensions Permissions
- NTFS Permissions

- Secure Sockets Layer (SSL)
- Client Certificates
- Database Security

The best way to implement security and make a site acceptably secure is to address each of these items in turn. The combination of these items yields a secure site that can deter all but the most determined hackers. It's always a trade-off, of course—the amount of time invested in applying security measures should be proportional to the sensitivity of your data. You'll also find that once you master these principles on one project, you can leverage your knowledge on future projects.

You should always keep security in the back of your mind as you develop Microsoft Visual InterDev applications—especially those that go out over the Internet to reach your customers and business partners.

SITE SECURITY

Site security restricts access to authorized users. You can take many different approaches to site security, and each has its advantages and disadvantages. In addition to the standard security options provided by a Web server such as Microsoft Internet Information Server (IIS), you can also add a software or hardware firewall system for additional security. Additionally, you can install a proxy server or other solution on top of the Web server and firewall system. The options are rapidly increasing as developers learn more about how people use the Web.

IP Filtering

IIS lets you filter based on the IP address. IP filtering is easily compromised once you obtain a valid IP address. Since the IP address is passed in an unencrypted form across both the Internet and private networks, it doesn't provide true security.

Figure 22-1 shows the dialog box that appears when you choose to edit IP Address And Domain Name Restrictions on the Directory Security tab in the Default Web Site Properties dialog box within the Microsoft Management Console (MMC). This dialog box lets you change the IP address access to IIS.

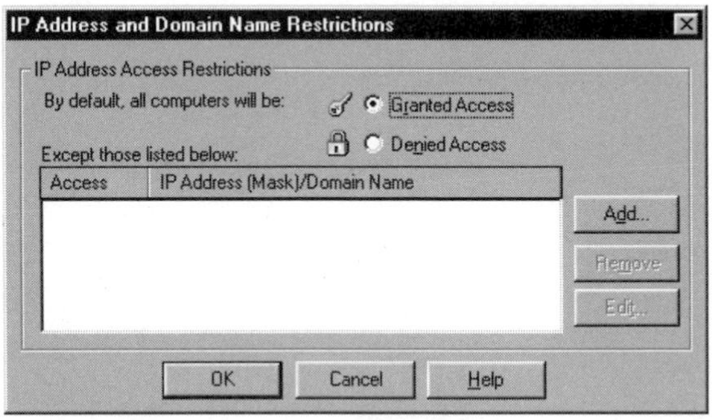

Figure 22-1. *The Microsoft Management Console (Internet Information Server) provides tools for filtering on either the IP address or DNS domain.*

NOTE IIS 4.0 provides much more fine-grained security than the IIS 3.0 Web server. A security tab within the Properties dialog box is present at several levels within the Internet Information Server snap-in in MMC. You can specify security settings at the directory level or file level by clicking on the appropriate node within the MMC, choosing Properties, and then choosing the relevant Security tab.

If you deny all other computers access to your Web server, you must enter the IP address of all computers that can access the Web server. To do this, click the Add button and enter the IP addresses in the Grant Access On dialog box shown in Figure 22-2. Or click the DNS Lookup button next to the IP address textbox, and IIS will prompt you for a domain name. The domain must be valid and reachable because IIS checks it as soon as you click OK to close the dialog box.

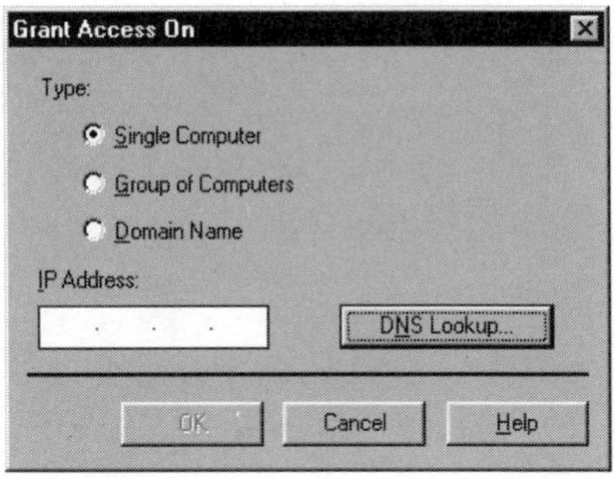

Figure 22-2. *The Grant Access On dialog box, used for granting IIS Web site access to IP addresses and/or domain names.*

You can, of course, allow access to some computers and disallow access to certain others by entering their IP addresses or domain names.

Either of these methods will work for many sites, but neither is very secure. The IP address is passed in clear text across the network (the Internet or an intranet), making it relatively easy to obtain. For instance, users with a sniffer application can usually pull the IP addresses. Through a process known as "spoofing," a user can make his or her message appear to the server as if originating from a valid address.

Windows NT User Access Rights

Windows NT provides flexible, industrial-strength security. Windows NT security is based on user IDs, passwords, and a robust challenge-and-response protocol that verifies user rights across a network without divulging any information that might compromise security. If your network is based on Microsoft Windows 95, Windows 98, or Windows NT and you use only an intranet, you have many options. You can actually meet your security needs by relying solely on Windows NT security features.

Each user account can be a member of one or more groups. You can assign Web access rights to a group instead of assigning them to individual user accounts. For instance, you can have a group named HR Web Admin that contains all the user accounts that can administer the Human Resources Web. This simplifies administration because you don't need to assign rights individually. You place all users with similar needs into a group, and then you assign the necessary rights once to that group. When new users are added to a group, they have all the rights granted to that group. When users are removed from a group, they lose any rights granted solely by their membership in the group—that is, they lose any rights that were not granted to them individually or through membership in another group. (Users can belong to any number of groups and can have the maximum combined rights granted through their membership in those groups.)

You can also assign other types of security beyond Web security to user groups. You can assign file and directory permissions as well as other permissions to a group, and the users of that group will have that level of access. The section titled "NTFS Permissions" later in this chapter provides more information on file and directory permissions.

Windows NT user access rights are checked whenever users try to access an IIS-hosted Web site. This is a powerful mechanism for controlling access to a site. Each time a user accesses any file or directory on the Windows NT system, that person's access to that object is verified.

Figure 22-3 shows the types of password authentication that the site administrator can select—Allow Anonymous Access, Basic Authentication (Password Is Sent In Clear Text), and Windows NT Challenge/Response.

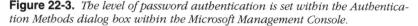

Figure 22-3. *The level of password authentication is set within the Authentication Methods dialog box within the Microsoft Management Console.*

Selecting Allow Anonymous Access lets anyone connect to the site. When a user tries to access the site, IIS uses the user name and password from the Anonymous Logon frame. The Anonymous User account is created automatically during IIS installation. The user name is in the form IUSR_*servername*, where IUSR stands for Internet User and *servername* is the name of the server on which IIS is installed. The password is pseudorandomly generated.

If the Windows NT Challenge/Response check box is the only one selected, access is limited to Microsoft Windows 95/Windows 98 and Windows NT clients. This is because a portion of the Challenge/Response protocol is implemented by code contained only in those operating systems. This is a very secure option because the password is never sent over the network. Rather, the server sends a request for information to the client that can be answered only if the client knows the password. Using the password, the client calculates the answer to the server's question and sends back only the answer—not the password. (The answer is even encrypted.) Each time the server confirms the client's authenticity, it uses a new question so that a previously captured answer cannot simply be played back. The Basic (Clear Text) option lets browsers on any operating system pass a user name and password to IIS. The Challenge/Response mechanism unique to Windows 95/Windows 98 and Windows NT is not used; the information is passed unencrypted. This provides minimal security because someone could easily extract the plain text user name and password from network data.

FrontPage Server Extensions Permissions

The FrontPage Server Extensions add another level of security to your IIS site. Each Web application you create with Visual InterDev has the FrontPage directory and file structure automatically added to it. This lets the FrontPage Server Extensions provide enhanced security for the site. The extensions use Windows NT users and groups in granting three types of rights to a Web site or application:

- **Browse**   Users can only browse content in the site.
- **Author**   Users can change, add, and delete content on an existing Visual InterDev or FrontPage site.
- **Administer**   Users can create, delete, and set permissions on sites.

Figure 22-4 shows the Groups tab of the Permissions dialog box—choose Web Project | Web Permissions... from the Visual InterDev Project menu—which lets an administrator assign access rights to Windows NT groups. (The FrontPage Server Extensions installation requests that you specify an administrator account.)

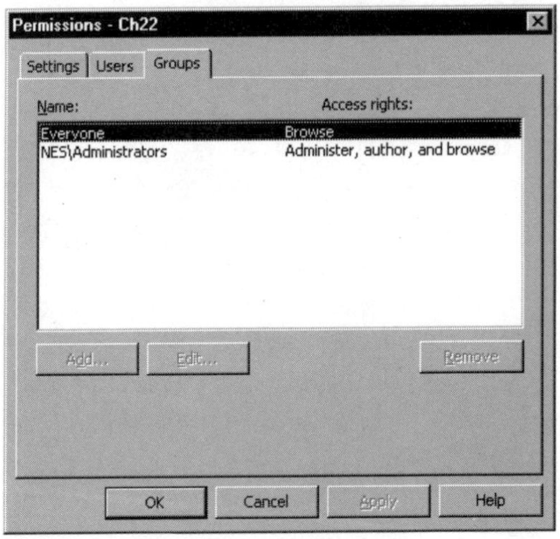

Figure 22-4. *Access rights can be assigned by user or by group.*

To ease the administrative burden, you can create Windows NT groups and use Windows NT to manage the users in each group. For instance, you can create groups named Web Authors, Web Administrators, and Web Browsers. Prefacing the group names with the word *Web* reduces the confusion with other Windows NT groups, especially the built-in Administrators group. If anonymous logon is permitted, you might not need the Web Browsers group.

By default, all sub-Webs created using the FrontPage Server Extensions (through FrontPage 98 or Visual InterDev) inherit their permissions from the root Web. To alter rights on only a sub-Web, take the following steps:

1. Select the project and make it the Active project.

2. Choose Web Project | Web Permissions from the Visual InterDev Project menu to display the Permissions dialog box.

3. On the Settings tab, select the Use Unique Permissions For This Web Application option.

4. Click the Apply button to activate unique permissions for this site.

5. Click the Users tab or the Groups tab to show the current security for this project.

6. Click the Add button to add a new user or group to the Access Control List (ACL) for this project.

7. In the Add Groups dialog box (shown in Figure 22-5), select the users or groups.

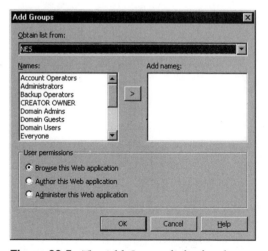

Figure 22-5. *The Add Groups dialog box lets you select users or groups to add to the list of authorized users or groups for a project.*

NOTE   The Web Project|Web Permissions... menu item under the Visual InterDev Project menu is available only if your Web project resides on an NTFS partition. If you are running your Web root under the FAT file system, are running Windows NT, and wish to convert to NTFS, you can do so by running the CONVERT program from the DOS Prompt. The CONVERT program converts FAT volumes to NTFS and has the following syntax,

CONVERT drive: /FS:NTFS [/V]

where

❑   drive specifies the drive to convert to NTFS. Note that you cannot convert the current drive.

❑   /FS:NTFS specifies to convert the volume to NTFS.

❑   [/V] specifies that Convert should be run in verbose mode.

To check the file system of your drives, you can choose Start|Programs|Administrative Tools (Common)|Disk Administrator. The Disk Administrator will tell you the format for each volume (logical drive) on your machine.

Connecting to a Proxy Server

A new feature in Visual InterDev 6.0 allows you to specify the settings for proxy servers. You can either have Visual InterDev use the same proxy server as the operating system or you can specify a particular proxy server just for your Web project.

To access the proxy server settings within Visual InterDev:

1.   Choose Options from the Visual InterDev Tools menu to open the Options dialog box.

2.   Expand the Projects node by clicking the plus sign (+).

3.   Select Web Proxy Settings under the Projects node.

Figure 22-6 shows the Options dialog box with the Web Proxy Settings displayed in the right-hand pane.

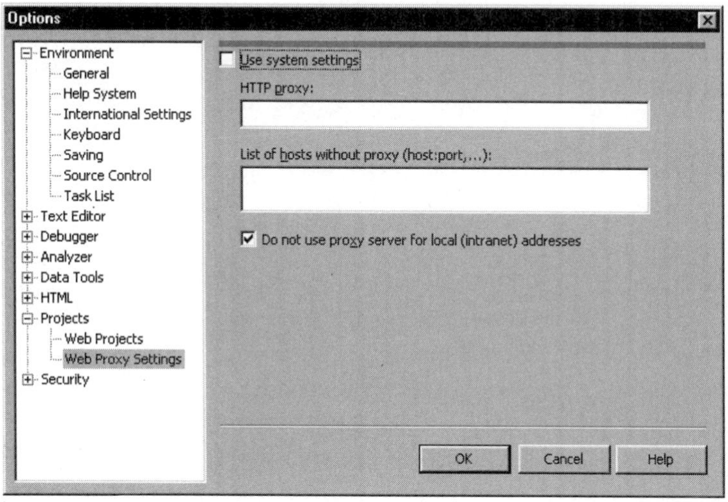

Figure 22-6. *The Options dialog box within Visual InterDev showing the Web Proxy Settings.*

Specifying the proxy server is useful when you are developing against a Web server that is outside of your corporate firewall on the Internet. Using the proxy can help to get you outside your intranet and onto the development Web server on the Internet.

To use the same proxy server as the operating system, simply check the Use System Settings check box. To use other customized settings, uncheck the Use System Settings check box and enter the name of the proxy server to use in the HTTP Proxy text box. Next enter the IP addresses of any hosts that should not use the proxy server in the List Of Hosts Without Proxy text box.

If you want all local IP addresses on your intranet to be accessed without using the proxy server you have just entered, check the Do Not Use Proxy Server For Local (Intranet) Addresses check box.

NTFS Permissions

The Windows NT File System (NTFS) supports the concept of user permissions through an Access Control List (ACL). The ACL contains information on which users and groups have permissions for specific files and directories.

Any member of the Windows NT Administrators group can modify the ACL for any file or directory. (It might be necessary to take ownership of that object first.) Removing the Anonymous User account from the ACL for a file or directory means that anyone trying to access that file is prompted for a valid Windows NT user name and password. If the user supplies a proper user name and password, the user is granted access; otherwise, access is denied.

NOTE   Windows NT supports the FAT file system in addition to NTFS. FAT does not support ACLs. You can use file and directory permissions only on disk partitions that use NTFS as the file system.

SECURE SOCKETS LAYER

Secure Sockets Layer allows secure browsing across an unsecured network by encrypting all information sent in both directions. To implement SSL, you must obtain a certificate from a certification authority such as VeriSign because SSL is built on a public-key cryptosystem. You then apply that certificate to the Web server. Once the certificate is applied, you can mark any virtual directory on that Web server as requiring SSL for access.

Figure 22-7 shows the Secure Communications dialog box within the Microsoft Management Console (Internet Information Server), where you can select the Require Secure Channel When Accessing This Resource check box. This check box is grayed out until you install a certificate on your Web server. In fact, if you have not yet installed a certificate and you try to access this dialog box (via the Secure Communications group box on the Directory Security tab of the Default Web Site Properties dialog box), you'll be presented with the Key Manager application. After installing your certificate on IIS, you'll also need to stop and restart the WWW service to have the check box enabled.

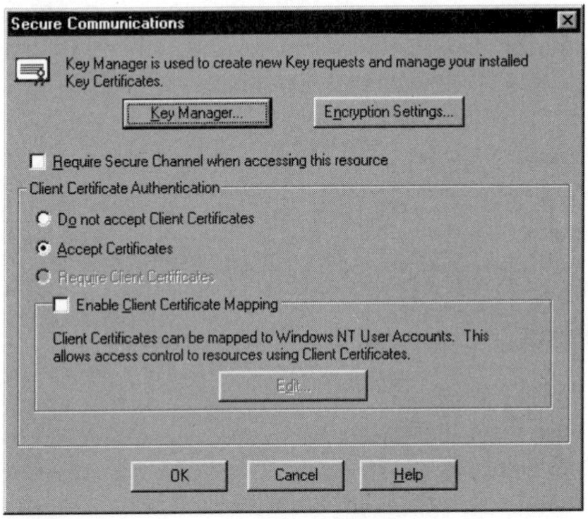

Figure 22-7. *The Secure Communications dialog box within the Microsoft Management Console (Internet Information Server) showing the Require Secure Channel check box.*

If you want to try out Secure Sockets Layer, VeriSign offers a two-week trial certificate that you can obtain from its Web site (at *http://www.verisign.com*). After you complete a form on that site, VeriSign will send you the free certificate via e-mail. This certificate will allow you to experiment with applying SSL to selected virtual directories on your Web server. Of course, it is intended for trial purposes only and is not for production use. Installing a server-side digital certificate on your Web server is a straightforward process and takes only a couple of minutes.

When you enter a secure area within your site, the padlock icon in the lower right corner of Microsoft Internet Explorer will appear locked. You'll also get a message from the browser that you are entering a secure area. The protocol listed in the URL address will also switch from *http:* to *https:*, which is known as Secure HTTP—the secure form of the HTTP protocol. To switch to HTTPS, you have to make this change to the URL in the hyperlinks within your Web pages.

For SSL to work, the user's browser must contain the requisite encryption software. Most popular browsers support SSL, including Netscape Navigator and Internet Explorer. Browsers that don't support SSL cannot access an SSL-secured site.

To better understand how the server and a browser engage in an SSL-secured session, imagine the following conversation:

> **Browser**: *I'd like to see your default.htm page, please.*

> **Server**: *I am a secure Web server and will let you look at that page only if you are an SSL-enabled browser—which I see you are. Here is a copy of my certificate issued by a certification authority, so you know that I am the server you are trying to reach. Do you accept it?*

> **Browser**: *Thank you. I have confirmed that your certificate is valid and was issued by a certification authority that I recognize. I also notice that it has not yet expired. I will encrypt all communications with you and show a special icon to my users so that they know that we'll keep their secrets. I will use the* https:// *prefix on my requests for pages.*

> **Server**: *I will also encrypt communications. Anyone who tries to figure out what we're saying to one another will be wasting time.*

NOTE Encryption is a processor-intensive activity. Thus, greater demands are placed on the CPU of both the client and the server when communicating via SSL. Furthermore, by definition the encrypted data appears to be completely random. Data compression is done through the exploitation of discernible patterns in that data. Because the data has no discernable patterns, any communications devices (modems) that rely on data compression to speed throughput will not offer the same high performance that they would with unencrypted data. In other words, SSL can significantly reduce throughput.

Cryptanalysis of the SSL protocol is beyond the scope of this book, but many security experts believe that SSL provides adequate protection for transactions by individuals.

NOTE   Publishing to an SSL-secured Web site via HTTP can be done only using SSL. Visual InterDev 6.0 and FrontPage 98 both support HTTP publishing through a secure SSL channel.

CLIENT CERTIFICATES

You might have noticed the Client Certificate Authentication group box in Figure 22-7 on page 554. If a Web browser uses the SSL3.0/PCT1 protocol (in other words, a URL starting with *https://* instead of *http://*) to connect to a server, and the server requests certification, the browser sends various certification fields to the server.

You can determine the values of the certification fields in the client certificate by using the *ClientCertificate* collection of the *Request* object. This collection provides numerous certification fields that are specified in the X.509 standard. Examples of some of the certification fields include user name, company name, issuer name, and the certificate's date of expiration. For more information on working with certificates, see Chapter 23.

DATABASE SECURITY

Web applications that provide access to data in a database typically have additional security requirements. Visual InterDev and Active Server Pages (ASP) provide certain features by default, as well as other options to enhance secure access to your application.

Visual InterDev uses two different types of database logins: design-time (that is, how Visual InterDev itself logs into the database) and run-time (how users log from the browser to the Microsoft ActiveX Data Objects [ADO] model).

You can set run-time logins to a default by using the Data Connection Properties sheet (on the Authentication tab). You can access the Data Connection Properties sheet by expanding the global.asa node within the Project Explorer, right-clicking the appropriate data connection, and then choosing Properties from the context menu. This login information, including the password, is cached as text in global.asa. If you use this option, database logins are protected from those browsing the site, but other site authors can see global.asa. This is fine for most situations because only authors can see the password, but some authors might not want any information cached in global.asa. Instead, they'll want a login screen that forces users to use their own user names or passwords for validation.

NOTE If someone tries to access the global.asa file from their Web browser, they will get the following error message:

HTTP/1.1 Requests for GLOBAL.ASA Not Allowed

This prevents people from attempting to read any username or password information that is stored in a global.asa file.

Database security starts with Web security. Before users can access a database over the Web, they must access the page that provides the database interface. If the page does not allow the user access, the user cannot get to the database.

The pages stored on a FrontPage Server Extensions site are subject to all the security of that site. After following the steps for setting browse security, you can extend security by adding a group for database users. A convenient and descriptive name for this group is Web Database Users. This group is then granted access to the pages that provide access to the database. For example, using FrontPage permissions, these pages can all be located in a separate site in which only the Web Database Users have browse privileges.

You can also use NTFS ACLs to restrict access to individual files or folders in a site. Using this technique, you must selectively assign permissions to all of the ASP files and any other files that provide database access.

Another approach is to use a custom login page to authenticate users. To do this, use the global.asa file and the *Session_OnStart* event to detect the start of a session, and then redirect the user to a login page. The following code does this:

```
<SCRIPT LANGUAGE=VBScript RUNAT=Server>
Sub Session_OnStart
    Response.Redirect "Login.asp"
End Sub
</SCRIPT>
```

The key line in the global.asa file is *Response.Redirect "Login.asp"*. This command redirects the user to the login.asp page for validation. The code in login.asp is as follows:

```
<%@ Language=VBScript %>

<HTML>

<HEAD>

<META NAME="GENERATOR" Content="Microsoft Visual Studio 6.0">
```

(continued)

```
<TITLE>VI-Bank - Login</TITLE>


<LINK REL="stylesheet" TYPE="text/css"
    HREF="_Themes/blueprnt/THEME.CSS" VI6.0THEME="Blueprint">
<LINK REL="stylesheet" TYPE="text/css"
    HREF="_Themes/blueprnt/GRAPH0.CSS" VI6.0THEME="Blueprint">
<LINK REL="stylesheet" TYPE="text/css"
    HREF="_Themes/blueprnt/COLOR0.CSS" VI6.0THEME="Blueprint">
<LINK REL="stylesheet" TYPE="text/css"
    HREF="_Themes/blueprnt/CUSTOM.CSS" VI6.0THEME="Blueprint">
</HEAD>
<BODY>

<TABLE>
<TR valign=top>
<TD width=125>
<!--#INCLUDE FILE="menu.htm"-->
</TD>
<TD>

<H2><FONT COLOR="navy"><I>VI-Bank - Login</I></FONT></H2>
<HR style="COLOR: navy">
<P>

<FORM METHOD="POST" ACTION="ValidateLogin.asp">
<TABLE>
<TR>
<TD>Username</TD>
<TD><INPUT TYPE="text" SIZE="20" NAME="username"></TD>
</TR>
<TR>
<TD>Password</TD>
<TD><INPUT TYPE="password" SIZE="20" NAME="password"></TD>
</TR>
</TABLE>
<P>
<INPUT TYPE="Submit" VALUE="Submit" NAME="Submit">
<INPUT TYPE="Reset" VALUE="Reset" NAME="Reset">
</FORM>

</TD>
</TR>
</TABLE>

</BODY>
</HTML>
```

(continued)

The login page accepts the username and password from the user via the appropriate form fields. When the user clicks the Submit button, control is transferred to ValidateLogin.asp. This sample code can be found under the Chap22 folder on the CD-ROM. The database used to validate the login is the VI-Bank Access database found under the VI-Bank folder. Here is the code for the Validate-Login.asp page:

```
<%@ Language=VBScript %>

<% Response.Buffer = True %>

<% ' VI 6.0 Scripting Object Model Enabled %>

<!--#include file="_ScriptLibrary/pm.asp"-->

<% if StartPageProcessing() Then Response.End() %>
<FORM name=thisForm METHOD=post>
<HTML>
<HEAD>
<META NAME="GENERATOR" Content="Microsoft Visual Studio 6.0">

<LINK REL="stylesheet" TYPE="text/css"
    HREF="_Themes/blueprnt/THEME.CSS" VI6.0THEME="Blueprint">
<LINK REL="stylesheet" TYPE="text/css"
    HREF="_Themes/blueprnt/GRAPH0.CSS" VI6.0THEME="Blueprint">
<LINK REL="stylesheet" TYPE="text/css"
    HREF="_Themes/blueprnt/COLOR0.CSS" VI6.0THEME="Blueprint">
<LINK REL="stylesheet" TYPE="text/css"
    HREF="_Themes/blueprnt/CUSTOM.CSS" VI6.0THEME="Blueprint">
</HEAD>
<BODY>

<!--METADATA TYPE="DesignerControl" startspan
...
<Recordset Design-Time Control>
...

<!--METADATA TYPE="DesignerControl" endspan-->

<%

' Get the user-entered username and password

username = Request.Form("username")
password = Request.Form("password")
```

(continued)

```
' Set the SQL String
sqlstring = "select ssn, userid, password from login where " + _
    "userid = '" + username + "'"
rsLogin.setSQLText(sqlstring)

' Open the recordset
rsLogin.open()

If rsLogin.EOF Then
    Response.Redirect("invalidusername.asp")
Else
    If Trim(rsLogin.fields.getValue("password")) = Trim(password) Then
        Session("ssn") = rsLogin.fields.getValue("ssn")
        Response.Redirect("main.asp")
    Else
        Response.Redirect("invalidpassword.asp")
    End If
End If

' Close the recordset
rsLogin.close()

%>
</BODY>
<% ' VI 6.0 Scripting Object Model Enabled %>
<% EndPageProcessing() %>
</FORM>
</HTML>
```

This file tries to validate the username and password. To retrieve the user name and password from the login.asp file, use the *Request* object to access the *Form* collection that contains the variables. The username and password are then stored in variables and the Recordset DTC is used to look up the username in the Login table in the database. If the user name is found and the password matches the password field in the database, the user can access the site via the main.asp file. If the user name is not found or the password does not match, the user cannot access the site and the appropriate error message Web page is displayed to the user. These error-message Web pages are named InvalidUser-name.asp and InvalidPassword.asp.

The database used in the previous example consists of one table named Login. This table has three text fields: SSN, Userid, and Password. You can use a separate database for a table such as Login, or you can add the table to an existing database. You can quickly extend this example by adding another table or two to build in group functionality. This way you can separate customers into different classifications or use the functionality to provide similar access to several users.

After you check the user's name and password, you can set a session variable to indicate that user's security level to future pages. In this case, you can take the username and set it in a *Session* variable with the same name. Then you can create a simple routine that checks this security level variable and either lets the user browse or execute the page, or redirects the user to a page indicating that access has been denied. The most effective way to do this is to write this routine in an include (.inc) file and simply include it at the top of the pages you want to protect.

You can also set the ADO connection string information (stored in the *Session* object). The passwords and user IDs passed in via the login page are then used for those users when they connect to databases using ADO throughout the site. This is convenient because the ID and password are stored in session variables to begin with. In this way, you can effectively grant different database access levels to different users—introducing another layer of security using the DBMS system. However, keep in mind that the more fine-grained the control, the more difficult it is to administer the site. In many cases, the best way to protect databases is to ensure that the access to database pages is appropriately restricted using any of the techniques we described.

Also, an obvious problem with using a login page is that the user name and password are passed as plain text in the HTTP stream. To protect this information, use SSL encryption.

NOTE The example above is just one technique for applying database security to your Web application. In general, when adding security to your applications, you should aim to minimize the number of areas where you need to maintain security information. Often developers tie the security back to the Windows NT security model. In other cases, developers tie the security back to the underlying database such as Oracle or Microsoft SQL Server. In this case, instead of maintaining a custom login table within your database, you would have the user enter an Oracle or SQL Server username and password. You then attempt to connect the user to the database. If the connection succeeds, the user has entered a valid login. If the connection fails, the user is not authorized to access your application and data.

Another technique is to always minimize the number of areas where you hard-code login information. Areas to watch out for include the global.asa file and any File DSNs. If you use a File DSN, you can always edit it with a text editor and remove any user name and password information after it has been created. That way, if the file is compromised, no user access information is given away.

Chapter 23

Using Certificates

In this final chapter, we'll finish our look at security with a topic that will become increasingly important and necessary over the next few years—the role of digital certificates as a form of user authentication. With organizations deploying extranets to tighten relationships with business partners, proper user authentication is critical. As the complexity of extranet applications increases and the sensitivity of the data being exchanged increases, organizations are looking beyond usernames and passwords for their user authentication mechanisms. Digital certificates can provide a more robust form of user authentication since they are installed into a user's browser and therefore tie authentication to an individual's PC rather than to a username and password that can be easily given out to others.

The Microsoft Windows NT 4.0 Option Pack includes Microsoft Certificate Server. This product allows organizations to become their own certification authority by managing the issuance, revocation, and renewal of digital certificates. These types of application are typically deployed in either intranets, extranets, or e-commerce applications where the data being exchanged is sensitive and can be accessed only by authorized individuals. Features in the Microsoft Internet Information Server (IIS) 4.0 Web server itself also allow for a more granular level of security setting than was previously possible in IIS 3.0 and earlier versions. This includes various configuration settings for how the Web server handles client-side certificates.

In this chapter, we'll start with some short background theory on public-key infrastructures and certification authorities and then progress through a discussion of Certificate Server, server-side and client-side certificates, and finally how to work with Active Server Pages (ASP) code to access both client-side certificates and Certificate Server functionality. At the end of this chapter, you'll be able to write applications using Microsoft Visual InterDev 6.0 that can leverage the full functionality of Microsoft Certificate Server and provide powerful user-authentication measures for your Web applications.

PUBLIC-KEY INFRASTRUCTURE

A public-key infrastructure (PKI) consists of all the people, processes, and technology that are required to apply security measures using public-key cryptography within an organization. The PKI usually includes digital certificates, a certificate server for issuing the certificates, and an administrator to manage the issuance, revocation, and renewal of the certificates.

A PKI can include many other components in addition to digital certificates, such as Smart Cards for user authentication and encryption. The PKI also relies upon industry standards such as X.500, X.509, and Lightweight Directory Access Protocol (LDAP).

CERTIFICATION AUTHORITIES

A certification authority (CA) is an organization that acts as a trusted third party to vouch for the authenticity of public keys within a PKI. When implementing a PKI, organizations can choose to either insource or outsource CA services. This decision needs to be made carefully since it takes a lot of planning to execute CA services. You need to develop a security policy; plan for the cost of the infrastructure; educate users; train staff to administer the certificate server (if insourcing); consider legal issues; and plan for every scenario in terms of how the certificates are issued, renewed, and revoked, if need be.

Outsourcing of CA services is often the preferred option if you have several thousand or more business partners or customers and you are satisfied with the third-party CA's experience and level of service for your specific applications. Examples of third-party CAs include GTE and VeriSign. Insourcing CA services is an excellent choice if you have a limited set of business partners (that is, hundreds or perhaps a few thousand) and if your data is highly sensitive. This is typical of extranet applications. In this case, you might well want to use Certificate Server and become your own CA.

CERTIFICATE SERVER

Microsoft Certificate Server is a general-purpose, highly customizable server application for managing the issuance, revocation, and renewal of digital certificates. Digital certificates are used for public-key cryptography applications such as server and client authentication under the Secure Sockets Layer (SSL) or Private Communication Technology (PCT) protocols. With Certificate Server, organizations can perform authentication in an Internet, intranet, or extranet environment through the use of these certificates.

Certificate Server is primarily for Web applications that require authentication and secure communication by using SSL. However, it is also applicable to other certificate-based applications such as Secure Mulitpurpose Internet Mail Extensions (S/MIME), Secure Electronics Transactions (SET) protocol, and Authenticode. Certificate Server can issue certificates for both clients and servers in the X.509 version 3 format.

Installing Certificate Server

Installation of Certificate Server is accomplished by using the Windows NT 4.0 Option Pack. The total disk space requirements for Certificate Server are just 11.8 MB. In fact, 9.9 MB of that space is occupied by the Certificate Server online documentation. The minimum hardware requirements for Certificate Server are the same as those for IIS 4.0. The installation is a wizard-driven process that takes only a couple of minutes to complete. During installation, you'll be prompted to either choose to create a root certificate for the certificate authority being created or to create a certificate request file that you can use to obtain a certificate from another CA. How you respond to this prompt should be based upon whether you want Certificate Server to be the root CA at the top of the CA hierarchy or you want it to be a nonroot CA that participates in an already established CA hierarchy.

After you have completed the installation of Certificate Server, you will need to either reboot your machine or manually start the Certificate Authority service. For a manual start, choose Start | Settings | Control Panel and then choose Services. You should then select the Certificate Authority service from the list in the Services dialog box and select Start, as shown in Figure 23-1.

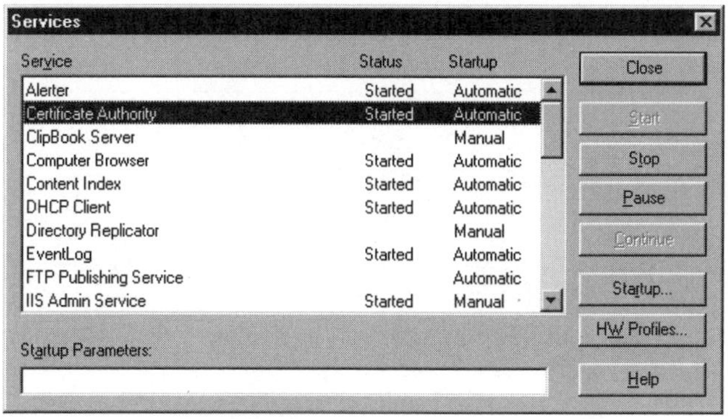

Figure 23-1. *The Certificate Authority service in the Services dialog box in the Windows NT 4.0 Control Panel.*

Certificate Server Architecture

Certificate Server has a server engine and database as well as other modules that communicate with the server engine to perform various tasks. External applications, such as those written in Microsoft Visual Basic, Microsoft Visual C++, Microsoft Visual J++, and Visual InterDev (Active Server Pages), can interact with the server engine via COM interfaces. The other modules in the architecture include administration tools, policy module, extension handlers, intermediary, and exit modules, as shown in Figure 23-2.

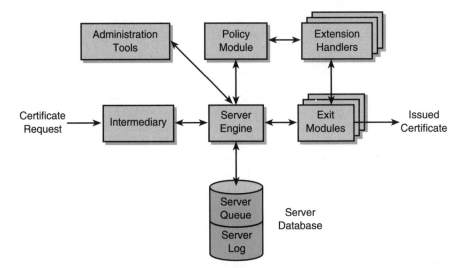

Figure 23-2. *The Certificate Server architecture, showing the server engine and the server database modules.*

Some of the interfaces available in Certificate Server are shown in Table 23-1. This will be of interest later on as we start writing ASP code within Visual InterDev 6.0 to programmatically access Certificate Server functionality.

Interface	Description
ICertConfig	Used by clients to get information about a server
ICertRequest	Used to send a request to the server and get the result of the request
ICertAdmin	Used by administration programs to manage requests, certificates, and revocation
ICertServerPolicy	Used by the policy module to get and set certificate and request properties

Table 23-1. *Interfaces imported and exported by the server engine of Certificate Server.* *(continued)*

Interface	Description
ICertServerExit	Used by exit modules to get and set certificate and request properties
ICertExit	Exported by exit modules; used by the server engine to deliver finished certificates and revocation information
ICertPolicy	Exported by the policy module; used by the server engine to check requests and get properties for certificates

To work with Certificate Server, you access it via the browser. You can get to the administration tools at *http://localhost/certsrv*. Figure 23-3 shows the main administration page for Certificate Server.

Figure 23-3. *The main administration page for Certificate Server.*

Here you can access four different items: the Certificate Administration Log Utility, the Certificate Administration Queue Utility, the Certificate Enrollment Tools, and the Certificate Server Documentation. Interestingly enough, many of these utilities are written in Active Server Pages. The database used to store certificate information is a Microsoft Access database named certsrv.mdb. As you can see in Figure 23-2, the server database is divided into two parts: the server queue and the server log. The server queue maintains a list of all certificate requests, and the server log maintains copies of all issued certificates. The certificate enrollment page has several links for installing CA certificates, processing certificate requests, and requesting client authentication certificates for Microsoft Internet Explorer and Netscape Navigator.

Installing a CA Certificate into Your Browser

A CA certificate is the digital certificate that authenticates the certificate authority that you are using. It's essentially the ID card for the CA. For your browser to enter into a dialog with a CA, the CA's certificate needs to be installed into your browser.

To install a CA certificate into your browser, you can either install a certificate from a third-party CA such as VeriSign or install the root CA certificate that has been generated for you by Certificate Server.

To install a root CA certificate into the Internet Explorer 4.0 browser from Certificate Server, follow these steps:

1. Make sure that Certificate Server is installed and has been configured as a root CA.

2. Go into the main administration page of Certificate Server at *http:// localhost/certsrv*, and click the Certificate Enrollment Tools hyperlink.

3. Select the Install Certificate Authority Certificates option.

4. Select the certificate that you have generated from Certificate Server by clicking the appropriate hyperlink, as shown in Figure 23-4.

5. In the File Download dialog box, choose Open This File From Its Current Location and click OK.

6. Click OK in the New Site Certificate dialog box.

Within Internet Explorer 4.0, you can check that the CA certificate has been installed correctly by choosing Internet Options from the View menu and then selecting the Content tab. Next click the Authorities button in the Certificates group box. You'll now be presented with a list of CAs whose certificates have been installed into your browser. From here you have the ability either to view the details of the certificate or to delete the certificate.

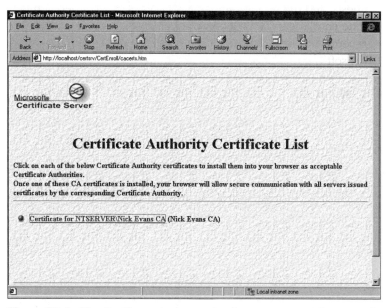

Figure 23-4. *The Certificate Authority Certificate List page. This page allows you to install a CA certificate into your browser.*

SERVER-SIDE CERTIFICATES

A server-side certificate is a certificate that is used to identify your Web server to end users. This type of certificate is often used on the Internet to provide SSL encryption for commercial Web sites, such as sites using Microsoft Site Server. In addition to providing SSL encryption so that communications between the browser and Web server cannot be easily captured and deciphered while in transit, digital certificates also authenticate the merchant you are dealing with.

To set up a Web page to use SSL, you need to take two steps. The first step involves installing the server-side digital certificate into IIS 4.0. The second step involves configuring your virtual directory and/or Web pages to require a secure channel. In the steps outlined below, we'll install a root CA certificate issued by Certificate Server into IIS 4.0.

1. Start Internet Service Manager by choosing Start | Programs | Windows NT 4.0 Option Pack | Microsoft Internet Information Server | Internet Service Manager.

2.   Select the Default Web site icon.

3.   Click the Key Manager button on the toolbar.

4.   Select Key | Create New Key from the Key Manager window.

5.   In the Create New Key dialog box, select the Automatically Send The Request To An Online Authority radio button and choose Microsoft Certificate Server from the drop-down list box. Click Next.

6.   Enter a name and password for the new key. Click Next.

7.   Enter your organization, organizational unit, and common name.

8.   Enter your country, state/province and city/locality.

9.   Click Finish, and the new key will be generated for you and added to the Key Manager window. (See Figure 23-5.)

10. Select the Server Bindings for this key. These settings determine which IP addresses and port numbers this certificate will be applied to. Click OK when finished.

Figure 23-5. *The Key Manager, showing a key and its distinguishing information, which are installed into the WWW service in Windows NT 4.0.*

To configure your Web application to require a secure channel, follow these steps:

1. Start Internet Service Manager by choosing Start | Programs | Windows NT 4.0 Option Pack | Microsoft Internet Information Server | Internet Service Manager.

2. Select the virtual directory or Web page that you want to secure.

3. Right-click the item, and choose Properties from the context menu.

4. In the Directory Security or File Security tab, click the Edit button in the Secure Communications group box.

5. Check the Require Secure Channel When Accessing This Resource check box.

When creating a page that has a hyperlink to the secure area of your site, be sure to use *https://* in the URL for the secure page instead of *http://*. This tells the Web server to use the secure HTTP protocol, HTTPS, and Secure Sockets Layer.

CLIENT-SIDE CERTIFICATES

Now that we have Certificate Server installed and we have installed a server-side digital certificate within IIS 4.0, two procedures remain before we can start working with client-side certificates within our Visual InterDev 6.0 Web projects. First we need to request a client-side certificate from Certificate Server and install it into our browser, and second we need to configure the Web server to accept or require client certificates for the relevant virtual directories or Web pages.

To request a client-side certificate from Certificate Server, follow these steps:

1. Make sure that Certificate Server is installed and has been configured as a root CA.

2. Go into the main administration page of Certificate Server at *http://localhost/certsrv/*, and click the Certificate Enrollment Tools hyperlink.

3. Select the Request A Client Authentication Certificate option.

4. Complete the Certificate Enrollment Form with your personal information, as shown in Figure 23-6 on the following page.

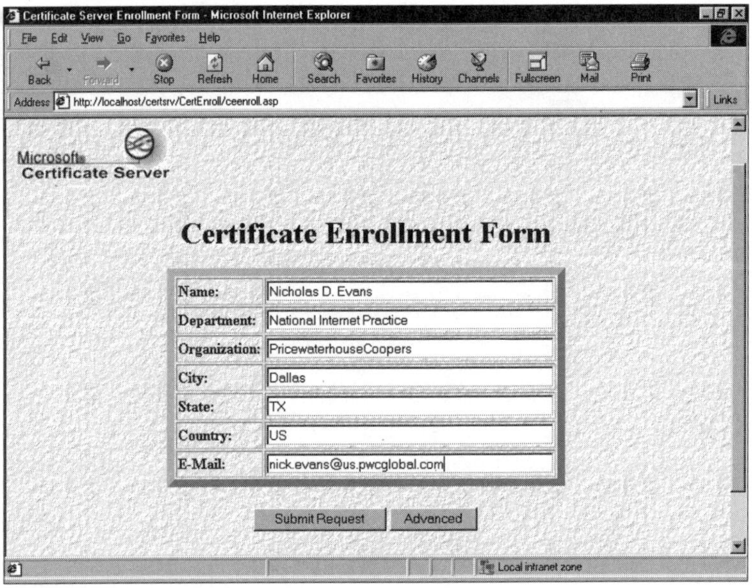

Figure 23-6. *Certificate Server's Certificate Enrollment Form page.*

5. Click Submit Request to submit the information to Certificate Server.

6. If all is successful, Certificate Server will present you with a Certificate Download page, as shown in Figure 23-7.

7. Click Download to download and install the new certificate. Certificate Server will remind you that you need to have the CA's root certificate installed as well.

Within Internet Explorer 4.0, you can check that the client certificate has been installed correctly by choosing Internet Options from the View menu and then selecting the Content tab. Next click Personal in the Certificates group box. You'll now be presented with a list of the client authentication certificates that have been installed into your browser. From here you have the ability either to view the details of the certificate or to import or export certificates. Figure 23-8 shows the certificate Properties dialog box if you click the View Certificate button. This dialog box shows the fields and their respective values within your certificate.

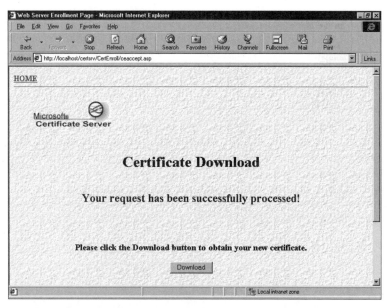

Figure 23-7. *Certificate Server's Certificate Download page.*

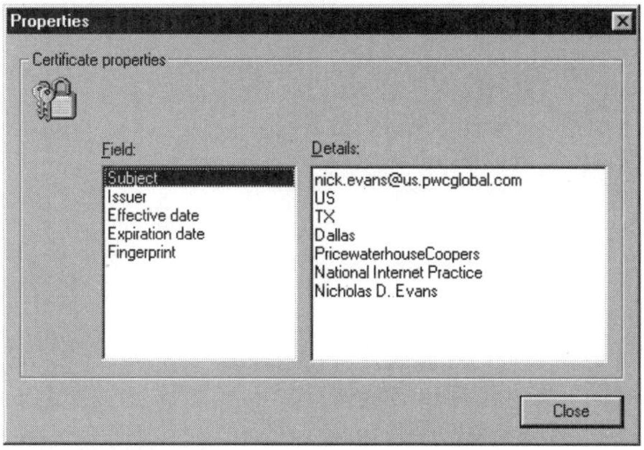

Figure 23-8. *The certificate Properties dialog box showing field names and their values for a client authentication certificate generated by Certificate Server.*

To configure IIS 4.0 to accept or require a client certificate, follow these steps:

1. Start Internet Service Manager by choosing Start | Programs | Windows NT 4.0 Option Pack | Microsoft Internet Information Server | Internet Service Manager.

2. Select the virtual directory or Web page that you want to secure.

3. Right-click the item, and choose Properties from the context menu.

4. In the Directory Security or File Security tab, click the Edit button in the Secure Communications group box.

5. Check the Require Secure Channel When Accessing This Resource check box.

6. Check either the Accept Certificates radio button or the Require Client Certificates radio button as required, as shown in Figure 23-9.

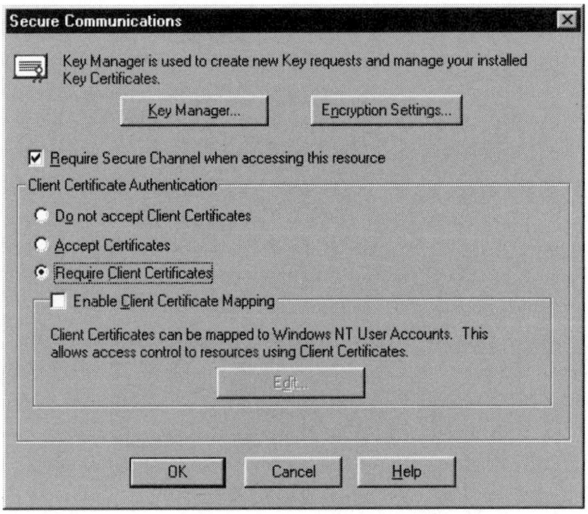

Figure 23-9. *The Secure Communications dialog box in the Internet Service Manager, showing the options for accepting or requiring client certificates.*

You'll also notice in Figure 23-9 that client certificates can be mapped to Windows NT user accounts. This allows you to control access to resources using standard Windows NT security. You can either specify direct one-to-one mapping of a certificate to a user account or specify wildcard mapping. In wildcard mapping, you can map any certificates that match certain criteria (such as the organization unit) to a single Windows NT user account or group. For example, you might map all client certificates with an organization code beginning with NIP to a Windows NT 4.0 group named NIP.

WRITING ASP CODE
TO READ CLIENT-SIDE CERTIFICATES

As you might recall, Active Server Pages has six built-in objects: *Request, Response, Application, Session, Server,* and *ObjectContext.* The *Request* object has a collection named *ClientCertificate.* This collection can be accessed via ASP to read the values in a client certificate.

If the Web browser is using Secure Sockets Layer to connect to your Web server and the server requests certification, a series of client certificate objects in this collection will contain information about the client's certification. You can tell when an SSL connection is being used because the address in the browser begins with *https://* instead of *http://.*

The syntax for retrieving these certificates is

```
Request.ClientCertificate( Key[SubField] )
```

Table 23-2 lists the possible key values, along with their uses.

Key	*Use*
Subject	A list of values that contain information about the subject of the certificate. Subfields are used with this key to extract the individual values from the list.
Issuer	A list of values that contain information about the issuer of the certificate. Subfields are used with this key to extract the individual values from the list.
ValidFrom	A valid date that indicates when the certificate becomes active.
ValidUntil	A valid date that indicates when the certificate expires.
SerialNumber	A string that represents the serial number. This string is a series of hexadecimal bytes separated by hyphens.
Certificate	The entire certificate (all the previous keys). It is represented in a binary format, so it's best to use the other keys to attain the values.
Flags	A set of flags that provide additional client certificate information. The following flags can be set: *ceCert Present*—a client certificate is present. *ceUnrecognized-Issuer*—the last certification in this chain is from an unknown issuer.

Table 23-2. *Key values in the* ClientCertificate *collection of the* Request *object.*

A variety of subfield values are available to extract specific information from the *Subject* and *Issuer* keys. Table 23-3 shows some of the common subfield values for these keys.

Subfield	Use
C	Specifies the name of the country of origin
CN	Specifies the common name of the user; only used with the *Subject* key
GN	Specifies a given name
I	Specifies a set of initials
L	Specifies a locality
O	Specifies the company or organization name
OU	Specifies the name of the organizational unit
S	Specifies a state or province
T	Specifies the title of the person or organization

Table 23-3. *Subfield values for the* Subject *and* Issuer *keys.*

The code below is taken from a sample Web page named ClientCertificate-.asp in the Certificate Web project included on the CD-ROM. This sample page shows how to read the values in a client certificate using the *Request* object and displays the values in the browser.

```
<%@ Language=VBScript %>
<HTML>
<HEAD>
<META NAME="GENERATOR" Content="Microsoft Visual Studio 6.0">
</HEAD>
<BODY>

<H2>Client Certificate Sample</H2>
<HR>

<%
If Len(Request.ClientCertificate("Subject")) = 0 Then
    Response.Write "No client certificate was presented"
Else
    Response.Write "<TABLE BORDER=1 CELLSPACING=5 CELLPADDING=5>"
    Response.Write "<TR><TD>Subject</TD><TD>" + _
        Request.ClientCertificate("Subject") + "</TD></TR>"
    Response.Write "<TR><TD>Issuer</TD><TD>" + _
        Request.ClientCertificate("Issuer") + "</TD></TR>"
    Response.Write "<TR><TD>ValidFrom</TD><TD>" + _
        CStr(Request.ClientCertificate("ValidFrom")) + "</TD></TR>"
```

(continued)

```
    Response.Write "<TR><TD>ValidUntil</TD><TD>" + _
        CStr(Request.ClientCertificate("ValidUntil")) + "</TD></TR>"
    Response.Write "<TR><TD>SerialNumber</TD><TD>" + _
        Request.ClientCertificate("SerialNumber") + "</TD></TR>"
    Response.Write "<TR><TD>Certificate</TD><TD>" + _
        Request.ClientCertificate("Certificate") + "</TD></TR>"
    Response.Write "<TR><TD>Flags</TD><TD>" + _
        CStr(Request.ClientCertificate("Flags")) + "</TD></TR>"
    Response.Write "</TABLE>"
End If
%>


</BODY>
</HTML>
```

Figure 23-10 shows an example of the resulting browser output from the ClientCertificate.asp page.

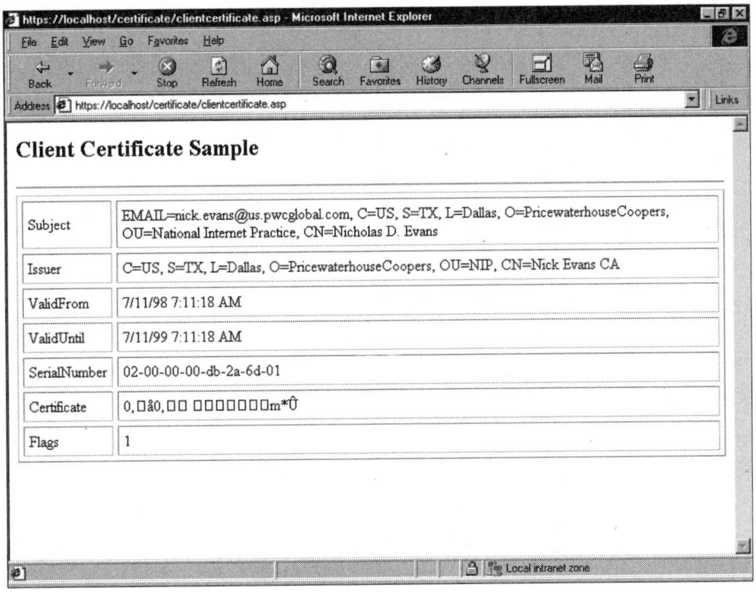

Figure 23-10. *The Internet Explorer 4.0 browser showing the output from the ClientCertificate.asp page that lists the values of the keys within a client certificate that has been presented to the Web server.*

Of course, in a real application you would read the values in the client certificate to determine whether the user is authorized to have access to your application instead of simply returning the values back to the browser. For example, you might use the common name (CN), organization name (O), or the organizational unit name (OU) subfield values of the *Subject* key to identify the user.

Once you have identified the user, you can take whatever next steps you need to within your particular application. This might include any of the following: redirection to a page specific to the user's role; performing a database lookup given one of the certificate subfield values to gather more information and ensure that the user is a valid business partner, customer, or employee; display a personalized welcome message; or many others. You could even read the EMAIL subfield value to send personalized e-mail messages (using the CDONTS NewMail server-side component) for cross-selling and other purposes.

To read a subfield value within ASP, you simply add the subfield to the key name, as shown here:

```
CommonName = Request.ClientCertificate("SubjectCN")
```

In this example, the common name subfield value of the *Subject* key is stored in a variable named *CommonName*.

The following code reads the e-mail address of the end user from their client certificate:

```
EMail = Request.ClientCertificate("SubjectEMAIL")
```

Using the *ServerVariables* Collection

In addition to using the *ClientCertificate* collection of the *Request* object to read client certificates, you can get a lot of useful information from the *ServerVariables* collection.

The code below is taken from a sample Web page named ServerVariables-.asp in the Certificate Web project included on the CD-ROM. This sample page shows how to read the values that relate to both client and server-side certificates using the *Request.ServerVariables* syntax and displays the values in the browser.

```
<%@ Language=VBScript %>
<HTML>
<HEAD>
<META NAME="GENERATOR" Content="Microsoft Visual Studio 6.0">
</HEAD>
<BODY>

<H2>Client Certificate (ServerVariables) Sample</H2>
<HR>

<%
Response.Write "<TABLE BORDER=1 CELLSPACING=5 CELLPADDING=5>"
Response.Write "<TR><TD>CERT_COOKIE</TD><TD>" + _
    Request.ServerVariables("CERT_COOKIE") + "</TD></TR>"
Response.Write "<TR><TD>CERT_FLAGS</TD><TD>" + _
```

(continued)

```
        Request.ServerVariables("CERT_FLAGS") + "</TD></TR>"
Response.Write "<TR><TD>CERT_ISSUER</TD><TD>" + _
        Request.ServerVariables("CERT_ISSUER") + "</TD></TR>"
Response.Write "<TR><TD>CERT_KEYSIZE</TD><TD>" + _
        Request.ServerVariables("CERT_KEYSIZE") + "</TD></TR>"
Response.Write "<TR><TD>CERT_SECRETKEYSIZE</TD><TD>" + _
        Request.ServerVariables("CERT_SECRETKEYSIZE") + "</TD></TR>"
Response.Write "<TR><TD>CERT_SERIALNUMBER</TD><TD>" + _
        Request.ServerVariables("CERT_SERIALNUMBER") + "</TD></TR>"
Response.Write "<TR><TD>CERT_SERVER_ISSUER</TD><TD>" + _
        Request.ServerVariables("CERT_SERVER_ISSUER") + "</TD></TR>"
Response.Write "<TR><TD>CERT_SERVER_SUBJECT</TD><TD>" + _
        Request.ServerVariables("CERT_SERVER_SUBJECT") + "</TD></TR>"
Response.Write "<TR><TD>CERT_SUBJECT</TD><TD>" + _
        Request.ServerVariables("CERT_SUBJECT") + "</TD></TR>"
Response.Write "</TABLE>"
%>

</BODY>
</HTML>
```

Figure 23-11 shows an example of the resulting browser output from the ServerVariables.asp page.

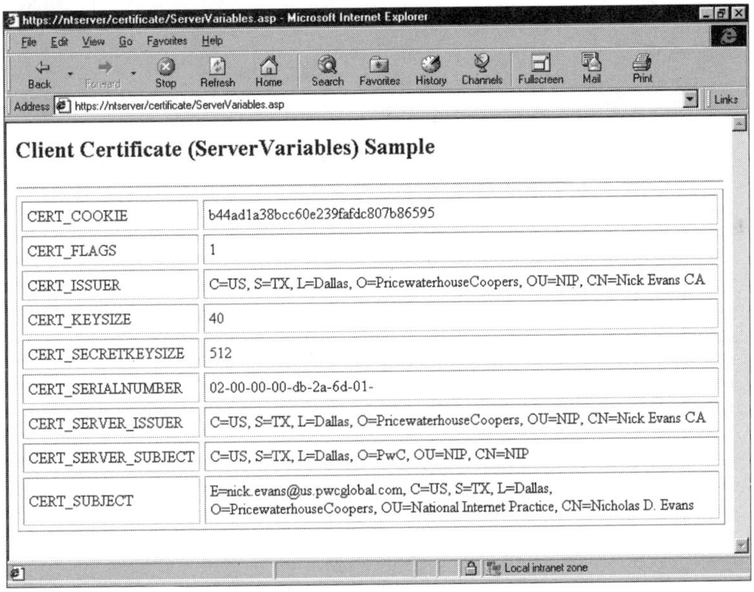

Figure 23-11. *The Internet Explorer 4.0 browser showing the output from the ServerVariables.asp page that lists several values of the keys from both a client certificate and server certificate.*

WRITING ASP CODE TO ACCESS CERTIFICATE SERVER FUNCTIONALITY

In addition to writing ASP code to read client certificates, you can also write ASP code to interface with Certificate Server itself. As we saw in the earlier section on Certificate Server architecture, the product exposes several COM interfaces for external applications to take advantage of. In this way, you can create specialized applications that truly extend Certificate Server and integrate your own business rules regarding the issuance, renewal, and revocation of digital certificates. By customizing Certificate Server in this way, you can also reduce the amount of manual administration that is required to run your Certificate Authority services.

In Table 23-1 on page 566, we saw some of the interfaces that Certificate Server exposes. To be able to call them from within our ASP code, we need to determine the program IDs (PROGIDs) for these components. Table 23-4 lists the PROGIDs for each of these interfaces.

Interface	*PROGID*
ICertAdmin	CertificateAuthority.Admin
ICertConfig	CertificateAuthority.Config
ICertGetConfig	CertificateAuthority.GetConfig
ICertPolicy	CertificateAuthority.Policy
ICertRequest	CertificateAuthority.Request
ICertServerExit	CertificateAuthority.ServerExit
ICertServerPolicy	CertificateAuthority.ServerPolicy

Table 23-4. *The PROGIDs for each of the interfaces exported or imported by the Certificate Server server engine. These PROGIDs can be used to communicate with Certificate Server via ASP Web pages.*

NOTE   One trick for finding the appropriate PROGIDs for any server-side components that you have installed on your machine is to use the Microsoft Transaction Server Explorer within the Microsoft Management Console. You can create a dummy package and then choose the option to add components that are already registered into the package. By doing this, you'll see a list of COM components that are registered on your system. When you have found the PROGIDs that you're looking for, simply choose to cancel the operation.

Determining Certificate Disposition

The code below shows how to use the CertificateAuthority.Admin and Certificate-Authority.Config components to determine the current disposition of a client certificate. Both of these components are instantiated by using the now familiar <OBJECT> tag with the appropriate PROGID. The code is taken from the Disposition.asp page included in the Certificate Web project on the CD-ROM.

```
<%@ Language=VBScript %>
<HTML>
<HEAD>
<META NAME="GENERATOR" Content="Microsoft Visual Studio 6.0">
</HEAD>
<BODY>

<H2>Client Certificate (Disposition) Sample</H2>
<HR>

<OBJECT RUNAT=server PROGID=CertificateAuthority.Admin
    id=objAdmin>
</OBJECT>
<OBJECT RUNAT=server PROGID=CertificateAuthority.Config
    id=objConfig>
</OBJECT>

<%
If Len(Request.ClientCertificate("Subject")) = 0 Then
    Response.Write _
        "This sample page requires a client certificate."
Else
    strSerialNumber = _
        Request.ClientCertificate("SerialNumber")
    strConfig = objConfig.GetConfig(0)
    disposition = _
        objAdmin.IsValidCertificate(strConfig, strSerialNumber)

    Select Case disposition
        Case 1
            strDisp = "Call did not complete"
        Case 2
            strDisp = "Call failed"
        Case 3
            strDisp = "Certificate revoked"
        Case 4
            strDisp = "Certificate still valid"
        Case 5
            strDisp = "Certificate never issued"
```

(continued)

```
        Case 6
            strDisp = "Taken under submission"
    End Select

    Response.Write "Configuration: " + strConfig + "<P>"
    Response.Write "SerialNumber: " + strSerialNumber + "<P>"
    Response.Write "Certificate disposition is <B>" + _
        strDisp + "</B>"
End If
%>

</BODY>
</HTML>
```

The page reads the client certificate presented by the browser and determines its *SerialNumber* key value by using the *Request.ClientCertificate("SerialNumber")* syntax. Next the *GetConfig* method of the CertificateAuthority.Config component is used to get the default configuration string for the certificate server. This configuration string uniquely identifies the certificate server by including the machine name and the name of the root CA. Next the *IsValidCertificate* method of the CertificateAuthority.Admin component is used to determine the disposition of the certificate. There are six disposition types, as shown in the code above. When calling the *IsValidCertificate* method, the serial number of the certificate and the configuration string for the certificate server are passed as arguments. Figure 23-12 shows an example of the resulting output from the Disposition.asp page.

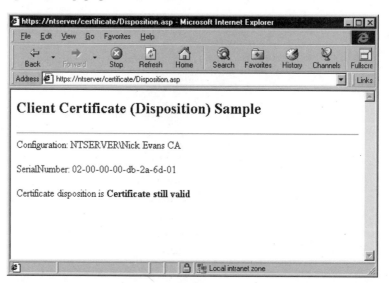

Figure 23-12. *Output from the Disposition.asp page showing the configuration string for the Certificate Server, the serial number of the presented client certificate, and the Certificate's disposition.*

Revoking a Certificate

When a certificate is revoked, a user can no longer use his or her certificate to access your application. Revoking a certificate is useful, and often highly necessary, in cases where employees leave a company or when you need to quickly deny access to your application.

Certificates are most commonly revoked using the Certificate Server Log Administration page. This page is accessible by clicking the Certificate Administration Log Utility hyperlink on the main administration page of Certificate Server. The list view of this page can be found at *http://localhost/certsrv/wcalist-.asp*. To revoke a certificate, you'll need to switch over to the form view by choosing a certificate to revoke. Figure 23-13 shows the Certificate Form Viewer with the Revoke button displayed at the bottom of the page.

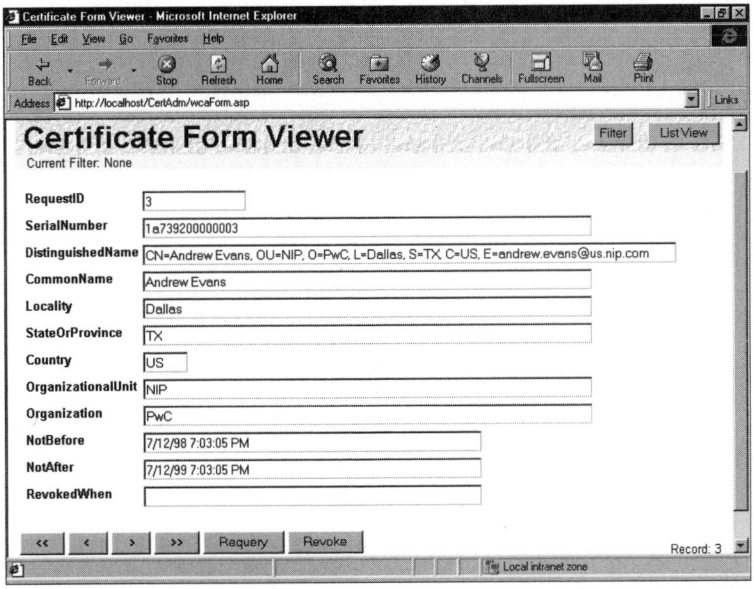

Figure 23-13. *The Certificate Form Viewer showing the details of a client certificate and the Revoke button for revoking the certificate.*

In your applications, you might want to automate features such as certificate revocation. You can do this from within your ASP code. For example, say you want to automatically revoke a certificate if your business partner becomes more than sixty days overdue in your accounts receivable database. To programmatically revoke a certificate, you can use the CertificateAuthority.Admin component, as shown in the code on the following page.

```
<OBJECT RUNAT=server PROGID=CertificateAuthority.Admin
    id=objAdmin>
</OBJECT>
<%
objAdmin.RevokeCertificate strConfig, strSerialNumber, 0, 0
%>
```

To revoke a certificate, call the *RevokeCertificate* method of the Certificate-Authority.Admin component and pass it four parameters:

- The configuration string for the Certificate Server

- The serial number of the certificate that you want to revoke

- The revocation reason (0 means an unspecified reason)

- The date at which the revocation becomes effective (0 means the current GMT time)

SUMMARY

In this chapter, we've covered a lot of material on Microsoft Certificate Server. This product will become more and more popular as organizations start to use it as part of a public-key infrastructure for their intranet and extranet applications. Visual InterDev 6.0 can be used to read client certificates for user authentication and also to extend the behavior of Certificate Server by calling the various COM components within the Certificate Server architecture. Client certificates are read using the *ClientCertificate* collection of the *Request* object. This makes it easy to access any of the certificate key or subfield values with just a single line of code. In addition to the *ClientCertificate* collection, the *Server-Variables* collection of the *Request* object can also be used to obtain information about both client and server certificates.

Appendix

What Works Where

Remote scripting is supported on the browsers and operating systems shown in the first table below. This is based upon the browser's support for invoking Java applets on the client.

Browser	*Operating System Required*
Internet Explorer 4.0+	Windows 95, Windows 98, or Windows NT Unix
Internet Explorer 3.02	Windows 95, Windows 98, or Windows NT
Navigator 4.0	Windows 95, Windows 98, or Windows NT

Design-time controls are supported on the platforms shown in this table:

Browser	*Operating System Required*
Internet Explorer 4.0+	Windows 95, Windows 98, or Windows NT
Internet Explorer 3.02	Windows 95, Windows 98, or Windows NT
Navigator 4.0	Windows 95, Windows 98, or Windows NT

Client-side database features are supported on Internet Explorer 4.0+ on Windows 95, Windows 98, and Windows NT.

Index

Page numbers in italics refer to figures, tables, or illustrations.

I

icons
  file status, 55–56
  Link View, 61
  padlock, 555
IDE. *See* integrated development environment
    (IDE)
id property, 342
if...else statement, 236–37
If...Then...Else statement, 225–27
IGetContextProperties interface, 501
Image Composer, 23
images, 12, 23
IMG element, 387
Immediate window, *68,* 76–77, *78*
importing
  content, 20
  existing Web sites, 58
  external style sheets, 171
@import statement, 171
include, server-side, 238–39
#INCLUDE directive, 239
Include DTC, 239
increment operator (++), 238
independent clients, 527
indexes, 302–3
Index Server Query component, 445–48
Index Server Utility component, 448–49
innerHTML property, 165–68
innerText property, 165–68
InputBox function, 232
INPUT element, 387
INPUT TYPE=RADIO element, 387
insertAdjacentHTML method, 164, *165*
insert queries, 308, *309*
insourcing CA services, 564
installation
  CA certificates into browsers, 568, *569*
  Microsoft Certificate Server, 565
  Microsoft Message Queue Server, 528–31
  server objects, 408
  Visual InterDev, 85
integrated development environment (IDE),
    4, 25–65
  configuring, 39–41
  Data View window, 12–13, *12,* 30, 127–28,
    291, 294–95

integrated development environment (IDE),
    continued
  drag-and-drop actions and popup menus,
    35–37
  Find command, 38
  Project Explorer window, 6, 26–28, *26, 117*
  projects and solutions, 32–34 (*see also*
    projects)
  Properties window, 28–30
  Task List, 41–43
  toolbars, 38–39
  Toolbox, 31–32 (*see also* Toolbox)
  using menus and keyboard, 34–37
  views and windows, 26–32 (*see also*
    windows)
IntelliSense statement completion, 5
  accessing page methods, 104
  accessing page properties, 101, *102*
  calling ActiveX server component, 456, *457*
  run-time properties and, 93
  using, 107
InterDev. *See* Microsoft Visual InterDev
interfaces
  Certificate Server, *566–67, 580*
  context object, 474, 500–501
  MTS, 472
Internet banking application. *See* VI-Bank
    example application
Internet Explorer. *See* Microsoft Internet
    Explorer
intranet applications, 3
IObjectContext interface, 474, 500
IP filtering, 546–48
isolation, 469
isolation, developer, 6, 52
isOpen method, 345
ISQL/W tool, 306
Item method, 497

J – K

Java, 6
Java applets, 265–66, 279–87
  ActiveX controls vs., 279
  inserting, into HTML and ASP files, 280–82
  scripting, 282–87
  Visual InterDev and, 18
  XML data source object, 385–86, 395–96, *397*

About the Authors

Nicholas D. Evans

Nicholas D. Evans is technical director of the National Internet Practice of PricewaterhouseCoopers. Nick is the author of a number of books on Web technology and writes a regular electronic commerce column in *Internet Week*. He can be reached at nick.evans@us.pwcglobal.com.

Ken Miller

Ken Miller is chief technology officer of 32X Tech Corporation, which specializes in providing courseware and training on Microsoft developer technologies, including Microsoft Visual InterDev, Microsoft Visual Basic, and Microsoft Visual J++. Ken can be reached at KenMiller@32X.com or through the 32X Tech Corporation's Web site at http://www.32X.com.

Ken Spencer

Ken Spencer is a senior instructor with 32X Tech Corporation. Ken also teaches seminars at professional conferences around the world and has authored and coauthored several books, including *OLE Remote Automation with Visual Basic* (Prentice Hall, 1995) and *Client/Server Programming with Microsoft Visual Basic* (Microsoft Press, 1996). Ken writes columns for a number of publications, including *Microsoft Interactive Developer*, *SQL Server Magazine*, and *Windows NT Magazine*. For more information on 32X training, visit the 32X Web site at http://www.32x.com.

The manuscript for this book was prepared using Microsoft Word 97. Pages were composed by Microsoft Press using Adobe PageMaker 6.52 for Windows, with text in Garamond and display type in Helvetica Black. Composed pages were delivered to the printer as electronic prepress files.

Cover Graphic Designer
Tim Girvin Design, Inc.

Cover Illustrator
Glenn Mitsui

Interior Graphic Artist
Rob Nance

Principal Compositor
Barb Runyan

Principal Proofreader/Copy Editor
Patricia Masserman

Indexer
Shane-Armstrong
Information Systems

Get the *complete picture* of database driven **Web development!**

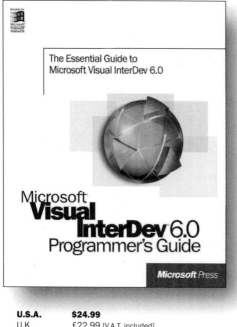

Microsoft® Visual InterDev™ 6.0 is the leader in Web tools and technology, and MICROSOFT VISUAL INTERDEV 6.0 PROGRAMMER'S GUIDE is the thorough, from-the-source guide that will enable you to unlock its full power. This comprehensive resource introduces you to the Visual InterDev 6.0 environment and guides you in creating Web projects and utilizing databases.

U.S.A.	**$24.99**
U.K.	£22.99 [V.A.T. included]
Canada	$35.99
ISBN 1-57231-867-8	

Microsoft®*Press*

Microsoft Press offers *comprehensive* learning solutions to help new users, power users, and professionals get the most from *Microsoft technology.*

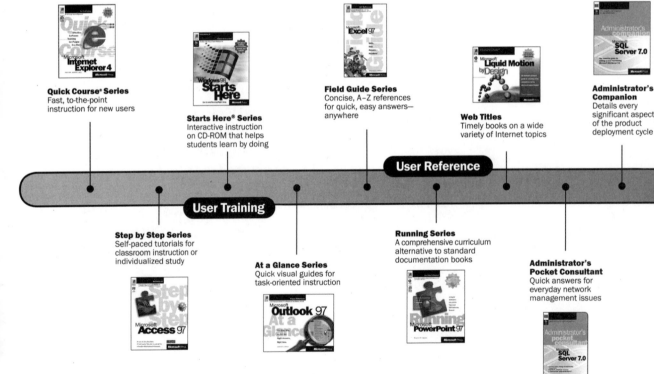

Quick Course® Series
Fast, to-the-point instruction for new users

Starts Here® Series
Interactive instruction on CD-ROM that helps students learn by doing

Field Guide Series
Concise, A–Z references for quick, easy answers—anywhere

Web Titles
Timely books on a wide variety of Internet topics

Administrator's Companion
Details every significant aspect of the product deployment cycle

User Reference

User Training

Step by Step Series
Self-paced tutorials for classroom instruction or individualized study

At a Glance Series
Quick visual guides for task-oriented instruction

Running Series
A comprehensive curriculum alternative to standard documentation books

Administrator's Pocket Consultant
Quick answers for everyday network management issues

Here's the
key to **building**
dynamic
Web applications

The Official Reference for
Microsoft Visual InterDev 6.0

Microsoft
Visual
InterDev 6.0
Web Technologies
Reference

***Microsoft** Press*

U.S.A.   **$39.99**
U.K.   £36.99 [V.A.T. included]
Canada $57.99
ISBN 1-57231-871-6

An indispensable set of resources collected in a single volume, the MICROSOFT® VISUAL INTERDEV™ 6.0 WEB TECHNOLOGIES REFERENCE offers essential reference guides to scripting languages on both the client and server sides, including:

- *Dynamic HTML Reference* describes the set of innovative features in Microsoft Internet Explorer 4.0 that enable you to easily add effects to your documents.

- *JScript® Reference* documents the fast, portable, lightweight interpreter for use in Web browsers and other applications that use ActiveX® controls, OLE Automation servers, and Java applets.

- *VBScript Reference* explains how you can bring Active Scripting to a wide variety of environments. The Visual InterDev development environment allows you to specify VBScript as your default scripting language for either client or server script.

- *Active Data Objects (ADO) Reference* shows you how to develop consistent, quick access to data, whether you're creating a front-end database client or middle-tier business object using an application, tool, language, or even a browser.

- *Visual InterDev Web Reference* lets you create the interface for your application using design-time controls and then write script to control the application using traditional object-oriented techniques.

Microsoft Press® products are available worldwide wherever quality computer books are sold. For more information, contact your book or computer retailer, software reseller, or local Microsoft Sales Office, or visit our Web site at mspress.microsoft.com. To locate your nearest source for Microsoft Press products, or to order directly, call 1-800-MSPRESS in the U.S. (in Canada, call 1-800-268-2222).

Prices and availability dates are subject to change.

Microsoft®Press

MICROSOFT LICENSE AGREEMENT

Book Companion CD

IMPORTANT—READ CAREFULLY: This Microsoft End-User License Agreement ("EULA") is a legal agreement between you (either an individual or an entity) and Microsoft Corporation for the Microsoft product identified above, which includes computer software and may include associated media, printed materials, and "on-line" or electronic documentation ("SOFTWARE PRODUCT"). Any component included within the SOFTWARE PRODUCT that is accompanied by a separate End-User License Agreement shall be governed by such agreement and not the terms set forth below. By installing, copying, or otherwise using the SOFTWARE PRODUCT, you agree to be bound by the terms of this EULA. If you do not agree to the terms of this EULA, you are not authorized to install, copy, or otherwise use the SOFTWARE PRODUCT; you may, however, return the SOFTWARE PRODUCT, along with all printed materials and other items that form a part of the Microsoft product that includes the SOFTWARE PRODUCT, to the place you obtained them for a full refund.

SOFTWARE PRODUCT LICENSE

The SOFTWARE PRODUCT is protected by United States copyright laws and international copyright treaties, as well as other intellectual property laws and treaties. The SOFTWARE PRODUCT is licensed, not sold.

1. GRANT OF LICENSE. This EULA grants you the following rights:

  a. Software Product. You may install and use one copy of the SOFTWARE PRODUCT on a single computer. The primary user of the computer on which the SOFTWARE PRODUCT is installed may make a second copy for his or her exclusive use on a portable computer.

  b. Storage/Network Use. You may also store or install a copy of the SOFTWARE PRODUCT on a storage device, such as a network server, used only to install or run the SOFTWARE PRODUCT on your other computers over an internal network; however, you must acquire and dedicate a license for each separate computer on which the SOFTWARE PRODUCT is installed or run from the storage device. A license for the SOFTWARE PRODUCT may not be shared or used concurrently on different computers.

  c. License Pak. If you have acquired this EULA in a Microsoft License Pak, you may make the number of additional copies of the computer software portion of the SOFTWARE PRODUCT authorized on the printed copy of this EULA, and you may use each copy in the manner specified above. You are also entitled to make a corresponding number of secondary copies for portable computer use as specified above.

  d. Sample Code. Solely with respect to portions, if any, of the SOFTWARE PRODUCT that are identified within the SOFTWARE PRODUCT as sample code (the "SAMPLE CODE"):

    i. Use and Modification. Microsoft grants you the right to use and modify the source code version of the SAMPLE CODE, *provided* you comply with subsection (d)(iii) below. You may not distribute the SAMPLE CODE, or any modified version of the SAMPLE CODE, in source code form.

    ii. Redistributable Files. Provided you comply with subsection (d)(iii) below, Microsoft grants you a nonexclusive, royalty-free right to reproduce and distribute the object code version of the SAMPLE CODE and of any modified SAMPLE CODE, other than SAMPLE CODE (or any modified version thereof) designated as not redistributable in the Readme file that forms a part of the SOFTWARE PRODUCT (the "Non-Redistributable Sample Code"). All SAMPLE CODE other than the Non-Redistributable Sample Code is collectively referred to as the "REDISTRIBUTABLES."

    iii. Redistribution Requirements. If you redistribute the REDISTRIBUTABLES, you agree to: (i) distribute the REDISTRIBUTABLES in object code form only in conjunction with and as a part of your software application product; (ii) not use Microsoft's name, logo, or trademarks to market your software application product; (iii) include a valid copyright notice on your software application product; (iv) indemnify, hold harmless, and defend Microsoft from and against any claims or lawsuits, including attorney's fees, that arise or result from the use or distribution of your software application product; and (v) not permit further distribution of the REDISTRIBUTABLES by your end user. Contact Microsoft for the applicable royalties due and other licensing terms for all other uses and/or distribution of the REDISTRIBUTABLES.

2. DESCRIPTION OF OTHER RIGHTS AND LIMITATIONS.

- **Limitations on Reverse Engineering, Decompilation, and Disassembly.** You may not reverse engineer, decompile, or disassemble the SOFTWARE PRODUCT, except and only to the extent that such activity is expressly permitted by applicable law notwithstanding this limitation.

- **Separation of Components.** The SOFTWARE PRODUCT is licensed as a single product. Its component parts may not be separated for use on more than one computer.

- **Rental.** You may not rent, lease, or lend the SOFTWARE PRODUCT.

- **Support Services.** Microsoft may, but is not obligated to, provide you with support services related to the SOFTWARE PRODUCT ("Support Services"). Use of Support Services is governed by the Microsoft policies and programs described in the user manual, in "on-line" documentation, and/or in other Microsoft-provided materials. Any supplemental software code provided to you as part of the Support Services shall be considered part of the SOFTWARE PRODUCT and subject to the terms and conditions of this EULA. With respect to technical information you provide to Microsoft as part of the Support Services, Microsoft may use such information for its business purposes, including for product support and development. Microsoft will not utilize such technical information in a form that personally identifies you.

- **Software Transfer.** You may permanently transfer all of your rights under this EULA, provided you retain no copies, you transfer all of the SOFTWARE PRODUCT (including all component parts, the media and printed materials, any upgrades, this EULA, and, if applicable, the Certificate of Authenticity), **and** the recipient agrees to the terms of this EULA.

- **Termination.** Without prejudice to any other rights, Microsoft may terminate this EULA if you fail to comply with the terms and conditions of this EULA. In such event, you must destroy all copies of the SOFTWARE PRODUCT and all of its component parts.

3. **COPYRIGHT.** All title and copyrights in and to the SOFTWARE PRODUCT (including but not limited to any images, photographs, animations, video, audio, music, text, SAMPLE CODE, REDISTRIBUTABLES, and "applets" incorporated into the SOFTWARE PRODUCT) and any copies of the SOFTWARE PRODUCT are owned by Microsoft or its suppliers. The SOFTWARE PRODUCT is protected by copyright laws and international treaty provisions. Therefore, you must treat the SOFTWARE PRODUCT like any other copyrighted material **except** that you may install the SOFTWARE PRODUCT on a single computer provided you keep the original solely for backup or archival purposes. You may not copy the printed materials accompanying the SOFTWARE PRODUCT.

4. **U.S. GOVERNMENT RESTRICTED RIGHTS.** The SOFTWARE PRODUCT and documentation are provided with RESTRICTED RIGHTS. Use, duplication, or disclosure by the Government is subject to restrictions as set forth in subparagraph (c)(1)(ii) of the Rights in Technical Data and Computer Software clause at DFARS 252.227-7013 or subparagraphs (c)(1) and (2) of the Commercial Computer Software—Restricted Rights at 48 CFR 52.227-19, as applicable. Manufacturer is Microsoft Corporation/One Microsoft Way/Redmond, WA 98052-6399.

5. **EXPORT RESTRICTIONS.** You agree that you will not export or re-export the SOFTWARE PRODUCT, any part thereof, or any process or service that is the direct product of the SOFTWARE PRODUCT (the foregoing collectively referred to as the "Restricted Components"), to any country, person, entity, or end user subject to U.S. export restrictions. You specifically agree not to export or re-export any of the Restricted Components (i) to any country to which the U.S. has embargoed or restricted the export of goods or services, which currently include, but are not necessarily limited to, Cuba, Iran, Iraq, Libya, North Korea, Sudan, and Syria, or to any national of any such country, wherever located, who intends to transmit or transport the Restricted Components back to such country; (ii) to any end user who you know or have reason to know will utilize the Restricted Components in the design, development, or production of nuclear, chemical, or biological weapons; or (iii) to any end user who has been prohibited from participating in U.S. export transactions by any federal agency of the U.S. government. You warrant and represent that neither the BXA nor any other U.S. federal agency has suspended, revoked, or denied your export privileges.

6. **NOTE ON JAVA SUPPORT.** THE SOFTWARE PRODUCT MAY CONTAIN SUPPORT FOR PROGRAMS WRITTEN IN JAVA. JAVA TECHNOLOGY IS NOT FAULT TOLERANT AND IS NOT DESIGNED, MANUFACTURED, OR INTENDED FOR USE OR RESALE AS ON-LINE CONTROL EQUIPMENT IN HAZARDOUS ENVIRONMENTS REQUIRING FAIL-SAFE PERFORMANCE, SUCH AS IN THE OPERATION OF NUCLEAR FACILITIES, AIRCRAFT NAVIGATION OR COMMUNICATION SYSTEMS, AIR TRAFFIC CONTROL, DIRECT LIFE SUPPORT MACHINES, OR WEAPONS SYSTEMS, IN WHICH THE FAILURE OF JAVA TECHNOLOGY COULD LEAD DIRECTLY TO DEATH, PERSONAL INJURY, OR SEVERE PHYSICAL OR ENVIRONMENTAL DAMAGE.

DISCLAIMER OF WARRANTY

NO WARRANTIES OR CONDITIONS. MICROSOFT EXPRESSLY DISCLAIMS ANY WARRANTY OR CONDITION FOR THE SOFTWARE PRODUCT. THE SOFTWARE PRODUCT AND ANY RELATED DOCUMENTATION IS PROVIDED "AS IS" WITHOUT WARRANTY OR CONDITION OF ANY KIND, EITHER EXPRESS OR IMPLIED, INCLUDING, WITHOUT LIMITATION, THE IMPLIED WARRANTIES OF MERCHANTABILITY, FITNESS FOR A PARTICULAR PURPOSE, OR NONINFRINGEMENT. THE ENTIRE RISK ARISING OUT OF USE OR PERFORMANCE OF THE SOFTWARE PRODUCT REMAINS WITH YOU.

LIMITATION OF LIABILITY. TO THE MAXIMUM EXTENT PERMITTED BY APPLICABLE LAW, IN NO EVENT SHALL MICROSOFT OR ITS SUPPLIERS BE LIABLE FOR ANY SPECIAL, INCIDENTAL, INDIRECT, OR CONSEQUENTIAL DAMAGES WHATSOEVER (INCLUDING, WITHOUT LIMITATION, DAMAGES FOR LOSS OF BUSINESS PROFITS, BUSINESS INTERRUPTION, LOSS OF BUSINESS INFORMATION, OR ANY OTHER PECUNIARY LOSS) ARISING OUT OF THE USE OF OR INABILITY TO USE THE SOFTWARE PRODUCT OR THE PROVISION OF OR FAILURE TO PROVIDE SUPPORT SERVICES, EVEN IF MICROSOFT HAS BEEN ADVISED OF THE POSSIBILITY OF SUCH DAMAGES. IN ANY CASE, MICROSOFT'S ENTIRE LIABILITY UNDER ANY PROVISION OF THIS EULA SHALL BE LIMITED TO THE GREATER OF THE AMOUNT ACTUALLY PAID BY YOU FOR THE SOFTWARE PRODUCT OR US$5.00; PROVIDED, HOWEVER, IF YOU HAVE ENTERED INTO A MICROSOFT SUPPORT SERVICES AGREEMENT, MICROSOFT'S ENTIRE LIABILITY REGARDING SUPPORT SERVICES SHALL BE GOVERNED BY THE TERMS OF THAT AGREEMENT. BECAUSE SOME STATES AND JURISDICTIONS DO NOT ALLOW THE EXCLUSION OR LIMITATION OF LIABILITY, THE ABOVE LIMITATION MAY NOT APPLY TO YOU.

MISCELLANEOUS

This EULA is governed by the laws of the State of Washington USA, except and only to the extent that applicable law mandates governing law of a different jurisdiction.

Should you have any questions concerning this EULA, or if you desire to contact Microsoft for any reason, please contact the Microsoft subsidiary serving your country, or write: Microsoft Sales Information Center/One Microsoft Way/Redmond, WA 98052-6399.